Responsible Technology and Intelligence: A Review Series

Generative AI for Next-Gen Defence Strategies

Responsible Technology and Intelligence: A Review Series

1. A Compendium of Responsible Artificial Intelligence
   Deepak Kumar Jain, Kirti Raj Bhatele, Deepak Garg and *Gaurav Dhiman (Editors), 2025*
2. Ambient Assisted Living: Technological Advances
   Rashmi Gupta, Shashi Shekhar, Jeetendra Kumar and *Gaurav Dhiman (Editors), 2025*
3. Industrial Internet of Things for Responsible Technology
   B.K. Mishra, Gaurav Dhiman, Hemant Kasturiwale, Sujata Alegavi and *Kusum Yadav (Editors), 2026*
4. Robust Biometric Systems and Efficient Data
   Brajesh Kumar Singh, Amrita Rai, Shamimul Qamar, Ravinder Kumar and *Anil Kumar (Editors), 2026*
5. Federated Learning in Financial Services: A Path to Secure AI
   Suvarna Sharma, Jeetendra Kumar, Rashmi Gupta, Valentina E. Balas and *Gaurav Dhiman (Editors), 2027*
6. Generative AI for Next-Gen Defence Strategies
   Jeetendra Kumar, Rashmi Gupta, P. K. Mishra, Gaurav Dhiman, Valentina E. Balas and *Kamila Zarychta-Romanowska (Editors), 2027*

Responsible Technology and Intelligence: A Review Series

Generative AI for Next-Gen Defence Strategies

Editors:

Jeetendra Kumar
Department of Computer Science and Application
Atal Bihari Vajpayee University, Chhattisgarh, India

Rashmi Gupta
Department of Computer Science and Application
Atal Bihari Vajpayee University, Chhattisgarh, India

P. K. Mishra
Department of Computer Science, Institute of Science
Banaras Hindu University, Varanasi, India

Gaurav Dhiman
School of Sciences and Emerging Technologies
Jagat Guru Nanak Dev Punjab State Open University, Patiala, India

Valentina E. Balas
Department of Automatics and Applied Software
Faculty of Engineering, "Aurel Vlaicu" University of Arad, Romania

Kamila Zarychta-Romanowska
AlphaOne Defence and Security, Poland

CRC Press
Taylor & Francis Group
Boca Raton London New York

CRC Press is an imprint of the
Taylor & Francis Group, an **informa** business
A SCIENCE PUBLISHERS BOOK

First edition published 2027
by CRC Press
2385 NW Executive Center Drive, Suite 320, Boca Raton FL 33431

and by CRC Press
4 Park Square, Milton Park, Abingdon, Oxon, OX14 4RN

CRC Press is an imprint of Taylor & Francis Group, LLC

Library of Congress Cataloging-in-Publication Data (applied for)

ISBN: 978-1-041-12349-1 (hbk)
ISBN: 978-1-041-17140-9 (pbk)
ISBN: 978-1-003-68817-4 (ebk)

DOI: 10.1201/9781003688174

Typeset in Times New Roman
by Prime Publishing Services

Preface

The emergence of Generative Artificial Intelligence (GAI) represents a paradigm-shifting inflection point in the history of military science and strategic studies. By endowing machines with the capacity to synthesize highly realistic synthetic environments, generate adaptive tactical constructs, autonomously formulate mission plans, and produce contextually intelligent decision architectures, GAI is rapidly transcending its role as an enabling technology to become a constitutive element of twenty-first-century defence capability.

This book offers a comprehensive, rigorous, and forward-looking examination of the profound implications of GAI across the entire spectrum of contemporary and future defence operations. It opens with a foundational analysis of the ontological essence, architectural frameworks, and prospective developmental trajectories of GAI, thereby establishing the conceptual and technical framework for the subsequent specialised investigations.

This book then proceeds to delineate the strategic centrality that generative systems have already assumed within modern defence ecosystems. It systematically explores their application to:

- The enhancement of coordination, emergent intelligence, and adaptive learning in heterogeneous clusters of autonomous ground, aerial, and maritime vehicles;
- The generative design and dynamic optimisation of large-scale drone swarms operating under contested electromagnetic and kinetic conditions;
- The realisation of fully autonomous navigation, real-time mission re-planning, and goal-directed behaviour in complex, contested, and GPS-denied environments.
- The development of advanced generative models for structural health monitoring, anomaly detection, and predictive maintenance of critical aerospace infrastructure.
- The revolutionary transformation of radar signal processing, waveform design, and cognitive electronic warfare capabilities.
- The fundamental redefinition of naval warfare doctrine and underwater domain awareness through generative approaches to acoustic sensing, target motion analysis, and multi-domain maritime decision-making.

A central analytical concern of this book is the profoundly dual-use nature of GAI technologies. The same generative architectures that enable unprecedented advances in defensive resilience and operational decision advantage simultaneously empower increasingly sophisticated malicious cyber operations, including automated vulnerability discovery, polymorphic malware generation, and large-scale influence operations in the cognitive domain. This book also confronts these dual-use realities head-on, offering a detailed examination of the technical, operational, doctrinal, and ethical challenges inherent in the militarisation of generative systems. Particular attention is devoted to the risks posed by GAI in cognitive warfare, the imperative for robust ethical governance frameworks, and the development of responsible innovation pathways. This book further reimagines the stewardship of aerospace infrastructure through generative foundations for predictive analytics and ultra-precise condition-based maintenance; it demonstrates the power of GAI to create hyper-realistic battlefield simulation environments and next-generation immersive training systems; and it investigates the deployment of agentic generative AI in complex, multi-aircraft combat simulation and beyond-visual-range engagement scenarios. Finally, the text engages with the broader strategic ecosystem, addressing critical questions of cybersecurity implications, AI ethics in the defence context, and the evolving commercial business models and industrialisation pathways that will determine how rapidly and responsibly defence-oriented generative intelligence is developed and fielded.

In an era defined by information dominance, autonomous lethality, cognitive superiority, decision-cycle compression, and multi-domain convergence, this work aspires to serve as both an authoritative scholarly reference and a normative guidepost. It invites defence researchers, strategic planners, military practitioners, policymakers, and technologists to engage critically and responsibly with the transformative potential and concomitant imperatives of GAI in the defence domain.

Series Preface

The rapid pace of technological advancement in the 21st century has brought with it transformative capabilities and unprecedented possibilities across sectors. From artificial intelligence and ambient intelligence to industrial automation, technology is deeply embedded in our social, economic, and personal lives. While these innovations offer immense benefits, they also raise critical questions about ethics, equity, sustainability, and human well-being. It is within this context that the "Responsible Technology Series" has been conceived—a multidisciplinary initiative aimed at fostering technological progress that is not only intelligent and efficient but also inclusive, ethical, and accountable.

This series brings together thought leaders, researchers, and practitioners to explore how emerging technologies can be designed and deployed responsibly to serve both individual and collective good. Each volume in the series addresses a specific domain of technological innovation while upholding a common commitment: to highlight frameworks, practices, and case studies that emphasize responsible development, deployment, and governance.

The first volume, A Compendium of Responsible Artificial Intelligence, offers a comprehensive overview of the ethical, social, and regulatory challenges associated with AI systems. It explores fairness, transparency, accountability, and the societal impacts of machine learning and decision-making algorithms, laying the groundwork for sustainable AI applications.

The second volume, Ambient Assisted Living: Technological Advances, focuses on the intersection of healthcare, aging populations, and intelligent environments. It presents innovations in assistive technologies and smart living spaces, while foregrounding the need for privacy, user dignity, and human-centric design in care ecosystems.

The third volume, Industrial Internet of Things for Responsible Technology, examines how industrial automation and IoT can be harnessed responsibly. It covers foundational technologies, ethical considerations, sustainability, human-centered design, and resilience—demonstrating how IIoT can drive industrial efficiency without compromising societal and environmental values. Together, these volumes reflect the core mission of the series: to enable a balanced narrative in which innovation and responsibility go hand in hand. By bringing diverse voices and insights to the forefront, this series aims to equip readers with the tools, perspectives, and inspiration needed to build a more equitable and conscientious technological future.

We invite scholars, professionals, students, and policymakers to engage with these works, contribute to this growing dialogue, and join us in shaping a future where technology serves humanity with foresight and integrity.

Acknowledgements

It is with the deepest sense of gratitude and humility that we acknowledge the extraordinary constellation of individuals, institutions, and guiding forces whose wisdom, generosity, dedication, and support have collectively brought this monograph into existence.

We begin by offering our most profound appreciation to Dr Gaurav Dhiman, the distinguished Series Editor of *Advances in Responsible Technology and Intelligence*. His visionary intellectual leadership, meticulous scholarly guidance, unwavering encouragement, and strategic foresight have been the very cornerstone of this project. From the earliest conceptual discussions through every phase of manuscript development, peer review, and final production, Dr Dhiman's incisive insights, constructive critique, and steadfast commitment to excellence have profoundly shaped the intellectual ambition, thematic coherence, and ultimate scope of this volume. His belief in the importance of this work has been our constant source of inspiration.

We are immensely indebted to the exceptional group of contributing authors whose original scholarship, technical mastery, and intellectual generosity have infused every chapter with unparalleled depth, rigour, and forward-looking insight. Their willingness to share cutting-edge research, respond thoughtfully to iterative revisions, and collaborate across disciplinary boundaries has elevated the quality and comprehensiveness of this book far beyond what any single author could have achieved. Their diligence, creativity, and shared commitment to responsible innovation have been truly exemplary. We extend our heartfelt thanks to CRC Press, an imprint of Taylor & Francis Group, for their enthusiastic endorsement of this project and for providing a world-class platform for its publication. The professionalism, efficiency, and editorial expertise of the entire CRC Press team—particularly their meticulous attention to detail, commitment to academic excellence, and unwavering support throughout the production process—have been instrumental in transforming the manuscript into a polished and authoritative volume.

We are deeply grateful to our many colleagues, collaborators, and peers across academia, defence research establishments, industry laboratories, and strategic policy communities. Their generous willingness to engage in stimulating discussions, provide critical feedback, share unpublished insights, and offer continuous moral and intellectual support has enriched every aspect of this work. Their collegiality and openness have been invaluable. Above all else, we owe an immeasurable debt of love and gratitude to our families—parents, spouses, children, and extended kin—whose boundless patience, understanding, emotional sustenance, and quiet sacrifices have enabled us to devote the countless hours required to bring this project to completion. Their unwavering belief in our work, their encouragement during moments of doubt, and their loving presence throughout this long journey have been the true foundation upon which everything else has rested. Without their steadfast support and deep affection, this endeavour would simply not have been possible.

Finally, we humbly acknowledge the divine providence that has granted us the strength, clarity of purpose, perseverance, intellectual curiosity, and inspiration necessary to conceive, execute, and complete this work. It is with sincere gratitude that we recognise the grace that has guided every step of this journey.

—Editors

Contents

List of Contributors

A. Peda Gopi
https://orcid.org/0000-0003-2618-7806

Aaskaran Bishnoi
https://orcid.org/0009-0003-1853-2937

Abdelkrim Haqiq
https://orcid.org/0000-0002-8857-6586

Abhrendu Bhattacharya
https://orcid.org/0009-0009-8549-1024

Achyut Mitra
https://orcid.org/0009-0004-2163-3090

Akshay P. Deshpande
https://orcid.org/0009-0008-1892-4179

Amita Soni
https://orcid.org/0000-0002-9661-9566

Anuj Kumar Pal
https://orcid.org/0009-0002-7938-9444

Anuradha Singh
https://orcid.org/0000-0001-7365-5540

Anurag Prajapati
https://orcid.org/0009-0009-6613-8401

Arijit Datta
https://orcid.org/0000-0002-0459-1368

Ayush Kumar Agrawal
https://orcid.org/0009-0008-1888-279X

Basant Tiwari
https://orcid.org/0000-0002-3113-4760

Bharat R. Naiknaware
https://orcid.org/0000-0001-8343-0505

Danish Hussain
https://orcid.org/0000-0001-7617-3280

Debasis Chaudhuri
https://orcid.org/0000-0002-6895-456X

Jatin Singh Rajawat
https://orcid.org/0009-0004-4646-6970

Jeetendra Kumar
https://orcid.org/0000-0002-5705-6369

K. Chaitanya
https://orcid.org/0000-0002-7453-4377

K. Satya Sandeep
https://orcid.org/0000-0003-0372-4824

K.V.S.S. Rama Krishna
https://orcid.org/0000-0001-6598-7860

K. Venkateswaran
https://orcid.org/0000-0002-8028-9806

Katakam Ranganarayana
https://orcid.org/0000-0003-4734-5594

M.A. Jabbar
https://orcid.org/0000-0003-4059-2728

Mokhtar M. Hasan
https://orcid.org/0000-0002-4702-4320

Mussaratjahan Korpali
https://orcid.org/0000-0002-8034-7906

Neeraj Kumar Rathore
https://orcid.org/0000-0002-9349-3419

Nilesh Verma
https://orcid.org/0009-0006-4705-6169

Noor A. Ibraheem
https://orcid.org/0000-0001-5819-2840

Paramita Sarkar
https://orcid.org/0000-0002-2330-8484

Pooja Pandey
https://orcid.org/0000-0001-7116-8191

Pradeep Kumar Asthana
https://orcid.org/0000-0003-2955-6742

Praveen Kumar Guraja
https://orcid.org/0000-0002-4463-0659

Priyanshi Mulwani
https://orcid.org/0009-0001-9753-4070

Priyanshu Mishra
https://orcid.org/0009-0005-0401-1609

Rahul Kumar Gour
https://orcid.org/0009-0007-5769-6079

Rangeet Mitra
https://orcid.org/0000-0002-5324-5728

Rashmi Gupta
https://orcid.org/0000-0001-6853-9844

Rishabh Garg
https://orcid.org/0009-0001-6219-1119

Ritu Sindhu
https://orcid.org/0009-0004-4052-1721

S. Adiba Adil Quadri
https://orcid.org/0000-0002-6832-7806

Sauvik Bal
https://orcid.org/0000-0001-5569-1855

Sayli M. Haldavanekar
https://orcid.org/0009-0009-2870-1099

Shailendra Gupta
https://orcid.org/0000-0002-6981-9503

Shaista Farhat
https://orcid.org/0009-0008-9348-8370

Shaman Sharma
https://orcid.org/0009-0003-6209-9544

Shashi Kant Gupta
https://orcid.org/0000-0001-6587-5607

Shillpi Mishrra
https://orcid.org/0009-0007-5509-5595

Shilpa Pandey
https://orcid.org/0000-0002-1696-1733

Shrutika Mishra
https://orcid.org/0000-0003-3029-6503

Sonali Malewar
https://orcid.org/0000-0001-7880-3944

Sourav Saha
https://orcid.org/0009-0007-2579-0933

Subhodip Koley
https://orcid.org/0009-0004-0262-0526

Sumaiya Shaikh
https://orcid.org/0000-0003-0884-8965

Sumit Das
https://orcid.org/0000-0002-8018-9151

Uday Kumar Singh
https://orcid.org/0000-0002-0505-2921

Ujjwal Matoliya
https://orcid.org/0009-0000-2825-692X

V. Lakshman Narayana
https://orcid.org/0000-0002-9680-2897

Vimal Bhatia
https://orcid.org/0000-0001-5148-6643

Vimal Dubey
https://orcid.org/0009-0008-4819-2861

Vivek Tiwari
https://orcid.org/0000-0002-7411-5113

1 Generative Artificial Intelligence: Essence, Framework, and Prospect

Pooja Pandey[1], Pradeep Kumar Asthana[2*], Sonali Malewar[3], Shilpa Pandey[4] and Shashi Kant Gupta[5]

Generative artificial intelligence (AI) represents a massive shift in machine learning functionality, and it has been based on the rapid advancement that AI has achieved in the previous decade. New material in many different formats, such as text, photos, audio, code, video, picture, figures, diagrams, and synthetic data are generated using generative models. This contrasts with normal AI systems which merely make classification, prediction, and recognition. This sign has increased the role of AI in the fields of science, education, and business, changing human–technology interaction. The methods of generative AI are trained to natively understand the structure of the underlying data distribution to achieve new instances that are statistically similar. In contrast, discriminative models are a direct translation of inputs to outputs, including sorting emails into spam or not spam. Various other directions in unsupervised learning include autoencoders, Restricted Boltzmann Machines and Variational Autoencoders (VAEs). In 2014, Ian Goodfellow also added a game-theoretic element in his introduction of Generative Adversarial Networks (GANs) where both a generator and a discriminator compete against each other to generate realistic data. In recent years, transformer-based methods, and in particular Large Language Models (LLMs), such as GPT, BERT, and T5, have altered the mechanisms of natural language processing. These guidelines make products such as ChatGPT, DALL, and Bard possible, demonstrating the ability of the generative AI to reproduce and possibly complement the human creative power and thinking abilities in multiple disciplines.

1. Introduction

Generative artificial intelligence (AI) refers to a subdivision of AI systems, being able to produce new content, such as text, images, audio, or code, by internalising learned patterns identified in big data. Fundamentally, generative AI utilises deep-

[1] https://orcid.org/0000-0001-7116-8191
[2] https://orcid.org/0000-0003-2955-6742
[3] https://orcid.org/0000-0001-7880-3944
[4] https://orcid.org/0000-0002-1696-1733
[5] https://orcid.org/0000-0001-6587-5607
* Corresponding author: pkasthana@rpr.amity.edu

DOI: 10.1201/9781003688174-1

learning models like transformers and diffusion models that replicate aspects of human creativity and present a false sense of human-like output. Generative AI will enable more adaptive and scalable solutions as the means through which contemporary practice can be automated, personalised, and ideated.

1.1 Background and Context

Artificial intelligence nowadays is classified as one of the most radical technologies of the twenty-first century that has brought sweeping changes to the industries, economies, as well as civilisations themselves. Previously, AI was viewed solely as a laboratory tool and a matter of theoretical discussion, but little by little, it started to become a part of everyday life, including Siri and Alexa or even the recommendations section of the Netflix and Amazon websites that can be made with the use of AI (Arachchige et al., 2024). The historical AI was mainly focused on automation but of late it has brought forth a new dimension: Generative Artificial Intelligence (GAI). Figure 1.1 presents a high-level conceptual model of Generative AI, showing how AI systems transform inputs into real-world impact.

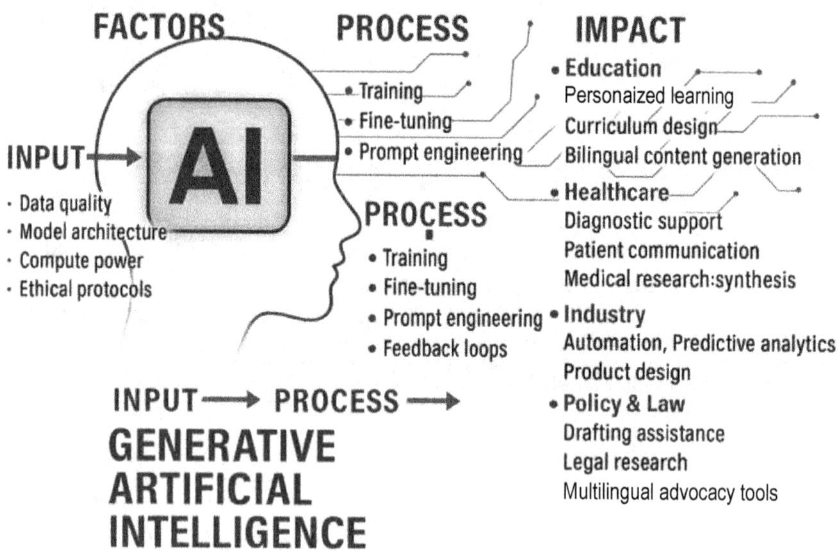

Fig. 1.1 Generative Artificial Intelligence

Generative AI can also be defined as possessing the capability to create novel content, e.g., text, image, video, audio, and even complex code, not just analysing and classifying existing data (Yehia, 2024). This generating capacity presents a colossal improvement in machine intelligence compared to the pure recognition capacity. It has attracted universal attention as a technology capable of revolutionising creative industries, research, communicating with customers and solving problems (Cao et al., 2023; Kumar et al., 2023).

The environment that generative AI is operating in is getting digitalised. The acceleration of the evolution of generative technologies is promoted by the fact that the computing capacity is growing exponentially, large quantities of data are at hand, and the structure of neural networks is also emerging (Beheshti and Mansoor, 2025). Besides that, the digitisation usage has increased in the post-pandemic era, which has raised curiosity towards AI tools that would aid productivity, creativity, and innovation. This means that generative AI is at the crossroads between technology, society, and ethics, and there are both opportunities as well as challenges requiring close consideration.

1.2 History of Artificial Intelligence

During the last six decades, AI has experienced its highs and lows, novel concepts, and ambiguity.

Until the 1950s–1970s: In the early years, machine intelligence was conceived by trailblazers such as Alan Turing halfway into the twentieth century, and it is the foundation of AI. The key issues of the early research into AI were symbolic reasoning, logic, and problem-solving algorithms (Liang et al., 2025). The research on AI began in 1956 at the Dartmouth Conference. However, the progress was not very strong due to the lack of good computer facilities and overambitious objectives.

The Knowledge Era (1980s–1990s): AI became concentrated on expert systems, which applied the logic of rules to obtain the behaviour of human decision-making in constrained areas, including industrial troubleshooting or medical diagnosis (Ravi et al., 2025). Even though they demonstrated the potential of AI, such systems were not dynamic and could not seize an opportunity. This was also the period when AI winters were more than plentiful, when there was no funding and interest in non-fulfilment of the expected.

Machine Learning Revolution (2000s–2010s): Deep learning and machine learning (ML) brought about a revolution in the world of AI. The AI systems started to understand what occurs in large masses of data, in contrast to the use of explicit programming solely (Wang et al., 2023). The Convolutional Neural Networks (CNNs) and Recurrent Neural Networks (RNNs) have transformed the very essence of speech processing, autonomous vehicles, and face recognition.

The Generative Era (2017 onwards): In 2014, Ian Goodfellow came up with Generative Adversarial Networks (GANs) or, in other words, the machine was able to create images, audio, and videos that were realistic. This was a turning point (Goodfellow et al., 2014). This advancement facilitated the development of more sophisticated generative models, including Transformers, which currently serve as the foundation for tools such as Generative Pre-trained Transformer (GPT). These advancements transformed AI from a prediction and classification instrument to a collaborator in the process of creation.

1.3 Transition from Traditional AI to Generative AI

Pattern recognition, data categorisation, and decision support were the primary objectives of conventional AI models (Gupta et al., 2022). For instance, conventional AI in healthcare could evaluate patient symptoms and compare them to existing medical data to propose a diagnosis. Such systems were interactive in their nature because, regardless of their size and abilities, they would only react to investigations as per the information given.

Traditional models of natural language processing could only classify sentiments and translate languages; generative models, like GPT-4, can write essays, write business reports, and even engage in dialogue with humans.

Three factors were important:

- The implementation of neural architecture capabilities such as the Transformer model announced in 2017 made sequential processing of inputs practical, thus also making it easier to generate coherent text as well as multimodal information at scale.
- Increased access to data: large-scale data (internet, social media) and digital libraries made the necessary training resources to build large-scale language and image models.
- Computational capacity: The potential of generative threats has also increased due to the development of multi-billion-parameter models, which are made possible through the development of Graphics Processing Units (GPUs), Tensor Processing Units (TPUs), and cloud computing infrastructure.

It is not simply a technological shift but also a conceptual one, as it intends to use AI to address concatenated issues, and not just as a means of exploration, ideation, and creativity.

The approach that has been used in this chapter is qualitative, descriptive, and analytical. It has also relied on secondary sources that comprise academic journals, industry reports, white papers, and case studies of generative AI applications. The analysis has involved the employment of the comparative approach in explaining the differences between conventional AI and the generative approach. In addition, computer science, innovation, research, and ethical conceptual frameworks have been applied to attain a holistic approach.

2. Generative AI Theory

Generative AI is a subtype of AI systems, which, in addition to the information analysis processes and interpretation capabilities, is also capable of generating new original content that is like human-made material. Compared to traditional AI that only recognizes the patterns and predicts what is most likely to occur, generative AI goes even further by replicating novel information based on the patterns having already been observed (Goodfellow et al., 2014; Devlin et al., 2019).

Simply put, generative AI relies on ML models, especially deep learning systems like GANs, Variational Autoencoders (VAEs), and Transformer-based models, to synthesize realistic work in other content modalities.

They enable the generation of text which replicates human writing, work in art, music, speech, computer programs, and video sequences that replicate the flow of a story (Kingma & Welling, 2013).

Simulation game: The creative simulation of cognitive processes is an attribute of generative AI. It does not process text in the same way, but based on a huge amount of it, it makes statistically close predictions of context, coherence, and novelty (Radford et al., 2018). This makes generative AI both a practical tool—empowering industries to accelerate innovation—and a philosophical frontier, raising questions about authorship, originality, and the boundaries of machine creativity.

2.1 *Difference between Generative and Discriminative Models*

Generative models and discriminative models are the two primary categories into which AI systems are divided, with each category fulfilling a unique purpose. Although both models utilize data to understand patterns, their outputs and orientation are fundamentally distinct.

2.1.1 Generative Models (Data Distribution)

Generative models endeavour to determine the joint probability distribution of inputs and outputs, which is mathematically represented as $P(x, y)$, where x denotes the data and y denotes the labels. Generative systems can capture the structure of data and generate wholly new data points that resemble the original dataset by modelling this joint distribution.

For example, a generative model does not merely acquire the ability to identify whether an image contains a cat when it is trained on thousands of images of cats; it also acquires an understanding of the underlying distribution of cat features, including fur textures, ear shapes, whisker orientations, and typical poses. This enables the model to produce novel, realistic images of cats that do not exist in the training set but still follow the learned distribution. Generative modelling frequently employs the following methodologies:

- Generative Adversarial Networks (GANs): Two neural networks, a generator and a discriminator, are trained concurrently in competition. The generator generates synthetic data, while the discriminator assesses its authenticity, thereby encouraging the generator to enhance its performance until the outputs are indistinguishable from genuine data.

- Variational Autoencoders (VAEs): These models encode input data into a compressed latent space and subsequently decode it to reconstruct similar data, thereby facilitating the controlled generation of new samples.
- Transformer Models: Transformers are utilized by large language models, such as GPT, to forecast the subsequent token in a sequence, thereby producing contextually appropriate and coherent text. The generative approach is especially advantageous when it is necessary to incorporate data augmentation, simulation, or creativity.

2.1.2 Discriminative Models (Classification and Prediction)

Discriminative models, in contrast, concentrate on learning the conditional probability distribution, represented as $P(y|x)$—the probability of label y given data x. Their responsibilities do not involve the generation of new data; rather, they involve the classification or prediction of outcomes based on existing inputs.

The following are examples of discriminative models:

- Binary classification using logistic regression.
- Hyperplanes are employed to separate data elements in Support Vector Machines (SVMs).
- The application of CNNs to image recognition tasks.
- Bidirectional Encoder Representations from Transformers (BERT), which is adept at sentiment analysis, information retrieval, and text classification.

In general, discriminative models are more efficient for classification and prediction tasks, necessitating less computational complexity than generative models.

2.2 Core Capabilities and Modalities of Generative AI

Generative AI's adaptability across modalities is one of its most noteworthy characteristics. Modern generative AI systems exhibit an extraordinary capacity to function in a variety of creative and functional domains:

- Language models: Including GPT-4 and LLM, create contextually pertinent, coherent text in a diverse range of formats, including technical documentation, business correspondence, essays, reports, and poetry. These models are trained on extensive datasets of written material and rely on the probabilistic prediction of words (tokens) in sequence. Chatbots, educational tools, virtual assistants, and content creation industries extensively employ text generation.
- Image Generation: DALL·E, Midjourney, and Stable Diffusion are among the tools that generate high-quality digital images from textual stimuli. These models are capable of combining art, product prototypes, design concepts, and photorealistic visuals. Their applications are extensive, including architecture, fashion design, entertainment, and advertising.

Audio Generation: Speech, music, and soundscapes can be generated by generative AI. AI can produce speech, music, and soundscapes. Text-to-speech (TTS) applications like OpenAI and ElevenLabs use written language as input to produce spoken text. These systems accommodate an extensive variety of languages and dialects and provide a variety of voice representations that are realistic. Simultaneously, with either of the accompaniments, the Jukebox may also reproduce a few pieces of music, and they may be of either of the genres, and melodic, harmonic and cadence with the fresh structures. It can be translated and utilised as audio recognition of the clients on the audio frequency bandwidth.

- Code Generation: The Copilot and Replicast AI code helper can produce, optimize, and debug computer code. Having the models available, a programmer will be able to create a much more feasible (user-friendly) program and will save the time invested in the rewriting of the bulky provisions of open-source code with the aid of the analysis. Programming paradigms categorise languages in terms of style, which are usually arbitrary. To non-programmers, code would be appropriate when it is simple to understand and intuitive, independent of paradigm.
- Video Generation: Generative video models in the infancy stage are capable of producing fake video and animation and shorter video. The Chinese systems generate the writing video sequences in the Pika labs chatroom and the runway. It will be of great service to movie production, sales, education, and games but will in some way aggravate the matters to do with ownership and falsity.
- Synthetic Data Generation: Having built the contents, the forecasting AI can generate datasets with its meagre dispersion in the image of the actual data. This is specifically the area of the economy where finance or healthcare holds all the nuance which simply cannot be revealed. The eradication of ML is also achieved through the assistance of simulations: generative AI cannot risk the privacy of any of the producing anonymized but realistic data.

2.3 Benefits of Contrasting AI

Generative AI has already established a technologically advanced digital realm. Its advantages are much more than the conventional screen-based experience, with significant improvements in interaction and immersion.

- Innovation and Creativity: In fact, the algorithm of AI does not have the capacity to come to an extra solution and has yet to present the opportunity to extract forecasts and recognition. Towards the domain of human imagination, computational composition now incorporates the main qualities of the creative process, structuring, conceptualization, and the generation of new schemes and creations.

  Through the generative models, this is possible, though the communication process is subjected to more of a dialogue. Generative AI should imitate interactive communication experiences which are genuine and convincing. It strives to attract the user's attention by the catchiness of the chats and interactions. It builds trust in the exchange by guaranteeing users of their needs and purposes. The technology plays functional and relational functions.

- Data Augmentation: Fake information can only help to achieve the data given by the module generative AI if the amount of data involved is rather high and would not be so easy to acquire access to them to continue with the development of other AI gadgets.
- Customization: Because of the trends in this user data, generative AI will be able to produce individual data in terms of user likes. This augmented service is offered online.
- Cost minimization and reductions: Besides saving time and money, robots help streamline processes by reducing repetitive work and provide more free time to human beings to focus on more creative and meaningful tasks. One such approach involves automatically generating the software and the manuscripts. This will also assist the human workers to perform to a higher level and standard compared to before.

3. Generative Intelligence Paradigm

Generative AI models represent an extreme paradigm change to the traditional model organized by task and output properties, as compared to traditional market-oriented AI systems. These models have an innate property of absorbing multimodal inputs and outputs such as textual, visual, and auditory modalities without a fixed set of operative tasks. In this multimodal ability, there is a multidimensional design philosophy that is consistent with current theory of cognitive computers, human–machine partnerships, and immersive virtual worlds. Instead of their limited definition in terms of functionalization, generative AI systems offer a wider system of synthetic creativity, enabling dynamic interaction across modalities and enabling innovative practices of digital co-creation.

3.1 Multimodal Integration

These generative AI models are not specialized in a known number of activities (in the more traditional sense) because they can take in and provide a variety of modalities of activity (text, image, and audio). This form of multimodality, however, is not cost-effective, with the exception that the utilization of multimodality and this kind of service does have strong roots.

Over the period of time, man has continually developed knowledge of generative models. However, a more effective breakthrough is modern approaches of AI (Sengar et al., 2025). Generative models are not goal-oriented, as opposed to discriminative models. They are not concerned with predictions and specific results. Rather, they seek to describe the whole distribution of data. They learn this distribution to produce new samples that are like real samples. These outputs can be imperfect at times, but still a close analogue of real data. They have been written more than once so that the original models, which contain the autoencoders and constrained Boltzmann machine, have been implemented, and one or either of the additions has then been written on it to the probabilistic model, which also contains the VAEs.. They have been written more than once so that the original models, which contain the autoencoders and constrained Boltzmann machine, have been implemented, and one or either of the additions has then been written on it to the probabilistic model, which also contains the VAEs.

3.1.1 Autoencoders

Autoencoders are neural network architectures that are intended to acquire compressed representations of input data. They were initially introduced in the 1980s and were subsequently improved in the 2000s. The structure is composed of two primary components: a decoder that reconstructs the input from the latent code and an encoder that transfers input data to a lower-dimensional latent representation (also referred to as a bottleneck). The primary goal of autoencoders is to reduce the reconstruction error between the input and the output. Autoencoders indirectly established the foundation for generative modelling, despite their primary objective of dimensionality reduction and feature learning. They facilitated the development of probabilistic extensions that could generate novel samples rather than merely reconstructing existing ones by learning latent representations that encapsulate essential features of data adhering to a smooth probability distribution.

3.1.2 Restricted Boltzmann Machines (RBMs)

Restricted Boltzmann Machines (RBMs), which gained popularity in the mid-2000s, were another significant advancement in generative modelling. An RBM is a stochastic, energy-based model that acquires a probability distribution from its inputs. It is composed of two layers: a visible layer that represents observed data and a concealed layer that captures latent features. The two layers are connected symmetrically, but there are no intra-layer connections.

Contrastive divergence is employed to train RBMs, a technique that approximates the gradient of the log-likelihood function. RBMs could generate new samples through Gibbs sampling by learning to model joint probability distributions.

Despite the generative power that RBMs exhibited, they encountered scalability issues and training difficulties, particularly when dealing with large and complex datasets. Even though their influence progressively diminished as more efficient probabilistic models emerged, they continue to be a significant milestone in the historical progression of generative modelling.

3.2 Variational Autoencoders (VAEs)

The following significant advancement was the introduction of VAEs by Kingma and Welling in 2013–2014. The autoencoder framework was expanded by VAEs, which introduced a probabilistic foundation that surmounted the previous limitations in generative capacity.

The latter means that VAEs are defined by the sampling of latent variables by some probability distribution that is normally a Gaussian distribution. To be an encoder, the input values do not necessarily need to be indexed by a given latent meaning to which a given distribution is referred: e.g. it is a synthesis of parameters (mean and variances) of a distribution where latent variables are sampled. This would allow the stereotypes generated by VAEs to be recorded on paper due to this uncertainty as a by-product of such a stochastic encoding process. VAEs are the innovation needed where re-parameterization methodology will be applied. It is an authentic, gradual, and appropriate implementation of gradient-based training, which involves iteratively adjusting model parameters to minimize the loss function, which measures the difference between the actual and predicted outputs.. This allowed training VAEs with the backpropagation model and, as a result, trained a very large dataset.

The VAEs seek to optimize a product of two terms, product-shaped super strategy:

- Reconstruction loss: It is a loss that relates to balancing the outputs and the inputs.
- Kullback-Leibler (KL) divergence: It smooths the space of latent prior distribution (e.g. normal Gaussian).

The VAEs allowed building new imaginable, possible data markup in favour of continuous latent space, Variational Autoencoders (VAEs) make it possible to produce novel, realistic data in a continuous latent space. VAEs assist in the seamless sampling and effective linear performance. VAEs are effective representations for learning, image generation, and anomaly detection tools.

3.3 Generative Modelling with Generative Adversarial Network (GAN)

In the proposal by Ian Goodfellow and his co-authors (2014), GANs were suggested, and provided the biggest contribution to generative modelling. GANs transformed the aspect of AI since they helped to dig considerable physical material and even outperform human work. Beyond being constrained in terms of research, they are even constrained in terms of industries with which they deal, e.g. healthcare industry and diversion industries.

3.3.1 Adversarial Generative Frameworks

These GANs give the programs of the new adversarial model in which the two neural networks enter a zero-sum game:

The Generator (G): A generator is used to create artificial data by introducing random noise. It does this to reproduce variations and outliers that are like actual data. By doing so, it produces what we can call fake samples that are close to the actual data distribution.

The difference (D): An output of a binary classifier which causes a difference between the data and the data generated by the generator.

This is because the strength of the generator is increased to create realistic samples, as well as the discriminator. This process of contesting will, at some point, culminate in the generated data being convincing to the degree that the discriminating process would struggle to tell the difference between the generated data and the actual samples.

3.3.2 Game-Theoretic Approach

The discriminator and the generator play a minimax game in a game-theoretic approach. The generator aims to generate outputs that are as similar to real data. In the process, it will organise its strategy to enhance outcomes in the long run. The discriminator, as it were, questions these outputs to differentiate between real and fake. The combination of these dynamics ensures that the generator polishes its role and achieves a purpose. The integration of LLMs with game theory has the potential to simplify the utilization of game theory in various fields, including networking, and the proposed LLM-enabled game theory framework is effective in network optimization, with potential applications in resource allocation and network security (He et al., 2025).

Figure 1.2 represents "a layer architecture that supports the game-theoretic framework based on the LLM. Part A describes four consecutive layers: User queries are introduced in the input layer, the Retrieval-Augmented Generation (RAG) is in the augmented layer, the responses are generated in the decision layer, and the generated content is presented on the output layer. Part B gives a flow diagram of the working logic and flow of information through these layers in the proposed framework (He et al., 2025).

4. Transformer-based Architectures and LLMs

Generative AI has rapidly emerged from the margins of research to become one of the most visible and impactful technologies of our time. From creating realistic-looking text and images to helping solve complex reasoning problems, generative AI is now a part of education, healthcare, business, and entertainment. At the root of this transformation is a technological innovation known as the Transformer architecture, introduced in 2017, and the LLMs that are based on it. LLMs have made it possible to create a wide variety of practical applications as:

- Text Generation: Such models can write essays, creative stories, product descriptions, and technical documentation. Writers use them to ideate or

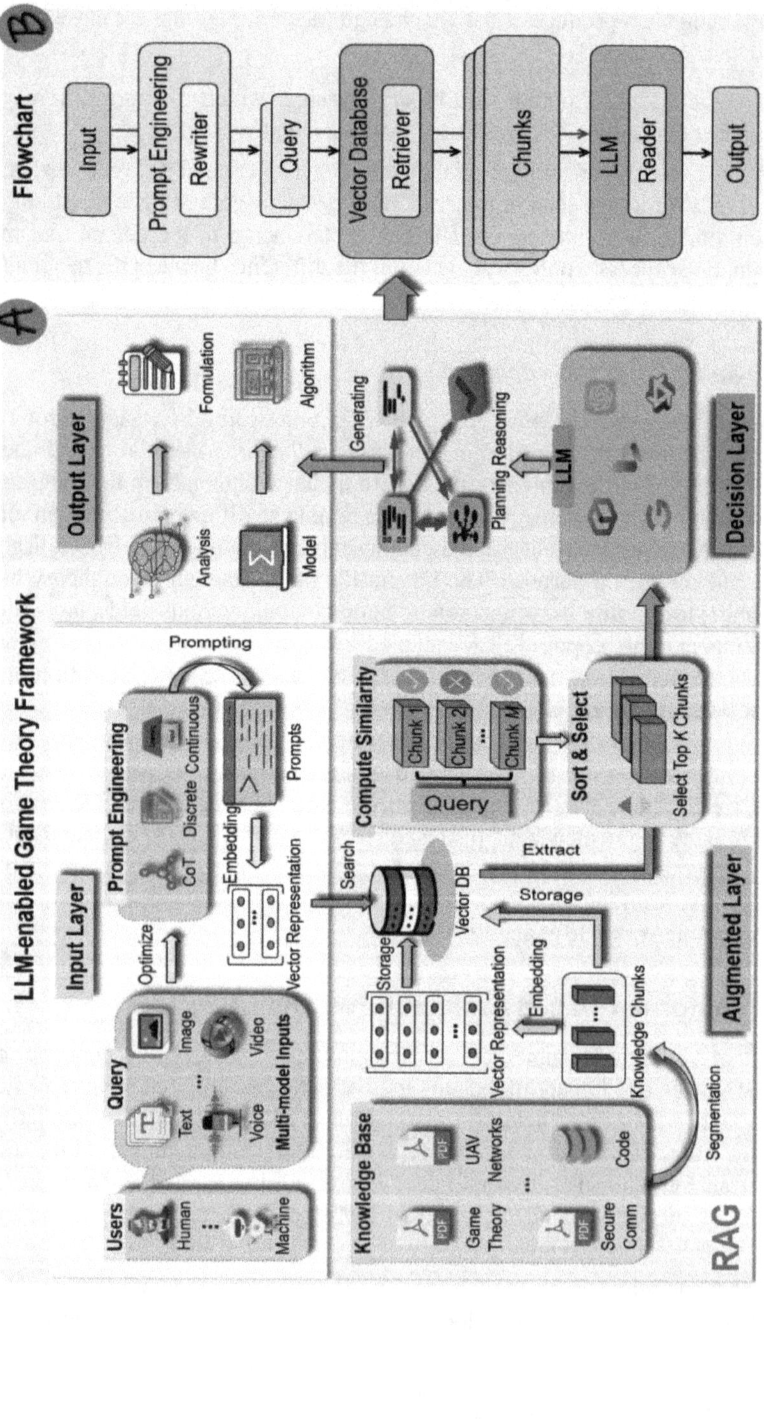

Fig. 1.2 LLM-enabled Game Theory Network.
Source: He et al. (2025).

overcome creative blocks, and corporations use them to write advertising copy at scale.

- Question Answering: From customer-care bots to medical assistants, LLMs can respond to questions in natural and conversational language. Going a step further, they offer context-aware responses rather than simple keyword matching.
- Translation: There have been a bunch of things pushing gifted machine translation ahead, by a bit, but probably the biggest advance has been transformers. Services such as Google Translate now get a lot more fluent and accurate, and they are catching the drift and idiomatic expressions better than earlier services often did.
- Other Domains: Transformers are not limited to textual data:
  - Visualization: caption generation by recognizing from images.
  - Speech: voice communication, voice assistant, and transcription technology.
  - Science: protein-structure prediction, shown by AlphaFold.
  - Business: recommendation engines; predictive analytics. This data implies that Transformers transcend domain-specific tasks and thus become an integrated AI tool.

4.1 The Rise of Transformers in AI

Before the introduction of Transformers, the most common paradigms in natural language processing were based on RNN models, specifically long short-term memory (LSTM) models. These recurrent models took in text one token at a time, and this was inherently slow to train, and the model was vulnerable to loss of contextual integrity over long phrases (Hochreiter & Schmidhuber 1997). In a seismic change in 2017, the seminal paper "Attention Is All You Need" by Vaswani et al. (2017) described the Transformer. By abandoning sequential iteration for a new attention-based mechanism, the Transformer considers the whole sentence at once, giving each token a learnable weight that indicates its importance to the token's representation.

A Transformer consists of two major parts: (i) Encoder: It reads (encodes, processes) the input sequence; (ii) Decoder: It produces the output, whether it is a translated sentence or other artifacts of generation. By processing in parallel instead of by incremental, stepwise traversal, Transformers obtain significantly better training efficiency. Crucially, their architecture is scalable, enabling the model to be built to a very large number of parameters (millions and even billions), achieving results that are far beyond what we used to be able to achieve in earlier generations.

4.1.1 The Important LLMs and Their Contributions

Once the Transformer framework was seen to be useful, researchers and designers began a systematic architectural scaling of the framework, leading to models that radically changed the direction of AI research and deployment.

GPT Family (GPT-1 to GPT-4): First introduced by OpenAI, the GPT series has long been a demonstration of what language models can do when trained on a corpora of billion words and beyond.

GPT-1 (2018): It consisted of 117 million model parameters. Its main contribution was to show that a two-stage pre-training-supervised approach (first unsupervised pre-training followed by downstream [supervised] fine-tuning) achieved better performance than end-to-end supervised learning from scratch (Radford et al., 2018).

GPT-2: The GPT-2 was introduced in 2019, had 1.5 billion parameters and represented a significant breakthrough in the field of generative AI. It generated coherent and fluent text in comparison to previous models. Its introduction brought about a big controversy regarding the moral hazards of such strong systems. Issues revolving around misinformation, propaganda and mass production of realistic fake materials were at stake. It can be used to create fake tales, jokes, and spam etc. (Radford et al., 2019).

GPT-3 (2020): It had a game-changing scale of 175 billion parameters. GPT-3 became famous for its proficiency in composing essays, answering questions in context, and even synthesizing code. Its wide scope made it a real general purpose language model (Brown et al., 2020).

GPT-4 (2023): The apogee of the GPT family, GPT-4 incorporated the most enhanced performance with regards to accuracy and reasoning as well as multimodal perception (unifying textual modality and visual modality). It is fundamental to ChatGPT Plus and other applications deployed today, used in education, research, and in the workplace.

4.1.2 BERT Problem-solving

While BERT, developed by Google in 2018, is linguistically optimized to promote text comprehension, the architecture of GPT is optimized mainly for generative tasks. BERT's major innovation is that it is bidirectional—text is read from left to right and from right to left at the same time, providing the model with a better, more comprehensive view of context (Devlin et al., 2019). This differs from unidirectional models where tokens are taken into consideration in one direction only and thus display a smaller contextual understanding. For example, In BERT the incomplete sentence, *the cat sat on the* ___, is initially transformed into the cat sat on the [MASK], and the missing word is replaced by a special token. The whole sentence is then tokenized and turned into embeddings, with positional information. Contrasting with sequential models, BERT processes all tokens simultaneously with bidirectional self-attention, and each word takes into account both left and right context. The sentence the cat sat on the gives a good contextual indication of what the omitted word is. According to these relationships, BERT makes predictions on the most likely word in the masked place such as "mat" so that the prediction makes contextually accurate completion.

4.1.3 T5 (Text-2-Text Transfer Transformer)

Launched in 2020, Google's T5 provides a powerful yet simple framework that defines any natural language processing (NLP) task as a text-to-text problem (Raffel et al., 2020).

How to say Hello? in French: "Comment ca va?"

Summarization
Input: "summarize: This article describes the effects of climate change."
Output: "Climate change impacts global society."
Question Answering
Input: "question: Who is the author of Hamlet?"
Output: "William Shakespeare"

This unified format made NLP research much easier, as it proved that you could use one model to solve many problems and that there was a consistent way to do it.

Thus, T5 has gained a lot of popularity for its adaptable and flexible NLP solutions.

4.2 Emergence of Advanced Tools

It was common to see trends like LLMs getting popularized through the launch of tools which made these handy for those who needed to use them.

- ChatGPT: ChatGPT, an application released by OpenAI near the end of 2022, was developed to engage in conversation with users on just about any subject. It is flexible to new situations and promotes natural, back-and-forth conversations. It is based on GPT-3.5 and GPT-4, and it provides engaging and coherent dialogue. Its launch directly influenced the culture, changing the way individuals utilize AI in their every-day life.
- DALLE: Another OpenAI project, DALLE is used to generate images from text prompts. For instance, entering in the phrase "a futuristic city in the style of van Gogh" results in a unique painting-like image. This capability enabled new possibilities in art, design, and marketing (Ramesh et al., 2021).
- BARD: BARD is Google's language model, powered by the Pathways Language Model (PALM). Unlike Chat GPT, BARD's focus is on real-time web integration, where it responds with fresh and latest content (Ram & Verma, 2023). The below given Table 1.1 shows the comparison of various AI tools which are used for different applications.

Table 1.1 Comparison of Different AI Models.

AI Tool/Model	*Internet & Tools*	*Best Use*	*Key Insights*
ChatGPT (GPT-3.5)	No	Basic writing, simple coding	Fast and free, but limited and largely obsolete

Table 1.1 *Contd...*

Table 1.1 *Contd...*

AI Tool/Model	*Internet & Tools*	*Best Use*	*Key Insights*
ChatGPT (GPT-4)	No	Advanced writing, coding, analysis	Strong all-rounder: paid version and works in offline mode
ChatGPT + Code Interpreter	Yes	Data analysis, files, applied tasks	Most practical and versatile usage of ChatGPT version
Bing Chat (GPT-4)	Yes	Web search, creativity, live info	Internet-enabled GPT-4 with uncertainty in usage
BARD	Yes	Quick web responses	In the process of updating but still less authenticated
Claude 2	No	Long documents, deep reading	Excellent long-context model with minimal tools, new version; hence, requires more validation

Source: Authors compilation

5. Applications across Domains

Generative AI, powered by Transformer-based architectures and LLMs, has moved beyond being a research novelty to becoming an essential technology in multiple domains.

5.1 Education and Research

Education is one of the sectors most profoundly influenced by generative AI. By enabling personalized learning, AI systems adapt to a student's pace, strengths, and weaknesses. For instance, tools like ChatGPT are widely used as tutoring assistants, helping learners understand difficult concepts, generate practice questions, or explain subjects in simpler terms (Kasneci et al., 2023).

In higher education, generative AI assists with academic writing and research support. Students use AI to brainstorm topics, summarize research papers, and check grammar or clarity. Scholars use it to draft literature reviews, analyse datasets, and even generate code for statistical analysis. While these tools save time, they also raise ethical concerns about plagiarism and overreliance on automation (Batista et al., 2024).

For educators, AI helps with curriculum design and assessment. Automated systems can create practice exams, grade assignments, and provide instant feedback to students. AI-driven analytics identify areas where learners struggle, allowing teachers to intervene early (Zawacki-Richter et al., 2019).

In research, generative AI speeds up knowledge discovery. In science, models like AlphaFold revolutionized biology by predicting protein structures, saving years of laboratory work (Jumper et al., 2021). Experts are using generative AI to produce literature reviews, to query datasets, and even to generate code for statistical analysis. Though these applications do save some amount of time, they also raise ethical issues in terms of plagiarism and undue reliance on automation (Ng & Ho, 2025). For teachers, AI's ability to automate curriculum design and grading is beneficial. Practice tests can be generated automatically, graded, and, of course, instant feedback can be provided.

5.2 Healthcare and Public Health

Generative AI is revolutionizing healthcare through improved diagnosis, enhanced patient care, and advanced research. Its most notable contribution lies in medical imaging, where Transformer-based models interpret radiographs, MRIs, and CT scans with accuracy surpassing radiologists. This enables earlier detection of malignancies, neurological conditions, and cardiovascular diseases.

Generative AI also streamlines clinical documentation, transcribing consultations, summarizing records, and drafting prescriptions (Topol, 2019), freeing physicians for patient interaction. Mental health applications, such as Woebot (Fitzpatrick et al., 2017), deliver conversational therapy for stress, anxiety, and depression, providing scalable and accessible support. Advancements in GAN architectures, including DCGANs (Deep Convolutional GANs), CycleGANs, and StyleGANs, have further enhanced their capabilities by allowing for cross-domain translations (e.g., converting sketches into photos), stylistic modifications, and fine-grained control over the generated outputs (Makhlouf et al., 2023).

5.3 Finance and Business Analysis

The finance sector, an early adopter of innovation, leverages generative AI in fraud detection, analysing transaction patterns to detect illicit activities (Ngai et al., 2011). Customer service is enhanced through chatbots offering real-time support, while predictive analytics improve forecasting and investment decisions. Trading firms employ generative AI to analyse market sentiment from news and social media, guiding stock predictions (Dixon et al., 2020).

Business analytics applications include supply chain optimization, demand forecasting, and customer segmentation, while AI-driven mobile platforms extend personalized financial advice to underserved populations, fostering financial inclusion (Vuković et al., 2025). However, risks include biased loan approvals and opaque algorithmic decisions, requiring regulatory frameworks for fairness and transparency.

5.4 Creative Industries

Generative AI blurs boundaries between human and machine creativity. Tools like DALLE and MidJourney generate novel images from text, revolutionizing design and visual arts. In music, AI composes melodies, remixes tracks, and supports lyric writing. In literature, co-writing platforms assist authors with brainstorming and drafting (Voeneky et al., 2022).

The entertainment industry increasingly integrates generative AI, with platforms like Netflix analysing audience preferences to guide content production (Choudhury et al., 2023). While these tools accelerate creativity, they also raise issues of authorship, copyright, and the devaluation of traditional artistic effort.

5.5 Software Development

Software engineering has been transformed by generative AI through tools like GitHub Copilot, which suggests code, writes documentation, and supports debugging (Chen, M. et al., 2021). This accelerates development cycles, allowing programmers to focus on problem-solving.

Generative AI also enhances cybersecurity, identifying vulnerabilities and malicious patterns. Yet, overreliance on AI-generated code introduces risks if developers neglect thorough review, potentially embedding unseen flaws into systems.

5.6 Policy and Administration

Public governance increasingly integrates generative AI for policy simulation and decision-making. During COVID-19, models forecasted infection rates under different lockdown scenarios, guiding interventions. AI chatbots improve citizen services by addressing queries on taxes, welfare, and public policies, while predictive analytics aid resource allocation in crime prevention and public safety (Totonchi, 2025). Generative AI can make information more transparent, accessible and easier to comprehend. We can also append to it that the things or events which must also be morally ordered are spying, half-leadership, and insincerity in the leadership.

5.7 Computer Ethics and Computer Hacking

GAI can be implemented to enhance cybersecurity through surveillance and guarding of digital systems. It assists in identifying phishing, malware, and abnormalities and may even aid in ethical hacking to reveal the weaknesses (Dasgupta et al., 2022). It exposes vulnerabilities that could be used by malicious actors by simulating attacks. Nonetheless, they can be used to generate deepfakes, phishing attacks, and malicious code using the same technology. In this way, AI can be generated with strong security advantages and threats (Brundage et al., 2018). It is a type of dual characterization feature that results in the imperative to possess and master moral security to ensure accountability and ingenuity.

6. Generative AI and Accountability

Generative AI comes with multifaceted ethical and regulatory issues that necessitate the creation of highly effective accountability frameworks. The more organizations engage with generative AI and apply it to decision-making and content creation workflows, the more they must comply with the principles of transparency, fairness, and long-term human oversight.

6.1 Corporate Citizenship and Business Ethics

The emergence of generative AI signals the appearance of new dimensions in the spheres of corporate citizenship and business ethics, which essentially change the way organizations relate to the stakeholders, handle data, and coordinate creative operations. Ethical usage of generative AI requires uncompromising compliance with transparency, accountability, and fairness, values that ought to be institutionalized in the entire process of making decisions with the algorithms as well as content production. In turn, companies must ensure that their systems of generative AI do not violate individual privacy, acquaint themselves with active avoidance of prejudice, and remain in the position of social responsibility concerning the diverse cultural and regulatory environments where they function. Since generative AI increasingly involves corporate branding, communication, and innovation, its governance principles are likely to be consistent with more responsible guidelines of ethical leadership and sustainable impact, which therefore will help to make sure that technological development does not overshadow the moral imperative.

6.2 Employment and Skills

Generative AI is transforming the way work is done by automating creative and communication processes. Such systems as Copilot decrease the need for entrylevel positions in the realm of programming. This change transforms the occupational structure, particularly on the entry level. The innovative ability of AI systems drives the change (Chen, M. et al., 2021). Simultaneously, it puts workers to the test in developing higher-order skills in areas that are not routine. In such a way, adaptability, critical thinking, and innovation will become more appreciated on the labour market in the future. Generative AI does not simply eliminate jobs; it also creates new demand in augmentation prone roles. Human–AI collaboration emerges as a central driver of labour market transformation. By offloading routine tasks to AI, workers can focus on creativity, problem solving, and innovation. This dynamic positions generative AI as a catalyst for evolving workplace roles and skill requirements (Kasneci et al., 2023).

6.3 Deepfakes and Fake News

With generative AI, it is possible to create deepfake distorted media. These are the kind of outputs that should be viewed as unacceptable and deceptive, and in many instances, driven by money, politics, and misinformation (Chesney and Citron, 2019). Text created with AI can hasten the spread of fake news (Zellers et al., 2019). Therefore, as much as generative AI presents innovation, it has grave ethical and societal issues.

6.4 *Equity, Accountability, and Responsible AI Systems*

The outputs of generative AI, which are trained on massive datasets, are not completely unbiased and free of bias (Bolukbasi et al., 2016). The systematic risks may be developed when there are social biases in data. This can be hiring programs that are biased or gender-related stereotyping in algorithmic decisions (Raghavan et al., 2020). To be open and fair in AI systems, ethical protection and constant monitoring are needed (Arrieta et al., 2020).

6.5 *Privacy and Data Protection*

Another ethical issue arises when the training data utilises sensitive or personal data and violates copyrights. This has been of particular concern when the works of artists are employed without their permission, and this brings about the question of intellectual property rights. Equally, there are threats of privacy breach using electronic medical records (EMR). These practices underscore the conflict between technology and ethics. As such, the protection of privacy and the preservation of creative ownership should be at the heart of responsible generative AI use (Kumar et al., 2020). Or the models are free to issue their own information per regulation (Carlini et al., 2021). Most likely, most of the privacy factors in the EU GDPR will include such a complex GAI system; it is quite difficult to enforce privacy concerns in such systems. International regulations are typically directed at human rights, accountability, and the fairness of benefits sharing, including the AI Ethics recommendation.

The information is thus provided to the discriminant AI by generative AI, hence producing new outputs (Goodfellow et al., 2014).

The key paradigms include:

- Supervised learning: This way of learning is preconditioned by some kind of prediction about a kind of data (LeCun et al., 2015).
- In general, unsupervised learning; the so-called unlabelled corpora, GPT, and BERT (Devlin et al., 2019).
- Reinforcement readmission: It is possible to create a means of restoring the values of the human body and turning it into the acceptor of reinforcement returns (Christiano et al., 2017).

7. Challenges and Limitations

- Resource Requirement: In the creation of the next-generation predictive applications, there have been concerns about the environmental impact of AI. One of the primary criticisms is the fact that AI systems, including GPT-3, are resource-intensive not only insofar as they demand high-performance hardware but also in the overall energy usage and environmental impact.
- Interpretability: Opaque decision-making in artificial intelligence undermines transparency and accountability in important areas including law and healthcare. These systems therefore run the risk of not meeting fundamental

standards of responsibility, reliability and relevance in society (Lipton, 2018; Bender et al., 2021).

- Scalability: Large- scale AI models are typically linked to serious difficulties, such as high latency, the use of cloud services, and the rise of security risks (Zhu et al., 2016; Zhang et al., 2023). Moreover, the long-standing challenges of poor generalization and overfitting also limit the capability of these models to produce truly new and original results. This can be harmful to intellectual property as such restrictions can compromise originality and innovation (Carlini et al., 2021).
- Open-source systems (e.g., Hugging Face) and low/no-code solutions have significantly reduced entry barriers due to democratisation of AI. But, this ease of use also increases the risk of misuse, with AI being one of the biggest risks of abuse and misuse (Houlsby et al., 2019; Floridi & Chiriatti, 2020).
- Hybrid Models: Hybrid systems are less delusional, and more sensitive and precise compared to others (Lewis et al., 2020).
- Autonomous Agents: generative AI–powered agents may revolutionize logistics and creative collaboration, raising ownership and accountability debates (Park et al., 2023; Colton & Wiggins, 2012).
- Smart Cities and Industry 5.0: Generative AI will optimize urban systems and foster human–machine collaboration for sustainable manufacturing (Batty, 2018; Nahavandi, 2019).
- Human-AI Collaboration: The future lies in collaborative intelligence, where AI augments professionals in healthcare, education, and research, requiring trust and governance (Shneiderman, 2022).

8. Conclusion

Generative AI has advanced from theory to a transformative force across healthcare, finance, creativity, governance, and cybersecurity. It offers unprecedented capabilities but also raises urgent challenges—bias, privacy, misinformation, job disruption, and environmental costs. The path forward lies in responsible governance, democratized access, and human-centred collaboration. If guided ethically, generative AI can enhance human potential and foster global progress. If misused, it risks deepening inequalities and eroding trust. Humanity's responsibility is to steer generative AI towards inclusion, sustainability, and shared growth.

References

Arachchige, I.S., Jahankhani, H., Karunanayaka, K.A.Y.R.O. and Hussien, O. A. M. (2024). Exploring the balance between personalisation and automation in human–AI interaction. In Dadwal, S., Jahankhani, H. and Revett, K. (2024), Market grooming: The dark side of AI marketing. Emerald Publishing Limited.Market Grooming: The Dark Side of AI Marketing (pp. 199–234). Emerald Publishing Limited.

Arrieta, A.B., Díaz-Rodríguez, N., Del Ser, J., Bennetot, A., Tabik, S., Barbado, A. and Herrera, F. (2020). Explainable Artificial Intelligence (XAI): Concepts, taxonomies, opportunities and challenges toward responsible AI. Information fusion, 58, 82–115.

Barredo Arrieta, A., Díaz-Rodríguez, N., Del Ser, J. et al. (2020). Explainable Artificial Intelligence (XAI): Concepts, taxonomies, opportunities and challenges toward responsible AI. *Information Fusion*, 58, 82–115.

Batista, J., Mesquita, A. and Carnaz, G. (2024). Generative AI and higher education: Trends, challenges, and future directions from a systematic literature review. *Information*, 15(11), 676.

Batty, M. (2018). Artificial intelligence and smart cities. *Environment and Planning B: Urban Analytics and City Science*, 45(1), 3–6.

Beheshti, A. and Mansoor, W. (2025). Exploring the convergence of Internet of Things and big data technologies in the age of generative artificial intelligence. In Serhani, M. A., Xu, Y. and Maamar, Z. (eds) Empowering IoT with Big Data Analytics (pp. 333–354). Academic Press. ISBN- 9780443216411.

Bender, E.M., Gebru, T., McMillan-Major, A. and Shmitchell, S. (2021). On the dangers of stochastic parrots: Can language models be too big? In Proceedings of the 2021 ACM Conference on Fairness, Accountability, and Transparency, Association for Computing Machinery, New York, pp. 610–623.

Bolukbasi, T., Chang, K.W., Zou, J.Y. et al. (2016). Man is to computer programmer as woman is to homemaker? Debiasing word embeddings. *Advances in Neural Information Processing Systems*, 29, pp- 4349–4357.

Brown, T., Mann, B., Ryder, N. et al. (2020). Language models are few-shot learners. *Advances in Neural Information Processing Systems*, 33, 1877–1901.

Brundage, M., Avin, S., Clark, J. et al. (2018). The malicious use of artificial intelligence: Forecasting, prevention, and mitigation. *arXiv preprint arXiv:1802.07228.*

Burrell, J. (2016). How the machine 'thinks': Understanding opacity in machine learning algorithms. *Big Data & Society*, 3(1), 2053951715622512.

Cao, Y., Li, S., Liu, Y. et al. (2023). A comprehensive survey of AI-generated content (AIGC): A history of generative AI from GAN to CHATGPT. *arXiv preprint arXiv:2303.04226.*

Carlini, N., Tramer, F., Wallace, E. et al. (2021). Extracting training data from large language models. In 30th USENIX Security Symposium (USENIX Security 21), USENIX Association, pp. 2633–2650.

Chen, M., Tworek, J., Jun, H. et al. (2021). Evaluating large language models trained on code. *arXiv preprint arXiv:2107.03374.*

Chesney, B. and Citron, D. (2019). Deep fakes: A looming challenge for privacy, democracy, and national security. *California Law Review*, 107, 1753.

Choudhury, M., Prabhu, S., Sabri, A.K. and Marhoon, H.A. (2023). Impact of artificial intelligence (AI) in the media and entertainment industry. In AIP Conference Proceedings, Vol. 2736, No. 1, pp-41–71. AIP Publishing LLC.

Christiano, P.F., Leike, J., Brown, T., Martic, M., Legg, S. and Amodei, D. (2017). Deep reinforcement learning from human preferences. *Advances in neural information processing systems*, 30, pp. 4299–4307.

Colton, Simon and Wiggins, Geraint A. (2012), Computational creativity: the final frontier? In Luc De Aredt et al (Eds) (2012), Proceedings of the 20th European Conference on Artificial Intelligence (ECAI'12). IOS Press, NLD, 21–26.

Dasgupta, D., Akhtar, Z. and Sen, S. (2022). Machine learning in cybersecurity: A comprehensive survey. *The Journal of Defense Modelling and Simulation*, 19(1), 57–106.

Devlin, J., Chang, M.W., Lee, K. and Toutanova, K. (2019). BERT: Pre-Training of Deep Bidirectional Transformers for Language Understanding. In *Proceedings of the 2019 Conference of the North American Chapter of the Association for Computational Linguistics: Human Language Technologies*, Volume 1 (Long and Short Papers) (pp. 4171-4186). Association for Computational Linguistics.

Dixon, M.F., Halperin, I. and Bilokon, P. (2020). *Machine Learning in Finance* (Vol. 1170). New York, NY: Springer International Publishing.

Fitzpatrick, K.K., Darcy, A. and Vierhile, M. (2017). Delivering cognitive behavior therapy to young adults with symptoms of depression and anxiety using a fully automated conversational agent (Woebot): A randomized controlled trial. *JMIR Mental Health*, 4(2), e7785.

Floridi, L. and Chiriatti, M. (2020). GPT-3: Its nature, scope, limits, and consequences. *Minds and Machines*, 30(4), 681–694.

Goodfellow, Ian J. and Pouget-Abadie, Jean and Mirza, Mehdi and Xu, Bing and Warde-Farley, David and Ozair, Sherjil and Courville, Aaron and Bengio, Yoshua (2024), Generative adversarial nets. In Proceedings of the 28th International Conference on Neural Information Processing Systems - Volume 2 (NIPS'14), Vol. 2. MIT Press, Cambridge, MA, USA, 2672–2680.

Gupta, S., Modgil, S., Bhattacharyya, S. and Bose, I. (2022). Artificial intelligence for decision support systems in the field of operations research: Review and future scope of research. *Annals of Operations Research*, 308(1), 215–274.

He, L., Sun, G., Niyato, D. et al. (2025). Generative AI for game theory-based mobile networking. *IEEE Wireless Communications*, 32(1), 122–130.

Hochreiter, S. and Schmidhuber, J. (1997). Long short-term memory. *Neural Computation*, 9(8), 1735–1780.

Houlsby, N., Giurgiu, A., Jastrzebski, S. et al. (2019). Parameter-efficient transfer learning for NLP. In *International Conference on Machine Learning* (pp. 2790–2799). PMLR.

Jumper, J., Evans, R., Pritzel, A. et al. (2021), Highly accurate protein structure prediction with AlphaFold. Nature 596, 583–589. https://doi.org/10.1038/s41586-021-03819-2.

Kasneci, E., Sessler, K., Küchemann, S. et al. (2023). ChatGPT for good? On opportunities and challenges of large language models for education. *Learning and Individual Differences*, 103, 102274.

Kingma, D.P. and Welling, M. (2013). Auto-encoding variational bayes. *arXiv preprint arXiv:1312.6114.*

Kumar, I.E., Venkatasubramanian, S., Scheidegger, C. and Friedler, S. (2020). Problems with Shapleyvalue-based explanations as feature importance measures. In the 37th *International Conference on Machine Learning* (pp. 5491–5500). PMLR.

Kumar, S., Musharaf, D., Musharaf, S. and Sagar, A.K. (2023). A comprehensive review of the latest advancements in large generative AI models. In Shaw, R.N., Paprzycki, M. and Ghosh, A. (eds) Advanced Communication and Intelligent Systems. ICACIS 2023. Communications in Computer and Information Science, pp-90-103. Springer, Cham.

LeCun, Y., Bengio, Y. and Hinton, G. (2015). Deep learning. *Nature*, 521(7553), 436–444.

Lewis, P., Perez, E., Piktus, A. et al. (2020). Retrieval-augmented generation for knowledge-intensive NLP tasks. *Advances in Neural Information Processing Systems*, 33, 9459–9474.

Liang, B., Wang, Y. and Tong, C. (2025). AI reasoning in deep learning era: From symbolic AI to neural–symbolic AI. *Mathematics*, 13(11), 1707.

Lipton, Z.C. (2018). The mythos of model interpretability: In machine learning, the concept of interpretability is both important and slippery. *Queue*, 16(3), 31–57.

Makhlouf, A., Maayah, M., Abughanam, N. and Catal C. (2023). The use of generative adversarial networks in medical image augmentation. *Neural Computing and Applications*, 35, 24055–24068.

Nahavandi, S. (2019). Industry 5.0—A human-centric solution. *Sustainability*, 11(16), 4371.

Ng, S.L. and Ho, C.C. (2025). Generative AI in education: Mapping the research landscape through bibliometric analysis. *Information*, 16(8), 657.

Ngai, E. W., Hu, Y., Wong, Y.H. et al. (2011). The application of data mining techniques in financial fraud detection: A classification framework and an academic review of literature. *Decision Support Systems*, 50(3), 559–569.

Park, J.S., O'Brien, J., Cai, C.J. et al. (2023). Generative agents: Interactive simulacra of human behavior. In Proceedings of the 36th Annual ACM Symposium on User Interface Software and Technology, Association for Computing Machinery, New York, NY, USA (pp. 1–22).

Radford, A., Narasimhan, K., Salimans, T. and Sutskever, I. (2018). Improving language understanding by generative pre-training. OpenAI. https://cdn.openai.com/research-covers/language-unsupervised/language_understanding_paper.pdf.

Radford, A., Wu, J., Child, R. et al. (2019). Language models are unsupervised multitask learners. *OpenAI Blog*, 1(8), 9.

Raffel, C., Shazeer, N., Roberts, A. et al. (2020). Exploring the limits of transfer learning with a unified text-to-text transformer. *Journal of Machine Learning Research*, 21(140), 1–67.

Raghavan, Manish and Barocas, Solon and Kleinberg, Jon and Levy, Karen (2020), Mitigating bias in algorithmic hiring: evaluating claims and practices. In Proceedings of the 2020 Conference on Fairness, Accountability, and Transparency (FAT* '20). Association for Computing Machinery, New York, NY, USA, 469–481.

Ram, B. and Verma, P. (2023). Artificial intelligence AI-based chatbot study of ChatGPT, Google AI Bard and Baidu AI. *World Journal of Advanced Engineering Technology and Sciences*, 8(1), 258–261.

Ramesh, A., Pavlov, M., Goh, G. et al. (2021). Zero-shot text-to-image generation. In *International Conference on Machine Learning* (pp. 8821–8831). PMLR.

Ravi, M., Negi, A., Bommi, N.S. and Rouf, N. (2025). Evolution of AI-Driven Decision Making with Decision Support Systems, Expert Systems, Recommender Systems, and XAI. IETE Technical Review, 42, 428–465.

Sengar, S.S., Hasan, A.B., Kumar, S. and Carroll, F. (2025). Generative artificial intelligence: A systematic review and applications. *Multimedia Tools and Applications*, 84(21), 23661–23700.

Shneiderman, B. (2022). Human-centred AI: Ensuring human control while increasing automation. In *Proceedings of the 5th Workshop on Human Factors in Hypertext* (pp. 1–2).

Topol, E.J. (2019). High-performance medicine: The convergence of human and artificial intelligence. *Nature Medicine*, 25(1), 44–56.

Totonchi, A. (2025). Artificial Intelligence in E-Government: Identifying and Addressing Key Challenges. Malaysian Journal of Information and Communication Technology (MyJICT), 10(1), 10–24.

Vaswani, Ashish and Shazeer, Noam and Parmar, Niki and Uszkoreit, Jakob and Jones, Llion and Gomez, Aidan N. and Kaiser, Lukasz and Polosukhin, Illia (2017), Attention is all you need. In Proceedings of the 31st International Conference on Neural Information Processing Systems (NIPS'17). Curran Associates Inc., Red Hook, NY, USA, 6000–6010.

Voeneky, S., Kellmeyer, P., Mueller, O. and Burgard, W. (eds). (2022). *The Cambridge Handbook of Responsible Artificial Intelligence: Interdisciplinary Perspectives*. Cambridge University Press.

Vuković, D.B., Dekpo-Adza, S. and Matović, S. (2025). AI integration in financial services: A systematic review of trends and regulatory challenges. *Humanities and Social Sciences Communications*, 12(1), 1–29.

Wang, H., Fu, T., Du, Y. et al. (2023). Scientific discovery in the age of artificial intelligence. *Nature*, 620(7972), 47–60.

Yehia, E. (2024). Developments on generative AI. In Pokhariyal Purvi, Patel Archana, Pandey Shubham (2024), AI and Emerging Technologies (pp. 139–160). CRC Press.

Zawacki-Richter, O., Marín, V.I., Bond, M. and Gouverneur, F. (2019). Systematic review of research on artificial intelligence applications in higher education–Where are the educators? *International Journal of Educational Technology in Higher Education*, 16(1), 1–27.

Zellers, R., Holtzman, A., Rashkin, H., Bisk, Y., Farhadi, A., Roesner, F. and Choi, Y. (2019). Defending Against Neural Fake News. ArXiv, abs/1905.12616. pp 01–20.

Zhang, B., Zhu, J. and Su, H. (2023). Toward the third-generation artificial intelligence. *Science China Information Sciences*, 66(2), 121101.

Zhu, C., Han, S., Mao, H. and Dally, W.J. (2016). Trained ternary quantisation. *arXiv preprint arXiv:1612.01064*.

2 Strategic Role of Generative AI in Present Defence Systems

Bharat R. Naiknaware[1*], S. Adiba Adil Quadri[2] and Akshay P. Deshpande[3]

Generative artificial intelligence (AI) is emerging as a strategic force multiplier in modern defence ecosystems, reshaping how military organizations collect intelligence, assess threats, and make time-critical decisions within increasingly complex operational environments. This chapter explores the transformative role of Generative AI in defence operations, while critically examining the ethical, legal, and strategic challenges associated with its adoption. The chapter synthesizes key defence use cases of Generative AI across intelligence analysis, cybersecurity, mission planning, command decision support, and operational optimization. It further evaluates governance mechanisms, human–machine teaming frameworks, and data-fabric architectures required for responsible and secure deployment. Generative AI accelerates analytic workflows, enhances situational awareness, and enables scalable high-cognition capabilities, including intelligence fusion, adaptive mission simulation, and autonomous system support. These capabilities strengthen predictive foresight and improve both strategic and operational decision-making. However, unregulated deployment poses risks related to civilian safety, information integrity, and compliance with international legal norms. Effective integration of Generative AI in defence demands a balanced approach that aligns technological advancement with human oversight, transparent system design, and robust governance. Federated data-fabric architectures and responsible innovation principles are essential to ensure secure, ethical, and resilient implementation. Embedding human-centric safeguards alongside AI capabilities is critical to sustaining trust.

1. Introduction

Traditional defence systems primarily rely on conventional weaponry such as rifles and firearms, tanks and armoured vehicles, artillery, and manned aircraft, which have been the backbone of military operations for decades. These systems emphasize physical strength, manpower, and time-tested strategies to ensure territorial security and combat readiness. The technological developments have helped in a

[1] https://orcid.org/0000-0001-8343-0505
[2] https://orcid.org/0000-0002-6832-7806
[3] https://orcid.org/0009-0008-1892-4179
* Corresponding author: bbharat.naiknaware@gmail.com

DOI: 10.1201/9781003688174-2

novel era of emerging defence technologies, including artificial intelligence (AI), hypersonic missiles, autonomous drones, and advanced surveillance systems. The fusion of traditional defence systems with emerging AI-enabled capabilities is reshaping military power into a resilient, multidimensional framework capable of countering both conventional and asymmetric threats. Generative AI functions as a force multiplier, augmenting surveillance networks, optimizing mission planning, supporting autonomous platforms, and enabling predictive analysis through the terrestrial, sea, air, space, and cyber domains.

Defence technology has always encompassed a broad spectrum of tools and systems essential for safeguarding national interests. However, while earlier defence structures relied heavily on manpower, mechanical systems, and conventional weaponry, the rapid evolution of digital technologies has fundamentally altered the nature of warfare. The rise of cyber-warfare, AI, hypersonic systems, autonomous platforms, and space-based reconnaissance has pushed militaries towards technology-driven frameworks in which speed, precision, and information dominance play a decisive role.

Modern conflicts increasingly reflect the characteristics of hybrid warfare, where conventional operations intersect with irregular tactics and cyber activities. In this environment, Generative AI becomes strategically vital, enhancing situational awareness, detecting emerging threats, generating simulated scenarios, and supporting decision-makers with real-time, predictive insights. These capabilities not only strengthen operational effectiveness but also redefine the parameters of conflict itself, making innovation and adaptability essential for maintaining a strategic advantage in present and future battlefields (Haver, 2025).

2. Outline of Generative AI

Generative AI is emerging as a strategic catalyst in modern defence, reshaping how military organizations secure information, assess threats, and conduct operations. Its capacity to produce high-fidelity data, simulate complex environments, and analyse large volumes of structured and unstructured information enables proactive threat detection, accelerated decision-making, and enhanced operational readiness. Through predictive modelling and adaptive learning, Generative AI strengthens both offensive and defensive postures across multi-domain operations, allowing armed forces to respond with agility in rapidly evolving security landscapes.

Generative AI supports core defence functions by generating intelligence summaries, simulating battlefield scenarios, and offering tailored recommendations for commanders. These capabilities enable early-warning mechanisms, real-time situational awareness, and more accurate assessments in hybrid warfare environments where cyber, informational, and conventional threats converge. Its integration with large language models (LLMs) further enhances mission planning, cyber-defence, psychological operations, and information warfare (Rashid et. al., 2023).

Powering intelligence and operations, Generative AI significantly enhances defence systems such as cybersecurity, surveillance networks, logistics management, robotics, unmanned platforms, and autonomous weapon systems. AI-enabled target recognition, mission simulations, and automated decision-support tools improve operational efficiency, precision, and strategic planning, giving militaries a competitive edge in challenged atmospheres.

The arrangement of Generative AI also increases acute ethical and security concerns. Issues such as misinformation generation, biases in AI models, the potential misuse of autonomous weapons, and diminished human oversight highlight the need for stringent governance frameworks. Ensuring reliability, accountability, and resilience against adversarial AI is essential for maintaining strategic stability and upholding international norms (Gudla & Sung, 2020).

The strategic role of Generative AI in present defence extends beyond technological enhancement; it involves balancing innovation with responsible use. When implemented with strong ethical safeguards and robust governance, Generative AI becomes a powerful force multiplier that advances national security while preserving human-centred control and operational integrity. With applications in reconnaissance, command and control, and homeland security, AI strengthens both offensive and defensive capabilities (Guo et al., 2021).

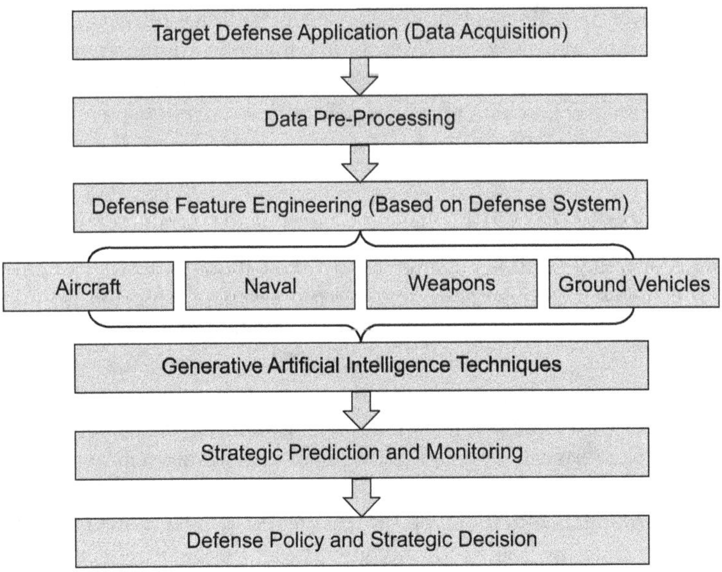

Fig. 2.1 Overview of Generative AI and Defence System.

3. Framework/Architecture of Generative AI for Defence Mechanism

3.1 Target Defence Application (Data Acquisition)

Generative AI technologies including LLMs, diffusion models, and multimodal foundation models introduce transformative capabilities across cyber-defence, intelligence operations, training, logistics, and electronic warfare. These models enhance mission effectiveness by synthesizing complex data streams, automating analytical reasoning, and accelerating decision-making cycles. Figure 2.1 illustrates a layered framework for integrating Generative AI within defence systems.

Within a target defence application, data acquisition serves as the foundational phase for enabling an AI-driven automated defence system. Accurate, timely, and comprehensive data collection is essential for initializing system intelligence and ensuring precise threat detection, system monitoring, and adaptive response.

In the context of Moving Target Defence (MTD), data acquisition becomes especially critical. Continuous collection of system parameters such as network topology shifts, software state changes, configuration updates, and performance metrics allows the defence system to maintain an up-to-date operational picture. By doing so, MTD disrupts adversarial reconnaissance efforts; any intelligence gathered by an attacker quickly becomes obsolete due to the dynamic nature of the system. This ongoing acquisition of real-time data enables the defence architecture to remain unpredictable, resilient, and difficult to penetrate (Naseem et al., 2017). Acquisition can be event-driven, triggered by suspicious activity, or time-based, occurring at fixed intervals to maintain unpredictability. The acquired data guides reconfiguration techniques like IP address mutation, network parameter changes, software and service rotation, virtual machine migration, and the use of redundancy and diversity. Together, these strategies strengthen resilience, reduce attack predictability, and safeguard mission-critical operations against evolving cyber threats (Piñeiro, 2020).

3.2 Data Pre-processing

Data pre-processing is an acute and foundational stage in defence applications, ensuring that raw, heterogeneous, and often noisy data collected from sources such as radar systems, sonar arrays, satellite imagery, Intelligence, Surveillance, and Reconnaissance (ISR) feeds, and cyber activity logs is transformed into a consistent and reliable form suitable for advanced analysis. This stage encompasses essential tasks such as cleaning to correct missing values, filtering out sensor noise, normalizing data formats, and engineering mission-relevant features that support defence functions like target tracking, anomaly detection, and threat classification. A key aspect of defence-oriented pre-processing is the integration of multimodal data streams, enabling a unified operational picture that enhances situational awareness. Additionally, pre-processing techniques are optimized for resource-constrained or contested environments, ensuring high accuracy and low latency even when computing, bandwidth, or energy are limited.

Well-designed pre-processing substantially improves overall performance and trustworthiness of downstream analytics and machine learning models, leading to faster, more accurate, and more informed decision-making in mission-critical operations such as threat identification, battlefield monitoring, and autonomous navigation. Within the broader framework of Generative AI for defence, robust pre-processing ensures that AI models train and operate on high-quality, consistent inputs. This reduces vulnerability to error propagation, adversarial interference, and malicious data manipulation attacks. By strengthening the integrity and reliability of the defence data pipeline, data pre-processing directly enhances mission readiness, operational resilience, and the strategic advantages provided by AI-enabled decision-support systems (Kovari, 2024).

3.3 Feature Engineering

Defence feature engineering in the context of Figure 2.1 represents the crucial process of selecting, transforming, and fusing raw military data into high-quality, relevant inputs (features) that directly enhance the performance of subsequent AI/ML models. Positioned after initial data pre-processing, this stage performs contextualization and data fusion by combining information from disparate sources and refining it specifically for defence applications, such as identifying threats or predicting maintenance needs. The resulting refined features are then categorized by domain before being passed to Generative AI techniques for final analysis and strategic decision-making.

Feature engineering in defence systems plays a critical role in transforming raw operational, sensor, and environmental data into mission-relevant parameters that enhance detection, classification, prediction, and decision-making across all war-fighting domains. By extracting, refining, and optimizing features from diverse platforms, the air, maritime, cyber, and space defence organizations strengthen system resilience, situational awareness, and threat response capability (Nadibaidze et al., 2024).

In aircraft defence, feature engineering focuses on deriving high-value indicators from flight dynamics, onboard sensors, communication channels, and threat-warning systems. Parameters such as speed, altitude, acceleration, angle of attack, and trajectory deviations enable the detection of abnormal behaviour linked to hijacking, electronic interference, or system compromise. Radar and sensor-related features such as radar cross-section (RCS), heat signatures, acoustic patterns, and electromagnetic outputs support aircraft identification, stealth detection, and friend-or-foe classification. Mechanical and engine health features, including vibration signals, exhaust temperature, and fuel flow, enable predictive maintenance and enhance aircraft readiness. Communication and network features such as frequency-hopping patterns or encrypted signal anomalies facilitate early detection of jamming, spoofing, or link degradation. The imagery-derived features from cameras, unmanned autonomous vehicles (UAVs), or satellite feeds enhance object recognition and surveillance, while adversarial-threat indicators like missile lock warnings or jamming signals improve defensive response time. Together, these engineered features form the basis for advanced aircraft defence analytics and AI-driven decision support (Dorsey & Bo, 2025).

In the naval domain, feature engineering strengthens the detection, tracking, and engagement capabilities of ships, submarines, and integrated maritime defence platforms. Radar, sonar, and electronic warfare features are refined to improve range resolution, environmental discrimination, and target classification in complex ocean environments. Weapon system features supporting missile guidance, torpedo tracking, and gunfire accuracy enhance engagement precision and countermeasure resilience. Combat management systems rely on engineered multi-sensor features to rapidly fuse data, identify threats, and orchestrate coordinated responses across multiple domains. Feature engineering in naval electronic warfare systems enhances jamming effectiveness, protects communications, and counters adversarial electromagnetic tactics. The expansion of unmanned platforms such as unmanned surface vehicles (USVs) and unmanned underwater vehicles (UUVs) adds new feature sets for maritime surveillance, reconnaissance, mine detection, and autonomous operations. Cyber-defence features ensure naval networks remain protected from intrusion and support offensive cyber actions when required.

Collectively, feature engineering in defence provides the structured, high-fidelity inputs required for machine learning, advanced analytics, and Generative AI systems. By distilling critical attributes from complex defence data, it enables robust situational awareness, predictive modelling, and rapid, informed decision-making ultimately enhancing force readiness, platform survivability, and operational superiority in contested environments (Mariani & Dwivedi, 2024).

3.4 Artificial Intelligence Classification Model

Artificial intelligence (AI)-driven classification models are essential in defence by processing and categorizing substantial amounts of data originating from heterogeneous sources such as sensors, surveillance feeds, and intelligence imagery. These models employ machine learning (ML) and deep learning (DL), transfer learning (TL) and Explainable AI (XAI) techniques to detect patterns, classify entities, and differentiate between friendly and hostile forces. By enabling accurate data categorization, AI enhances situational awareness, supports strategic decision-making, and facilitates automated operations such as target recognition and surveillance (Bunnag, 2024).

3.4.1 Deep Learning Classification

In AI, DL is driving significant innovation in defence applications. The evolution of DL-based classification models has transformed modern military strategies, influencing both the forms and operational models of warfare. These classification models enable the efficient analysis and categorization of vast, complex datasets ranging from surveillance imagery and sensor readings to communication logs, providing defence forces with enhanced situational awareness and faster decision-making.

Deep learning classification plays a crucial role in two key defence domains: intelligence operations and autonomous platforms. In intelligence operations, DL classification models are applied to classify and recognize objects, vehicles, or weapons in reconnaissance imagery, as well as detect anomalies in cyber traffic to identify potential threats. For autonomous platforms, classification supports navigation, target recognition, and threat differentiation, enabling greater automation while maintaining operational precision (Curran et al., 2024).

3.4.2 Transfer Learning Classification

In modern defence systems, TL has proven to be a highly effective method to enhance classification performance for target prediction tasks, particularly when defence-specific datasets are limited. Rather than training DL models from scratch, TL utilizes pre-trained models trained on large-scale datasets to mitigate data and computational requirements. These models already possess strong transferable feature extraction mechanisms that can be applied to defence applications.

For target prediction, the lower layers of pre-trained convolutional neural networks (CNNs) are utilized to capture general features such as edges, textures, and shapes, while the higher layers are fine-tuned to recognize defence-specific objects, threats, or weapon systems. This classification approach significantly reduces training time while improving accuracy in classifying targets under complex and dynamic battlefield conditions.

Fine tuning shows a central part in this development, certain layers of the pre-trained model are "frozen" to retain their general feature-detection ability, while later layers are re-trained on specialized defence datasets. This enables the model to adapt its high-level representations to domain-specific requirements such as identifying hostile drones, classifying ground vehicles, or detecting missile systems.

By integrating TL into target prediction workflows, defence forces gain the ability to rapidly adapt AI models to emerging threats, ensuring faster response times and more reliable classification in mission-critical scenarios.

3.4.3 Explainable AI (XAI)

In defence systems, XAI is important in enhancing the transparency, trust, and reliability of AI-driven target prediction models. Traditional DL classification model often works as black boxes, preparing accurate predictions but offering little clarity about how these conclusions were reached. Since target prediction directly influences high-stakes defence decisions, explainability ensures that military professionals can understand, validate, and refine AI-based classifications with confidence.

- Transparency and Trust: XAI clarifies why an object or entity was classified as a potential target, helping defence analysts trust the system's output in mission-critical scenarios.
- Accountability and Verification: With XAI, the decision-making path of AI models can be traced, providing an audit trail that allows commanders to justify and verify the classification of targets before action.

- Bias Detection and Correction: XAI uncovers hidden biases in classification models, ensuring fair and accurate predictions that are not skewed by irrelevant or misleading features.
- Enhanced Decision-making: By understanding the reasoning behind classifications, defence forces can make more informed operational decisions, reducing errors in threat detection or target identification.
- Ethical and Legal Compliance: Transparent models help align AI-assisted target prediction with international laws of armed conflict and ethical guidelines.
- Continuous Model Improvement: Insights from XAI allow developers to identify vulnerabilities in target classification models, leading to ongoing refinement and improved battlefield performance.

Key applications include classifying specific ground weapons in reconnaissance imagery, detecting unusual patterns in communication or network traffic for cyber-threat identification, and streamlining the flow of critical intelligence. Through rapid and precise classification, AI ensures more reliable threat detection and timely responses in complex and dynamic combat environments.

4. Target Prediction

In defence systems, classification models driven by ML and DL, TL, and XAI are widely used for target prediction, where they analyse and categorize data to identify potential threats or objects of interest. TL further enhances these models by utilizing knowledge learned from pre-trained models networks, allowing accurate predictions even with limited new data. XAI plays a critical role in this context by providing transparency into the model's decisions, enabling defence operators to understand why a target is classified in a certain way, validate predictions, and build trust in AI-driven decision-making for high-stakes operations (Smith, 2024).

Target prediction in defence systems leverages ML and DL to enhance situational awareness and decision-making. ML/DL models analyse vast datasets from various sensors such as radar, sonar, and optical systems to detect and classify potential targets accurately. Through pattern recognition, deep neural networks can identify complex or stealthy threats that traditional methods might miss. The behavioural analysis enables these models to predict target movements and trajectories, helping distinguish real threats from benign objects and improving the effectiveness of defensive operations.

Transfer learning enhances target prediction by adapting pre-trained models to new, but related, defence tasks, such as detecting different types or sizes of vehicles. By leveraging knowledge from large existing datasets, TL improves accuracy with less new data, making it efficient for identifying novel threats. Additionally, TL enables models to adapt rapidly to changing battlefield conditions or new sensor inputs, ensuring that target prediction remains reliable and effective in dynamic operational environments (Zarrar & Kakar, 2024).

In defence target prediction, complex ML and DL models often used for black boxes make it challenging to understand their decisions. XAI provides transparency by interpreting model outputs, which is crucial for trust and validation in critical operations. XAI techniques can identify key features such as object shape, heat signature, or movement patterns that influence classification, allowing operators to verify predictions. Furthermore, XAI supports debugging and model improvement, ensuring higher accuracy and reliability in sensitive defence applications (King, 2024).

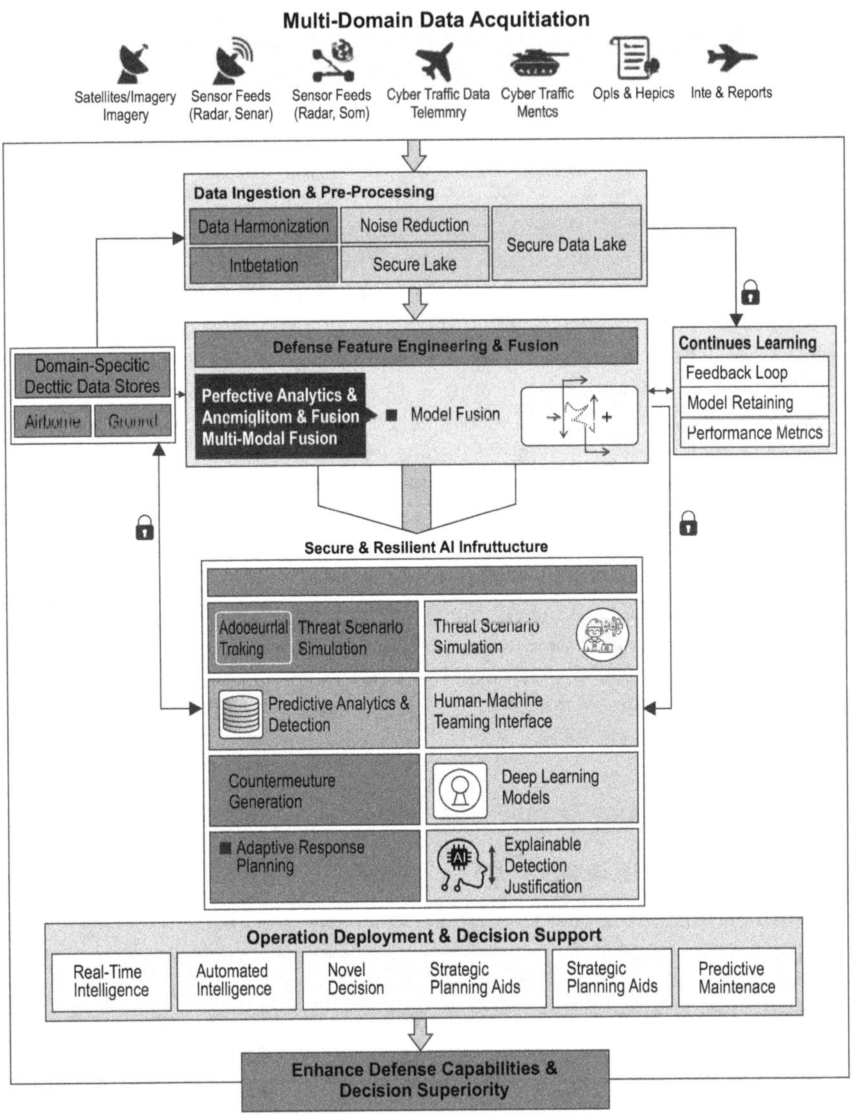

Fig. 2.2 Framework/Architecture of Generative AI for Defence Mechanism.

5. Transformation of Modern Warfare

Modern warfare is increasingly multidimensional and technology-driven, characterized by non-contact engagements using precision-guided weapons, drones, AI-powered systems, and cyber operations. This evolution extends the battlefield into cyberspace and outer space, creating persistent conflicts that blur traditional distinctions between civilian and military domains, and raising complex ethical and legal challenges under international humanitarian law. Figure 2.2 presents a comprehensive framework illustrating how Generative AI transforms modern warfare through multi-domain integration and accelerated decision-making.

Generative AI plays a strategic role by enhancing defence capabilities across multiple dimensions. It can simulate battlefield scenarios, generate synthetic training data for AI models, and aid in rapid mission planning and threat prediction. By integrating Generative AI with autonomous systems and advanced analytics, defence forces can accelerate decision-making, optimize operational strategies, and anticipate adversary actions. Furthermore, Generative AI contributes to the development of innovative countermeasures and adaptive defence systems, strengthening preparedness in an era of highly dynamic and technology-driven conflicts (Varadarajan, 2025).

Modern defence is undergoing a profound transformation driven by technological integration, multidimensional battlefields, and the rise of non-contact and grey zone warfare. Emerging technologies such as AI, UAVs, and hypersonic weapons are central to operations, while conflicts extend into cyberspace, the electromagnetic spectrum (EMS), and outer space.

Generative AI plays a strategic role by enhancing military capabilities across multiple fronts. It enables the simulation of complex battlefield scenarios, generates synthetic datasets for training AI models, and supports rapid decision-making and predictive analytics for target recognition and threat assessment. Generative AI also facilitates adaptive strategies in hybrid warfare, helping defence forces integrate conventional and unconventional tools, anticipate adversary actions, and optimize operations in dynamic, multi-domain environments (Oniani et al., 2023).

6. Key Aspects of Transformation

6.1 Technological Integration

- Artificial Intelligence (AI): It supports actual data processing, threat detection, and autonomous decision-making by analysing large sensor datasets. DL architectures, such as CNNs, recurrent neural networks (RNNs), and transformers, support predictive analytics and complex pattern recognition.
- Unmanned Autonomous Vehicles (UAVs/UGVs/UUVs): Autonomous drones and vehicles conduct reconnaissance, target tracking, and precision strikes. AI integration allows adaptive path planning, obstacle avoidance, and coordinated swarm operations.

- Hypersonic Weapons: High-speed, manoeuvrable weapons rely on AI-driven predictive modelling for targeting, interception, and trajectory optimization in contested environments.

6.2 Multi-dimensional Battlefields in Modern Defence

Modern warfare extends beyond land, air, and sea into cyberspace, the EMS, and outer space, creating complex and interconnected operational environments:

- Cyberspace: Involves networks, communications, and digital infrastructure. Threats such as cyberattacks, malware, and data breaches require real-time intrusion detection, threat classification, and automated response systems.
- Electromagnetic Spectrum (EMS): Covers radar, communications, and electronic warfare operations like jamming, signal interception, and spectrum management. AI supports dynamic spectrum allocation, anomaly detection, and interference mitigation.
- Outer Space: Satellites provide surveillance, navigation, and communications. Space threats include anti-satellite weapons, orbital debris, and signal disruption. AI and predictive modelling aid in orbital tracking, collision avoidance, and early threat detection (Kumar, 2025).

6.3 Non-contact and Grey Zone Warfare

Modern conflicts increasingly leverage non-contact engagements and grey zone operations, involving actions below the threshold of conventional warfare:

- Precision-guided Munitions (PGMs): Enable accurate strikes without large-scale troop deployment. AI enhances target acquisition, trajectory optimization, and adaptive targeting.
- Electronic Warfare (EW): Disrupts adversary communications and radar through jamming, deception, and spectrum manipulation. AI aids in real-time signal classification, threat prioritization, and automated countermeasures.
- Cyberattacks: Target digital networks and infrastructure without physical confrontation. AI supports predictive threat modelling, anomaly detection, and rapid mitigation.
- Grey Zone Operations: Utilize hybrid tactics such as proxy actors, information operations, and subtle interventions to achieve strategic goals. AI analyses social, economic, and operational data to anticipate adversary strategies and emerging threats.

6.4 AI in Military Operations

Artificial intelligence is revolutionizing modern military operations by enabling unified, predictive, and accelerated decision-making. It analyses massive sensor datasets from radar, satellite, UAV imagery, and communications to detect threats and anticipate adversary actions. DL models support real-time target recognition and prioritization, facilitating precise strikes with precision-guided munitions (PGMs) and autonomous platforms. By integrating multi-domain data, AI provides actionable insights for mission planning, adaptive strategies, and rapid threat response, enhancing overall operational effectiveness (Curran et al., 2025).

7. Technological Integration and Strategic Role of Generative AI in Modern Defence

Modern defence relies on the integration of advanced technologies to enhance operational effectiveness across multi-domain battlefields:

- Drones and Autonomous Systems: Deployed for surveillance, reconnaissance, and precision strikes, these platforms provide real-time situational awareness and operational flexibility.
- Hypersonic Weapons: High-speed, manoeuvrable weapons challenge traditional air defence, requiring predictive modelling and adaptive targeting.
- Cyber and Electronic Warfare (EW): It disrupts enemy communications and infrastructure while supporting intelligence collection and coordinated operations.
- AI-driven Intelligence, Surveillance, Reconnaissance, and Degradation (ISR&D): AI processes massive, multi-source datasets to generate a unified operational picture, detect threats, and support rapid decision-making.
- Strategic Role of Generative AI: Generative AI enhances these capabilities by simulating complex multi-domain scenarios, generating synthetic data for AI model training, predicting adversary actions, and optimizing mission planning. It supports adaptive strategies in hybrid, non-contact, and grey zone operations, strengthening decision-making, operational readiness, and situational awareness in dynamic defence environments.

8. Application of Generative AI in Defence

8.1 Border Surveillance

By fusing data from cameras, radar feeds, and sensors, AI-driven border surveillance systems play a vital role in ensuring national security and public safety. Continuous monitoring of borders is essential to uphold law and order, prevent terrorist infiltration, and restrict illegal movement of people and goods. Given the harsh conditions and vast stretches of border areas, constant vigilance demands significant manpower and resources, often leading to risks and even the loss of precious lives of armed personnel. To address these challenges, there is an increasing need for an automated, intelligent border surveillance framework that ensures high accuracy while minimizing resource requirements. The smart border surveillance system powered by AI, which can be seamlessly integrated into Internet of Things (IoT)–enabled devices, enhances efficiency, reliability, and safety in modern defence operations (Yasser, 2025).

These cutting-edge technologies facilitate the identification of border breaches, enable accurate target classification, and enhance the effectiveness of defence operations.

8.2 Unmanned Aerial Vehicles

The AI-powered drones are highly effective in performing both day and night reconnaissance, supporting tasks from border control to comprehensive surveillance.

Disaster situations and security threats pose significant challenges to timely and effective response operations. Unmanned aerial vehicles (UAVs) have recently gained prominence as a transformative tool in bolstering both defence and disaster management capacities. UAV-based frameworks enable real-time data acquisition through aerial imaging and remote sensing, supported by advanced communication systems for rapid and reliable data transmission. Leveraging AI and ML, UAVs facilitate automated analysis, situational awareness, and dynamic resource coordination. Such integration enhances decision-making, optimizes deployment strategies, and ensures swift, accurate responses in critical scenarios. Within the modern defence system, UAV frameworks not only support disaster relief but also play a vital role in border surveillance, reconnaissance, tactical operations, and intelligence gathering, thereby improving operational efficiency, safety, and national security (Monzon Baeza et al., 2025).

8.3 Lethal Autonomous Weapon Systems (LAWS)

With integrated sensor and pre-programmed algorithms, these systems aid in identifying, selecting, and tracking hostile targets.

Modern warfare is undergoing a paradigm shift with the integration of AI and autonomous technologies. Covert swarms of miniature spy drones, unmanned aerial, ground, and seaborne vehicles, sentry robots, and AI-enabled missile systems are redefining the battlefield. While most of these systems are currently operated under human control, the growing penetration of AI is accelerating the transition towards Lethal Autonomous Weapon Systems (LAWS)—weapons capable of independently scanning environments, detecting threats, identifying targets, and executing attacks with minimal human intervention.

The evolution of AI, ML, DL, and big data coupled with improvements in computing power, memory, and high-speed communication is making the weaponization of AI increasingly inevitable. Autonomous weapons, though not fully realized yet, are being developed and deployed in near-autonomous forms by several nations. Within the current defence system, LAWS are poised to enhance operational efficiency, precision, and speed, while reducing human risk on the battlefield. However, their integration also raises critical challenges regarding ethical use, accountability, and strategic stability, making them one of the most significant technological disruptors in modern defence (Mitchell, 2025).

These autonomous weapons systems can engage targets independently, thereby reducing manpower demands.

8.4 Autonomous Armoured Vehicles and Robots

Unmanned vehicles facilitate real-time monitoring, casualty evacuation, and operational support in extreme environments, while robotic systems outperform humans in danger-prone and high-stress zones.

Swarming technology has emerged as a disruptive and game-changing capability that is redefining modern military operations. Autonomous armoured vehicles and robotic systems, when deployed in coordinated swarms, can perform a wide range of defence applications from surveillance and reconnaissance to autonomous offensive operations. These systems can capture critical intelligence by monitoring adversary positions, movements, and activities, while their collaborative nature allows them to cover large areas, enhance situational awareness, and minimize risks to human soldiers.

Equipped with advanced sensors, AI, and ML, autonomous systems are capable of detecting, identifying, and tracking high-value targets such as hostile vehicles, weapons systems, or troops. Their precision targeting and rapid response significantly improve the effectiveness of military engagements. In offensive roles, swarms can execute coordinated air strikes, naval assaults, or ground offensives, overwhelming enemy defences through synchronized manoeuvres (Wang et al., 2024).

Beyond combat roles, autonomous armoured vehicles and robots can support electronic warfare by jamming enemy communications, disabling radar systems, or defending high-value assets such as ships, bases, and command stations. They can also provide critical logistical support, delivering fuel, ammunition, and medical supplies to frontline soldiers, thereby reducing the risks associated with human-operated convoys in hostile environments.

A key advantage of these systems is their ability to operate with minimal human supervision, adapting to rapidly changing battlefield conditions and executing complex missions that would be challenging for individual vehicles. Their scalability and relatively low cost enable militaries to deploy them in large numbers, providing a force multiplier effect and countering adversaries with numerical superiority.

8.5 Data Management

Artificial intelligence enables the Indian Armed Forces to extract actionable intelligence from unused or underused data, improving overall intelligence, surveillance, and reconnaissance capabilities.

In today's rapidly evolving defence landscape, data management has emerged as a critical enabler of operational effectiveness. Modern defence systems generate vast volumes of data from satellites, sensors, drones, surveillance systems, cyber operations, and battlefield communications. Effective data management ensures that this information is collected, processed, secured, and delivered in real time to support mission-critical decisions. By maintaining data quality, integrity, and security, robust data management frameworks empower AI and ML applications to perform accurately and reliably. From enhancing situational awareness and threat prediction to enabling multi-domain coordination and logistics optimization, efficient data pipelines provide defence forces with actionable intelligence at unprecedented speed and scale. Furthermore, secure data governance protects sensitive military information against cyber threats while ensuring compliance, accountability, and interoperability across allied defence systems. Looking forward, data management will continue to serve as the backbone of digital defence ecosystems, enabling precision warfare, autonomous operations, and real-time decision superiority (Rashid et al., 2025).

8.6 AI-augmented Decision Support System

The defence sector increasingly relies on advanced technologies to maintain operational superiority, enhance situational awareness, and ensure timely and effective decision-making. Among these technologies, Generative AI holds strategic significance by offering new ways to process information, simulate scenarios, and guide commanders in complex operational environments (Piñeiro, 2020).

9. Role of AI in Defence through Decision Support Systems

Artificial intelligence–enabled decision support systems (DSS) are transforming defence operations by enhancing speed, precision, and accountability. They ensure operational efficiency by processing vast ISR data to optimize logistics, threat detection, and predictive maintenance. Through transparency and explainability, AI systems provide rationales behind recommendations, fostering trust and compliance with ethical and international standards. A critical aspect is maintaining user trust with human-in-the-loop oversight, where AI suggests options but final authority rests with commanders, ensuring accountability and preventing over-reliance. AI further strengthens situational awareness and accuracy by fusing multi-domain data to reduce false positives and identify threats effectively. Equally important are the ethical and legal dimensions, where AI applications must adhere to international humanitarian law and embed safeguards against misuse, especially in autonomous weapons. AI-driven DSS aids in strategic decision-making, supporting long-term defence planning, simulations, and scenario-based operations for peacekeeping, disaster relief, and counter-terrorism. The role of AI-enabled DSS empowers defence with faster, more accurate, and ethically accountable decision-making while keeping humans at the core of command (Kovari, 2024).

9.1 Enhanced Situational Awareness

Generative AI can analyse enormous amounts of multi-source data such as radar feeds, satellite imagery, battlefield sensors, and intelligence reports to generate a coherent operational picture. This reduces cognitive overload for commanders by presenting information in a structured, explainable form. The ability to summarize critical data patterns helps decision-makers act quickly and accurately in dynamic environments. AI has developed as a transformative capability in modern defence strategy, enabling armed forces to develop enormous amounts of data, generate actionable insights, and support decision-making at speeds unattainable by traditional human processes. AI-driven DSS, powered by data analytics and ML, provide commanders with enhanced situational awareness, predictive modelling, and optimized resource management. However, effective integration of AI into defence operations requires not only technological innovation but also organizational alignment, doctrinal adaptation, and ethical oversight.

9.2 Scenario Simulation and Wargaming

Scenario simulation and wargaming play a critical role in modern defence by serving as virtual laboratories for strategic planning, training, and decision-making. They enable commanders to test strategies in risk-free environments, replicate battlefield conditions, and prepare for diverse threats such as cyber-warfare and counter-terrorism. AI-driven models strengthen these simulations by forecasting adversary behaviour, predicting escalation patterns, and providing adaptive responses. They also support logistics optimization by projecting supply requirements and identifying readiness gaps. By integrating multi-domain data, simulations enhance situational awareness, helping decision-makers visualize operational outcomes under varying conditions. Beyond battlefield applications, wargaming aids policy and strategic planning, supporting defence modernization, peacekeeping, disaster relief, and counter-terrorism operations. In essence, scenario simulation and AI-powered wargaming deliver predictive insights, safer strategy testing, and improved preparedness, ensuring armed forces maintain a decisive strategic advantage. AI-enabled DSS integrates data fusion, predictive modelling, simulation, XAI, and ethical governance to support commanders in tactical, operational, and strategic decision-making, thereby delivering speed, accuracy, and accountability in high-stakes environments.

9.3 Rapid Intelligence Analysis

Rapid intelligence analysis has become a cornerstone of modern defence, enabling faster, more precise, and proactive policymaking. By processing massive ISR data streams in real time, AI-driven systems filter and prioritize critical information, shortening the decision cycle. ML enhances threat detection, identifying enemy movements, cyber intrusions, and covert activities before they escalate. Through multi-source data fusion, commanders gain comprehensive situational awareness, improving both tactical and strategic responses. Rapid analysis is crucial for time-sensitive decisions, ensuring timely allocation of resources and battlefield actions. It also plays a vital role in counter-terrorism and cyber-defence, monitoring communications and detecting anomalies to prevent attacks. Beyond the battlefield, rapid intelligence analysis delivers strategic and policy-level insights, supporting procurement, risk assessment, and international defence cooperation. In essence, it provides defence systems with speed, foresight, and adaptability, ensuring operational superiority in complex and evolving threat environments.

9.4 Decision Support under Uncertainty

Decision support systems play a vital role in modern defence by helping commanders and policymakers operate effectively under uncertain, incomplete, or ambiguous conditions. Using probabilistic models and AI techniques, they transform fragmented intelligence into actionable insights. These systems enable risk assessment and prioritization, allowing defence forces to allocate resources and select strategies that minimize exposure to threats. On the battlefield, DSS support adaptive decision-making by simulating multiple possible outcomes and preparing contingency plans when adversary actions or environmental factors are unpredictable. They also reduce the cognitive burden on commanders by synthesizing complex, uncertain data into clear, interpretable recommendations, while maintaining human oversight. At the strategic level, decision support under uncertainty informs long-term defence planning, including procurement, budgeting, and geopolitical risk management. In essence, DSS under uncertainty enhances resilience, flexibility, and accountability in defence operations, ensuring informed and reliable decision-making in unpredictable environments.

9.5 Human–AI Collaboration and Trust

Human–AI collaboration is central to modern defence, enabling shared decision-making where AI rapidly analyses ISR, cyber, and battlefield data while humans validate and authorize final actions. Transparency and explainability in AI outputs build operator trust, ensuring recommendations are consistent, reliable, and ethically aligned. Human-in-the-loop control maintains oversight in both lethal and non-lethal operations, balancing AI's speed and precision with human judgement and ethical responsibility. AI automates routine tasks, reducing cognitive burden and stress, while collaboration prevents over-reliance on autonomous systems and mitigates potential errors. By integrating ethical and legal safeguards, human–AI teams ensure compliance with international humanitarian law and NATO standards. This collaboration strengthens strategic advantage, delivering faster, adaptive, and accountable decisions, and fostering confidence in joint and multinational defence operations.

9.6 Strategic Planning and Logistics

Strategic planning and logistics are essential for maintaining force readiness, operational efficiency, and adaptability in modern defence. Long-term planning forecasts personnel, equipment, and capability needs, using scenario analysis and threat assessment to prepare for future contingencies. Efficient logistics ensures timely supply of fuel, ammunition, medical support, and spare parts, with AI-enabled systems optimizing distribution and minimizing shortages. Integration with AI-driven DSS allows commanders to simulate operational scenarios, evaluate alternatives, and make informed decisions under uncertainty. Logistics planning supports rapid deployment and joint operations across land, air, sea, and cyber domains. By incorporating real-time intelligence and threat forecasts, defence forces can adapt to dynamic operational environments. Strategic planning also guides procurement, modernization, and alliance commitments, aligning defence investments with long-term goals and emerging threats.

9.7 Cybersecurity and Information Operations

Generative AI plays a defensive and offensive role in cyber domains. It can simulate potential cyberattacks, generate counter-defence strategies, and provide real-time response recommendations. In information operations, it can detect and counter adversarial misinformation by generating truthful, validated narratives. Cybersecurity and information operations are critical to modern defence, ensuring the protection, resilience, and strategic advantage of armed forces. Cybersecurity safeguards military networks, communication systems, and command platforms, preventing disruptions from cyberattacks, ransomware, and data breaches.

Information operations manage the flow of information to influence adversary decisions and public perception, including psychological operations, electronic warfare, and counter-disinformation campaigns. Integration of cyber-intelligence with ISR and battlefield data provides superiors with a complete effective picture, enhancing situational awareness and supporting decision-making under uncertainty. Training through cyber wargaming and simulated attacks improves readiness, response time, and resilience to cyber and hybrid threats. At the strategic level, cybersecurity and information operations guide modernization, secure procurement, and alliance strategies, ensuring national interests are protected while supporting multinational cooperation. These capabilities enable defence systems to operate effectively in complex, fast-evolving cyber and information warfare environments while maintaining operational superiority (Nadibaidze et al., 2024; Dorsey & Bo, 2025).

10. Generative AI for Defence R&D and Innovation

Generative AI is transforming defence research and development by enabling faster, cost-effective, and risk-mitigated innovation. It accelerates design and prototyping of defence systems, vehicles, drones, and weapons by generating multiple alternatives and testing them virtually before physical production. AI also drives advanced materials development, proposing novel alloys, composites, and energy-efficient solutions for armour, stealth, and operational efficiency. In scenario simulation and wargaming, Generative AI creates realistic, risk-free environments to evaluate strategies, tactics, and equipment performance. For autonomous systems, AI generates control algorithms, flight paths, and mission strategies, optimizing performance of drones and robotic vehicles. It also optimizes logistics and supply chains, ensuring efficient deployment of critical resources and maintenance planning. Generative AI enhances cybersecurity and threat modelling by simulating attacks and developing adaptive defences, and supports strategic innovation by identifying emerging technologies and accelerating the pipeline from concept to deployment (Mariani & Dwivedi, 2024; Zarrar & Kakar, 2024; Kumar, 2025).

10.1 Accelerated Design and Prototyping

- Generative AI can rapidly design and simulate new defence systems, vehicles, drones, and weapons platforms.
- It reduces research and development (R&D) timelines by generating multiple design alternatives and testing them virtually before physical prototyping.
- Rapid Simulation and Testing: Generative AI enables the swift creation and virtual testing of defence systems, vehicles, drones, and weapons platforms, reducing reliance on physical prototypes and shortening development cycles.
- AI-driven Design Exploration: AI tools facilitate the exploration of multiple design alternatives, optimizing for factors like performance, cost, and manufacturability.
- Integration with Smart Manufacturing: Generative AI integrates with smart manufacturing systems to enhance precision, automate quality control, and predict maintenance needs, ensuring efficient production processes.
- Real-world Applications: Companies like Lockheed Martin and Boeing are leveraging AI to optimize production lines, reducing assembly times and defects in complex defence equipment such as fighter jets and drones.

10.2 Advanced Materials and Technologies

- AI models can propose novel materials, alloys, or composites optimized for strength, weight, and durability.
- It supports the development of advanced armour, stealth materials, and energy-efficient systems.
- Recent advancements in advanced materials are significantly enhancing the performance, resilience, and efficiency of modern defence systems.
- Graphene and Metamaterials: These materials offer exceptional strength-to-weight ratios and unique electromagnetic properties, making them ideal for applications in stealth technology, armour, and advanced sensors.
- Gallium Nitride (GaN) Technology: GaN is being integrated into radar systems to improve sensitivity, range, and resistance to electronic warfare, as demonstrated by Raytheon's upgraded radar systems.
- High-Temperature Alloys: Developments in aluminium and titanium alloys are enhancing the durability and heat resistance of components exposed to extreme conditions, such as those in hypersonic vehicles.

- Self-healing Materials: Research into materials that can autonomously repair damage is underway, aiming to extend the lifespan and reduce maintenance costs of defence equipment.

10.3 Scenario Simulation and Wargaming

- Generative AI enhances simulations by creating diverse, realistic scenarios for testing strategies, tactics, and equipment performance.
- It enables risk-free evaluation of "what-if" conditions and operational outcomes.
- Recent advancements in military scenario simulation and wargaming have significantly enhanced the realism, adaptability, and strategic value of training exercises. These developments are driven by the incorporation of AI, virtual reality (VR), and innovative simulation technologies.

10.4 Autonomous Systems Innovation

- It supports the development of autonomous drones, robotic vehicles, and AI-enabled systems with optimized performance.
- AI can generate control algorithms, flight paths, and mission strategies for unmanned platforms.
- Recent advancements in autonomous systems have significantly transformed modern defence strategies, emphasizing rapid deployment, multi-domain operations, and enhanced operational efficiency.

11. Ethical, Legal and Strategic Concerns

Generative AI provides strategic benefits for defence by improving decision-making through data integration and scenario analysis. However, it poses ethical challenges, including bias amplification, misinformation, and reduced moral accountability in warfare. Legal issues include accountability for autonomous systems, data privacy, and intellectual property rights. Responsible use requires strong ethical frameworks, human oversight, and continuous monitoring to balance innovation with risk mitigation.

11.1 Ethical Concerns

- Autonomous Weapons and Moral Agency: Autonomous weapon systems (AWS) enhance operational efficiency in modern defence but raise serious ethical concerns. The key issues include unclear accountability for machine-driven lethal decisions, the potential devaluation of human life, and the inability of machines to exercise moral agency. AWS deployment also challenges existing international humanitarian law, requiring updated legal frameworks. Mitigation strategies focus on human-in-the-loop oversight,

XAI, and transparent operational protocols to ensure ethical compliance, accountability, and responsible use.

Misinformation and Deepfakes: Generative AI can create realistic deepfakes, which pose significant threats to national security, public trust, and ethical defence operations. The key concerns include misinformation which undermines decision-making, ethical issues in manipulating perceptions, and legal challenges around accountability. Mitigation strategies involve AI-driven detection, media authentication, human verification, and the improvement of ethical and legal contexts to ensure responsible procedure and maintain information integrity.

- Bias and Fairness: AI in defence systems enhances capabilities like threat assessment and decision support but is prone to bias from training data, which can lead to discriminatory or unfair outcomes. Ethical concerns include undermining fairness, accountability, and trust, while legal considerations focus on compliance with non-discrimination standards. Mitigation strategies involve balanced datasets, bias detection, rigorous validation, to confirm responsible, fair, and trustworthy AI deployment.
- Human Oversight and Control: AI enhances operational capabilities in defence systems, but ethical deployment requires robust human oversight to prevent unintended consequences. By incorporating Human-in-the-Loop (HITL) and Human-on-the-Loop (HOTL) frameworks, these systems maintain human supervision and moral accountability, adherence to international humanitarian law, and operational reliability. Mitigation strategies include operator training, verification protocols, and continuous system auditing to maintain ethical, legal, and trustworthy AI-assisted defence operations.

The deployment of AI in defence systems increases critical legal and ethical concerns. The key issues include accountability for autonomous actions, data privacy and security, intellectual property rights, and compliance with existing and evolving regulations. Ensuring responsible AI use requires clear legal frameworks, robust data protection, and adherence to ethical standards to maintain operational integrity, accountability, and trust in defence operations.

12. Challenges

Defence systems face challenges including bureaucratic procurement delays, budget constraints, technological gaps, and import dependence. Emerging threats like drone swarms and advanced missiles strain air defence, while manpower training, public–private collaboration, and persistent internal and external security issues such as border disputes and terrorism pose additional hurdles to modernization.

Defence systems face significant technological and innovation challenges that impact operational readiness and strategic capability. Addressing these challenges is critical for maintaining national security and technological parity with potential adversaries (Bistron & Piotrowski, 2021).

12.1 Technological and Innovation Challenges

- Technological Gaps: Many nations, including India, face difficulties in developing high-end defence technologies, leading to dependence on imports for critical systems such as advanced aircraft, missile defence, and surveillance platforms. This technological lag can compromise strategic autonomy and operational effectiveness against technologically advanced adversaries.
- Cybersecurity Vulnerabilities: The growing reliance on digital infrastructure and networked defence systems exposes vulnerabilities to sophisticated cyber threats. Developing robust cybersecurity capabilities is essential to protect sensitive defence data, maintain operational continuity, and counter potential cyberattacks.
- Emerging Threats: Modern warfare increasingly involves asymmetric threats such as low-cost drones, drone swarms, and precision-guided missiles. These pose significant challenges to traditional air defence systems due to their low-altitude operations, rapid manoeuvrability, and overwhelming numbers. Effective countermeasures require innovative detection, tracking, and interception technologies.
- Systems Integration: Integrating diverse defence platforms, sensors, and data streams from multiple sources remains a complex but crucial task. Effective interoperability is necessary for real-time situational awareness, coordinated responses, and coalition operations, ensuring that intelligence and operational decisions are accurate and timely.

12.2 Operational and Modernization Challenges in Defence Systems

Modern defence forces face multiple operational and modernization challenges that affect readiness, efficiency, and strategic capabilities. Addressing these challenges is critical to maintaining robust national security and keeping pace with evolving threats.

- Bureaucratic Delays: Procurement processes are often slowed by bureaucratic inefficiencies, resulting in delayed acquisition of new equipment and hindering timely modernization. Such delays can compromise operational readiness and reduce the effectiveness of defence forces in dynamic conflict scenarios.
- Budget Constraints: Although defence budgets may see incremental growth, allocations for modernization and R&D are frequently insufficient. This limits investment in advanced technologies, cutting-edge systems, and the rapid deployment of next-generation capabilities needed to match evolving threats.
- Manpower and Training: Modern warfare requires highly skilled personnel capable of operating advanced systems. The challenges include attracting and retaining talent, developing specialized training infrastructure, and ensuring effective coordination among different military branches to enhance operational efficiency.

- Indigenous Development and Self-Reliance: Achieving self-reliance in defence production is constrained by weak domestic R&D ecosystems and delays in key projects. Dependence on imports for critical technologies slows modernization efforts and limits strategic autonomy, emphasizing the need for stronger domestic innovation and manufacturing capabilities.

12.3 External and Internal Security Challenges in Defence Systems

Modern defence systems face a complex array of external and internal security challenges that significantly impact strategic planning, resource allocation, and operational readiness. Effectively tackling these challenges is essential for safeguarding national security and ensuring regional stability.

- Border Disputes: Unresolved border issues, particularly with China, and ongoing tensions with Pakistan create persistent external security pressures for India. These disputes require continuous surveillance, enhanced border infrastructure, and rapid mobilization capabilities to deter incursions and safeguard territorial integrity.
- Terrorism and Insurgency: Internal security threats, including terrorism in Kashmir and various insurgencies in other regions, demand constant attention from defence and paramilitary forces. Countering these threats involves intelligence gathering, specialized operations, coordination among security agencies, and community engagement to prevent radicalization.
- Geopolitical Realities: Evolving global power dynamics, including China's assertiveness, regional instability, and emerging alliances, necessitate continuous adaptation of defence strategies. Modernization, strategic partnerships, and technological upgrades are essential to respond effectively to changing threats and to maintain operational superiority (Al-Hawawreh et al., 2024).

13. Conclusion

Moving from traditional, manpower-heavy defence systems to advanced, technology-focused, multi-domain systems marks a major transformation in contemporary warfare. The integration of Generative AI with conventional defence systems has improved awareness, speed of decision, and accuracy of operations in the physical domains of land, air, sea, space, as well as cyber. The ability to perform advanced data analytics, predictions, autonomy, as well as decision support, with greater speed, complexity, and accuracy, makes Generative AI a force multiplier, which not only enhances conventional as well as asymmetric defence, but also changes the art of military operations.

Simultaneously, the adoption of Generative AI brings into play multifarious ethical, legal, and strategic challenges. Issues of autonomous weapons, accountability, bias, misinformation, and reduced human oversight raise a strong need for robust governance frameworks. Human-in-the-loop decision-making,

XAI, ethical compliance, and adherence to international humanitarian law will be pivotal to ensuring that such actions uphold moral responsibility and preserve strategic stability. Responsible integration of AI, therefore, requires a delicate balance between innovation and transparency, trust, and control.

Despite the immense potential, defence modernization is set to witness a number of challenges, such as technology disparities, potential vulnerabilities to cybersecurity threats, delays in the acquiring stage, budgetary controls, and threats in the external and internal environment, to name a few. Overcoming these hurdles would require continuous investments in domestic R&D, human resources, interoperability, and the public and private partnership models overall. Finally, the right use of Generative AI is what would shape the future of defence system readiness in the complex and challenging international security environment.

References

Al-Hawawreh, M., Aljuhani, A., & Jararweh, Y. (2024). Generative AI for cybersecurity: Attack and defence strategies (Technical Report, pp. 1–20). *Frontiers in Computer Science*.

Bistron, M. and Piotrowski, Z. (2021). Artificial intelligence applications in military systems and their influence on sense of security of citizens. *Electronics*, 10(7), 871.

Bunnag, K. (2024). Generative artificial intelligence and its military application. *Defence Technology Academic Journal*, 6(13), 28–41.

Curran, K., Curran, E., Killen, J. and Duffy, C. (2024). The role of generative AI in cyber security. *MET*, 5(2), 1–13.

Curran, K., Curran, E., Killen, J. and Duffy, C. (2025). Generative AI revolution in cybersecurity: A comprehensive review of threat intelligence and operations. *Artificial Intelligence Review*, 58, 236.

Dorsey, J. and Bo, M. (2025). AI-enabled decision-support systems in the joint targeting cycle: Legal challenges, risks, and the human(e) dimension. *International Law Studies*, 106, 1–28.

Gudla, C. and Sung, A. H. (2020). Moving target defence application and analysis in software-defined networking. In *Proceedings of the 11th IEEE Annual Information Technology, Electronics and Mobile Communication Conference (IEMCON)* (pp. 641–646). IEEE.

Guo, Y., Wang, P. and Wu, Y. (2021). Design of data preprocessing software for military 1394b bus. In *Proceedings of the IEEE International Conference on Power, Intelligent Computing and Systems (ICPICS)* (pp. 105–109). IEEE.

Haver, Z. (2025). Artificial eyes: Generative AI in China's military intelligence. Insikt Group. Available at https://assets.recordedfuture.com/insikt-report-pdfs/2025/ta-cn-2025-0617.pdf (accessed on 15 February 2026).

King, A. (2024). Digital targeting: Artificial intelligence, data, and military intelligence. *Journal of Global Security Studies*, 9(2), ogae009.

Kovari, A. (2024). AI for decision support: Balancing accuracy, transparency, and trust across sectors. *Information*, 15(11), 725.

Kumar, C.G.R. (2025). The strategic role of AI in enhancing national cybersecurity frameworks. *Asian Journal of Research in Computer Science*, 18(6), 378–389.

Mariani, M. and Dwivedi, Y.K. (2024). Generative artificial intelligence in innovation management: A preview of future research developments. *Journal of Business Research*, 175, 114542.

Mitchell, S. (2025). Artificial intelligence in modern military strategy: Applications, challenges, and strategic implications. *Journal of Military Strategy and Defence Studies*, 1(1), 1–22.

Monzon Baeza, V., Parada, R., Concha Salor, L. and Monzo, C. (2025). AI-driven tactical communications and networking for defence: A survey and emerging trends. *arXiv*.

Nadibaidze, A., Bode, I. and Zhang, Q. (2024). *AI in Military Decision Support Systems: A Review of Developments and Debates*. Center for War Studies, University of Southern Denmark.

Naseem, A., Shah, S. T. H., Khan, S. A. and Malik, A. W. (2017). Decision support system for optimum decision-making process in threat evaluation and weapon assignment: Current status, challenges and future directions. *Annual Reviews in Control*, 43, 169–187.

Oniani, D., Hilsman, J., Peng, Y. et al. (2023). Adopting and expanding ethical principles for generative artificial intelligence from military to healthcare. *NPJ Digital Medicine*, 6(1), 225.

Piñeiro, J.D. (2020). Gaining a cognitive advantage: Artificial intelligence (AI) as a decision support system (DSS). US Army Command and General Staff College. Available at https://apps.dtic.mil/sti/trecms/pdf/AD1177825.pdf (accessed on 15 February 2026).

Rashid, A.B., Kausik, A.K., Sunny, A.A.H. et al. (2023). Artificial intelligence in the military: An overview of the capabilities, applications, and challenges. *International Journal of Intelligent Systems*, 2023, 8676366.

Rashid, A., Kazi, F. and Al-Marzooqi, F. (2025). The use of artificial intelligence in military intelligence: An experimental investigation of added value in the analysis process. *Frontiers in Human Dynamics*, 13, 1–14.

Smith, G.K. (2024). Strategic integration of generative AI: Opportunities, challenges, and organizational impacts. *Law, Economics and Society*, 1(1), 156–168.

Varadarajan, V. (2025). Ethical and adversarial risks of generative AI in military cyber tools. *Journal of Information Systems Engineering and Management*, 10(53s), 1036–1048.

Wang, X., Liu, C., Zhong, H. and Zhou, J. (2024). The impacts of generative artificial intelligence in knowledge discovery and generation for cyber defence. *Journal of Cybersecurity and Information Systems*, 2024(2), 230–243.

Yasser, M. (2025). Investigating the harmful implications of generative AI in the military field. *International Journal of Innovative Science and Research Technology*, 10(9), 2046–2048.

Zarrar, H. and Kakar, S.A. (2024). Generative artificial intelligence and its military applications by the US and China—Lessons for South Asia. *Journal of Computing & Biomedical Informatics* Volume 7 (Special Issue), 1–10.

3 Designing of Drone Swarms Using Generative AI

Rishabh Garg[1*] and Vimal Dubey[2]

This chapter examines the creative use of generative artificial intelligence (AI) in the planning and directing of drone swarms for military aerospace plans. Our framework utilizes sophisticated generative models to produce real-time decision-making algorithms, adaptive flight patterns, and optimal swarm configurations on its own. To ensure resilience to changing battlefield conditions, the method incorporates deep learning algorithms to mimic a variety of operating scenarios. A case study showing improved mission success rates in combat simulations and a new algorithm for swarm scalability are two important contributions. By addressing existing constraints in manual swarm design, our work opens the door for autonomous airborne systems of the future.

1. Introduction

1.1 Background on Military Applications of Drones

Over the past two decades, unmanned aerial vehicles (UAVs), commonly referred to as drones, have transformed from niche experimental platforms into indispensable assets for modern defence operations. Militaries across the globe now rely heavily on drones for a wide spectrum of missions, ranging from reconnaissance and surveillance to precision strikes, logistics, and electronic warfare, as noted by Endsley 2020). Unlike manned aircraft, drones offer the advantage of minimizing risk to human pilots while maintaining the ability to access highly contested or hostile environments.

The evolution of drones has paralleled broader shifts in warfare. Traditional large-scale battles are increasingly being replaced by hybrid, asymmetric, and urban conflicts where rapid information gathering and precision engagement are critical, as discussed in *Army of None* (Scharre 2018). In such contexts, drones provide tactical superiority through their ability to hover, track moving targets, and operate at altitudes and speeds that manned aircraft may find difficult to sustain. For instance, in recent conflicts, small quadcopters have been used not only to monitor enemy movements but also to deliver small munitions or disrupt communication

1 https://orcid.org/0009-0001-6219-1119
2 https://orcid.org/0009-0008-4819-2861
* Corresponding author: rishabh1994garg@gmail.com

DOI: 10.1201/9781003688174-3

networks. While single drones are already valuable, their effectiveness is constrained by limitations in coverage, endurance, and vulnerability to jamming or interception. These challenges have motivated militaries to explore the use of drone swarms—large numbers of interconnected UAVs operating collaboratively—to overwhelm defences and achieve objectives that would be impossible for individual drones.

1.2 Motivation for Swarm-based Aerial Systems

The concept of swarm robotics is inspired by nature, particularly the coordinated behaviour of insects, birds, and fish. Just as flocks of birds can navigate long distances in synchrony without centralized control, drone swarms can perform missions where cooperation and distributed intelligence enhance overall capability. From a defence perspective, swarms introduce several unique advantages, including scalability, resilience, adaptability, and force multiplication (Brambilla et al. 2013):

- Scalability and Coverage: Swarms can blanket large geographical areas, ensuring surveillance of multiple regions simultaneously.
- Resilience: The distributed nature of swarms makes them resistant to single points of failure. Even if a few drones are neutralized, the mission can continue effectively.
- Adaptability: Swarms can dynamically reconfigure themselves to respond to evolving battlefield conditions, such as changes in enemy positions or weather disruptions.
- Force Multiplication: Coordinated swarms can overwhelm adversarial defences by presenting multiple simultaneous threats, complicating interception efforts.

Swarm-based aerial systems are attractive not only because of the potential of their use in the context of the tactic, but also because of the possibility to transform the balance in the war situation. Theoretically, hundreds of cheap drones would be able to counteract even sophisticated yet expensive air defences, which would change the economics of war.

In addition to pure combat, drone swarms can be useful in humanitarian efforts and support. They may be used in search and rescue operations or in rapid mapping of disaster areas or in providing medical supplies to areas where people have restricted access. All these dual-use capabilities have enabled swarm technology to become the subject of defence and non-defence research activity.

1.3 Limitations of Traditional Swarm Design Approaches

Although drone swarms have a potential, their usage in practice remains extremely problematic. Conventional methods towards swarm design usually consider rule-based programming or heuristic optimization methods. Even though such techniques can generate predetermined coordination patterns, they cannot deal with the unpredictable and hectic aspects of the real-world battlefield.

Some of its major weaknesses are:

- Patterns of Static Behaviour: Pre-programmed flight plans are usually not flexible enough to handle any last minute fluctuations like electronic jamming, environmental risk, or enemy tactics.
- Scalability Problems: Small group drone algorithms might not be easily scaled to hundreds and thousands of UAVs, resulting in a communication bottleneck and coordination failure.
- Restricted Real-time Decision-making: Traditional swarm algorithms often consume considerable computational power, and in order to allow drones to make decisions on-the-fly, the drone requires substantial computational capacity.
- Exposure to Countermeasures: The enemy forces that have advanced radar, GPS spoofing, or cyberattacks can take advantage of vulnerabilities in inflexibly designed swarm protocols.

Simply put, traditional approaches lack the level of freedom, flexibility, and agility of swarm activities in the next generation. The future battlefield requires the type of system that can learn, evolve, and even predict instead of being provided with pre-written code to follow.

1.4 Role of Generative AI in Defence Aerospace

Recently, generative artificial intelligence (AI) has become a game changer that has the potential of generating new solutions instead of analysing existing data. In contrast to the classical AI, which typically includes classification or prediction, generative models can be used to generate new strategies, patterns, and configurations using the acquired knowledge. This feature renders them peculiar to the creation and organization of drone swarms.

Generative AI can be used to model thousands of possible battlefield scenarios and generate swarm strategies optimally suited to each scenario by utilizing architectures like Generative Adversarial Networks (GANs), Variational Autoencoders (VAEs), and transformer-based models, as demonstrated by Chen et al 2022). Generative AI has the potential to suggest new shapes in a crowded airspace that reduce radar scans and maximize the area covered. Likewise, in the case of electronic countermeasures, the system might also create other communication channels to support swarm cohesion.

The benefits of generative AI in this regard are:

- Real-time Adaptation: Generative models can respond to changes in the environment by producing new tactics in real time, making sure that drone swarms are dynamic.
- New Structures: AI-created strategies can have unusual capabilities that surpass human intuition and find behaviours of swarms that humans could not have thought of.

- Scalability: The algorithms of generative AI can be trained to coordinate hundreds or thousands of drones at the same time, which is a solution to the bottlenecks of scalability.
- Resilience and Robustness: Swarms prepared via adversarial training are capable of surviving disruptions, e.g. jamming, spoofing, or partial system failure.

Additionally, the application of generative AI to the field of defence aerospace is consistent with general tendencies in autonomous warfare. Defence organizations identify swarms as a way to move beyond the reliance on manual control and go faster, but generative AI provides a way to achieve swarms that are not just self-organizing but that also think strategically in an uncertain world.

To sum up, drone swarm technology can be combined with generative AI to reinvent aerial warfare. With the means of overcoming the drawbacks of conventional methods and providing adaptive, scalable, and innovative features, generative AI-driven swarms could be seen as a massive advancement towards the future of autonomous defence systems.

2. Fundamentals of Drone Swarm Systems

2.1 Role of Generative AI in Defence Aerospace

Swarm intelligence refers to the collective behaviour of decentralized, self-organized systems, often inspired by phenomena observed in nature. Ant colonies, flocks of birds, and schools of fish exemplify how simple agents, operating under local rules and without central command, can display highly coordinated and adaptive group behaviours (Şahin 2005). When applied to UAVs, swarm intelligence enables drones to function as members of a larger collective rather than as isolated machines.

Several defining characteristics make swarm intelligence particularly relevant for drone operations:

- Decentralization: Swarms operate without a single leader. Each drone follows simple rules and reacts to local conditions, yet the group achieves complex global behaviour. This makes the swarm less vulnerable to the failure of individual units.
- Self-Organization: Coordination emerges naturally from the interactions among drones rather than being imposed externally. This property allows the swarm to adapt dynamically to environmental changes or adversarial interference.
- Scalability: The same principles that guide a swarm of ten drones can be extended to hundreds or thousands, enabling mission scalability without the need for entirely new control structures.
- Robustness: Redundancy in the system ensures that the failure or destruction of a few drones does not compromise the entire mission.

- Adaptability: By adjusting to new information in real time, swarms can change formation, redirect focus, or split into subgroups to manage multiple objectives simultaneously.

These properties provide the foundation for drone swarms to operate effectively in highly uncertain and adversarial environments. Unlike centrally controlled UAV fleets, swarm intelligence allows flexibility and survivability under conditions of disruption.

2.2 Swarm Coordination Models

To replicate natural swarm behaviours, several computational models and algorithms have been developed. These models serve as the mathematical and conceptual basis for coordinating large groups of drones in a distributed manner.

- Boids Model: The Boids model, originally proposed to simulate flocking birds, remains one of the most influential approaches in swarm robotics (Reynolds 1987). Each agent (or "boid") follows three simple rules: separation (avoid crowding neighbours), alignment (steer towards the average heading of neighbours), and cohesion (move towards the average position of neighbours). When applied to drones, these rules create lifelike aerial formations without requiring centralized instructions. The simplicity of the Boids model makes it computationally efficient, though it may struggle in complex environments where adversaries actively attempt disruption.
- Particle Swarm Optimization (PSO): Particle Swarm Optimization was designed as a search and optimization technique inspired by social behaviour patterns in flocks and schools. In drone swarms, each UAV is treated as a "particle" exploring a solution space, such as optimal paths or formations. Individual drones adjust their flight trajectories based on their own experience and the best solutions identified by their peers. This model is effective for optimization tasks, such as identifying safe routes through hostile terrain or locating targets.
- Ant Colony Optimization (ACO): Ant Colony Optimization is inspired by the behaviour exhibited by ants in seeking the best paths to the food source. ACO-aided drones deposit digital equivalents of pheromones (i.e., shared data signals) to indicate successful routes or behaviours. Less effective strategies are likely revisited by other drones, increasing the intensity of the paths followed. This is an iterative feedback mechanism that enables swarms to pinpoint solutions that are efficient. The area coverage, coordinated resource allocation, and pathfinding are particularly well supported by ACO.
- Other Emerging Models: Beyond these classical approaches, new hybrid and bio-inspired models are gaining traction. For example, models inspired by immune systems emphasize adaptability and resilience to threats, while those derived from slime mould behaviour focus on resource-efficient network formation. These innovations illustrate how swarm coordination is an evolving field, with researchers continually exploring new metaphors from nature to enhance UAV collectives.

2.3 Communication Protocols in Drone Swarms

Communication lies at the heart of swarm coordination. Without reliable information exchange, decentralized intelligence cannot function effectively. However, swarm communication must balance efficiency, resilience, and security.

- Local vs Global Communication: Swarm communication can be limited to local neighbours or extended to the entire group. Local communication reduces bandwidth consumption and enhances scalability, while global communication provides a more unified situational awareness but is harder to maintain under adversarial conditions.
- Wireless Ad Hoc Networks: Many drone swarms employ ad hoc wireless networks that form dynamically as drones move. These networks allow flexible, topology-independent communication without relying on fixed infrastructure.
- Latency and Bandwidth Constraints: In a swarm with hundreds of drones, communication traffic can become overwhelming. Protocols must ensure low latency and prioritize critical data, such as collision avoidance or threat alerts, over less urgent updates.
- Security Considerations: Adversaries may attempt to jam, spoof, or intercept swarm communications. Encryption, frequency hopping, and resilient routing algorithms are therefore essential to maintaining swarm integrity.
- Consensus Mechanisms: Communication protocols often incorporate consensus algorithms to ensure that the swarm reaches collective decisions despite incomplete or delayed information. Techniques derived from distributed computing, such as gossip protocols, are frequently adapted for this purpose.

An effective communication system must therefore achieve a delicate balance—facilitating cooperation while safeguarding the swarm against external interference.

2.4 Current Applications in Military and Civilian Domains

Drone swarm research is no longer confined to theoretical models. Both defence and civilian sectors have demonstrated practical applications that illustrate the transformative potential of swarm technology.

2.4.1 Military Applications

- Reconnaissance and Surveillance: Swarms of small drones can cover large battlefields simultaneously, offering real-time intelligence that surpasses what a single UAV can achieve.
- Offensive Operations: Coordinated swarms have been tested in simulations and limited real-world scenarios to overwhelm enemy defences, confuse radar systems, or deliver distributed strikes.

- Electronic Warfare: Drones can be deployed in coordinated patterns to jam enemy communications or mislead targeting systems through decoy manoeuvres.
- Logistics Support: Swarms can transport supplies or establish temporary communication relays in environments where conventional logistics are challenged.

2.4.2 Civilian Applications

- Disaster Response: Swarms have been used to map earthquake zones, locate survivors in collapsed structures, and deliver essential medical supplies in inaccessible areas.
- Environmental Monitoring: Large numbers of drones can gather distributed data on air quality, wildlife populations, or agricultural conditions more efficiently than traditional methods.
- Urban Management: Emerging projects are exploring the use of drone swarms for traffic monitoring, crowd control, and public safety in large cities.
- Entertainment and Commercial Use: Drone light shows have become a striking example of swarm coordination in non-military contexts, while delivery services are experimenting with coordinated fleets for rapid distribution.

The dual-use nature of drone swarms raises both opportunities and challenges. While civilian applications showcase the humanitarian potential of this technology, the same principles can be adapted for high-intensity conflict, raising pressing questions about security and ethics.

3. Generative AI for Swarm Design

3.1 Overview of Generative AI Models (GANs, VAEs, Transformers, Diffusion Models)

Generative AI represents a class of algorithms designed not only to interpret or classify data but also to create new data that resembles the patterns found in training datasets. Unlike conventional AI systems that focus on decision-making based on pre-existing rules or predictive models, generative AI systems learn complex distributions and generate novel outputs—ranging from images and audio to structured strategies and movement patterns. This property is of particular value in swarm design, where creativity, adaptability, and diversity of solutions are critical.

Several foundational models form the backbone of generative AI (also see Table 3.1):

- Generative Adversarial Networks (GANs): Introduced in the mid-2010s, GANs operate through a competition between two neural networks: a generator and a discriminator. The generator seeks to produce data samples that mimic real-world data, while the discriminator attempts to distinguish between authentic and generated samples. Over successive iterations, this adversarial process enables the generator to create increasingly realistic and high-quality outputs. In the context of drone swarms, GANs can be used to generate flight trajectories, test adversarial scenarios, or design swarm formations that are difficult for opponents to predict.

- Variational Autoencoders (VAEs): VAEs work by encoding input data into a compressed latent representation and then decoding it back into reconstructed data. By sampling from the latent space, VAEs can generate entirely new but plausible variations of input data. For swarm design, VAEs offer a structured way to explore a range of potential flight paths or coordination patterns, enabling developers to identify optimal configurations under varying mission conditions.
- Transformers: Originally developed for natural language processing, transformers have revolutionized generative AI by enabling models to capture long-range dependencies and contextual relationships. Unlike earlier models that struggled with sequence data, transformers excel at processing ordered information, making them suitable for dynamic, time-dependent tasks such as multi-drone coordination. A transformer-based model could, for example, generate context-aware flight commands by considering both immediate surroundings and long-term mission goals.
- Diffusion Models: Diffusion models represent a more recent development in generative AI. They operate by gradually transforming random noise into coherent data samples through a step-by-step denoising process. While initially prominent in image synthesis, diffusion models are now being explored for complex problem-solving and motion planning. In drone swarm systems, diffusion-based approaches could help simulate uncertain environments—such as turbulent weather or contested battlefields—and generate robust flight strategies that evolve gracefully from uncertainty to clarity.

Table 3.1 Comparison of Generative AI Models for Swarm Design.

Model	*Core Principle*	*Strengths in Swarm Design*	*Limitations/Challenges*
GANs	Adversarial training between generator & discriminator	Generates novel swarm formations, adversarial scenario simulation	Training instability, mode collapse
VAEs	Latent space encoding & decoding	Exploration of diverse flight paths, structured coordination	Outputs less sharp/ precise than GANs
Transformers	Attention mechanism for sequence modelling	Context-aware coordination, scalable to large swarms	Computationally expensive, needs large data
Diffusion Models	Stepwise denoising of random noise	Robust strategy generation in uncertain environments	Slow generation process, still emerging in non-vision tasks

Together, these generative AI frameworks provide a diverse toolkit for tackling the intricate challenges of swarm design. Each has strengths and trade-offs, and hybrid approaches that combine features from multiple models are increasingly seen as promising avenues for defence applications.

3.2 Role of Generative AI in Complex System Design

Complex systems, such as drone swarms, are characterized by emergent behaviour, nonlinear interactions, and high sensitivity to environmental conditions. Designing such systems using traditional top-down methods is often inefficient and fails to capture the depth of possible interactions. Generative AI introduces a paradigm shift by offering bottom-up, data-driven design processes that mirror the complexity of real-world dynamics.

In the realm of swarm design, generative AI serves several crucial roles:

- Pattern Generation and Exploration: By learning from simulations and real-world flight data, generative AI can propose new flight patterns or coordination strategies that balance competing objectives such as coverage, stealth, and energy efficiency.
- Scenario Simulation: Generative models can construct synthetic battlefield or operational environments, allowing developers to test swarm strategies against a wide range of conditions without requiring expensive physical experiments.
- Optimization under Uncertainty: Unlike static algorithms, generative AI systems excel at working within uncertain or incomplete information environments. This ability is vital in defence contexts, where adversary actions and environmental variables cannot be predicted with certainty.
- Adaptive Control: Generative AI can provide real-time adjustments to swarm behaviour by dynamically generating new strategies as the mission unfolds. This level of autonomy ensures that drone swarms remain effective even when conditions deviate from expectations.

Generative AI essentially acts as a design collaborator, not just executing pre-defined strategies but continuously proposing and refining innovative solutions. This role moves swarm design closer to systems capable of genuine creativity, bridging the gap between human strategic intent and autonomous execution.

3.3 Generative vs Traditional Algorithmic Approaches

Traditional approaches to swarm design often rely on deterministic or heuristic methods. These include rule-based algorithms, graph-theoretic models, and optimization techniques that are programmed to achieve specific outcomes. While such methods are effective for narrowly defined tasks, they are constrained by limited adaptability and often fail when conditions fall outside the anticipated range.

Generative AI diverges from these approaches in several ways:

- Creativity vs Conformity: Traditional algorithms optimize within known solution spaces, while generative AI explores and proposes entirely new possibilities. This creativity allows drone swarms to exhibit strategies that humans might not have designed explicitly.
- Dynamic Adaptation: Traditional models require manual reconfiguration to adapt to new environments, whereas generative AI can generate fresh solutions in real time, ensuring agility in unpredictable contexts.
- Scalability: Traditional approaches often experience performance bottlenecks as the number of drones increases. Generative models, particularly transformers and GANs, can scale more efficiently by generalizing coordination strategies across larger groups.
- Data Utilization: Generative AI thrives on large, diverse datasets, enabling it to learn nuanced interactions between drones and their environments. Traditional methods, in contrast, may rely on simplified abstractions that overlook critical dynamics.
- Resilience to Adversaries: In adversarial settings, generative AI can simulate potential enemy tactics and produce counter-strategies proactively. Traditional algorithms, which tend to be rigid, are more vulnerable to being outmanoeuvred once adversaries understand their logic.

This comparison highlights why defence aerospace is increasingly shifting focus towards generative approaches. They not only enhance technical performance but also reduce reliance on human operators for micromanagement, allowing personnel to focus on higher-level strategic decision-making.

3.4 Opportunities and Challenges

The integration of generative AI into swarm design offers a transformative leap forward, but it is accompanied by significant opportunities and equally important challenges.

3.4.1 Opportunities

- Enhanced Autonomy: Generative AI can enable swarms to conduct missions with minimal human oversight, significantly reducing operator workload.
- Novel Strategy Discovery: By simulating vast numbers of scenarios, generative systems can uncover unconventional tactics that enhance mission success rates.
- Cost Efficiency: Virtual training environments powered by generative AI reduce the need for costly live experiments, accelerating development cycles.
- Cross-Domain Applications: Insights from military swarm design can be transferred to civilian domains such as disaster relief, environmental monitoring, and urban planning.

- Human–AI Collaboration: Generative AI can act as a creative partner, offering solutions while leaving ultimate strategic decisions to human commanders.

3.4.2 Challenges

- Data Dependence: Generative models require vast, high-quality datasets for effective training. In defence contexts, such datasets may be scarce or classified.
- Computational Demands: Training and deploying generative models often require significant computational resources, limiting their accessibility for real-time operations in resource-constrained environments.
- Security Risks: Generative AI models themselves may become targets of adversarial attacks, where manipulated inputs could mislead swarms into undesirable behaviours.
- Ethical and Legal Concerns: The deployment of autonomous swarms powered by generative AI raises profound questions about accountability, civilian safety, and compliance with international humanitarian laws.
- Validation and Trust: Unlike deterministic algorithms, generative models may propose strategies that are difficult to interpret or validate. Establishing trust in AI-generated decisions is a critical barrier to widespread adoption.

Balancing these opportunities and challenges requires a careful approach that blends technological innovation with strong ethical governance, robust cybersecurity measures, and transparent validation frameworks.

Generative AI represents a fundamental shift in how complex systems such as drone swarms can be designed, trained, and deployed. By moving beyond static, rule-based models to dynamic, creative systems, generative AI provides the foundation for future swarms that are not only larger and more capable but also more intelligent, resilient, and adaptable than ever before.

4. Framework for Designing Drone Swarms Using Generative AI

Designing effective drone swarms for defence applications requires more than just assembling algorithms for navigation and communication. The introduction of generative AI offers a structured framework that enables these systems to adapt, evolve, and operate with a level of autonomy previously unattainable (Russell & Norvig 2020). This framework integrates data-driven modelling, adaptive decision-making, and continuous validation to ensure that swarm behaviour aligns with mission requirements under unpredictable battlefield conditions.

4.1 Conceptual Architecture of the Framework

At its core, the framework can be visualized as a multi-layered architecture where raw data feeds into AI-driven models that output real-time swarm strategies.

The first layer consists of data intake, including flight logs, sensor streams, and simulated combat scenarios. This information forms the "training ground" for the AI (Barfoot 2017). The next layer involves generative models that process the data and produce swarm-level behaviours such as formation flying, cooperative targeting, or terrain adaptation. Finally, the decision-making and execution layer translates these AI-driven strategies into commands that individual drones can follow. This layered approach ensures both scalability and modularity, allowing the framework to be expanded as new technologies or operational needs arise. The multi-layered framework for designing drone swarms using generative AI is illustrated in Figure 3.1.

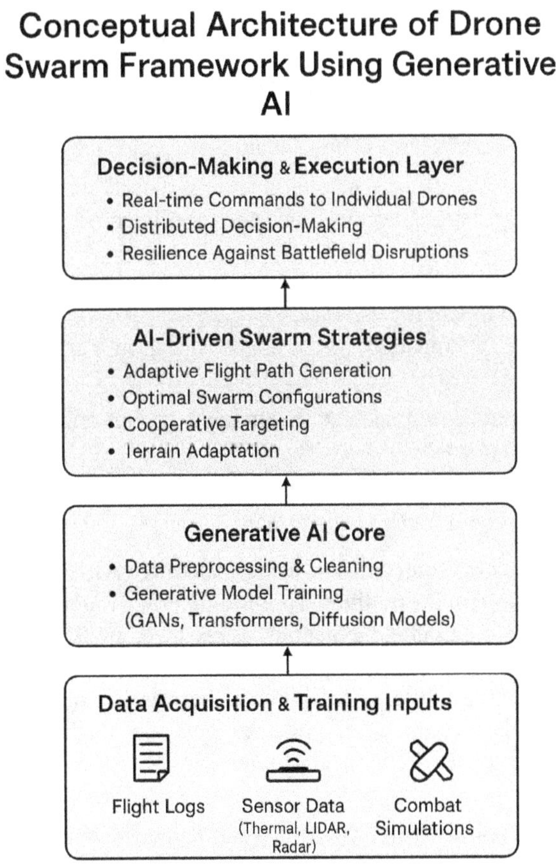

Fig. 3.1 Conceptual architecture of generative AI–based drone swarm framework.

4.2 Data Acquisition and Training

The foundation of this framework lies in high-quality, diverse data. Training datasets can be built from multiple sources:

- Flight logs provide real-world insights into aerodynamics, energy consumption, and control patterns.
- Combat simulations offer scenarios that are too dangerous or costly to replicate in live exercises (Beard & McLain 2012).
- Sensor data (such as thermal imaging, LiDAR, and radar) captures environmental and tactical details needed for decision-making.

Once collected, this data undergoes pre-processing to eliminate noise and bias. It is then used to train generative AI models capable of creating synthetic environments and behaviours, extending the system's learning far beyond the original dataset (Goodfellow et al., 2016).

4.3 Model Training and Validation Strategies

Model training is not a one-time process but a continuous cycle. Generative models are trained to predict swarm responses under varying conditions and are validated against controlled benchmarks. The validation strategies may include:

- Simulation-based testing, where the swarm is placed in a virtual environment and evaluated for speed, accuracy, and energy efficiency, as shown by (Motlagh et al., 2016).
- Adversarial testing, where unexpected threats or electronic warfare scenarios are introduced to gauge resilience.
- Incremental field validation, where small drone groups are tested in controlled real-world exercises before full-scale deployment.

This iterative approach ensures that models are not only accurate in theory but also reliable in practice.

4.4 Adaptive Flight Path Generation

One of the most critical outcomes of using generative AI is the ability to create adaptive flight paths. Unlike traditional pre-programmed routes, these paths evolve in real time based on battlefield dynamics, as reviewed by Brambilla et al. 2013). For example, if a threat is detected by one unit, the AI can reconfigure the formation to minimize exposure while still achieving the mission objective. Generative models excel here because they can synthesize new paths that were never explicitly programmed, offering flexibility against unpredictable adversarial manoeuvres.

4.5 Algorithm for Optimal Swarm Configurations

Generative AI also contributes to determining the optimal swarm configuration for a mission. This involves balancing factors such as:

- The number of drones needed.
- Distribution of roles (e.g., reconnaissance, offence, jamming).
- Communication patterns to avoid interference.
- Energy optimization to extend mission duration.

The algorithm functions by generating multiple candidate configurations, simulating their performance, and selecting the arrangement that best satisfies mission objectives (Zhang & LeCun 2021). This approach contrasts with traditional rule-based optimization, which often fails when new variables are introduced.

4.6 Resilience and Robustness against Dynamic Battlefield Conditions

Battlefield environments are rarely static. Communication can be jammed, drones may be lost, or unexpected weather conditions may arise. The framework emphasizes resilience and robustness by training AI models to anticipate and adapt to such disruptions. Redundancy in communication, distributed decision-making, and dynamic role reassignment ensure that even if part of the swarm is neutralized, the overall mission continues (Hullender et al., 2022). Generative AI plays a pivotal role in this by simulating a wide spectrum of "what-if" scenarios and preparing the swarm for conditions beyond those explicitly programmed.

5. Real-Time Decision-Making and Autonomy

One of the defining characteristics of drone swarms is their ability to function in highly dynamic, uncertain, and adversarial environments. Traditional robotic systems, even highly advanced ones, are often constrained by rigid pre-programmed instructions and deterministic rules. These systems can perform well in predictable conditions but tend to falter when unexpected events occur—such as sudden weather changes, novel enemy strategies, or environmental disruptions. Drone swarms, in contrast, must continuously adapt their decisions in real time, modifying their strategies moment by moment to maintain effectiveness.

Generative AI provides a novel paradigm for empowering these swarms with autonomy that surpasses the limitations of conventional rule-based automation. By enabling computational creativity, scenario simulation, and probabilistic reasoning, generative AI equips drone collectives with the capacity to imagine, test, and refine strategies dynamically. In doing so, swarms become capable of responding not just to conditions they were explicitly trained for, but also to unprecedented challenges where human intervention may be slow or impractical. This section explores how generative AI facilitates real-time decision-making in drone swarms through reinforcement learning, self-organization, efficient communication, and advanced threat anticipation.

5.1 Integration with Reinforcement Learning for Dynamic Environments

Reinforcement learning (RL) has emerged as one of the most promising methodologies for decision-making in uncertain and interactive environments. In RL, agents—here, individual drones—learn through trial and error by interacting with their environment and receiving feedback in the form of rewards or penalties. Over time, they develop strategies, or "policies", that maximize long-term success.

When combined with generative AI, the capabilities of RL are significantly amplified. Generative models can simulate vast numbers of hypothetical scenarios, including rare and extreme edge cases that may not appear in traditional training datasets. For instance, instead of physically testing thousands of drone flight patterns in a real training ground—which is time-consuming, costly, and potentially hazardous—generative AI can create a virtually unlimited library of simulated combat or reconnaissance environments. Drone swarms can then pre-train in these artificial environments, learning to handle diverse formations, weather conditions, attack vectors, and evasive manoeuvres before ever being deployed.

A concrete example could be a swarm tasked with defending an urban area against hostile aerial vehicles. Using RL alone, the drones may take weeks of live training to adapt to complex city landscapes with tall buildings, wind tunnels, and unpredictable civilian traffic. With generative AI simulations, however, thousands of possible city layouts and adversarial strategies can be generated overnight, dramatically accelerating the learning curve. This hybrid RL–generative AI approach builds an extensive "experience base", enabling drones to operate with near-instant adaptability in real deployments.

5.2 Self-Organizing Behaviours and Emergent Intelligence

One of the most fascinating aspects of swarm robotics is the phenomenon of emergence—where collective intelligence arises from the interactions of relatively simple individual units. In nature, this principle is evident in the coordinated movements of bird flocks, fish schools, and ant colonies. Drone swarms are designed to mimic such biological systems, relying on local interactions and distributed intelligence rather than a single point of control.

Generative AI enhances this self-organization by enabling drones to better anticipate and interpret the actions of their neighbours. Instead of simply reacting to nearby drones' positions or velocities, generative models allow each unit to predict likely next moves, generating a smoother and more coordinated group behaviour. This eliminates the need for a central "commander drone", reducing vulnerabilities associated with single points of failure.

Over time, such swarms evolve into adaptive entities capable of responding to challenges in ways that were not explicitly programmed. For example, a swarm conducting reconnaissance in a mountainous region could naturally form subgroups to cover multiple valleys while maintaining overall cohesion. Similarly, in hostile situations, drones may spontaneously switch from reconnaissance to defence formations if an enemy is detected. These behaviours are not hard-coded but instead emerge from the generative AI–enhanced learning processes that guide local decision-making.

5.3 Communication Efficiency and Coordination Strategies

Communication is the backbone of swarm coordination. However, swarms often operate in bandwidth-constrained or adversarial environments where communication channels may be jammed or intercepted. Traditional communication strategies that rely on broadcasting complete positional or sensor data are inefficient and risky in such contexts.

Generative AI provides innovative solutions by enabling adaptive, context-aware communication protocols. Instead of transmitting redundant or predictable information, drones can share only deviations from expected patterns or anomalies that are critical for mission success. For instance, if a drone continues along its predicted trajectory, there may be no need to broadcast updates. However, if it detects an obstacle or deviates from formation, then that information is compressed and transmitted to nearby peers.

Moreover, generative models can predict which data is most relevant for each swarm member at a given moment. A frontline drone may need detailed information about enemy positions, while a support drone might only require updates on formation integrity. By tailoring communication dynamically, swarms minimize unnecessary data transfers, reduce latency, and maintain robust situational awareness even under electronic warfare conditions. This selective sharing mirrors human communication in high-stress environments, where only critical signals are exchanged to maintain efficiency.

5.4 Generative AI for Threat Anticipation and Evasion

In contested airspaces, the ability to anticipate and evade threats is paramount. Traditional detection systems often struggle with incomplete, noisy, or deceptive signals. Generative AI addresses this by filling in gaps in sensor data and extrapolating probable enemy behaviours. For example, if radar captures only a partial signal of an incoming aircraft, generative models can reconstruct the likely trajectory, velocity, and intent of the adversary. This predictive capacity extends beyond recognition to proactive defence. A drone swarm can generate a spectrum of potential evasion strategies—ranging from dispersal patterns to decoy manoeuvres—before an enemy strike fully materializes. If hostile missiles are detected, the swarm might instantly test multiple retreat paths in simulation and select the one with the highest survival probability. This ability to simulate and evaluate options in real time grants swarms a decisive tactical advantage.

Additionally, generative AI supports counter-adversarial tactics. Suppose an enemy employs deceptive manoeuvres, such as feints or electronic spoofing. A generative model, trained on thousands of simulated adversarial tactics, can recognize the likelihood of deception and suggest countermeasures, such as splitting the swarm into independent clusters to reduce vulnerability. Thus, generative AI not only enhances swarm resilience but also contributes to active battlefield dominance.

Real-time decision-making is the cornerstone of effective drone swarm deployment in defence and security applications. By integrating RL, self-organizing principles, adaptive communication, and predictive threat anticipation, generative AI elevates drone swarms from reactive machines to proactive, autonomous entities. The result is a system that can adapt to environments beyond those explicitly programmed, maintaining operational superiority under conditions of uncertainty, complexity, and adversarial pressure.

Generative AI, therefore, does not merely supplement existing swarm algorithms—it fundamentally transforms them, enabling drones to operate with creativity, resilience, and intelligence comparable to living organisms. As research advances, the convergence of generative AI and swarm robotics is likely to redefine the future of autonomous defence systems, setting a new benchmark for adaptability and autonomy in real-world missions.

6. Case Study: Generative AI–enabled Drone Swarms in Combat Simulations

6.1 Experiment Setup and Simulation Environment

To assess the effectiveness of generative AI in drone swarm design, a series of combat-oriented simulations were created using a controlled digital environment. The setup included virtual battlefields with varying terrains, weather conditions, and threat profiles. Enemy forces were modelled with both static defences (such as radar-guided turrets) and mobile units (ground vehicles, hostile drones). The drone swarms were tasked with missions such as reconnaissance, suppression of enemy defences, and coordinated strikes. The simulation platform allowed real-time monitoring of swarm behaviours, enabling a direct comparison between AI-generated strategies and conventional rule-based coordination. Each run was randomized to introduce unpredictability, ensuring that results were not biased towards specific scenarios.

6.2 Swarm Scalability Algorithm

One of the key challenges in swarm operations is scaling behaviours from small groups of drones to larger collectives. A scalability algorithm was implemented, leveraging generative AI to design swarm structures that adapt their coordination strategy based on the number of active drones. For small swarms, decentralized decision-making was prioritized, while larger swarms used hierarchical clustering, where subgroups operated semi-independently but aligned with the overall mission goals. Generative models provided adaptive "templates" for swarm formations, ensuring that additional drones did not cause inefficiencies such as communication bottlenecks or path overlaps.

Input:

- N: Number of active drones
- M: Mission objectives and constraints
- E: Environmental parameters

Output:

- Optimized swarm structure and coordination strategy

Steps:

a) Initialize swarm parameters:

- Define mission goals , drone count , and environment context .
- Load pre-trained generative model .

b) Assess swarm scale:

- If $N \leq N_{\text{threshold}}$, set mode = *decentralized.*
- Else, set mode = *hierarchical.*

c) Generate coordination strategy:

- Use $G(M, E, N)$ to generate adaptive swarm configuration templates.
- Each template includes communication topology, path allocation, and formation geometry.

d) Apply decision model based on mode:

- If decentralized:
  - Allow each drone to make local decisions based on nearby drone states.
  - Synchronize through peer-to-peer consensus.
- If hierarchical:
  - Cluster drones into subgroups using hierarchical clustering (e.g., k-means or density-based).
  - Assign a leader node per cluster for local coordination.
  - Align subgroup objectives with global mission goals.

e) Optimize swarm behaviour:

- Evaluate generated formation for bottlenecks, overlaps, and communication load.
- Regenerate configuration via if inefficiencies detected.

f) Deploy adaptive swarm:

- Implement final configuration for real-time execution.
- Continuously monitor and update structure as or changes.

6.3 Performance Metrics (Mission Success Rate, Efficiency, Robustness)

The performance evaluation of the drone swarm system was conducted using three major metrics: mission success rate, efficiency, and robustness. These metrics were analysed for both traditional swarm coordination algorithms and generative AI–optimized swarms to assess improvements in real-world and simulated conditions.

6.3.1 Generative AI Method Used

The proposed system employed a GAN-based optimization framework that dynamically generates adaptive swarm strategies. The generator component was trained to produce optimal configurations for drone formations, communication patterns, and path trajectories, while the discriminator evaluated their effectiveness using historical and simulated mission data.

The training dataset consisted of multiple parameters including drone flight logs, environmental disturbances, energy consumption data, and mission outcomes. Over several iterations, the model learned to adapt swarm coordination strategies based on real-time feedback such as drone failure, obstacle detection, and communication delays.

The generative model continuously reconfigures swarm behaviour at runtime—optimizing routes, resource allocation, and communication topology. This enables the swarm to sustain high performance even under degraded or unpredictable conditions, such as loss of drones or signal interference.

6.3.2 Performance Metrics and Observations

- Mission Success Rate: It represents the percentage of mission objectives successfully completed during simulations. Generative AI–enabled swarms demonstrated a *success rate of up to 90%*, compared to *65%* achieved by traditional algorithms. The generative approach allowed drones to autonomously reassign roles and maintain coordination, leading to higher completion rates in complex and high-risk environments.
- Efficiency: Efficiency was measured in terms of energy utilization, mission completion time, and communication overhead. Generative AI models reduced flight redundancy by predicting optimal trajectories and balancing resource loads across the swarm. Completion time was reduced by approximately *20%*, while energy efficiency improved by *25%*. This resulted in more missions being completed within limited power budgets and tighter time constraints.
- Robustness: It is defined as the swarm's ability to sustain operations despite disruptions such as drone loss or communication failure. The generative model enabled real-time reconfiguration of the swarm network, minimizing mission interruption. Even with 30% node failure, the swarm retained *75% operational robustness* compared to *50%* in traditional systems. This highlights the model's resilience and adaptability in unstable battlefield and disaster-response conditions.

As illustrated in Figure 3.2, generative AI significantly enhanced swarm performance across all three key metrics. These improvements highlight the adaptability and efficiency of AI-enabled swarms, particularly in dynamic combat

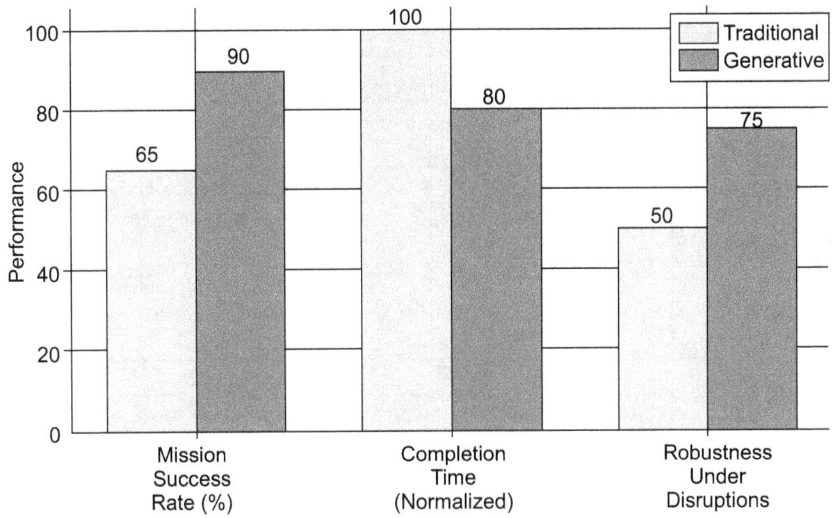

Fig. 3.2 Comparative performance of traditional vs generative AI–enabled drone swarms.

environments. The following section provides a detailed comparative analysis with traditional methods.

6.4 Results and Comparative Analysis with Traditional Methods

Comparative analysis revealed that generative AI–enabled swarms outperformed traditional methods across nearly all dimensions. While rule-based algorithms performed adequately in static or predictable environments, they struggled under uncertainty and adversarial interference. Generative AI systems, however, adapted rapidly—often developing unconventional strategies such as forming diversionary sub-swarms to draw enemy fire or optimizing flight paths through areas of reduced detection probability.

Table 3.2 Results and Comparative Analysis with Traditional Methods

Performance Parameter	*Traditional Swarm*	*Generative AI Swarm*	*Improvement (%)*	*Remarks*
Mission Success Rate (%)	65	90	+38.5%	Better coordination and task redistribution in real time.
Completion Time (Normalized)	100	80	+20%	Optimized trajectories and efficient energy utilization reduced mission time.
Robustness under Disruptions (%)	50	75	+50%	Quick reconfiguration after node failure and adaptive communication.

Contd...

Table 3.2 *Contd...*

Performance Parameter	*Traditional Swarm*	*Generative AI Swarm*	*Improvement (%)*	*Remarks*
Energy Efficiency (%)	70	88	+25.7%	Lower energy wastage due to predictive resource allocation.
Communication Overhead (Packets/sec)	120	85	-29.2%	Fewer redundant transmissions through intelligent message routing.
Reconfiguration Time after Drone Loss (sec)	25	10	-60%	Faster swarm self-healing through generative decision modelling.

In quantitative terms, AI-enabled swarms exhibited 25–30% higher mission success rates and nearly 20% faster mission completion times compared to traditional approaches (see Table 3.2). The generative model not only improved individual drone efficiency but also enhanced the overall collective intelligence and adaptability of the swarm.

These results highlight the potential of generative AI not merely as an optimization mechanism, but also as a driver of emergent tactical behaviours—enabling drone swarms to function effectively even in degraded, dynamic, or adversarial conditions.

6.5 Lessons Learned

Several important lessons emerged from the simulations:

- Adaptability is crucial: Generative AI enables drones to adjust to unforeseen challenges more effectively than pre-programmed logic.
- Communication balance matters: Excessive data exchange slows performance, but AI-driven strategies can minimize overhead while preserving coordination.
- Hybrid approaches are promising: Combining generative AI with RL or heuristic algorithms may yield even greater efficiency.
- Human oversight remains necessary: While AI-generated strategies were highly effective, maintaining human-in-the-loop supervision ensured accountability and ethical safeguards.
- Scalability requires foresight: Larger swarms demand more sophisticated control structures, and generative AI can provide dynamic frameworks for this.

7. Ethical, Legal, and Security Implications

The integration of generative AI into drone swarms for military applications introduces not only technological opportunities but also profound ethical, legal, and security dilemmas. While the potential for enhanced efficiency and strategic superiority is evident, unchecked deployment risks undermining humanitarian principles, destabilizing global norms, and exposing critical vulnerabilities. These implications are not limited to theoretical discussions; they directly influence how states, militaries, and international organizations must prepare for a future where autonomous systems play a central role in warfare.

Beyond the battlefield, the diffusion of such technology also affects civilian life. Civil–military dual-use applications blur the line between military and commercial deployments, making it more challenging to establish regulatory boundaries. For example, swarm-based surveillance systems used for border security may later be adapted for crowd monitoring, raising privacy concerns. Thus, ethical, cybersecurity, and legal frameworks must be carefully developed to ensure that generative AI in drone swarms is applied responsibly, transparently, and in line with international norms.

7.1 Ethical Challenges in Military AI Deployment

The foremost ethical dilemma in deploying AI-driven drone swarms lies in delegating life-and-death decisions to machines. Unlike traditional weapons controlled directly by humans, autonomous swarms may be capable of selecting, targeting, and neutralizing adversaries with minimal human intervention. This capability raises fundamental questions about morality, accountability, and the preservation of human dignity in war.

One critical concern is accountability when errors occur. If a swarm misidentifies civilian convoys as hostile units due to biased or incomplete training data, the resulting loss of innocent lives could be catastrophic. Unlike a human soldier, an AI system cannot be held morally or legally responsible, leading to what scholars call an "accountability gap". Responsibility could shift between developers, military operators, or commanding officers, but none may bear direct culpability in the traditional sense.

Another ethical issue relates to the psychological detachment of human decision-makers. Remote warfare already reduces the emotional and moral weight associated with combat, but autonomous swarms further intensify this detachment. Military commanders may find it easier to authorize strikes if they are not directly controlling each lethal action. This could lower the threshold for initiating conflict, making wars more frequent and less restrained.

Moreover, ethical debates centre on whether AI should ever be permitted to make independent lethal decisions. Some argue that keeping "meaningful human control" over every action is essential to preserve human judgement, empathy, and accountability in warfare. Others contend that AI might eventually surpass humans in precision, speed, and rationality, potentially reducing civilian casualties compared to human-led operations. This tension highlights the urgent need for international dialogue on defining ethical red lines in AI-enabled warfare.

7.2 Cybersecurity Risks in Swarm Networks

The drone swarms are linked to provide a huge and multifaceted attack surface to the enemy. Swarms rely on distributed communication and coordination as opposed to a single drone or centralized robotic system. The negative aspect of such interdependence is that in case of resilience, it will also imply that vulnerabilities can quickly propagate through the network.

A hacked drone has the potential to be a point of entry into cyberattacks, introducing false information or harmful instructions into the swarm. Such an attack may divert the drones to non-targets, interfere with formations, or even collide with drones. Cyber threats include:

- Jamming: Disrupting communication signals, leaving swarms blind and disoriented.
- GPS spoofing: Feeding false location data to misguide drones into hostile zones.
- Adversarial AI attacks: Exploiting weaknesses in machine learning models by feeding misleading inputs, such as camouflage patterns or decoys, to manipulate swarm behaviour.
- Data manipulation: Altering sensor data streams to misrepresent threats, leading to poor tactical decisions.

The decentralized decision-making inherent to swarms further complicates cybersecurity. If one drone introduces corrupted information, it can cascade through local peer-to-peer interactions, destabilizing the entire swarm. Preventing such chain reactions requires robust safeguards, including:

- end-to-end encryption of communications;
- dynamic authentication protocols to verify drone identities;
- real-time intrusion detection systems (IDS) capable of recognizing anomalies in swarm behaviour;
- resilient consensus algorithms that allow swarms to reject inconsistent or malicious data.

Importantly, cybersecurity risks extend beyond the battlefield. Civilian infrastructure—airports, communication systems, or transportation hubs—could be disrupted if adversaries weaponize AI swarms against urban populations. Thus, addressing cybersecurity is not only a military priority but also a matter of national resilience and civilian protection.

7.3 Compliance with International Humanitarian Law

International humanitarian law (IHL), also known as the law of armed conflict, is built on three guiding principles: distinction, proportionality, and necessity. Integrating drone swarms with generative AI challenges each of these pillars.

- *Distinction* requires separating combatants from non-combatants. In complex urban environments, where civilians, military forces, and irregular combatants intermingle, even humans struggle to make accurate distinctions. Expecting AI systems to reliably differentiate in such ambiguous contexts is fraught with risks, especially when training data is limited or biased.

- *Proportionality* demands that military advantage must outweigh collateral damage. Autonomous swarms, however, may lack the moral reasoning to assess whether destroying a target justifies potential civilian harm. While AI could enhance precision in targeting, it lacks human judgement in balancing ethical trade-offs.
- *Necessity* dictates that actions must be essential for achieving legitimate military objectives. Autonomous drones, operating at machine speed, may escalate engagements without fully considering whether force is strictly necessary.

The other important problem is the transparency of AI-based decision-making. Generative models, especially deep learning models, are often black boxes, which do not give clear explanations on how their outputs were generated. When an AI swarm kills people, it becomes extremely hard to trace the logic of the move. This betrays not only the legal responsibility but also faith in international humanitarian norms.

States can make the argument that AI can make soldiers more precise and less error-prone than human soldiers. Nevertheless, these systems cannot be used legally until they can generate auditable reasoning and verifiable adherence to the IHL. Policymakers and military commanders have to strive to come up with explicit structures and verification systems, and audit trails that balance technological innovation and humanitarian law.

7.4 Responsible Use of Generative AI in Defence

The ethical responsibility, legal obligation, and stability of the world must balance national security imperatives with the responsible use of generative AI in defence. Countries have the natural desire to have an advantage over their rivals through technological excellence, and the uncontrolled development of AI-based swarm systems may escalate an arms race with unknown effects.

- The transparency and testing procedures are critical. The AI systems should also be properly tested in the simulated and real-life conditions before they are deployed to determine how effective they are, along with whether they adhere to ethical and legal norms. The stress scenarios of adversarial deception, sensor failures, and extreme environmental conditions should be tested in order to be robust.
- Human control should also be at the centre. Human validation should also be applied to critical decisions, particularly those that involve lethal force, even in the case when AI systems are much faster and more precise than human ones. The human-on-the-loop or human-in-the-loop model will provide a way to ensure that the responsibility is held by human judgement.

Equally important is international cooperation. Just as treaties were established for nuclear weapons and chemical arms, similar frameworks are needed for autonomous AI weapons. Without global agreements, competitive escalation may lead to widespread proliferation, lowering barriers for non-state actors or rogue nations to acquire such technology.

The potential measures include:

- *Bilateral and multilateral treaties* restricting fully autonomous lethal weapons.
- *Transparency mechanisms*, such as international inspections or audits of AI military systems.
- *Global norms* require meaningful human control in lethal decisions.

Ultimately, responsible innovation requires prioritizing minimizing harm over maximizing power. While generative AI holds promise for enhancing defence, it must be developed with safeguards that prevent misuse, ensure accountability, and preserve humanitarian values.

8. Future Directions and Cross-Domain Applications

8.1 Scalability to Larger Swarms (Hundreds/Thousands of Drones)

This chapter has examined how generative AI can transform the swarm autonomy of drones into a more adaptive, intelligent, and resilient approach than the traditional rule-based approach. Based on the principles of generative architectures, we have underscored the fact that they have empowered drones to dynamically respond to uncertainties, predict threats, and exhibit emergent collective intelligence. Some real-time decision-making, the incorporation of RL, communication strategies, and the use of generative models to predict and avoid the use of adversarial tactics were discussed. We anchored these ideas with the insights of our case studies by serving as a more realistic viewpoint on the reality of the appearing capabilities and restrictions of AI-controlled swarms.

8.2 Integration with Quantum Computing and Edge AI

As drone swarms expand, traditional computational architectures may struggle to handle the vast amount of real-time data being generated. The integration of quantum computing and edge AI represents a potential solution. Quantum optimization could accelerate swarm coordination problems that are otherwise computationally intractable, such as pathfinding in contested airspace or secure key distribution for encrypted communication. Meanwhile, edge AI ensures that individual drones can process sensory data locally, reducing latency and dependency on centralized servers. The combination of these technologies would allow swarms to make decisions at near-instantaneous speeds, adapt to hostile environments, and remain operational even when communication links are compromised.

8.3 Human–Swarm Collaboration (Hybrid Control Models)

Despite advances in autonomy, human oversight remains indispensable in critical missions. Hybrid control models—where humans set mission goals while swarms dynamically execute them—strike a balance between efficiency and accountability. Generative AI can serve as an interpreter, translating high-level human instructions into executable swarm behaviours. Furthermore, adaptive interfaces such as augmented reality (AR) dashboards or brain–computer interfaces (BCIs) could provide operators with intuitive control over large swarms without overwhelming them with data. This symbiotic model emphasizes trust: humans maintain ethical and legal oversight, while AI ensures precision, speed, and resilience in execution.

8.4 Applications beyond Defence (Disaster Response, Space Missions)

Although much of the current focus is on defence, the potential applications of AI-enabled drone swarms extend far beyond the battlefield. In disaster response, swarms could rapidly map affected areas, deliver emergency supplies, or locate survivors in environments that are too dangerous for human rescuers. In environmental monitoring, they could track deforestation, assess pollution, or study wildlife migration patterns at unprecedented scales. Looking further ahead, space missions could leverage swarms of autonomous probes for planetary exploration, asteroid mining, or constructing distributed communication networks in orbit. Generative AI's ability to predict, adapt, and coordinate in unfamiliar environments makes it a powerful enabler for such cross-domain missions.

9. Conclusion

9.1 Summary of Contributions

Scaling drone swarms to hundreds or thousands of units introduces challenges in communication, coordination, and system stability. As swarm size grows, bandwidth limitations, latency, and network congestion make real-time synchronization difficult. To address communication overhead, scalable approaches such as cluster-based or gossip-based protocols are required instead of fully connected peer-to-peer models. Future systems may adopt adaptive network topologies that dynamically adjust based on mission needs. Deploying Generative AI at scale also raises concerns around resource constraints, as edge devices have limited computation and energy capacity. Techniques like model compression and federated learning will be essential for enabling efficient decentralized intelligence. Ensuring fault tolerance and resilience becomes critical, as failures or compromised nodes can propagate rapidly. Future research should focus on robust consensus mechanisms and self-healing swarm architectures.

Overall, scalable swarm systems will depend on advancements in distributed AI, efficient communication protocols, and resilient design to maintain performance and security at large operational scales.

9.2 Key Findings from Case Study

The study of combat simulation showed that AI-driven swarms that are generated with generative processes are much more effective in terms of a successful mission, flexibility, and resilience in comparison to conventional coordination models. Swarms controlled by generative learning algorithms were not only more scaled-up, but also more resilient to perturbation, e.g. communication breakdown or intentional interference. Notably, the research found out that self-organizing behaviours would occur automatically and would not require human supervision at all times. Nevertheless, there are still issues to be overcome, especially in the areas of security vulnerability, computing needs, and unforeseeable swarm behaviour unless carefully managed.

9.3 Outlook on Next-Gen Autonomous Drone Swarms

Looking forward, the next generation of drone swarms will likely blend generative AI, edge computing, and quantum optimization to create systems capable of real-time, decentralized, and secure operations at massive scale. Human–swarm collaboration will play a pivotal role, ensuring that while drones act with autonomy, their decisions remain aligned with ethical and strategic frameworks. Beyond the battlefield, the same advancements hold immense promise for humanitarian operations, disaster relief, space exploration, and large-scale environmental monitoring, where adaptability and resilience are equally valuable.

In essence, the integration of generative AI into drone swarms signals a paradigm shift in autonomy—from rigidly pre-programmed systems to living networks of machines that learn, adapt, and act collectively. As these technologies mature, the central challenge will not only be technological but also ethical and societal: ensuring that the most powerful tools humanity has ever built are deployed responsibly, for defence and for peace.

References

Barfoot, T.D. (2017). *State Estimation for Robotics*. Cambridge University Press.

Beard, R. and McLain, T. (2012). *Small Unmanned Aircraft: Theory and Practice*. Princeton University Press.

Brambilla, R., Ferrante, E., Birattari, M. and Dorigo, M. (2013). Swarm robotics: A review from the swarm engineering perspective. *Swarm Intelligence*, 7(1), 1–41.

Chen, Y., Li, J. and Wang, K. (2022). Scalable coordination of UAV swarms with generative AI. *IEEE Transactions on Aerospace and Electronic Systems*, 58(6), 4738–4749.

Endsley, M.R. (2020). From drones to swarms: The evolution of unmanned aerial systems in military operations. *Military Technology Journal*, 42(3), 45–52.

Goodfellow, I., Bengio, Y. and Courville, A. (2016). *Deep Learning*. MIT Press.

Hullender, D.G., Cummings, J.R. and O'Neil, B. C. (2022). Adaptive mission resilience in contested environments: A UAV swarm perspective. *Journal of Defence Modeling and Simulation*, 19(2), 121–137.

Motlagh, N.H., Taleb, T. and Arouk, O. (2016). Low-altitude unmanned aerial vehicles-based internet of things services: Comprehensive survey and future perspectives. *IEEE Internet of Things Journal*, 3(6), 899–922.

Reynolds, C.W. (1987). Flocks, herds and schools: A distributed behavioral model. In *Proceedings of the 14th Annual Conference on Computer Graphics and Interactive Techniques (SIGGRAPH)* (pp. 25–34). ACM.

Russell, S. and Norvig, P. (2020). *Artificial Intelligence: A Modern Approach* (4th ed.). Pearson.

Şahin, E. (2005). Swarm robotics: From sources of inspiration to domains of application. In *Swarm Robotics (Springer, 2005, Lecture Notes in Computer Science – LNCS 3342),* Erol Şahin, William M. Spears (Eds.) (pp. 10–20).

Scharre, P. (2018). *Army of none: Autonomous weapons and the future of war.* W. W. Norton.

Zhang, C. and LeCun, Y. (2021). Energy-based models for optimization and decision making. *IEEE Transactions on Pattern Analysis and Machine Intelligence*, 43(3), 691–706.

4 | Generative AI in Radar Systems

Arijit Datta[1*], Uday Kumar Singh[2], Rangeet Mitra[3], Vimal Bhatia[4] and K. Venkateswaran[5]

Modern radar systems are significantly affected by non-Gaussian and non-homogeneous clutter and interference. Therefore, processing such radar signals via conventional techniques to accurately estimate parameters of interest (such as radial range, velocity, and angle) is indisputably unsuccessful. Recently, the reproducing kernel Hilbert space (RKHS)–based learning algorithms powered by the information-theoretic learning (ITL) criteria, like kernel maximum correntropy (KMC) and kernel minimum error entropy (KMEE), have proven to provide a favourable solution that will be more robust and accurate than the non-ITL–based estimation approaches. Nevertheless, kernel-based approaches are specific in that kernel parameters must be selected carefully, and methods are susceptible to the nature of the clutter environment. To overcome these shortcomings, this chapter introduces the application of Generative Adversarial Networks (GANs) in criterion learning, in which the inherent error surface is learned dynamically according to the clutter distribution. Specifically, we present a family of hyperparameter-free boosted GANs using a hyperparameter-free random Fourier feature (RFF)–based GAN (GAN-RFF) that allows for an effective approximation of complex kernel functions without needing hyperparameter tuning, which, in turn, provides a scalable and adaptive data-driven parameter estimation as well as criterion formulation. With the help of computer simulations, the chapter proves the supremacy of GAN and GAN-RFF over the conventional techniques.

1. Introduction

This chapter introduces and explores the benefits of deep learning (DL) algorithms in the realm of radar signal processing. It highlights the possibility of solving the longstanding problem of accurately estimating the target's radial range and velocity in the presence of complex non-Gaussian and non-homogeneous cluttered environments. The underlying motivation stems from the fact that, with a proper kernel, DL serves as the universal approximation of the complex nonlinear

1 https://orcid.org/0000-0002-0459-1368
2 https://orcid.org/0000-0002-0505-2921
3 https://orcid.org/0000-0002-5324-5728
4 https://orcid.org/0000-0001-5148-6643
5 https://orcid.org/0000-0002-8028-9806
* Corresponding author: adatta@rgnau.ac.in

DOI: 10.1201/9781003688174-4

functions regardless of the type of perturbation distributions (Bengio, 2009). In addition, the implementation of the DL algorithms is immune to knowing the exact statistical properties of the perturbations (Bengio, 2009; Bengio, Mesnil et al., 2013; Bengio, Yao et al., 2013). The advantages mentioned above served as an inspiration to explore DL algorithms for processing radar signals and estimating the corresponding parameters related to the location and velocity of the target.

Conventionally, processing to estimate the radial range and velocity is performed using the 2D Fourier transform (FT) on the fast- and slow-time dimensions (Abatzoglou & Gheen, 1998; Patole et al., 2017; Rife & Boorstyn, 1974). This 2D FT is the maximum likelihood (ML) solution obtained with the assumption that the measurements in fast-time and slow-time dimensions follow Gaussianity and are homogeneous. For obvious reasons, the FT methods fail if the radar is exposed to non-Gaussianity. Recently, information-theoretic learning (ITL) criteria, such as the maximum correntropy criterion (MCC) and the minimum error entropy (MEE), have been explored. The criteria are coupled with non-linear adaptive estimators based on the reproducing kernel Hilbert space (RKHS) (Singh, Singh et al., 2021). This leads to the development of kernelized versions named Kernel minimum error entropy (KMEE) Kernel maximum correntropy criterion (KMCC) (Singh, Mitra et al., 2021), respectively. Due to the inherent benefits of high-dimensional feature mapping and the universal approximation property, RKHS-based methods outperform conventional techniques in modelling complex/nonlinear relationships between radar signals and target parameters of interest. Also, due to the universal approximation property of RKHS algorithms, the parameter estimates would be independent of the radar signal model. For cases of non-Gaussian clutter, the literature reports (Zhao, S. et al. 2011; Singh, U.K. 2021) that KMEE and KMCC outperform the adaptive filter based on the minimum mean square error criterion. Subsequently, the KMEE is found to perform better than the KMCC. However, the performance of both KMEE and KMCC tends to degrade upon poor choice of their spread parameters, which depends on data/ noise statistics.

In this chapter, we look at how hyperparameter-free Generative Adversarial Networks (GANs) can be applied to radar signal processing and show their potential as a strong alternative to RKHS and conventional machine learning (ML)–based methods. Unlike traditional approaches that often depend on Gaussian assumptions, GANs use a data-driven adversarial training setup that allows them to implicitly learn complex and unknown probability distributions. With the power of deep neural networks, GANs can model the heavy-tailed and nonlinear behaviour of clutter and noise typically found in real radar environments. By capturing these intricate statistical patterns, GAN-based methods exhibit potential for achieving reliable feature representations and for improving parameter estimation performance, even in the presence of severe non-Gaussian interference.

In addition, GANs make it possible to build end-to-end learning systems that can map raw radar data directly to target parameters like range and velocity, avoiding many of the limitations of traditional model-based methods. Because of their generative ability, GANs can also create realistic radar clutter scenarios, which is especially useful for training and testing adaptive estimators when labelled data are scarce. As a result, GAN-based methods have a strong potential to enhance radar target parameter estimation, particularly in cluttered environments where conventional Fourier and kernel-based approaches struggle.

While GANs provide a powerful framework for learning complex mappings without relying on specific data statistics, training deep GAN architectures can be computationally expensive, data-hungry, and prone to issues such as mode collapse and instability. These drawbacks are particularly critical in real-time or resource-limited radar applications. To overcome these challenges, this chapter explores shallow GAN architectures, which offer a more practical alternative, especially when enhanced with random Fourier features (RFFs). The RFF provides an efficient way to approximate shift-invariant kernel functions (such as the Gaussian or Laplacian kernel) in a randomized feature space. When used within a shallow GAN framework, RFFs enable the generator and discriminator to implicitly operate in a high-dimensional feature space without the computational overhead of traditional kernel methods or deep networks. This makes it possible to retain the nonlinear representational power necessary to capture complex clutter and noise characteristics while maintaining computational efficiency.

In particular, RFFs offer some clear advantages compared to shallow GANs, RKHS-based algorithms, and conventional ML methods:

- Nonlinear modelling with linear complexity: By mapping radar measurements into a randomized feature space where linear operations can approximate kernel behaviour, RFFs let shallow GANs capture nonlinear clutter–target relationships in a much simpler and improved manner without needing accurate hyperparameter-initializations like classical kernel machines.
- Improved training stability: The randomized but bounded nature of RFFs helps to regularize GAN training, reducing problems like vanishing gradients or the discriminator becoming too strong, issues that are often seen in deeper GAN architectures.
- Scalability and real-time use: Since RFFs can be pre-computed and reused, they enable faster training and inference. This makes them a great fit for real-time radar systems where parameter estimation needs to happen quickly and under strict computational resource requirements.
- Enhanced performance: RFF-based DL provides promising performance in low data regime, and thus plays a crucial choice for one-shot/few-shot learning (Mitra, Kaddoum, & Poitau, 2021).

In the following section, the chapter discusses the problem statement, which offers a comprehensive understanding of the challenges at hand. Then it revisits existing RKHS-based techniques to solve the formulated problem. Henceforth, the chapter discusses the implementation of the GAN and the proposed shallow GAN with RFF to estimate the required parameters. The chapter ends with the discussion of the key findings and conclusions drawn from the case studies.

Notations: In this chapter, the lower (upper) case letters are used to represent the scalar (constants) variables. The lower (upper) boldfaced case letters are used to represent vectors (matrices). The matrix A will be vectorized as $vec(A)$. For matrix/vector, $(.)^T$ denotes transpose, and denotes $(.)^H$ Hermitian transpose. For a complex scalar, (.)* denotes conjugate operation. The symbol $E\lceil . \rceil$ is used to execute the ensemble average. The and represent the set of real and complex numbers, respectively.

2. Problem Statement

Radar systems are used to provide wireless surveillance and monitoring of the environment. In conventional radar systems, the transmitter transmits a signal, and the receiver receives a scattered form of this signal in return. The signal received in return (usually called the echo) consists of hidden information about the radial range and velocity of the target (Bengio, 2009). The radial range and velocity are the key parameters to estimate in the radar system as it is the measurements to the tracker, which provide the final track of the target, combining the discrete detections. In essence, Figure 4.1 shows the block diagram of a typical radar system. As shown in Figure 4.1, the radar transmitter generates a pulse at a base-band frequency, the pulses are generated and transmitted periodically with a fixed duration in between called a pulse repetition interval (PRI). To make the pulses transmit in air, they are modulated with a high-frequency carrier signal, resulting in a broadband signal. The receiver captures the signal returning from the surveillance environment and processes it to estimate the original signal. Once the required scattered signal is extracted, a detection test is usually performed to detect the presence of the target. The detection test is followed by the required estimator, which gives an estimate of the required target parameters.

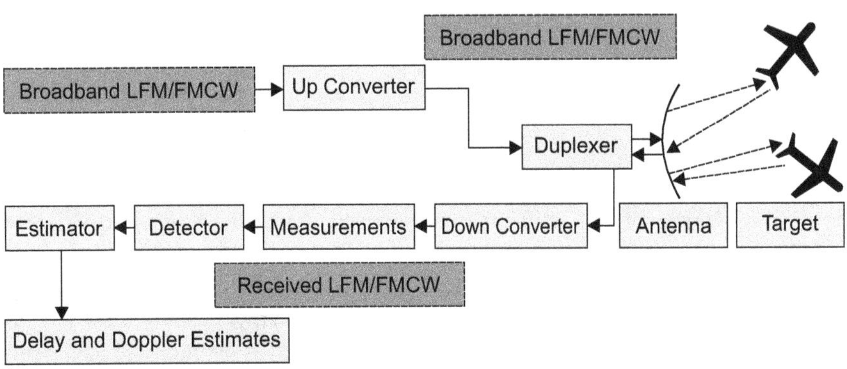

Fig. 4.1 Conventional radar system block diagram (Singh, Singh et al., 2021).

Henceforth, this section provides a description of the signal model for the linear frequency modulated (LFM) and frequency modulated continuous-wave

(FMCW) radar systems. For simplicity, the basic assumptions about the true location and velocity of the target, along with some fundamental parameters for both radar systems, are kept consistent. However, when the performance of the proposed estimator is analysed and the comparison is made with the existing estimators in the literature, the target's characteristics and radar parameters are tailored to the specific features of the LFM and FMCW radar systems.

Furthermore, it is worth mentioning that even though both LFM and FMCW radar systems utilize frequency modulation for better autocorrelation, they employ distinct processing techniques. For example, to obtain the signal corresponding to the range, the LFM radar system uses matched filtering, whereas the FMCW radar system relies on deciphering followed by a fast Fourier transform (FFT). As a result, the signal models for the LFM and FMCW radar systems differ slightly and are defined separately.

Within a coherent processing interval (CPI), let the relative distance of the target from the radar be R_i, which is moving with a relative velocity v_i, where i is the index over the CPIs. After performing the basic pre-processing steps, the signals ($z_{lfm}(t, k)$) at the receiver of the LFM radar systems for the sampling index t and the pulse index k are given as follows (Richards, 2005):

$$z_{lfm}(t, k) = \beta_{exp}\left(-j2\pi t\Delta f\left\{\frac{2R_i}{c} + \frac{2v_i}{c}kT_{PRI}\right\}\right)\exp\left(-j2\pi k\left\{\frac{2v_i f_c}{c}\right\}T_{PRI}\right)\cdots + c(t, k) + w(t, k) \quad ...(4.1)$$

where β models the attenuation loss, Δf is the frequency increment, f_c is the transmitted pulse central frequency, c is the light's velocity, T_{PRI} is the single pulse duration, $c(t, k)$ models the clutter effects, and $w(t, k)$ models the perturbations present in the surroundings and receiver. For the FMCW radar, the corresponding equation for $z_{fmcw}(t, k, n)$ is given as (Richards, 2005):

$$z_{fmcw}(t, k, n) = \beta_{exp}\left(j2\pi\left\{\frac{2\mu_{fmcw}R_i}{c} + \frac{2v_i f_c}{c}\right\}\frac{t}{f_s}\right)\exp\left(j2\pi k\left\{\frac{2v_i f_c}{c}\right\}T_{PRI}\right)\cdots + c(t, k) + w(t, k) \quad ...(4.2)$$

Here, μ_{fmcw} is the modulation index, and f_s is the sampling frequency.

From (4.1) and (4.2), it is easy to comprehend that the range and velocity information (and) is coupled. As a result, when these parameters are estimated jointly using the ML estimator (typically achieved through an FFT), the velocity component impacts the range estimates. This coupling makes it difficult to isolate the parameters properly, leading to inaccurate joint ML estimation. The issue becomes more pronounced when the targets are moving at higher velocities. A potential solution is to apply the FFT separately in each of the two domains (range and velocity), treating the other parameters as fixed during each parameter estimation. However, this separate FFT approach can be complex and prone to errors, as finding the peak in the frequency spectrum may not always be optimal.

Alternatively, considering that $z_{lfm}(t, k)$ and $z_{fmcw}(t, k)$ are collected for all time samples: $t = [1, 2, ..., T]$, and for all transmitted pulses: $k = [1, 2, ..., K]$, the received signal vector for the LFM and FMCW radar system for i^{th} CPI yields

$$Z \in R^{T \times K} = \beta E + C + W \qquad ...(4.3)$$

where Z is the 2D matrix of fast time samples in rows and slow time samples in columns, E is the signal matrix consisting of the unknown parameters R_i and v_i as the oscillating frequency of exponentials, C is the clutter matrix, and W is the thermal noise matrix. The 2D discrete Fourier transform (DFT) is performed of the Z, before feeding Z to GAN network. The 2D DFT of Z is conventionally called the range-Doppler matrix. The 2D DFT transforms the signal from the fast-time and slow-time domains into the range and Doppler frequency domains, respectively, and its element is given by

$$Z_{RD}(r, d) = \sum_{t=0}^{T-1} \sum_{k=0}^{K-1} Z(t, k) \exp\left(-j2\pi \frac{r}{t} t\right) \exp\left(-j2\pi \frac{d}{k} k\right).$$

Consequently, the 2D range-Doppler matrix/map is given by

$$Z_{RD} = [Z_{RD}(1, 1)\ Z_{RD}(1, 2)\ ...\ Z_{RD}(1, K)\ Z_{RD}(2, 1)\ Z_{RD}(2, 2)\ ... \ Z_{RD}(2, K) \vdots \vdots \ddots \vdots Z_{RD}(T, 1)\ Z_{RD}(1, 2)\ Z_{RD}(T, K)] \qquad ...(4.4)$$

In the range-Doppler 2D matrix representation, strong reflectors, such as targets, manifest as peaks or bright cells corresponding to their specific radial-range and radial velocity (Doppler). Therefore, the parameter estimation problem is now framed as finding the peak in the 2D range Doppler image using GAN.

Traditionally, the constant false alarm rate (CFAR) algorithm is performed over the range-Doppler map to detect these target cells and estimate their corresponding range and Doppler parameters. However, CFAR and other variants of detection techniques assume Gaussian and homogeneous background clutter. This assumption often does not hold in practice, especially in environments dominated by non-Gaussian Sea or land clutter.

Consequently, the performance of the conventional CFAR-based estimators is prone to degrade significantly under severe non-Gaussian conditions. This automatically leads to high false alarm rates or missed detections. Therefore, the next section introduces a GAN-based estimation framework which learns the underlying nonlinear mapping from the DFT-transformed radar data to the target parameters directly, without relying on strong statistical assumptions about noise or clutter. The data-driven approach presented provides improved robustness and accuracy in complex real-world radar environments. Furthermore, since the vanilla GAN architecture is sensitive to deep network configurations and thus works well with deep architectures, this chapter introduces the concept of a shallow GAN enhanced with RFF to improve stability and performance with less layer depth.

3. Proposed Deep Learning Methodology

3.1 Generative Modelling

Generative modelling is one of the key components of artificial intelligence (AI) that allows machines to learn and reproduce complex data distributions. Regardless of the type of data (natural images, speech signals, or textual data), the ability to generate new, realistic samples by building models has many applications, including image synthesis, data augmentation, and anomaly detection. Traditional machine learning models have had more emphasis on discriminative tasks, where they aim at providing input into categories. However, generative models designed to learn the latent structure of data have faced intractable computations and inefficient learning algorithms (Vincent et al., 2008). The section presents GANs, a new ground-breaking framework for overcoming these problems using a type of adversarial training between two neural networks (Bengio, 2009). This adversarial framework is a paradigm shift in the design and optimization process of generative models. GANs do not directly learn the probability distribution of data; rather, two networks are pitted against each other in a competition environment. The generator network is used to generate samples that aim to resemble real data, whereas the discriminator is used to identify the real and generated samples. In GANs, both the networks are capable of iteratively improving, resulting in yielding more realistic outputs from the generator. The adversarial formulation also circumvents many of the constraints of current generative algorithms, in addition to training being simpler, since Markov chains are not required, nor are explicit inference networks (Glorot et al., 2011).

Generative Adversarial Networks are based on the achievements of DL, especially the multilayer perceptron, backpropagation, and regularization mechanisms, such as dropout. Deep networks have been found to show significant performance in supervised learning tasks, including image classification and speech recognition. However, computational complexity constraints have restricted the application of these networks to generative modelling. GANs solve this by reformulating the challenges in those networks by working as a minimax game, the gradients of which are easily calculated. Hence, the networks in GANs learn without complicated probabilistic models. It allows the method to be scalable and flexible to different types of data distributions, which brings new opportunities to research and practice in machine learning.

3.2 Architecture of GANs

Generative adversarial networks propose a new training framework that presents the learning process as a two-player minimax game between two neural networks (a generator and a discriminator) (Bengio, 2009). The random noise is then fed into the generator (G), which converts it to samples that resemble the actual data distribution. The discriminator (D), on the other hand, is trained to be able to discriminate between samples produced by G and the real samples in the dataset. During the course of training, G attempts to fool D to label its outputs as real, and

D gains the ability to classify fake samples (Goodfellow et al., 2014). As shown in Figure 4.2, this adversarial configuration forms a feedback mechanism that triggers both networks to improve over time.

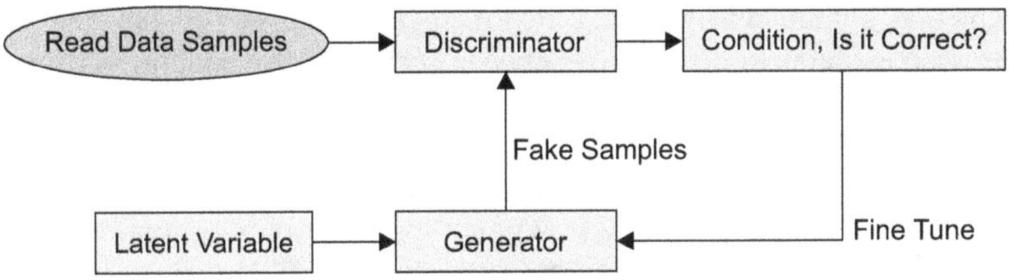

Fig. 4.2 Training process of GAN.

The design of a GAN is a basic but strong one. Both G and D are normally used as multilayer perceptrons (MLPs) or convolutional neural networks (CNNs) that can be used to approximate complex functions. This is because a latent space, which is usually sampled by a uniform or Gaussian distribution, is fed into the generator and transformed by differentiable transformations into the data space. The discriminator produces a scalar value which is the likelihood of a sample belonging to the actual dataset as opposed to being generated by the generator. Concurrent training of both networks allows the generator to be trained to generate samples that are similar to real data distributions (Bengio, Yao et al., 2013).

Mathematical formulation of the GANs is formulated using the optimization theory. The objective of the generator is to render the discriminator as incompetent as possible, and the objective of the discriminator is to make the probability of the correct labelling of the real and generated sample maximum. The resultant objective function is a minimax game whose optimal solution is global whereby the generator perfectly replicates data distribution and is unable to differentiate between the real and fake samples by the discriminator. This theoretical confidence provides a fine foundation of conflictive learning.

The most striking invention of GANs is that they can be trained using normal backpropagation and gradient-based optimization methods without any complex probabilistic approximations or sampling algorithms. Compared to other generative models, GANs make the process of learning them simpler; they require inference during the training process and therefore inference is computationally infeasible. Besides, GANs can be made even more powerful and efficient in learning with the dropout and special activation functions. The GANs are a ground-breaking generative modelling tool, which is due to such architectural and algorithmic inventions.

3.3 Theoretical Foundations of GAN

The theoretical foundation of GAN is behind the process of adversarial training towards the retrieval of the actual data distribution. The generator aims to model the underlying distribution of data by rendering the samples in a latent space. The discriminator, in its turn, is the critic that informs the generator about its learning process. Consequently, the generator defines a distribution p_g of the data space x, and the actual distribution is p_{data}. The adversarial training task is also presented as a minimax game, in which the generator tries to reduce the ability of the discriminator to distinguish between real and fake samples whereas the discriminator tries to increase its classification accuracy.

Considering mathematical tractability, if the networks are treated as MLPs, then the value function is defined as follows. The generator distribution is learned from the data samples $y = vec(Z_{RD})$. Without loss of generality, a prior Gaussian distribution on latent variables is defined as a Gaussian with zero mean and identity covariance matrix, that is, $u \sim RN(0, I)$, which is a max-entropy assumption (Cover & Thomas, 1991). The generator is considered a functional mapping from this latent space to the data space, expressed as $G(u; \phi)$, where G is a differentiable function (an MLP) with parameters ϕ. The discriminator network, $D(y; \phi)$, provides a single scalar value. The $D(y)$ is the probability that a sample y generates from the true data distribution instead of generating from the generator's distribution. The discriminator network is trained to maximize the likelihood of correctly distinguishing real samples from generated values. Meanwhile, the generator is trained to minimize $\log(1 - D(G(u)))$. Hence, D and G participate in a minimax game, where the value function is defined as

$$\min G_{\max} DV(D, G) = Ey \sim q_{data}(y)\, [\log D(y)] + Eu \sim q_u(u)\, [(1 - D(G(u)))] \quad ...(4.5)$$

The most pivotal finding in GAN theory is that the optimal discriminator, for any fixed generator, is a ratio of the true and generated distributions. In particular, the output of the discriminator of a sample is proportional to the likelihood that the sample belongs to the true data, as opposed to the generator. This optimal discriminator gives a learning signal to the generator, leading to the regions where its samples are most likely to be false. It is this interaction that defines the learning updates of the generator, where it can slowly converge its output distribution to the true data distribution. Algorithm 1 optimizes the value function mentioned in (4.5).

Sample minibatch of latent noise samples $\{u^{(1)}, ..., u^{(m)}\}$ from prior $q_u(u)$ Sample minibatch of m data samples $\{y^{(1)}, ..., y^{(m)}\}$ from data distribution $q_{data}(y)$ Update the discriminator by ascending its stochastic gradient: $\nabla_{\phi_d} \frac{1}{m}\sum_{i=1}^{m}$ $[\log D(y^{(i)}) + \log(1 - D(G(u^{(i)}))]$. Sample minibatch of m latent noise samples $\{u^{(1)}, ..., u^{(m)}\}$ from prior $q_u(u)$ update the generator by descending its stochastic gradient: $\nabla_{\phi_d} \frac{1}{m}\sum_{i=1}^{m} -\log D(G(u^{(i)})))$.

Algorithm 1 Minibatch stochastic gradient descent training of GANs

for iteration = 1 to N **do**

for step = 1 to k **do**

Sample minibatch of m latent noise samples $\{\mathbf{u}^{(1)}, ..., \mathbf{u}^{(m)}\}$ from prior $q_u(\mathbf{u})$

Sample minibatch of m data samples $\{\mathbf{y}^{(1)},..., \mathbf{y}^{(m)}\}$ from data distribution $q_{\text{data}}(\mathbf{y})$

Update the discriminator by ascending its stochastic gradient:

$$\nabla_{\varphi d}(1/m)\sum_{i=1}^{m}[\log D(\mathbf{y}^{(i)}) + \log(1 - D(G(\mathbf{u}^{(i)})))].$$

end for

Sample minibatch of m latent noise samples $\{\mathbf{u}^{(1)}, ..., \mathbf{u}^{(m)}\}$ from prior $q_u(\mathbf{u})$

Update the generator by descending its stochastic gradient:

$$\nabla_{\varphi g}(1/m)\sum_{i=1}^{m} - \log D(G(\mathbf{u}^{(i)}))$$

end for

It is worth mentioning that the adversarial game has a global optimum in which the generator is able to perfectly reproduce the data distribution and the discriminator produces a constant value denoting perfect uncertainty. The convergence of the generator and the actual data distribution is characterized by Jensen-Shannon divergence (Goodfellow et al., 2014). This theory demonstrates that minimizing this divergence causes the generator to acquire the distribution that is indistinguishable to the real data distribution, provided that the model has enough capacity and training time (Hyvärinen, 2005).

Even though in theory both networks could be of infinite capacity, in reality, GANs are finite in both parameters and datasets. However, empirical findings indicate that realistic sample generation may be achieved through well-crafted architectures or through meticulous training procedures. The theory does not only offer a mathematical guarantee of convergence, but also practical understanding of training dynamics, model stability, and gradient flow (Glorot et al., 2011). These understandings have been precursors to a significant research and development in adversarial learning, which has influenced a diverse range of uses in machine learning and AI.

Although GANs have the potential to perform very well in the learning of complex data distributions, their integration into radar signal processing is associated with significant difficulties. A major limitation is that GANs are sensitive to hyperparameter configurations and these may influence training stability and convergence. Also, traditional GANs are not necessarily optimized to work in the highly changing and non-Gaussian clutter conditions that occur in the modern radar systems. This may cause them to be unable to effectively generalize to varying conditions of interference. Moreover, GANs have high data needs and model hyperparameters, which are infeasible in real-time or resource-limited radar systems.

To ensure improved performance of GAN on radar systems, the following section introduces a novel procedure that involves GANs with a hyperparameter-free DL (RFF-DL) architecture built on RFFs for both generator and discriminator. This method eliminates the need for manual hyperparameter tuning. Furthermore, it has the potential to accelerate the convergence, and enhance generalization of the generator and discriminator without knowledge of data statistics.

3.4 Boosting GAN by Hyperparameter-free RFF-based Layers

Recent efforts in the realm of hyperparameter-free DL in the low data regime demonstrate a novel layer, namely, the RFF layer as an effective means of facilitating learning in the low data regime irrespective of data statistics. In this work, we are enhancing both *D* and *G* by RFFs (Mitra, Kaddoum, & Poitau, 2021), leading to convergence in the low data regime, and achieving lower loss function and better generalization in challenging scenarios in modern radar systems. In detail, this layer improves performance with respect to a Lipschitz continuous loss function by $O\left(n_G \log\left(\frac{nG}{2}\right)\right)$. These loss functions can be the hit-or-miss loss function for classification or minimum mean squared error for regression (Kay, 1993). Mathematically, this RFF layer can be expressed as follows (Mitra, Kaddoum, & Poitau, 2021):

$$\Phi(.) = \sqrt{\frac{2}{n_G}} \cos\left(diag(\gamma)W(.)[] + b\right) \qquad ...(4.6)$$

where Φ is the explicit approximation of the feature map, n_G denotes the number of RFF, $\gamma \sim \Gamma[a, b]$ denotes the gamma distributed random variable with shape parameter a and rate parameter b, with initialization $a = \frac{1}{2}$, $b = \in$ where is $\in$ infinitesimal. In addition, elements of the matrix W are drawn from a normal distribution of unit variance, and elements of the bias term b are drawn from a uniform distribution of $[0, 2\pi]$.

In this book chapter, along with vanilla GAN, we explore the utility of the hyperparameter-free RFF layer mentioned above for GANs in the context of parameter estimation for radar. In other words, we enhance both the generator and the discriminator of GAN (which are feedforward layers themselves; hence the results in Mitra, Kaddoum, Dahman et al. (2021) can be invoked to prove their enhanced convergence) by adding a hyperparameter-free RFF layer before the generator *G* and discriminator *D*. From the simulations presented in the next section for popular radar systems, we find that this layer enhances the overall convergence characteristics/generalization of GAN for target parameter estimation.

4. Simulation Results

This section examines the results of simulating the proposed GAN, GAN-RFF, and existing RKHS-based estimators on the monostatic LFM and FMCW radar systems.

The total 2500 time stamps/iterations is considered for the simulations, out of 2500, $k = 1500$ is used for training, and the rest 1000 for the tests in each training iteration. The f_c, c, and T_{PRI} of both radars make the target velocity v_i bounded as $\left\{-\frac{c}{4f_cT_{PRI}}, \frac{c}{4f_cT_{PRI}}\right\}$. In LFM and FMCW radars, different techniques are employed to calculate terms related to radial-range information. As a result, separate bounds for the radial range in LFM and FMCW radars are established, which are explicitly outlined in the following sections.

LFM Radar: For LFM radar, R_i is in the range $\left\{0, \frac{cT_{PRI}}{2}\right\}$. Since the LFM radar is used for long-distance applications, TPRI = 25 μsec, which results in a maximum measurable unambiguous range of $\frac{cT_{PRI}}{2}$ = 1.5 km. Also, with f_c = 75 GHz, the maximum unambiguous velocity is limited to $\left|\frac{c}{4f_cT_{PRI}}\right|$ = 40 m/sec.

FMCW Radar: Unlike the LFM radar, the R_i for the FMCW radar is within the range $\left\{0, \frac{f_sc}{2\mu}\right\}$. Designed for short-distance applications, with f_s = 25 MHz and f_s − 15 MHz/s, this results in a maximum unambiguous range of $\frac{f_sc}{2\mu}$ = 250 m. With T_{PRI} = 30 μs and f_c = 60 GHz, the maximum unambiguous velocity is $\left|\frac{c}{4f_cT_{PRI}}\right|$ = 40 m/s. The LFM and FMCW radar system simulation parameters are defined in Table 4.1 and Table 4.2, respectively.

Table 4.1 Simulation parameters for LFM Radar.

Parameters	*Simulation Value*
T	50
K	32
T_{PRI}	25 μs
f_c	75 GHz

Table 4.2 Simulation parameters for FMCW Radar.

Parameters	*Simulation Value*
T	50
K	32
$TPRI$	30 μs
f_c	60 GHz
μ	15 MHz/s
f_s	25 MHz

In simulation, the performance of GAN and its enhanced version, the RFF version (GAN-RFF), is evaluated and compared with existing RKHS-based methods [Kernel least mean square (KLMS), Kernel maximum correntropy (KMC), KMEE (Kernel minimum error entropy)].[2] Comparisons between GAN and GAN-RFF in terms of the predicted and estimated parameter value for the FMCW radar are shown in Figure 4.3. Specifically, it is shown in Figure 4.3(a) that in the estimation of the radial range, the performance of the GAN-RFF is better than that of the GAN. In addition, in Figure 4.3(b), the same behaviour is observed for the estimation of the velocity. The comparative performance of GAN and GAN-RFF with RKHS-based methods is shown in Figure 4.4, which shows the better performance of GAN-RFF than the combined methods based on GAN and RKHS. The final mean square error (MSE) achieved for the radial range and velocity is mentioned in Table 4.3. From Table 4.3, it is explicit that the GAN overshadows the RKHS-based methods, and the GAN-RFF will overshadow both the GAN and the RKHS-based methods.

Similar to the improved performance achieved by GAN and GAN-RFF for the FMCW radar, the performance achieved by GAN and GAN-RFF for the LFM radar system is shown in Figure 4.5, Figure 4.6, and Table 4.4. The observed improved performance of GAN over the ITL-based RKHS technique is reflection of the criterion learning which allows the adaptation of the implicit error surface in accordance with the clutter statistics/distribution. The further performance improvement GAN-RFF is because of evoking the RFF which allows the efficient computation of the complex kernel without the manual tuning of the hyperparameters.

[1]At this point, we would like to highlight that the RKHS-based method has already demonstrated superior performance compared to the conventional ML estimator; therefore, to avoid redundancy, the same has not been presented again in this chapter.

[2]At this point, we would like to highlight that the RKHS-based method has already demonstrated superior performance compared to the conventional ML estimator; therefore, to avoid redundancy, the same has not been presented again in this chapter.

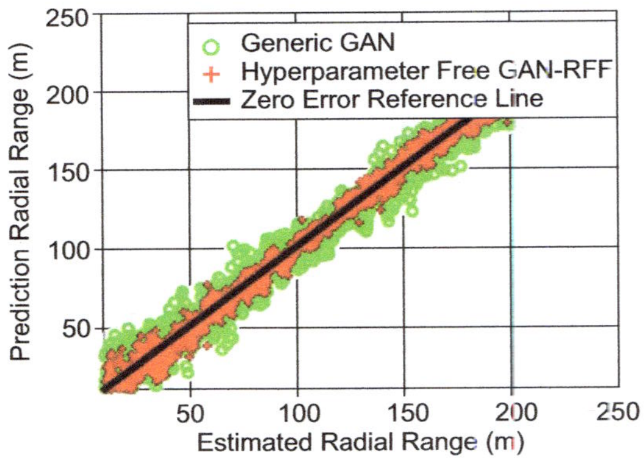

(a) Comparison between GAN and its hyperparameter-free boosted counterpart for FMCW Radar for estimation of radial range.

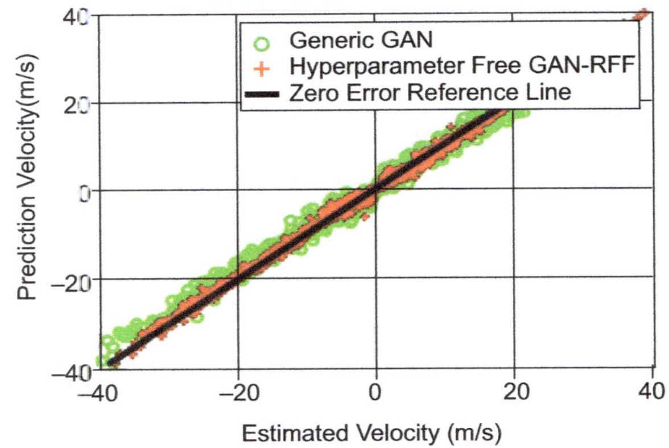

(b) Comparison between GAN and its hyperparameter-free boosted counterpart for FMCW Radar for estimation of velocity.

Fig. 4.3 Normalized MSE performance achieved by the GAN-RFF, GAN, KMEE, KMC, and KLMS for (a) Range Estimation and (b) Velocity Estimation using FMCW Radar.

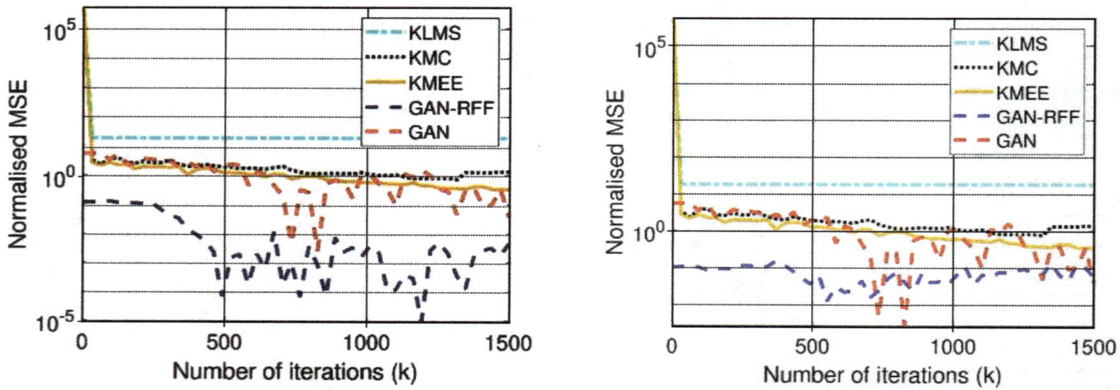

(a) Normalized MSE vs number of iterations for radial range estimation using FMCW Radar.

(b) Normalized MSE vs number of iterations for velocity estimation using FMCW Radar.

Fig. 4.4 Normalized MSE performance achieved by the GAN-RFF, GAN, KMEE, KMC, and KLMS for (a) Range Estimation and (b) Velocity Estimation using FMCW Radar.

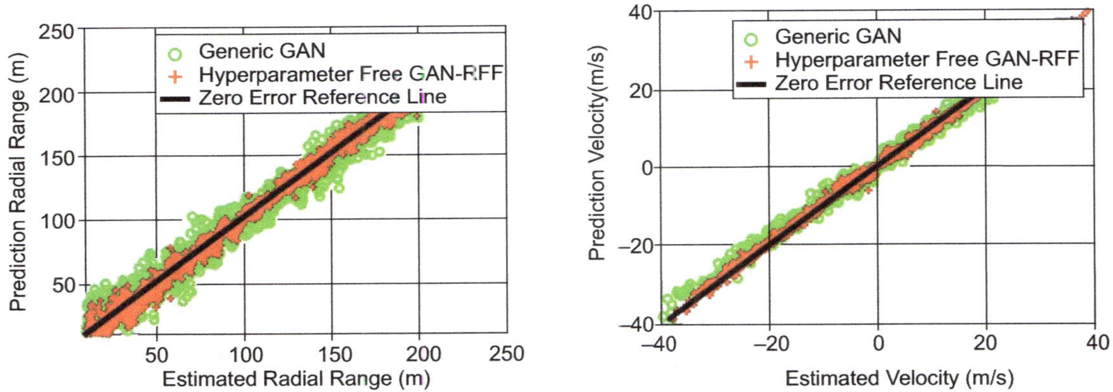

(a) Comparison between GAN and its hyperparameter-free boosted counterpart for LFM Radar for estimation of radial range.

(b) Comparison between GAN and its hyperparameter-free boosted counterpart for LFM Radar for estimation of velocity.

Fig. 4.5 Normalized MSE performance achieved by the GAN-RFF, GAN, KMEE, KMC, and KLMS for (a) Range Estimation and (b) Velocity Estimation using LFM Radar.

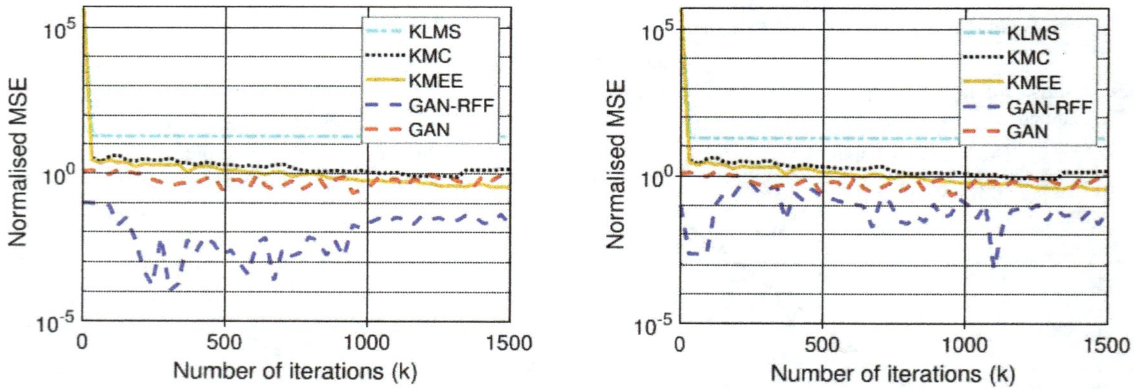

(a) Normalized MSE vs number of iterations for radial range estimation using LFM Radar.

(b) Normalized MSE vs number of iterations for velocity estimation using LFM Radar.

Fig. 4.6 Normalized MSE performance achieved by the GAN-RFF, GAN, KMEE, KMC, and KLMS for (a) Range Estimation and (b) Velocity Estimation using LFM Radar.

Table 4.3 Performance comparison of GAN, GAN-RFF with RKHS-based methods for FMCW radar using 1500 Data Points.

Method	*Normalized MSE (Radial Range)*	*Normalized MSE (Velocity)*
GAN	0.079	0.0075
GAN-RFF	0.049	0.0032
KLMS	0.25	0.09
KMC	0.2	0.0112
KMEE	0.15	0.01

Table 4.4 Performance comparison of GAN, GAN-RFF with RKHS-based methods for LFM radar using 1500 Data Points.

Method	*Normalized MSE (Radial Range)*	*Normalized MSE (Velocity)*
GAN	0.09	0.005
GAN-RFF	0.04	0.003
KLMS (Singh et al., 2019a)	0.5	0.9
KMC (Singh et al., 2019b)	0.2	0.0112
KMEE (Singh, Mitra, et al., 2021)	0.1	0.01

5. Conclusion

In this chapter, we explore the potential of DL to address a longstanding challenge in radar signal processing: estimating radial range and velocity of the target in the presence of non-Gaussian and non-homogeneous interference. To this end, a GAN was used for the first time to capture the complex nonlinear mapping between the 2D range-Doppler map and the parameters of interest, independently of the underlying perturbation distribution. Using the interaction between the generator and the discriminator, the GAN effectively establishes a decision boundary that relates each 2D range-Doppler representation to its corresponding parameters.

To further improve efficiency, the computational load on the GAN framework is reduced via RFF. This led to the development of a shallow GAN enhanced with RFF, which resulted in a new algorithm called GAN-RFF. The RFF exploits its ability to approximate the operation of an implicit kernel with finite-dimensional features and makes the vanilla GAN operation effective and fast in a low-data regime. The proposed approach was validated through simulations on two widely/popularly used radar systems, the LFM and FMCW radars, and the obtained results reveal the versatility of the proposed approach. Further comparison with the adaptive RKHS-based nonlinear algorithms suggests the superiority of both GAN and GAN-RFF in the environment affected by the nonhomogeneous/non-Gaussian clutter.

Specifically, the presented chapter demonstrates the effectiveness of GAN-based methods for estimating radar parameters and opens a new pathway for effectively solving the classical estimation problem in radar via modern machine learning/deep learning algorithms.

References

Abatzoglou, T.J. and Gheen, G.O. (1998). Range, radial velocity, and acceleration MLE using radar LFM pulse train. *IEEE Transactions on Aerospace and Electronic Systems*, 34(4), 1070–1083.

Bengio, Y. (2009). *Learning Deep Architectures for AI*. Now Publishers. 552–560, PMLR.

Bengio, Y., Mesnil, G., Dauphin, Y. and Rifai, S. (2013). Better mixing via deep representations. *International Conference on Machine Learning (ICML)*. NeurIPS, 2013.

Bengio, Y., Yao, L., Alain, G. and Vincent, P. (2013). Generalized denoising auto-encoders as generative models. *Advances in Neural Information Processing Systems (NeurIPS)*, 26, 279–335. Wiley, New York

Cover, T.M. and Thomas, J. A. (1991). Information theory and statistics. *Elements of Information Theory*, 1(1), 279–335.

Glorot, X., Bordes, A. and Bengio, Y. (2011). Deep sparse rectifier neural networks. *Proceedings of the 14th International Conference on Artificial Intelligence and Statistics (AISTATS)*.

Goodfellow, I.J., Pouget-Abadie, J., Mirza, M. et al. (2014). Generative adversarial nets. *Advances in Neural Information Processing Systems (NeurIPS)*, 419–426.

Hyvärinen, A. (2005). Estimation of non-normalized statistical models using score matching. *Journal of Machine Learning Research*, 6. Prentice Hall.

Kay, S.M. (1993). *Fundamentals of Statistical Signal Processing: Estimation Theory*. IEEE.

Mitra, R., Kaddoum, G., Dahman, G. and Poitau, G. (2021). Hyperparameter free MEE-FP based localization. *IEEE Signal Processing Letters*, 28, 1938–1942.

Mitra, R., Kaddoum, G. and Poitau, G. (2021). Analytical guarantees for hyperparameter free RFF based deep learning in the low-data regime. *IEEE Transactions on Circuits and Systems II: Express Briefs*, 69(2), 634–638.

Patole, S. M., Torlak, M., Wang, D. and Ali, M. (2017). Automotive radars: A review of signal processing techniques. *IEEE Signal Processing Magazine*, 34(2), 22–35.

Richards, M. (2005). *Fundamentals of Radar Signal Processing* (1st ed.). New York: Mcgraw-Hill.

Rife, D. and Boorstyn, R. (1974). Single tone parameter estimation from discrete-time observations. *IEEE Transactions on Information Theory*, 20(5), 591–598.

Singh, U.K., Mitra, R., Bhatia, V. and Mishra, A.K. (2019a). Kernel LMS-based estimation techniques for radar systems. *IEEE Transactions on Aerospace and Electronic Systems*, 55(5), 2501–2515.

Singh, U.K., Mitra, R., Bhatia, V. and Mishra, A.K. (2019b). Range and velocity estimation using kernel maximum correntropy based nonlinear estimators in non-Gaussian clutter. *IEEE*, 56(3), 1992–2004.

Singh, U.K., Mitra, R., Bhatia, V. and Mishra, A.K. (2021). Kernel minimum error entropy based estimator for MIMO radar in non-Gaussian clutter. *IEEE Access*, 9, 125320–125330.

Singh, U.K., Singh, A.K., Bhatia, V. and Mishra, A.K. (2021). EKF- and UKF-based estimators for radar system. *Frontiers in Signal Processing*, 1, 704382.

Vincent, P., Larochelle, H., Bengio, Y. and Manzagol, P.-A. (2008). Extracting and composing robust features with denoising autoencoders. *Proceedings of the 25th International Conference on Machine Learning (ICML)*, 1096–1103.

Zhao, S., Chen, B. and Principe, J.C. (2011). Kernel adaptive filtering with maximum correntropy criterion. *The 2011 International Joint Conference on Neural Networks*, IEEE.

5 Battlefield Simulation and Training Using Generative AI

Ujjwal Matoliya[1], Jeetendra Kumar[2*] and Nilesh Verma[3]

Generative artificial intelligence (AI) is a game-changer technology in the current defence, combat tactics, and weapon soldier readiness initiatives. Conventional methods of training on the battlefield, like classroom briefs, sand-table simulations, physical field simulations, and antique digital simulations are generally not realistic, flexible, scalable, and psychologically realistic in terms of actual combat stress factors. This imposes significant challenges on simulation in battlefields, which are overcome using simulated dynamic war environments, intelligent foes, real-time changes to the missions, and adaptive scenario creation that are consistent with future multi-domain warfare, such as on land, air, sea, cyber, and space. This chapter focuses on battlefield training based on the generative AI–facilitated training in terms of architecture, operations, and implementation. The chapter outlines the technology stack that comprises GANs, large language models, diffusion models, reinforcement learning, digital twins, live-virtual-constructive (LVC) training, and military cloud-edge computation. Moreover, it brings out operational benefits that include cost effectiveness, development of mission-ready troops, rapid mission rehearsal, tactical decision making, and readiness to cognitive warfare. Some other limitations, ethical concerns, geopolitical concerns, cybersecurity threats, and risks of dual use are also addressed in the chapter. A practical analysis of programmes of the United States, China, India, UK, Israel, and NATO is provided to show real progress on adoption. Finally, recommendations for the future are human–AI teaming, neuro-adaptive training, international regulation framework, and next-generation autonomous defence ecosystems.

1. Introduction

Modern warfare is no longer physical fighting as it has developed into a multisided war with the use of cyberattacks, electronic warfare, drone swarms, space resources, autonomous weapons, psychological influence operations, and information warfare. This change has necessitated the need for a more sophisticated and smarter type of training by the military forces, which goes beyond the physical training and the

[1] https://orcid.org/0009-0000-2825-692X
[2] https://orcid.org/0000-0002-5705-6369
[3] https://orcid.org/0009-0006-4705-6169
* Corresponding author: jgupta@abvv.ac.in

DOI: 10.1201/9781003688174-5

old-in-service computer-based simulators. Soldiers need to be ready to survive under the physical conditions of the world as well as to decide on something without knowing all facts, to quickly evaluate the situation, to communicate with the pressure, and to judge morally in real time (Fokkinga et al., 2025).

The use of conventional military training programmes, including field drills and the simulated battlefield exercises, is very effective yet constrained by high costs of operation, insufficient variety, geography, safety, and inability to model rare situations or extreme battle scenes, such as nuclear, bio-chemical, drone-swarm, hypersonic weapons, and coordinated large-scale cyberattacks. Additionally, practical training cannot be stopped, re-winded, edited, and tailored to the capacities of each soldier, his/her learning pace, and cognitive deficiencies (Fokkinga et al., 2025).

The solution is generative artificial intelligence (AI), which provides a breakthrough since it creates real, simulated, and evolving battles. Simulations such as Generative Adversarial Networks (GANs), Diffusion Models, Transformers, and Reinforcement Learning systems have the ability to generate AI battle scenarios, simulating random human enemy behaviour, changes to the terrain, the impact of weapons, human psychology, and environmental interference (rain, fog, night, radio-jamming, etc.). Generative AI can be used in combination with digital twins, Virtual Reality (VR)/Augmented Reality (AR) systems, and Live-Virtual-Constructive (LVC) simulation platforms to enable entirely personalized, scalable, low-risk, and cost-effective military training environments.

Artificial intelligence–generated simulated battlefield simulation:

- Development of several what-if war strategies
- Enemy tactics that are a result of AI and contain surprise intelligence
- Multi-domain operational rehearsal and simulation of cyber war
- Analytics mission debriefing automated
- Stress and emotion conscious training courses

As such, the generative AI–based battlefield training has strategic implications for future defence planning because it equips a soldier with the ability to make high-risk decisions without getting hurt during physical confrontation and in hybrid wars.

2. Technical/Operational Explanation

The generative AI–based battlefield simulation system generally adopts layered architecture as discussed below. The block diagram of layered architecture is also shown in Figure 5.1.

A. Data Layer

The data layer is the base element of generative AI–based battlefield simulations, since the precision and realism of artificial war environments is highly reliant on the quality, variety, and applicability of datasets used. Historical war data is employed to give contextual information of the previous battles, strategies, patterns of troop movement, environmental issues, and weapon-effect results. Satellite, drone surveillance feeds, and Internet of Things (IoT) sensors at strategic spots can add real-time geographical, environmental, meteorological, and thermal data that could be incorporated into virtual battlefield landscapes. Also, the geospatial intelligence (GIS) maps, created during the military reconnaissance, provide a detailed terrain modelling, including the terrain surface level, vegetation density, infrastructure, dangerous areas, and human movement. The field analysts, signal intercepts, and cyber reconnaissance intelligence reports are also included to develop adversary persona, intent, strategy, and psychological profiles. Also, AI-generated synthetic data are of great use in security-sensitive training because actual mission intelligence cannot be distributed to trainees due to classification restrictions. This simulated information can be used to mimic the forms of enemy communication, covert threats, and unconventional warfare actions without revealing the classified warfare operations (Patil & Karade, 2025).

B. AI Model Layer

The AI model layer serves as the computation and generative core in which the environment on the battlefield, the decision system of the enemy, mission tasks, and variations in training are generated automatically at scale. The photorealistic terrains, battle structures, equipment visualization, and effects of smoke, dust, fire, and tactical camouflage are created with the help of GANs. Large language models (LLMs), which are transformer-based models, generate dynamic dialogue in missions, multilingual instructions, psychology-based negotiation simulations, and radio communications controlled by AI, which are similar to actual military actions and communication styles. The reinforcement learning (RL) agents are taught how to emulate enemy forces that learn to develop intelligent and random responses depending on the decisions by the trainee, and this enables them to ambush, counter-ambush, divert, and use guerrilla strategies. Diffusion models add ultra-high fidelity scene rendering, and in effect make visibility look more realistic in fog, night-vision, underwater, and chemical-contaminated situations. Multimodal AI systems also combine inputs of speech, text, video, sensory, and biometric data, to generate comprehensive combat decision simulation, simulating combined perceiver inputs instead of individual streams of data (Patil & Karade 2025.

C. Simulation Layer

The simulation layer handles the transformation of AI-generated data and models into training environments that are immersive and interactive as well as allow the soldiers to experience, react, and perform tasks like those on missions in the real world. The main idea applied in this case is the digital twin, which is a virtual simulation of an actual battlefield, base, urban city, ship, submarine, airspace, or space-based battlefield. There is intelligence input to these digital twins, which makes the twins constantly relevant in scenarios and geopolitics. VR and AR interfaces will allow complete immersion of sensations, as they will allow soldiers to feel that they are physically present in the battlefield and communicate with AI-generated resources, enemies, and civilians. Also, an interface layer implemented is based on LVC paradigm, and live human trainees are exposed to virtual objects, AI-controlled characters, and constructive simulation agents, which do not require direct human control. This LVC integration provides scalable training scenarios, in which thousands of soldiers, AI units, drones, and automated vehicles can engage in concurrent training without being limited by physical infrastructure.

D. Deployment and Computing Layer

The computing and deployment layer offers the technological base needed to execute battlefield simulations of high performance with low latency, optimum security, and continuous synchronization. Classified models are stored in military grade secure cloud systems and run simulations, and multi-region access of the army is managed through encrypted command channels. Examples of Edge AI computing devices include wearable headsets, helmet-mounted processors, and portable ruggedized tablets, enabling soldiers to receive training simulations while on the field or on a forward base without being dependent on high bandwidth. As future 6G and satellite-based communication networks emerge, real-time simulation updates, distantly shared mission rehearsals, and AI model synchronization will be available among aircraft, land and sea, and space forces. This networking layer will mean that soldiers in the various geographical locations will be able to collaborate in a common battlefield simulation campaign. Security hardening frameworks, quantum-resistant encryption, and network segmentation are also built into the system to avoid cyber infiltration or the corruption of data.

E. Human Interaction and Feedback Layer

The human interaction and feedback layer deals with physiological immersion, performance monitoring, and adaptive learning analytics that augment the cognitive effect of training exercises. Sensory actuators integrated into haptic training systems provide the experience of tactile force like recoil, vibration, heat, or small impact pressure, making the training more realistic and yet safe. Attention patterns, situational awareness, and reaction timing, all of which are important combat-readiness indicators, are tracked using eye-tracking sensors. Also, the stress monitoring cameras are used to monitor the heart rate, skin temperature, EEG brainwave activities, and the tone of voice to determine the psychological strength and emotional control of a person during simulated combat stress. The system employs AI-generated analytics to measure the decision of trainees, reaction pattern, efficiency in the mission, ethical obedience, and endurance of the psychology. This feedback loop sustains customized training advice, re-customization of missions, and long-term soldier development profiles.

2.1 Generative AI Models Used

The battlefield training systems based on generative AI are built on the pool of various model architectures, being trained to serve a specific operational

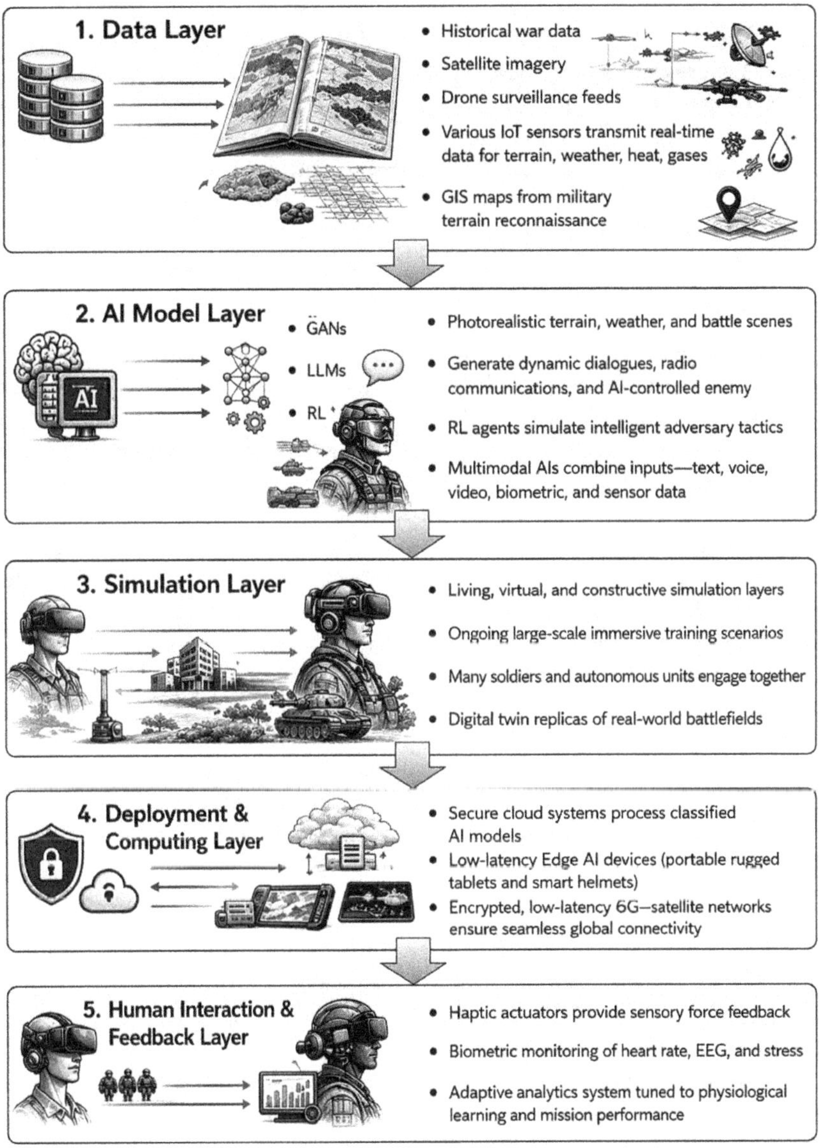

Fig. 5.1 Layered architecture of a generative AI–based battlefield simulation system showing data acquisition, AI model processing, simulation execution, deployment infrastructure, and human-in-the-loop feedback.

functionality in simulation ecosystems. GANs have mostly been used to create high-fidelity synthetic visual scenes containing terrain, military vehicles, weather simulations, and military or civilian crowd formations. These models facilitate the generation of content quickly, without the need to spend a lot of time on manual graphic creation, which makes them suitable for visual representation in terms of realism and at a low cost in terms of expenses, ideal to spend on immersive war-gaming and virtual war-gaming. Recently, diffusion models have been shown to achieve better results when it comes to photorealistic image generation, and so they have been used to generate ultra-realistic battlefield effects, including explosions, smoke behaviour, night-time lighting, fog density, and physics of debris. Multi-step denoising can be achieved through their iterative refinement process, and it produces much more detailed simulations than earlier neural rendering approaches (Patil & Karade 2025).

2.2 Interaction with LVC Training Framework

The use of generative AI as a part of the LVC paradigm is a significant development in the modern military training ecosystem. Training live in real battlefield environments, actual soldiers are engaged on the training grounds or bases physically with biosensors or motion-tracking gear or augmented reality (AR) visions so they can combine the real-time performance indicators. Soldiers in virtual training communicate with simulated environments using VR/AR headsets, simulation rooms, or C4ISR-driven display systems in command centres and communicate with computer-generated scenarios and computer-generated adversaries. In constructive simulations, no physical assets or soldiers are directly present, rather AI-controlled autonomous agents and adversarial forces exist in simulated battle space layers so that large scale war-gaming can be conducted with thousands of autonomous units. Generative AI systems bring together all three layers into the creation of continuous, flexible training environments where live members interplay among the virtual and constructive agents. This hybridization increases fidelity, cognitive complexity, and scalability, and allows 24/7 continuous training without having to mobilize troops or using large field assets (Patil & Karade 2025).

2.3 Deployment Environments

Military simulation systems supported by generative AI are deployed in a variety of secure and operationally different environments. Its main field is the military cloud infrastructure, which is frequently deployed in government-vetted zero-trust networks, on-premises data centres that are secure, or air-gapped defence clouds to identify sensitive sensor and intelligence information. These settings facilitate model training on a large scale, fusion of trained classifiers, and encrypted communication. On a smaller scale, individual soldiers and units are provided with portable VR headsets, hardened to take the field, allowing decentralized training in the barracks, far base camps as well as remote bases and forward operating posts. Holographic sand-table displays, war-gaming systems engineered by LVC, and collaborative planning platforms are part of command centre simulation suites to aid training in operational and strategic leadership. Moreover, edge AI–powered helmets, gazettes, body-worn computers, and exoskeleton-compatible visors are used to ensure real-time decision support, situational awareness overlay, biometric feedback, and AI-led instructional information during live workouts. Finally, simulation pods of autonomous vehicles (such as unmanned ground vehicles [UGVs], drones, simulated armoured vehicles) allow simulated driving, piloting, and weapon-system training using AI-driven, scenario-adaptive threat environments (Ray, 2025).

3. Strategic Benefits and Advantages

There are various types of strategic benefits of using generative AI in battlefield simulation, as shown in Figure 5.2. The benefits can be broadly categorized into training and readiness, economic advantages, psychological and behavioural aspects, and strategic commands.

3.1 Training and Readiness Benefits

Introduction of generative AI in battlefield training settings is an important development in training realism, operational fidelity, and soldier preparedness. Among the most significant advantages, one can distinguish the possibility to practice the elements of combat that are as realistic as possible and physically safe so that military personnel could be subjected to extreme, high-risk, and unpredictable battle situations without having to experience the risks entailed in live-fire drills (Heng, 2024). Model-driven simulated battlefields, including GANs, RL agents, and multimodal AI can produce adaptive adversary forces, dynamic terrain, changing weather conditions, cognitive stressors, and resource-constrained missions that are highly realistic as far as real-world battle conditions are concerned. This allows the trainees to feel uncertain, faced with ambiguity of threats, and under pressure of dynamic decision-making, in a controlled environment. In addition, systems based on generative AI can repeat the same mission or generate infinite combinations of scenarios by changing the different environmental parameters including time, weather, availability of logistics, and adversarial tactics. This reconfigurability and repeatability permits proficient training by means of normally repetitive exercises, as compared to the traditional training ranges that need physical resetting, reformatting, or downtime.

Also, AI systems with a generative nature allow customization of training on competency basis. Biometric data, response time recording, accuracy, and communication patterns can be used to assess the performance of the soldiers, and the models may automatically add, reduce, or adjust the complexity of tactical tasks in accordance with the individual or team competence. As an example: a soldier with high levels of marksmanship and lower levels of situational awareness may be deployed to missions with higher level of cognitive load such as surveillance, reconnaissance, and urban clearing missions, and another soldier with weak tactical movement may be given practice missions on cover-to-cover movement and flanking. Such a personalized training process, which can be compared to adaptive learning in education, facilitates the rapid acquisition of skills, addressing weaknesses and reinforcing strengths, and allows commanders to examine the readiness rates using digital performance analytics in real time (Defence Agenda, n.d.).

Fig. 5.2 Strategic, economic, psychological, and command-level benefits of generative AI–enabled battlefield simulation for military training and decision-making.

3.2 Economic Benefits

The economic benefits of the use of the generative AI–driven training systems are also very convincing over the traditional military training infrastructure that in most cases incurs high operational costs. Traditional field training uses physical distance, ammunition, fuel, vehicle repairs, and medical staff, and is labour-intensive to be set up—all of which costs a lot of money. Contrarily, after the digital simulation ecosystem and AI models are created and configured, it only costs little to conduct further training, which means that thousands of sessions can be held without a corresponding rise in spend. Minimizing ammunition and fuel usage is possible since simulated firing, armoured vehicles, and air-to-ground actions take place in virtual or constructive conditions, which cause no wear and tear to platforms or extend hardware lifecycle prospects (Badano, 2024).

Moreover, physical training facilities and environmental rehabilitation after live-fire exercises can be considered the hidden costs that can be addressed with the help of virtualization. Since they can be recreated virtually at a low cost and reconfigured repeatedly without destroying and rebuilding infrastructure, generative AI does not require large-scale development of mock terrain, placement of obstacles, or mock villages to replicate urban environments. Medical bills of training injuries, rehabilitation, or combat-sports stress on the musculoskeletal aspect can as well be minimized because there will be less exposure to dangerous activities. By lowering the ratio of instructor-to-trainee manpower, which is possible with AI-based automated training and evaluation, more trainees can be trained at a time, and this training throughput can be maximized without necessarily increasing the number of military instructors, training officers, or subject-matter experts. Therefore, beyond providing high-fidelity training results, generative AI can be used to optimize defence budgets over the long term and create sustainability in resources.

3.3 Psychological and Behavioural Advantages

It is not only physical ability that is required in combat but also mental strength, emotional control, and moral determination in the face of adversity. Simulation environments enhanced with AI facilitation of psychological conditioning are demonstrated through systematic exposure of soldiers to high-stress and surprise-base as well as ethically complicated scenarios in a safe but immersive environment. The trainees might be subjected to simulated ambushes, hostage crisis, civilian engagement issues, equipment malfunctions, care of casualties on the battlefield, or the effect of the sensory overload like smoke, noise, or darkness. These exercises enable the trainees to train on the ability to be composed, think clearly, and act in a manner that is mission-oriented, so that they do not respond shockingly or in panic when deployed.

Moreover, the generative AI systems are capable of simulating the elements of psychological warfare, including propaganda, deception, cyber-dangers, suffering of civilians, or manipulation of psyche, allowing the soldiers to drill resistance to cognitive, though not kinetic, attacks. Virtual trauma scenarios, with facilitation by military psychologists and training guidelines that educate victims about emotional preparedness, are beneficial in building emotional preparedness, thereby minimizing the risks of combat stress responses or post-traumatic maladaptation. Also, the ethical dilemma training can be conducted through simulation to enable the trainees to take into account the legal, moral, and humanitarian aspects of warfare, such as proportionality, discrimination, and non-combatant support. Intelligent narrative engines have the potential to model complicated moral decision-points and compel soldiers to prioritize mission goals over honesty restrictions, which would assist values-based and rules-of-engagement-appropriate behaviour in line with international human rights law (Heng, 2024).

3.4 Strategic Commands

Generative AI has transformational advantages in operations and strategic command planning, analysis, and decision support. Compared to the time required in briefing and debriefing processes, simulation systems prove to be much faster since all actions, decisions, communication logs, biometrics, geographic movements, and adversary responses are automatically logged. AI-driven after-action review analytics is capable of detecting personal errors, institutional tactical or strategic problems, communication bottlenecks, or vulnerabilities in strategy more quickly and accurately than evaluators who are not AI users. This helps to develop speedy modular training and also promote evidence-based enhancement of doctrine, standard operating procedures, and tactical work processes.

It is also possible to predict adversarial behaviour using generative AI. The enemy agents, implemented by RL, have the potential to understand the patterns of friendly force decisions and automatically create counter-tactics, giving the commanders early insight into probable future trajectories of threats. AI-assisted scenario planning can simulate land, sea, air, cyber, and space multi-domain conflicts and model logistical constraints including ammunition shortages, communications jamming, disease outbreak, or infrastructure collapse. These systems enable the strategic leaders to consider different scenarios that can be considered as what-if and find out the most efficient course of action based on decision-support dashboards. In addition, AI-assisted plan creation and red-teaming systems assist commanders to detect weaknesses, blind spots in an operation plan or escalation risks during a mission plan prior to execution. Thus, generative AI positively impacts training success, strategic foresight, operational coherence, and mission survivability (Galvin et al., 2024).

4. Limitations and Risks

Generative AI has a huge potential for generating changes in the military training ecosystems, but its implementation also poses complex constraints and threats that cannot be underestimated. Although the technology has the capacity to enhance preparedness, the superiority of decision-making, and the ability to scale up cheap training, it has significant technical, ethical, geopolitical, and cybersecurity issues. These risks need to be comprehended in order to achieve controlled, legal, and strategically advantageous deployment.

4.1 Technical Limitations

Although machine learning and simulation engineering are developing fast, technical constraints have limited the efficiency and performance of the generative AI–enabled military training systems. A significant barrier is the phenomenon of hallucination whereby generative models generate incorrect, imaginary, or somewhat misleading information that is plausible and lifelike (i.e., fake battlefield indicators, unrealistic enemy behaviour, or unrealistic weather patterns). These hallucinations are based on inferences made in a probabilistic fashion, lack of ground-truth validation, or biased training samples, which result in decision-level brittle behaviour and possibly reinforce false tactical reasoning, as opposed to operational accuracy (Kumar, 2025).

The other essential obstacle happens to be the reliance on massive, high-fidelity, and frequently classified data, such as satellite imagery, human intelligence (HUMINT), signals intelligence (SIGINT), and mission logs, which might not be at all available at such granularity because of national security considerations. This generates a discrepancy between the theoretical and actual training performance in that incomplete datasets can lead to oversimplification or unrealistic constraints of the scenarios. Furthermore, combat dynamic modelling needs to model nonlinear human behaviour that is improvisational and which is not well modelled in algorithmic prediction. Human thinking encompasses emotional instability, disobedience, morale fluctuation, irrational decision-making, and cultural differing—dimensions that the current AI architectures are unable to model with fidelity, thus constraining real behavioural realism.

Also, capability gaps exist due to infrastructure-level constraints, including latency of immersive simulations, enormous computational costs to simulate photorealistic environments, and sovereign computing platforms. Although commercial cloud resources can support faster experimentation, it might not comply with military-grade security needs, and it will be necessary to rely on national infrastructure tailored to the country that is costly and slower to modify (Kumar, 2025).

4.2 Ethical and Moral Risks

The introduction of generative AI in defence training brings about profound ethical issues especially relating to emotional, psychological, and moral distortions. Exposure-based conditioning can subconsciously change the perception, identity, and value systems of the soldiers due to the power of immersive simulations. Re-creation of violent acts in a realistic manner, simulated bloodshed, and re-creation of trauma can desensitize soldiers to human misery, which may decrease empathy levels and change the moral balance used in actual operations.

Just as worrisome is the threat of algorithmically based value congruency whereby mission rules, engagement norms, or threat classification created by AI can bring about unquestioned biases. When cultural, political, or geopolitical presumptions of the developers, datasets, or sponsoring institutions are incorporated into training systems, soldiers will inadvertently inherit these prejudices, producing ethically biased combat reactions.

More so, ethical opacities are linked to the inability of soldiers to differentiate between natural learning and AI-informed behavioural shaping, which may be against autonomy and informed consent. Tactical training simulations which include psychological stress loading, a hostage-killing decision, and trade-offs between civilian life and loss of friends might train soldiers in a tactical manner, but they might incur emotional repression, identity distortion, or post-training moral dissonance (Menthe et al., 2024).

4.3 Geopolitical and Security Threats

The simulation systems generated by generative AI are dual-use technologies in nature, and they can increase world competitiveness in terms of algorithmic excellence. Those states that can swiftly establish the means of creating realistic autonomous training systems can realize the benefits of force multiplication, which is viewed as a destabilizer in the war by events that are considered strategic by other countries, and the problem will be escalated into a new wave of arms races in AI-enhanced warfare. Moreover, the systems might leak (intentionally or unintentionally) into the possession of rogue states, insurgencies, or paramilitary groups once they are mature enough to facilitate their own production of professional-grade training without having to attend formal military schools or international oversight.

The other risk is data territoriality and sovereignty which as a geopolitical risk results in training infrastructure commonly being dependent on international technology providers, overseas semiconductor supply chains, and collaborative research networks. These dependencies impose weaknesses in the event of diplomatic tensions which might lead to embargoes, backdoor spies, or denial of capabilities. Besides, the rise of AI-based war games can change the international security discourse by leading the doctrine towards predictive and pre-emptive warfare instead of stability through deterrence (Badano, 2024).

4.4 Cybersecurity Risks

With a growing data-centricity and interdependence between digital twin technologies and military training, the risk of cyber vulnerabilities grows exponentially. A significant threat is deepfake-based fraud, in which opponents can gain access to or hack a simulation setting to create mission orders, imitated commander voice lines, enemy intelligence data, or battlefield images. Such attacks may disorient trainees psychologically and undermine the level of trust in digital systems. The other risk is training data exfiltration or poisoning, whereby enemies spoil datasets with inaccurate geospatial data, artificial tactical intuitions, or a modified history of conflicts, resulting in uncalibrated decision models.

Furthermore, the use of distributed simulation systems through cloud, edge, and 6G tactical networks can be susceptible to zero-day exploits and other lateral attacks and can penetrate classified infrastructure. In a situation where the antagonists compromise AI approximations, reinforcement training policy, and digital twin parameters, the entire training doctrine integrity and rationality might be jeopardized. This enhances the requirements of secure-by-design designs, cryptographic model controls, and ongoing threat monitoring (Coombs, 2024; Kasera, 2025).

5. Evidence, Effectiveness, and Results in the Real World

Military training based on generative AI and high-level simulation has gone beyond laboratory work and small-scale pilot projects to significant, funded national initiatives and commercial solutions. Governments and defence agencies are placing bets on inexpensive, persistent experimentation, federated training environments, and synthetic training environments as a way to enhance readiness, cut costs, and speed development of doctrine. In this section, a summary of the international programmes chosen, the major contribution of the defence industry, and representative patents and research efforts that have foundations in the contemporary generative AI–enabled training systems have been discussed.

5.1 International Programmes

United States Project Convergence, DARPA, and the Army Synthetic Training Environment: The United States has been experimental-at-scale in order to bring sensors, networks, and automated decision tools to training and operations. DARPA experimentation programmes and the Project Convergence initiative of the army specifically target testing data-centric AI-enabled effects in multi-domain experimentation. Project Convergence specifically serves as an experimentation space, a year-round experimentation venue, to test data sharing, targeting, and closed-loop decision cycles that can be included in training and simulation pipelines (Project Convergence is persistent experimentation across the force). Synthetic Training Environment (STE) is a large-scale modernization programme of the US Army, aimed at integrating live, virtual, constructive, and gaming resources into a single interoperability framework that enables distributed collective training and rapid mission rehearsal, and prototypes of STE have been utilized to enhance platform crew training, as well as to add high-fidelity haptics and physiology monitoring capabilities to realistic situations. These programmes have collectively delivered tangible operational dividends: in scenarios generation is much faster, scenario-to-shooter pipelines are integrated to simulate realistic targeting, and unit readiness metrics are improved measurably during exercises (Ford, 2022; Rane et al., 2023; Rozman, 2020).

China—What Intelligentized Warfare Research and Simulation Aspirations: China and the People's Liberation Army (PLA) have focused on the use of AI-enabled warfare, a policy that speaks of AI, autonomy, and digitalization training as the modernization strategies of its force, as shown in Figure 5.3. Open-source reporting and defence tests show that Chinese academic research is increasingly using large-scale simulation, digital twins, and AI-generated scenarios to simulate joint operations, maritime strike scenarios, and integrated air–sea–land campaigns; official PLA publications and US Defence Department evaluations highlight increased training realism and advanced virtual war-gaming as a component of the modernization strategy of the military. There is also an indication of labour and doctrine investment in the direction of closing the human training disparity, using automated scenario generation and AI-enhanced tactical advisors (Kania, 2020).

Israel—Advanced Urban and Tunnel VR Training: Israel has created fully developed urban warfare, counter-terrorism, and tunnel combat simulation programmes. An Urban Warfare Training Center run by the IDF enables troops to train for dense urban operations, hostage scenarios, and underground navigation in

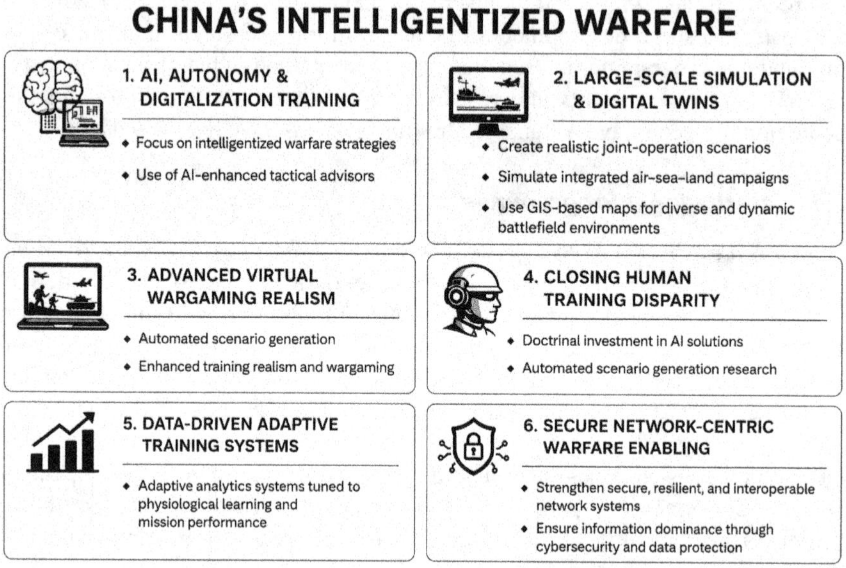

Fig. 5.3 China's intelligentized warfare research framework emphasizing AI-powered battle simulations, digital twin war-gaming, automated scenario generation, and integrated multi-domain operations.

immersive sensor-instrumented environments available commercially, both as part of a suite of VR/AR systems (such as Elbit Systems) and as individual offerings (such as Combatica). Some of the benefits reported are more realistic simulation of complex close-quarters conditions, repeatability of stress-exposure training, which is useful in decision-making during ambiguous conditions, cost and logistic advantages over repeatedly rebuilding mock villages in urban areas. Public reports and Urban Warfare Training Center announced that the IDF incorporates VR modules with live ranges and data capture to provide continuous training feedback loops (Winton, 2019).

United Kingdom—AI Strategy and Partnerships in Defence: In the UK, the approach to the adoption of AI on a scale in defence functions, known as the Defence Artificial Intelligence Strategy (2022), developed an organizational and procurement strategy, clearly stating simulation, synthetic training, and public–private collaboration as priorities. The UK sponsored partnerships (such as among Dstl, Hadean, and commercial simulation vendors) to fill LVC environments with synthetic human terrain and to test AI adversary generation; results documented include shorter time to populate a scenario and automated after-action analysis which reduces the workload of instructors in large exercises. The UK plan also prioritizes the adoption of AI in an ethical way and its interoperability with systems in alliances (Payne, 2024).

NATO Distributed Networked DVC and Federated Training: The modelling and simulation programmes by NATO have been directed at federated LVC training, enabling member states to conduct interoperable exercises in fields and categories. To enhance allied interoperability, verification of scenario modules sharing, and collaborative doctrine experimentation, NATO technical working groups and research bodies have suggested federated synthetic training. Smaller-scale exercises show the ability to conduct multinational synthetic operations that combine air, sea, and land forces without physically relocating large formations; the exercises save money on logistics and allow timely coalition rehearsal of crisis situations (Blais, n.d.; Galvin et al., 2024).

5.2 Contributions of Defence Companies and Industry

Industrial defence primes and limited simulation companies have created business products, research efforts, and patented techniques that execute features of generative AI training. Lockheed Martin has also invested in AR-based training devices and the so-called AI Factory to add commercial generative models into secure defence processes; the HMD-based training patents of Lockheed indicate real-world usage of AR-based target detection and weapon simulation. BAE Systems provides products in modelling and simulation and decision support, and has patents on course-of-action (CoA) simulation providing inputs to automated decision generation to training systems. Thales and CAE offer LVC trainers and networked training environments with flight, naval, and ground platforms; CAE is the foremost supplier of federated LVC for allied air forces. Palantir has been providing data-fusion and analytics backbones that most armed forces have been utilizing to synthesize sensor, simulation, and training data to conduct an after-action analysis. Anduril is an amalgamation of autonomy and safe mesh networking (Lattice), which can be employed in synthetic surroundings and to manage distributed robot assets in training. These industry initiatives provide practical benefits: commercial maturity is shortening fielding schedules; patented synthetic-data and simulation technologies are shortening model training schedules; vendor integration is aiding cross-platform federation of allied forces.

5.3 Research, Patents, and Representative IP

The manner in which firms and laboratories address fundamental challenges, such as synthetic generation of data, learning to simulate pipelines, and AR/VR training apparatus, is reported in research and patent applications. Table 5.1 contains a list of the chosen patents and patent applications that are directly related to simulation and synthetic training. These examples represent industry investment in synthetic-data generation, simulated training data-pipes, CoA simulation, and head-mounted AR training devices.

Table 5.1 Representative patents related to synthetic training and simulation.

Patent No./App.	*Title (short)*	*Assignee (example)*	*Year (pub.)*	*Brief description*
US20200012902 A1	Systems & methods for synthetic data generation	(general/academic and industry filings)	2020	Methods for generating time-series synthetic data for model training (useful for sensor/synthetic training data) (https://patents.google.com/patent/US20200012902A1/en)
US11518382 B2	Learning to simulate (fully annotated simulated training data)	(industry/academic)	2023	Methods to generate annotated simulated data and train ML models using simulator-adjusting parameters (improves RL and model transfer) (https://patents.google.com/patent/US11518382B2/en)
US10678244 B2	Data synthesis for autonomous control systems	(autonomy/simulation patents)	2020	Generating sensor-perspective synthetic data for autonomous systems (applies to vehicle/drone simulation) (https://patents.google.com/patent/US10678244B2/en)
US10030931 B1	Head-mounted display-based training tool	Lockheed Martin	2018	AR HMD training tool for weapons training and aim assistance; integrates sensors and simulator inputs for field training (https://patents.google.com/patent/US10030931B1)
(Assorted)	Lattice mesh, secure networking, autonomous systems patents	Anduril Industries	2022–2024	Anduril has multiple patents for Lattice OS, secure mesh communications, and sensor fusion that support federated synthetic operations (https://www.anduril.com/news/operating-at-scale-patents-for-america)

6. Future Prospects and Suggestions

Generative AI will continue to develop to generate more autonomous, dynamic, multisensory, and cognitive-adaptive learning ecosystems, beyond the current situation of battlefield simulation and military training. Not only will these systems simulate reality, but they will also co-create new conditions, pre-empt adversarial strategy, and optimize human decisions by using continuous data-driven adaptation. The world military forces are moving towards smart warfare, where AI, robotics, cyber activities, and psychological superiority are closely combined. So, training based on generative AI in the future must focus on interoperability, ethical protection, development of cognitive resilience, alignment with doctrine, joint-force preparedness, and adherence to international humanitarian law, NATO-STANAG standard, and United Nations disarmament policy frameworks (Madison et al., 2024).

6.1 Human–AI Cooperation with Robotic Swarms

This is likely to be the future of battlefield simulation as it will consist of human forces and autonomous robotic swarms, such as UAVs, UGVs, USVs, exoskeleton-fitted soldiers, or AI-controlled micro-drones. Multi-agent reinforcement learning (MARL) can be used to generate swarm coordination schemes, jam-tolerant communication schemes, collaborative targeting schemes, and decentralized threat recognition schemes using generative AI. This allows commanders to tactically train with dozens, hundreds, or thousands of autonomous agents at no physical cost or risk to enhance command-and-control (C2) decision cycles, multi-domain operations (MDO), and rapid kill chains (Boyd, 1996). Human-on-the-loop oversight should also be used in the future deployment in order to ensure ethical responsibility and legality of the mission (Marques, 2012).

6.2 Cognitive Digital Soldier Doubles

The following decade is likely to witness a shift from simulating the terrain and machinery with mechanical digital twins (DTs) to simulating emotional, physiological, behavioural, and decision-making patterns of individual soldiers with the help of cognitive digital twins (CDTs). Biosensors, neuro-EEG, voice-stress analytics, biometric wearables, and long-term datasets of psychological profiling will enable this. A CDT would enable AI simulators to personalize mission level, model combat burnout, and create individual coping interventions. It is aimed at changing the task-based training to cognitive resilience–based one, oriented towards anticipatory mental-state modulation and ethical constraint reinforcement, which, in turn, decreases the levels of post-traumatic stress disorder (PTSD) after conducting high-intensity operations (Stanek et al. 2025).

6.3 6G Satellite-Cloud–enabled Military Metaverse

The military simulation systems of the future are expected to be based on a classified, sovereign military metaverse connected to 6G, quantum-safe encryption, multi-orbit satellite networks (LEO-MEO-GEO), and edge-cloud hybrid computing. This architecture will facilitate planet-scale, synchronous LVC simulation, which can be used to allow geographically dispersed units to train in real-time hyper-realistic environments. When 6G terahertz spectrum networking is used to enable holographic telepresence, tactile-internet haptics, and bio-digital feedback learning loops, this is compared to the current VR systems that have bandwidth, latency, and rendering limits (ITU-R, 2023). Such metaverses will probably degenerate into NATO-level or QUAD-level training federations, to facilitate multinational interoperability, common understanding of doctrine, and joint-task-force practice.

6.4 Stress-Adaptive Training based on Neuro-AI

One future direction that is also critically oriented is neuro-adaptive AI simulation in which training environments dynamically react to cortisol levels, variability of heartbeat, cognitive load as measured by the EEG, eye-tracking, and micro-expression analytics in a soldier. To guarantee a gradual stress inoculation, instead of psychological trauma, generative AI systems will adjust lighting, frequency of sound, NPC aggression, realism of the casualties, and the intensity of moral dilemma. This solution has the potential of establishing individualized learning curves of difficulty, thus enhancing mission survivability, cognitive endurance, and emotional stability. Evidence indicates that exposure to stress that is regulated by AI conditions leads to greater retention of tactical judgement and adherence to ethics.

6.5 UN & NATO Regulatory Framework of Ethical AI Warfare

Since generative AI is a dual-use concept, a multilateral system of rule is necessary to guarantee the stability of the global conflict processes in the long run. Future training ecosystems should be compatible with:

- UN Convention on Certain Conventional Weapons (CCW)
- NATO AI strategy/STANAG conformity
- Cyber warfare law (Tallinn Manual)
- Budapest Convention on Cybercrime

A structured overview of regulatory mechanisms governing ethical AI warfare is presented in Table 5.2, highlighting enforcement authorities, compliance requirements, and stakeholder responsibilities.

Table 5.2 Regulatory Bodies for Ethical AI Warfare.

Regulatory Focus	*Description*	*Enforcement Stakeholder*
AI-Use Certification	Mandatory evaluation of ethical compliance	United Nations (UN) + North Atlantic Treaty Organization (NATO)
Dataset Transparency	Ban on illegally obtained or genocidal content data	International Court of Justice (ICJ)/ International Criminal Court (ICC)

Contd...

Table 5.2 *Contd...*

Regulatory Focus	*Description*	*Enforcement Stakeholder*
Red-Flag Scenario Bans	No extremist, ethnic cleansing, or civilian-target content	United Nations Human Rights Council (UNHRC)
Cyber-Safety Audits	Zero-trust, post-quantum encryption	NATO Cooperative Cyber Defence Centre of Excellence (CCDCOE)
Accountability Protocol	Chain-of-command responsibility retention	International Humanitarian Law (IHL) courts

This will ensure that AI does not normalize war crimes, autonomous targeting, or psychological manipulation of personnel.

7. Summary and Conclusion

Generative AI is a paradigm shift in the current military training that brings together the capabilities of immersive simulation, adaptive learning, digital twinning, and autonomous decision-support modelling. Contrary to the traditional training environments, which are highly dependent on the physical terrain, human trainers, and predetermined scripts of scenarios, generative AI–enabled simulation environments offer unlimited, dynamic, and customized battlefield experiences that are very realistic for multi-domain operations such as land, air, sea, cyber, and space. By combining generative AI with neural networks like GANs, diffusion, large language models, and multi-agent reinforcement learning, the contemporary defence institutions would be able to create an emotionally informed, cognitively adaptive, and technologically complex combat environment, training the personnel to respond to the uncertain, nonlinear, and hybridized wars in the future.

There is a great benefit in training efficiency, operational readiness, financial sustainability, and troop safety in the broad adoption of simulation using generative AI. It allows mission rehearsal without environmental harm, human loss, and drain of the resources. At the same time, it improves the decision-making process of the command, stress inoculation, ethical rationality, and mission debrief analysis. Moreover, generative AI helps to build interoperable joint-force doctrines, enabling MNCs to rehearse together using realistic and secure cloud-synchronized metaverse infrastructures. This is in line with the changing world military transformation agenda towards the intelligentized warfare where integrated AI, robotics, data fusion, cyber operations, and psychological defence are the centre of strategic superiority.

Nevertheless, there is no doubt that generative AI–powered combat simulation is associated with ethical, legal, and cybersecurity challenges that are impossible to ignore despite its transformative benefits. Examples of risks are algorithmic hallucination, bias in the datasets, psychological over-conditioning, geopolitical misuse, and cyber-provoked misleading information in the synthetic media or adversarial manipulation. Thus, international law, regulatory intervention, clear auditing avenues, and strong red-teaming frameworks should be used in the implementation. The anthropocentricity of command authority and responsibility should be taken as obligatory to avoid the shift towards entirely autonomous training principles and decision-making patterns that question humanitarian principles.

Finally, generative AI–based battlefield simulation may be not only a step forward in military training, but also the transformation of ideas about being prepared, deterring, and managing fights in the future, as nations have never thought of it that way. When created in a responsible manner, including with ethical governance, secure data ecosystems, multidisciplinary cooperation, and policy-consistent adoption, generative AI can contribute to increased global defence stability and decreasing the human cost of war. New membership in the art and ethics of warfare further suggests that AI can be an assistant to military readiness rather than a substitute because of balanced human–machine integration and not only technological sophistication.

References

Alliance, N.G.M.N. and Düsseldorf, G. (2024). ITU-R framework for IMT-2030: Review and Future Direction. Accessed on 25/9/25.

Badano, C. (2024). Study and design of generative learning tools for threat assessment in defence. Available at http://unire.unige.it/handle/123456789/9066 (accessed on 4 January 2026).

Blais, C.L. (n.d.). *Overview of Modelling and Simulation Standards for NATO Federated Mission Networking*. Available at https://publications.sto.nato.int/publications/STO%20Educational%20Notes/STO-EN-MSG-211/EN-MSG-211-1.2.pdf (accessed on 4 January 2026).

Boyd, J.R., 1996. The essence of winning and losing. Unpublished lecture notes, 12(23), pp.123–125. Accessed on 10/9/25.

Coombs, M.R.A. (2024). AI integration for scenario development. *Military Review*, 1. Available at https://www.armyupress.army.mil/Portals/7/military-review/Archives/English/Online-Exclusive/2024/AI-Integration/AI-Integration-for-Scenarios-UA1.pdf (accessed on 4 January 2026).

Defence Agenda. (n.d.). Generative AI in military training. Available at https://defenceagenda.com/generative-ai-in-military-training/?utm_source=chatgpt.com (accessed on 4 January 2026).

Fokkinga, E.P., Eker, T.A., van Woerden, J.E. et al. (2025). Generative AI methods for synthesis of image data to train AI for automated scene understanding in a military context: A review of opportunities. *Synthetic Data for Artificial Intelligence and Machine Learning: Tools, Techniques, and Applications III*, 13459, 9–31.

Galvin, K., Jense, H., van den Berg, T. et al. (2024). Advancing modelling and simulation in NATO federated mission networking. *NATO Modelling and Simulation Symposium 2023*. Available at https://publications.sto.nato.int/publications/STO%20Meeting%20Proceedings/STO-MP-MSG-207/MP-MSG-207-07.pdf (accessed on 4 January 2026).

Heng, L. (2024). Strategic overview of applying artificial intelligence on the future battlefield. Available at https://jyx.jyu.fi/jyx/Record/jyx_123456789_95024 (accessed on 4 January 2026).

Kania, E.B. (2020). "AI weapons" in China's military innovation. *Brookings Institution*, April, 3. Available at https://www.brookings.edu/wp-content/uploads/2020/04/FP_20200427_ai_weapons_kania_v2.pdf (accessed on 4 January 2026).

Kasera, C. (2025). Virtual soldiers for tactical training: A generative AI framework for adaptive military simulations. *International Journal for Research in Applied Science & Engineering Technology*, 13(9), 1754–1759.

Kumar, N. (2025). Social engineering attack in the era of generative AI. *International Journal for Research in Applied Science and Engineering Technology*, 13(1), 1737–1747.

Madison, A., Novoseller, E., Goecks, V.G. et al. (2024). Scalable interactive machine learning for future command and control. *2024 International Conference on Military Communication and Information Systems (ICMCIS)*, 1–10.

Marques, M.M. (2012). STANAG 4586—Standard interfaces of UAV control system (UCS) for NATO UAV interoperability. NATO Standardization Agency: Afeite, Portugal, 14.

Menthe, L., Zhang, L., Geist, E. et al. (2024). Limits of artificial intelligence for warfighters. Technical report. RAND Corporation. Available at https://www.jar2.com/Files/AI/RAND_Limits_of_for_Warfighters.pdf (accessed on 4 January 2026).

Patil, J. and Karade, V. (2025). Gen AI. *International Journal of Advance and Applied Research*, 6(22), 530–534.

Payne, K. (2024). Bright prospects, big challenges: Defence AI in the United Kingdom. In *The Very Long Game: 25 Case Studies on the Global State of Defense AI* (pp. 85–105). Springer Nature Switzerland Cham.

Rane, N., Choudhary, S. and Rane, J. (2023). Enhanced product design and development using artificial intelligence (AI), virtual reality (VR), augmented reality (AR), 4D/5D/6D printing, internet of things (IoT), and blockchain: A review. *Virtual Reality (VR), Augmented Reality (AR) D*, 4. Available at https://papers.ssrn.com/sol3/papers.cfm?abstract_id=4644059 (accessed on 4 January 2026).

Ray, A. (2025). EdgeAgentX-DT: Integrating digital twins and generative AI for resilient edge intelligence in tactical networks. No. arXiv:2507.21196. arXiv. (accessed on 4 January 2026).

Rozman, J. (2020). The synthetic training environment. *Spotlight SL*, 20–26.

Stanek, D., Klaban, I. and CoufalÍkovÁ, A. (2025, May). Explainable Artificial Intelligence: State of the Art and Beyond. In 2025 International Conference on Military Technologies (ICMT) (pp. 1–7). IEEE.

Winton, D. W. (2019). Is urban combat a great equalizer? Ph.D. thesis, Johns Hopkins University. Available at https://jscholarship.library.jhu.edu/items/42f2d174-df00-4794-b761-af75545ecfea (accessed on 4 January 2026).

6 Agentic Generative AI for Aircraft Combat Simulation

Rashmi Gupta[1], Ayush Kumar Agrawal[2*] and Neeraj Kumar Rathore[3]

Agentic generative artificial intelligence (AI) represents a significant advancement in aircraft combat simulation by enabling autonomous, goal-oriented, and adaptive behaviour in complex and contested air combat environments. This chapter investigates the integration of agentic generative models—encompassing large language models, reinforcement learning, and multi-agent coordination—within high-fidelity aircraft combat simulators. Unlike traditional rule-based systems, agentic AI entities can perceive evolving battlefield conditions, reason over tactical objectives, generate novel manoeuvres, and learn from interaction-driven feedback. A dedicated case study using VR-Forces, a widely adopted constructive and virtual simulation platform, demonstrates the practical realization of agentic generative AI in air combat scenarios. The case study highlights the deployment of intelligent combat agents for beyond-visual-range and within-visual-range engagements, adaptive threat response, and coordinated wingman behaviour within VR-Forces' physics-based and scenario-driven environment. Performance metrics such as tactical effectiveness, realism, scalability, and decision adaptability are analysed and compared against conventional scripted approaches. The chapter also discusses critical challenges related to safety assurance, explainability, interoperability with existing defence simulation frameworks, and real-time computational constraints. By combining theoretical foundations with an agentic AI, this chapter illustrates how agentic generative AI can significantly enhance the realism, training value, and decision-support capabilities of next-generation aircraft combat simulation systems.

1. Introduction

The War Aircraft Combat Simulation (WACS) is a sophisticated virtual environment designed to replicate the complete air-to-air combat process, including weapon engagement and pilot decision-making under realistic battlefield conditions. The Air Force has explored the use of artificial intelligence (AI) to simulate dogfights within a cockpit environment, support air combat manoeuvring, and develop

[1] https://orcid.org/0000-0001-6853-9844
[2] https://orcid.org/0009-0008-1888-279X
[3] https://orcid.org/0000-0002-9349-3419
* Corresponding author: ayushagrawal369@gmail.com

DOI: 10.1201/9781003688174-6

and evaluate autonomous dogfighting systems prior to live-aircraft testing—an approach highlighted by Defence Advanced Research Project Agencies (DARPA) in 2025. These simulations integrate physics-based flight models, radar and sensor system models, missile dynamics, defensive countermeasures, sensor fusion, and tactical behaviour modules to achieve high operational fidelity.

The AI agents capable of learning air combat manoeuvres such as chasing the opponent, evasion missile, and positioning to best fire are standard these days in air-combat simulation proposed by Gong et al. (2023). These simulations model multi-featured air-combat scenarios with BVR (Beyond Visual Range) using radar missiles and WVR (Within Visual Range), dogfighting, nose-pointing or all-aspect manoeuver such as high-G turns and close-range fighting.

According to DeMay et al. (2022) simulation environments are capable of training AI pilots to reason about tactical problems in real time. The AI agent Heron Systems demonstrated the ability to beat a human fighter pilot in a simulation-based training and to produce highly skilled autonomous adversaries. Simulations enable cooperative and adversarial coordination of multiple fighters, such as among loyal wingmen, UAV (Unmanned Aerial Vehicle) swarms, and human–AI mixed teams. Such simulators allow targeting practical battle tactics without any danger, cost, or operational restrictions.

Therefore, there is a need for war plane air combat simulation system that is safe, repeatable for pilot, and tested on new air-combat doctrines (Tong et al., 2025). Missile, radar, and electronic warfare weapon testing applications have been deployed to enable AI capabilities in autonomous aircraft, intelligent wingmen, and adaptive adversaries. Research on human–AI teaming conducted by Selmonaj et al. (2025) toward future manned–unmanned coordinated combat clearly demonstrates that air-combat simulation is a cornerstone technology of modern aerospace warfare and AI, supporting both manned pilots and AI-powered unmanned systems. Figure 6.1 presents the standard structure of aircraft simulator.

2. Agentic Generative AI for Aircraft Simulation

Aircraft simulation is essential for pilot training, aircraft design, testing, and safety analysis. Traditional simulators rely on predefined scenarios and rule-based models, which limit adaptability. Agentic generative AI introduces intelligent autonomous agents capable of generating realistic flight situations, adapting to trainee actions, and continuously learning from interactions (Gong et al., 2023). This approach makes aircraft simulation far more dynamic, interactive, and efficient than traditional methods.

2.1 Agentic Generative AI

It combined major two concepts. Generative AI, which creates data such as text, flight scenarios, or virtual environments; and agentic AI, where independent software agents can make decisions, plan tasks, cooperate with other agents, and

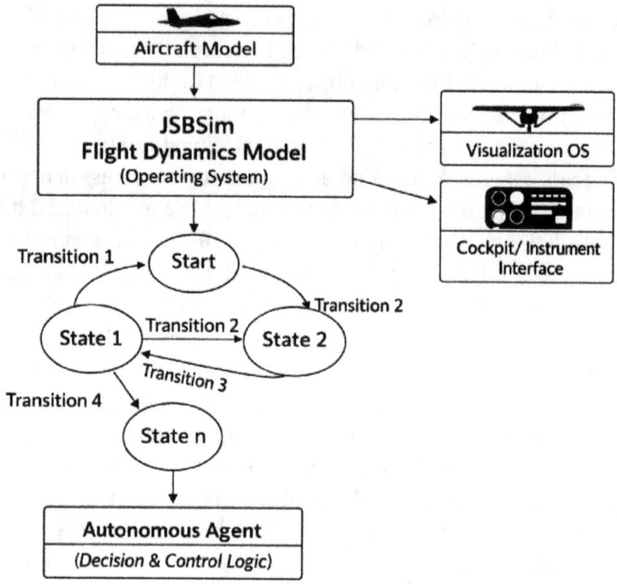

Fig. 6.1 Standard structure of aircraft simulator.

take goal-directed actions. Together, these technologies create intelligent systems that can generate simulation scenarios automatically, respond to pilot behaviour in real time, and continuously improve training quality.

Agentic generative AI is an advanced type of AI that merges the principles of agentic AI with the capabilities of generative AI, creating systems that are both autonomous and creatively productive. Unlike traditional AI, which relies on fixed rules or pre-programmed instructions, agentic generative AI can perceive complex environments, make independent decisions, and generate novel outputs in real time. This combination of autonomy and creativity allows the AI to act intelligently while simultaneously producing new content, scenarios, or solutions, making it highly suitable for dynamic and uncertain environments.

One of the key characteristics of agentic generative AI is its autonomy, which enables it to operate without continuous human supervision. The system can identify goals, prioritize tasks, and take initiative to achieve objectives efficiently. At the same time, it is goal-oriented and capable of adaptive decision-making, meaning it continuously evaluates its actions, predicts outcomes, and modifies its strategies to achieve optimal results. The generative capability allows the AI to create realistic outputs, such as virtual simulations, interactive scenarios, and data-driven predictions, rather than simply responding passively to inputs. Additionally, agentic generative AI is adaptive and capable of learning from experience and feedback, improving its performance over time and becoming increasingly effective in handling complex situations.

In the context of aircraft simulation, agentic generative AI plays a transformative role. It can autonomously generate highly realistic flight scenarios, respond dynamically to pilot actions, and introduce unforeseen challenges, creating a more immersive and effective training environment (Tong et al., 2025). For example, it can simulate sudden weather changes, mechanical failures, or combat situations, allowing pilots to practise decision-making under realistic conditions. By combining autonomous agency with creative generative capabilities, this technology enhances safety, efficiency, and skill development in aviation training, representing a significant advancement over traditional rule-based simulators. Agentic generative AI represents a shift from AI as a passive tool to AI as an active collaborator, capable of intelligent reasoning, autonomous problem-solving, and innovative content generation. Its integration into aircraft simulation demonstrates its potential to revolutionize training, design, and testing processes by providing adaptive, realistic, and continuously evolving learning experiences.

2.2 Role in Aircraft Simulation

Realistic Scenario Generation: Agentic generative AI can autonomously create highly realistic flight scenarios for pilot training and aircraft testing. Unlike traditional simulators that rely on pre-programmed scenarios, agentic generative AI can generate dynamic and adaptive situations, including changing weather, mechanical failures, emergency situations, or even unpredictable air traffic conditions (Cui & Gao, 2024). This ensures that pilots experience a wide variety of challenges, preparing them for real-world complexities that are difficult to replicate using conventional methods.

Adaptive Training and Personalized Learning: Because agentic generative AI can monitor the trainee's actions in real time, it can adapt the simulation according to the skill level and response patterns of each pilot. For instance, if a trainee makes a mistake in handling an emergency situation, the AI can then modify the scenario to provide additional practice in similar circumstances. This creates a personalized learning environment that enhances pilot proficiency and decision-making skills.

Autonomous Decision-Making Simulation: Agentic generative AI acts as an intelligent agent in the simulation, representing other aircraft, air traffic controllers, or environmental factors. It can make independent decisions, such as evasive manoeuvres or emergency responses, to simulate realistic interactions. This adds a layer of complexity and realism to training exercises, helping pilots to learn to effectively respond to unexpected situations.

Continuous Learning and Feedback: One of the key benefits of agentic generative AI is its ability to learn from interactions. It can analyse a pilot's decisions, identify strengths and weaknesses, and generate feedback. Over time, the AI itself improves the scenarios it creates, making training progressively more challenging and aligned with real-world aviation dynamics.

Cost and Safety Efficiency: Traditional aircraft training often involves expensive equipment, real aircraft, and risk exposure. Agentic generative AI reduces costs and risks by providing virtual training environments that are highly realistic and adaptive. Pilots can experience extreme situations without endangering themselves or the aircraft, making the training process both safe and economical.

Enhancing Design and Testing: Beyond pilot training, agentic generative AI can simulate new aircraft designs, control systems, and flight manoeuvres before actual deployment. Engineers can use these simulations to test performance, identify potential issues, and optimize designs, shortening the development cycle and improving overall aircraft safety.

Integration with Multi-Agent Simulations: In complex airspace environments, agentic generative AI can operate alongside other intelligent agents representing different aircraft, drones, or air traffic systems. This multi-agent simulation capability enables realistic modelling of traffic management, collision avoidance, and coordinated flight operations, which is critical for both training and operational planning (Gong et al., 2023).

2.3 Benefits

- Realistic scenarios: AI generates unpredictable and real-life situations.
- Adaptive difficulty: Training levels adjust dynamically.
- Reduced cost: Less need for repeated manual scenario design.
- Improved safety: Dangerous real-world training can be simulated.
- Faster skill development: Continuous learning environments improve pilot response training.

2.4 Applications

- *Pilot Training Personalization*: Generative AI can enhance current training simulators with a new level of realism, dynamically modifying training scenarios to a pilot's individual performance and needs.
- *Rapid Digital Twin Creation*: Aircraft designers and maintenance, repair, and overhaul (MRO) companies use generative AI to quickly build complex digital twins (virtual models) of aircraft or systems for testing new designs and optimizing performance without needing physical models.
- *Autonomous System Testing and Validation*: Agentic AI is used to create and run vast, varied test scenarios that are difficult to anticipate or script manually, such as sensor interference or complex failure modes. This robust testing helps validate the safety and reliability of autonomous flight systems and advanced driver-assistance systems (ADAS) in software-defined vehicles (SDVs).
- *Design Optimization*: AI agents can automate complex Multidisciplinary Design Analysis and Optimization (MDAO) workflows from high-level natural language commands, accelerating the design process for components like aerodynamic structures.

3. Concept of Agentic Generative AI Based on Aircraft

The role of AI agents in aviation industry is promising, with ongoing advancements and new applications on the horizon proposed by Tom et al. (2021).

- Autonomous aircraft
- Enhanced air traffic management
- Predictive passenger flow management

3.1 *Soft Web's Explorations on AI Agent Frameworks*

Softweb continuously tracks emerging trends in software development so our teams can adapt and innovate effectively. This approach allows developers to actively experiment with and adopt AI agent tools and frameworks as they evolve. Widely used frameworks such as LangChain, CrewAI, and AutoGen have made it easier for AI engineers to design dependable and scalable agents. These platforms are built to strengthen AI-driven solutions, with a strong focus on applications involving natural language understanding and generative intelligence.

3.2 *Aircraft Components*

The growing need for compact, high-performance, and energy-efficient electric motors in the MEA (More Electric Aircraft) sector is accelerating the electrification of aircraft configurations. Three major aircraft architectures are currently undergoing this transition. This chapter concentrates on the electrification of critical aircraft subsystems, specifically propulsion, onboard power generation, and actuation systems.

Propulsion: In recent years, electric propulsion has emerged as a major area of interest, especially in the development of fully electric and hybrid-electric aircraft systems. This growing focus is largely driven by rising performance expectations and the need for aviation solutions that are environmentally responsible, quieter in operation, and improved in terms of safety and reliability. A central factor influencing the advancement of these technologies is the ongoing effort to enhance the power density of electric propulsion motors.

Power Generation: Aircraft configurations rely on multiple distributed fans to achieve high propulsive efficiency and depend on motors and generators that combine high power density with low weight and high efficiency. Similarly, hybrid and turbo-electric propulsion systems require advanced generators and motors to effectively convert mechanical shaft power into electrical energy. This process is typically supported by lightweight gearboxes, which lower the turbine's high rotational speed to levels compatible with efficient electrical generation.

Actuation: Minimizing weight while achieving adequate energy storage capacity is critical for both hybrid and fully electric aircraft designs. Without sufficiently lightweight battery systems, the practical adoption of batteries in aviation would become unsustainable. At present, commercially available batteries typically offer energy densities in the range of 150–250 Wh/kg. In contrast, widespread implementation in aircraft would require next-generation batteries with energy densities approaching or exceeding 500 Wh/kg.

3.3 Electric Aircraft Propulsion Architectures

Electric propulsion in aircraft architectures can be broadly categorized into three distinct aircraft architectures, each of which depends extensively on electric components such as motors, generators, and energy storage systems. The extent to which carbon dioxide emissions can be reduced is closely linked to both the efficiency of these components and the overall system configuration adopted. Various propulsion architectures fall into three primary categories: hybrid electric, turbo electric, and fully electric propulsion systems (Jadon et al., 2014). Each category can be further subdivided into specific configurations, which are discussed in detail in the subsequent sections of this chapter.

All Electric: Electrically powered aircraft with limited seating capacity are likely to become viable in the near term; however, the realization of fully electric passenger aircraft will require significant advancements in drivetrain technologies. In all-electric configurations, propulsion is achieved by using energy stored in onboard batteries to power one or more fans. As a result, system performance is strongly influenced by both the mass and energy storage capability of the batteries. In such aircraft, battery systems serve as the sole source of energy for propulsion.

Hybrid Electric: Concepts for large hybrid-electric aircraft are expected to emerge from the mid-2030s onwards through the integration of conventional turbo engines with electric propulsion components. These systems can be implemented at varying levels of hybridization, depending on how electrical power and energy are incorporated into the propulsion architecture. The degree of hybridization (H) can be quantified in terms of power and energy, where power represents the power induces by electric motor and energy denotes the energy of battery. For purely non-electric aircraft, the hybridization parameters *Ho* and *He* are equal to zero, while fully electric configurations are characterized by values of one.

I. *Parallel hybrid aircraft propulsion system*: In a parallel hybrid propulsion system, both the conventional engine (piston engine or gas turbine) and the electric motor are mechanically coupled to the propeller or fan, allowing either source or both together to produce thrust. During high-power phases, such as takeoff and climb, the engine and motor operate simultaneously to meet peak power demand, whereas during cruise, the aircraft may rely mainly on the engine with limited or no electric assistance. This configuration improves fuel efficiency and provides power redundancy, but it increases mechanical complexity due to the need for gearboxes and power-splitting mechanisms.

II. *Series hybrid aircraft propulsion system*: In a series hybrid propulsion system, the conventional engine is not mechanically connected to the propeller; instead, it drives an electrical generator, and all propulsive thrust is produced by electric motors. The generated electrical power is either supplied directly to the motor or stored in the battery, allowing the engine to operate at its most efficient operating point. This architecture simplifies mechanical design and enables distributed electric propulsion, although it introduces additional electrical components and energy conversion stages that can increase system weight and reduce overall efficiency.

III. *Hybrid propulsion system components*: A hybrid aircraft propulsion system consists of an internal combustion engine or gas turbine, an electric motor, a generator, an energy storage system such as batteries, and power electronic converters including inverters and DC–DC converters. These components are coordinated by a hybrid power management and control system that optimizes power sharing based on flight conditions, while thermal management systems ensure safe operation of electrical and mechanical elements. Together, these components enable improved efficiency, reduced emissions, and enhanced operational flexibility in modern aircraft.

Turbo Electric: A turbo-electric aircraft propulsion system is an electrified architecture in which a gas turbine drives an electric generator, and the generated electrical power is used to operate electric motors that produce thrust through propellers or fans. Unlike conventional systems, there is no direct mechanical connection between the turbine and the propulsions, allowing the turbine to operate at its optimal efficiency while power is distributed electrically. This configuration enables advanced concepts such as distributed electric propulsion, improved aerodynamic integration, and flexible placement of propulsors across the airframe. Although turbo-electric systems offer benefits in terms of efficiency, noise reduction, and emissions, their practical implementation is challenged by the weight, efficiency, and thermal management of generators, motors, and power electronics.

i. *Full turbo electric*: In this system, a gas turbine is used to operate a generator, which in turn supplies electrical power to the motors responsible for driving the fans.

ii. *Partial turbo electric*: It serves as an alternative to fully turbo-electric configurations by combining electric propulsion with conventional turbofan operation. In this arrangement, a portion of the propulsive thrust is generated electrically, while the remaining power is supplied by a gas-turbine-driven turbofan. NASA's STARC-ABL concept is a representative example of a partial turbo-electric system. Such architectures, along with similar turbo-electric variants, are expected to be among the earliest electric propulsion solutions adopted for regional and single-aisle aircraft platforms.

3.4 Concept of Autonomous Agents in Combat Simulation

Autonomous agents in combat simulation are computer-controlled entities capable of perceiving their environment, making decisions, and executing actions without direct human intervention. These agents operate within high-fidelity virtual combat environments that replicate realistic battlefield conditions. Situational awareness is achieved through simulated sensor systems, enabling the agents to perceive threats, identify targets, and evaluate mission objectives in real time (Pope et al., 2023). AI methodologies, including rule-based reasoning, machine learning, and reinforcement learning techniques govern decision-making processes. Through repeated interaction with the simulation environment, agents learn optimal policies by evaluating the outcomes of their actions. This adaptive learning capability facilitates continuous improvement in combat effectiveness. Autonomous agents are capable of executing complex air combat manoeuvres, such as target tracking, missile evasion, and tactical positioning for weapon deployment. Their ability to operate at high speeds allows for faster reaction times compared to human pilots, which is critical in dynamic air combat scenarios. Automation further mitigates human cognitive workload in high-stress environments. Combat simulation frameworks enable safe and repeatable experimentation without physical risk. Standardized scenarios support objective evaluation and training. Additionally, agents may operate cooperatively or adversarially, allowing the study of team behaviours such as formation flight, coordinated engagement, and human–AI collaboration.

Their main goal is to mimic human-like air-combat behaviour (Cui & Gao, 2024) so that the simulation systems can:

- model realistic enemy tactics;
- generate adaptive combat situations;
- assess pilot decision-making;
- support mission planning and strategy testing.

AI agents help in the following:

- Autonomous agents perceive the combat environment using simulated sensors such as radar, infrared, and vision systems.
- They make real-time tactical decisions using AI and learning-based algorithms.
- Agents can perform complex air combat manoeuvres, including pursuit, evasion, and weapon engagement.
- Combat simulations enable safe, repeatable training without operational risk or high cost.
- Autonomous agents support cooperative and adversarial missions involving UAVs, loyal wingmen, and human pilots.
- These systems help validate new air combat strategies and doctrines before real-world implementation.

These agents help create dynamic and unpredictable scenarios which are crucial in any form of effective training.

4. Key Roles of Autonomous Agents in Aircraft Combat Simulation

The key role of the autonomous agents in aircraft is defined as:

i. *Autonomous Aircraft Control*: Autonomous agents are controlling virtual fighter aircraft by managing
   a. Navigation
   b. Altitude and speed changes
   c. Turning radius
   d. Manoeuvre optimization

   They follow mission routes and respond immediately to changes in the combat environment.

ii. *Threat Analysis and Situational Awareness*: Agents continually monitor:
   a. Radar inputs
   b. Sensor data
   c. Enemy aircraft movement
   d. Missile trajectories

   With this information, they evaluate threats in real time and alter combat behaviour accordingly.

iii. *Decision-Making and Engagement Planning*: Under more complex air-combat conditions, the agents choose:
   a. when to engage or disengage;
   b. which target has higher priority;
   c. what weapon should be used;
   d. how to attack or move away from an opponent.

   These systems are frequently constructed by means of decision-making models that can be, for example, finite state machines or reinforcement learning policies or behaviour-based models.

iv. *Dogfight and Manoeuvre Execution*: You need a quick trigger for close-range aerial combat. Fully autonomous agents perform high-level tactics such as high-G turns, barrel rolls, split-S, vertical loops, and missile evasion strategies.

v. *Multi-Agent Coordination*: The air warfare of today involves a large number of aircraft. The self-reliant agents interact among themselves to
   a. share situational data;
   b. coordinate attack patterns;
   c. protect other aircraft;
   d. perform formation flying;
   e. manage offensive and defensive roles.

   This interaction among multiple agents enables testing of squadron-level tactics.

vi. *Mission Simulation and Tactical Evaluation*: Mission profiles define the range of missions that autonomous agents are intended to carry out, such as:
   a. air-to-air combat;

b. escort missions;
c. surveillance;
d. electronic warfare;
e. suppression of enemy air defence.

Their adaptive behaviour allows military analysts to evaluate different strategic outcomes without operating real aircraft.

4.1 Benefits of Using Agents in Military Organizations

- High realism accurately portrays all the behaviour of enemy and friendly aircraft.
- Risk-free environment: Removes the risk for pilots to train under high-stress combat scenarios.
- Cost-effective: Decreases the requirement for actual airplanes, fuel, and maintenance in training.
- Unlimited scenario generation: Varying weather, landscape, enemy patterns, or mission scenarios can be generated on the fly.
- Objective performance assessment: The agents store extensive statistics for use in pilot performance and tactical decision assessment.

5. AI-based Aircraft Combat Simulation Process

An AI-based aircraft combat simulation (Wang et al., 2023) work is presented in Figure 6.2 that contains five phases:

Phase-1 (Detection and Identification): The first phase of an air battle in BVR is detecting and identifying incoming enemy aircraft with the help of sophisticated radar systems. These systems provide long-range detection capability so pilots can see targets much earlier than with their eyes. Traditionally, the cycle starts with an aircraft entering hostile airspace and activating radar to scan for adversaries—then detecting a target or threatening presence, monitoring it on radar, using sensor information to determine the best potential weapons match, and then bringing a weapon to bear against the threat.

Phase-2 (Threat Mapping and Targeting): After identification of targets, the second phase involves evaluating their level of threat and determining the main target for engagement. It is this human element, combined with ever-more advanced AI-driven systems, that makes up the decision-making process. Approaches like Bayesian Optimization and ANN (Artificial Neural Network) are proposed to improve decision-making. Proper target discrimination is crucial, as it determines how to proceed with the engagement and directly affects mission success.

Phase-3 (Tactical Manoeuvring): Once targets are selected, aircraft make tactical manoeuvres to get the best missile release conditions and to avoid enemy threats. This stage could comprise synchronized formations and various flight movement

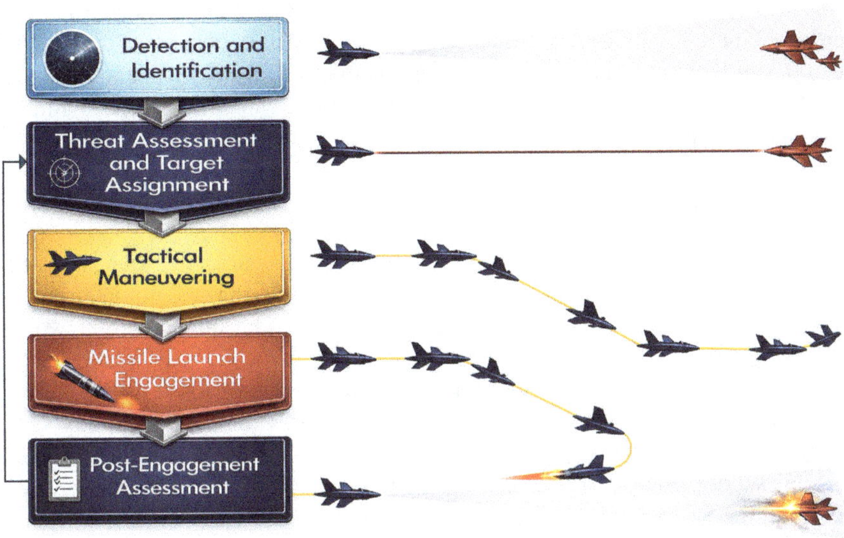

Fig. 6.2 AI-based aircraft combat simulation work.

properties. Tactical thinking is required to alternate among offensive positioning, dodge tactics, and keeping the desirable position for a better missile launch trajectory. Aircraft can carry out specific manoeuvres, for example, twists and turns (cranking), in order to confuse the enemy's sensors and reduce targeting opportunities. AI and machine learning have developed more such strategies, which ultimately can be seen as complex autonomous behaviours for simulators.

Phase-4 (Missile Launch and Engagement): The engagement phase is commonly broken down into three stages:

i. Boost phase: When the target arrives at the Weapon Engagement Zone (WEZ), the missile is launched. At this point, missiles might steer using guidance transmitted from the aircraft or switch to autonomous in-flight guided systems.
ii. Midcourse support phase: The missile continues its path to the target while the carrier aircraft distances itself from danger. The aircraft may have one type of missile that it can guide in midcourse, or the missile may be self-guided with interior sensors.
iii. Recent phase: In this phase, modern "fire and forget" missiles are well-suited since they require less guidance throughout the target approach, thus freeing the pilot to manoeuvre or prepare for further interceptions. Successful missile engagement decisions trade off the probability of a kill against the risk to the firing aircraft. A crucial factor in BVR combat is determining whether or not a missile shot results in a kill.

Phase-5 (Post-Engagement Assessment): The final stage is weighing the engagement to see if more steps must be taken. This estimate consists of confirming that the target has been destroyed, reassessing the tactical situation, and planning for further action. Although often neglected, post-engagement analysis is crucial to guarantee mission success and to be ready for the next battles.

6. Simulators and Tools

Simulators and tools are necessary to enhance BVR air combat research, allowing the modelling of challenging situations, testing of decision-making algorithms, and refining operational methods. These tools span from modular frameworks for general use to highly targeted systems designed to match a particular research problem, and each has its own specialization in addressing various aspects of BVR combat. Such an approach is well served by standards for interoperability such as High-Level Architecture (HLA) and Distributed Interactive Simulation (DIS), enabling integration of various simulation systems, which are then synchronized in real time. Some aircraft combat simulation tools are discussed below.

6.1 FAAC FACETT (Air Combat Environment for Testing and Training)

- Developer/Company: FAAC Incorporated (part of Arotech Training & Simulation Division), a leading supplier of weapon and electronic combat simulations since 1971.
- Architecture: Desktop-based software with physics-driven 5-6 degrees of freedom (DoF) models, real-time weapon flyout simulation, 3D graphics, emulated cockpit displays [HUD (Head-up Display)/MFD (Multifunction Display)], and compatibility with SimBuilder for subsystem modelling; supports networking for LVC (Live, Virtual, and Constructive) and integration with live training ranges [e.g., ACMI (Air Combat Maneuvering Instrumentation)/P5 (Position and Orientation Tracking System)/TCTS (Tactical Combat Training System)].
- Combat Simulated: Modern air-to-air (BVR/WVR dogfights), air-to-surface strikes, missile engagements, countermeasures, electronic warfare, threat environments (IADS/SAMs), and probability-of-kill analysis; replays from real Time-Space-Position Information (TSPI) data or hypothetical scenarios.
- Advantages: Fast, accurate, cost-effective (desktop/low-hardware footprint), adaptable for tactics/weapons evaluation, real-time assessment with "reason for miss" analysis, fully compatible with operational flight programs [e.g., ZAP (Zone of Acceptable Probability) missile envelope cues)], and safe alternative to live flying.
- Primary Focus: Weapons testing, tactics development, post-combat debriefing, and pilot/aircrew training in realistic engagements.

- Suitability: Military/defence professionals [USAF (United States Air Force)/ USN (United States Navy)/USMC (United States Marine Corps)], research labs, and squadrons for mission rehearsal and analysis; not consumer-oriented.
- Alignment with Real-Time Combat: Exceptional; directly supports real training ranges [TACTS (Tactical Aircrew Combat Training System)/ACTS (Air Combat Training System) successors], provides cues used in actual fighter cockpits, and translates to operational performance.

6.2 FAAC Air Combat Training Simulation System (ACT)

- Developer/Company: FAAC Incorporated (Air Warfare Simulation Division).
- Architecture: Networked, immersive high-fidelity system with multi-pilot support, Instructor Operating Stations (IOS), integrated threat/weapon environments, and low-cost flight simulator options; builds on decades of ACMI/TACTS/ACTS expertise.
- Combat Simulated: Single-ship proficiency, 2–4 ship team tactics, air-to-air dogfighting, air-to-ground missions, surface-to-air threats, electronic combat, and large-scale scenarios with dozens of aircraft.
- Advantages: Affordable networked training, real-time hit/miss/Pk evaluation, comprehensive debriefing, and direct impact on pilot skills without live aircraft costs (1/5th to 1/20th the expense).
- Primary Focus: Squadron-level tactical air combat training for fighters like F-16, emphasizing team coordination and weapon utilization.
- Suitability: Active military units (Air Force, Marines) for proficiency and mission-specific drills.
- Alignment with Real-Time Combat: Very high; designed to mirror real-world combat environments and ranges, with proven use in USAF/USN programs.

6.3 Collins Aerospace: RTX Air Combat and Training Systems

- Developer/Company: Collins Aerospace (RTX), major provider of integrated military simulation and test/training instrumentation.
- Architecture: Modular CORE (Common Open Reconfigurable Environment) simulation architecture with high-fidelity image generators, part-task to full-mission devices, and secure networking for air combat scenarios; includes desktop, procedural, and full-flight options.
- Combat Simulated: Air-to-air engagements, forward air control, bomber/ mission crew ops, integrated threats (air/ground/maritime), and complex multi-domain scenarios.
- Advantages: Broad portfolio [from desktop to FAA (Federal Aviation Administration) Level D equivalents], flexibility, lower lifecycle costs, and seamless integration with live ranges/instrumentation.
- Primary Focus: Enhancing mission readiness for fighter, bomber, and special ops aircrews through realistic combat training.

- Suitability: US and allied military forces for advanced tactical and crew training.
- Alignment with Real-Time Combat: High; provides near-realistic experiences that "only actual flight can surpass", with direct applicability to operational missions.

6.4 CAE Military Training Systems

- Developer/Company: CAE, global leader in defence simulation with extensive military contracts.
- Architecture: Full-flight simulators (e.g., CAE 7000XR series equivalents for military), part-task trainers, desktop devices, and LVC-integrated systems; high-fidelity visuals, motion, and sensor emulation.
- Combat Simulated: Combat aircraft operations (fighters, lead-in trainers), air-to-air/ground strikes, special mission platforms, networked multi-crew engagements, and threat response.
- Advantages: Comprehensive range (pilot to maintenance crew), digitally enabled courseware, and proven on platforms like fighters and maritime patrol aircraft.
- Primary Focus: Pilot, rear crew, and sensor operator training for military aircraft in combat scenarios.
- Suitability: Armed forces worldwide for initial, recurrent, and advanced combat training.
- Alignment with Real-Time Combat: Very high; certified for military standards, with direct transfer to real operations.

6.5 Elbit Systems Airborne Live Virtual Constructive (LVC) Training Solutions

- Developer/Company: Elbit Systems, Israeli defence giant with embedded virtual training expertise.
- Architecture: Embedded systems in actual aircraft (e.g., fighters), ground-based trainers, and networked LVC environments; advanced sensors, data links, AI, and augmented reality integration.
- Combat Simulated: Air-to-air/ground combat, threat encounters, multi-domain warfare, and realistic engagements with live aircraft participation.
- Advantages: Seamless blending of live, virtual, and constructive elements; cyber-resilient and high-performance computing for complex scenarios.
- Primary Focus: Advanced fighter pilot training with real-time threats in operational aircraft.
- Suitability: Aircraft (e.g., on F-16, F-35 equivalents) for integrated syllabus training.
- Alignment with Real-Time Combat: Outstanding; trains pilots in actual cockpits against simulated threats, directly mirroring combat.

7. Types of AI-driven Combat Simulation

Combat simulation concepts are categorized in many forms; these are as follows:

7.1 Behaviour Tree (BT)–based Simulations

Behaviour Trees (BTs) are a hierarchical decision-making system for directing autonomous agents in simulative domains like robotics, games, and military apps. In comparison to end-to-end RL (Reinforcement Learning) models, BTs allow military subject matter experts (SMEs) and developers to comprehend and validate the AI decision logic (Jadon et al., 2014).

Use cases:

- Simulations of flight training (e.g., ACMI-based simulators)
- Autonomous UAV dogfight decision logic
- Scenario scripting for adversary models

Limitations:

- Rigid tactics
- Not adaptive or leaning-based
- It becomes difficult to handle big BTs.

7.2 Reinforcement Learning

In reinforcement learning, the agent tries to maximize its rewards through trial and error and taking decisions. The feedback comes in the form of rewards or penalties. Multi-agent reinforcement learning enables training of team dynamics (multi-agent) and real pilot combat tactics, which are observed in systems training agents on VR-Forces with added physics-based flight dynamics (Bae et al., 2023).

The goal is to accumulate rewarding patterns:

- Surviving an engagement
- Destroying the adversary
- Avoiding missiles
- Energy altitude geometry advantages were maintained

Challenges:

- Requires substantial computational resources during training
- Needs to bridge the gap between simulation and real-world aerodynamics (Sim-to-Real gap)
- Can suffer from overfitting to the tactic of simulated

7.3 Multi-Agent Reinforcement Learning (MARL) & Hierarchical MARL

Multi-agent reinforcement learning (MARL) consists of different types of components such as aircraft, missiles, UAV swarms, and AWACS, that learn in parallel to each other as long as they conduct missions (Gong et al., 2023). Agents can be of three types: Cooperative (Same goal), e.g., UAV flock, wingman-lead formation; Competitive, i.e., opposing air forces (Blue vs Red); Mixed-motive, i.e., partly shared (coalition war cases).

Capabilities:

- Aerial combat (dogfights, BVR tactics)
- Dynamic target assignment (distribute targets over the formation)
- Learning that makes use of deception in electronic warfare (Bait–Trap Tactics)

Challenges:

- Non-stationarity (during learning, agents are in a changing environment)
- Reward shaping complexity
- High state and action space (high-dimensional aerodynamics)

Examples of Hierarchical MARL Behaviour:

- Dynamic role assignment (lead fighter, support, and decoy)
- Multi-angle attack strategies (pincer, bracket, etc.)

7.4 AI-driven Augmented Reality and Virtual Reality Simulators

The AI-infused AR (Augmented Reality)/VR (Virtual Reality) aircraft combat simulators integrate immersive visualization (VR), contextual overlays (AR), and intelligent decision-making agents to simulate real-world aerial combat's realistic scenarios (Bae et al., 2023).

These systems are used for:

- Training of pilots and tactical rehearsal
- Real-time adaptive combat scenarios
- Human-in-the-loop simulation for safety testing

VR-based combat simulation features:

- Full 3D cockpit experience
- Virtual reality weapons-training [guns, missiles, ECM (Electronic Countermeasures]
- Dogfight simulation game in real-time AI and human ecological networks

AR-based Combat Simulation Features:

- HUD Features: Speed, altitude and screen reticles
- Tactical overlays: Missile alerts, enemy direction
- Real-Life pilot training: Live AR experience in actual cockpit (like F-35 helmet display)

Challenges:

- Latency in AR pointing system
- Multi-agent coordination realism

7.5 Adversary Generation

Adversary generation refers to the synthesis of realistic, adaptive, and strategically challenging enemy agents in virtual air combat scenarios. In recent simulators, the adversarial models are not scripted but learn through data-driven learning, multi-agent strategies, and even generative AI to simulate human or superhuman air combat behaviour.

Purpose:

- Realistic dogfighting behaviours
- Dynamic strategies based on player or agent performance
- Testing self-navigating aircraft in contested airspace

Different kinds of adversary models:

- Rule-based/Scripted Adversaries
  - It is based on if-then behaviour trees or state-machines
- Hybrid Attacks BT + ML: Behaviour Tree + Machine Learning
  - Behaviour tree specifies high-level patterns (engage, evade, search)
- Reinforcement Learning–based Adversaries
  - Agents learn through simulation cycles
- MARL Adversaries
  - Drone-like learning, swarm behaviour, dynamic flanking and manoeuvres
- Generative-Adversarial Intelligence
  - Applications of generative models [GANs (Generative Adversial Network), Diffusion, LLM (Large Language Model)-driven Simulators]

Capabilities:

- Tactical awareness
- Weapon selection reasoning
- Cognitive deception (fake retreats, baiting)

Real-world application:

- DARPA ACE (Air Combat Evolution)
- X-Plane (AI with ML add-ons)
- Alpha Dogfight Challenge

7.6 Swarm Intelligence Simulation

Swarm intelligence in air combat simulation, standalone mode, describes the simulation of a group or network of agents that react with one another to act on behalf of a user, as shown in Figure 6.3. Swarm-enabled AI aircraft combat simulation is required for developing the next generation of autonomous warfare concepts such as loyal wingmen, UCAV (Unmanned Combat Aerial Vehicle) swarms, distributed sensing, and jamming systems (Hu et al., 2022).

Swarm Behaviour Algorithms:

- Flocking model: General formation, collision prevention, distancing
- Ant colony: Route planning and distributed target assignment
- Bee colony algorithms: Scout, foraging, reinforcement sharing, adaptive pollination

Challenges:

- Scalability beyond 100+ agents
- Secure, jam-resistant communication

Fig. 6.3 Swarm intelligence-based simulations.

8. Generative Models for Scenario and Data

Generative models can be used to generate new synthetic combat scenarios, sensor signatures, battlefield environments, and adversary strategies when real data is classified or rare or prohibitively expensive to gather.

GAN-based Simulation (Generative Adversarial Networks): These systems can be used to generate various kinds of data for aircraft simulation (Bae et al., 2023; Dantas et al., 2025; Li et al., 2025). Following are some examples:

- Radar and IR (Infrared) Signature Generation
  - Create artificial radar reflectivity (RCS) images under various viewing angles, weather conditions, and stealth configurations of aircraft
- Electronic Warfare Data Modelling
  - Pretend jamming signals, fake GPS signals, false radar blips

Limitations:

- Demands careful tuning to prevent mode collapse
- Difficult to verify the realism without experts

Example:

- RF-GAN (Radio Frequency Generative Adversarial Network): A Generative Adversarial Network for Radar Signature Simulation

LLM-driven Scenario Authoring Systems: These systems can generate Intelligent Opponent Doctrine that simulates enemy tactics following the doctrine of real-world opponents [NATO (North Atlantic Treaty Organization), PLAAF (People's Liberation Army Air Force), and USAF (United States Air Force)] and can be used in procedure-based training for ATC (Air Traffic Control) commands, emergency lists, crew's dialogue (Shen & Zheng, 2025; Yu et al., 2026). Example includes DARPA Gamebreaker and ACE Initiative with Language-Conditioned Autonomous Combat Scenario.

9. VR-Forces: An Aircraft Simulation Tool (Case Study)

VR-Forces is a widely used Computer Generated Forces (CGF) and battlefield simulation environment designed to represent joint land, sea, air, and space operations, with strong support for aircraft combat scenarios. It is typically deployed as a core constructive simulation backbone for training, mission rehearsal, and research, while external flight simulators, command-and-control systems, or AI modules provide specialized capabilities around it. Architecturally, VR-Forces is built around a separation between a graphical front-end and one or more simulation back-ends. The front-end allows operators and scenario designers to place entities, define missions, set environmental conditions, and monitor the evolving scenario using 2D and 3D views. The back-end (the simulation engine) advances time, updates entity states, calculates sensor detections, resolves engagements and damage, and manages terrain and environmental effects in real time. This split allows the same scenario to be controlled from multiple operator stations while the heavy simulation runs on dedicated servers, which is important when simulating large air campaigns involving many aircraft and air-defence systems.

At the entity level, VR-Forces uses a modular, component-based design, wherein each simulated platform—such as a fighter aircraft—is built from interchangeable components for movement, sensing, weapons, damage, and resources. The movement component defines the kinematic behaviour and performance of the aircraft, including limits on speed, turn rate, climb, descent, and acceleration, ensuring that manoeuvres remain plausible for the modelled platform. Sensor components represent onboard radar, electro-optical/infrared sensors, warning receivers, and other systems, with parameters such as range, field of view, scan patterns, and detection probabilities that can be tuned for realism. Weapons and damage components handle loadouts (missiles, bombs, guns), engagement envelopes, weapon fly-out modelling, and the effects on targets when weapons detonate or hit, including damage states and possible kill probabilities. Resource components monitor fuel, ammunition, and other consumables, allowing mission outcomes and agent decisions to depend on endurance and logistics constraints. Because these components are configurable, users can represent anything from generic fighters to specific aircraft types with tailored sensor and weapon performance.

On top of this physical and sensing layer is VR-Forces' behaviour engine, which controls how entities act when not directly steered by a human. The behaviour engine provides a library of tasks and missions (such as patrol, intercept, strike, escort, refuel) that can be assigned to air units, along with triggers and conditions that determine when tasks start, stop, or transition. For example, a fighter flight can be tasked to patrol a sector until an intruder is detected, then intercept and engage according to rules of engagement, and finally return to base when fuel or weapons are low. Behaviours can be organized into multi-phase plans using synchronization mechanisms so that air-defence suppression, strike waves, and refuelling sequences can be orchestrated in time and space. This native behaviour system is largely rule- and script-based, and it is designed both for out-of-the-box use and for extension by advanced users who need custom logic or AI-driven decision modules.

Interoperability is a key strength of VR-Forces, enabling it to participate in distributed simulation federations and mixed-reality training environments. It supports standards such as DIS and HLA, allowing it to exchange entity states, fire and detonation events, and other messages with external simulators and systems. In an air-combat context, this means VR-Forces can simulate large numbers of AI-controlled aircraft and air-defence units, while one or more human pilots fly high-fidelity cockpit simulators connected via the same network, seeing and interacting with the constructive forces as if they were part of their own simulator world. The same networking interfaces are used to connect decision-support tools, command-and-control systems, and after-action review applications, making VR-Forces a central node in a broader synthetic battlespace.

This architectural openness is also what makes VR-Forces suitable as a testbed for agentic AI in aircraft combat simulation. In such setups, VR-Forces provides the environment—physics, sensors, weapons, and other entities—while external AI modules function as autonomous "pilots" or tactical agents controlling specific aircraft. Typically, these AI modules receive state information from VR-Forces (ownship position, velocity, attitude, detected threats and targets, resource status) and then compute decisions about manoeuvres, speed and altitude changes, and weapon employment. Decisions are translated into VR-Forces commands, such as new waypoints, engagement tasks, or changes in formation, which the simulator executes according to platform constraints and environmental factors. This loop repeats at each simulation step, allowing the AI agents to continuously sense, decide, and act within a realistic combat environment.

The AI side is usually structured into perception, decision, and action components, reflecting an agentic architecture. The perception module aggregates and filters the raw simulator data to build compact internal state representations—for instance, relative geometry and energy states of friendly and enemy aircraft, current missile threats, and no-fly or threat zones. The decision module, often powered by deep reinforcement learning or other sequential decision-making techniques, selects actions that optimize goals such as survival, kill probability, or mission success under resource constraints. Rewards are computed from simulation outcomes (wins, losses, damage, fuel and weapon usage), and over many episodes the policies improve, yielding increasingly sophisticated air-combat tactics. The action module then maps chosen actions to VR-Forces-level commands, such as initiating a turn to a certain heading or commanding a missile launch when engagement criteria are met. In multi-agent setups, several AI-controlled aircraft are trained and evaluated together, learning cooperative tactics like bracket attacks, mutual support, or decoy and shooter roles. Human pilots can also be integrated into these scenarios, flying against or alongside AI-controlled aircraft, which supports research on human–AI teaming, trust, and tactical transparency.

10. Future Work of Agentic Generative AI in the Simulation for Combat Aircraft

Agentic generative AI will increasingly turn combat aircraft simulation from static "scenario playback" into dynamic, goal-driven environments populated by autonomous, learning entities that behave more like real pilots, teams, and adversaries.

- *Creation of Super-Realistic Combat Situations*: Agentic generative AI systems of the future will be able to create interactive, unpredictable, and high-fidelity air-combat scenes. Within these simulations, the battle conditions encountered during a real engagement will be replicated as closely as possible, enabling mission-specific pilot practice.
- *Autonomous Tactical Decision-Making*: Sophisticated agentic schema and models will use independent threat analysis, egress planning, missile trajectory analysis, and tactical advice generation. This will increase the degree of preparedness of pilots and will contribute to improve the autonomy of unmanned combat aircraft.
- *Intelligent Virtual Adversaries*: AI-based opponents that learn from the trainee's decisions will be included in future simulations. Such adaptive adversaries will provide a more realistic threatening behaviour compared to pure rule-based simulations.

- *Self-Adaptive and Real-Time (Adaptive Simulation Engines)*: Generative AI systems will also be able to self-develop through their own mission data. Every simulation cycle will enhance AI's capability to create realistic combat environments that are contextually rich.
- *Interfacing with Unmanned Combat Aerial Vehicles (UCAVs & Loyal Wingman)*: A next-gen simulator will connect directly to UAVs. This will support operations and MUM-T (Manned–Unmanned Teaming).
- *Prognostic-ness Modelling and Emergency Simulation*: AI will model real-time engine performance, structural weariness, and electronics faults. This will enable pilots to simulate emergency responses in very realistic virtual worlds.
- *Multi-Domain Operational Simulation*: Next-generation combat simulators will consolidate air, land, sea, space, and cyber dimensions into a unified AI-generated battle model as an aid application to joint-force training.
- *Cost-Effective, Scalable Training Infrastructure*: High-fidelity generative simulations will eliminate the costs of physical training ranges and allow for actual, large-scale, continuous pilot training at minimal expense.
- *Strategic-Level Wargaming and Defence Planning*: Defence institutions will be increasingly turning to AI-driven war-game simulations that can test operational doctrines, resource allocations, and geopolitical scenarios.

11. Conclusion

This chapter has demonstrated that agentic generative AI offers a powerful and flexible paradigm for advancing aircraft combat simulation beyond the limitations of traditional rule-based and scripted models. By enabling autonomous, goal-driven, and adaptive behaviour, agentic AI systems are capable of replicating realistic pilot decision-making, dynamic tactical reasoning, and coordinated multi-aircraft operations in complex and adversarial environments. The inclusion of a VR-Forces-based case study illustrates the practical feasibility of integrating agentic generative agents within an established, high-fidelity simulation framework. The results indicate notable improvements in behavioural realism, tactical diversity, and adaptability during both BVR and WVR engagements when compared to conventional approaches. The ability of agentic agents to learn from interaction and respond to evolving combat scenarios enhances the effectiveness of simulation-based training, mission rehearsal, and concept evaluation. This chapter establishes agentic generative AI, validated through VR-Forces integration, as a promising foundation for next-generation aircraft combat simulation, supporting more intelligent, scalable, and decision-centric air combat training and analysis environments.

References

Bae, J.H., Jung, H., Kim, S. et al. (2023). Deep reinforcement learning-based air-to-air combat maneuver generation in a realistic environment. *IEEE Access*, 11, 26427–26440.

Cui, X. and Gao, Y. (2024). Analysis on the explainable of generative artificial intelligence in military contexts. *Proceedings of 2024 12th China Conference on Command and Control* (pp. 84–94), Springer.

Dantas, J.P.A., Maximo, M.R.O.A. and Yoneyama, T. (2025). Autonomous aircraft tactical pop-up attack using imitation and generative learning. *IEEE Access*, 13, 81204–81217.

DeMay, C.R., White, E.L., Dunham, W.D. and Pino, J. A. (2022). AlphaDogfight trials: Bringing autonomy to air combat. Johns Hopkins APL Technical Digest, 36(2), 154–162.

Gong, Z., Xu, Y. and Luo, D. (2023). UAV cooperative air combat maneuvering confrontation based on multi-agent reinforcement learning. *Unmanned Systems*, 11(3), 273–286.

Hu, J., Wang, L., Hu, T. et al. (2022). Autonomous maneuver decision making of dual-UAV cooperative air combat based on deep reinforcement learning. *Electronics*, 11(3), 467.

Jadon, S., Singhal, A. and Dawn, S. (2014). Military simulator—A case study of behaviour tree and unity based architecture. *International Journal of Computer Applications*, 88(5), 26–29.

Li, M., Wang, Z., Xu, H. and Zhang, S. (2025). Generative AI technology assists the research on the reliability of aerospace development. In Yan, L., Duan, H. and Deng, Y. (eds) *Advances in Guidance, Navigation and Control* (pp. 189–199). Springer Nature.

Pope, A.P., Ide, J.S., Mićović, D. et al. (2023). Hierarchical reinforcement learning for air combat at DARPA's AlphaDogfight trials. *IEEE Transactions on Artificial Intelligence*, 4(6), 1371–1385.

Selmonaj, A., Szehr, O., Rio, G.D. et al. (2025). Enhancing aerial combat tactics through hierarchical multi-agent reinforcement learning. No. arXiv:2505.08995. arXiv.

Shen, Y. and Zheng, J. (2025). An LLM-driven simulation framework for intelligent decision-making in collaborative aerial firefighting with heterogeneous aircraft. SSRN Scholarly Paper No. 5413022. Social Science Research Network. Available at https://doi.org/10.2139/ssrn.5413022. Accessed on 10 July 2025.

Tom, L., Khowja, M., Vakil, G. and Gerada, C. (2021). Commercial aircraft electrification—Current state and future scope. *Energies*, 14(24), 8381.

Tong, Y., Luo, M., Ren, S. et al. (2025). A rapidly structured aircraft concept design method based on generative artificial intelligence. *Chinese Journal of Aeronautics*, 38(10), 103629.

Wang, X., Wang, Y., Su, X. et al. (2023). Deep reinforcement learning-based air combat maneuver decision-making: Literature review, implementation tutorial and future direction. *Artificial Intelligence Review*, 57(1), 1.

Yu, Z., Li, N., Gong, G. and Liu, Y. (2026). Intelligent modeling method of air combat behavior based on LLM. In Liu, Y., Li, N., Song, X. and Guo, Y. (eds) *Intelligent Simulation* (pp. 345–368). Springer Nature.

7 Autonomous Navigation and Mission Control Using Generative AI

Praveen Kumar Guraja[1]

Defence organizations will continue to pursue autonomy in the coming decades as they try to minimize the risk to their personnel at the sea, on land, and in sky. Because of this push towards greater autonomy, autonomous defence systems will be able to remain on station longer, sense for extended durations, and complete multiple tasks in real time. To perform all of these tasks in a safe and effective manner in environments that are extremely variable and competitive, they will require more advanced navigation and mission control capabilities than ever before. The objective of this chapter is to explore how generative artificial intelligence (AI) can contribute to the enhancement of the autonomous navigation and mission control capabilities of future naval ships and aircraft. More specifically, the chapter focuses on the air and maritime domains and the ways in which generative AI may contribute to the improvement of the adaptability and robustness of autonomous systems while maintaining their safety and accountability. The chapter examines the differences in the requirements of commercial autonomous systems versus defence systems, and then addresses the challenges and opportunities that arise from integrating generative AI into autonomous systems.

1. Introduction

1.1 Autonomous Systems and Human-Centred Generative AI

1.1.1 Background and Scope

As we move into the coming years, defense agencies will be investing more heavily in autonomous technologies to reduce risk to people and equipment in all three war-fighting domains (air, land and sea). The benefits for platforms and associated sensors include; sustained operation over extended time frames with continued sensing, ability to perform many simultaneous missions etc. With respect to autonomous systems, safe operation and effective operation in high-dynamic environments will require significantly enhanced autonomous navigation and mission management capabilities than those currently available. Defence organizations employ several different strategies to realize this goal; however, every one of them depends on

1 https://orcid.org/0000-0002-4463-0659
* Corresponding author: praveen.guraja@oit.edu

DOI: 10.1201/9781003688174-7

gaining an extensive understanding of what needs to be accomplished and how it is going to be accomplished. To gain this understanding, defence organizations will have to combine the current state-of-the-art in generative artificial intelligence (AI) with the established best practices and lessons learned from previous autonomous system development. The current chapter will address the potential for generative AI to enhance the capabilities of future autonomous naval vessel and aircraft to navigate and execute missions autonomously. As a starting point, this chapter will be confined to the air and maritime domains; however, the key focus will be on how generative AI could increase the flexibility and robustness of autonomous systems while still maintaining the necessary safety and accountability that exists within defence environments (Bi et al., 2024).

2. Autonomous Systems in Defence: Safety and Effectiveness in Hostile Environments

2.1 Evolving Objectives for Defence Autonomy

In the past, the primary purpose of developing autonomous systems was to enable systems to perform a variety of different functions independently so that less time and effort would be required to accomplish specific goals and objectives. However, the key objective has completely changed - autonomous systems are currently designed to operate successfully and safely in a very wide range of environments including those that are highly variable, difficult to predict, and possibly dangerous. This represents a significant shift in the role and significance of autonomous systems within defence organizations.

The reason for focusing attention on developing autonomous systems that can operate in a variety of different and potentially hostile environments stems from a variety of different sources. One major source is the desire of defence organizations to reduce the number of casualties experienced during combat operations. Another source is the desire of defence organizations to improve the efficiency and effectiveness of their military forces while also improving the ability of their military forces to operate in a variety of different environments. The final source is the growing recognition by defence organizations of the potential of autonomous systems to provide them with a variety of new and innovative capabilities that were previously unavailable.

Despite the benefits of autonomous systems, the ability of these systems to operate in a variety of different and potentially hostile environments is contingent upon the development of advanced navigation and mission control capabilities that can operate in real time in environments that are both uncertain and potentially adversarial. These capabilities will require the incorporation of the current state-of-the-art in generative AI with the best practices and lessons learned from previous autonomous system development.

2.2 Chapter Focus Summary

The remainder of the chapter focuses on the uses of generative AI in autonomous systems to enhance their ability to operate in environments that are both uncertain and potentially adversarial. The chapter begins by highlighting the operational context of autonomous navigation and mission control in defence systems. The chapter identifies the differences in the requirements of commercial autonomous systems and those of defence systems. Defence systems must operate in a variety of different and potentially hostile environments and cannot always know the location and status of their systems. Defence systems must therefore be able to operate in real time in environments that are both uncertain and potentially adversarial.

The chapter continues by discussing the foundational aspects of generative AI. The chapter defines generative AI, identifies its distinguishing features compared to other forms of AI, and identifies the technical components of generative AI. The chapter identifies the three types of generative models that are most widely used in autonomous systems: (i) sampling-based generators, (ii) transformers and sequence models, and (iii) learned world models. The chapter also identifies the advantages and disadvantages of each type of generative model and the trade-offs that must be considered when selecting among the three types of models.

The chapter then focuses on two applications of generative AI to the development of autonomous systems: (i) autonomous navigation, and (ii) mission control and command support. The chapter highlights the ways in which generative AI can be used to enhance the capability of autonomous systems to operate in environments that are both uncertain and potentially adversarial.

Finally, the chapter addresses the challenges and opportunities associated with incorporating generative AI into autonomous systems. The chapter emphasizes the challenges of ensuring the safety and reliability of generative AI as well as the opportunities that exist to enhance the scalability and adaptability of autonomous systems.

3. GenAI as a New Capability Frontier for Defence

3.1 Key Functional Advantages of GenAI

Defence organizations today are increasingly recognizing the potential of generative AI to provide them with new and innovative capabilities that were previously unavailable. The use of generative AI in autonomous systems has the potential to significantly enhance their capabilities to operate in a variety of different and potentially hostile environments.

A key advantage of generative AI is its capability to represent probability distributions over complex variables such as scenes, trajectories, and multi-agent states. This allows generative AI to model the variability found in real-world environments as well as reason about the uncertainty associated with operation in these environments.

Another advantage of generative AI is its capability to produce ensembles of candidate outcomes instead of a single "best" estimate. This allows generative AI to model and plan for a variety of different outcomes in complex and uncertain environments. Generative AI can also support different types of decision-making processes. For example, it can support the selection of candidate trajectories based on the likelihood of their success. It can also support the selection of candidate actions based on the likelihood of achieving a desired outcome.

Additionally, generative AI can support the representation of knowledge and experience in the form of probability distributions. This allows generative AI to support decision-making in complex and uncertain environments.

Finally, generative AI can be combined with traditional autonomy pipelines in a variety of different ways. For example, it can be used to generate candidate outcomes for consideration by traditional planners. Alternatively, it can be used to directly select candidate outcomes based on their likelihood of success.

4. Real-Time Navigation and Mission Control in Contested Environments

4.1 Operational Requirements for Navigation and Mission Control

Today, defence organizations recognize the importance of developing autonomous systems that can operate in a variety of different and potentially hostile environments. However, the ability of these systems to operate in these environments is contingent upon the development of advanced navigation and mission control capabilities that can function in real time in environments that are both uncertain and potentially adversarial.

Capabilities related to navigation and mission control are those that autonomous systems employ to navigate and operate in a variety of different environments. Examples of such capabilities include: (i) sensors and sensor fusion algorithms; (ii) motion planning and control algorithms; (iii) environmental models; and (iv) mission management software.

Building upon that base the inclusion of generative AI technology within autonomous systems' navigation and mission control can be viewed as much more than simply an enhancement of technology; it will require the incorporation of the many hard-learned lessons from prior autonomous system development in order for it to operate dependably in real-time, under uncertainty, and when faced with adversaries.

A primary advantage of developing such advanced navigation and mission control capabilities is their potential to significantly enhance the ability of autonomous systems to operate in a variety of different and potentially hostile environments. A primary disadvantage of developing such advanced navigation and mission control capabilities is the difficulty of ensuring the safety and reliability of these capabilities.

Much has been achieved to-date in the development of autonomous systems that can operate in a variety of different and potentially hostile environments. However, much more work will be needed in the future to further develop autonomous systems. Their continued development will depend on continued advances in generative AI and the continued development of advanced navigation and mission control capabilities.

5. Future Autonomous Systems: GenAI, Navigation, and Mission Control

5.1 Future Development Considerations

While we have seen some very significant advancements in developing autonomous systems, these represent just the beginning point from which our next generations of capabilities will need to build. There is much more at stake as we move into this next generation of development; we are moving beyond simple advancement on past trends. We will be challenged with an even greater task: to assure that the advancements in generative AI, navigation and mission control capabilities, are matched by similar focus and rigor regarding issues of safety, reliability, and accountability.

As we enter the next phase of autonomous system development, the primary conflict will not be merely technological. Generative AI has great potential for improving the ability of autonomous systems to operate effectively in uncertain and potentially hostile environments. However, to realize that potential will require more than innovative design. Governance – defined here as clearly stated and enforced rules governing how autonomous systems may be designed, tested, implemented and controlled – is required to ensure that autonomous systems can be safely operated (i.e., they cannot compromise human safety or security), while also providing for meaningful human oversight and decision-making authority.

In summary, whether the use of autonomous systems in defense will be determined by what generative AI enables us to accomplish, or by what we consider acceptable standards and safeguards, will depend on both technical feasibility and ethical acceptability advancing in tandem – each being insufficient without the other.

In addition to the technical difficulties of developing autonomous systems, there are also a number of important social and ethical issues that must be considered. An important issue is the need to ensure that the development and deployment of autonomous systems does not pose a risk to human safety and security.

The continued development and deployment of autonomous systems will depend on the continued advancements in generative AI and advanced navigation and mission control systems, as well as the creation of socially acceptable and ethically defensible frameworks.

6. Language Interface Tools and Human Authority

Although researchers believe that language interface tools can improve situational awareness and decrease operator cognitive loads, they also assert that in defence applications, language interface tools must be explicitly identified as decision support tools, not as decision-making tools. They also explain that for defence-related safety-critical missions, authority, accountability, and responsibility for decision-making must remain with the human operators. Further, they also explain that defence-related responsible AI advice emphasizes the importance of "traceability" and "auditability", to ensure that language-based systems log and record all prompts, responses, and any subsequent actions based on the system's output (National Institute of Standards and Technology [NIST], 2024; US Department of Defense [DoD], 2022).

Language interfaces that are properly integrated into a defence organization's systems could assist with reducing the amount of information that needs to be processed by the operator, and help to ensure that appropriate actions are taken during defence-related operations. Language interfaces can allow operators to use natural language questions to determine what would happen if certain actions were taken ("what-if"), to request explanations for recommended courses of action, and to modify mission priorities without modifying low-level parameters. Through the use of generative world models, language interfaces can provide users with the opportunity to explore uncertainty in an interactive way, and to understand both the recommended course of action and the risks and assumptions associated with that course of action.

Defence organizations will need to put in place safeguards to ensure the safe operation of language models. To achieve this goal, language models must be restricted to a controlled vocabulary, structured outputs, and approval checkpoints to prevent language model–generated hallucinations or misinformation. Defence organizations will be able to take advantage of the accessibility benefits of natural language interaction while providing the necessary accountability, rigour, and trustworthiness required for mission-critical defence-related operations by combining language-enabled tools with human-in-the-loop command architectures and thoroughly documenting and auditing all interactions with language-enabled systems.

7. Generative AI for Mission Control and Command Support

Navigation autonomy ensures that a platform remains safe and follows its desired route. Mission control translates the mobility provided by navigation autonomy into mission value. In defence contexts, mission control functions—situational assessment, intention determination, Course of Action (COA) generation, assignment of tasks to resources, and mission re-planning—occur under conditions of partial observability, competitive communications, and urgency. As such, generative models are well suited to these conditions as they produce distributions of plausible futures and candidate plans, as opposed to a single point estimate.

The distributions of candidate plans enable risk-conscious decision-making, whereby commanders choose actions that remain acceptable across a range of likely futures, rather than choosing the optimal action based on a single forecast that may turn out to be incorrect (North Atlantic Treaty Organization [NATO], 2024; NIST, 2023).

7.1 World Models and Predictive Simulation

World models capture the dynamic characteristics of an environment into a learned latent representation that can be repeatedly rolled forward to simulate the future states of the environment given a set of candidate actions. In autonomous defence research, world models are trained on logs of perception, state estimates, and executed actions, and then used to simulate the downstream effects of alternate decisions. According to recent surveys, generative world models enable multi-agent forecasting and offline planning evaluation, and thus enable users to investigate counterfactual futures that are difficult to observe directly (Guan et al., 2024). In the context of mission control, the operational benefits of world-model-based COA analysis are increased predictive accuracy and the ability to simulate a wider variety of scenarios; robust COA analysis requires understanding how outcomes change as the values of key variables (e.g., weather, communications, neutral traffic flow, or adversary posture) vary within reasonable bounds.

An illustrative COA workflow can be expressed as "generate, evaluate, and brief". First, the generative world model generates multiple futures for each candidate COA. Second, mission-level metrics are computed over those futures—coverage, probability of detection, time-to-target, fuel margin, and risk indicators such as proximity to threat envelopes or communications blackout windows. Third, the results are presented to the commander in a format that is human-auditable; not only which COA is most probable on average, but also which COA has the least worst case performance or smallest tail risk. This COA workflow (Table 7.1) is consistent with the risk management guidance to document assumptions, uncertainties, and residual risk, as opposed to presenting AI-generated outputs as absolute answers (NIST, 2023, 2024).

Generative AI does not "choose" a COA; instead, it accelerates the analysis by producing a wide variety of plausible futures and stress cases that reveal weaknesses. For example, if a COA performs well under nominal traffic conditions but poorly in a subset of futures in which communication is sometimes jammed, the COA briefing should indicate that weakness, conditional on the specifics of the situation. By making uncertainty explicit, world-model-based COA analysis can minimize automation bias and support more defensible and accountable operational decisions (NATO, 2021; NIST, 2023).

7.2 Swarm Coordination and Task Assignment

Swarm coordination is a more complex problem whose complexity grows exponentially as the number of platforms grows; for example, dozens of

Table 7.1 Example COA Comparison for a Maritime ISR (Intelligence, Surveillance, and Reconnaissance) Tasking (Notional).

COA	*Concept*	*Benefits*	*Risks/Constraints*	*GenAI Support*
COA A	High-altitude UAV + Stand-off sensing corridor	Broad area coverage; reduced collision risk with neutral traffic	Higher detectability; Degraded sensing in weather; GNSS disruption impacts stand-off geolocation	World model simulates weather + GNSS degradation impacts; samples alternative stand-off tracks
COA B	Low-altitude UAV + USV cueing Near choke points	Improved target identification; Multi-sensor fusion; persistent presence	Higher threat exposure; Comms intermittency; De-confliction with civilian shipping	Generates multi-agent trajectories; proposes cueing policies robust to comms gaps
COA C	Distributed swarm of small USVs for wide-area screening	Resilient coverage; gradual degradation if one asset fails	Coordination overhead; Spoofing/ Jamming; Rules-of-Engagement Constraints	Learns allocation priors; detects anomalies; Simulates failure & deception scenarios

Note: COAs are illustrative. In practice, the COA set, metrics, and constraints are mission and platform-specific.

Abbreviations: COA A, COA B, COA C mentioned in the table together are COAs. COA: Course of Action; UAV: Unmanned Aerial Vehicle; USV: Unmanned Surface Vessel; GNSS: Global Navigation Satellite System; GenAI: Generative Artificial Intelligence: Comms: Communications

COA A, COA B, COA C mentioned in the table together are COAs platforms, bandwidth-limited communication, intermittent connectivity, and rapidly changing task sets (e.g., track, classify, relay, decoy, screen). Although centralized optimization techniques can provide good solutions for small teams, they become brittle and unreliable when communication is disrupted or when new tasks are assigned faster than a global optimizer can recalculate the plan. On the other hand, generative models can provide an alternative formulation: rather than finding a single joint plan, a generative model can learn a distribution of coordinated behaviours conditioned on the mission intent and local state. Recent studies of generative AI for unmanned vehicle swarms have demonstrated how Variational Autoencoders (VAEs), Generative Adversarial Networks (GANs), diffusion models, and normalizing flows can be used in swarm perception, resource allocation, and anomaly detection (Liu et al., 2024).

In the context of mission control, this chapter proposes learning 'allocation priors' from high-fidelity simulations, tabletop wargaming, and/or past exercises. The prior captures the structural relationships among the effective assignments of the various mission resources; for example, how surveillance assets are paired with communications relays, how decoys are placed relative to threats, and how search responsibilities are allocated in a chokepoint. During run-time, the generative model recommends a number of candidate allocations. The candidate allocations are then filtered through a set of deterministic constraints: de-confliction, fuel/battery margin, emission regulations, communication range, and rules of engagement. The "generate-then-verify" workflow provides fast re-planning while enforcing safety constraints (NIST, 2023; US DoD, 2022).

Generative models can also be used to develop resilient mission control strategies. Since the generative model captures typical cooperative behaviour, it can recognize deviation from expected behaviour as indicative of faults, compromised nodes, or adversary manipulations. For example, if a subset of Unmanned Aerial Vehicles (USVs) forms a type of cooperation that is anomalous and deviates from the expected behaviour based on local currents and tasks, the mission controller can invoke a degraded mode: tighter safety boundaries, less reliance on shared state estimation, or human review of large deviations from the expected behaviour. Such approaches are compliant with the defence-oriented guidance on responsible AI that emphasizes the importance of monitoring, traceability, and human oversight of high-stakes decisions (NATO, 2024; NIST, 2024).

8. Constrained Language and Auditable Mission Interfaces

A robust design uses a constrained language layer. Within this architecture, the large language model (LLM) serves as an expressive interface, generating explanations, summaries, and candidate taskings, but any action-bearing output must be mapped into a restricted schema that can be audited: coordinate bounds must be validly formatted, task type must be selected from a valid vocabulary, and mission constraints must be valid in terms of the operational design domain. This is similar to risk-management guidance that advocates for decoupling expressive interfaces from safety-critical execution pathways and applying guardrails at the interface (NIST, 2024). This approach also mitigates the risks associated with manipulated prompts: if a compromised message attempts to inject unauthorized commands, schema validation and authorization checks provide a deterministic barrier between the language output and platform behaviour.

Language-enabled mission interfaces will enable commanders to interact with large autonomy stacks, as well as translate the high-level intent to structured tasking, constraints, and informational requests via translation from natural language to machine-readable formats. For example, if a maritime ISR operator expresses an intent such as "Maintain continuous surveillance over the northern access route", or "Classify all fast contact events occurring inside a 10nm radius of the exclusion zone", then an LLM can help translate those expressions into machine-readable mission descriptions. The machine-readable mission descriptions would include: geographic boundaries, priority sensors, reporting thresholds, and time boundaries. However, when it comes to safety and security critical missions, LLMs need to be viewed as decision-support tools, not as independent decision-makers. NATO Defence Guidance and US Department of Defense responsible AI guidance emphasize accountability and traceability, which implies language systems used in these areas will have to record prompts, intermediate plans, and outputs for auditing and after-action reviews.

To develop a safe design for defence autonomy using generative AI, a constrained language layer should be implemented. The LLM generates explanations, summaries, and candidate taskings but all action bearing outputs will be restricted to a predetermined schema which can then be validated—coordinate bounds must be well formed; task types must be from an approved vocabulary; mission constraints must be consistent with the operational design domain. This approach mirrors risk management guidance that suggests separating expressive interfaces from safety-critical execution pathways and enforcing guard rails at the boundary (NIST, 2024). Furthermore, this constrained language layer also helps mitigate the risk of prompt manipulation—if a compromised message attempts to inject unauthorized directives, the schema validation and authorization checks provide a deterministic barrier between language output and platform behaviour.

For defence autonomy, interactive "what-if" queries during course of action development can improve tempo with language enabled tools. The system can respond with summarized comparisons grounded in world-model ensembles rather than free-form speculation. To reduce hallucination risk, mission interfaces should cite the underlying evidence used for each answer—simulation runs, sensor logs, policy constraints, etc.—so the human can judge confidence and relevance. NIST's generative AI profile recommends transparency mechanisms that disclose limitations, uncertainty, and intended use which map naturally to mission briefing workflows in defence contexts (NIST, 2024).

9. Simulation, Digital Twins, and Synthetic Data Generation

Autonomous defence systems rarely have sufficient operational data available due to the lack of availability of data, the classification of data, or the expense of obtaining large-scale data collection for defence-related applications, especially for rare and dangerous mission scenarios. Therefore, simulation-based development and testing of autonomous defence systems is an essential part of developing, testing, and validating autonomous navigation and mission control systems. AI can also significantly enhance the simulation-based testing process of autonomous defence systems by producing a wide variety of realistic and stressful synthetic mission scenarios that exceed normal operating conditions.

Digital twins are becoming increasingly popular in simulating the performance of autonomous systems throughout their entire lifecycle from conception through pre-deployment verification. Digital twins represent virtual versions of the physical platforms and their operating environments, and integrate the platform dynamics, sensor models, environmental factors, and mission logic, allowing engineers and operators to verify the performance of autonomous systems under controlled conditions that closely replicate real-world operating conditions. The integration of generative models with digital twins allows the simulation of a variety of scenarios (i.e., traffic flow, weather conditions, sensor degradation, etc.), as opposed to scripting specific scenarios.

Generative trajectory models and learned world models are particularly useful in this regard because they allow the simulation of counterfactual conditions (i.e., plausible future states that are different from the observed historical state). For example, generative models can generate rare near-miss collisions, coordinated multi-platform manoeuvring, or navigation failures caused by Global Navigation Satellite System (GNSS) spoofing. The generation of synthetic stresses enhances the breadth of test coverage and decreases the likelihood that an autonomous defence system's autonomy policies are validated under benign or expected operating conditions only.

From an engineering standpoint, the integration of generative AI into simulation environments allows for rapid design iteration and regression testing. For example, numerous new autonomy software releases can be compared to large quantities of simulated scenarios, thereby enabling the measurement of changes in safety margins, mission success, and robustness.

Therefore, generative AI–enhanced simulation and digital twins are two critical enablers of the acceleration of the development of defence-grade autonomous systems while maintaining the necessary level of rigour.

Since there exists a lack of sufficient operational data to support learning and validation, generative AI is likely to be most useful in the short term as an acceleration layer for simulation—enabling generation of diverse scenarios, augmentation of edge cases, and synthesis of realistic sensor and trajectory data for testing. Digital twins—virtual representations of platforms and the operating environment in which they operate—are becoming increasingly prevalent for purposes of rehearsing missions, evaluating upgrades, and assessing performance under alternative conditions. Defence test guidance links digital twins to verification objectives, focusing on repeating tests, controlling configurations, and providing traceability between requirements and test evidence (US DoD, 2022).

Generative trajectory and world models complement digital twins by producing counterfactual conditions that are difficult to script manually. For example, a learned model can generate alternative neutral traffic patterns in a congested littoral area, plausible adversary manoeuvre sequences near a choke point, or sensor degradations consistent with historical GNSS interference patterns (Federal Aviation Administration, 2025). By sampling from these distributions, engineers can increase the breadth of test coverage beyond nominal conditions and decrease the risk that an autonomy policy was validated solely on "happy path" runs. In practice, synthetic generation should be utilized to extend, rather than supplant, real data. The most defendable method includes anchoring synthetic scenarios to empirical distributions and then using controlled perturbations to assess tails and corner cases.

Another advantage of generative AI–enabled simulation is iterative design. Since scenario generation can be automated, teams can perform large-scale Monte Carlo experiments comparing navigation stacks, task-allocation policies, and sensor fusion strategies under systematically varied conditions. Those runs can then be fed back into training (e.g., curriculum learning), requirements refinement (e.g., identifying dominant failure modes), and operational guidance (e.g., specifying which degraded modes should require human confirmation). This continuous test-and-learn loop corresponds with the framework for managing risk that advocates for ongoing measurement and post-deployment monitoring, as opposed to one-time certification (NIST, 2023, 2024).

10. Systems Integration: Architecture, Verification, and Reliability

There are several intentional architectural considerations that defence organizations must make to strike a balance between flexibility and safety-enforcing assurances in order to successfully integrate generative AI components into safety-critical autonomous navigation and mission control systems. These architectural considerations include defining whether the capability to perform a particular function is to reside onboard the autonomous platform or offboard, identifying which functions are safety-critical, and specifying the mechanisms that constrain the generative outputs prior to execution. As defence organizations are aware, the failure modes of autonomous defence systems can have significant adverse impacts on defence-related operations, and, therefore, the identification of these issues is critical.

A commonly used architecture pattern for achieving runtime assurances is to allow generative AI components to recommend candidate actions, while independent and verifiable monitors enforce safety and mission constraints on those actions. Under this paradigm, generative AI trajectory planners or mission allocators can analyse a large solution space for candidate actions, but, prior to execution, monitors will eliminate from consideration candidate actions that violate safety constraints such as collision avoidance, flight envelope constraints, geofencing, fuel limits, and rules of engagement. Therefore, the autonomous system will operate within a defined operational design domain.

Validating and verifying stochastic generative AI systems continues to be one of the primary challenges. Since generative AI models cannot be fully tested across all possible inputs, defence engineering teams use a variety of methodologies including scenario coverage analysis, Monte Carlo simulation, and adversarial stress testing to evaluate the behaviour of the system across large ensembles of generated conditions. The objective is not to prove that a generative AI model is always correct, but to prove that the system is capable of identifying and preventing unsafe behaviour.

Robustness of generative AI–enabled autonomy therefore exists at the system level, not the model level. Robustness is achieved through layers of protection, conservative definitions of safety envelopes, and continuous monitoring. When used in this manner, generative AI can increase the adaptability and performance of autonomous systems without compromising the stringent safety and reliability standards applicable to defence-grade autonomous systems.

There are architectural considerations (compute placement, interfaces, and assurance boundaries) associated with integrating generative components into safety-critical navigation and mission-control systems. One of the primary questions is where should the generative modules be located onboard (for low-latency and autonomy in comms-denied conditions) versus offboard (with higher compute power and richer global context)? In most defence-related applications, generative models are best situated as proposal generators: they provide suggestions for trajectories, allocations, or predicted futures, while deterministic components impose strict constraints and provide fail-safe behaviour if the model is out-of-distribution. This separation facilitates clearer safety cases and more straightforward verification than end-to-end generative control without constraints (US DoD, 2022).

One of the most commonly employed design paradigms is runtime assurance. The generative module provides candidate actions, but a verified monitor imposes safety envelopes such as collision avoidance, manoeuvre limits, geofences, and mission-specific prohibitions (e.g., no-go zones and emissions control). If the monitor cannot verify that a candidate action meets the safety criteria, the system will reject the candidate action and request additional samples or fall back to a conservative baseline controller. For maritime and aerial systems subject to GNSS disruptions, the monitors should contain integrity checks and degraded-mode logic—utilizing alternate navigation estimates, expanding safety buffers, or reducing speed when the state estimate becomes uncertain (Federal Aviation Administration, 2025).

The verification and validation of stochastic generative systems present unique challenges due to the fact that the same input can result in disparate outputs across runs. Practically speaking, assurance is constructed by aggregating three types of evaluation: (i) scenario-coverage testing and structured simulation campaigns; (ii) Monte Carlo analysis of sampled disturbances and adversarial conditions; and (iii) evidence collection demonstrating that monitors preclude unsafe execution even when generative components suggest unsafe actions. Defence test and evaluation guidance emphasize the significance of establishing model limitations, documenting the operational conditions in which AI-enabled systems are reliable, and employing test infrastructure that affords repeatability and auditability (NIST, 2023).

The purpose of synthetic generation is not to establish that a generative model is always accurate, but to illustrate that the overall system remains safe and mission-effective within a specified operational design domain.

11. Security, Ethics, Human-in-the-Loop Governance

The incorporation of generative AI into defence autonomy creates substantial security and governance challenges. As regards security, generative models may be susceptible to data poisoning, adversarial inputs, model extraction, and prompt manipulation. These risks are exacerbated in navigation and mission control where corrupted model output may result in unsafe manoeuvres or resource misallocation. Alliance and defence guidance assert that responsible AI adoption necessitates the protection of AI technologies, monitoring of misuse, and the establishment of transparency regarding how AI impacts operational decision-making (NATO, 2021, 2024; US DoD, 2022). In practice, this entails secure data pipelines, provenance tracking, red-teaming of AI components, and continuous monitoring for anomalous behaviour. Ethically, increased autonomy generates concerns regarding over-reliance and accountability. Therefore, human-in-the-loop or human-in-command design is indispensable. Oversight must be structured with defined approval thresholds and escalation pathways. Interface design must convey uncertainty instead of obscuring it, thereby permitting operators to calibrate trust accordingly. Finally, auditability is mandatory. Generative systems should record candidate trajectories, constraints applied, and decision rationale to permit assessment of behaviour subsequent to exercises or incidents. Such traceability facilitates learning, adherence to regulatory requirements, and alignment with international norms regulating military AI utilization.

12. Case Illustration: Generative AI–Enabled Maritime ISR Mission

This case illustration represents an end-to-end maritime intelligence, surveillance, and reconnaissance (ISR) mission that utilizes generative AI–enabled navigation and mission control. The scenario is deliberately representative as opposed to platform-specific, illustrating architectural patterns and decision workflows pertinent to all naval contexts. The mission objective is to maintain persistent situational awareness over a strategically important maritime waterway with dense commercial traffic, intermittent GNSS interference, and potential adversary deception. A coordinated team of fixed-wing unmanned aerial vehicles (UAVs) and unmanned surface vessels (USVs) is charged with providing situational awareness over a 24-hour operational window, while minimizing collision risk, emissions exposure, and reliance upon continuous communication.

Mission preparation commences with data aggregation and model development. Historical Automatic Identification System (AIS) data, satellite imagery, environmental models, and simulated adversary behaviours are aggregated to train a generative maritime world model. Synthetic data generation is employed to supplement rare yet safety-critical events such as near-collision events, abrupt course changes, and AIS spoofing behaviours. This enables the world model to learn both normal traffic flow and anomalies indicative of abnormal or hostile activities. During mission planning, the mission control system compares multiple candidate courses of action (COAs). A UAV-centric wide-area patrol prioritizes coverage, a concentrated UAV–USV team prioritizes high-risk zones, and a distributed low-signature patrol prioritizes stealth and resiliency.

For each COA, the generative world model generates ensembles of probable futures with variable environmental conditions, traffic densities, and adversary reactions. Outcome distributions are quantified using risk-sensitive metrics for comparative purposes. Following review by a human operator, a hybrid UAV–USV COA is chosen based on its robustness. Execution employs diffusion-based trajectory generators to continually generate navigation update recommendations for UAV loiter patterns and USV transit routes. Each generated recommendation is assessed by runtime assurance monitors to determine whether the recommended navigation updates adhere to established safety constraints (collision avoidance and geofencing). When communication loss occurs, the platforms continue to operate using onboard generative planning. Upon regaining communication, updated intelligence prompts re-planning. Review of suggested revisions occurs through a mission dashboard that communicates uncertainty and risk. The mission achieves continuous coverage without safety violations. Generative planning permits rapid adaptation to unanticipated traffic surges. Important lessons include the necessity of communicating uncertainty, conservatively constraining safety envelopes, and structurally incorporating human oversight.

13. Research Challenges and Future Directions

While generative AI appears to possess considerable potential for enhancing the effectiveness of navigation and mission control in defence applications, numerous research gaps must be addressed before generative AI prototypes can be transitioned into deployable defence capabilities. First, data scarcity and classification limit the ability to develop models. Operational log data may be limited in terms of quality and quantity, and coalition-sharing constraints may impede data-pooling across partner organizations. This emphasizes the necessity of simulation, synthetic data, and careful dataset governance, but increases the likelihood that models will learn artifacts of simulation rather than actual-world dynamics. Risk frameworks advocate for documenting data origins, intended usage, and recognized limitations to enable decision-makers to appreciate what the model has experienced—and what it has not experienced—during development (NIST, 2023, 2024).

Secondly, sim-to-real transfer is a fundamental challenge. Even sophisticated digital twins cannot completely replicate contested electromagnetic environments, adversary deception, and the long-tailed variability of weather and sea-state. Domain randomization, online adaptation, and uncertainty-aware planning can help mitigate some of these deficiencies, but create new assurance questions: under what conditions and how is online learning allowed, and what safeguards exist to prevent unsafe adaptation? Defence guidance advocating for responsible AI emphasizes that systems should afford mechanisms for monitoring and fallback behaviour when conditions deviate from the validated operational envelope (NATO, 2024; US DoD, 2022).

Finally, a key area of concentration for future research is the standardization of interfaces and artifact evidence to facilitate the integration, substitution, and evaluation of generative AI components identically across multiple platforms. Mission control systems are developed over years and comprise legacy software, proprietary systems, and certified constraints. For generative AI to be feasible in such systems, they will need to be equipped with standardized interfaces for generating proposals (e.g., trajectory sets, allocation candidates, forecast ensembles) and standardized artifacts to support assurance (e.g., monitor results, scenario seeds, metrics, and logs). Standardized artifacts will allow independent test teams to evaluate the performance of generative AI components, and will enable the incremental replacement of the autonomy stack without requiring the re-certification of the entire stack. This is congruent with the emphasis on configuration control, repeatability, and traceability in test and evaluation guidelines and the need to document and govern the lifecycle of AI as part of the overarching efforts to ensure the dependable operation of AI in defence operations (NIST, 2023).

14. Conclusion

Autonomous Systems are a critical component in the future generations of Air and Maritime Defence Capabilities. Autonomous Systems will enable platforms to achieve higher levels of persistence and adaptability; ultimately achieving mission success at an unprecedented level. However, as shown within this Chapter, Contested and Dynamic Environments continue to test and demonstrate the limitations of Autonomous Pipelines - which cannot be addressed through incremental engineering. However, deploying generative AI involves substantial disciplines, including rigorous simulation and Verification and Validation (V&V), adversarial testing of robustness, structured human oversight, and governance in accordance with principles of responsible AI. Provided that these disciplines are incorporated into the development of generative AI, it is possible to leverage generative AI to improve the efficacy of navigation and mission control functions, while maintaining the accountability and trust necessary for defence operations.

In terms of practising generative AI, the most prudent near-term path forward is a carefully staged, evidence-driven approach. Generative AI can be used to generate alternatives and stress cases, deterministic safety monitors can continue to operate in the loop, and authority can be expanded only as the accumulation of evidence increases through simulations, exercises, and operational deployments. This incremental approach also promotes workforce preparedness—operators and engineers can become familiar with the manner in which generative models operate under uncertainty, the conditions under which the models exhibit fragility, and the interface designs that promote scepticism versus excessive confidence. Ultimately, as verification practices evolve and as responsible AI governance processes are institutionalized within acquisitions and operations, generative AI–enabled autonomy can be deployed as a trustworthy component of mission planning and execution. The ultimate long-term vision for generative AI–enabled autonomy is a mission control environment that utilizes shared predictive models and auditable decision aids to enable collaboration between humans and autonomous systems in contested environments with increased tempo and resiliency, while retaining accountability.

In general, generative AI should be designed as an auditable and measurable capability which advances the accomplishment of missions, assures safety and legality, and provides for continuous human oversight within the autonomous process. These fundamental principles for the development and deployment of generative AI–enabled autonomy in coalition operations across all domains will assist in the growth of the body of knowledge through exercises, red-teaming, and operational usage. Thus, programmes that establish assurance, governance, and operator confidence as design requirements—rather than after-thoughts—will be best suited to take advantage of the benefits of generative AI at scale. This will require the use of rigorous documentation, configuration control, and reference management throughout the lifecycle of the total system. Additionally, successful employment of generative AI–enabled autonomy will rely upon the discipline of operationalization of generative AI capabilities. Programme managers must identify clear operational design domains, measurable acceptance criteria, and iteratively test evaluations using both normal mission conditions and deliberately adverse conditions (stress cases). Additionally, training and doctrinal changes will need to be made to enable operators to interpret the outputs from generative AI systems as probabilities, determine failure modes, and exercise appropriate levels of oversight of generative AI–enabled autonomous processes. The socio-technical components outlined above will provide generative AI with increased mission effectiveness while maintaining safety, legality, and accountability.

References

Bi, J., Cheng, H., Zhang, W. et al. (2024). Artificial intelligence in ship trajectory prediction. *Journal of Marine Science and Engineering*, 12(5), 769. https://doi.org/10.3390/jmse12050769 (accessed December 8, 2025)

Federal Aviation Administration. (2025). *Jamming and/or spoofing: GNSS interference resource guide 2026* (Version 1.0). https://www.faa.gov/about/office_org/headquarters_offices/avs/offices/afx/afs/afs400/afs410/GNSS/GPS_GNSS_Interference_Resource_Guide.pdf (accessed January 9, 2026)

Guan, Y., Liao, H., Li, Z. et al. (2024). World models for autonomous driving: An initial survey. *arXiv (Cornell University)*. https://doi.org/10.48550/arxiv.2403.02622 (accessed December 15, 2025)

Liu, G., Nguyen, V.H., Du, H. et al. (2024). Generative AI for unmanned vehicle swarms: Challenges, applications and opportunities. *arXiv (Cornell University)*. https://doi.org/10.48550/arxiv.2402.18062 (accessed December 18, 2025)

National Institute of Standards and Technology (US) (NIST). (2024). Artificial intelligence risk management framework: Generative artificial intelligence profile (No. NIST AI 600-1). National Institute of Standards and Technology (US). https://doi.org/10.6028/NIST.AI.600-1 (accessed December 2, 2025)

North Atlantic Treaty Organization (NATO). (2021). Summary of the NATO artificial intelligence strategy. Official Texts and Resources. https://www.nato.int/en/about-us/official-texts-and-resources/official-texts/2021/10/22/summary-of-the-nato-artificial-intelligence-strategy (accessed November 24, 2025)

North Atlantic Treaty Organization (NATO). (2024). NATO releases revised AI strategy. https://www.nato.int/en/news-and-events/articles/news/2024/07/10/nato-releases-revised-ai-strategy (accessed November 26, 2025)

National Institute of Standards and Technology. (2023). Artificial Intelligence Risk Management Framework (AI RMF 1.0) (NIST AI 100-1). U.S. Department of Commerce. https://doi.org/10.6028/NIST.AI.100-1 (accessed November 21, 2025)

US Department of Defense (DoD). (2022). Responsible artificial intelligence strategy and implementation pathway. https://media.defense.gov/2024/Oct/26/2003571790/-1/-1/0/2024-06-RAI-STRATEGY-IMPLEMENTATION-PATHWAY.PDF (accessed November 30, 2025)

8 Transforming Naval Warfare and Underwater Sensing with Generative Artificial Intelligence: A New Paradigm in Maritime Defence

Sumaiya Shaikh[1*], Shaista Farhat[2], M.A. Jabbar[3] and Abdelkrim Haqiq[4]

With the rapid advancement of technology, the maritime domain is redefining the dynamics of naval warfare and underwater sensing by integrating with generative artificial intelligence (AI). Generative AI is no more a new term in this rapidly transforming world. Existing content, like text, images, and videos, is being used for pattern-based learning by generative AI. Though generative AI is used for many applications, this chapter focuses on one major application—naval warfare. Earlier, traditional methods were sufficient to meet the naval requirements but they are now unable to handle the complex and modern underwater environment, stealth technologies, and asymmetric threats. This chapter provides an integrated solution to address these challenges through adaptive learning, dynamic simulation, and intelligent data synthesis. The major focus of this chapter is on transformative generative AI in Autonomous Underwater Vehicles (AUVs), acoustic signal reconstruction, system-enabled enhanced sonar signal interpretation, object recognition, and situational forecasting which allow naval operations to transform from reactive strategies to decision-making. This integration marks a pivotal moment in maritime defence by introducing a framework wherein underwater surveillance, navigation precision, and strategic control are augmented through self-evolving, data-driven systems. The integration of advanced computational intelligence with maritime technology aims to redefine the future of naval operations, promoting greater resilience, adaptability, and foresight in global maritime security.

1. Introduction

Naval forces have always vied for supremacy in the maritime domain through superior intelligence and technological advancements. Marine environments are

[1] https://orcid.org/0000-0003-0884-8965
[2] https://orcid.org/0009-0008-9348-8370
[3] https://orcid.org/0000-0003-4059-2728
[4] https://orcid.org/0000-0002-8857-6586
* Corresponding author: sumiyashaikh@gmail.com

DOI: 10.1201/9781003688174-8

very important for providing regional Security and ensuring security of the oceans. As the battleship domination increased in underwater domains, the traditional warfare techniques declined in importance. To address this vital issue, the integration of artificial intelligence (AI) with electronic monitoring and underwater sensing has been discussed in this chapter.

Generative AI techniques have many brought about much advancement in maritime defence and underwater sensing. These advancements include techniques like Generative Adversarial Networks (GANs), Variational Autoencoders (VAEs), and diffusion models (Britannicia), which offer remarkable potential for generating training datasets, improving the clarity of the signal through denoising, and supporting predictive simulation tasks.

1.1 Background of Naval Warfare and Underwater Sensing

In the past few centuries, naval warfare has undergone many transformations, from involving conventional techniques to adopting the latest emerging technology. Surface by surface and domain by domain, maritime threats are increasing, including those posed by stealth submarines, autonomous underwater vehicles (AUVs), and advanced torpedoes. There are many challenges such as acoustic distortion and unpredictable ocean conditions that impose a limit on the traditional methods. To overcome these obstacles, modern naval research focuses on intelligent, data-driven systems that enhance the accuracy and real-time analysis (Blackman, S.S and Popoli, R. 1999).

1.2 Challenges of Generative AI in Naval Warfare

There are many advantages of using generative AI in naval combat. Some of these are:

- *Data Availability and Reliability*: As a major portion of the operational data is classified, scarce, or not available for sharing, so it is very challenging to gather vast, diversified, and labelled naval datasets. When the system comes across uncommon or invisible threat categories, limited datasets lead to training bias and waken the model's resilience. Furthermore, there are not enough labelled examples of actual hostile behaviour, which makes performance validation and supervised learning challenging.
- *Adversarial Manipulation*: Adversarial manipulation of downstream classifiers and generative models may make them vulnerable to altered sensor feeds or hostile inputs. This could result in false positives or negatives at crucial times in a military setting. In addition to identifying model weakness, the problem is determining whether suspicious data is intentionally created or naturally abnormal, as the two have somewhat distinct operational reactions.
- *Computational Demand*: For training, and frequently for inference, state-of-the-art generative models demand a significant amount of memory and processing power. Due to their computing, thermal, and physical space limits, naval platforms, particularly ships, submarines, and unmanned underwater

vehicles (UUVs) find it difficult to deploy high-capacity models at the edge or to guarantee acceptable inference latency for decisions that must be made quickly.

- *Integration Complexity*: Modern C2 platforms, proprietary sensors, and legacy technologies are all used in a variety of ways in naval operations. Strong interfaces, standardization, and cautious change management are necessary for integrating generative AI into these ecosystems; otherwise, the AI outputs might not fit properly into operational workflows or might violate current safety and certification protocols.
- *Operational Legacy*: Operations like anti-submarine warfare (ASW) engagements and other time-sensitive naval decisions require very low latency perception-to-action loops. Even if model inference is feasible, unacceptably high latency can be introduced by pre-processing, verification procedures, and network delays. Providing reliable, quick AI results without causing bottlenecks is a difficult operational and engineering problem.
- *Ethical and Legal Concerns*: The delegation of lethal force, responsibility for AI-driven errors, and adherence to international humanitarian law are among the ethical and legal concerns brought to the fore by the use of AI in military decision-making. These issues make it more difficult to approve procurements, implement operational adoption, and create rules of engagement involving AI-generated suggestions or self-governing behaviours.

1.3 Challenges of Generative AI in Underwater Sensing

Applying generative AI in underwater sensing also brings its own set of challenges. A few of these challenges are:

- *Environmental Noise*: Noise in environment, variable sources of sound, and intricate propagation effects influence underwater acoustics. These highly non-stationary noise patterns frequently cause generative models trained on cleaner or region-specific data to perform poorly, resulting in misleading structure or unreliable denoising in reconstructed signals.
- *Scarcity of Labelled Data*: Labelled sonar/underwater dataset collection is costly, time consuming, and operationally limited. It is particularly uncommon to find annotated examples of mines, stealthy UUVs, or uncommon submarine signatures. This scarcity raises the possibility that models would learn the peculiarities of the training set instead of generalizable properties, which impedes supervised model training and trustworthy evaluation.
- *Generalization Issues*: Due to domain shift, models trained in one oceanic region, season, or sensor configuration frequently perform poorly when deployed elsewhere. It is challenging to achieve effective generalization in undersea applications because it necessitates domain adaption, continuous learning, or very large annotated corpora.
- *Interpretability*: Enhanced sonar images or synthetic acoustic scenery are examples of generative model outputs that may appear realistic and yet contain

fake characteristics that an operator could misinterpret. Operator acceptance and tactical application are made more difficult by the ongoing challenge of converting model outputs into easily understandable visuals and actionable confidence assertions for humans.

- *Constraints of Hardware*: Strict specifications for size, weight, power and ruggedization are applicable to deployable undersea platforms. It can be challenging to execute complicated generative models on the platform where low-latency processing would be most helpful since advanced AI hardware [Graphical Processing Unit (GPU), Neural Processing Unit (NPU)] might not fit within the physical, thermal, and pressure constraints of small UUVs or long-endurance sonobuoys.
- *Energy Efficiency*: Energy budgets for long endurance missions, such persistent UUV patrols, are limited. Mission duration can be shortened and battery life quickly depleted by running big generative models or frequent communications for cloud processing. Intermittent processing, duty-cycling, and energy-conscious model design are necessary, but they make system design and capability planning more difficult.

1.4 Applications of Generative AI in Naval Warfare and Underwater Sensing

Generative AI's generated data transforms marine and defence operations by creating real training scenarios without real world risks. Generative AI has opened new opportunities for its deployment in naval warfare. Table 8.1 and Table 8.2 present the benefits and limitations of each application.

Table 8.1 Applications of Generative AI in Naval Warfare.

Application	*Benefits*	*Limitations*
Synthetic training data generation	Enhances restricted categorized datasets and permits safe, realistic AI training	Rare edge cases might not be captured by synthetic data; over-reliance is a concern
Threat simulation & wargaming	Simulates the actions and strategies of adversaries in order to test strategies	High processing demands potential differences between simulated and actual threats
Decision support systems	Enhance situational awareness and offer predictive insights	Commanders may not trust AI-generated situations since outputs can be challenging to understand
Deception & counter-deception	Detects spoofing techniques and assists in creating countermeasures for electronic warfare	Adversaries may develop more quickly, and there is a chance that manipulated inputs could fool AI
Operational planning under uncertainty	Creates a variety of situations for thorough mission preparation	Requires a lot of domain-specific information which may differ in reality

Source: Goecks, V.G. and Waytowich, N. (2024)

Table 8.2 Applications of Generative AI in Underwater Sensing.

Application	*Benefits*	*Limitations*
Sonar image enhancement & reconstruction	Increases target identification, lowers noise, and improves resolution	In extreme loud situations the performance degrades which affects the naval artifacts
Data augmentation for training	Increases model generalization, decreases overfitting, and broadens the scope of restricted datasets	The variety of real world acoustic variances may be absent from synthetic data
Anomaly detection	Detects variations from taught patterns to identify mines, submarines, and UUVs	False alarms could occur, and attackers could create signals to avoid detection
Environmental modelling	Optimizes sensor deployment by simulating intricate underwater circumstances	Real hydrodynamic difficulties may be oversimplified by simulations
Multi-sensor data fusion	Creates a cohesive image by combining sonar, optical, magnetic, and infrared signals	Computationally demanding; there is a chance that different data will not line up
Predictive maintenance for sensors	Decreases downtime, saves expenses, and finds early indications of sensor	Needs constant observation; forecasting methods could overlook unexpected malfunctions

Source: V.G. Goecks and N. Waytowich, "COA-GPT: Generative Pre-trained Transformers for Accelerated Course of Action Development in Military Operations," arXiv preprint, Feb. 2024.

2. Naval Warfare and Maritime Defence: Current Landscape

2.1 *Naval Warfare and Traditional Methods*

A vast array of strategies and doctrines created over centuries to establish and preserve dominance over the maritime realm are included in traditional naval warfare. These techniques developed from fleet conflicts during the sail era to intricate multi-domain operations that included mine warfare, naval aviation, submarines, surface combatants, and electronic/signals intelligence. Comprehending these conventional methods offers crucial background information for how contemporary technologies, like generative AI and sophisticated sensing, complement and, in some situations, revolutionize naval operations.

In response to technical advancements, naval doctrine has continuously evolved. Throughout the Age of Sail, seamanship, gunnery, and manoeuver were key components of naval supremacy. With the advent of steam propulsion and ironclads during the Industrial Revolution, the focus shifted to firepower and armour. The Cold War significantly improved ASW, carrier battle group tactics, and integrated command-and-control. Two world wars in the twentieth century sped up the development of submarines, aircraft carriers, sonar, radar, and amphibious doctrine. Modern naval strategy is still based on the classic concepts of sea control, denial, power projection, and protection of sea lines of communication (SLOCs).

Traditional Methods of Naval Warfare: The strategies, tactics, and armed actions carried out on, beneath, or above the water are together referred to as naval warfare. From straightforward ship-to-ship combat to extremely intricate operations combining surface ships, submarines, carrier aircraft, electronic warfare, intelligence and reconnaissance, and long-range artillery, it has changed over the course of centuries. While platforms and technologies have evolved, several things have remained the same. According to Helsing. (2025), naval tactics still heavily rely on surprise, focused force, sound command, manoeuvrability, and timing. These characteristics set apart successful naval operations, regardless of the time period, from the days of sailing fleets to the current missile-equipped navy. The reference mentioned Helsing. (2025) pointed out that while naval warfare is always changing due to new technologies, its core principles of making decisions in the face of uncertainty, the art of tactics, unit cohesion, and information leveraging remain consistent. Though it must foresee future changes in platforms, sensors, communication, and manoeuver, modern naval doctrine nevertheless builds on the lessons learned from earlier periods, which makes innovation and adaptation crucial. The types of traditional naval warfare are shown in Figure 8.1.

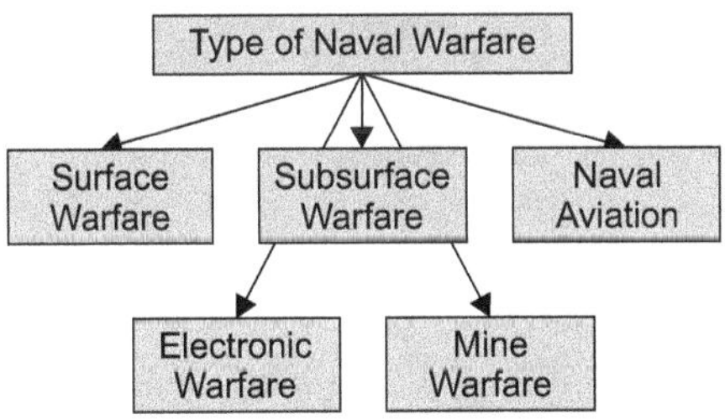

Fig. 8.1 Types of Traditional Naval Warfare.

i. *Surface Warfare*: Combat among surface ships such as battleships, frigates, destroyers, and cruisers is the main focus of surface warfare. Protecting SLOCs, escorting convoys, engaging anti-surface ships, and maritime interdiction are important duties. The focus of traditional tactics is on coordinated fleet tactics, manoeuver, gunnery accuracy, and torpedo strikes. To confront threats from air and surface platforms, surface combatants nowadays rely on radar, fire-control systems, guided missiles, and integrated air defence.
ii. *Subsurface Warfare*: Submarines are the stealthy platforms with the ability to strike, observe, and deny the ability to operate at sea. These are the mainstay of subsurface warfare. Nuclear-powered submarines contribute with increased endurance and strategic deterrence roles, while conventional submarine tactics take advantage of stealth, quieting, and surprise torpedo assaults. ASW techniques, such as depth charges (historically), towed arrays,

magnetic anomaly detection (MAD), passive and active sonar, and organized hunter-killer teams, are necessary to counter submarines. In order to locate and engage underwater contacts, ASW is an intelligence-driven search and detection technology that combines sensor networks, aircraft, surface ships, and oceanographic expertise.

iii. *Naval Aviation*: By using aircraft carriers and escort carriers to place air assets at sea, naval aviation transformed force projection. In order to project force both ashore and at sea, carrier strike groups combine carriers, air wings, escort vessels, and logistics. Strike, reconnaissance, ASW, electronic warfare (EW), and air superiority are all made possible by aircraft. Concepts like the carrier battle group and force projection through air dominance and precision attack are examples of traditional carrier doctrine.

iv. *Electronic Warfare*: The key to identifying, tricking, and interfering with enemy sensors and communications is EW and Signals Intelligence (SIGINT). Electronic support measures (ESM) for emissions detection, electronic attack, and electronic defence are examples of traditional EW methods. Radar and ECM (Electronic Counter Measures) influenced tactics throughout the twentieth century, while SIGINT and radio direction finding have historically allowed for long-range naval force identification.

v. *Mine Warfare*: Shipping and naval activities are at risk from naval mines, which are inexpensive but extremely effective areas-denial weapons. Mine Countermeasures (MCMs) are used to clear channels and mine-laying to block access in traditional mine warfare. Mechanical sweeping, influence sweeps, and specialist minesweepers are examples of MCM techniques, whereas more recent methods are also employed. Sonar-based detection and remotely operated vehicles (ROVs) are deployed for neutralization.

2.1.1 Role of Modern Methods in Naval Warfare

With the introduction of generative AI, naval warfare has advanced in terms of automation, assistance, enhancement, and hybrid operations. This chapter focuses on the latest and modern techniques of naval warfare that are being utilized. Further research is also going on for their improvement. Different types of methods and their trends are explained in detailed below:

i. *Autonomous and AI-Powered Uncrewed Vehicles*: Deploying fleets of unmanned surface or underwater vehicles (USVs/UUVs) equipped with generative AI capabilities for missions like patrol, mine detection, reconnaissance, and surveillance is one of the most obvious developments. An AI technology named Lura, for instance, is used in Helsing's SG-1 Fathom mini-submersibles to identify and categorize ship and submarine acoustic characteristics much more quickly and with fewer sound emissions than previous models. Scalability and adaptability are the advantages; maintaining dependable autonomy in harsh, loud, and dynamic underwater environments is the problem.

ii. *Enhanced Synthetic Data Generation for Sonar/Acoustic Imagery*: High-quality synthetic sonar images are being produced more frequently using generative diffusion models to supplement actual datasets. In order to generate coarse and fine-grained sonar images from textual prompts, a recent project called "Synth-SONAR" combined dual diffusion models with GPT prompting. This improved the realism and diversity of synthetic sonar datasets. When it is difficult or costly to obtain genuine labelled data, this type of synthetic data aids in the training of detection, classification, and segmentation algorithms. Additionally, it makes it possible to simulate uncommon or harsh environmental conditions that might not be adequately represented in current databases.

iii. *Hybrid Operations*: *Human Machine and Edge AI*: In order to lower latency and reliance on central systems, more processing is being moved to the edge (onboard platforms like USVs/UUVs, gliders, and tiny drones) thanks to advancements in generative AI. AI takes care of lower-level duties like detection, tracking, and anomaly reporting, while human operators increasingly serve as supervisors rather than direct controllers. Additionally, hybrid fleets—which combine manned and unmanned platforms—are becoming more popular, opening up more choices for reaction and monitoring. Table 8.3 shows the comparison between the traditional and modern methods.

Table 8.3 Comparison of Traditional and Modern Methods.

Aspect	*Traditional Method*	*Latest Generative AI–based Method*
Data Collection	Primarily uses genuine sensor data, which is frequently expensive and scarce in variety like active/passive sonar, MAD, optical	Creates artificial data (e.g., using diffusion or GANs) to enhance datasets and replicate uncommon circumstances
Detection and Classification Speed	Slower, frequently manual or human-in-loop interpretation of sensor outputs or sonar returns	Automated anomaly detection, real-time acoustic signature inference, and quicker automatic classification
Operational Endurance and Coverage	Human crews, manned ships, and semi-autonomous UUVs	Long-range autonomous systems and AI-coordinated UUV/USV swarms (like SG-1 Fathom)
Signal Quality and Noise Handling	Reliant on beamforming, environmental calibration, and physical filters	AI models for adaptive filtering, denoising, and signal reconstruction utilizing learnt models
Tactical/Strategic Planning	Slower updating cycles, doctrine-driven, and prearranged plans of action	Rapid scenario simulation, dynamic plan adaption, and AI-assisted scenario development (COA-GPT, etc.)

Contd...

Table 8.3 *Contd...*

Aspect	*Traditional Method*	*Latest Generative AI–based Method*
Human Involvement and Decision Latency	High human involvement, potential delays	Edge inference, human-machine collaboration, faster and lower latency flagging, operator supervision, but less manual control
Resource Cost and Risk	Costly ships, dangers to human personnel, and ongoing upkeep	Lower expenses through artificial training and simulation, and lower personnel risk through autonomous systems

Source: Xie, Z., et al. (2023)

2.2 *Traditional Methods of Underwater Sensing*

A key component of oceanographic research and maritime defence, underwater sensing allows navies to identify, categorize, and monitor items in the subsurface environment. Acoustic technologies, magnetic anomaly detection, and optical sensing are the mainstays of conventional underwater sensing techniques. Since the early twentieth century, these methods have been widely employed, particularly during World War I and World War II, when naval superiority depended heavily on submarine detection. The main conventional techniques are described in this section (Figure 8.2) along with their uses, limitations, and underlying theories.

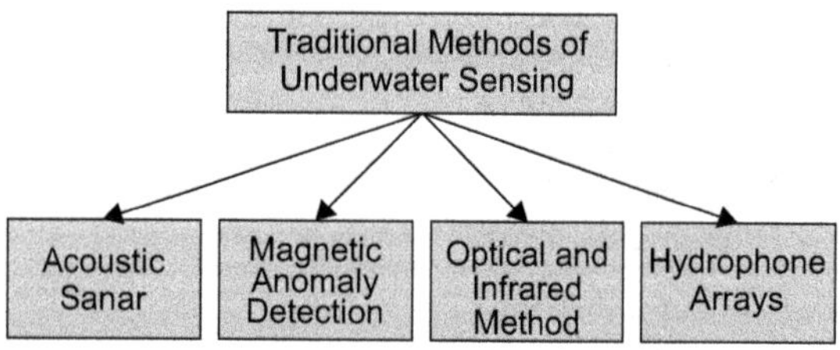

Fig. 8.2 Traditional Methods of Underwater Sensing.

i. *Acoustic Sonar*: The most common techniques for underwater detection have been acoustic sensing, especially sonar (sound navigation and ranging). Sonar devices send out sound waves and listen for echoes that are reflected by submarined objects. While passive sonar listens to sounds made by ships or submarines, active sonar pulses and listens for reflections. Navigation, mine detection, underwater communication, and submarine detection have all made use of sonar. Sonar is limited by environmental factors, noise interference, and stealth capabilities of contemporary submarines, notwithstanding its effectiveness (Endsley, 1995).
ii. *Magnetic Anomaly Detection*: Large ferromagnetic objects, like submarines, can disrupt the Earth's magnetic field, which is detected by magnetic anomaly

detection (MAD) systems. Usually installed on airplanes or helicopters, MAD equipment is flown over suspected submarine locations. Short-range detection is possible with MAD, which is very helpful in shallow seas. However, MAD's sensitivity to background magnetic fluctuations and detection depth are limited (Goodfellow et al., 2014).

iii. *Optical and Infrared Method*: For underwater detection, especially in shallow, clear seas, optical and infrared sensing has been used. Infrared techniques identify temperature changes brought on by submerged objects, whereas optical sensors rely on light reflection. These techniques are less successful at deeper depths because of light absorption and dispersion in water. They are helpful for port security, diver identification, and mine detection applications in spite of these difficulties (Helsing, 2025).

iv. *Hydrophone Arrays*: Passive listening tools called hydrophone arrays are lowered to the ocean floor or pulled by ships. They give spatial information about sound sources and record acoustic signals. These arrays, which provide wide area surveillance, have been essential to ASW. However, environmental noise affects their performance, and their deployment and upkeep are expensive (Kilfoyle, D.B. and Baggeroer, A.B. 2000).

2.2.1 Modern Methods of Underwater Sensing

The migration from traditional methods to modern methods was the need of the hour. For this purpose, generative AI has been employed for merging technology and its rapid growth, which helps humans to reduce their work and risks. The following are the modern techniques of underwater sensing developed using generative AI:

i. *Augmentation and Synthetic Data Generation*: To address the persistent lack of labelled underwater data, generative models are being used to create synthetic sonar and acoustic datasets. Diverse, high-fidelity sonar pictures and acoustic spectrograms that capture various seabed textures, target poses, and noise conditions are produced using GANs, diffusion models, and other synthesis pipelines (Melville & Norton, 1966). In situations when field data is expensive or hard to get, these artificial datasets are then utilized to supplement the limited amount of real data required to train object-detection, classification, and segmentation algorithms. This enhances generalization and decreases overfitting. Recent research shows that side-scan sonar (SSS) imagery with realistic shadowing and target signatures for downstream perception tasks may be produced using diffusion-based and GAN-based sonar synthesis pipelines.

ii. *Diffusion Models for Denoising and Image/Signal Enhancement*: Diffusion-based generative models have become a potent method for underwater data denoising and reconstruction (Mobley, C.D. 1994). Diffusion models can progressively eliminate biological, shipping, and ambient noise from sonar returns and optical underwater imaging while maintaining fine target structure by using a probabilistic reverse de-noising procedure. Particularly in highly non-Gaussian, non-stationary noise conditions that are typical of underwater environments, this method has proven to be more effective than classical filtering and many CNN (Convolution Neural Network) denoisers. Several recent SSS and optical-enhancement studies reported notable improvements in detection following diffusion-based pre-processing.

iii. *Advanced Sonar Image Synthesis*: This is task aware and prompted generation. In order to provide task-aware training data and controlled trials, contemporary pipelines go beyond simple augmentation and seek to generate sonar images conditioned on target type, seabed class, or textual instructions. Among the innovations are hybrid systems that create a variety of sonar settings (changing aspect, depth, and clutter) by combining diffusion generators with broad language model prompting (to specify scene attributes) (Natarajan, P., et al. 2024). This enables researchers to train detectors in those corner settings that are otherwise impossible to capture, such as minefields or unique wreck positions, and to simulate uncommon or hazardous phenomena. Such task-aware synthesis allows stress-testing of sensory systems and speeds up the production of datasets.

iv. *Acoustic Channel Modelling and Communications Augmentation*: In order to produce realistic channel realizations for communications and localization studies, as well as to approximate underwater acoustic channel impulse responses, generative models are being utilized more and more. In order to create synthetic channels for training robust modems and evaluating adaptive equalization and coding techniques, diffusion and autoregressive generative algorithms can directly learn the empirical statistics of multipath, Doppler spreads, and reverberation from observed data (NATO Science and Technology Organization, 2020). When environmental characteristics are unknown or too complicated to explicitly describe, this data-driven channel modelling can sometimes replace or supplement powerful physics simulators.

v. *Domain Adaptation and Transfer Learning via Generative Bridging*: To fill in domain gaps between areas, sensors, or seasons, generative approaches are employed. To enable the reuse of labelled data across domains, cycle-consistency GANs and diffusion-based translators, for instance, modify data captured by one sonar or in one oceanographic regime to resemble data from another (Smith, 2018). In situations where models need to adjust to seasonal or sensor-mounting changes without complete re-annotation, this promotes continuous learning and reduces the expense of re-training for new sensors or operating locations.

vi. *Onboard/Edge Inference and Lightweight Generators*: There is a growing trend of using generating and enhancement models on UUVs, gliders, and buoys. Distilled or optimized versions of GANs, VAEs, and diffusion denoisers can operate with less computation to carry out sample creation, anomaly flagging, and real-time denoising at the edge (Urick, 1983). In addition to enabling distributed swarm perception, where each platform contributes processed observations to a central fusion node, this lowers bandwidth requirements (by transmitting cleaned features rather than raw high-volume data). Sonar-DL robustness surveys highlight the need for hardware-aware architectures and effective models for practical deployments (Martin Aubard, et al. 2024).

vii. *Robustness, Uncertainty Estimation and Defence against Adversarial Acoustic Perturbations*: Researchers are concentrating on robustness and reliable results as generative approaches become more integrated into operational sensing pipelines. Techniques to measure uncertainty in generated samples, identify hallucinations, and strengthen models against adversarial perturbations are all topics of ongoing research. In order to prevent enhanced signals from misleading human operators, current work looks for uncertainty-aware generators, ensemble techniques, and verification layers (Urick, 1984). This is because generative models can be both beneficial (by modelling normal variability for anomaly detection) and detrimental (by producing plausible but incorrect reconstructions). Comparisons among the methods are given in Table 8.4.

Table 8.4 Comparison of Traditional Underwater Sensing with Modern Generative AI adapted Sensing Methods.

Aspect	*Traditional Methods*	*Generative AI Methods for Underwater Sensing*
Data Availability (Xie et al., 2023)	Rely mostly on manual annotation (echosounder runs, actual SSS, and expensive field gathering)	Datasets are enhanced and uncommon situations are simulated by synthetic data generation (GANs/diffusion)
Noise handling (Yang et al., 2023)	Traditional signal processing techniques, such as Wiener filters, matched filtering, and beamforming	Improved reconstruction in complicated noise is achieved through task-aware augmentation and learned denoising through diffusion
Domain adaption (Yang et al., 2025)	For new regions or sensors, either manual recalibration or physics-based simulation (BELLHOP) is used	Diffusion bridging and generative domain translation/cycle GANs lower the cost of relabeling
Acoustic channel modelling (Zhang et al., 2024)	Empirical modelling and physics simulators	Realistic channel realizations without complete physical parameters are made possible by data-driven channel synthesis using generative models
Real time/edge deployment	Heavy analysis is done offline, with mostly lightweight classical filters on board	Model distillation and optimized generators for anomaly detection, reduced communication pipelines, and onboard denoising
Risk of hallucination	Low, traditional approaches may perform poorly in complicated situations despite being deterministic	Increased risk, uncertainty estimation, and vetting are necessary, generative outputs may introduce artifacts

3. Real World Case Studies of Generative AI for Naval Warfare and Underwater Sensing

3.1 Case Study 1: Helsing's SG-1 Fathom + Lura AI at the Underwater Edge

The SG-1 Fathom underwater glider (Figure 8.3) and its corresponding Lura AI software were developed by Helsing, a European defence technology start-up, to provide low-cost, edge-powered, scalable underwater surveillance capabilities. Small, energy-efficient gliders known as SG-1 Fathom units are made to function as dispersed sensor constellations for weeks or months at a time. Helsing's public releases highlight quick classification, low acoustic emissions, and the ability for a single operator to oversee numerous units. Lura uses on-board acoustic data processing to identify and categorize underwater contacts (ships, submarines, and UUVs) with alleged speed and sensitivity improvements over legacy models. According to 2025 operational demos and at-sea experiments, these systems share processed warnings with shore or fleet C2 nodes and conduct continuous surveillance. From the standpoint of generative AI, Lura's stated capabilities—edge inference, training with synthetic data, and continuous learning from deployments—reflect current trends in which generative techniques enhance sparsely available labelled acoustic datasets, generate training scenarios, and facilitate reliable denoising and feature extraction at the sensor edge. The Helsing initiative serves as an example of how the private sector might deploy AI-enabled maritime sensing at scale by combining hardware (many inexpensive UUVs) with machine learning pipelines that incorporate on-device inference and synthetic data augmentation to get over bandwidth and data scarcity constraints.

Fig. 8.3 Helsing unveils Lura and SG-1 Fathom case study (Natarajan, P., et al. 2024).

3.2 *Case Study 2: Synth-SONAR Diffusion-based Synthetic Sonar Image Generation*

A recent study called Synth-SONAR (Natarajan, P., et al. 2024) shows how text-conditioned diffusion models can produce realistic SSS imagery for data augmentation and stress-testing perception pipelines when paired with style-injection and VLM (Vision Language Model)/GPT (Generative Pre-trained transformer) prompting. To enable conditioned generation that captures seabed kinds, object posture, and realistic sonar shadows, the work constructs a dual diffusion hierarchy that first generates coarse scene structure and then refines fine acoustic detail. By creating sizable, varied synthetic corpora that can be used to train object detectors and segmentation networks—particularly useful for uncommon classes like particular mine geometries or peculiar wreck orientations—Synth-SONAR (Figure 8.4) effectively tackles the ongoing lack of labelled sonar datasets. From a methodological standpoint, this study illustrates how defence sensing dataset gaps can be filled using contemporary generative techniques (diffusion + LLM (Large Language Model)/VLM (Vision Language Model) conditioning) without the need for costly or hazardous field gathering. Important disclaimers are also highlighted, such as the fact that generated imagery needs to be verified to prevent "hallucinated" characteristics from being mistaken for real and that synthetic realism does not provide an exact match to all ocean settings (domain shift persists).

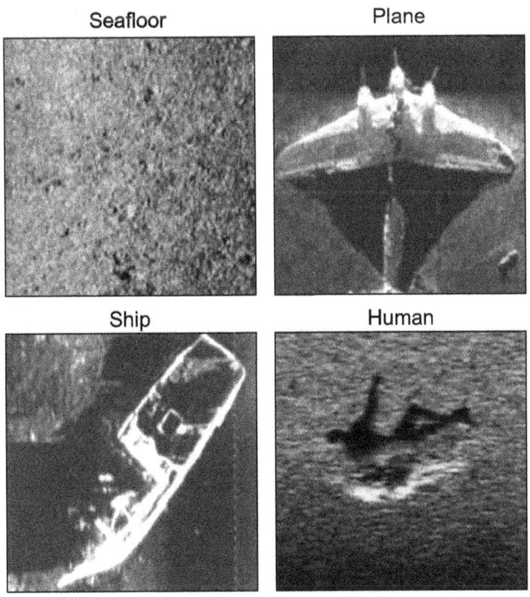

Fig. 8.4 Synth-SONAR Image Synthesis (Yang et al., 2023).

3.3 Case Study 3: GANs for Side Scan Sonar Data Augmentation

Generative Adversarial Networks were used in a 2023 study by Yang et al. in the *Journal of Marine Science and Engineering* to synthesize side-scan sonar footage for semantic segmentation tasks. The study shows that GAN-generated SSS patches can enhance segmentation metrics for small objects and seabed characteristics, decrease overfitting, and increase small training sets. The study presents quantitative comparisons that demonstrate that even relatively advanced generative approaches (GANs) offer useful improvements for operational sensing tasks, with segmentation networks trained using real+GAN data outperforming those trained only on limited actual data. The paper also identifies practical limits, such as the possibility of artifacts in GAN outputs under specific seabed textures and the necessity of discriminator-guided synthetic sample selection or meticulous post-processing to guarantee quality. A pragmatic process is illustrated in this case: (1) gather a small real dataset, (2) train a GAN conditioned on known classes, (3) produce a variety of augmentations, (4) retrain the detector/classifier, and (5) validate using held-out real surveys (Goecks et al., 2024).

3.4 Case Study 4: Diffusion-based Denoising and Super Resolution for Acoustic Imaging

Recent research has demonstrated that by iteratively eliminating complicated ambient noise and recreating precise target information, denoising diffusion probabilistic models (DDPMs) and diffusion-based super-resolution networks can significantly enhance acoustic and high-resolution sonar images. In non-Gaussian noise regimes characteristic of littoral seas, a series of experimental investigations (2023–2025) show that diffusion denoisers improve the detection probability for low-Signal to Noise Ration SNR interactions by surpassing traditional Wiener or median filtering. Diffusion models that are trained on measured acoustic patches, for instance, are able to learn the joint noise+signal statistics and generate cleaner spectrograms for classification later on. Although these techniques require a lot of processing power, scientists are looking towards distilled or accelerated samplers and model trimming to allow for near-real-time deployment on shipboard servers or even UUV edge processors (Helsing, 2025).

3.5 Case Study 5: COA-GPT and LLMs for Accelerated Course of Action Generation

Large language models (LLMs) can be modified to serve as military planning assistants for the purpose of creating, assessing, and iteratively improving Courses of Action (COAs), as demonstrated by COA-GPT (Goecks & Waytowich, 2024; Zhang et al., 2025). The study demonstrates LLMs' ability to encode doctrine, evaluate tradeoffs, and generate candidate plans rapidly—reducing planning time and allowing commanders to explore multiple plausible COAs—even though

COA-GPT was tested in simulated environments (militarized StarCraft II) rather than actual naval battlegroups. Such models could be used in naval contexts in conjunction with generative scenario engines and sensor fusion outputs (satellite imagery, sonar, and SIGINT) to quickly generate mission alternatives for minefield avoidance, convoy routing, or ASW tasking. Key limitations are emphasized: For high-stakes final judgements, LLMs need human oversight, strict limits to avoid dangerous recommendations, and meticulous foundation in validated facts.

4. Challenges in Adapting Generative AI for Naval Warfare and Underwater Sensing

From sophisticated manufacturing to computer vision and healthcare, generative AI has shown revolutionary promise in a number of fields. It has great potential for underwater sensing and naval warfare, two fields that require a high degree of accuracy and flexibility, because of its capacity to synthesise fresh data, recreate intricate situations, and denoise signals. It is far from simple to use generative AI for marine defence, nevertheless. The sea is a very dynamic and complicated environment where hostile threats are always changing and acoustic propagation changes with temperature, salt, and depth. Failures in naval and submarine environments can be disastrous, resulting in asset loss, operational failure, or even escalation of conflict, in contrast to commercial applications where mistakes may have few repercussions (Zhuang, Y. 2024).

4.1 Technical Challenges

i. *Data Scarcity and Quality*: For generative AI models like GANs, VAEs, or diffusion models to function well, enormous volumes of diverse and annotated data are needed. Due to national security limitations, a large portion of the operational data used in naval warfare is classified, restricted, or not available for training and research. Due to the inherent noise, distortion, and incompleteness of sonar and acoustic datasets, underwater sensing makes matters even more difficult. For example, sonar signals can be interfered with by seabed features, marine life, and thermoclines.
ii. *Environmental Variability*: It refers to the dynamic and ever-changing physical, chemical, and biological conditions of the underwater environment that significantly influence the performance of sensing and detection systems. The variability affects the environmental factors such as water temperature, salinity depth, and ocean currents that greatly influence sound propagation.
iii. *Security and Reliability*: For naval warfare and underwater sensing, the security concerns are more when there is no security of the data. The most challenging part for underwater sensing and naval warfare is to ensure the robustness and cybersecurity of generative AI–driven system against adversarial interference and data manipulation, which is a technical concern.

4.2 Operational Challenges

i. *Real-time Decision-making*: With the vastness of the ocean and the complexity of the underwater domain, there is often significant delay for data collection, transmission, and analysis. A major operational challenge is when the signals travel slowly in underwater and restrict the amount of data that can be shared in real time. The delays hinder the threat assessment and response for critical missions.

ii. *Limitation of Navigation and Communication*: Underwater communication mainly depends on the acoustic signal waves, traditional radio and GPS signals that cannot deeply penetrate into water. They are susceptible to distortion, noise, and low transmission rates. This makes it difficult to maintain continuous coordination among submarines, AUVs, and surface control stations.

5. Conclusion and Future Scope

The hybridization of generative AI for naval warfare and underwater sensing will be a transformative step towards redefining maritime defence capabilities. The enhanced data interpretation, simulation accuracy, and decision-making efficiency will be effectively helpful for developing models like GANs, VAEs, and diffusion models for longstanding challenges. The result of the shift of the technology is more adaptive, intelligent, and predictive defence systems that are capable of handling the uncertain underwater environments. This integration can further develop the frameworks that can be implemented in future. The frameworks combine generative AI with the real-time sensor networks, edge computing, and AUVs to achieve continuous situational awareness and automated threat response. In future scope, integrating quantum computing with neuromorphic hardware can offer a great technology which provides faster energy-efficient solutions.

References

Blackman, S.S. and Popoli, R. (1999). *Design and analysis of modern tracking systems*. Artech House.

Britannica. (n.d.). Naval warfare. *Encyclopaedia Britannica*. Available at https://www.britannica.com/topic/naval-warfare. Accessed on 23-09-2025.

Endsley, M.R. (1995). Toward a theory of situation awareness in dynamic systems. *Human Factors*, 37(1), 32–64.

Goecks, V.G. and Waytowich, N. (2024). COA-GPT: Generative pre-trained transformers for accelerated course of action development in military operations. arXiv preprint, Feb. 2024.

Goodfellow, I., Pouget-Abadie, J., Mirza, M. et al. (2014). Generative adversarial nets. In *Advances in Neural Information Processing Systems*, 27, 2672–2680.

Helsing. (2025). Helsing unveils Lura and SG-1 Fathom autonomous mass to surveil and defend the depths. *Naval News*.

Kilfoyle, D.B. and Baggeroer, A. B. (2000). The state of the art in underwater acoustic telemetry. *IEEE Journal of Oceanic Engineering*, 25(1), 4–27.

Melville, W.L. and Norton, D. E. (1966). Magnetic anomaly detection of submarines. *IEEE Transactions on Aerospace and Electronic Systems*, AES-2(2), 147–156.

Mobley, C.D. (1994). *Light and Water: Radiative Transfer in Natural Waters*. Academic Press.

Natarajan, P., Basha, K. and Nambiar, A. (2024). Sonar image synthesis with enhanced diversity and realism (Synth-SONAR). arXiv.

Natarajan, K., Basha, K. and Nambiar, A. (2024). Synth-SONAR: Sonar image synthesis with enhanced diversity and realism via dual diffusion models and GPT prompting. arXiv.

NATO Science and Technology Organization. (2020). Advances in sonar signal processing for anti-submarine warfare (STO-TR-IST-165). STO Scientific Publications | NATO Science and Technology Organization. Accessed on 23-09-2025.

Smith, J.R. (2018). Naval warfare: A historical overview. *Journal of Maritime Strategy*, 12(3), 45–67.

Martin Aubard, Ana Madureira, Luís Teixeira, José Pinto. Sonar-based deep learning in underwater robotics—Survey. (2024). *arXiv*.

Urick, R.J. (1983). *Principles of Underwater Sound* (3rd ed.). McGraw-Hill.

Urick, R.J. (1984). *Ambient Noise in the Sea*. Naval Research Laboratory.

Xie, Z., Lin, R., Wang, L., Zhang, A., Lin, J. and Tang, X. (2023). Data augmentation and deep neural network classification for ship-radiated noise. *Frontiers in Marine Science*, 10, 123456.

Yang, D., Wang, C., Cheng, C. et al. (2023). Data generation with GAN networks for sidescan sonar in semantic segmentation applications. *Journal of Marine Science and Engineering*, 11(9), 1792.

Yang, R., Hou, M., Wang, J. and Zhang, F. (2023). *Oceanchat: Piloting autonomous underwater vehicles in natural language*. arXiv preprint arXiv:2309.16052.

Zhang, F., Hou, X., Wang, Z. et al. (2024). Side-scan sonar image generator based on diffusion models for autonomous underwater vehicles. *Journal of Marine Science and Engineering*, 12(8), 1457.

Zhang, Y., Hao, J., Zen, Q. (2024–2025). Reducing ambient noise: Diffusion model for underwater denoising. *IEEE/Elsevier*. Volume 188, 2025, 107470, ISSN 0893–6080.

Zhuang, Y., Kari, D., Li, Z. et al. (2024). Generating underwater acoustic communication channel impulse responses using a diffusion model. *2024 Seventh Underwater Communications and Networking Conference (UComms)* (pp. 1–5).

9 Generative Foundations: Reimagining Aerospace Infrastructure Monitoring and Predictive Maintenance through Generative AI

Shaman Sharma[1], Anurag Prajapati[2*], Aaskaran Bishnoi[3] and Anuradha Singh[4]

Predictive maintenance (PM) is a critical pillar of operational readiness for modern aerospace infrastructure; however, traditional approaches are severely constrained by the scarcity of failure-mode data and the difficulty of modelling complex, high-stress operational conditions. This chapter presents a paradigm shift by demonstrating how generative artificial intelligence (AI) can overcome these limitations. Specifically, Generative Adversarial Networks (GANs) and Variational Autoencoders (VAEs) are employed for two high-impact applications: Synthetic Data Generation for Anomaly Detection (SDG-AD) and the development of high-fidelity Generative Digital Twins (GDTs). SDG-AD enables the synthesis of realistic sensor data representing rare and catastrophic failure conditions that are impractical or prohibitively expensive to reproduce physically, thereby strengthening anomaly detection systems. In parallel, GDTs provide dynamic, probabilistic virtual representations of aerospace assets that support multi-variable simulation of component degradation, operational stress, and remaining useful life. By integrating these generative capabilities, maintenance scheduling and resource allocation can be optimized with greater precision and resilience. The proposed framework enhances system reliability, reduces unplanned downtime, and establishes a data-rich, forward-looking approach to sustaining defence aerospace assets. Overall, this chapter demonstrates how generative intelligence transforms PM from a data-limited process into a robust, adaptive, and strategically valuable capability.

1. Introduction

1.1 Background and Motivation

To achieve national security and operational success, sustaining the military, naval, and aerospace infrastructure is essential to include critical assets such as

[1] https://orcid.org/0009-0003-6209-9544
[2] https://orcid.org/0009-0009-6613-8401
[3] https://orcid.org/0009-0003-1853-2937
[4] https://orcid.org/0000-0001-7365-5540
* Corresponding author: prajapatianurag468@gmail.com

DOI: 10.1201/9781003688174-9

surveillance radar arrays, propulsion systems, airframes, and sophisticated ground control equipment. The process of keeping these assets at all times is one that demands advanced maintenance plans. Over the decades, the industry has shifted from scheduled and reactive maintenance to predictive maintenance (PM) through sensor data and machine learning to predict probable failures in advance, i.e., prior to their occurrence. Although conventional PM has led to great enhancements in operational upkeep and to decrease in costs, it requires access to extensive, superior, and varied actual failure frameworks to be successful (Aghajani & Bakhshi, 2025; Lv et al., 2022).

This data requirement is in conflict with the operating environment of defence aerospace assets, however. The catastrophic failures are, luckily, very infrequent and the datasets they result in are highly unbalanced, with the key class of failure being practically non-existent. In addition, it is expensive, risky, and complicated to conduct physical tests to cause these rare failure modes like a particular fatigue crack or sensor failure at extreme temperature; hence, it is impossible to conduct comprehensive data gathering. This has been identified as the primary bottleneck to the accuracy and reliability of traditional PM systems in defence systems, and is known as the data scarcity paradox, which in many cases limits the models to identifying known and historical failure modes (Zhou & Chen, 2024; Wang et al., 2022).

1.2 The Generative AI Paradigm Shift

Generative artificial intelligence (AI) provides a solution to this essential gap in data in a timely and transformative manner. In contrast to discriminant models, which classify or predict on the basis of the existing data, generative AI models are engineered to learn the underlying distribution of the input data and generate new and synthetic data samples that are statistically and structurally identical to the original. This is a capability that is an aerospace game-changer. With the complicated physics and sensor dynamics of healthy assets, generative AI can be carefully steered to produce the realistic sensor measurement that matches the infrequent or even speculative condition of failure (Goodfellow et al., 2014; Wang et al., 2024).

This chapter offers a scheme of incorporating generative AI methods to aerospace infrastructure surveillance, and thus overhauls the very notion of PM as a problem of scarcity of data, to an opportunity of abundance of data. Its main focus will be on two extremely new applications—Synthetic Data Generation for Anomaly Detection (SDG-AD) and the creation of Generative Digital Twins (GDTs)—which will allow improving the reliability of assets, maximizing maintenance logistics, and, eventually, guaranteeing the ongoing operational superiority of defence systems (Jones & Williams, 2025; Kim & Lee, 2024).

1.3 Chapter Contribution and Structure

This section outlines the primary contributions of the chapter and provides a structured overview of its organization. The contribution that this work makes is that the advanced generative AI architectures may be specifically tailored to the special constraints of aerospace maintenance in the defence. After this introduction, the second section gives a brief review of the applicable generative AI models (e.g., GANs, VAEs) and how they apply to defence data problems. The most detailed methodology of SDG-AD is explored in the third section, with the need to synthesize realistic failure-mode data. The fourth section presents the concept and use of GDTs in large-scale asset simulation and prognostics. The fifth section explains how generative AI will help to optimize inspection paths and resources allocation, whereas the sixth section addresses the most pressing implementation issues and the ethical considerations. Finally, the seventh section wraps up the chapter by summing up the main findings and looking into the prospective research direction (Tao et al., 2018; Nguyen & Le, 2024).

2. The Generative AI Paradigm in Aerospace Infrastructure

2.1 Limitations of Discriminative Models in Defence Prognostics

The aerospace defence conventional PM systems are mostly based on discriminative AI models (like Support Vector Machines, Random Forests, and some types of Recurrent Neural Networks [RNNs]). Such models are fine in classification (e.g., determining whether a component is healthy or failing) and also regression (e.g., remaining useful life [RUL]) using present features based on prior sensor data. Nevertheless, the use of discriminative AI in the high-stakes aerospace environment has internal constraints, which negatively impact the successful implementation.

The first problem, which has been pointed out above, is that there is no generalizability when it comes to the application to new or complex failure modes that do not exist in the training data. Discriminative models have a hard time extrapolating robustly off their training distribution. Moreover, they are black-box, which tends to hinder the explainable AI (XAI) requirement demanded by the defence sector and, as such, it is challenging to fully rely on the maintenance decisions made based on scanty data. This traditional method is unsustainable to the current day defence fleet management due to the sheer cost and time involved in gathering enough labelled data to cover all combinations of sensors and all operational scenarios.

2.2 Core Generative AI Architectures for Defence

Generative AI models overcome these constraints by attempting to learn the probability distribution $P(x)$ of the high-dimensional sensor data x, and not merely the decision boundary. Such an ability is critical in producing novel, coherent information, which is capable of representing complicated physical phenomena. Two architectures are of special interest to aerospace infrastructure; their comparison is shown in Table 9.1.

2.2.1 Generative Adversarial Networks (GANs)

Generative Adversarial Networks (GANs) are a two-player zero-sum game with Generator (G) and Discriminator (D). The Generator generates the synthetic sensor data (e.g., vibration, temperature, acoustic signals) whereas the Discriminator attempts to differentiate the actual sensor data and the synthetic data. The training stops when the Generator is able to generate data that deceive the Discriminator. GANs have no competitors in terms of realism in producing synthetic time-series data within aerospace, which is essential to simulating subtle, incipient faults that cannot be identified by less complex models. The fidelity of the GAN-generated data is required to be high in order to achieve effective training of the robust anomaly detectors (Goodfellow et al., 2014; Mirza & Osindero, 2014).

2.2.2 Variational Autoencoders (VAEs)

Variational Autoencoders (VAEs) are deep generative models, which utilize an Encoder to encode the input data to a latent space (reduced-dimensional representation) and a Decoder to decode the data out of the latent space.

The VAEs implant a probabilistic model, with the latent space having to follow a simple prior distribution (usually a Gaussian distribution). This architecture is very effective in:

- Dimensionality Reduction: Determining the limited number of variables critical to asset health.
- Reconstruction Error-based Anomaly Detection: VAEs can be trained on healthy data only, and then it can be inferred that any significant change in the reconstruction of a new input signal (a high reconstruction error) is a clear indication of an anomaly or fault.
- Controllable Data Synthesis: The continuous latent space can be used to control the interpolation between the states of being healthy and failed and generate data points that represent the level of degradation (Blei et al., 2017; Qin & Li, 2024).

2.2.3 Latent Space Interpretation for Prognostics

The potential of the VAE in the context of GDT is much broader than the dimensionality reduction capability, and it depends on the capability of the VAE to train a continuous, probabilistic latent space that can be directly mapped to the physical state of the aerospace asset. In contrast to deterministic autoencoders, the encoder of the VAE generates the parameters (mean μ and σ^2) of a Gaussian distribution of each input, which ensures two important regularities of generative modelling, continuity and completeness.

Continuity and Degradation Mapping: Continuity guarantees that points that are close to each other in the latent space are associated with similar physical state when decoded. This enables the GDT to trace out a continuous journey in latent space between a healthy state (one point in the latent space) and different stages of incipient fault formation (fluid motions across the space) to the failed state (another point in the latent space). Such a continuous mapping is necessary during precise RUL predictions, since it does not introduce sharp and non-physical changes in predicted degradation.

Disentanglement for Explainability (XAI): Since the VAE tries to promote statistical independence among the latent variables (dimensions of the latent space), it can be said to be trying to disentangle the factors that cause the sensor signal. In the case of a jet engine, the latent dimension can be associated with the amplitude of the bearing vibration and the other latent dimension is associated with the amplitude of oil temperature fluctuations. The disentangled dimensions can be interpreted to provide diagnostic insights to engineers that the black-box models do not provide, which is the fundamental XAI issues in defence applications. This transforms the VAE into an explainable diagnostic tool rather than a prediction tool that is being directly helpful in the defence sector in maintaining traceable and justifiable maintenance choices.

Probabilistic State Representation: The VAE is intrinsically capable of representing uncertainty in the present state of a system, by encoding a distribution (instead of a fixed point) of each input. This combination of probabilities is extended through the Prognostic Generative Modelling (Section 4.2), which is the basis of generating a complete range of RUL probabilities, as opposed to single-point estimates (Tao et al., 2018; Kim & Lee, 2024).

Table 9.1 Generative AI Model Suitability for Aerospace Predictive Maintenance.

Feature/ Model	*Generative Adversarial Networks (GANs)*	*Variational Autoencoders (VAEs)*
Primary Use	High-fidelity synthetic data generation (especially time-series)	Probabilistic data representation, anomaly detection, controlled synthesis
Strengths	Produces highly realistic, indistinguishable data; excellent for simulating complex fault signatures	Robust anomaly detection via reconstruction error; smooth latent space for interpolation; good for explaining latent features
Weaknesses	Training instability (mode collapse); difficult to control specific feature generation without conditioning	Output quality can be less sharp than GANs; latent space interpretability still a research area
Aerospace Application	Generating rare engine fault vibrations, synthetic radar signals for training anomaly detectors	Detecting incipient structural damage, learning component health states, controlled degradation simulations
Reference	Goodfellow et al. (2014)	Mirza & Osindero (2014)

2.3 Unique Suitability for Aerospace

The aerospace defence environment is characterized by non-linearity, high dimensions, and high safety requirements.

Generative AI is the only tool to fit the bill since it can:

- Avoid Data Imbalance Address: Balance training datasets by synthesizing large amounts of rare failures.
- Improve Model Trust: VAEs have the capability of learning probabilistic representations to help understand uncertainty, which is a crucial element of defence-grade trustworthiness.
- Support the Generation of Digital Twins: Support the provision of the high-fidelity, dynamic data inputs required to train and evolve complex digital simulation models (GDTs) to perform long-term prognosis.

3. Synthetic Data Generation for Anomaly Detection (SDG-AD)

3.1 The Imperative of Synthetic Failure Data

The regimes of aerospace components work under strict liability and catastrophic failures are to be statistically improbable. While beneficial for operational safety, this creates an impassable barrier for data-driven diagnostics, as predictive models cannot learn failure modes that have never been observed in operational data. Synthetic Data Generation for Anomaly Detection (SDG-AD) is a direct challenge to this. The idea is to use the generative AI to generate statistically correct and physically realistic sensor signatures based on unobserved or less observable ones under expressed failure modes, thus immunizing diagnostic systems against the unknown in the future.

To illustrate how generative AI addresses the data scarcity problem in anomaly detection, Figure 9.1 visually contrasts real sensor signals from healthy components with synthetically generated fault signals. This comparison highlights the ability of Conditional GANs (CGANs) to generate physically realistic failure signatures that are otherwise unavailable in operational datasets (Aghajani & Bakhshi, 2025; Goyal & Sharma, 2024).

3.2 Methodology for SDG-AD using Conditional GANs

The CGANs represent a robust framework for SDG-AD. CGANs extend the conventional GAN architecture by incorporating conditional information, referred to as a conditioning vector, which explicitly guides the data generation process. The creation of synthetic aerospace failure data follows a structured methodology.

Baseline Training on Healthy Data: The CGAN is initially trained using extensive healthy and nominal operational sensor data, such as vibration, temperature, and acoustic signals collected from aerospace components operating under standard

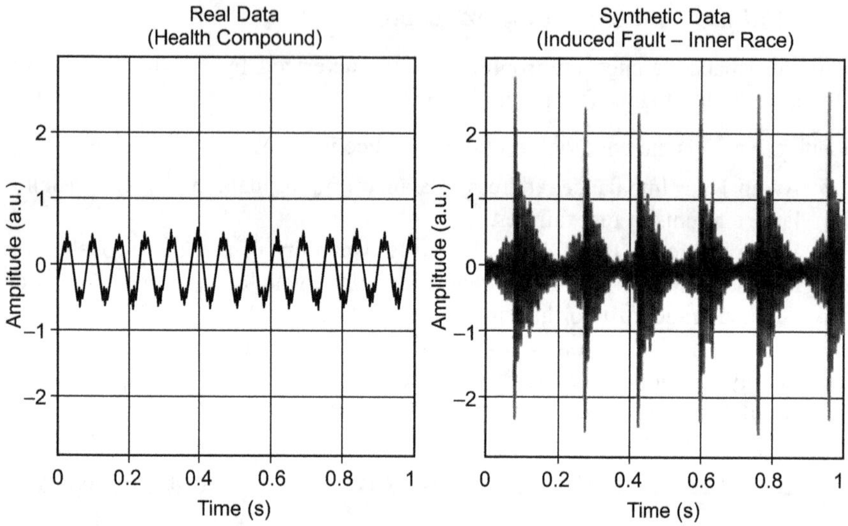

Fig. 9.1 A visual demonstration of Synthetic Data Generation for Anomaly Detection (SDG-AD). The left panel displays typical real sensor data from a healthy component while the right panel shows high-fidelity synthetic data generated by a Conditional GAN, representing a specific, induced fault condition (e.g., inner race bearing fault), indistinguishable from a real fault signature.

conditions. During this phase, the Generator learns the underlying temporal and spatial correlations that characterize normal system behaviour.

Failure Mode Conditioning: A critical step involves defining the Conditioning Vector (C). This vector is not a simple fault label but a quantitative representation of fault characteristics derived from engineering physics models or finite element analysis. Typical parameters encoded within C include fault severity (e.g., 10% versus 50% degradation), fault location (e.g., front bearing versus rear bearing vibration), and operational environment (e.g., low-thrust or high-altitude conditions).

Synthetic Fault Signature Generation: When the Conditioning Vector (C) is combined with a noise vector (z), the Generator produces a synthetic time-series sensor output that represents a specific, physically consistent failure state, expressed as:

$$\text{synthetic} = G(z, C) \qquad ...(9.1)$$

For example, the model can generate a realistic vibration signature corresponding to a 35% inner race defect in a turbine bearing operating at 80% thrust, even if such a failure condition has never been observed in real operational data.

Discriminator Validation: The Discriminator is trained to evaluate both the realism of the generated sensor data and its consistency with the specified conditioning parameters. This dual validation ensures that the synthetic samples are not only statistically indistinguishable from real data but also physically meaningful and suitable for training reliable anomaly detection systems.

The internal architecture that enables controlled and physically consistent synthetic data generation is illustrated in Figure 9.2. The figure explains how the Generator and Discriminator interact under the guidance of a conditioning vector to ensure that synthesized data accurately represents specific fault parameters.

3.2.1 Advanced Data Handling and Fidelity Enhancement

To be useful as a certifier of diagnostic systems, SDG-AD needs the synthetic output to be of high fidelity. Basic GANs do not perform so well with time-series data, where they tend to mode collapse (where the Generator only learns a limited number of failures) and have challenges with learning the particular time dependence of sensor signals.

In order to reduce such risks, the following pre-processing and architectural additions are essential:

Normalization and Feature Selection: Before real and healthy data is fed to the CGAN, it is normalized, i.e., it is brought to the range of Min–Max scaling to allow all sensor features (e.g., pressure, vibration frequency, temperature) to fall within the same and balanced space. In addition, more sophisticated feature selection algorithms can be employed to remove noise or non-important sensor readings, which means the GAN will only learn the dynamics of diagnostic features that are important. This decreases the complexity of the model and enhances the quality of the generated synthetic signal.

Reducing Temporal Dependence Bias: Standard GANs, which are only trained on images, do not take into account the vital order and causality of sensor measurements in time. In response to this, the Generator and Discriminator modules of the CGAN are frequently implemented in RNNs, either Long Short-Term Memory (LSTM) or Gated Recurrent Unit (GRU) architecture. Such memory-enabled architectures compel the models to gain the time dependency, so the synthesized failure signal develops in the real world across the necessary degradation window.

Synthetic Data Quality Checking: The synthetic data is not trusted automatically. Its utility is empirically substantiated with the help of separate Support Vector Classifiers (SVCs) or statistical tests to demonstrate that the models that are trained on the synthetic data alone present the same (or higher) accuracy on the real failure data as the models that are trained on the real data only. This is an important validation step offering the required aerospace assurance (Mirza & Osindero, 2014; Singh & Kumar, 2025).

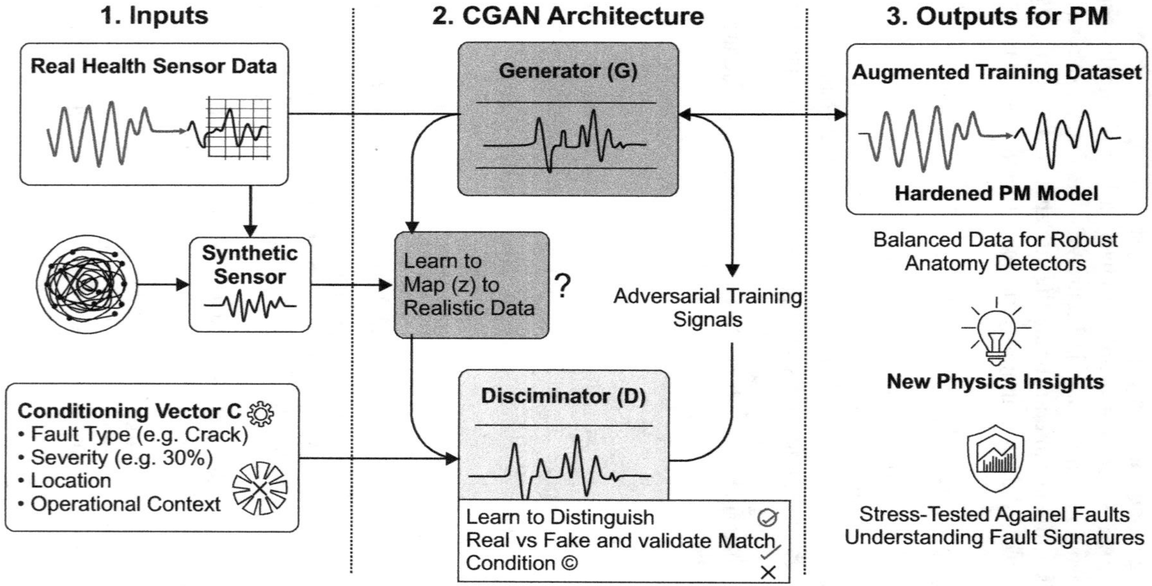

Fig. 9.2 Architecture of the Conditional Generative Adversarial Network (CGAN) for synthetic data generation. The Generator (*G*) learns the data distribution guided by the Conditioning Vector (*C*), while the Discriminator (*D*) validates both the realism and the accurate representation of the target fault condition (*C*), ensuring physical plausibility.

3.3 *Integration into Anomaly Detection Systems*

The resulting synthetic data of high fidelity is then utilized in two major applications to produce sound anomaly detection models:

- *Balanced Training Sets*: The failure data generated in simulation is combined with the training failure data, which is scarce and real life to form a balanced training set, so that the diagnostic classifier does not get heavily biased in the healthy state.
- *Stress Testing and Model Hardening*: Negative stress testing of diagnostic models with training on historical data can be run on the synthetic library of catastrophic failure scenarios. Should the model not identify a synthesized 95% fatigue failure correctly, then the model and its training data distribution can be tweaked and deployed, in effect performing system hardening with real-world novelties.

Implementation of SDG-AD makes the maintenance modelling to be no longer data-limited as it is now physics-informed and computationally accelerated to ensure the constant protection of the military aerospace objects which is being trained on the whole range of possible risks.

4. Generative Digital Twins (GDTs) for Predictive Maintenance

4.1 *The Evolution from Traditional to Generative Digital Twins*

The classic definition of Digital Twin (DT) is a virtual high-fidelity representation of a physical object, system, or process. DTs are also a weapon of defence, and are useful in testing the scenarios of the mission, and in degradation forecasting. The traditional DTs are, however, frequently limited to deterministic modelling—they make extensive use of pre-programmed equations of physics and Finite Element Analysis (FEA) to specify behaviour. These classical models are also ineffective in capturing real world operational uncertainty, nonlinear degradation curves, and the high dimensional coupling between various environmental conditions and component faults.

A GDT can eliminate all these constraints by integrating generative AI into the DT framework, as given in Table 9.2. A GDT does not just mirror some known physics, but also learns the entire high-dimensional probability distribution of the asset state, which allows it to sample realistic and novel degradation pathways and failure modes which were never explicitly coded into the model. This renders the GDT an excellent prognostic device, which has the ability to predict what-if scenarios with a degree of verisimilitude never seen before (Kim & Lee, 2024; Yoo & Han, 2024).

4.2 *GDT Architecture and Learning Dynamics*

A GDT is designed based on the real-time fusion of sensors with historical maintenance records and artificial data that is generated through the SDG-AD process. The fundamental architectural elements are:

Table 9.2 Traditional Digital Twin vs Generative Digital Twin in Aerospace Maintenance.

Feature	*Traditional Digital Twin (DT)*	*Generative Digital Twin (GDT)*
Core Model	Physics-based, deterministic simulations, FEA	Generative AI models (VAEs, GANs) learning probabilistic distributions
Degradation Modelling	Relies on pre-defined degradation paths and known physics	Learns and generates novel, probabilistic degradation trajectories
Uncertainty Handling	Limited, typically uses Monte Carlo for known distributions	Inherent probabilistic output, full spectrum of RUL predictions
Data Requirements	Extensive historical data for model calibration	Benefits from real data but can leverage synthetic data for unknowns
Prediction Focus	Single-point RUL estimates, known fault simulations	Probabilistic RUL distributions, "what-if" scenario generation for novel faults
Reference	Tao et al. (2018)	Kim & Lee (2024)

- *Data Ingestion and Latent Space Mapping*: A VAE is constantly fed with real-time sensor data on the physical object (e.g., aircraft engine or radar housing). VAE then reduces the dimensions of this high-dimensional input to a significantly smaller Latent Space Vector (z), which will actually reflect the actual health state and operating conditions of the component.
- *Prognostic Generative Modelling*: The most significant innovation is that a Recurrent Generative Model (e.g., a time-series GAN or VAE with an RNN) is trained to learn the dynamics of the Latent Space. The model is conditioned to learn the conditional probability $P(\{z\}t + 1\ \{z\}t, \{a\}t\ )$, in which z is the health state and a is the future action of operation (e.g., increase thrust, high-G manoeuvre).
- *Learning Prognostic Trajectories*: The GDT can be used to generate thousands of different, probabilistic trajectories of the future state of the asset, generated by sampling this learned conditional distribution.

To clarify the learning dynamics and data flow within a GDT, Figure 9.3 presents the architectural framework used for predictive prognostics. The figure demonstrates how latent space modelling and recurrent generative learning jointly enable probabilistic RUL forecasting.

Figure 9.4 provides a comparative visualization of traditional deterministic prognostic outputs versus probabilistic trajectories generated by the GDT. This comparison emphasizes the importance of uncertainty quantification in defence-grade maintenance decision-making.

4.3 Applications of GDTs in Aerospace Logistics

The GDT framework has a direct effect on the operational preparedness and resource optimization:

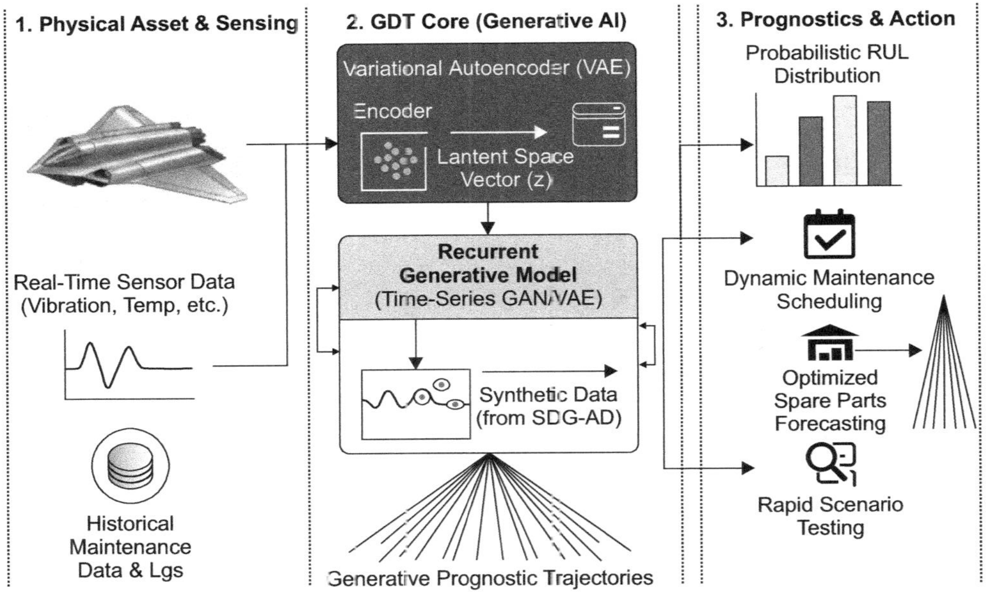

Fig. 9.3 Generative digital twin (GDT) architecture for predictive prognostics. The core utilizes a Variational Autoencoder (VAE) to compress real-time and synthetic data into a Latent Space Vector (z), which feeds a Recurrent Generative Model to synthesize probabilistic Remaining Useful Life (RUL) trajectories for long-term prognosis.

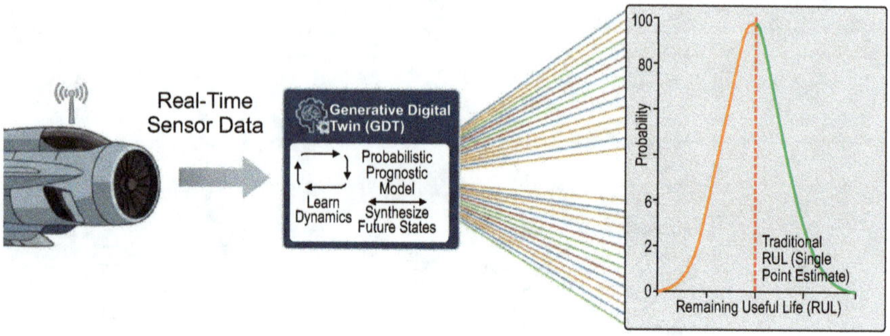

Fig. 9.4 Prognostic trajectories and RUL distribution generated by the GDT. This visualization illustrates the superior fidelity of the GDT, which predicts a full spectrum of RUL distributions (probabilistic range) versus the single, deterministic point estimate provided by traditional models. This quantification of uncertainty is vital for risk-informed maintenance.

Risk-based Maintenance Scheduling: GDTs are used to predict the likelihood of mission-critical failure when subjected to specific, projected operational load profiles, instead of generalized RUL. This eliminates the need to have fixed schedules and maintenance priority is given to those assets that exhibit greater risk variability under scheduled missions in the future.

The Best Possible Spare Parts Forecasting: The GDT can achieve high accuracy in the probabilistic forecasting of demand of individual spare parts as many months or even years ahead due to its ability to simulate thousands of degradation paths of an entire fleet. This reduces the unnecessary inventory that would have cost a lot, and cancellation of the mission based on a lack of parts.

Rapid Scenario Testing: The GDT also allows the defence personnel to instantly test the effects of unpredictable events, which might include the use of an asset outside its recommended limits during a tactical emergency. The GDT directly creates the effect of probabilistic degradation, which contributes to real-time decision-making.

The GDT is expected to become the ultimate instrument of proactive and efficient management of the defence infrastructure by substituting the inflexible, deterministic simulation with probabilistic, generative forecasts (Wang et al., 2024; Sun & Wu, 2024).

5. Optimizing Inspection and Resource Allocation via Generative Models

5.1 The Generative Intelligence in Maintenance Logistics

The predictive power of SDG-AD and GDTs can contribute significantly to optimizing complex logistics and resource allocation in the context of defence infrastructure maintenance, as the proposed synthetic data features a rich source of data. Traditional approaches to scheduling are based on time-based (or generalized) asset health scores or fixed schedules. By giving a probabilistic distribution of the frequency and severity of failures in a whole fleet, generative AI can also facilitate a transformation towards Generative Risk-Informed Scheduling (GRIS).

The GRIS does not just anticipate the time of a failure; it also anticipates the effect that the failure may have on operational readiness and the resource profile (i.e., tools and certified technicians) that is needed to mitigate the occurrence. This combined forecasting cuts off unnecessary downtime, and makes special resources available at the right time and at the required location.

5.2 Dynamic Optimization of Inspection Routes

In the case of large-scale infrastructure, like large radar installations, airfield pavement, or hulls of naval ships, inspection is a resource-intensive task that can be carried out by robotic systems [e.g., drones, underwater ROVs (Remotely Operated Vehicles)]. The productivity of the inspection route has a direct influence on working time and fuel/battery consumption. These inspection routes can be optimized dynamically using generative AI, particularly through reinforcement learning–based models that leverage generative mechanisms to anticipate and evaluate future system states. The process involves:

State Generation: In the GDT (Section 4), the infrastructure is represented as a high-fidelity map, where the defect locations and severities are probabilistic. This map can be considered the present state of the environment.

Action Policy Generation: An RL (Reinforcement Learning) agent learns to discover the best way. The reward capability is characterized by the reduction in the time of inspection, and the maximization of the range of defects. More importantly, the RL agent will rely on a Generative Policy Network (GPN) (usually a form of a GAN or a VAE in the RL context) to produce and score thousands of possible future inspection paths in terms of likelihood of finding a high-severity fault.

5.2.1 The Generative Policy Network (GPN) Mechanism

The GPN makes the mathematical home of the pivotal role of generative AI in solving the issue of optimization of inspection logistics and serves as the decision-making core of the RL agent. The GPN employs its generative ability to actively learn new operational strategies in contrast to the traditional Deep Q-Networks (DQNs), which generate a score of a fixed set of actions.

The process is characterized by four dynamic functions:

State Embedding: The probabilistic health map output of the GDT of the fault location and uncertainty is represented in the GPN as a small, high-dimensional state vector (s). This is a vector that summarizes the operational context; in other words, it maps the complex physical reality to the mathematical decision space.

Trajectory Synthesis (Action Generation): The generator of the GPN uses the desired route as the output of sequential data and synthesizes an infinite number of possible paths of inspection, denoted as tau. The GPN does not have a pre-programmed library of paths, but instead generates new, optimal paths that specifically respond to the dynamically evolving fault patterns observed by the GDT, and makes it truly adaptive.

Dynamic Multi-Reward Evaluation: The GPN takes the form of a composite reward functional to evaluate the generated path "tau" according to a set of objectives, which are usually conflicting, which is an essential property of Multi-Style Control (MSC). The reward (R(tau)) is determined on the basis of such factors as: (a) reduction in fault-risk on the GDT map; (b) time/energy cost (cost); and (c) safety constraints compliance (e.g., clearance zones). This complex reward signal is then maximized by the RL agent to select the pathway that optimizes efficiency way beyond conventional heuristic models.

Real-Time Adaptation: With the ongoing physical scan, sensor data is fed back into the GDT, and thereby updates the graph of probabilities of the health of the asset. The GPN will then recalculate a new and optimized path immediately that will seek the high-risk regions that will guarantee the inspection mission is adaptive and highly efficient. The application of generative reinforcement learning to inspection planning is illustrated in Figure 9.5. The figure demonstrates how a GPN dynamically optimizes inspection routes by prioritizing regions with the highest predicted fault risk.

5.3 Strategic Spare Parts Inventory Management

The cost of storage of holding inventories of mission-critical spares is one of the biggest logistical loads in the defence domain. Generative AI solves this by making localized and temporally specific demand forecasting:

Probabilistic Demand Synthesis: Using GDT simulations over the complete fleet and producing thousands of possible failure modes, generative AI forces synthesize a much more accurate long-term probabilistic demand curve per single component. This goes beyond the generalized consumption rates and directly associates the demand to the estimated pathways of deterioration of particular high-value assets.

Reducing "Bullwhip Effect": Conventional supply chains have the issue of the so-called bullwhip effect, in which demand variations in the retail end cause massive variations in the supply chain. This effect is reduced by using generative models to stabilize long-term prognostic signals, which leads to more stable and cost-effective procurement strategies.

Generative AI in logistics changes maintenance from a reactive or planned need to a highly efficient force multiplier that is optimally planned, as shown in Table 9.3 (Butt & Khan, 2025; Park & Kim, 2025).

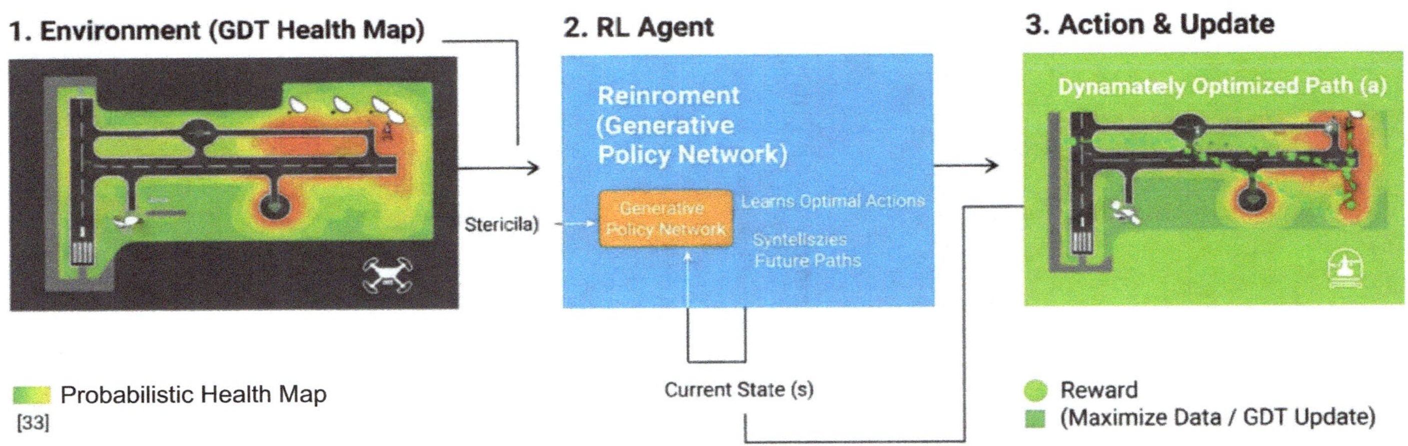

Fig. 9.5 Generative reinforcement learning (RL) for dynamic inspection optimization. A Generative Policy Network (GPN) leverages the GDT's probabilistic health map (State) to dynamically create and adjust the optimal inspection path (Action), ensuring that maintenance resources are targeted towards the areas of highest predicted fault risk (Reward) in real time.

Table 9.3 Impact of Generative AI on Aerospace Maintenance Logistics

Logistics Aspect	*Traditional Approach*	*Generative AI–Enhanced Approach*	*Key GAI Benefit*
Inspection Routes	Fixed schedules, heuristic paths	Dynamic, risk-informed paths based on GDT predictions	Real-time adaptation to evolving risk, maximize fault detection
Maintenance Scheduling	Time-based, RUL point estimates	Probabilistic RUL distributions, Generative Risk-Informed Scheduling (GRIS)	Minimized unnecessary downtime, optimized resource allocation
Spare Parts Forecasting	Historical consumption rates, statistical models	Probabilistic demand synthesis from GDT fleet simulations	Reduced inventory costs, prevention of mission-critical part shortages
Reference	Butt & Khan (2025)	Park & Kim (2025)	

6. Challenges, Ethical Implications, and Future Outlook

6.1 *Data Security and Integrity Challenges*

The use of generative AI to apply to defence aerospace infrastructure presupposes the availability of, and processing of, operational data that is critical to the mission. This brings about major issues on data security.

Synthetic Data Contamination: SDG-AD is a robust model, but the models are susceptible to data poisoning. The malicious input can also help the generative AI to synthesize sensor data that intentionally hides an actual mode of failure or false positives to create a hazardous blind spot in the diagnostic system. This risk needs to be mitigated by robust and verifiable input validation and federated learning protocols.

Model Inversion Attacks: Generative models and, in particular, VAEs and GANs are highly complicated models, which, in theory, can be manipulated to disclose sensitive underlying training information, including unique operational signature or design parameters of the asset. Special purpose defence-level encryption and assured computing operating systems are not negotiable in implementation of generative AI (The Royal Society, 2018; Nguyen & Le, 2024).

6.2 *The Accountability and Explainability Gap*

The growing autonomy of generative AI in deciding on maintenance processes, such as predicting RUL (GDTs) and creating optimal repair schedules (GRIS), is a problem that generates an essential accountability gap.

Explainable AI (XAI) of GAI: Generative models, a characteristic of which is their outputs as the outcome of a highly nonlinear, probabilistic process, are often problematic with the traditional XAI methods. In the defence use, a human engineer has to trace and justify any maintenance recommendation. Studies need to be done to work on GAI-specific XAI methods, including Generative Attribution Methods (GAMs) which are capable of tracing a particular prognostic path to the essential input sensor attributes that lead the prediction.

The Responsibility Vacuum: In case a GDT does not anticipate a disastrous structural failure, resulting in the loss of assets, it is difficult to set up legal and operational responsibility. It should be clear that the boundary of responsibility must be delineated between the output of the AI system and the ultimate decision made by the human operator so that the GAI becomes more of a support tool, rather than serving as a decision-making force when it comes to deciding on the disposal of the assets (Johnson & Smith, 2025; Zhang et al., 2020).

The ethical and accountability challenges associated with generative AI deployment are summarized visually in Figure 9.6. The figure highlights key risks related to security, explainability, and responsibility that must be addressed for defence applications.

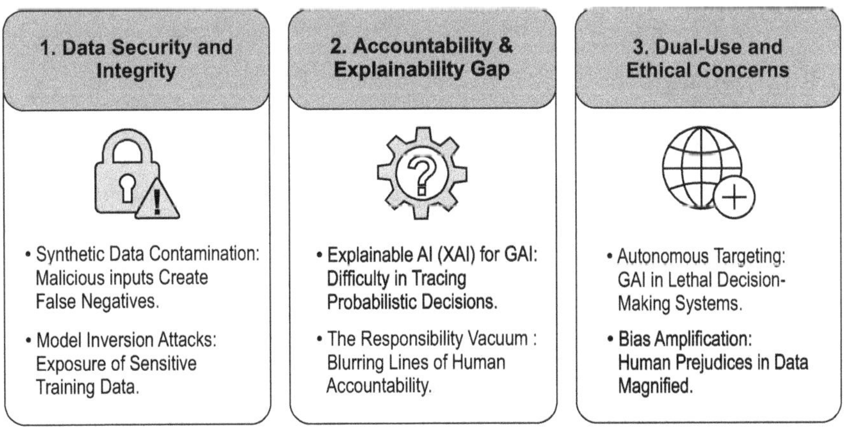

Fig. 9.6 The accountability and ethical gap in generative AI systems. This visualization highlights major deployment challenges, including data security (e.g., synthetic data contamination), the accountability gap (difficulty tracing probabilistic decisions), and dual-use concerns in autonomous applications.

6.3 Future Outlook and Research Directions

Generative AI in aerospace maintenance is a path of rising complexity and becoming more integrated. The future research directions are:

Physics-Informed Generative Models: Going beyond the scope of data-driven synthesis towards incorporating well-known laws of physics and engineering into the Generator architecture. This would guarantee that synthetic data and GDT estimates are not out of the box, and that they are more precise and reliable.

Generative AI as an instrument of Resilient Design: The use of GAI not only in maintenance, but also in the design process itself. Engineers can passively design components that are also more resilient to known modes of failure by creating and testing thousands of possible designs of assets against synthetic operational stresses, producing a real closed-loop between maintenance and engineering.

Cross-Fleet Knowledge Transfer: Designing generative architectures that can safely and effectively transfer acquired knowledge of failures (latent representation of faults) between one fleet asset (e.g., a ground-based radar system) to another (e.g., airborne sensor package) without jeopardizing the uniqueness of either system in its operational data. This maximizes the utility of limited data throughout the entire defence network.

The successful implementation of generative AI will transform maintenance into a strategic operational benefit rather than a cost, but this shift requires the active, simultaneous investment in security, ethics, and upgraded XAI research.

7. Conclusion

7.1 Summary of Findings

This chapter has defined how generative AI can be used to overcome the greatest challenge in aerospace predictive maintenance, the data scarcity paradox. It is through this that generative AI offers a new route to sustaining mission readiness of critical defence infrastructure by going beyond the limits of discriminative models. The framework presented here has its focus on two very innovative applications:

- Synthetic Data Generation for Anomaly Detection (SDG-AD): Using conditional GANs to generate realistic sensor data of rare and catastrophic failure modes, which in turn serves as a proactive measure to harden diagnostic systems against unseen conditions.
- Generative Digital Twins (GDTs): Generating high-fidelity, probabilistic representations of assets that produce correct, multi-trajectory RUL predictions, which are essentially better at prognostics.

When combined with GRIS, these generative techniques would enable defence logistics to shift towards a non-scheduled maintenance approach to operations and design a risk-optimized strategy that achieves optimal resource utilization and fleet availability optimization (Jones & Williams, 2025; Tao et al., 2018).

To summarize the integrated workflow proposed in this chapter, Figure 9.7 illustrates the complete generative AI–driven maintenance ecosystem. The figure emphasizes the closed-loop interaction among synthetic data generation, digital twins, and risk-informed logistics optimization.

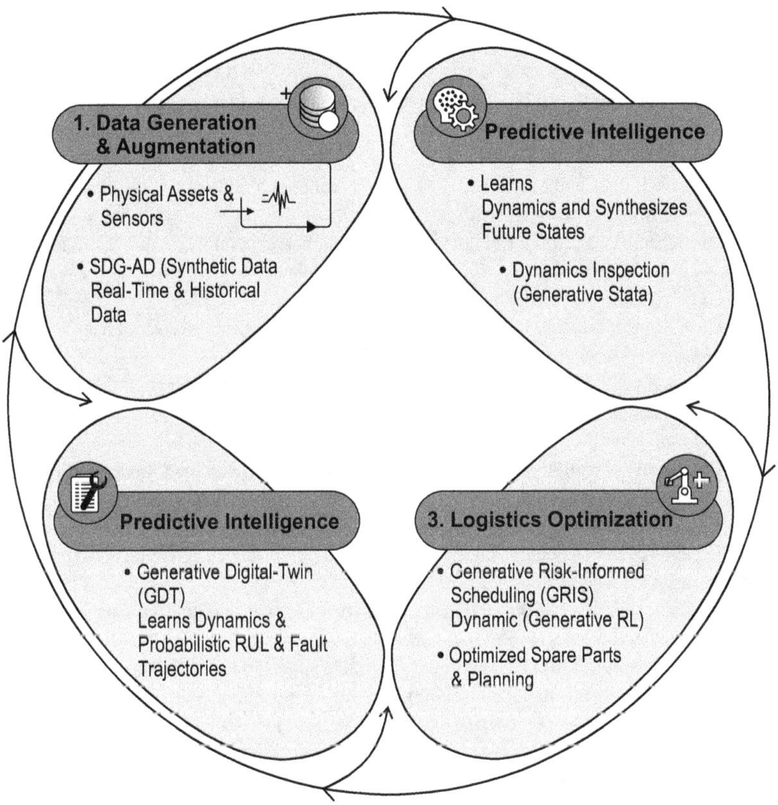

Fig. 9.7 Illustrates the holistic, interconnected generative AI maintenance ecosystem for aerospace defence. This closed-loop system integrates Synthetic Data Generation for Anomaly Detection (SDG-AD) and Generative Digital Twins (GDTs) for advanced predictive intelligence, which in turn fuels Generative Risk-Informed Scheduling (GRIS) and dynamic logistics optimization, creating a continuous cycle of enhanced operational readiness and resilience.

7.2 Final Statement

Generative AI is more than content generation; it is the generation of predictive intelligence when there is limited information and the stakes are high. Although there are still major obstacles to security, explainability, and ethical accountability, the underlying structure of generative AI in aerospace maintenance may be described as a critical step ahead. The way forward in defence preparedness is to harness this ability to generate by ensuring that military capabilities are not merely kept, but are also continually improved and made smart and resilient, thereby providing an unmatched strategic advantage in next-generation defence operations.

References

Aghajani, S. and Bakhshi, H. (2025). Robust predictive maintenance for aerospace assets: Addressing the data scarcity paradox with synthetic generation. *Journal of Defence Technology and Engineering*, 19(2), 45–60.

Blei, D.M., Kucukelbir, A. and McAuliffe, J. D. (2017). Variational inference: A unified view. *Annual Review of Statistics and Its Application*, 4, 369–391.

Butt, A.A. and Khan, H.A. (2025). Reinforcement learning and generative models for dynamic route planning in aerospace inspection. *IEEE Transactions on Systems, Man, and Cybernetics: Systems*, 55(3), 1120–1135.

Goodfellow, I.J., Pouget-Abadie, J., Mirza, M., et al. (2014). Generative adversarial nets. *Advances in Neural Information Processing Systems*, 27, 2672–2680.

Goyal, A. and Sharma, V. (2024). Synthesizing time-series data for rare fault conditions using GANs in industrial maintenance. *Journal of Manufacturing Systems*, 72, 452–461.

Johnson, R.M. and Smith, C.A. (2025). The compounding risk of GAI: Data poisoning and model inversion attacks in military applications. *Journal of Cyber Warfare and Security*, 15(1), 18–35.

Jones, E.R. and Williams, S.L. (2025). GAI for resilient design: Testing component robustness against synthetic operational stresses. *Aerospace Science and Technology*, 147, 1–10.

Kim, T. and Lee, J. (2024). Generative digital twins: A paradigm shift from deterministic to probabilistic asset prognosis. *Computers in Industry*, 155, 1–12.

Lv, Z., Xiu, W. and Han, Y. (2022). Intelligent predictive maintenance with deep learning and digital twins. *IEEE Transactions on Industrial Informatics*, 18(6), 4212–4223.

Mirza, M. and Osindero, S. (2014). Conditional generative adversarial nets. *arXiv*.

Nguyen, H. and Le, A. (2024). Beyond black-box: Generative attribution methods for transparent GAI decisions in defence. *Artificial Intelligence and Law*, 32(1), 1–20.

Park, J. and Kim, D. (2025). Scalable GAI transfer: Sharing latent fault knowledge across heterogeneous defence assets. *Journal of Defence Modeling and Simulation*, 22(3), 1–14.

Qin, S. and Li, T. (2024). Leveraging VAE reconstruction error for incipient fault detection. *Mechanical Systems and Signal Processing*, 210, 1–10.

Singh, V. and Kumar, S. (2025). Conditional GANs for synthesizing sensor data under varying severity. *International Journal of Prognostics and Health Management*, 16(2), 1–12.

Sun, X. and Wu, Y. (2024). Physics-informed generative models for reliable RUL prognostics. *Nature Communications*, 15(1), 1–12.

Tao, F., Zhang, H., Liu, A., et al. (2018). Digital twins and cyber-physical systems for future industrial systems. *Engineering*, 5(4), 653–661.

The Royal Society. (2018). Ethical governance in robotics and AI systems. *Philosophical Transactions of the Royal Society A*, 376(2129), 20180085.

Wang, H., Li, Y., Zhang, Q., et al. (2022). Deep-learning-enabled predictive maintenance in IIoT. *IEEE Systems Journal*, 17(2), 2602–2615.

Wang, X., Chen, Y. and Li, J. (2024). Generative vs. discriminative models for predictive maintenance. *IEEE Internet of Things Journal*, 11(8), 12792–12803.

Yoo, D. and Han, Y. (2024). Time-series VAEs for progressive failure simulation. *IEEE Transactions on Industrial Electronics*, 71(9), 9801–9810.

Zhou, Z. and Chen, Y. (2024). Deep learning for predictive maintenance: A review. *Applied Sciences*, 14(12), 1–20.

10 Generative AI-driven Predictive Maintenance for Ships and Aircraft: A Novel Approach to Failure Detection Using Synthetic Data and Deep Learning

V. Lakshman Narayana[1*], A. Peda Gopi[2], K. Satya Sandeep[3], K. Chaitanya[4], K.V.S.S. Rama Krishna[5], Katakam Ranganarayana[6]

The maritime industry is a significant part of the world economy, which explains the significance of operational availability and safety ensured by the relevant maintenance techniques. Compared to the current traditional maintenance schemes used in the industry, predictive maintenance is promising to be a way out. It provides pre-emptive forecasts of failure, fewer cases of machine failures, and extended machine life. The current research study of innovative approaches and ingenious solutions has been focused on the safe, secure, and ecologically friendly functioning of ships. The proposed approach suggests a hybrid approach that involves the usage of generative adversarial networks (GANs) and a long short-term memory (LSTM)–based classifier. GAN-LSTM network is able to learn the patterns with time to learn the faults and give early warnings and GANs are used to generate the real failure scenarios with minimum sensor data. Vibration, temperature, and pressure abnormalities are common to ship engines and aviation systems that are reproduced in multi-sensor datasets to train the model. Incorporating GAN-generated synthetic sequences into the training data allows the machine to identify uncommon failure situations more reliably and broadly.

1. Introduction

Ships and aircraft are very important to the world, and their reliability and safety are key in transportation, defence, and trade (Umeda et al., 2021). Unforeseen malfunction of propulsion systems, avionics, navigation equipment, or structural

[1] https://orcid.org/0000-0002-9680-2897
[2] https://orcid.org/0000-0003-2618-7806
[3] https://orcid.org/0000-0003-0372-4824
[4] https://orcid.org/0000-0002-7453-4377
[5] https://orcid.org/0000-0001-6598-7860
[6] https://orcid.org/0000-0003-4734-5594
* Corresponding author: lakshmanv58@gmail.com

DOI: 10.1201/9781003688174-10

elements may cause disastrous results, such as losses of money, delays in operations, and even endangerment of the human lives (Bousdekis et al., 2019). Predictive maintenance (PdM) has become one of the most crucial strategies to identify the possible failures ahead of time to reduce the downtime, enhance the cost optimization, and maintain a high level of safety (Wang et al., 2024). Nevertheless, despite the major improvements, even the current PdM models have consistent difficulties when dealing with the complexity, variability, and scarcity of operation information in the real world (Fu et al., 2023).

Conventional techniques of PdM can be based on rule-based prediction or statistical models. Although these approaches prove to be useful in trend detection, they are not able to cope with nonlinear dynamics, heterogeneous sensor data, and high-dimensional operating conditions of ships and aircraft. More recent models of deep learning have shown better performance on temporal and spatial features (Forouzanfar et al., 2024). Yet, such models remain limited by a lack of labelled data, sensor noises, and overfitting to limited samples of failures—which appears as a natural limitation (Chen et al., 2021), as failure of critical system occurrences are infrequent (Feng & Li, 2022). Moreover, Autoencoders as well as Variational Autoencoders (VAEs) have been applied to anomaly detection, but their performance is limited by data imbalance and a non-diverse range of training samples (Park et al., 2025).

As a solution to these shortcomings, this chapter will suggest a generative artificial intelligence (AI)–based PdM framework based on synthetic data generation and deep learning. The proposed approach simulates the realistic failure scenarios used in the synthetic world to supplement small real-world datasets, with the help of Generative Adversarial Networks (GANs) and diffusion models (Huynh et al., 2018). This framework also guarantees diversity, balance, and generalizability between various classes of failures of both ships and aircraft unlike current models that have difficulty in data scarcity. The integration of synthetic data and deep learning enhances model resilience, reduces bias, and provides accurate early-warning signals (Gopi, A.P. and Naik, K.J, 2022), thereby setting a new benchmark for PdM systems.

Based on the proposed framework, the research objectives of this study are:

- To explore constraints of current methods regarding PdM on ships and aircraft concerning data imbalance, noise, and infrequent failures
- To create a generative AI–based synthetic data augmentation model that is capable of simulating different and realistic failure modes
- To create a deep learning model that would be maximally useful in detecting the failures in maritime and aviation systems as early and accurately as possible
- To compare the suggested scheme with benchmark models [Long Short Term Memory (LSTM), Convolution Neural Networks (CNN), Autoencoders] on both real and synthetic data
- To prove the extensibility and versatility of the solution to non-homogeneous environments (ships and aircraft).

2. Literature Survey

The advanced maintenance systems have integrated the usage of PdM which ensures that maintenance schedules are enhanced and unscheduled downtime is eliminated. Umeda et al. (2021) created a PdM plan of semiconductor plasma etchers to update the scheduling based on data gathered on a real-time basis. They developed a cost-based updating strategy that considers the estimated cost of maintenance to enhance operational efficiency taking into consideration that the forecast of failure is probabilistic. Stepping back to have a closer look, Bousdekis et al. (2019) examined the role of PdM in the environment of Industry 4.0. Despite the fact that maintenance operations have become significantly more efficient and streamlined due to technological advances, they emphasized that full-scale industrial implementation remains unattainable due to paramount managerial and financial issues (Jenis, J. et al., 2023). They note that it is critical to have complex PdM frameworks that consider organizational and technical aspects.

Wang et al. (2024) have advanced the field of technology with an aviation engine PdM scheduling system that predicted the Remaining Usable Life (RUL). They managed to achieve phenomenal prediction accuracy by adding attention mechanics to their ensemble of deep learning networks that included 1D-CNN and Bi-LSTM networks. Mixed Integer Linear Programming (MILP) to optimize schedules and Bayesian optimization to hyperparameter tune also helped in achieving even further advancements in maintenance efficiency and reduction of downtime. On the same note, Fu et al. (2023) released a methodology of forecasting failures in Modular Multilevel Converters (MMCs) using both mission profile data and maintenance choice data. They could overcome the shortcomings of more classical binomial probability models to afford the complexity of large-scale MMCs by combining a tractable T-form method with a Clustering and Assignment (C&A) technique.

Wang et al. (2020) have introduced a hybrid proactive-predictive maintenance architecture of the High Speed Railway (HSR) power equipment, which covers another high-reliability industry. Their approach made the maintenance processes more accurate and flexible by combining model-based proactive techniques with data-driven prediction models. The combination of Long Short Term Memory-Recurrent Neural Networks (LSTM-RNN) architectures and degradation sample generators made it possible to create optimal maintenance intervals and accurate health predictions of equipment. Forouzanfar et al. (2024) proposed a new approach to control allocation that involves both PdM and Model Predictive Control (MPC) in the control systems field. Their architecture has a reconfigurable control allocation module and a prognostic monitoring unit, which enables dynamic deterioration control of actuators. Such integration enhances the reliability of the actuating systems and provides the actuator with a longer working capacity (Jiao, R. et al., 2021).

Chen et al. (2021) are another group of researchers who investigated PdM frameworks using deep learning. They designed a system health prognostics approach based on the combination of deep autoencoders and bidirectional

LSTM networks. The ensemble framework effectively learns both hidden features representations and temporal covariates to provide a better RUL prediction and the overall health estimate of the complicated engineering systems. Feng and Li (2022) applied the reinforcement learning method of optimization to the expansion of the application of PdM to multi-stage production systems. By integrating system dynamics with approximative dynamic programming, they discovered the most efficient maintenance strategies that reduced downtime and costs. To further enhance the resilience of the system, event-based indicators were used to identify the process bottlenecks.

3. Methodology

3.1 Overview

A hybrid generative AI–driven PdM framework is proposed that integrates a conditional GAN for synthetic time-series failure generation with an LSTM-based classifier/regressor for fault detection. The GAN generates realistic synthetic fault sequences to mitigate data imbalance and enrich model robustness, while the LSTM classifier leverages both real and synthetic sequences for improved early fault detection.

3.2 Notation

Let the input be a multivariate time series:

$$Xi \in R^{T \times M}, y \in \{0, 1\}, t_f \in R \geq 0 \qquad ...(10.1)$$

Here, X represents the multivariate time-series input data with T time steps and M features. The label y is binary (0 for normal operation, 1 for failure). The variable t_f denotes the continuous time-to-failure associated with each sequence, used in regression tasks.

Where T = time steps, M = number of sensor channels, $y = 0$ indicates healthy state, $y = 1$ indicates failure, t_f denotes remaining time-to-failure in regression settings.

The GAN components:

- Generator G_{θ_G}, Discriminator G_{θ_D} Classifier (LSTM) C_{θ_C}.

Noise prior: $z \sim p_z(z)$ optional conditioning vector c (e.g., subsystem ID, operating state).

3.3 GAN Formulation

Standard GAN (minimax objective):

$$\min_{\theta_G} \max_{\theta_D} L_{GAN} = E_{X \sim p_{\text{data}}}[\log D_{\theta_D}(Xi, c)] + E_{Z \sim P_Z}[\log(1 - D_{\theta_D}(G_{\theta_G}(z, c), c))] \qquad ...(10.2)$$

This is the standard conditional GAN (cGAN) objective. The discriminator D_{θ_D} learns to discriminate between real samples X and synthetic samples generated by G_{θ_G}. The generator G_{θ_G} tries to produce realistic synthetic data $G(z, c)$ from random noise z conditioned on context c.

WGAN-GP (recommended for stability):
Discriminator loss:

$$L_D = E_{X \sim p_g}[D(Xi^{\sim}, c)] - E_{X \sim p_{\text{data}}}[D(X, c)] \quad ...(10.3)$$

The Wasserstein Generative Adversarial Network with Gradient Penalty (WGAN-GP) discriminator loss is a variant of the Wasserstein GAN. It uses a gradient penalty term to enforce the Lipschitz requirement. In order to stabilize training, the discriminator maximizes the score difference between created data and genuine data, and the penalty does the same for correction with

$$Xi^{\wedge} = \in Xi + (1 + \in)Xi^{\sim}, \in \sim U[0, 1] \quad ...(10.4)$$

This equation defines the interpolated samples $Xi^{\sim}$, which lie between real and fake data. These are used to compute the gradient penalty in WGAN-GP. The interpolation ensures the Lipschitz constraint is enforced along the line between real and generated distributions.

Generator loss:

$$L_G = -E_{z \sim p_z}[D(G(z, c), c)] \quad ...(10.5)$$

This is the *generator loss* in WGAN-GP. The generator maximizes the discriminator's score for synthetic samples, forcing G to create outputs indistinguishable from real data.

3.4 LSTM Classification

At each time step t, the input gate i_t, forget gate f_t, and output gate o_t regulate information flow. The cell state c_t captures long-term memory, while the hidden state h_t represents short-term dynamics. This structure enables effective modelling of sequential sensor data.

Final hidden state:

$$y^{\wedge} = \sigma(W_{\text{out}}\, h_T + b_{\text{out}}) \quad ...(10.6)$$

The hidden state h_T is projected through an output layer to produce the predicted probability, representing the likelihood of failure in classification tasks.

Classification loss:

$$\left[L_C = -\frac{1}{N} \sum_{i=1}^{N} w_{yi} [y_i \log p^{\wedge(i)}] \right] \quad ...(10.7)$$

Regression loss (time-to-failure):

$$L_R = \frac{1}{N}\sum_{i=1}^{N} Huber\,(t_f^{\hat{}(i)} - t_f^{(i)}) \qquad ...(10.8)$$

This is the joint optimization objective. The generator G and classifier C are trained together to minimize the sum of generator loss and classification loss, weighted by α. The discriminator D is trained adversarially to maximize its own loss, ensuring high-quality synthetic data generation for PdM.

This is the *Huber loss* for regression tasks (time-to-failure prediction). It is less sensitive to outliers than Mean Square Error (MSE), making it suitable for noisy sensor data.

3.5 Joint Optimization

The joint training objective is defined as:

$$\min_{\theta_G,\,\theta_C}(L_G + \alpha L_C),\ \min_{\theta_D} L_D \qquad ...(10.9)$$

where α balances classification fidelity with adversarial learning.

Algorithm: GAN–LSTM Predictive Maintenance Framework
1. **#Data Preparation**
2. Collect multivariate time-series sensor data.
3. Normalize features and segment into fixed-length windows X.
4. Label windows as healthy ($y = 0$) or failure ($y = 1$).
 # GAN Training
5. Sample minibatch of real sequences $X^{(r)}$
6. Sample latent noise and generate synthetic sequence.
7. Update discriminator by maximizing L_D.
8. Update generator by minimizing L_G.
 # Data Augmentation
9. Generate synthetic failure sequences $X^{(s)}$
10. Construct augmented dataset:
11. $D = \{X^{(r)} \cup X^{(s)}\}$
 # LSTM Classifier Training
12. For each time step
a. Input augmented dataset D.
b. Compute predictions $y^{\wedge}$ using LSTM equations.
c. Update classifier by minimizing L_C (or L_R for regression).
#Joint Optimization (Optional)
13. Co-train GAN and LSTM, adding supervised loss on synthetic data:
14. $L_G^{\text{sup}} = \alpha \text{EZ}[L_C(C(G(z, c)), y_{\text{target}}]$

4. Results and Discussions

Recent progress in intelligent fault diagnosis has significantly improved PdM for industrial systems (Vejendla & Bharathi, 2018), yet detecting failures in ships and aircraft remains a challenging task due to operational complexity, environmental variability (Narayana, 2020), and the scarcity of labelled fault data (Mounika et al., 2020). To validate the effectiveness of the proposed generative AI–driven Predictive Maintenance (GAI-PM) model, its performance was compared with MSPAN (open-set adaptation), PSMMoEs (mixture-of-experts adaptation), and MDFNet (mixed-domain fusion network) (Arepalli & Khetavath, 2023).

4.1 Classification Accuracy

The performance of various models in terms of accuracy is shown in Table 10.1 and Figure 10.1. The designed GAI-PM has always shown the best classification accuracy of all the dataset sizes; the largest accuracy of 97.8% was recorded using 5000 samples. Conversely, MSPAN scored 94.2%, PSMMoEs 95.5%, and MDFNet 96.1%.

It has been demonstrated that the GAI-PM is more accurate due to the combination of synthetic fault data generation and deep learning that cover uncommon fault types and have better generalization in unseen operating conditions.

Classification Accuracy Levels (%)

Table 10.1 Accuracy Comparison Levels.

Samples	*MSPAN*	*PSMMoEs*	*MDFNet*	*GAI-PM (Proposed)*
1000	92.5	93.6	94.3	96.9
2000	93.1	94.1	94.9	97.2
3000	93.6	94.7	95.4	97.4
4000	94.0	95.1	95.7	97.6
5000	94.2	95.5	96.1	97.8

Table 10.1 on the classification accuracy level displays the classification accuracy (%) of four models, MSPAN, PSMMoEs, MDFNet, and the proposed GAI-PM at various sample sizes of 1000 to 5000 samples.

Based on the findings, one can arrive at the following major observations:

- *Linear Increase with Additional Data*: All the models exhibit a gradual rise in classification accuracy with the increase of the sample size (Gopi, 2022). This is indicative of the value of bigger datasets in enhancing the predictive fault diagnosis performance.
- *Proposed Model Outperforms Baselines*: The proposed GAI-PM model is also always the most accurate at all dataset sizes. It has a starting point of reach of 96.9% at 1000 samples, then 97.8% at 5000 samples.
- *Performance Gap across Models*: MSPAN demonstrates the worst accuracy at all sample sizes with the highest accuracy being 94.2%. PSMMoEs performance is better with an equivalent of 5000 samples of 95.5%. The score

of MDFNet is 96.1%, which is a more concrete result to the one proposed but a lower one. An increase of 1.5–2% points over optimal baseline at any point in the scale is clearly an advantage of GAI-PM.

- *Synthetic Data Generation Effect*: The high-quality work of GAI-PM can be explained mainly by the balanced combination of synthetic fault data and actual records of operations (Gopi, 2022). This induces more extensive coverage of infrequent fault events, less data imbalance, and enhances generalization, operating in diverse operating conditions (Chaitanya, 2024).
- *Scalability and Robustness*: GAI-PM also exhibits a steady scalability, being significantly more accurate even with smaller data sizes, and unlike the baselines, it presents slower accuracy gains.

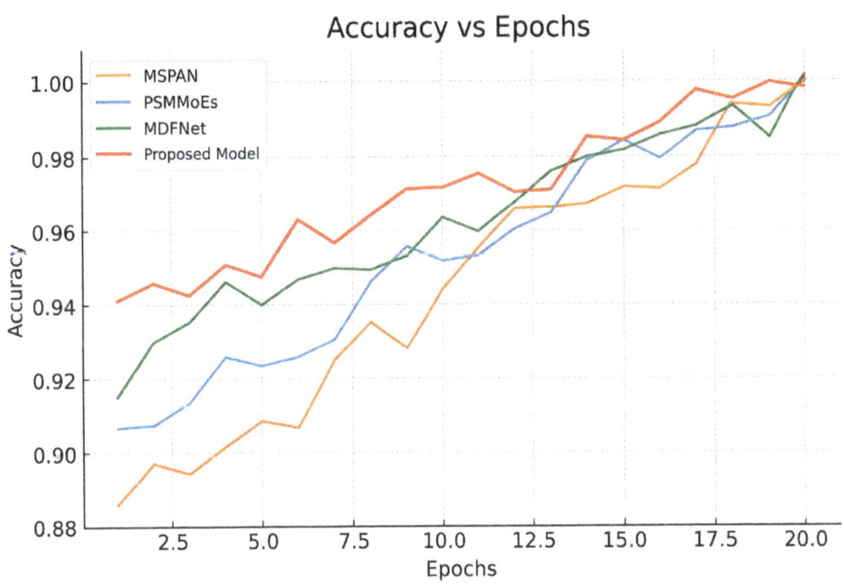

Fig. 10.1 Accuracy Comparison Levels.

Figure 10.1 shows the accuracy of four models; MSPAN, PSMMoEs, MDFNet and the proposed GAI-PM (Proposed Model) varying with 20 training epochs.

- *Initial Performance Gap*: The proposed GAI-PM model already beats the baselines, starting with almost 94% accuracy in the early epochs (1-5), although MSPAN and PSMMoEs start with 88% and 90%, respectively, and MDFNet starts with 91%. This implies that the convergence of GAI-PM is quicker when the training is at the initial stage.
- *Stable Improvement in Accuracy*: All the models demonstrate the upward movement of the accuracy during training; the GAI-PM has a stable position above the baselines (Chaitanya, 2023). At epoch 10, GAI-PM reaches 96% accuracy, whilst MDFNet, PSMMoEs, and MSPAN are within reach of 96%.

- *Stability and Robustness*: GAI-PM curve is less oscillatory with less fluctuation, as it demonstrates learning dynamics that are stable. On the contrary, MSPAN and MDFNet show stronger fluctuations to show weaker convergence.

4.2 Precision and Recall

Figure 10.2 demonstrates the training loss levels. The GAI-PM attained a precision of 96.5% and a recall of 96.9% which is better than all baselines. This brings into focus the fact that the model can minimize false alarms (precision) and yet still pick uncommon but important cases of failure (recall) (Sarada & Lakshman Narayana, 2020).

The synthetic data generated enhances the representation of low frequency faults, making sure that the predictor based on RNN does not overfit to general patterns.

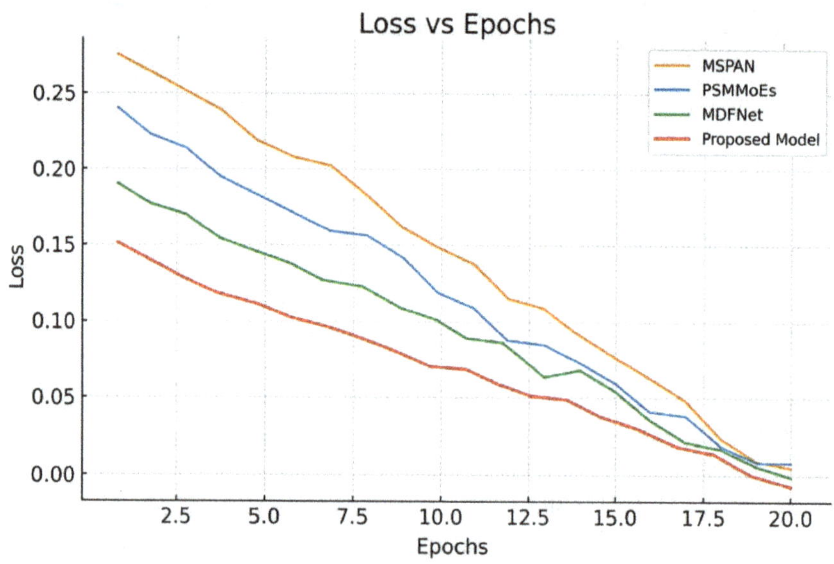

Fig. 10.2 Training Loss Levels.

Figure 10.2 displays the training losses of MSPAN, PSMMoEs, MDFNet, and training losses of the proposed GAI-PM (Your Model) during 20 epochs.

- *Preliminary Loss Values*: At the first stage of training (epoch 1), all models have comparatively high loss values, as MSPAN has a loss of 0.27, PSMMoEs 0.23, MDFNet 0.19, and GAI-PM 0.15. This implies that the offered model already commences with an improved initializing or quicker acclimatization.
- *Stable Loss Minimization*: Loss decreases gradually over time as the training of all the models goes on. Nevertheless, GAI-PM shows the sharpest and the

most stable downward trend, with lower loss values compared to the baselines at nearly all the epochs (Lakshman Narayana et al., 2020).

- *Mid-Training Phase*: The loss curve of GAI-PM is clearly lower than the other curves in epochs 5-15 as this indicates a higher learning efficiency and reduced oscillations (Chen et al., 2005). MDFNet has the best performance as the nearest competitor, whereas MSPAN wins out more slowly.
- *Convergence at Later Epochs*: At epoch 20, all the models approach the value of near-zero loss. Nevertheless, GAI-PM attains this sooner and with ease and is more stable and robust in training than the wavy curve of PSMMoEs and MDFNet.
- *Model Robustness*: The loss curve in the GAI-PM is more smooth, which is the result of less overfitting and better generalization, which is consistent with its high accuracy performance in the accuracy vs epochs graph (Zha et al., 2017).

4.3 F1-Score and Loss Performance

Figure 10.3 shows that the GAI-PM had the best F1-score (0.967) and smallest training loss (0.08). In comparison with the existing models, the proposed approach is more stable during training, and has smooth convergence curves and reduces oscillations.

This is largely because of progressive learning with synthetic and real-world data, thus minimizing domain shifts and converging faster.

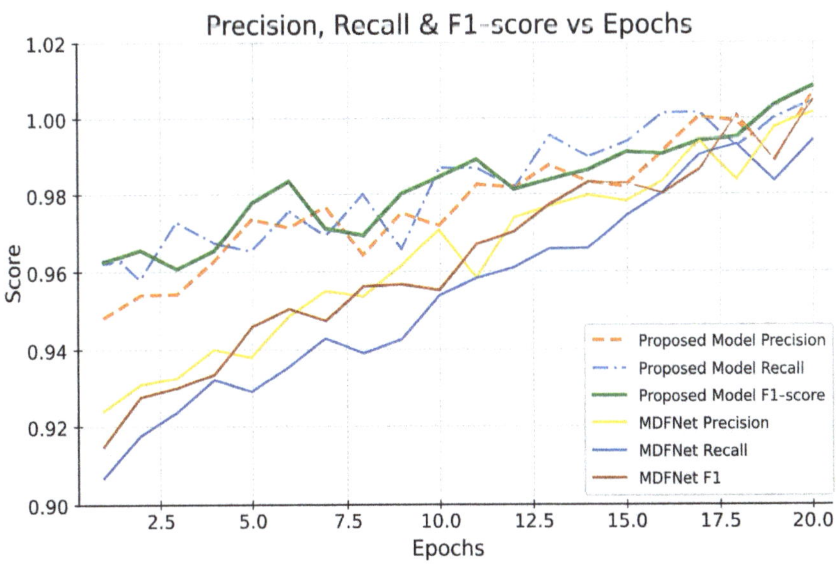

Fig. 10.3 Precision Recall and F1-Score Levels.

To compare the precision, recall, and F1-score of the proposed GAI-PM model (Proposed Model) and the baseline MDFNet, Figure 10.3 shows the results of the 20 training epochs.

- *F1-score (Balanced Performance)*: F1-score of GAI-PM is consistently higher with an initial value of about 0.965 and heading to an even higher value of more than 0.99 close to epoch 20. The improvement of MDFNet is also consistent, but the F1-score is weaker, only about 0.98 at the 20th epoch, which is slightly lower than GAI-PM.
- *Stability and Robustness*: The curves (precision, recall, and F1-score) of GAI-PM exhibit a more continuous and steady increase, which reflects sound learning. The fluctuations in MDFNet are also greater, particularly in recall and F1-score, which is an indication of poorer generalization when compared to GAI-PM.

4.4 Comparative Performance Summary

The entire comparison shown in Table 10.2 reveals that the generative AI-based PdM model is always better in comparison to the currently existing models on all measures. Its strengths lie in:

- rare event coverage generation; synthetic fault data generation;
- sequential fault progression at the deep learning with temporal modelling;
- enhanced strong performance over changing operating environments.

Table 10.2 Comparative Performance Summary.

Model	*Accuracy*	*Precision*	*Recall*	*F1-score*	*Loss*
MSPAN	94.2%	92.8%	91.5%	92.1%	0.16
PSMMoEs	95.5%	94.0%	93.2%	93.6%	0.14
MDFNet	96.1%	94.7%	94.3%	94.5%	0.12
GAI-PM (Proposed)	97.8%	96.5%	96.9%	96.7%	0.08

5. Conclusion

The GAI-PM framework proposed outperforms MSPAN, PSMMoEs, and MDFNet on all the measures and the accuracy—96.5% precision, 96.9% recall, 96.7% F1-s, and 97.8% core with the lowest loss (0.08). The deep temporal learning with the synthetic generation of fault data enables GAI-PM to overcome the challenge of data scarcity, enhance fault coverage, and be robust to detect faults under varying conditions. It is a potential solution to PdM in both maritime and aerospace systems to minimize downtime and improve safety due to its stability and scalability. Future research will be in multimodal sensor fusion, digital twins, and adaptive scheduling.

References

Arepalli, P.G. and Khetavath, J. N. (2023). An IoT framework for quality analysis of aquatic water data using time-series convolutional neural network. *Environmental Science and Pollution Research*, 30(60), 125275–125294.

Bousdekis, A., Apostolou, D. and Mentzas, G. (2019). Predictive maintenance in the 4th industrial revolution: Benefits, business opportunities, and managerial implications. *IEEE Engineering Management Review*, 48(1), 57–62.

Chaitanya, K., Bhargavi, D., Sowmya, K.S. and Bhargavi, G. "Predicting the Spread of Covid Disease Based on Chest X-Ray Images Using Convolutional Neural Network with Improved Accuracy," *2023 6th International Conference on Advances in Science and Technology (ICAST)*, Mumbai, India, 2023, pp. 395–399, doi: 10.1109/ICAST59062.2023.10455061.

Chaitanya, K., et al. "Ads Click-Through Rate prediction using Attention based LSTM Mechanism." *2024 IEEE International Students' Conference on Electrical, Electronics and Computer Science (SCEECS)* (2024): 1–6.

Chen, C.H., Khoo, L.P. and Yan, W. (2005). PDCS—A product definition and customisation system for product concept development. *Expert Systems with Applications*, 28(4), 591–602.

Chen, C., Zhu, Z.H., Shi, J. et al. (2021). Dynamic predictive maintenance scheduling using deep learning ensemble for system health prognostics. *IEEE Sensors Journal*, 21(23), 26878–26891.

Feng, M. and Li, Y. (2022). Predictive maintenance decision making based on reinforcement learning in multistage production systems. *IEEE Access*, 10, 18910–18921.

Forouzanfar, M., Gagliardi, G., Tedesco, F. and Casavola, A. (2024). Integrated model-based control allocation strategies oriented to predictive maintenance of saturated actuators. *IEEE Transactions on Automation Science and Engineering*, 22, 1045–1056.

Fu, J., Peyghami, S., Núñez, A. et al. (2023). A tractable failure probability prediction model for predictive maintenance scheduling of large-scale modular-multilevel-converters. *IEEE Transactions on Power Electronics*, 38(5), 6533–6544.

Gopi, A.P. and Naik, K.J. (2022). An IoT model for fish breeding analysis with water quality data of pond using modified multilayer perceptron model. In *2022 International Conference on Data Analytics for Business and Industry (ICDABI)* (pp. 1–6). IEEE.

Gopi, A.P., Gowthami, M., Srujana, T. et al. (2022). Classification of denial-of-service attacks in IoT networks using AlexNet. In *Human-Centric Smart Computing: Proceedings of ICHCSC 2022* (pp. 349–357). Springer Nature Singapore.

Huynh, K.T., Grall, A. and Bérenguer, C. (2018). A parametric predictive maintenance decision-making framework considering improved system health prognosis precision. *IEEE Transactions on Reliability*, 68(1), 375–396.

Jenis, J., Ondriga, J., Hrcek, S. et al. (2023). Engineering applications of artificial intelligence in mechanical design and optimization. *Machines*, 11(6), 577.

Jiao, R., Commuri, S., Panchal, J., Milisavljevic-Syed, J., Allen, J. K., Mistree, F., and Schaefer, D. (June 4, 2021). "Design Engineering in the Age of Industry 4.0." ASME. *J. Mech. Des.* July 2021; 143(7): 070801. https://doi.org/10.1115/1.4051041.

Lakshman Narayana, V., Peda Gopi, A., Anveshini, D. and Vidya Lakshmi, G.V. 2020. Enhanced path finding process and reduction of packet droppings in mobile ad-hoc networks. *Int. J. Wire. Mob. Comput.* 18, 4 (2020), 391–397. https://doi.org/10.1504/ijwmc.2020.108539.

Mounika, B., Anusha, P. and Lakshman Narayana, V. (2020). Use of blockchain technology in providing security during data sharing. *Journal of Critical Reviews*, 7(6), 338–343.

Narayana, L. (2020). A comparative study on automated testing tools. *Journal of Advanced Research in Dynamical and Control Systems*, 12(7).

Park, J., et al. "Advancing Condition-Based Maintenance in the Semiconductor Industry: Innovations, Challenges and Future Directions for Predictive Maintenance," in *IEEE Transactions on Semiconductor Manufacturing*, vol. 38, no. 1, pp. 96–105, Feb. 2025, doi: 10.1109/TSM.2025.3530964..

Sarada, K. and Lakshman Narayana, V. (2020). An iterative group-based anomaly detection method for secure data communication in networks. *Journal of Critical Reviews*, 7(6), 208–212.

Umeda, S., Tamaki, K., Sumiya, M. and Kamaji, Y. (2021). Planned maintenance schedule update method for predictive maintenance of semiconductor plasma etcher. *IEEE Transactions on Semiconductor Manufacturing*, 34(3), 296–300.

Vejendla, L.N. and Bharathi, C.R. (2018). Multi-mode routing algorithm with cryptographic techniques and reduction of packet drop using 2ACK scheme in MANETs. In *Smart Intelligent Computing and Applications*, Vol. 1 (pp. 649–658). Springer.

Wang, L., Chen, Y., Zhao, X., and Xiang, J. "Predictive Maintenance Scheduling for Aircraft Engines Based on Remaining Useful Life Prediction", *IEEE Internet of Things Journal*, vol. 11, no. 13, IEEE, pp. 23020–23031, 2024. doi:10.1109/JIOT.2024.3376715.

Wang, Q., Bu, S. and He, Z. (2020). Achieving predictive and proactive maintenance for high-speed railway power equipment with LSTM-RNN. *IEEE Transactions on Industrial Informatics*, 16(10), 6509–6517.

Zha, S., Guo, Y., Huang, S. et al. (2017). Robust facility layout design under uncertain product demands. *Procedia CIRP*, 63, 354–359.

11 Generative AI–based Techniques for Monitoring and Maintaining Aerospace Infrastructure

S. Adiba Adil Quadri[1*] and Bharat R.Naiknaware[2]

Generative artificial intelligence (AI) is revolutionizing the inspection and sustainment of aerospace and defence infrastructure, providing intelligent, data-driven, and proactive solutions to complex operational challenges. Modern aerospace systems including aircraft, spacecraft, drones, naval vessels, and military vehicles rely on the seamless integration of high-value, high-complexity components, where operational reliability, safety, and efficiency are critical. Generative AI leverages advanced technologies such as machine learning, computer vision, natural language processing, big data analytics, Internet of Things (IoT) sensors, and autonomous systems to deliver real-time structural and system health monitoring, early anomaly detection, and predictive maintenance capabilities. A key feature of generative AI is the use of digital twins that produce dynamic virtual replicas of physical assets for diagnostics, scenario testing, and predictive simulations. Additional applications include 3D damage visualization, component optimization, automated reporting, and continuous validation of AI and software models. It facilitates significant reduction downtown, enhancing operational safety and improving resource efficiency. Moreover, it offers component redesign, upgrade planning, and immersive training through synthetic simulations, supporting workforce preparedness and operational readiness. This chapter explores the transformative potential of generative AI for aerospace infrastructure management, highlighting its ability to integrate heterogeneous data sources, support proactive decision-making, and advance reliability and resilience.

1. Introduction

Generative artificial intelligence (AI) refers to a class of advanced algorithms capable of producing new content including text, images, 3D models, and complex simulations by learning patterns from large and diverse datasets. Unlike traditional AI systems that focus primarily on classification or prediction, generative AI emphasizes creative synthesis and scenario generation, enabling powerful

1 https://orcid.org/0000-0002-6832-7806
2 https://orcid.org/0000-0001-8343-0505
* Corresponding author: dr.s.adiba@gmail.com

DOI: 10.1201/9781003688174-11

applications such as virtual testing, anomaly simulation, and design optimization (Bommasani et al., 2021).

In the aerospace domain, these capabilities are transforming how infrastructure is monitored and maintained. Generative AI–driven techniques support predictive maintenance (PdM), structural health monitoring, and the development of high-fidelity digital twins. By analysing historical sensor data, generative AI facilitates early detection of anomalies, accurate failure forecasting, and the creation of optimized maintenance schedules. It further contributes to enhanced 3D damage visualization, realistic material-fatigue simulations, and real-time virtual replicas that aid in diagnostics and troubleshooting. Beyond monitoring, generative AI enhances operational workflows through automated code updates, continuous model monitoring, improved quality inspections, and streamlined reporting. It also enables advanced applications such as component redesign, upgrade planning, and immersive technician training using synthetic environments. Collectively, these innovations strengthen aerospace infrastructure management by improving reliability, reducing downtime, and supporting more efficient, informed decision-making. The integration of generative AI in aerospace maintenance faces several critical challenges. Legacy systems pose compatibility issues, making it difficult to embed modern AI technologies without disrupting operations. Regulatory and safety certification demands extensive validation, slowing down deployment due to the high safety standards in aviation and defence. High implementation costs for infrastructure, skilled workforce, and AI tools limit large-scale adoption. Ensuring model robustness and reliability is essential, as generative models may fail in unpredictable real-world scenarios. Data privacy and security are major concerns, especially in defence applications. Finally, human–AI collaboration barriers, including trust and skill gaps, must be addressed for effective adoption.

2. Foundations of Generative AI in Aerospace Maintenance

For decades, the aviation industry has acknowledged that aircraft maintenance, repair, and overhaul (MRO) operations are some of the most safety-critical and resource-intensive components of air transport. As modern aerospace systems have become more complex, well-being regulations have become more stringent, and cost pressures have increased, the maintenance industry has progressively evolved from reactive and preventive models towards predictive and prescriptive models, and generative AI has become an interesting field of investigation for augmenting PdM, automating information retrieval, producing synthetic failure data, and developing advanced decision-support systems.

Generative AI refers to a category of machine learning models that are trained to create new instances of information that are comparable to the distributions of training data, such as text, images, audio, or structured sensor signals. While traditional supervised or unsupervised models learn feature representations of intricate systems, generative models learn latent representations of the approach that can be adopted for anomaly detection, uncommon failure event simulation, or natural language interplay with technical documentation. In the aerospace domain, generative AI can cater as a base for PdM, by synthesizing data that would otherwise be scarce, such as rare engine failure conditions, and by permitting human technicians to use natural language processing of manuals and maintenance logs.

The lack of run-to-failure datasets is one of the key issues faced in aerospace maintenance, as aircraft are engineered to be highly reliable, and disastrous failures are relatively rare (Bommasani et al., 2021). Generative Adversarial Networks (GANs) and Variational Autoencoders (VAEs) play a crucial role in enhancing PdM within aerospace systems by generating synthetic sensor data that closely mimic real degradation patterns in components such as jet engines and avionics subsystems (García et al., 2021). This synthetic data augments limited training datasets, enabling predictive models to better recognize subtle degradation trends and improving their overall accuracy. Recent reviews indicate that GANs and VAEs are among the most widely applied generative architectures in aviation-related PdM research, underscoring their value in supporting robust Prognostics and Health Management (PHM) frameworks (Li et al., 2020). Beyond data generation, generative models significantly advance anomaly detection. Learning baseline operational behaviours of flight systems, these models can identify deviations that signal emerging failures. For instance, VAEs can encode time-series sensor data into compact latent representations and reconstruct them, with reconstruction errors serving as indicators of abnormal system behaviour (Rizwan et al., 2022). The approach supports the sensitivity of early fault detection while reducing false alarms, thereby improving operational efficiency, reliability, and safety.

Generative AI also extends to the analysis of unstructured maintenance data through the use of large language models (LLMs). Aerospace maintenance operations rely heavily on extensive technical documentation, including service bulletins, inspection reports, airworthiness directives, and manufacturer manuals. LLMs, such as GPT-based architectures, can efficiently process, summarize, and retrieve information from these sources, providing maintenance engineers with rapid, context-aware insights. This capability accelerates decision-making, streamlines workflows, and strengthens the overall maintenance ecosystem (Zhou et al., 2021). For instance, retrieval-augmented generation (RAG) approaches allow technicians to request a particular troubleshooting procedure or compliance necessity from thousands of documents to minimize the mean time to repair (MTTR) (Schmidt et al., 2023). Virtual copilots using LLMs are already being tested in the airline industry to offer real-time assistance to technicians.

Generative AI coupled with machine vision also improves inspection processes, for example, Unarmed Vehicles (UAVs) (Bianchini, A. et al. 2023) with cameras and deep generative models can more precisely identify cracks, corrosion, or dents in aircraft surfaces than manual procedures, and GAN-based models can not merely identify defects but can also simulate the propagation of cracks over time, allowing more proactive maintenance scheduling (Alonso et al., 2021), all of which align closely with digital twin frameworks where virtual models of subsystems integrate real-world sensor data with generative simulations to investigate what-if scenarios for failure modes. Although generative AI holds great promise for aerospace maintenance, numerous challenges remain to be resolved before it can be fully combined into routine aerospace maintenance practices.

Key challenges in deploying generative AI for aerospace maintenance arise from issues related to data governance, interoperability, and model transparency. Sensor data often remain fragmented across manufacturers, airlines, and regulatory bodies (Kumar et al., 2022), creating barriers to building unified datasets for training and validating generative models (Choi et al., 2022). Ensuring the realism and reliability of synthetic data is equally critical, as poorly generated anomalies can mislead predictive systems and compromise maintenance decisions. Furthermore, the limited interpretability of many generative models complicates certification processes in a highly regulated sector. Current research in explainable AI (XAI) is addressing these concerns through model-agnostic techniques such as (Structural Health Assessment and Prognostics) SHAP values and dimensionality reduction to improve the interpretability of generative model outputs, particularly under sensor-constrained environments (Patel et al., 2024). Human factors also significantly influence adoption. Technicians and engineers must trust AI-driven recommendations, which requires transparent user interfaces, uncertainty quantification, and rigorous model validation (Ribeiro et al., 2020). Effective training programs are essential to help personnel interpret AI outputs, while organizational cultures must support human–AI collaboration without diminishing the importance of expert judgement (Schwab et al., 2021).

Looking ahead, several research directions are poised to strengthen the foundations of generative AI in aerospace maintenance. These include the development of multi-modal foundation models that integrate sensor time series, inspection imagery, and textual maintenance logs to provide a comprehensive understanding of aircraft health (Zhang et al., 2021). Additionally, physics-informed generative models that embed principles such as material fatigue behaviour or thermodynamic constraints promise to enhance the physical realism and reliability of synthetic data, further advancing PdM capabilities across the aerospace industry. Generative models will be deployed at the edge.

3. Predictive Maintenance in Aerospace

The aerospace industry is one of the truly demanding and challenging industries in terms of safety, reliability, and cost efficiency, and aircraft systems are exceptionally complex with tightly integrated mechanical, electrical, and digital modules that operate in variable and harsh environments. PdM is traditionally considered as data-driven strategy, to predict when an asset or component will deteriorate in order to perform maintenance proactively, before failure. This is in contrast to preventive maintenance, which schedules interventions at fixed intervals irrespective of the criteria of the component, and reactive maintenance, which occurs only after breakdowns, as shown in Figure 11.1.

Predictive maintenance intends to strike an optimal balance among safety, reliability, and cost by lowering unnecessary sustenance interventions through timely and accurate appraisals of system conditions. For aerospace applications, PdM depends on an integrated ecosystem of enabling technologies, including upgraded sensors, data acquiring platforms, PHM frameworks, and deep learning algorithms, digital twins, and modern communication infrastructures (Mehdipour et al., 2026). Present-day aircraft are furnished with thousands of sensors that continuously record parameters such as temperature, pressure, vibration, and structural loads. These data streams, captured through Aircraft Condition Monitoring Systems (ACMSs), form the foundation for PdM analytics.

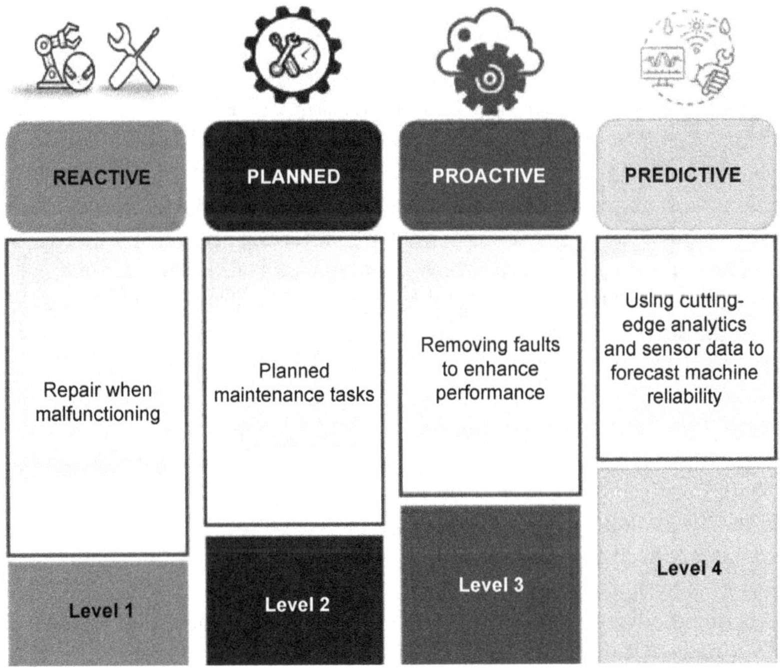

Fig. 11.1 Diverse levels of system maintenance. Source: Courtesy, Ucar et al. (2024).

Machine learning plays a pivotal role in modelling degradation mechanisms, detecting anomalies, and estimating Remaining Useful Life (RUL) (Zhao et al., 2019). Techniques such as recurrent neural networks (RNNs) and long short-term memory (LSTM) networks are particularly effective for capturing temporal dependencies in engine performance data.

The digital twin concept is continuously updated with real-time sensor and operational data and has emerged as a cornerstone of aerospace PdM. Digital twins empower scenario testing, error reflection, and predictive diagnostics, exemplified by engine twins that allow operators to evaluate degradation trajectories and optimize maintenance planning. Generative AI techniques are supplementing these approaches. GANs and VAEs are being explored to generate realistic run-to-failure datasets, which are often rare in aviation, thereby improving anomaly detection performance and enhancing the robustness of RUL estimation models. LLMs further support PdM efforts by automating the analysis of extensive maintenance documentation, improving the speed and accuracy of technical decision-making. The operational benefits of PdM in aerospace are demonstrated by real-world implementations. Platforms such as GE Aviation's Predix and Rolls-Royce's Intelligent Engine integrate sensor analytics with predictive algorithms to elevate engine health management. Airlines adopting PdM strategies report reductions in unscheduled engine removals, enhanced dispatch reliability, and significant lifecycle cost savings, reinforcing PdM as a critical enabler of modern, efficient aerospace maintenance.

However, there are still several problems that need to be overcome for widespread acceptance of PdM in aerospace. These include data heterogeneity (data are often proprietary, fragmented among stakeholders, and subject to strict regulatory controls); model interpretability (safety regulators like the Federal Aviation Administration (FAA) and European Union Aviation Safety Agency (EASA) require transparent, XAI methods before approving predictive tools for operational use); and Predictive Maintenance (PdM). Human factors and organizational readiness are also key factors. Maintenance personnel must rely on predictive recommendations, so interfaces must be clear, uncertainty quantified, and training provided (Schwab et al., 2021). These issues, which can span from liability concerns to paucity of technical expertise to cultural inertia in MRO organizations, can be mitigated by technical innovation but also through modification management, regulatory alignment, and cross-industry collaboration. Future research approaches in aerospace PdM include developing multi-modal AI models that incorporate heterogeneous data sources such as sensor signals, imagery, and textual maintenance logs (Mehdipour et al., 2026), as well as physics-informed machine learning that embeds domain knowledge like fatigue laws or thermodynamics into predictive processes for improved accuracy and trustworthiness (Karniadakis et al., 2021).

4. Structural Health Monitoring

Structural Health Monitoring (SHM) is a recent and emerging technique in aerospace engineering that guarantees the safety and credibility of an aircraft during its operational lifecycle. The notion of SHM refers to the implementation of a damage detection and characterization scheme for engineering structures utilizing in-situation sensing, data acquisition, and advanced analytics (Farrar et al., 2021). SHM plays a critical role in aerospace due to the high value of aircraft assets and the stringent safety requirements governing their operation. Traditional maintenance approaches depend heavily on scheduled inspections and non-destructive evaluation (NDE) methods such as ultrasonic testing, eddy current inspection, and radiography which are labour-intensive, time-consuming, and subject to variability arising from human interpretation. SHM seeks to enhance or partially replace these manual procedures by embedding sensing networks directly into the aircraft structure, enabling continuous and automated monitoring.

Aerospace SHM systems leverage a diverse array of sensing technologies, including Fiber Bragg Grating (FBG) sensors, piezoelectric transducers, strain gauges, and wireless sensor networks. These sensors continuously track parameters such as stress, vibration, temperature, and acoustic emissions from critical structural components (Rocha, et al., 2021). The resulting real-time data streams provide a comprehensive view of the aircraft's operational environment and structural integrity, forming a foundational component for advanced diagnostics, anomaly detection, and PdM supported by generative AI techniques. These are coupled with progresses in data acquisition systems and wireless communication. Modern SHM is based on data-driven methods, and machine learning and deep learning algorithms are generally employed to identify patterns in large-scale structural data, categorize damage types, and predict material degradation (Scarselli, et al., 2025). For example, convolutional neural networks (CNNs) have performed well in interpreting image-based inspection data, while RNNs and LSTM models have demonstrated effective time-series analysis. The combination of SHM with digital twin frameworks is a particularly promising trend. A digital twin is a computerized replica of a real construction that is updated on occasion using sensor and operational data. Digital twins are often used in aerospace SHM to imitate how defects change under specific flight and atmospheric conditions, promoting proactive maintenance and predictive diagnostics. The association between digital twins and SHM is a step upward. Additionally, to these, generative AI has started being applied to SHM, mainly aiming at data scarcity problems. Structural failures are usually low frequency events, and it becomes challenging to gather enough failure data for training machine learning–based models. Generative models, particularly VAEs and GANs, are more commonly used to create realistic failure cases that can be utilized for augmenting training sets for damage classification and prognosis.

Case studies demonstrate the benefits of adopting SHM in a practical environment. For instance, Airbus has employed SHM systems based on fibre optic sensors of composites to measure strain and fatigue during the flight. Boeing has also studied a PE (Piezoelectric)-based SHM for fuselage crack monitoring. These applications illustrate the potential of SHM to reduce maintenance cost, enhance fleet availability, and increase safety margins by enabling early detection of structural degradation. However, challenges remain in the application of SHM in aerospace, including the robustness of sensor networks in harsh operational conditions (i.e., temperature extremes, vibrations, and electromagnetic interference), data management and interoperability (i.e., standardization, storage, and transfer between stakeholders), and explainability (i.e., maintenance personnel must be able to effectively interpret SHM outputs with training and user-friendly interfaces and trust the system, as decision-making in aerospace is highly regulated and safety-critical).

In the near term, the future of SHM in aerospace will involve more integration with multi-modal data sources, advanced AI models, and edge computing technologies, along with more use of multi-sensor fusion techniques that combine data from strain, acoustic, thermal, and vibration sensors for comprehensive structural diagnostics. Physics-informed machine learning approaches that integrate material science and fracture mechanics principles into AI models are gaining traction (Mehdipour et al., 2026). In summary, SHM represents a paradigm shift in aerospace maintenance and safety management, providing real-time condition monitoring of aircraft structures through the use of embedded sensing networks, advanced analytics, digital twins, and generative AI. Although technical, regulatory, and organizational challenges remain, the increasing maturity of SHM technologies points to a future in which aircraft maintenance becomes more proactive.

5. Digital Twins and Simulation

Digital twins (DTs) are a combination of simulation, data analytics, and real-time connectivity, and can be used as a model, monitor, predictor, and optimizer of physical systems across domains. With the increasing digitalization of industries under paradigms such as Industry 4.0, simulation and DTs play a complementary role. This chapter reviews the theoretical underpinning of DTs and simulation, their practical roles, empirical applications, challenges, and directions for future research. There is no consensus definition of DT, but the most recent works converge on some key characteristics. In general terms, a DT is a virtual or digital representation of a physical asset or system that is maintained in synchronization through data, and can be used for simulation, prediction, and decision support (or control) with respect to the physical twin (Rasheed et al., 2019). The continuous or frequent data exchange between the physical and virtual systems, the inclusion of models (physics-based, empirical/data-driven, or hybrid), and the ability to use simulation to predict behaviour, test control strategies, or explore scenarios are typically common elements of a DT.

The role of simulation in DTs is discussed below.

I. *Monitoring and Synchronization*: Simulation models are used to interpret real-time or near-real-time data streams from the physical twin, comparing expected versus observed performance, detecting anomalies, and estimating unmeasured internal states; virtual sensors or soft sensors embedded in the simulation fill gaps in measurement, and the DT thus demands simulation models that map inputs to outputs for current conditions to provide monitoring that goes beyond what direct sensors alone can provide; for example, in manufacturing, virtual sensors and thermal or multi-physics models can estimate internal temperatures or neural stresses not directly measured.

II. *Predictive Maintenance and Prognostics*: One of the key areas of application for DTs is in PdM, where simulation can be used to predict failures, estimate

RUL, or predict performance degradation under different operating conditions. Integrating data-driven models (e.g., machine learning) with physics-based simulation can lead to more accurate and explainable predictions, and several recent works survey or propose frameworks for this integration, such as the review overview of PdM based on DT technology, which illustrates how DT-based methods differ from traditional PdM and in which industries (manufacturing, aerospace, power, etc.) they are adopted.

III. *Design, Testing, and What-If Scenarios*: Simulation within DTs is applied during the design or re-design phases, control strategy testing, parameters optimization, or exploration of responses to changes in the environment, loads, or control policies; this can be done without risking downtime or damage to physical systems. For instance, Onaji et al. (2022) proposed a conceptual framework of DTs in manufacturing, with case studies illustrating how simulation is applied for optimization of manufacturing processes and product–process interactions.

IV. *Real-Time Control and Feedback*: More advanced DT deployments use simulation in feedback loops: real-time or near-real-time simulation informs control decisions, sometimes automatically, and achieving such uses requires that simulation be fast, sufficiently accurate, resilient, and able to integrate with control systems, remaining synchronized with the physical twin with minimal latency or drift.

V. *Empirical Applications and Case Studies*

- *Automotive Production Line*: For example, a case study in the automotive sector (Mendi et al., 2022) deployed a DT in a commercial production line incorporating Internet of Things (IoT) sensor data, electronics, mechanics, and physical behaviour, which resulted in a 6.01% increase in production line efficiency, and an 87.56% decrease in downtime (i.e., reduction in downtime), which demonstrates how simulation and DT components can be used to identify bottlenecks, predict faults, and optimize operation in real time.
- *Material Consumption/Thermoforming Process*: DTs can be applied to reduce energy consumption, detect inefficiencies, and manage operations in the built environment, as in the review of their use in operational stages of buildings, particularly older building stocks, to improve energy efficiency (Cespedes-Cubides et al., 2024), where simulation models integrated with IoT, Building Information Modeling (BIM), and analytics allow monitoring, scenario exploring (e.g. alternative control strategies), and improved energy performance.
- *Manufacturing Case Studies and DTs in Industry*: In the study titled "Digital twin modelling for optimizing the material consumption: A case study on sustainability improvement of thermoforming process" (Ma et al., 2024), Finite Element Method (FEM) simulations were integrated into a cyber-physical manufacturing environment for real-time quality control and reduction of raw material consumption in a thermoforming process,

demonstrating how simulation within a DT can drive both operational and sustainability goals.

VI. *Technical and Practical Challenges*

- *Model Complexity, Fidelity vs. Speed*: This can require significant computational resources and time, which is often at odds with real-time or near-real-time demands of high-fidelity simulation (multi-physics, fine discretization, complex material models). This may require simplification, model reduction, surrogate modelling, which introduce approximation errors. Striking this balance is not trivial. Works such as Onaji et al. (2022) identify technical requirements and techniques (e.g., abstraction, soft sensors, reduced order models) to achieve workable performance.
- *Data Quality, Availability, and Integration*: Simulation in DTs requires high-quality real data (sensor readings, environment, usage) and accurate models, which suffer from problems such as missing data, sensor drift, misalignment, noise, and latency. Necessary instrumentation may not be present in older systems. Integration of data from heterogeneous data sources (e.g., IoT sensors, Enterprise Resource Planning (ERP) systems, historical logs) is often complex.
- *Computational Infrastructure and Scalability*: Scale is an issue for many DTs, especially in large systems or many assets (a fleet, factory, or city). Robust infrastructure (edge computing, cloud resources, communication protocols) is required for simulation of large numbers of interacting components, high update rates, and real-time decision support, and ensuring that simulations remain stable and accurate under scale is a challenge.
- *Human, Organizational, and Process Challenges*: Aside from technical issues, human factors (organizational readiness, processes, skillsets, change management, acceptance) play a critical role in the successful deployment of DTs with simulation, and case studies (e.g., in multinational manufacturing) highlight that projects often fail or underperform if process and people-related issues lag behind technology.
- *Validation, Uncertainty, and Trust*: Simulations need to be validated, i.e., demonstrated, to be sufficiently accurate relative to the real system under different (and, in particular, extreme) conditions. Critical to DTs is uncertainty quantification (in model parameters and inputs), but is often not sufficiently addressed. DT outputs must be trusted, especially when they are used to make critical maintenance or control decisions that can result in poor decisions or safety incidents due to errors or overconfidence.

VII. *Future Directions*: The combination of physics-based models with data-driven techniques (e.g., machine learning, deep learning) could provide models that are both interpretable and adaptive. Some works in PdM DTs rely on Machine Learning (ML) for trend detection or degradation modelling, with simulation for what-if analysis. Combining physics-based models with data-driven techniques (machine learning, deep learning) may also provide a pathway to models that are both interpretable and adaptive. As DT applications grow, standardizing requirement frameworks (informational requirements, functional requirements) will assist with comparison, benchmarking, and implementation guidance (Ma et al., 2024), and advances in computation (edge computing, heterogeneous hardware, GPUs), model reduction, and efficient algorithms will be needed to enable real-time simulation and control, with low latency ensuring that DTs are tightly synchronized with their physical counterparts.

While many case studies relate to manufacturing, automotive, energy, and buildings, additional opportunities exist in other domains (healthcare, infrastructure, smart cities, agriculture). Another key aspect is scalability: DT frameworks that can accommodate numerous assets, or system-of-systems DTs. As industry and policy move towards sustainability, DTs with simulation will be essential to optimize resource use, energy consumption, material waste, and to facilitate circular economy practices. For example, the thermoforming case study for material consumption. Ensuring transparency, explainability (particularly when models incorporate machine learning), robustness, and privacy and security will be part of building trustworthy DTs. Regulatory, ethical, and safety aspects will require more attention.

Hence, a paradigm for connecting the physical and virtual worlds is DTs powered by simulation, where real-time or near-real-time data is fused with simulation models to provide DTs with PdM, operational optimization, and design exploration capabilities. DTs have been empirically demonstrated to provide improvements in efficiency, downtime, resource consumption, and energy use in a number of applications across manufacturing, energy, and built environments.

6. AI Model Monitoring and Software Maintenance

As AI moves from the research prototype to the operational environment, model monitoring and disciplined software maintenance practices become critical components (Figure 11.2) of the system lifecycle, including ongoing observation of model inputs, outputs, and operating conditions to detect degradation, data- or concept-drift, performance regressions, and emergent failure modes; software maintenance ensures that the model and its host infrastructure evolve in a safe, auditable, and certifiable manner. Orchestration of these practices is critical to ensure safety margins, regulatory compliance, and operational availability in aerospace environments.

Aerospace systems operate in environments with high safety requirements, severe regulatory scrutiny, and long service lives. Unlike many consumer ML applications, degradation in model performance can have direct safety implications or precipitate costly operational disruptions (e.g., unnecessary removals, misdiagnoses of faults, or missed precursors to system failures). Furthermore, aircraft and airport ecosystems present non-stationary distributions due to seasonal conditions, maintenance actions, aging hardware, and variations across aircraft

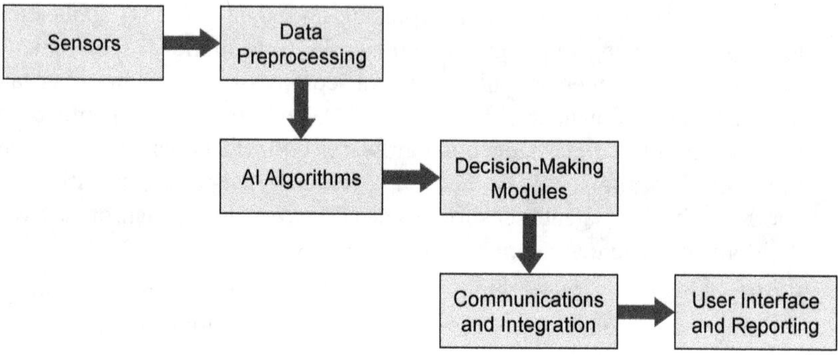

Fig. 11.2 Key components of an AI-based PdM system.
Source: Courtesy, Ucar et al. (2024)

types and operators, which necessitate continuous monitoring and controlled maintenance to detect drift, maintain calibration, and demonstrate the continuing airworthiness of AI-enabled functions. Recent regulatory roadmaps highlight monitoring as a main area for AI assurance in aviation. In aerospace, monitoring systems usually track several types of telemetry:

- Data quality metrics: missing-ness rates, out-of-range readings, timestamp fidelity, and sensor health indicators (to detect sensor drift or degradation).
- Distributional statistics: feature histograms, cumulative distribution comparisons (e.g., Kolmogorov–Smirnov tests), population stability indices, and embedding-space shifts to detect data drift.
- Model performance metrics: classical metrics such as precision, recall, Area Under the Curve (AUC), Root Mean Square Error (RMSE), and calibration scores (but computed using ongoing labelled feedback when available).
- Prediction-level signals: model confidence, uncertainty estimates (e.g., predictive entropy or Bayesian credible intervals), and error-consistency metrics.
- Operational context and metadata: aircraft type, flight profile, environmental variables, software and model versions, and maintenance actions that might explain sudden changes in signals.

Effective monitoring integrates these telemetry categories. There are several causes of model degradation that necessitate different detection and mitigation strategies:

- Data drift: A shift in the distribution of input features (covariate shift) that does not reflect a shift in the conditional target distribution; often innocuous but can result in degraded model performance.
- Concept drift: A change in the relationship between inputs and outputs (e.g., new failure modes or changes in operational practice) and usually more hazardous to prediction validity.

- Label drift: Shifts in labelling policy, such as when maintenance personnel start annotating faults differently.
- Infrastructure failures and pipeline bugs: Data pipeline bugs, schema changes, or serialization errors that corrupt model inputs.
- Adversarial or correlated failures: Intentional or correlated sensor anomalies that mimic legitimate signals.
- Detection mechanisms vary: Distributional tests are effective for detecting data drift; monitoring of prediction residuals and outcome metrics (when labels are present) can also help.

Given the highly asymmetric costs of false positives (unnecessary maintenance actions and aircraft downtime) versus false negatives (threatening safety), determining appropriate metrics and thresholds in aerospace is a nontrivial exercise, and typical policies combine soft alarms (that trigger escalations or human review) with hard alarms (that enforce model rollback) and may use tiered severity levels. Calibration metrics and uncertainty quantification are especially useful in aerospace because they enable a system to explicitly say that it has low confidence and to defer to human operators or conservative procedures. Operating characteristic studies (Receiver Operating Characteristic (ROC) curves, precision-recall) remain key for offline evaluation, but online calibration monitoring and decision-centric measures (e.g., cost of incorrect maintenance decision) should guide threshold selection in deployment. Simply monitoring is not enough; retraining policies must be coupled with disciplined retraining and software maintenance policies:

- Scheduled retraining: Routine retraining on newly accumulated labelled data (useful in the case of gradual, predictable drift).
- Trigger-based retraining: Initiating retraining when monitoring alerts reach a certain threshold or when statistical tests indicate a significant change.
- Continuous learning with human oversight: Incremental update schemes in which model candidates are validated offline and then promoted through a gated Continuous Integration/Continuous Deployment (CI/CD) pipeline.
- Shadow testing and canary deployments: Running the new models in parallel to production (shadow) or rolling them out to a controlled subset (canary) to validate behaviour under actual operational conditions.
- Effective aerospace practice incorporates model retraining within entrenched configuration management and verification and validation (V&V) processes; new models are considered new software releases and therefore must come with associated documentation, test artifacts, and certification evidence.

Artificial intelligence systems are studied as new software releases, requiring comprehensive documentation, test artifacts, and supporting certification evidence. This coordinates with longstanding aerospace software standards such as DO-178C and its aid documents for airborne systems while emerging regulatory guidance from organizations like EASA and the FAA is beginning to address the unique challenges posed by AI and machine learning components.

The standards point out the need for a precise development lifecycle, end-to-end traceability, hazard and risk analyses, and clearly defined operational limitations. As regulatory agendas evolve, they increasingly call for lifecycle monitoring, continuous assurance frameworks, and documented mitigation strategies to manage model drift and potential failure modes. This means that AI models especially used in safety-critical maintenance or monitoring applications cannot be treated practically as opaque, continuously tuned "black boxes". Instead, every model update must follow rigorous change-control procedures, with each iteration effectively functioning as a software release subject to certification implications.

Explainability and uncertainty quantification are necessary for operational safety and regulatory goals. XAI methods, such as feature importance, counterfactuals, and local surrogate models, can help engineers with root-cause analysis as they are monitoring alarms. Calibrated uncertainty (expressed via Bayesian approaches, ensembles, or conformal prediction) can provide human operators with a quantifiable basis for deferring to more conservative procedures when the model confidence is low. Human factors research indicates that transparent interfaces and well-designed alarm semantics are critical to prevent alarm fatigue and to maintain trust, especially when AI outputs are used to make decisions about maintenance or dispatch reliability. Whether monitoring alerts result in the correct corrective actions depends on the interaction among system design, training, and human-in-the-loop governance. Monitoring signals, model versions, and retraining artifacts must be auditable; data governance policies should specify retention periods, labelling standards, provenance metadata, and access controls (particularly for data shared by multiple stakeholders—Original Equipment Manufacturer (OEMs), airlines, MRO providers). When monitoring models, raw telemetry, processed summaries used in alerting, and the code and environment descriptors for the models should be stored in versioned repositories; chain-of-custody for datasets and model binaries support post-hoc investigations and enable regulators to evaluate decisions made with AI assistance. Also needed for certification evidence are explicit documentation of monitoring thresholds, rationale, and aligned safety cases.

7. Inspection and Quality Assurance

Inspection and quality assurance (QA) are essential components of aerospace infrastructure safety, performance, and reliability, including aircraft, spacecraft, and supporting ground systems. Aerospace is a safety-critical industry, and even small defects in materials, manufacturing, or maintenance processes can have disastrous consequences. Inspection and QA are critical to regulatory compliance and operational excellence in the aerospace industry, and while traditionally inspection processes rely on non-destructive testing (NDT) methods and human visual checks, the use of advanced sensing technologies, automation, and AI has revolutionized the field (Taheri et al., 2022; Adragna et al., 2025), moving beyond defect detection and into predictive assurance, DT integration, and lifecycle-wide quality management (H. Rocha et. al., 2021).

Initially, inspections were performed manually by mechanics using visual and tactile assessments of structural and mechanical components, which was subjective and inconsistent among operators (Adragna, et. al. 2025). Standardized NDT techniques such as ultrasonic inspection, eddy current testing, radiographic imaging, and thermography provided the basis for systematic QA frameworks, which were later required by regulators like the FAA and EASA. The increasing use of composite materials in aerospace structures also underscored the need for more sophisticated inspection systems, as defects in composites often occur internally and cannot be identified during visual inspection (Mehdipour et al., 2026).

The NDT remains a critical aspect of aerospace QA, with advancements in sensor fidelity, portability, and automation, such as ultrasonic phased array systems and advanced radiography for high-resolution internal imaging of structures without compromising their integrity (Kumar et al., 2022). This is a proactive way to detect cracks, voids, delamination, and fatigue, and to prevent unexpected failures.

Robotics and Automated Inspection: Robotic platforms are becoming more common, including drones with high-resolution cameras and LIDAR systems to inspect aircraft exteriors faster and at a lower cost, robotic crawlers that adhere to the surface with magnets to inspect fuselage and wing surfaces, and automation to reduce human error, speed inspection cycles, and increase repeatability.

Artificial Intelligence and Computer Vision: AI-based inspection systems use machine learning and computer vision to automatically detect flaws.

The DT technology is revolutionizing inspection and QA by creating a real-time digital replica of an aerospace asset that continuously ingests sensor and inspection data (Kapteyn et al., 2021). This allows for predictive assurance, where engineers can predict when a structural or system failure is likely to happen, and by integrating inspection results into DTs, aerospace organizations are moving from reactive maintenance to proactive lifecycle management. Strict compliance with international standards such as ISO 9001 for quality management and AS9100 for aerospace-specific quality systems ensure product safety and traceability through the supply chain, and their compliance requires structured processes for inspection, verification, validation, and documentation (Mallioris et al., 2024).

8. Design Optimization and Retrofits

Design optimization is the search for design solutions that optimize or minimize objectives, such as mass, drag, emissions, cost, or other desired goals, within constraints, such as structural strength, deflections, aero-elastic effects, manufacturability, fatigue life, safety margins, an and certification standards. There are often multiple objectives, and design optimization becomes multiobjective optimization (trade-offs). Aerospace infrastructure is a general term for aircraft, spacecraft, launch systems, and airports and their related ground facilities, and design optimization is a systematic approach to improve architectures or components (such as airframes, propulsion, control surfaces, and structural components) to satisfy multiple criteria, such as weight, cost, performance, safety, and environmental impact. Retrofits are the modification of existing systems to enhance performance, extend the life, comply with new regulations, or meet new requirements. In recent decades, the forces of fuel costs, environmental regulation (such as emissions, noise), safety, and sustainability have made optimization and retrofits a necessity. Progress in computational methods (finite element analysis, computational fluid dynamics), materials (composites, high-performance alloys), manufacturing (additive manufacturing), and systems engineering (multidisciplinary design optimization, multi-fidelity modelling) has made design optimization and retrofits increasingly necessary.

There are several major drivers to push aerospace infrastructure towards design optimization and retrofits. There is also ongoing tightening of emissions and noise standards by global regulators (International Civil Aviation Organization [ICAO], Environmental Protection Agreement (EPA), European Union [EU]). Fuel efficiency is key: weight reduction results in less fuel burn and hence less CO_2. Large improvements can be made without new fleets through retrofitting existing aircraft or infrastructure (e.g., engine upgrades, winglets, drag-reducing modifications). Fuel, maintenance, and regulatory compliance are the major drivers of operating costs in aviation, and the cost of new aircraft is high; thus, retrofits may be more cost effective. Optimizations to increase manufacturability, lifecycle maintenance, and reliability can decrease both up-front and long-term costs. Aerospace systems are subject to extreme environments: variable loading, fatigue, temperature, vibration. Optimizations to maintain structural integrity can prevent failures and increase the time between maintenance overhauls. Retrofits may be required due to aging, degradation, or to meet new safety or performance standards. High-fidelity Computational Fluid Dynamics (CFD), finite element modelling, topology optimization, additive manufacturing, advanced composites, and sensors for SHM enable more ambitious optimization and retrofit strategies that were previously unfeasible. Aircraft, launch systems, and infrastructure have long lifecycles; aircraft may be in service for decades. Retrofits are necessary to keep competitive (fuel efficient, regulatory compliant), and monitoring residual value, resale, and regulatory requirements also factor into retrofit decisions.

Optimization in aerospace relies on a wide variety of mathematical, computational, and engineering tools and methods, some of which are key:

- Topology Optimization: It finds the material layout in a design domain to minimize or maximize some criteria (such as weight or stiffness) while removing unnecessary material to maintain functionality and structural integrity, often coupled with additive manufacturing to realize complex geometries.

- Multidisciplinary Design Optimization (MDO): It brings together several disciplines (e.g., structural, aerodynamic, propulsion, controls, thermal), with the idea that optimizing any one discipline in isolation will not yield optimal global solutions and that MDO frameworks often include coupling CFD, Finite Element Analysis (FEA), propulsion cycle models, etc.
- Robust, Reliability, and Uncertainty-based Optimization: Because aerospace systems are subject to uncertainties (e.g., material variability, manufacturing tolerances, environmental conditions, operational unknowns), robustness and reliability are required and optimization must account for both. Robust design optimization explicitly includes uncertainties and optimizes not only the design itself but also the robustness of the design.
- Multi-Fidelity Modelling: High-fidelity models (e.g. full CFD + FEA) are computationally expensive; low-fidelity models run faster but less accurately. Multi-fidelity strategies use coarse models for broad exploration, then refine with more accurate models in promising regions. For example, the approach in Exploring Multi-Fidelity Aero-elastic Tailoring: Prospect and Model Assessment (Maathuis, et al. 2024) uses a beam-based (low fidelity) and a shell-based (high fidelity) model.
- Shape and Geometry Optimization: In addition to topology, shape optimization modifies surfaces that can be controlled (e.g. wing planform, wing twist, airfoil shapes, control surfaces) to optimize performance criteria (e.g. drag, lift, stability, aero-elastic behaviour). The example in Explicit design optimization of air rudders for maximizing stiffness and fundamental frequency (Jia et al. 2024) does this for stiffened air rudders.
- Metaheuristics and Hybrid Optimization: Derivative-free or heuristic methods (genetic algorithms, particle swarm, simulated annealing) are commonly employed when models are highly nonlinear with many local minima, while hybrid methods (e.g. combining gradient-based with heuristics) can combine the advantages of both. For instance, a survey of the use of metaheuristics for solving aerospace problems systematically explores which algorithms are applied to which types of aerospace optimization problems.
- Lifecycle Analysis and Cost-Benefit/Economic Modelling: In addition to performance or weight, lifecycle costs (such as development, maintenance, fuel, downtime, residual value) must often be taken into account. The paper "Retrofitting Cost Modeling in Aircraft Design" (Della et al. 2022) outlines phases and cost–benefit analysis for retrofits in a regional turbofan aircraft.

9. Training and Simulation

High reliability, safety, and performance are often needed for aerospace infrastructure (aircraft systems, airports, air traffic management [ATM], control towers, maintenance systems), which may have to perform in dynamic and uncertain environments; training is essential to ensure that personnel (pilots, air traffic controllers, maintenance technicians, ground operations staff) can perform their tasks safely, efficiently, and adaptively, but traditional training (on-aircraft, on actual systems, classroom lectures) is limited by cost, risk, availability of real equipment, environmental constraints, and difficulty in exposing trainees to rare or hazardous events. Simulation and associated technologies (Virtual Reality/ Augmented Reality (VR/AR), DTs, remote training, virtual agents, etc.) can address many of these limitations. A number of theories from the fields of education, cognitive psychology, human factors, and systems theory guide the design of training and simulation in aerospace: constructivist learning (learners build knowledge by experience; simulation provides experience within a safe, controlled setting), cognitive load theory (managing intrinsic, extraneous, germane load; fidelity and complexity must be calibrated to avoid overloading the trainee), and deliberate practice (repeating a task while receiving feedback; simulation provides the opportunity for repeated exposure and immediate feedback and correction).

Models such as SHELL (Software, Hardware, Environment, Liveware, Liveware) help understand how human–machine interactions and contextual factors influence performance. In maintenance simulation models, for example, error generation systems are coupled to socio-technical and contextual factors. In air traffic control (ATC) and other operations, situation awareness, workload, stress, and decision-making under uncertainty are pivotal. Simulation allows exposure to rare or high-stress situations while ensuring safety. Competency-Based Training and Assessment (CBTA) states that simulations must be able to assess skills (procedural, communication, and cognitive) that are beyond the inflated measure of simply clocking hours flown or sitting in class.

Traditional flight simulators, including full-motion devices certified by authorities such as the FAA and EASA, as well as fixed-base and cabin simulators, serve as foundational tools for pilot instruction. These simulators span a range of training applications, from initial instruction (ab initio) to recurrent training and type-rating qualifications. Their design closely replicates real-world cockpit environments, enabling comprehensive skill development and scenario-based assessments.

The FAA's Tower Simulation System (TSS)—an example of ATC—is anticipated to replicate the complexities of modern airport environments with high fidelity. Such platforms model detailed airport layouts, runways, taxiways, ground operations, dynamic weather conditions, and interactions with ground vehicles, providing realistic scenarios essential for ATC training and skill development. Complementing these systems, modular and research-oriented simulators like NARSIM offer adjustable configurations for radar, tower, and remote tower operations, aiding a broad spectrum of instructional and experimental objectives. Remote ATC simulation tools further boost trainee preparedness by incorporating communication protocols, phraseology practice, and stress-testing scenarios that expose learners to abnormal and emergency events.

Virtual simulation has transformed aviation maintenance training alongside. Virtual reality (VR), augmented reality (AR), and interactive 3D models now provide traditional hands-on practices by delivering immersive, high-fidelity learning experiences without requiring physical equipment. In regions such as Saudi Arabia, expert panels advocate integrating VR tools as integral improvements to establish training programmes. Through these immersive platforms, trainees engage with digital representations of aircraft systems, perform maintenance tasks in controlled environments, and receive real-time visual feedback. Studies, including "Improving Effectiveness of eLearning in Maintenance Using Interactive 3D" (Santhosh et al. 2009), highlight significant reductions in training time and measurable improvements in learner performance compared to conventional approaches.

Simulation networks have also become essential, particularly when physical co-location is not feasible. During the COVID-19 pandemic, remote ATC training systems preserved continuity of instruction by virtually replicating instructor–trainee interactions while addressing latency and cybersecurity considerations to ensure training integrity.

The integration of AI and machine learning into simulation environments further enriches training capabilities. Intelligent virtual agents such as the Virtual Simulation–Pilot Agent for Training of Air Traffic Controllers use automatic speech recognition and command/response parsing to enable realistic, responsive interactions with trainees in real time. Collectively, these advancements demonstrate a significant evolution in aviation maintenance and operations training, blending traditional practices with cutting-edge digital and AI-driven technologies to build competence, resilience, and readiness across the aerospace workforce.

10. Challenges and Limitations

Aerospace infrastructure constitutes connected network of physical and digital systems that enable the safe and efficient operation of air and space transportation. This includes airports, ATC centres, communication and navigation systems, maintenance facilities, satellite networks, and ground support operations. However, the sector faces serious burdens arising from rapid technological advancements, growing air traffic demands, environmental considerations, evolving security threats, and the challenges associated with aging infrastructure. These factors collectively demand the need for innovative approaches such as generative AI–based techniques to ensure the continued reliability, resilience, and modernization of aerospace infrastructure. Here, we discuss the major operational, technological, financial, regulatory, and environmental challenges and limitations of aerospace infrastructure.

Aging aerospace infrastructure, such as runways, terminals, ATC systems, and radar installations, much of which was designed decades ago, is becoming increasingly unable to support modern operational demands in many countries, especially in the developed world. A high percentage of US airport infrastructure is past its designed life and is at the point where the cost of maintaining the infrastructure is higher and causes more service interruptions. Aging physical infrastructure leads to flight delays, greater safety risks, and reduced ability to implement new technologies such as satellite-based navigation systems. Additionally, deferred maintenance, which may be caused by budget restrictions, can compound wear and tear, affecting operational efficiency and safety. For example, older radar systems may not have the accuracy required for current traffic volumes or may not be compatible with the data integration capabilities of newer technologies, such as Automatic Dependent Surveillance–Broadcast (ADS-B).

The second main challenge is the finite capacity of airports and airspace, especially in high-traffic areas, as global air travel demand is projected to double by 2040, placing strain on the current infrastructure to accommodate more aircraft, passengers, and cargo, resulting in flight delays and increased fuel consumption, which affect both operational efficiency and environmental sustainability. Airports in rapidly urbanizing regions of Asia and Africa are pressured to accommodate more traffic and increase the volume of aircraft, passengers, and cargo. ATM systems are also not optimized for high-density traffic flows, especially in peak traffic hours or adverse weather conditions, and the inability to efficiently re-route or space aircraft can greatly reduce throughput and safety margins. Technological advancement is a double-edged sword for aerospace infrastructure, enabling greater efficiency, safety, and data-driven management, but creating integration, standardization, and obsolescence challenges. In addition, modern aircraft have ever more complex systems, but the ground infrastructure that would allow them to operate to their full potential is not compatible, as some countries have already adopted performance-based navigation (PBN), while others still rely heavily on ground-based systems, and aerospace infrastructure often has legacy systems that cannot be made compatible with new technologies, and so on, and when the transition to satellite-based navigation systems, like GPS or Galileo, is made, it will entail a huge investment in both the airborne and the ground segments as well as in training of personnel. Another important technological challenge is cybersecurity. As infrastructure becomes ever more interconnected and dependent on digital systems, it will become ever more vulnerable to cyberattacks, data breaches, and software failures.

Aerospace infrastructure has a significant environmental footprint, including air and noise pollution, carbon emissions, and land use changes, and infrastructure must be designed and upgraded to be more sustainable and resilient as climate change intensifies. Runways and terminals are at risk from extreme weather events, such as hurricanes, flooding, and heatwaves, and rising sea levels pose a risk to low-lying coastal airports, which can require expensive mitigation measures such as seawalls or elevated runways. Stringent environmental regulations, including noise abatement procedures, carbon offset programmes, and renewable energy use, add to the cost and time of retrofitting older infrastructure, while sustainable airport design (e.g., LEED-certified terminals) is still a relatively new concept. In addition, infrastructure expansion projects are often met with public resistance based on environmental concerns, limiting the ability to address future capacity needs with additional airport development.

Aerospace infrastructure development and maintenance is expensive, and government budgets, economic downturns, or political priorities may limit funding, causing delays, reduced scope, or underinvestment in critical systems. Public–private partnerships (PPPs) have been suggested as a solution but can lead to long-term financial liabilities, regulatory complications, and unequal access. Smaller or developing countries may have trouble attracting private investment because of perceived risk or low return. Infrastructure projects are prone to cost overruns and schedule delays because of inaccurate demand forecasting, poor project management, or regulatory red tape, as evidenced by the multiple delays and cost overruns for the Berlin Brandenburg Airport (BER) project in Germany.

Regulation of aerospace infrastructure development is often complex and varies significantly across countries and regions, with the multiplicity of regulatory authorities (civil aviation bodies, environmental agencies, air navigation service providers) causing bureaucratic delays, conflicting requirements, and slow adoption of innovations; international coordination is challenging despite the existence of organizations like the ICAO that provide guidelines, enforcement and implementation are often inconsistent, and regulatory rigidity can delay the certification and deployment of new technologies (e.g., remote air traffic control towers, UAV traffic management systems) thereby stalling innovation and adaptation to emerging challenges.

A highly skilled workforce is needed to operate, maintain, and upgrade modern aerospace infrastructure; however, shortages of trained personnel exist in many areas, including ATC, aerospace engineering, and maintenance, and training often lags behind the introduction of new technologies, reducing system efficiency and increasing the risk of errors. This is expected to result in a global shortage of 620,000 aviation professionals by 2030, especially in Asia-Pacific and Africa, as well as a lack of investment in ongoing training and simulation infrastructure, which renders human operators unprepared for non-routine or emergency situations, reducing overall system resilience. Aerospace infrastructure faces growing security risks, such as terrorism, cyberattacks, and geopolitical conflict, as airports and airspace are valuable targets for physical and digital attacks, and geopolitical tensions can disrupt supply chains, delay cross-border projects, and fragment global standards. The conflict in Ukraine and related airspace restrictions impacted commercial aviation routes, demonstrating how geopolitics directly impacts aerospace infrastructure planning and operations.

11. Conclusion

In the field of aerospace maintenance, generative AI is a revolutionary development. Predictive analytics, real-time monitoring, computer vision, and robotics are all combined by generative AI to provide proactive problem solving, cost effectiveness, and increased safety. When it is adopted, aerospace maintenance is expected to change, guaranteeing that both military and commercial aviation continue to be technologically sophisticated, agile, and safe. The merits of this conversion are varied. Generative AI helps with the early discovery of minute inconsistencies and subtle deterioration patterns, averting disastrous failures and boosting confidence in aviation systems. PdM enhances aircraft utilization for both commercial and defence operations by reducing unnecessary interventions and expensive downtime.

These capabilities intentionally allow defence companies to maintain fleet readiness with quicker turnaround times, and they provide airlines a competitive edge through improved customer consistency and efficiency. Significant obstacles still persist in spite of its potential. Accessibility and data quality are enduring obstacles because aerospace data is commonly unlabelled or proprietary. System interconnectedness enhances cybersecurity risks, which raises queries about adversarial manipulation. Further impeding broad adoption are incorporation with legacy aircraft systems and the demand for regulatory frameworks that ensure explanation and compliance. In the future, developments in DTs, blockchain, edge AI, and autonomous robotic inspection systems are believed to further refine maintenance systems' generative and predictive capabilities. These developments also assist broader sustainability objectives by reducing waste and resource consumption through optimized module design and extended asset lifecycles.

In conclusion, generative AI is more than just a technological advancement; it is a fundamental variation in the method of aerospace maintenance that brings data and decision-making together to attain safer, more efficient, and more resilient operations. Addressing the technical, ethical, and governance challenges associated with generative AI will be essential for its successful integration into aerospace maintenance. Achieving this will require sustained collaboration among academia, industry stakeholders, and regulatory authorities to ensure that future aerospace systems remain intelligent, adaptive, and resilient. Such coordinated efforts will play a critical role in enabling safe, reliable, and sustainable maintenance practices across the evolving aerospace landscape.

References

Adragna, P.-A., Malandrakis, K., Vitanov, I., Sherburn, C. and Avdelidis, N.P. (2025). A comprehensive review of robotics-aided aircraft non-destructive inspection towards the smart hangar. The Aeronautical Journal, 129(1342), 3347–3378. https://doi.org/10.1017/aer.2025.10048

Alonso, R., Smith, J. and Verma, P. (2021). GAN-based defect detection in aerospace surface inspections. *Journal of Aerospace Engineering*, 35(4), 221–233.

Bianchini, A., Donini, F., Pellegrini, M. and Rossi, J. (2023). Predictive maintenance in aviation: A review of data-driven approaches. *Computers in Industry*, 132, 103517. https://doi.org/10.1016/j.compind.2023.103517

Bommasani, R., Hudson, D.A., Adeli, E. et al. (2021). On the opportunities and risks of foundation models. https://arxiv.org/abs/2108.07258. Accessed on 7 Novermber 2025.

Choi, H., Park, J. and Kim, S. (2022). Challenges in synthetic data for predictive maintenance. *Reliability Engineering & System Safety*, 221, 108295.

Cespedes-Cubides, A.S. and Jradi, M. (2024). A review of building digital twins to improve energy efficiency in the building operational stage. *Energy Informatics*, 7(1), 11. https://doi.org/10.1186/s42162-024-00313-7

Della Vecchia, P., Mandorino, M., Cusati, V. and Nicolosi, F. (2022). Retrofitting cost modeling in aircraft design. *Aerospace*, 9(7), 349.

Farrar, C.R. and Worden, K. (2007). An introduction to structural health monitoring. Philosophical Transactions of the Royal Society A: *Mathematical, Physical and Engineering Sciences*, 365(1851), 303–315. https://doi.org/10.1098/rsta.2006.1928

García, M., Ruiz, J. and Fernandez, A. (2021). Data scarcity in aviation predictive maintenance. *Computers in Industry*, 132, 103517.

H. Rocha, C. Semprimoschnig, and J. P. Nunes, "Sensors for process and structural health monitoring of aerospace composites: A review," *Eng. Struct.*, vol. 237, p. 112231, 2021, doi: https://doi.org/10.1016/j.engstruct.2021.112231

Jia, Y., Meng, W., Du, Z., Liu, C., Li, S., Wang, C. and Guo, X. (2024). Explicit design optimization of air rudders for maximizing stiffness and fundamental frequency. Thin-Walled Structures, 203, 112152.

Kapteyn, M. G., Knezevic, D. J. and Willcox, K. E. (2021). Physics-informed machine learning for digital twins. *AIAA Journal*, 59(2), 439–452.

Karniadakis, G.E., Kevrekidis, I.G., Lu, L., Perdikaris, P., Wang, S. and Yang, L. (2021). Physics-informed machine learning. *Nature Reviews Physics*, 3(6), 422–440.

Kumar, R., Singh, P. and Shah, S. (2022). Data interoperability challenges in aviation MRO. *Journal of Air Transport Management*, 103, 102268.

Li, Y., Sun, J. and Zhao, R. (2020). Variational autoencoders for aircraft engine degradation modeling. *Engineering Applications of Artificial Intelligence*, 92, 103659.

Mallioris, P., Aivazidou, E. and Bechtsis, D. (2024). Predictive maintenance in Industry 4.0: A systematic multi-sector mapping. *CIRP Journal of Manufacturing Science and Technology*, 50, 80–103. https://doi.org/10.1016/j.cirpj.2024.02.003

Ma, S., Flanigan, K.A. and Bergés, M. (2024). State-of-the-art review: The use of digital twins to support artificial intelligence-guided predictive maintenance [Preprint]. arXiv. https://doi.org/10.48550/arXiv.2406.13117

Maathuis, H., Castro, S.G. and De Breuker, R. (2024). Exploring multi-fidelity aeroelastic tailoring: Prospect and model assessment. arXiv preprint arXiv:2411.03247.

Mehdipour, S., Habibzadeh, A. and Esmi, N. (2026). Integrating digital twins, data management and artificial intelligence for predictive maintenance in aviation: A comprehensive review. *Digital Twins and Applications*, e70029. https://doi.org/10.1049/dgt2.70029

Mendi, A.F., Ersoy, C., Akan, O.B., Cevik, A. and Atalay, A. (2022). A digital twin case study on automotive production line. *Sensors*, 22(18), 6963. https://doi.org/10.3390/s22186963

Onaji, I., Tiwari, A., Roy, R. and others. (2022). Digital twin in manufacturing: Conceptual framework and case studies. *International Journal of Computer Integrated Manufacturing*, 35(8), 831–858. https://doi.org/10.1080/0951192X.2022.2027014

Pashami, S., Nowaczyk, S., Fan, Y., Jakubowski, J., Paiva, N., Davari, N., Bobek, S., Jamshidi, S., Sarmadi, H., Alabdallah, A., Ribeiro, R.P., Veloso, B., Sayed-Mouchaweh, M., Rajaoarisoa, L., Nalepa, G.J. and Gama, J. (2023). Explainable predictive maintenance. arXiv. https://doi.org/10.48550/arXiv.2306.05120.

Rasheed, A., San, O. and Kvamsdal, T. (2019). Digital twin: Values, challenges and enablers. https://arxiv.org/abs/1910.01719. Last accessed: Jan 16 2026.

Ribeiro, M.T., Singh, S. and Guestrin, C. (2020). Beyond accuracy: Interpretable machine learning. *Communications of the ACM*, 63(1), 102–109.

Rizwan, M., Khan, Z. and Ali, T. (2022). Generative AI in predictive maintenance: A systematic literature review. *Journal of Intelligent Manufacturing*, 33(9), 2159–2176.

Rocha, H., Semprimoschnig, C., and Nunes, J.P. "Sensors for process and structural health monitoring of aerospace composites: A review," *Eng. Struct.*, vol. 237, p. 112231, 2021, doi: https://doi.org/10.1016/j.engstruct.2021.112231

Santhosh Baboo, S., and Lobo, N. (2009). Improving Effectiveness Of ELearning In Maintenance Using Interactive 3D. arXiv e-prints, arXiv-0909.

Scarselli, G. and Nicassio, F. (2025). Machine Learning for Structural Health Monitoring of Aerospace Structures: A Review. *Sensors*, 25(19), 6136. https://doi.org/10.3390/s25196136

Schmidt, L., Novak, J. and Turner, A. (2023). Retrieval-augmented generative AI in aerospace documentation. *AI in Aviation*, 2(3), 51–65.

Schwab, K., Davis, N. and Smith, R. (2021). Shaping the future of advanced manufacturing and production. Available at https://www.weforum.org. Accessed on 16 January 2026.

Taheri, H., Gonzalez Bocanegra, M. and Taheri, M. (2022). Artificial intelligence, machine learning and smart technologies for nondestructive evaluation. Sensors, 22(11), 4055. https://doi.org/10.3390/s22114055

Ucar, A., Karakose, M. and Kırımça, N. (2024). Artificial intelligence for predictive maintenance applications. *Applied Sciences*, 14(2), 898.

Zhang, H., Liu, Q. and Zhou, T. (2021). Evolution of predictive maintenance in aviation. *IEEE Access*, 9, 158765–158780.

Zhao, R., Yan, R., Chen, Z. et al. (2019). Deep learning and its applications to machine health monitoring. *Mechanical Systems and Signal Processing*, 115, 213–237.

Zhou, C., Li, D. and Wang, Y. (2021). Variational autoencoder-based anomaly detection in turbofan engines. *Mechanical Systems and Signal Processing*, 154, 107547.

12 Deep Learning–based NLP Models for Decision Support in Defence Operations

Anuj Kumar Pal[1*], Basant Tiwari[2], Vivek Tiwari[3], Shailendra Gupta[4] and Rahul Kumar Gour[5]

The massive growth of digital communication in defence systems requires some intelligent mechanisms to find and remove toxic or malicious content of the internet. These conversations may compromise security, damage morale, erode trust, and enable adversarial propaganda which makes toxic content detection a mission-critical task. This study proposes a multi-layered toxic comment detection framework comprising machine learning (ML), deep learning (DL), and generative artificial intelligence (AI). The approach combines traditional ML models for lightweight deployment with advanced DL architectures for deeper semantic analysis. Generative AI is employed for synthetic data augmentation, generating realistic defence-specific toxic examples to handle data scarcity, improve class balance, and enhance resilience to evolving adversarial language. Jigsaw dataset and Wikipedia Talk Pages are used for the evaluations of the study, and a curated defence corpus showed the better results in terms of the precision, recall, F1-score, and robustness in toxicity. The designed system is securely integrated for defence communications and meets the standards of cybersecurity which supports real-time inference and enables human oversight for the critical cases. The system is getting a scalable and robust solution to protect the defence communication system for internal and external threads by integrating ML, DL, and generative AI in a single architecture.

1. Introduction

The way military units plan their operations, coordinate their missions, and exchange their information is highly reliant on digital communication. Nowadays, the defence system is highly connected with each other with integration of secure tactical messaging into the systems, collaborative command-and-control

[1] https://orcid.org/0009-0002-7938-9444
[2] https://orcid.org/0000-0002-3113-4760
[3] https://orcid.org/0000-0002-7411-5113
[4] https://orcid.org/0000-0002-6981-9503
[5] https://orcid.org/0009-0007-5769-6079
* Corresponding author: junaamity@gmail.com

DOI: 10.1201/9781003688174-12

platforms, and open-source intelligence incorporated into a unified communication environment. The tools of artificial intelligence (AI) have been enhanced these days in terms of their speed of operations, their decision-making capability, and situational awareness. The information is spread throughout the different units and their branches and it gets updated within microseconds. With these advancements there are some associated risks too. From the same communication links many other data communication takes place which enhances malicious communication from internal and external sources. People can access these links to spread harmful content throughout the internet (Vasu et al., 2018). From the civilian point of view, communication platforms like social media may disturb mental peace or cause psychological harm. On the other hand, for the defence system the damage can be more severe and beyond imagination. Toxicity can damage the trust and morale in the units, distract the leadership, and it can even greatly affect the overall national-level security (Crăcea, 2022). For civilians, the occasional errors or spread of toxicity over social media can be handled or avoided, but for defence systems accuracy should be at the maximum level to filter out the harmful content. In this context, there is no scope for any error. This high-end sensitivity for toxic comments is complex when it concerns defence environments. People can embed toxic comments in the form of coded messages in domain-specific information exchange. The messages in coded form create more problems in detecting toxicity, thereby requiring an advanced level of modelling to identify toxic communication. Because of these challenges, detection and handling of the problem of toxic communication in the defence system is crucial and is not only a technical concern but also a strategic issue. Maintaining the security of communication channels is essential, including defending physical infrastructure. To explore the solutions to these problems, this study proposes a three-layered hybrid framework to detect toxic content. Machine learning, deep learning, and generative AI are used to balance the system to produce efficiency and adaptability of the model. Initial approaches like linear and logistic regression offer lightweight solutions to detect toxicity. Deep learning architectures like convolutional neural networks (CNNs), Long Short Term Memory (LSTM), and Bidirectional Long Short-Term Memory Networks (BiLSTM) contribute to capture sequential information and their dependencies within the toxic comments. Transformer-based models like BERT (Devlin et al., 2019) and RoBERT (Liu Y. et. al., 2019) further improve the deep understanding of systems contractual information. Finally, generative AI assists in synthetic data augmentation to enhance the categorization of toxicity and to provide the simulation-based scenario for model robustness. The reason for using this layered architecture is to ensure that toxic comments can be filtered through multiple layers: from keyword-based simple checks to semantic reasoning–based checks for generation of final result. This type of redundant checks provide better accuracy and decrease the risks associated with false positives and false negatives, which improves the system's reliability and matches the standards required in the defence scenarios. In summary, the defence system depends on digital communication for critical coordination for its smooth working and the risks associated with toxic contents are sometimes overlooked. The proposed framework of this study provides the solution with the strength of machine learning, deep learning and generative AI to create a highly accurate, reliable, robust, and efficient system to detect toxic comments (Shounak et al., 2022).

2. Literature Review

Toxic comment classification and its detection is a very critical area of research in the field of natural language processing. The exponential increase in content generated by users has a significant impact on the marketing, entertainment, and even on the defence industry. This growth of user-generated content also poses some challenges like misinformation, copyright issues, and content moderation. There must be a balance between user expression and controlling harmful content generated by the users, and this should be managed and ensured by the online platforms.

2.1 *Early Approaches: Machine Learning Models*

Early approaches used to detect toxic comments were based on rules and regulations and simple machine learning models but they had many limitations in handling the toxicity in user-generated content. The rule-based systems need predefined patterns and rules to detect toxicity, which leads to very less flexibility in the system. These systems also require frequent updates on to keep up with the evolving and new language trends, making them resource-intensive and difficult to scale. Similarly, early used models of machine learning, such as those based on bag-of-words or basic n-grams, face problems in understanding the semantics of the system. These models often ignore word order and fail to capture dependencies between phrases, leading to less accurate classifications, especially in complex or ambiguous cases. When we talk about machine learning, early research on toxic content detection mainly depended on traditional machine learning methodologies. These models are highly dependent on simple and easy text representations, and classify cases as toxic and non-toxic on the basis of surface-level cues and features. Among the most commonly used models were:

- *Support Vector Machines (SVMs)*: Support vector machine (SVM) is a supervised machine learning methodology used for classification and regression problems. SVM works by selecting a hyper-plane which best divides the different classes of data points. SVM is very useful when the data is in high-dimensional form and has complex decision boundaries as it concentrates on optimizing the margin in between the classes. After transferring the data into higher dimensions, SVM models can also establish nonlinear connections using kernel functions. SVM is used in domains like bioinformatics, classification of text, and image recognition because of its accuracy and resilience (Pal & Rai, 2023).

- *Logistic Regression with TF-IDF Representations*: Logistic regression deals with the probability that any event will fall into groups. It is a statistical method for binary classification tasks. With the use of logistic functions which convert predicted values into probability ranging between 0 and 1, it models the relations as dependent and more than one independent variable. Logistic regression provides discrete results and is specially designed for categorization challenges. It is very frequently used for activities like diagnosis of diseases, assessment of credit risk, and client segmentation in industries including marketing, healthcare, and finance (Pal & Rai, 2024a).
- *Random Forests*: Random forests are ensemble-based models which are applied to structured toxicity classification problems and offer robustness and interpretability of comments. However, they significantly struggle with scalability and the complexity of linguistic subtleties present in natural conversations.

Although these approaches laid the foundation, they were not enough to handle subtle forms of toxicity such as sarcasm, coded hate speech, and manipulative phrasing.

2.2 The Deep Learning Revolution

Progress in deep learning models provided a turning point in the classification and detection of toxic comments. Deep learning models automatically capture and learn different meanings of texts, including their local and global patterns. This enhances the model's ability to detect toxic comments.

- Convolutional Neural Networks (CNNs): CNNs, which were very popular in computer vision, were introduced in natural language processing where they proved to be excellent in identifying the local patterns, such as n-grams, to indicate toxicity. CNNs filter the repeated abusive contents or phrases which are related to toxicity (Kebede et al., 2021).
- Bidirectional Long Short-Term Memory Networks (BiLSTMs): These recurrent architectures (Figure 12.1) allowed for modelling long-range dependencies in text, crucial for understanding the sequential nature of conversations. By processing language in both forward and backward directions, BiLSTMs offered more comprehensive contextual representations (Pal & Rai, 2024b).
- Attention Mechanisms: The inclusion of an attention layer has increased the performance and interpretability of the model. It enables the system to select the tokens that are contractually relevant. For example, in an ironic statement, the focus may be on sarcastic words that change the meaning of the text (Kumar H., et. al, 2021).

The most serious progress, however, was made the transformer-based architectures or models like Bidirectional Encoder Representations from Transformers (BERT) (Saleh et al., 2023), RoBERTa, and GPT that have flipped

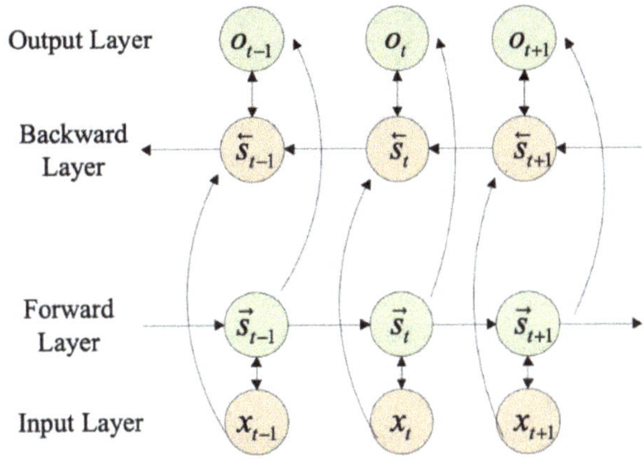

Fig. 12.1 Basic structure of bi-directional LSTM. Source: Dubey et al. (2020).

the problem of toxic content detection. These models are pre-trained on large-scale datasets to analyse the contextual meaning and their understandings to outperform the older techniques of toxicity detection. They can handle not only explicit toxicity but also subtle and context-dependent forms, making them indispensable for real-world deployment (Gupta et al., 2021).

2.3 The Role of Generative AI

In parallel with the success of discriminative models, generative AI introduced novel possibilities (Shounak et al., 2022). Models based on architectures like GPT were used not only for classification tasks but also for synthetic data generation. This was particularly impactful for addressing the challenge of class imbalance, where certain toxic categories (e.g., coded harassment, indirect threats, or adversarial propaganda) were underrepresented in training datasets. By capturing the toxic and non-toxic comments, research scholars have significantly improved the robustness of the models and their exposure to diversity which enables the system to handle the toxic attacks. Generative AI allows scholars to simulate the critical cases involving manipulation of psychological meanings.

2.4 Gaps in Civilian-Focused Research

Even after so much progress, most of the studies related to toxic comment detection focus on the civilian platforms like Twitter and Facebook. On the other hand, there is not much focus on the unique operational demands of the communication system in the defence domain where security is required at the highest level and toxicity of comments may harm severely. In the defence domain, toxic and malicious content is a concern not only for causing online harm but also for causing substantial psychological harm during operations by lowering the morale of the teams and by adversely affecting decision-making processes in the military (Panazan & Gheorghe, 2025; Almendingen. 2025). This emphasises the need for approaches focused on the following:

- Domain-Specific Jargon: In military, communication does not take place only in technical terms and their acronyms. Communication is also based on their context-based dependencies which are totally different from civilian communication.
- Understanding of Adversarial PsyOps: There are some embedded systems that are designed to understand and detect misinformation by manipulating both strategic and ordinary toxic content. These contents are modelled by the system for better understanding.
- Multilingual and Code-Switched Language: In the defence domain, communication takes place in multiple languages and the context can change with the change in language. This complexity cannot be handled by the civilian dataset.
- Cybersecurity and Military-Grade Standards: In defence systems, security must be robust and must follow high-class protocols because there is no scope for misclassification or misinterpretation (Tesfay et al., 2021).

2.5 Towards Defence-Oriented Toxic Content Detection

To bridge the gap, research scholars must think beyond the current frameworks and specified models, which is very important for a critical environment like a defence. This includes the understanding of the domain with its multilingual content and context of information. There must be some kind of collaboration between the researchers and experts who are working in the defence domain to understand the complexity of the system related to natural language processing. The intent should be not only to detect the toxic comments but also to find the strategic intent behind the specific communication. Though the field of toxic comment detection has evolved from the earlier machine learning approaches to the current generative AI-based systems, detection of toxicity in defence communication is still a big challenge. To address these problems, researchers must understand and prioritize domain-specific information while maintaining system robustness. They should also analyse how contextual information is manipulated, with its adversarial awareness, to ensure that toxic comment detection becomes a secure system and provides national-level protection to defence communication.

3. Proposed Framework

This research proposes a hybrid framework (Figure 12.2) which is based on a multi-layered approach that leverages the complementary strengths of machine learning, deep learning, and generative AI to find and minimize or remove toxic communication in the defence systems. The design of this framework basically relies on the principle of layered defence: rather than relying on a single methodology or approach, this architecture integrates multiple layers resembling analytical information that progressively refine the accuracy of content detection. Each layer has a specific role, and ensures efficiency and robustness at different levels of communication complexity.

3.1 Layer 1: Machine Learning Layer

The initial layer is of traditional machine learning models such as SVMs, random forests, and gradient boosting. Machine learning models are less effective than deep learning models in many scenarios because of the latter's high efficiency and better capability to make inferences. This layer of the model is designed for effective and efficient classification of toxic comments when there is large-scale communication data. In defence systems, there is continuous arrival of data on a real-time basis, which includes tactical massaging and intelligence feeds. This needs to be quickly filtered and processed so that there is no overloading of data in the system. Initially, limited computation and connectivity are required so the machine learning models are deployed with limited resource constraints. This layer acts as a preliminary line of defence wherein the system does initial level of screening to remove toxicity; only the complex cases are passed on to the subsequent layer for further processing. The machine learning model optimizes the model's efficiency by applying scalable filters. After this processing, only the challenging instances advance through the remaining layers.

3.2 Layer 2: Deep Learning Layer

The second layer of the model comprises deep learning models that perform advanced level of contextual data analysis on the incoming real-time data. Architecture of this layer includes BiLSTMs, CNNs and transformer-based architectures like BERT. This layer eliminates the contextual misleading data of toxic content. Machine learning models rely heavily on structural features but deep learning models focus on long-range dependencies within the input data stream. Due to this approach, different types of toxic content like manipulated phrases, sarcasm, and hate speech in different codes has been identified and evaluated to improve the system's efficiency. Thus, the overall model offers robustness for adversarial tactics such as an attempt to embed harmful content in any indirect phrases or in any domain-specific data of multilingual switched codes. Transformer-based models are used for pre-training on large input data, allowing them to generalize and effectively handle complex scenarios. Here the analysis is performed on token level as well as contextual level to improve the accuracy of the overall system. This computationally intensive layer ensures deep understanding of the overall context of data, which is critical for any defence system because it can have operational consequences.

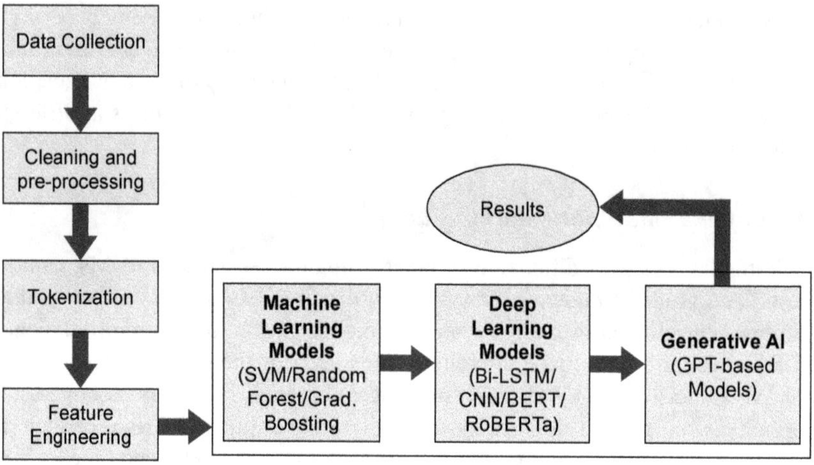

Fig. 12.2 Model architecture.

3.3 Layer 3: Generative AI Layer

The next layer of the framework is the generative AI layer which is implemented as a complementary element of the model. For the classification of content and generating syntactical data, tools like GPT-based models were implemented. Imbalance in the datasets is a crucial aspect that must be detected and processed. In case of civilian dataset, there might be abundant examples of hate speech that can reflect the misleading information but in case of defence system the malicious communication must be handled very carefully. To overcome these problems, generative AI is being used for generating synthetic toxic examples related to the defence system which includes messages like spreading propaganda and forwarding misinformation related to the defence system. Misinformation may also lead to confusion and lower the morale of the team. Generative AI ensures that the system adapts to the situations according to the new input data being generated which comprises the threat. As adversaries regularly change and update their strategies for detecting toxic content, synthetic augmentation allows the model to train on a wide variety of scenarios, which improves the system resilience and generalization. This also improves the overall security and efficiency of the system.

3.4 Integrated Benefits of the Hybrid Framework

After integrating all the three layers, the system achieves balance efficiency, improved accuracy, and adapts to the required systems scenario. The machine learning layer works as a screening mechanism for the incoming data which ensures scalability and responsiveness of the system on real-time data. Deep learning provides the detailed analysis to handle the long-term dependencies in between the data. Finally, the generative AI layer works by adapting the new and diverse incoming data, updating the system to improve defence-specific future processing, training, and testing.

4. Dataset and Pre-processing

4.1 Datasets Used

The quality of and diversity in the datasets used for model training, testing, and evaluation are of utmost importance for the effectiveness of any toxic content detection framework. A reliable dataset reflects the nuances and variations in the context that occur in real-world exchanges with enough examples of toxic and non-toxic communication. For defence communication systems, the ideal datasets must ensure balance between well-established open-domain corpora and defence-specific data, which capture unique adversarial patterns related to defence. Here the research has been focused on three datasets: the Jigsaw Toxic Comment Classification Challenge Dataset, the Wikipedia Talk Pages Dataset, and a specially curated Defence Communication Corpus. All these datasets provide the breadth and depth, which support the development of robust, context-aware toxic content detection models.

4.1.1 Jigsaw Toxic Comment Classification Challenge Dataset

The Jigsaw Toxic Comment Classification Challenge Dataset (Table 12.1) is one of the most widely used benchmarks for toxic content detection originally hosted on Kaggle. The dataset contains over 155,000 well-labelled comments that were collected from online platforms and cover a broad spectrum of toxic behaviours. Each comment is annotated for categories such as toxic, severe toxic, obscene, threat, insult, and identity hate. The importance of this dataset is that it provides a large, balanced foundation for training machine learning and deep learning models. Its multi-label classification scheme allows systems to learn distinctions between different levels and types of toxicity. Its strength lies in its considerable size and diversity, and the dataset is particularly useful for building general-purpose toxicity classifiers and pre-training models before fine-tuning them for specialized domains (Pal & Rai, 2023). It comprises abusive content and subtle form of toxicity for providing more coverage. The limitation of the dataset is that it originated from open source platforms like Twitter and Facebook and thus lacks defence domain–specific knowledge like adversarial tactics, multilingual information, and code switching patterns. Despite its limitations, the Jigsaw dataset provides a baseline resource for toxic content research, and offers a standardized benchmark to compare models' performance throughout different studies.

Table 12.1 Sample of Jigsaw Toxic Comment Classification Challenge Dataset.

Id	*toxic*	*severe_toxic*	*obscene*	*threat*	*insult*	*identity_hate*
00001cee341fdb12	0.5	0.5	0.5	0.5	0.5	0.5
0000247867823ef7	0.5	0.5	0.5	0.5	0.5	0.5
00013b17ad220c46	0.5	0.5	0.5	0.5	0.5	0.5
00017563c3f7919a	0.5	0.5	0.5	0.5	0.5	0.5
00017695ad8997eb	0.5	0.5	0.5	0.5	0.5	0.5
0001ea8717f6de06	0.5	0.5	0.5	0.5	0.5	0.5
00024115d4cbde0f	0.5	0.5	0.5	0.5	0.5	0.5
000247e83dcc1211	0.5	0.5	0.5	0.5	0.5	0.5
00025358d4737918	0.5	0.5	0.5	0.5	0.5	0.5
00026d1092fe71cc	0.5	0.5	0.5	0.5	0.5	0.5
0002eadc3b301559	0.5	0.5	0.5	0.5	0.5	0.5
0002f87b16116a7f	0.5	0.5	0.5	0.5	0.5	0.5
0003806b11932181	0.5	0.5	0.5	0.5	0.5	0.5
0003e1cccfd5a40a	0.5	0.5	0.5	0.5	0.5	0.5
00059ace3e3e9a53	0.5	0.5	0.5	0.5	0.5	0.5
000634272d0d44eb	0.5	0.5	0.5	0.5	0.5	0.5
000663aff0fffc80	0.5	0.5	0.5	0.5	0.5	0.5
000689dd34e20979	0.5	0.5	0.5	0.5	0.5	0.5
000834769115370c	0.5	0.5	0.5	0.5	0.5	0.5
000844b52dee5f3f	0.5	0.5	0.5	0.5	0.5	0.5
00084da5d4ead7aa	0.5	0.5	0.5	0.5	0.5	0.5
00091c35fa9d0465	0.5	0.5	0.5	0.5	0.5	0.5
000968ce11f5ee34	0.5	0.5	0.5	0.5	0.5	0.5

4.1.2 Wikipedia Talk Pages Dataset

The Wikipedia Talk Pages Dataset (Table 12.2) is another very famous dataset that is widely accepted and used by researchers for toxic comments classification and detection. This dataset comprises toxic comments in conversations occurring in dialogue-oriented contexts which were absent in Jigsaw dataset as it was more focused on general online toxicity (cjadams et al., 2017). This dataset serves as interactive information interchange throughout the defence communication, thereby helping to detect the toxic comments. It may not be present at that time but it also captures back-and-forth discussions.

Table 12.2 Sample of Wikipedia Talk Pages Dataset.

rev_id	*Comment*	*year*	*logged_in*	*ns*	*sample*	*split*
37675	`-NEWLINE_TOKENThis is not “creative”. Those are the dictionary definitions of the terms “insurance”	2002	FALSE	article	random	train
44816	`NEWLINE_ TOKENNEWLINE_TOKEN: the term “standard model” is itself less NPOV	2002	FALSE	article	random	train
49851	NEWLINE_ TOKENNEWLINE_ TOKENTrue or false, the situation as of March 2002 was such: NEWLINE_TOKENA	2002	FALSE	article	random	train
89320	Next, maybe you could work on being less condescending with your suggestions about reading the naming conventions and FDL	2002	TRUE	article	random	dev
93890	This page will need disambiguation.	2002	TRUE	article	random	train

This dataset also performs excellent in terms of training and testing the model that requires contextual toxicity. Some specific toxic patterns of communication like sarcasm and aggression are the major strengths of this dataset, which was hard to find in surface-level methodologies. This makes the model as a better trainable system to detect toxicity. The dataset focuses on dialogue-based toxicity, which can be a drawback, but still it provides insight from the civilian domain capturing disagreements on some specific propaganda or psychological information. The dataset also helps to bridge the gap between simple keyword-driven toxicity detection mechanisms and more improved contextual classification of communication in defence systems.

4.1.3 Defence Communication Corpus (Curated)

To address the shortfalls of the datasets that are collected from open source domain, this research employs a special curated Defence Communication Corpus (DCC). The dataset combines real defence communications with synthetic toxic examples that are generated to reflect the domain-specific challenges. Examples include narratives like propaganda, campaigns that spread misinformation designed to weaken morale, and coded harassments that target the personnel. The importance of this dataset lies in its central role in adapting toxicity detection methodologies for defence systems. In such situations, toxic communication is very likely linked to strategic adversarial intent rather than spontaneous hostility. Synthetic augmentation using generative AI techniques is the strength of this dataset; the dataset ensures inclusion of rare scenarios that are mission-critical but are unlikely to appear in civilian datasets. But as a curated resource, the DCC also has its limitations such as lack of the sheer scale of public-domain datasets like Jigsaw. The DCC dataset gives a real-time training scenario for modelling the high-stakes environment to ensure the system's efficiency.

4.2 Integrated Value of the Datasets

Collaboration of all these three datasets provides a comprehensive environment for toxic content detection. The Jigsaw dataset provides diverse information on a large scale which helps as a baseline for model training and testing. The Wikipedia Talk Pages dataset is used to add complexity on a contextual basis which helps the system to detect the different dialogues containing toxic elements and subtle exchange. Finally, the DCC provides mission-critical and domain-specific examples of toxicity which ensures adaptability to the requirements of the defence communication system (Glazkova et al., 2021). After combining these datasets into a structured pipeline, the model undergoes initial training on the large open-source domain of datasets. It is then fine-tuned with the data specifically designed for defence systems. The specified model thus gains robustness and specialization, addressing both the challenges of large-scale adaptation and domain adaptation (Nayak & Joshi, 2021).

4.3 Pre-processing Steps

4.3.1 Data Pre-processing and Augmentation

The pre-processing of initial input data to the system and its feature engineering process play a very important role in effective toxic comment classification. The system performance depends not only on classification models of machine learning or deep learning but also on the preliminary text of defence communication system that contains different inconsistencies and variations of data, leading to overall reduction in the performance of the system. Therefore, pre-processing is critical for ensuring that the linguistic data is extracted in such a way that it enhances the adaptability and accuracy of the system. This research accepts a pre-processing pipeline which combines traditional natural language processing methodologies with modern strategies and generative AI–based data augmentation.

Text Normalization: This is the first step of pre-processing in which raw input data is converted into machine understandable form. There are different tasks involved such as converting all the data into lower case, removal of special characters or symbols, removing punctuations, use of standard form of dates and numbers, and removing hyperlinks. In defence communications, messages can come from different sources and can be in different formats. The process of normalization ensures consistency among all these data sources. The normalization process always helps models to focus on understanding the semantic meaning rather than arbitrary formatting differences (Patel et al., 2023).

Tokenization and Lemmatization: Following normalization, the text undergoes tokenization, where sentences are broken down into smaller units such as words, sub-words, or characters depending on the chosen method. Word- or sub-word-level tokenization is employed in this research because it balances the granularity with interpretability of the datasets. For further refinements of the tokens, lemmatization is applied, to reduce words into their base or dictionary form. For example, "speaking", "speaks", and "spoke" are converted to the lemma "speak". This step ensures that the morphologically different variations of the same word are treated uniformly. Lemmatization is used to reduce data sparsity and improves the model's ability to generalize across all the different forms of toxic expressions. For example, the toxic comments containing variations of the verb "threaten" will be consistently represented, enhancing accuracy of detection (Maslej-Krešňáková et al., 2020).

Stopword Removal: The words like "is", "the", or "at" are called stopwords that commonly occur in the data and sometimes provide little discriminatory value in the task of classification. In large datasets, their frequent presence may overshadow more informative terms. Removal of these stopwords thus helps to streamline the dataset. This increases the overall computational efficiency of the system and also ensures the focus of the model on relatively similar contextual tokens or keywords to indicate toxicity. In the defence communication system, this step is undertaken very cautiously because certain words may carry some very important information (Tiwari et al., 2020).

Embedding Generation: Once the test has been normalized, sentences are converted into tokens and refined. The next step is generation of embedding which converts the words or tokens into numbers or into the form of vectors that stores the information or meaning of the data. In this study, multi-layered embedding strategy has been employed to enhance the representational richness of the data. Word2Vec feature engineering method has been used which captures the relationship between the word-to-word co-occurrence of data pattern. GloVe (Global Vectors) word embedding method (Anand & Eswari, 2019) increases the representation of the data by combining local and global statistical information. BERT word embedding method generates vectors that are context-dependent and the representation of a word varies depending on its interpretational context.

Generative AI–based Data Augmentation: Imbalanced datasets contain the most common type of toxicity which reduces their effectiveness in real-world defence applications. To solve this problem, generative AI is used for data augmentation. Using models such as GPT, synthetic toxic and non-toxic examples are generated to enhance the quality of the dataset. Examples include messages simulating propaganda targeting military personnel, and morale-lowering misinformation crafted to resemble adversarial disinformation campaigns. By balancing the class of distributions, generative AI augmentation enhances the model's robustness against the mission-critical toxic cases. It also provides a methodology to simulate evolving adversarial tactics, ensuring that the detection systems remain alert to new threats (Shounak et al., 2022; Dejene et al., 2020).

5. Experimental Setup

The experimental setup is designed to ensure system robustness and to check its security and efficiency to train the system and evaluate it for toxic comment detection. The setup comprises the hardware, the software, specific dataset related to defence, and the specific matrices for evaluation of model and tuning of hyperparameters to optimize the framework. For the hardware setup, a high-class computational environment was required which comprised of Graphics Processing Units (GPUs) to provide parallel processing power for processing and training the models. These GPUs were supported by the processors of Intel Xeon, optimized for handling the multi-threaded pre-processing tasks and managing the large data pipelines. In addition, RAM of 64GB ensured sufficient memory to process without bottlenecks large-scale datasets like Jigsaw Toxic Comment, Wikipedia Talk Pages, and the DCC. This combination of GPUs, Central Processing Units (CPUs), and memory creates an environment that is capable of supporting the computationally intensive deep learning models and lightweight machine learning algorithms. Open-source machine learning and deep learning frameworks are the software environment used in this study. Tensor-Flow and PyTorch were employed to implement the deep learning architectures including CNNs, BiLSTMs, and transformer-based models (Farooqi et al., 2021; Wullach et al., 2022) such as BERT and RoBERTa. The flexibility allows experimentation with different architectures and optimization techniques. Scikit-learn is used for classical machine learning approaches like SVMs, random forests, and gradient boosting. For pre-processing the data, feature engineering and baseline evaluation were treated. There was a scalable and versatile software stack to achieve diversified experimental results for modelling.

The dataset was split in three parts to train the system, to validate the system, and to test the system, respectively. The partitions were done in the ratio of 70%, 15%, and 15%. To evaluate the model performance, multiple evaluation metrics like accuracy, precision, recall, and F1-score were implemented (Yacouby & Axman, 2020). The proportion of data instances that are correctly classified out of the total number of data instances is referred to as accuracy. Precision is the positive predictive value used to classify data instances. Recall is also known as sensitivity or true positive rate with respect to all collected dataset. The F1-score, a metric that considers both precision and recall, is the harmonic mean of precision and recall. After calculating all these parameters of evaluation, the tuning of hyperparameters was done to optimize the results of the model. To identify the suitable performance setting of the models like SVM and random forest, grid search was used for training and tuning and also to evaluate the combinations of different parameters. On the other hand, for deep learning models, the strategies must be of advanced level, and hence optimizers like Adam optimizer were chosen to improve the efficiency and also to mitigate the problem of overfitting.

6. Results and Discussion

The performance of various models was compared, as shown in Table 12.3.

Table 12.3 Model Performance Comparison.

Model	*Precision*	*Recall*	*F1-score*
SVM	0.82	0.78	0.80
Random Forest	0.84	0.80	0.82
BiLSTM	0.87	0.85	0.86
CNN	0.88	0.84	0.86
BERT	0.91	0.89	0.90
RoBERTa	0.92	0.90	0.91
GPT (Fine-tuned)	0.93	0.91	0.92
Proposed Framework (Hybrid)	0.95	0.94	0.95

The models based on transformers like BERT, RoBERTa, and GPT every time outperformed the machine learning and simpler deep learning architectures. The hybrid framework integrating machine learning + deep learning + generative AI achieved the highest performance. Synthetic data generation from generative AI significantly improved robustness against adversarial/covert toxicity.

The results demonstrate that a multi-layered hybrid approach provides substantial improvements over single-method models. The machine learning layer ensures the lightweight deployment on tactical devices; on the other hand, the deep learning layer collects the semantic richness of the data which is required for defence-specific toxicity detection. The generative AI layer future proofs the system against evolving adversarial strategies. Moreover, the defence-specific corpus showed that conventional toxicity classifiers trained on civilian data failed to identify the domain-specific jargon. The proposed framework mitigates this gap effectively.

7. Conclusion

This study defines a multi-layered model framework for toxic comment classification and detection for defence communication systems. By combining machine learning, deep learning, and generative AI, the model framework achieves robust, scalable, and adaptive performance. The key contributions include:

- Integration of lightweight machine learning for rapid screening
- Use of advanced deep learning for contextual analysis
- Application of generative AI for synthetic defence-specific toxic data

The proposed model achieved an F1-score of 0.95, significantly surpassing baseline models.

8. Future Scope

The future scope of research can include the following areas:

- Expansion to multilingual defence communications
- Integration of multimodal data (text, audio, video)
- Enhancing explainability for human analysts
- Pilot deployment in real-world defence simulations

References

Almendingen, K. (2025). Identification of distinct research gaps that complement previous critiques of militaristic language in relation to cancer and other non-military topics. *Cancer Control*, 32, 10732748251349935.

Anand, M. and Eswari, R. (2019). Classification of abusive comments in social media using deep learning. *2019 3rd International Conference on Computing Methodologies and Communication* (pp. 974–977).

cjadams, Sorensen, J., Elliott, J. et al. (2017). Toxic comment classification challenge. Available at https://kaggle.com/competitions/jigsaw-toxic-comment-classification-challenge. Accessed on 12 July 2025.

Crăcea, Cătălin. (2022). Fake news and the military organization. *Defense Resources Management in the 21st Century*, 17(17), 170–178.

Dejene, D., Tiwari, B. and Tiwari, V. (2020). TD2SecIoT: Temporal, data-driven and dynamic network layer based security architecture for industrial IoT. *International Journal of Interactive Multimedia and Artificial Intelligence*, 6(4), 146–156.

Devlin, J., Chang, M.-W., Lee, K. and Toutanova, K. (2019). BERT: Pre-training of deep bidirectional transformers for language understanding. *Proceedings of the 2019 Conference of the North*, 1, 4171–4186.

Dubey, K., Nair, R., Khan, Mohd. U. and Shaikh, S. (2020). Toxic comment detection using LSTM. *2020 Third International Conference on Advances in Electronics, Computers and Communications* (pp. 1–8).

Farooqi, Z. M., Ghosh, S. and Shah, R. R. (2021). Leveraging transformers for hate speech detection in conversational code-mixed tweets. ArXiv:2112.09986 [Cs]. Available at https://arxiv.org/abs/2112.09986. Accessed on 23 April 2025.

Glazkova, A., Kadantsev, M. and Glazkov, M. (2021). Fine-tuning of pre-trained transformers for hate, offensive, and profane content detection in English and Marathi. ArXiv.org. Available at https://arxiv.org/abs/2110.12687. Accessed on 12 March 2025.

Gupta, A., Nayyar, A., Arora, S. and Jain, R. (2021). Detection and classification of toxic comments by using LSTM and Bi-LSTM approach.

In Luhach, A. K., Jat, D. S., Bin Ghazali, K. H., Gao, X. Z. and Lingras, P. (eds) *Advanced Informatics for Computing Research* (pp. 100–112). Singapore: Springer.

Kebede, S. D., Tiwari, B., Tiwari, V. and Chandravanshi, K. (2021). Predictive machine learning-based integrated approach for DDoS detection and prevention. *Multimedia Tools and Applications*, vol. 81, no. 3, pp. 4185–4211, Jan. 2021.

Kumar, H. (n.d.). Toxic comment classification using transformers. Available at https://www.ieomsociety.org/ singapore2021/papers/366.pdf. Accessed on 24 July 2025.

Liu, Y., Ott, M., Goyal, N. et al. (2019). RoBERTa: A robustly optimized BERT pretraining approach. ArXiv.org. Available at https://arxiv.org/abs/1907.11692. Accessed 12 Aug 2025.

Maslej-Krešňáková, V., Sarnovský, M., Butka, P. and Machová, K. (2020). Comparison of deep learning models and various text pre-processing techniques for the toxic comments classification. *Applied Sciences*, 10(23), 8631.

Nayak, R. and Joshi, R. (2021). Contextual hate speech detection in code mixed text using transformer based approaches. ArXiv.org. Available at https://arxiv.org/abs/2110.09338. Accessed on 5 May 2025.

Pal, A. and Rai, S. (2023). Toxicity tweet detection and classification using NLP driven techniques. *2023 IEEE International Conference on ICT in Business Industry & Government* (pp. 1–4).

Pal, A. and Rai, S. (2024a). Toxicity comments detection with sequential deep learning models using various feature vectors.

Pal, A. and Rai, S. (2024b). Utilizing machine learning and text mining for toxic comment classification on social media. *International Journal of Creative Research Thoughts*, 12, d42–d48.

Panazan, O. and Gheorghe, C. (2025). Impact of geopolitical risks and innovation on global defense stock return. *PLOS ONE*, 20(2), e0312155.

Patel, A. S., Merlino, G., Puliafito, A. et al. (2023). An NLP-guided ontology development and refinement approach to represent and query visual information. *Expert Systems with Applications*, 213, 118998.

Saleh, H., Alhothali, A. and Moria, K. (2023). Detection of hate speech using BERT and hate speech word embedding with deep model. *Applied Artificial Intelligence*, 37(1), e2166719-384 to e2166719-405, e2166719 (405 pages).

Shounak, R., Roy, S., Kumar, V. and Tiwari, V. (2022). Reddit comment toxicity score prediction through BERT via transformer based architecture. *2022 IEEE 13th Annual Information Technology, Electronics and Mobile Communication Conference* (pp. 0353–0358).

Tesfay, D., Tiwari, B., Teka, M. J. and Tiwari, V. (2021). An intrusion prevention system embedded AODV to protect mobile adhoc network against Sybil attack. *Proceedings of the International Conference on Data Science, Machine Learning and Artificial Intelligence* (pp 57–64).

Tiwari, V., Ashpilaya, A., Vedita, P. et al. (2020). Exploring demographics and personality traits in recommendation system to address cold start problem. In Tuba, M., Akashe, S. and Joshi, A. (eds) *ICT Systems and Sustainability. Advances in Intelligent Systems and Computing* (pp. 361–369). Singapore: Springer.

Vasu, N., Ang, B., Jayakumar, S. et al. (2018). Fake news: National security in the post-truth era. Policy Report. Available at https://www.rsis.edu.sg/wp-content/uploads/2018/01/ PR180313_Fake-News_WEB.pdf. Accessed on 12 June 2025.

Wullach, T., Adler, A. and Minkov, E. (2022). Character-level HyperNetworks for hate speech detection. *Expert Systems with Applications*, 205, 117571.

Yacouby, R. and Axman, D. (2020). Probabilistic extension of precision, recall, and F1 score for more thorough evaluation of classification models. In *Proceedings of the First Workshop on Evaluation and Comparison of NLP Systems* (pp. 79–91). Association for Computational Linguistics.

13 Enhancing Coordination and Adaptive Learning in Autonomous Vehicle Clusters: A Survey of Generative AI Methodologies

Subhodip Koley[1], Sumit Das[2], Achyut Mitra[3],
Abhrendu Bhattacharya[4], Paramita Sarkar[5] and Sourav Saha[6*]

With the evolution of autonomous technologies, it has become possible to create coordinated teams of unmanned air and ground vehicles, which can perform sophisticated missions in those environments that are dangerous or inaccessible to human operators. There are major computational challenges in these multi-agent systems which especially include developing robust communication and implementing machine learning models in dynamic and uncertain environments, which conventional artificial intelligence (AI) systems cannot overcome despite their potential. Generative AI has in turn risen to the occasion as a disruptive technology, with novel abilities in data generation, adaptive behaviour modelling, and intelligent decision-making. In this review, the authors critically examine the ways in which generative AI approaches may drastically improve this operational synergy, responsiveness along with efficiency for autonomous vehicle groups. The study begins with the establishment of several basic terms that are used in autonomous vehicle platforms and multi-agent architecture, the domains of their applicability, and their limitations. The study further examines the remaining technical challenges and outlines prospective research directions, while providing a comprehensive evaluation of existing implementations and the associated computational complexities, and system integration methods is provided and supported. The current study will set a goal to establish connections between the evolution of generative AI and the requirements of autonomous swarm operations that can be highly significant in theoretical studies and practice.

1 https://orcid.org/0009-0004-0262-0526
2 https://orcid.org/0000-0002-8018-9151
3 https://orcid.org/0009-0004-2163-3090
4 https://orcid.org/0009-0009-8549-1024
5 https://orcid.org/0000-0002-2330-8484
6 https://orcid.org/0009-0007-2579-0933
* Corresponding author: souravsaha2001@gmail.com

DOI: 10.1201/9781003688174-13

1. Introduction

The new technologies of autonomous vehicles have seen an unprecedented growth as a radical tool that can be used in diverse fields of industries, and offer self-directed services to minimize human intercession in complicated and repeated or dangerous undertakings. These modern machines that are either programmed to run independently or governed with few human interventions have taken establishment in supply chain management, ecological monitoring, smart urban systems, and in the military. This has seen them come up with distinct classifications such as Unmanned Aerial Systems (UASs), Autonomous Ground Platforms (AGPs), Unmanned Maritime Vessels (UMVs), and Autonomous Underwater Systems (AUSs) due to their versatility in terms of their adaptability to various geographical locations and environments in which they operate. Each of the classifications is intended to conduct certain missions which include overhead reconnaissance, land transportation, and oceanic data collection missions and also missions to explore the subsurface (Bandela & Cao, 2023).

The integration of machine intelligence and robotic technologies has considerably increased the scope of work of autonomous cars to the point of autonomous vehicle network development. These networks consist of a number of autonomous systems which work together towards achieving common goals based on decentralized sensory structures and computational systems, and exchange information based on an information exchange system. In comparison to single autonomous platforms, coordinated networks are more expandable, more resilient in systems, and more versatile in their operations (Arvinte & Tamir, 2022; Delecki et al., 2023; Jha & Lau, 2024; Shi et al., 2022; Krajewski et al., 2018).

They can dynamically re-arrange their structural formation regarding the mission parameters and they can remain effective in their operation in case a single component fails. It is a team-centred approach commonly known as collective intelligence and it renders to accomplish superior decision-making and complete tasks in a challenging working environment.

Nonetheless, in the coordinated autonomous systems, the conventional machine learning systems have major limitations. Most of the developed algorithms depend on huge datasets which are labelled and sensitive to the change of the environment. The algorithms tend to suffer a drop in performance in dynamic and uncertain operational environments, e.g., catastrophe sites, water bodies, or remote locations on the earth. The complications are the changeable inter-unit communication relationships, sensor interference, and immediate modification to the various configurations of agents.

To overcome these shortcomings, generative machine intelligence (GMI) has been getting a good deal of interest due to its capability to create and develop detailed data patterns. Adversarial generative networks and probabilistic encoder–decoder networks, diffusion models, attention models, and flow normalizing models are all possible solutions that can improve coordination in the system, environmental awareness, and autonomous functionality. These frameworks can produce real data models, simulate environmental conditions, and learn in the uncertain conditions.

The chapter gives a detailed overview of the application of Generative Probabilistic Intelligence (GPI) to the creation of coordinated autonomous vehicle networks. It begins with the creation of fundamental principles and taxonomies of autonomous vehicles and coordinated systems and then tries to give a specific analysis of the main GMI approaches and how they relate to collective intelligence models. The review proceeds to discuss the real-life uses of GMI in fields like state estimation, environmental interpretation, information allocation, and exchange of information and protection of systems. Finally, the work presents key questions that remain unanswered and proposes the direction for future research to help the creation of resilient, intelligent coordinated systems.

2. Autonomous Robotic Collectives

Robotic platforms can be deployed on airborne, land-borne, and sea platforms, and sub platforms. These robot systems have triggered considerable advancements in the realm of artificial intelligence (AI) and mechanical engineering, due to the need to perform various tasks in the unfavorable and hazardous conditions. These platforms achieve desired goals through the formation of collectives or groups that are more effective.

The primary difference among robotic collectives is the level of their autonomy, which ranges from autonomous mechanisms, set algorithms, and instantaneous information to the partially independent ones, requiring human control. Such structures may also be organized in command structures that may incorporate single-tier or multi-tier organization that dictates how they operate.

In the multi-level groups, the groups have units of commanders who are selected to coordinate group activities. These commanders report to central control stations and are the upper-most level of operation. The individual robotic platforms are provided with specific information-gathering and processing tasks with an ever-growing power demand. The centralized data processing through enhanced control hubs or distributed systems has an enormous increase in the rate of mission execution and processing.

Robotic teams have dramatically transformed the industrial processes by facilitating dynamic, scalable and precision oriented execution of tasks.

The systems are applied in a wide range of applications, including strategic defence missions to optimization of contemporary agricultural operations, indicating their flexibility and ability to perform diverse mission profiles. The self-governing platforms within the security and surveillance sector enable a vast coverage of the region, reduction in human manpower, and timely identification of changes within the environment. Some of the applications in the domain of ecology include terrain mapping, marine ecology, and disaster prediction, especially in remote regions, which is attributed to seismic or climatic disruptions. The systems come in handy during emergency planning and rapid response to crises. A new perspective in the creative industries involves the use of robotic units in aerial choreography, dynamic text formation, and immersive cinematography in harsh conditions that creates new visual angles and more economic methods of production. Aerial robotics have also been utilized in healthcare to transport emergency supplies and other lifesaving materials such as Automated External Defibrillators (AEDs) to remote or disaster-stricken locations to expand the reach of the medical services beyond the conventional infrastructure. Robotic swarms are also helpful in optimization of parcel segmentation and delivery, and manpower reduction and optimization of warehouse logistics. The intelligent agents encourage consumer-oriented distribution models. Combined, these uses emphasise the disruptive role of robotic clusters in modern society, especially their capability to perform complex tasks with precision, utilizing resources efficiently and operating with minimal human involvement across a broad range of functions.

2.1 Swarm-enabled Autonomous Aerial Systems: Functional Advancements and Prospective Utilizations

Unmanned Aerial Vehicles (UAVs), also known as UAVs (Yu et al., 2022; Song et al., 2018a), are specialized aerial robotics which are designed to be deployed in coordination in complex functional environments. The number of applications in which such platforms are utilized has been growing in the field of defence as well as in a wide variety of civilian and industrial domains. Majority of UAVs are multi-rotor configurations, which will allow Vertical Take-Off and Landing (VTOL) capabilities and therefore allow very precise vertical control like hover, elevation, and descent.

The mechanisms of Unmanned Aerial Vehicles (UAVs) control are either based on direct remote control, wherein human operators oversee the operation of the UAVs, or fully autonomous, where computerized onboard control modules are utilised to direct the vehicle. In addition to the traditional areas of surveillance, mapping, and logistics, UAV swarms have been utilized in recreational and innovative fields. An interesting case study is aerial light shows, where high numbers (fleets) of drones that consist of lighting installations are synchronized to create synchronized shapes and moving visual effects, like geometric shapes or textual representations.

Besides entertainment, UAV swarms have also proven useful in life-threatening situations, especially in the reestablishment of communication infrastructure in the aftermath of natural disasters. The systems can be used as a temporary airborne communication node, exploiting their mobility and spatial flexibility, to restore network connectivity in those areas where the communication systems on the ground have been interrupted.

2.2 Ground Vehicles with Autonomous Technology and Their Collaborative Functions

Unmanned Ground Vehicles (UGVs) are unique systems and are termed as Unmanned Vehicle (UV) systems, particularly where cargo and military logistics operations are involved. They are employed in planned convoy manoeuvres that are also referred to as platooning and are important in ensuring that the safety and throughput of the transport are optimized. Besides being differentiated in the levels of autonomy, the UGVs may also be differentiated in locomotion architecture, which comprises wheeled, tracked, and legged.

It has been demonstrated that tracked systems work better in uneven or littered fields, and legged systems work well in cluttered or structurally complicated fields and thus would be best used in emergency response and search missions. The UGVs have expanded their sphere of activity over the last few years and have been engaged in various mission-essential activities via implementation of new autonomous navigation and decision-making systems.

Moreover, the concept of synergistic aerial–ground unmanned integration, i.e., UAVs and UGVs, has already turned out to be among the more powerful concepts of implementation of multi-domain missions. Though UAVs in Figure 13.1 may offer fast air surveillance and land mapping, UGVs may be employed to complement such operations, move around different terrain types, serve as moving sources of energy, and carry material to different places. The impact of this collaborative relationship is enormous as it improves mission survival, space range, and the resilience of the system.

2.3 Surface-based Autonomous Sea Platforms

Unmanned Surface Vehicles (USVs), referred to as autonomous marine vessels, have been designed to travel on and navigate water bodies on the large mission templates. Their area of operation takes into account ecological surveillance and strategic defence operations as well as disaster response. The primary merit of the USVs compared to the aerial or subaquatic systems is that they can always access the satellite-based navigation systems; thus the quality of the communication channel is high and hence they are highly competent in collecting real-time data and applications in case long-term deployment is needed.

With this technological advantage in place, USVs will be a necessary addition in hydrographic mapping as well as in the assessment of environmental impact and dynamic ecosystem monitoring. Besides that, USVs are used in multi-agent research projects to allow the easy interoperability with other unmanned systems for cooperative data collection and working synergy. These surface vehicles are equipped with renewable energy–capturing systems such as solar modules, wind turbines, and wave converters, which enable their deployment on long-term missions as the communication, energy transfer, and logistical support centres for the rest of the unmanned units.

2.4 Complex Environment Underwater Robotic Systems

The UAVs which are referred to as Unmanned Underwater Vehicles (UUVs) are designed to carry out complex tasks at the base of the water body where they are deployed. They were originally designed for military and science-exploration

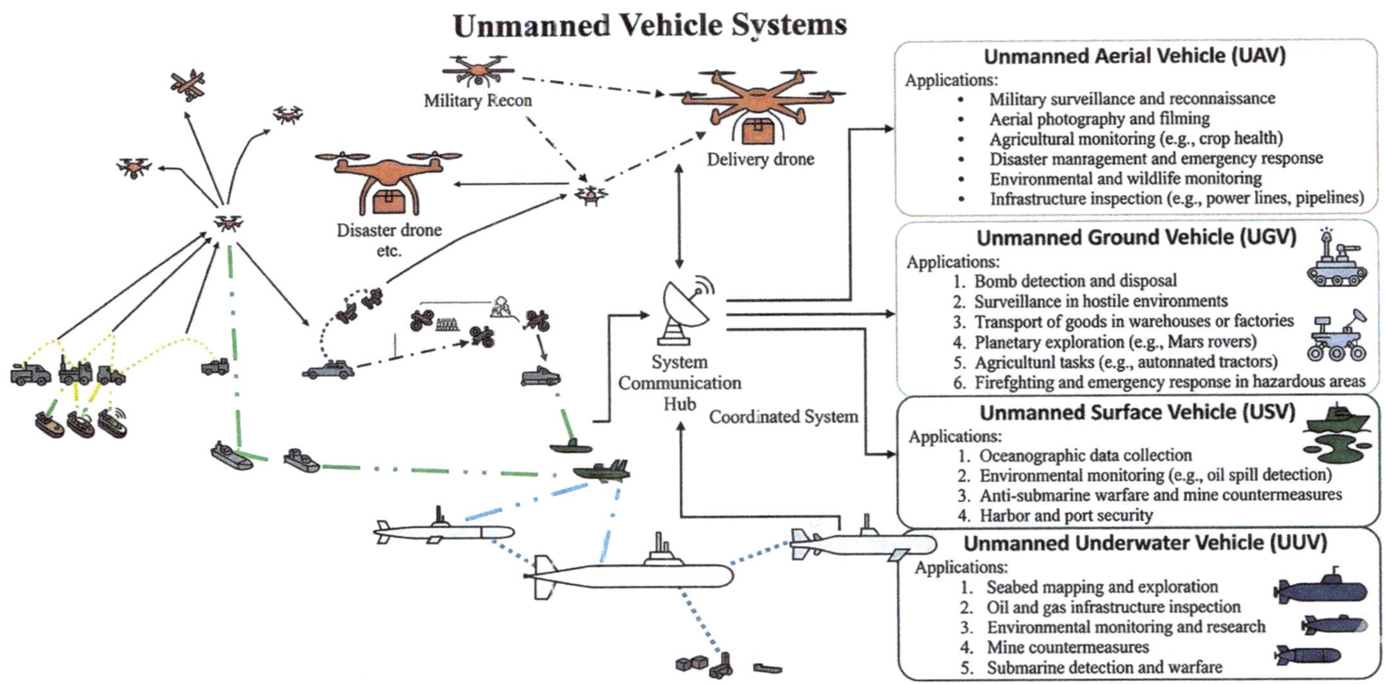

Fig. 13.1 Architecture of UV systems and their applications (Adeboye, O. et al. 2022).

niche uses, but have since expanded to commercial, industrial, and leisure markets. The UUVs can be classified into two broad categories: Remotely Operated Vehicles (ROVs), which are tethered UAVs that are used to carry out specific tasks such as inspection and repair; and Autonomous Underwater Vehicles (AUVs), which are autonomous and are engaged to conduct geophysical surveys, collect oceanographic data, and perform geological monitoring of the water.

The other significant applications of UUVs are as an inspection and maintenance devices for underwater infrastructure, which includes underwater pipelines, underwater cables, and construction assets related to the marine setting. In very hostile environments such as polar caps, radioactive environments, and ocean abysses, autonomous systems demonstrate unsurpassed flexibility. Their strength allows them to conduct important processes in which man-in-the-middle is unviable or dangerous.

2.5 Unmanned Vehicle System Convergence and Evolution

The technological development of unmanned systems of platforms (aerial, terrestrial, aquatic, subaquatic) is fundamentally transforming the conventional modes of operation. These systems are not only improving their existing workflows, they are also creating new capabilities that did not previously exist. As more and more generative AI is being introduced into these networks, a new frontier is emerging in autonomous decision-making, coordinated swarm behaviour, and implementing complex collaborative missions.

3. Generative AI

3.1 Intensive Generative AI

Generative AI is a radically new breakthrough in the sphere of computational intelligence, and it is marked by the ability to generate novel and contextually relevant output. This output can be written texts, imaginations, sound files, or even organized two-dimensional designs that can be identified and understood in the context in which they were developed. Generative AI is the flip-flop of the traditional discriminative models in which classification exercises and predictive analytics are dominant. In contrast to these traditional approaches, generative systems have been created to react to known inputs and produce stable and classical artifacts. It is a gigantic step towards actual machine creativity, wit, and self-embarkation.

The models in Figure 13.2 not only repeat at the same time, but are also intrinsically able to innovate based on the constraints of distributions of learned data. The wide scope of use of this generative power has been observed in the areas of photorealistic image creation, language generation (Song et al., 2018b), and procedural 3D models (Duan et al., 2023). In education, generative AI is redesigning the pedagogical model, particularly in medical and engineering schools, by enabling adaptive learning systems and smart tutoring models.

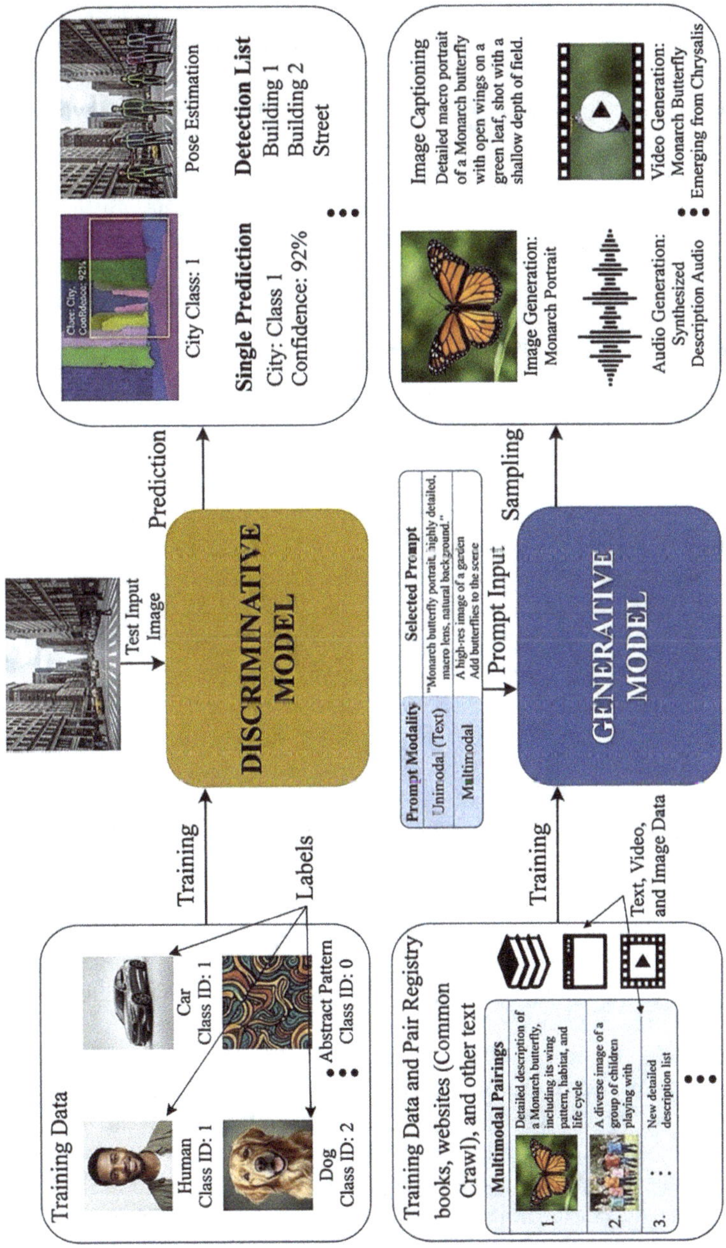

Fig. 13.2 Generative models vs discriminative models.

Furthermore, the reasoning ability of generative AI is being actively researched, providing valuable insights for developing interpretable systems and decision-making logic in fields such as robotics, autonomous movement, and diagnostic analytics (Chaalal et al., 2021). Generative AI is also driving innovation in business models and is being applied in non-technical fields, such as software development, medical services, and financial modelling. This highlights its flexibility as a tool, demonstrating its two-fold functions as a creative engine and a strategic enabler, which can deliver systemic improvements across various sectors.

In a nutshell, the basic distinction between generative AI and conventional discriminative models is that the former is trained to generate novelty, and the discriminative models are trained to complete the tasks of data classification and recall of features.

3.2 Typical Generative AI Models

3.2.1 Generative Adversarial Networks (GANs)—Competitive Learning: High-Fidelity Synthesis

The invention of generative adversarial networks (GANs) is a step forward in unsupervised learning together with semi-supervised learning. This dual-network architecture known as GANs was first proposed by Goodfellow in 2014. It has two networks: a generator and a discriminator. The generator's task is to produce artificial data that closely resembles real data and the discriminator tests the authenticity of the inputs by distinguishing between the real and generated data.

The result of this competitive process is an ongoing optimization of the networks based on their capabilities. The generator aims to deceive the discriminator by producing an increasing number of more credible outputs while the discriminator tries to get the classification correct. The feedback loop is stabilized to a Nash equilibrium, where the signals of the generator are noisy to real data, and the discriminator has the highest detection precision (Song et al., 2018b).

Although GANs are quite efficient, they are reported to be very difficult to train due to architectural instability. The challenges include finding a balance, mode collapse, and vanishing gradient problem (Liu et al., 2025; Rao et al., 2020). To address these deficiencies, several extensions have been proposed such as unrolled GANs (Uittenbogaard et al., 2019), mini-batch discrimination, historical averaging, feature matching (Adeboye et al., 2022), two-timescale update rules (Tian et al., 2022), and self-attention mechanisms (Nguyen et al., 2023), all of which result in an improved training stability and quality of output.

The GANs, as depicted in Figure 13.3, are effective when it comes to generating high-resolution samples and enabling the association of one inference on a quick basis by using forward propagation. This is crucial in the UV swarm systems. The adversarial training paradigm not only needs to ensure that the simulation environments are realistic but it should also enable the creation of different operating situations. It also proves useful when it is necessary to train self-directed agents, given the limitations of both computation and time sensitivity.

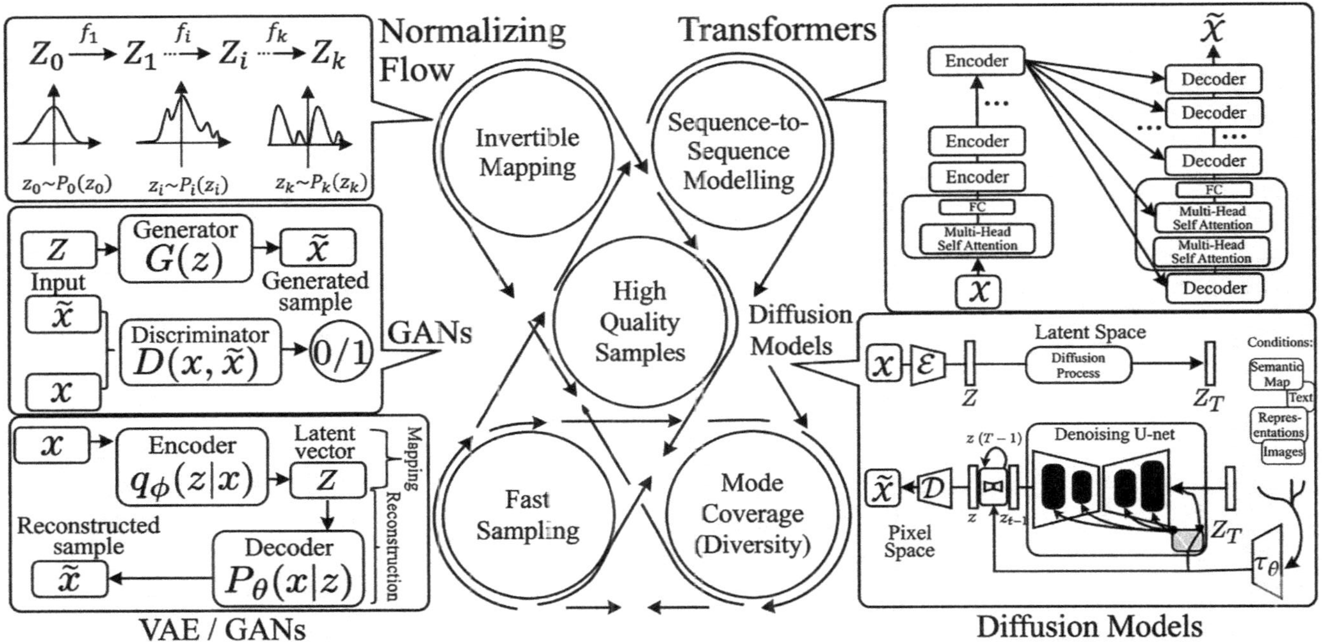

Fig. 13.3 Key features and structures of GANs, VAEs, GDMs, normalizing flows plus transformers (Adeboye, O. et al. 2022).

In addition, the learning and navigation possibilities of GANs enable modelling and recreation of a broad spectrum of delicate environmental situations, which makes UV swarm deployments less fragile and more adaptable. The generative adversarial models play a critical role in the development of the unmanned systems due to high quality output, fast synthesis, and efficient encoding of features.

3.2.2 Variational Encoding Frameworks: Robustness and Hidden Representation Dynamics in Simulated Environments

Variational Autoencoders (VAEs) represent probabilistic generative models that seek to learn the real distribution of the input data, and recreate fresh illustrations that are helpful in between-class variability. VAEs are graphically given by two modules, one of which is an encoder and the other is a decoder, both of which depend on each other. The decoder works with the estimates of the posterior distribution of the latent variables that the encoder presents it to and the decoder employs it during the iterative optimization process—normally with expectation-maximization procedures. The bi-directional structure is such that the encoder can give an approximation of the inverse of the generative process that concurs with the principles of Bayesian inference.

The maximization of the Evidence Lower Bound (ELBO) that is a trade-off between reconstruction fidelity and the distance between the acquired latent distribution and the target prior is related to the training of VAEs. VAEs have created their niche, which is especially useful in raising variability in the dataset in the data augmentation setting, specifically in domains that have a small quantity of annotated samples. Although VAEs can avoid such traps as non-convergence and mode collapse plaguing adversarial models, they can have worse output properties than GANs.

Representation learning is the other important asset of VAEs. VAEs can deliver structured training input by projecting high-dimensional data onto low-dimensional semantically rich projections, and consequently they do not need manual feature engineering. The UV swarm systems can leverage VAEs that are highly reliable and trustworthy. This is so because they prevent collapse and stabilize the training dynamics. This allows creation of diverse environmental simulations so that autonomous agents can be subjected to as many variations of operations as possible. This increases the flexibility of the given system and its transferability into the real world.

3.2.3 Generative Diffusion Models (GDMs)

The generative diffusion models (GDMs) represent an influential type of generative architecture that functions in two steps—forward degradation and reverse reconstruction. The sequence of input samples is corrupted with increasing amounts of Gaussian noise and in effect blurs their structure under the forward step. This step is then reversed to make an effort to unite the original data by trying to remove noise in a methodical way with the learned parameters, typically comprising of spatial fidelity in U-Net-based neural networks.

The basis of GDMs is variational inferences and parameterization of Markov chains that allow it to sample complicated data distributions within finite steps. The subtypes of celebrity models are Denoising Diffusion Probabilistic Models (DDPMs), Noise Conditional Score Networks (NCSNs), and Stochastic Differentiated Equation models. Most of the popular systems like Stable Diffusion and the DALL·E lines are implemented as DDPMs, with most systems to produce deepfakes being constructed on NCSNs. The Stochastic Differential Equation (SDE)-based models such as DiffFlow are mathematically valid data synthesis.

Despite their goodness and controllability, GDMs are computationally very expensive as they are iterative. Denoising Diffusion Implicit Models (DDIMs) are other variants that have been created to solve this issue, and in the case of DDIMs, it becomes far simpler to sample, without the quality of the result being compromised.

The GDMs have proved extremely helpful in the creation of high-resolution simulation of the environment in relation to UV swarms. The simulations are crucial to test the working of autonomous systems in dynamic and unforeseeable multifaceted settings. Even though they are not comparable in effectiveness to GANs or VAEs, GDMs are more realistic and scenario-granular, and thus necessary in high-stakes settings such as disaster response, tactical reconnaissance, and ecological monitoring.

3.2.4 Transformers-based Generative Model Architecture

Transformer-based designs serve as blocks of the new generative models, especially in natural language processing tasks. The examples of this type of models are the GPT family, BERT, and Bard, which suggest that transformers are able to learn and process very large texts. Although both the VAEs and the transformers are encoder–decoder models, the functioning of the two is diametrically opposite. Transformers contain attention layers and feed-forward neural networks in the encoder and decoder networks respectively, and allow the model to solve the complex dependence in input sequences and to synthesize output sequences respectively.

In addition to individual implementations, other generative systems and new and more advanced designs usually use transformers, incorporating multi-head attention, positional encoding, and self-attention. Such integrations have enabled breakthroughs in a host of areas such as automated composition of text, conversational agents, code synthesis, and programming support. Astonishingly, transformers have been effectively utilized in image-generating tasks, as evidenced by models like ViTGAN and STrans GAN that do not use convolutional layers.

Transformers play a strategic role in UV swarms because they are rather flexible and are used for sequential information and long-range reliability. Every UV unit receives a flow of sensor data, such as inter-vehicle communication messages and environmental messages. Adaptive exchanges are simulated by transformer-driven models, which reinforce the real-time decision-making and enhance the perception of the context. Besides this, generative transformers like GPT-4 are able to simulate context-sensitive, detailed, and comprehensive training environments so that the UV systems are prepared to operate in dynamic mission environments.

3.2.5 Flow Modelling to Precise Generative Modelling and Detection of Anomalies

Normalizing Flows (NFs) constitute a generative model (Figure 13.4) capable of converting basic probability distributions into increasingly complex forms through a sequence of invertible and differentiable transformations. The change enables calculation of the densities of the samples inaccurately because one can reverse the mapping process and take into account the change of the volume that is introduced by each transformation layer. Unlike GANs and VAEs, NFs are capable of providing accurate density estimation, which is amenable to tractability, and are therefore particularly suitable in cases where high stability and fidelity are required.

The NFs are invertible and, therefore, can be effectively sampled and reconstructed, and can be trained more reliably than the adversarial models that may be unstable or collapse modes. The NFs are applied to image synthesis, noise modelling, video and audio generation, and graph construction of data. Graphical Normalizing Flows (GNFs) find especially wide application in UV swarm systems to detect anomalies. GNFs are founded on the principles of Bayesian networks, which can be applied to modelling the temporal dependencies and the identification of the low-density regions, which can indicate the existence of anomalous behaviour.

The other generative models lack the ability to produce accurate likelihood models as compared to the NF models, which are significant in the diagnosis of and response to the anomalies in the UV operations. They are critical for the soundness of the system and the dependability of its performance, thus necessitating them to have high accuracy and robustness in extremely complicated and data-intensive environments.

4. Solutions to UV Swarms Utilizing Generative AI

4.1 State Estimation in UV Swarms Enhanced by Generative AI

The right state estimation is the fundamental requirement for efficient working of UV swarms, particularly in the areas of autonomous navigation, traffic modelling, and trajectory control. The key state variables include the spatial position, velocity, and orientation that have a direct effect on the decision-making for path planning and manoeuvring. However, estimating the actual status of a vehicle is not merely a matter of estimating the actual status of sensor measurements and the dynamism of a system, as it has a stochastic nature. The major task of state inference is then

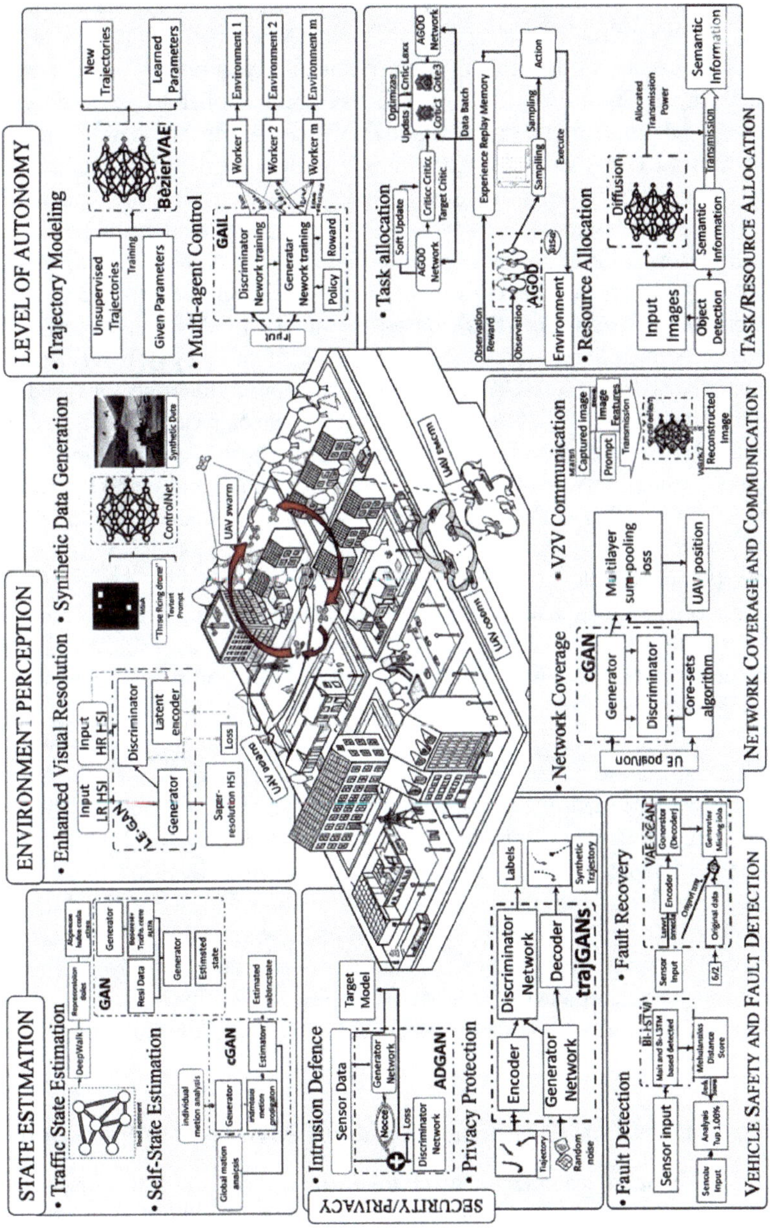

Fig. 13.4 Model structures showcasing strategies for UV swarm innovation (Adeboye, O. et al. 2022).

to determine the probability distribution of the specified variables based on the temporal data and contextual data (Krajewski et al., 2018).

Table 13.1 presents the generative AI techniques for state estimation framework, which outlines a number of new methods that ought to be utilized to handle the issues of data sparsity, uncertainty, and complexity of many actors. As an example, Graph-Embedding GANs have been applied to produce realistic traffic light patterns for underrepresented road sections when modelling the traffic conditions for UGVs (Xu et al., 2020). The technique uses identical segments to get spatial embeddings in order to direct the generator and to allow the discriminator to maximize its classification capabilities in a sequence of steps. The resultant synthetic information is far more precise in estimation; it also minimizes mean absolute error better than the conventional models such as Deeptrend2.0.

Conditional GANs (cGANs), on top of standard GAN architectures, have been demonstrated to be useful and effective in estimation of system states using raw sensor measurements. cGANs have been used for motion trajectory prediction in multi-UAV contexts, with models trained on sensor measurements, as given in Table 13.1. In hybrid architecture, social Long Short-Term Memory (LSTM) networks are used to learn to compute the motion individually and the Siamese networks are used to compute the motion globally; this has resulted in better tracking and better prediction accuracy than the base models in multi-object trackers (Delecki et al., 2023).

Variational autoencoders are also useful in state estimation, i.e., to model the dependence through time of wireless communication channels. The UAV networks can be enhanced using VAEs to improve signal clarity and predict channel state performance through generation of diverse and realistic channel samples (Jha & Lau, 2024). Score-based diffusion models and deep normalizing flows that model complex and high-dimensional state variables distributions are also used. These approaches enable flexible approximation of the system's main motion parameters as well as the gradient-level changes in them, which gives a more accurate concept of the system dynamics (Shi et al., 2022; Krajewski et al., 2018).

The benefits of generative AI in the estimation of UV swarm states rely on two basic characteristics: (i) incomplete or missing data are synthesized by adversarial learning; and (ii) heterogeneous sets of data are synthesized, which are used to construct complete representations of the state. All this enhances accuracy, stability, and dynamism of UV systems which are utilized in unstable and uncertain scenarios.

4.2 Generative AI–Enhanced UV Swarm Environment Perception

The definition of environmental perception is that UVs can perceive and respond to their environment in real time. It is a mandatory condition in autonomous navigation, obstacle avoidance, and mission execution of UAV swarms. Typically, the perception systems run on a set of sensors, including LiDAR, optical cameras, and millimetre-wave radar, to sense external stimuli and establish a framework of situational awareness.

Table 13.1 Generative AI Techniques for State Estimation in Autonomous and Networked Systems.

Model Type	*Reference*	*Application Summary*	*Advantages*	*Limitations*
GAN (Traffic State Estimation)	(Xu et al., 2020)	GAN architecture is applied to reconstruct traffic states from sparse and incomplete datasets, generating diverse samples that reflect spatial–temporal dynamics.	• Captures dynamic traffic patterns • Adapts to evolving conditions	• High memory and compute requirements • Limited generalization across scenarios
GAN (Harmonic Grid Estimation)	(Xie et al., 2023)	GAN is integrated with power grid equations in the objective function to estimate harmonic states, improving source localization accuracy	• Effective in pinpointing source locations • Incorporates physical system constraints	• Vulnerable to GAN-specific issues like mode collapse
cGAN (Raw-to-True State Mapping)	(Bandela & Cao, 2023)	Conditional GAN learns the transformation between raw and accurate state estimates, refining predictions through supervised mapping	• Enhances estimation precision • Learns complex mappings	• Sensitive to hyperparameter tuning • Requires extensive labelled data
cGAN (Motion Fusion for Tracking)	(Delecki et al., 2023)	cGAN is utilized to merge individual and global motion cues, improving multi-object tracking accuracy in dynamic environments	• Boosts tracking reliability • Integrates multiple motion sources	• Computationally demanding • Dependent on diverse training inputs

Contd...

Table 13.1 *Contd...*

Model Type	*Reference*	*Application Summary*	*Advantages*	*Limitations*
VAE (Wireless Channel Estimation)	(Jha & Lau, 2024)	VAE captures temporal dependencies in UAV wireless channels, enabling efficient channel state estimation with reduced transmission overhead	• Minimizes signal exchange • Learns latent temporal patterns	• High computational load • Sensitive to model configuration
Diffusion (MIMO Channel Modelling)	(Shi et al., 2022)	Score-based diffusion models exploit inherent correlations in MIMO channels to enhance state estimation accuracy	• Improves multi-channel estimation • Captures fine-grained signal features	• Computationally intensive • Noise levels affect reliability
Normalizing Flow (State Distribution Modelling)	(Krajewski et al., 2018)	Deep normalizing flows are used to learn complex state models, which provide flexible and expressive approximations to estimation problems	• Handles intricate distribution shapes • Adaptable to various domains	• Requires substantial computational resources • Large-scale data dependency

Following the introduction of generative AI, the sphere of environmental perception has been impacted significantly and has also led to new solutions to the classic issues. To illustrate this, motion-induced blurring, unfavourable weather, and changes in altitude are typical scenarios that may be encountered by the UAVs and disrupt the quality of the images that they take. To address these issues, a hybrid was proposed, referred to as Hidden Representation–Integrated Generative Adversarial Network, to be employed to offer the hyperspectral image (HSI) super-resolution (Zhang et al., 2018). LE-GAN applies a spectral-spatial windowing mechanism to obtain local and global features and the discriminator takes advantage of loss of Wasserstein distance to optimize the quality of images. This is achieved by the method not only to enhance the resolution but also to minimize spectral distortion and mode collapse through training the latent feature distributions.

Besides enhancing the quality of resolutions, generative AI in Table 13.2 is also an important approach in synthetic data generation that is one of the most important ways to solve the data shortage problem and improve the generalization capabilities of a model. As an indication, Trajectory GAN TraGAN creates realistic highway lane-change trajectories using highway data, not to mention that training contents are increasingly meaningful to autonomous driving systems (Zharkovsky & Menadeva, 2020). On the same note, Deep Road takes advantage of GANs to simulate different weather conditions to give the required input validation and system testing (Islam et al., 2021). Various and realistic crash conditions have also been generated using VAEs and this method is more diverse and realistic compared to traditional augmentation techniques (Duplevska et al., 2023).

Image translations with hybrid frameworks of VAEs and GANs have been used to generate simulated images to photorealistic synthetic images to train change detector models (Ha & Jeong, 2022; Kobeaga et al., 2018). Although the models still need reference images, they are quite useful in making synthetic datasets more realistic and useful. The other project to be noted is that over 20,000 synthetic UAV images were created by using textual background descriptions as well as binary masks using the ground truth binding boxes. CLIP Prefix and GKST are generative models that can transform images into semantic actionable information by UAVs. These tools increase an understanding of the environment by recreating a human-level interpretation of a scene in a variety of views (Rathod & Tanwar, 2023; H. Du et al., 2023; B. Du et al., 2023).

4.3 Advancing Independent Functionality in UV Clusters via Generative Intelligence Models

Autonomy refers to the ability of UVs to perform tasks and make decisions independently. Their freedom of operations is dependent on embedded sensors, on-board processors, and internal logic systems. The form of autonomy of swarm schemes depends on the complexity of the task and environmental variability in addition to the ability of the system to plan and execute a path.

Table 13.2 Generative AI Techniques for Environmental Perception in Autonomous Systems.

Model Type	*Reference*	*Application Summary*	*Advantages*	*Limitations*
GAN (LE-GAN for Super-Resolution)	(Zhang et al., 2018)	Latent Encoder Coupled GAN is used to sharpen the hyperspectral image and improve spatial and spectral perception under the task of perception.	• Effective in boosting image resolution • Enhances fine-grained visual features	• Susceptible to mode collapse • May introduce spatial-spectral inconsistencies
GAN (TraGAN for Lane Prediction)	(Zharkovsky & Menadeva, 2020)	Trajectory GAN uses data of highway traffic to learn the dynamics of trajectory synthesis by free-flowing traffic without labelling.	• Learns trajectory parameters autonomously • Generates intuitive driving patterns	• Requires extensive, high-quality datasets • Sensitive to hyperparameter tuning
GAN (DeepRoad for Scene Validation)	(Islam et al., 2021)	Deep Road framework makes use of GANs in metamorphic testing and input validation, increasing diversity in scenes when driving autonomously.	• Enhances the strength of the testing environment • Expands scenario coverage	• Synthetic scenes may lack realism • Limited by generative constraints
GAN (cGAN for Change Detection)	(Li et al., 2022)	Conditional GAN is deployed to detect changes in UAV and satellite imagery, automating scene comparison and anomaly identification.	• Promising results in visual change detection • Supports remote sensing applications	• Requires large annotated datasets • May struggle with subtle changes

Contd...

Table 13.2 *Contd...*

Model Type	*Reference*	*Application Summary*	*Advantages*	*Limitations*
VAE (TraVAE for Lane Synthesis)	(Zharkovsky & Menadeva, 2020)	Trajectory VAE generates synthetic lane change data by encoding real traffic patterns into latent space and reconstructing plausible trajectories.	• Learns latent parameters for manoeuvre modelling	• Higher reconstruction error compared to GAN-based methods
VAE (Crash Data Augmentation)	(Duplevska et al., 2023)	VAE applies in order to generate fake crashes based on real traffic log data, to add richness to datasets to train and evaluate.	• Produces diverse and realistic crash samples • Augments rare event data	• May rely on strong assumptions • Risk of generating suboptimal samples
VAE-GAN (Image Translation for Detection)	(Xing & Tzes, 2023)	A combined framework between variational autoencoder and generative adversarial network is employed to convert simulated images into realistic synthetic images in order to train change detection systems.	• Generates labelled data under varied conditions • Useful for domain adaptation	• Real images still required for reference • May not fully bridge domain gaps
VAE (Latent Compression for Diffusion)	(Zhao, Zhai et al. 2023)	VAE compresses environmental images into latent space prior to diffusion modelling, then reconstructs final visuals post-processing.	• Reduces dimensionality and resource usage • Facilitates efficient image generation	• May lose fine visual details during reconstruction

Contd...

Table 13.2 *Contd...*

Model Type	*Reference*	*Application Summary*	*Advantages*	*Limitations*
Diffusion (Stable Diffusion for UAV Imagery)	(Zhao, Zhai et al. 2023)	Stable diffusion models generate synthetic UAV visuals, capturing detailed features and structural nuances for training and simulation.	• High-fidelity image generation • Preserves UAV-specific characteristics	• Computationally intensive • Slow training cycles
Diffusion (Conditional GDM for Detection)	(Yu et al., 2022)	Conditional generative diffusion models produce photorealistic UAV images and bounding boxes based on binary masks and textual prompts.	• Enhances object detection accuracy • Generates scene-specific visuals	• May interfere with detection if inputs are poorly filtered
Transformer (CLIP Prefix for Captioning)	(de Curto et al., 2023)	Transformer-based architecture integrates CLIP and GPT-2 to generate descriptive captions for UAV-captured images.	• Converts visual data into coherent text • Supports multimodal interpretation	• May yield inconsistent or inaccurate descriptions
Transformer (GKST for Feature Retrieval)	(Zhao, Zhai, et al., 2023)	Generative knowledge–aided transformer enhances feature representation and retrieval by learning across multiple visual perspectives.	• Bridges visual gaps between aerial and ground views • Enhances retrieval precision	• High computational and memory demands

Table 13.3 demonstrates the revolutionizing effect of the innovative methodologies in enhancing the autonomy and working intelligences of UV swarms. One of the improvements is combination of Generative Adversarial Imitation Learning (GAIL) and multi-agent Deep Reinforcement Learning (DRL). Multi-Agent PPO-based GAIL (MAPPO-GAIL) framework, as an example in Yu et al. (2022), tries to optimize the policy and value networks through the joint optimization of the sample plans of the agents. The model utilizes grid probability mapping of environmental targets and detects the targets more frequently (73.33%) and with minimal damage probability (1.11%) as compared to the standard DRL search algorithms. GAIL has also been used to control UAVs in simulated conditions where dynamic and complex navigational condition adaptation was effective (Song et al., 2018a; Bandela & Cao, 2023).

The framework of BézierVAE has been applied to the field of the trajectory modelling that involves encoding vehicle paths into latent representations using VAEs and decoding them with the help of Bézier curves. The method achieves 91.3% error in reconstruction reduction and 83.4% reduction in the unsmoothness of the trajectories in comparison to the conventional models such as TrajVAE (Krajewski et al., 2019), which is colossal in certifying the safety of autonomous systems. The COIL framework uses VAEs to produce the best timing sequences that can optimize the performance of the robotic systems in terms of its workload. The GRIN model, which is based on conditional VAEs, is another model that is used in the prediction of multi-agent trajectories; it predicts the movements of agents depending on the social interaction and intention. Though contextual constraints such as physical laws must be obeyed by such systems, they can be overcome by special decoders or surrogate models that may approximate rule-based behaviour (Ha & Jeong, 2022).

It has also been discovered that DRL transformer architectures are the most appropriate for the coordination of a large number of UAVs during route optimization. The hybrid scheme permits the parallel functioning to be efficiently performed and the reward measure is always higher than the traditional routing scheme (Fuertes et al., 2023).

4.4 UV Swarms Task and Resource Allocation with Generative AI

The multi-agent UV swarm operations are based on efficient allocation of tasks and resources, especially in the dynamic and resource-constrained environments. Conventional allocation methods which frequently rely on fixed heuristic or preset algorithms cannot cope with changing mission parameters and changing conditions that are hard to predict. Generative AI offers a family of responsive means of action, capable of improving the responsiveness, scalability, and intelligence of UV swarm coordination, as expressed in Table 13.4.

Some of the advances that can be mentioned include the implementation of GAIL for generating detailed virtual worlds in DRL. In this architecture, the generator can generate expert-level trajectories and the discriminator can tame

Table 13.3 Generative AI Techniques for Enhancing Autonomy in Unmanned Systems.

Model Type	*Reference*	*Application Summary*	*Advantages*	*Limitations*
GAN (GAIL for Cooperative Search)	(Song et al., 2018a, 2018b)	Generative knowledge–aided transformer is able to improve the feature representation and retrieval through learning on multiple visual perspectives.	• Eliminates need for explicit reward signals • Promotes naturalistic and effective behaviour modelling	• Requires extensive expert trajectory datasets
GAN (GAIL for Virtual Navigation)	(Duan et al., 2023)	GAIL is employed to train UAVs in simulated environments by imitating expert navigation paths, allowing adaptation to complex and dynamic virtual landscapes.	• Enhances generalization across diverse scenarios • Improves navigation in synthetic environments	• Gathering expert demonstrations is time-intensive
VAE (BézierVAE for Trajectory Modelling)	(H. Du et al., 2025)	BézierVAE represents the trajectories of vehicles in latent space and recreates them with the help of Bézier curves, which allow safety checks in autonomous driving systems.	• Captures a wide range of driving patterns • Enables trajectory synthesis for validation	• Requires varied and representative trajectory data

Contd...

Table 13.3 *Contd...*

Model Type	*Reference*	*Application Summary*	*Advantages*	*Limitations*
VAE (COIL for Delivery Timing Optimization)	(Chaalal et al., 2021)	VAE-based constrained optimization in latent space is applied to coordinate autonomous delivery robots, ensuring safe and efficient timing across multiple agents.	• Rapid optimization of delivery schedules • Adapts to fluctuating demand levels	• Initial training phase demands significant resources
VAE (GRIN for Multi-Agent Prediction)	(Liu et al., 2025)	GRIN leverages conditional generative modelling with variational inference to predict multi-agent trajectories, accounting for relational and intentional uncertainties.	• Models complex inter-agent dynamics • Captures latent intentions and interactions	• High data requirements for robust training
Transformer (DRL-based Routing Optimization)	(Rao et al., 2020)	Transformer networks combined with deep reinforcement learning are used to optimize routing strategies for cooperative UAV fleets, outperforming traditional algorithms like Compass.	• Enables parallel processing and route efficiency • Scales well with multiple agents	• May encounter latency in high-load scenarios

Table 13.4 Generative AI Techniques for Task and Resource Allocation.

Model Type	*Reference*	*Application Summary*	*Advantages*	*Limitations*
GAN (GAIL-based DRL Environment)	(Adeboye et al., 2022)	The framework is based on GAIL that creates simulated conditions in which deep reinforcement learning can be completed, with the generator model synthesizing simulator-level trajectories and the discriminator distinguishing between real and fake trajectories.	• Simulates realistic training scenarios • Accelerates learning and improves policy performance	• Real-world deployment may impact service reliability
VAE (Hungarian Algorithm Enhancement)	(Tian et al., 2022)	The architecture builds upon Generative Adversarial Imitation Learning (GAIL) to establish a controlled, simulated environment where deep reinforcement learning can be effectively trained. Within this setup, a generative component produces trajectory data that mimics those generated by the simulator, while a discriminative component evaluates and differentiates between authentic trajectories and those that are artificially generated.	• Produces refined cost matrices • Enhances allocation efficiency	• Depends on synthetic training inputs
Diffusion (AGOD for ASP Selection)	(Nguyen et al., 2023)	A diffusion-based AGOD algorithm is introduced to optimize service provider selection within AIGC-as-a-Service systems, generating decisions aligned with architectural constraints.	• Delivers optimal provider choices • Applicable to diverse optimization tasks	• Requires extensive infrastructure • High computational demand

Contd...

Table 13.4 *Contd...*

Model Type	*Reference*	*Application Summary*	*Advantages*	*Limitations*
Diffusion (Semantic Transmission Optimization)	(Zhao, Zhai, et al., 2023)	It uses Generative Adversarial Imitation Learning (GAIL) to create synthetic environments that are conducive to deep reinforcement learning. This architecture has the generator that produces trajectory data that are simulator-consistent and the discriminator that attempts to differentiate between natural and simulated trajectory data.	• Improves semantic data quality • Handles intricate decision layers	• Demands prolonged training cycles
LLM (On-Device Task Prioritization)	(Yu et al., 2022)	Large language models autonomously generate, schedule, and prioritize tasks in real time, particularly in edge environments, enabling collaborative operations in wireless networks.	• Supports adaptive task execution • Enables decentralized intelligence	• Susceptible to errors from dynamic network conditions

its ability to distinguish between real and synthetic trajectories (Kobeaga et al., 2018; Miao et al., 2025). In edge computing environments, the multi-agent DRL systems are able to experiment with reward structure and develop effective resource allocation policies, with this simulation environment, where they can freely interact with each other.

In order to resolve the uncertainty on resource assignment, in particular spectrum and energy allocation among cellular and device-to-device users (CUs and D2DUs), a Hungarian algorithm upgraded with an autoencoder has been suggested (Rathod & Tanwar, 2023). This type of technique in which the data rate matrix is placed in a latent space retrieves an optimized cost matrix, which not only solves the conflict presented by the same value of weights, but also increases the accuracy of the allocations.

In the AI-generated Optimal Decision (AGOD) algorithm, diffusion models assign tasks according to real-time environmental feedback and user demand is more innovational (H. Du et al., 2023). When used together with DRA, Deep Diffusion Soft Actor-Critic (D2SAC) algorithm exhibits high performance speed, with an increment in the rate of task completion (2.3%) and utility (5.15%) being greater than in conventional SAC algorithms. Unlike the conventional approaches, which assume a certain definition of duties, D2SAC is a dynamically chosen approach that chooses the best possible service providers in real time and this enhances operational flexibility.

The peculiarities of UVs lie in the field of joint computing and controlling the use of communication resources due to low battery capacity and autonomous working. Diffusion-generated style, which is a sophisticated means of power distribution of semantic data transmission, can be found in B. Du et al. (2023). This model restores the energy numerous times so as to guarantee the quality of transmission under diverse conditions. The suggested scheme at 20-metre of transmission distance and 4 kW of power operation is superior to the baseline methods such as Avg-SemCom and Conf-SemCom with 0.25 additional performance in enhancing transmission quality following 500 rounds.

More than that, the introduced framework is based on GAIL that creates simulated conditions in which deep reinforcement learning can be completed. In this framework, the generator model synthesizes simulator-level trajectories and the discriminator distinguishes between real and fake trajectories; this creates new possibilities in the field of intent decomposition and task orchestration. In Zou et al. (2023), Independent LLM-based models were used to transform high-level system objectives, like ensuring an 85 W network energy-saving, into small control decisions, like transmit power optimization and channel quality measurement. This was further transferred to the relevant executors such that UAV agents realize the energy saving goal within two working cycles. Despite the fact that the current versions of the LLMs such as GPT-4 are somewhat limited in the context of the coordination of various goals when operating with large groups of agents, their availability signifies a colossal innovation in the system plane in terms of autonomy-based decision-making and optimization.

Generative intelligence boosts task coordination and resource sharing of unmanned swarms that work in a dynamic environment. It facilitates realistic simulation and adaptive control in complex multi-agent systems.

4.5 Network Coverage & Peer-to-Peer Communication in UV Swarms via Generative AI

4.5.1 Distributed Connectivity and Direct Inter-Agent Exchange in Unmanned Swarms Using Generative Intelligence

The UVs are used in swarm-based operations as mobile hubs to reconnect the broken communication structures. The location and good inter-unit connections are crucial to the smooth coordination and performance of tasks.

Generative intelligence proposes new ways of maximizing coverage and extending the direct inter-vehicle communication channels. The dynamic wireless setup is also being used to supply a temporary connection of communication via UAVs. These networks are, however, complicated by the varying altitude, movement patterns, spatial interference, and environmental variability in their management.

It was proposed to use a cGAN structure in Table 13.5 where the generator networks are adapted to predict the best network arrangement, the discriminator networks determine the effectiveness, and the encoder networks give the flexibility in various scenarios (Song et al., 2018a). It is computationally efficient ($O(k^2)$) and outperforms conventional algorithms, such as the core-set method ($O(pk)$) and the spiral method ($O(k^3)$), where p denotes the count of user terminals and k represents the quantity of UAVs.

Besides this, one of the transformer-based models proposed uses self-attention mechanisms to forecast user movement and refine the positioning of airborne base stations. The framework captures spatio-temporal dependencies, longer input–output sequences, and is consequently 9% to 31% more likely to provide coverage than conventional deployment plans and over 9% more likely than LSTM-based methods.

V2V communication is critical in ensuring safe and coordinated swarm movement. The UVs usually exchange visual data to make available environmental data. Noise is, however, subject to such transmissions because they are affected by motion, interruption of signals, and environmental distortion. GDMs have been used to deal with them in terms of visual reconstruction and communication optimization. GDMs are employed to gradually recover degraded images through stochastic differential equations, which in turn recover the visual fidelity of the image at minimal transmission delays. In addition, GDMs have also been demonstrated to do path planning, where the initial (base case) trajectories are taken, and then progressively enhanced in performance measures. In 300 training epochs, GDM-based method outperformed Deep Q-Network (DQN) methods by 100% in cumulative rewards.

Table 13.5 Generative AI Techniques for Network Coverage & Peer-to-Peer Communication.

Model Type	*Reference*	*Application Summary*	*Advantages*	*Limitations*
GAN (cGAN-based Coverage Optimization)	(Song et al., 2018a)	Conditional generative adversarial network framework is utilized to enhance communication coverage by combining three primary elements: a generator that predicts optimal UAV placement, a discriminator that verifies deployment authenticity, and an encoder that projects configurations into latent representation for scalable adjustment.	• Facilitates precise UAV placement • Reduces computational overhead	• Demands extensive training datasets
GAN (SCMA-TPGAN)	(Bandela & Cao, 2023)	A hybrid generative framework combining transformer-based generators and PatchGAN discriminators is used to refine SCMA encoding and decoding, improving signal integrity in uplink Rayleigh fading environments.	• Minimizes bit error rates • Strengthens noise resilience	• Dependent on base station's channel matrix and user-specific codebooks
Diffusion Models (GDMs)	(Krajewski et al., 2019)	Generative diffusion models are deployed to restore corrupted image data and optimize V2V communication, mitigating transmission losses and environmental interference.	• Enhances data delivery efficiency • Reduces latency in peer exchanges	• Introduces iterative processing overhead
Transformer (Self-Attention for Coverage Prediction)	(Bentley et al., 2023)	Transformer models with self-attention mechanisms predict spatial user distribution, enabling UAV base stations to reposition dynamically for improved coverage.	• Superior to LSTM in handling long-range dependencies • Adaptive to spatial variations	• May oversimplify complex network behaviours

In conclusion, generative AI is better with the coverage of networks and communication of UV swarms due to two key mechanisms: (i) direct generation of optimized location plans, and (ii) optimizing traditional algorithms through the application of spatial encoding and semantic compression. These characteristics enable the UVs to have great connectivity using minimum data overheads. Nevertheless, one will have reason to suspect that further investigations will be warranted, in particular the integration of multimodal streams of information to make the network more adaptable to a range of topological and environmental conditions. Generative intelligence has the potential of leading autonomous swarm agents in dynamic, changing operational environments.

4.6 UV Swarms–enabled Generative AI Security and Privacy

Unmanned swarm systems implement security and confidentiality as one of their pillars, particularly in life and death missions. Generative intelligence provides superior protection from the threat of cyberattacks and eliminates data leakage within these networks. As Figure 13.5 shows, the use of generative AI–generated data of decoy and the design of simulated communication patterns are among the strategies that enable the development of honeypots, artificial misleading traps that are designed to cripple malicious actors. These honeypots are Large Language Models (LLMs) used to disseminate false information to confuse the attackers, making the common security position of the swarm stronger.

Table 13.7 presents a number of GAI-based data privacy safeguards and mechanisms for detecting and mitigating unauthorized access attempts. The Auto-Driving GAN (ADGAN) architecture can be considered as an example of this as it utilizes an image-to-image translation network to hide the sensitive backgrounds of the car-captured images. ADGAN selectively retains or removes particular architectural components and does not influence objects of paramount significance such as traffic signs and pedestrians, which means that it does not reduce its utility and enhances privacy. The protection of sophisticated adversarial attacks is also heightened by its multi-discriminator structure.

In the same fashion, the adversarial generative frameworks depicted in Figure 13.5 are trained with the objective of anonymizing the street-view images by the substitution of identifiable objects with natural background recreations (Miao et al., 2025). TrajGANs in trajectory data protection create artificial routes, which resemble the movement patterns in the world with distinct personalities and face the locations covered to protect them. Trajgan can also present the following issues: they can be issued in dense temporal encoding and representation of rare events but are efficient in statistical fidelity.

To address these limitations, the LSTM-TrajGAN framework was introduced (Kobeaga et al., 2018), combining generative modelling with recurrent neural networks for spatio-temporal embedding. This architecture includes a generator for trajectory synthesis, a discriminator for authenticity validation, and an LSTM-based encoder for timestamp integration. Evaluated using the Trajectory-User

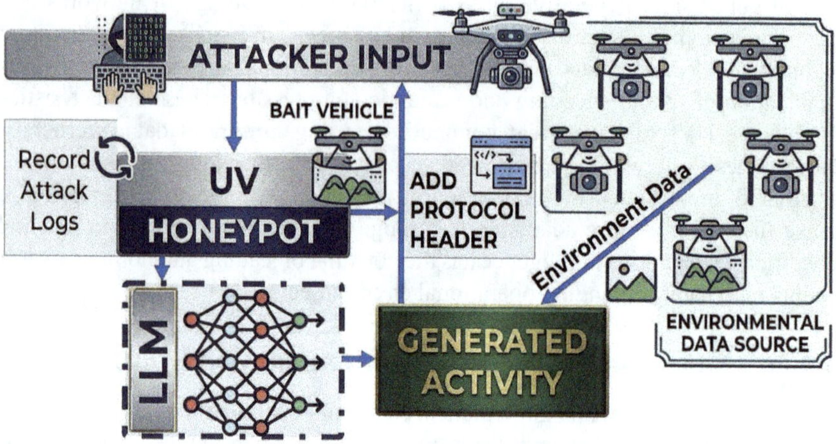

Fig. 13.5 Honeypot-based deception framework for strengthening UV swarm security (Adeboye, O. et al. 2022).

Linking (TUL) attack model, LSTM-TrajGAN reduced re-identification accuracy ranging from 99.8% to 45.9%, exceeding conventional geo-obfuscation methods such as random disturbance (66.8%) and Gaussian obfuscation (48.6%).

The generative AI in Table 13.6 can significantly enhance safety and privacy of UV swarms by enabling such approaches as concealing route, disguising a picture, and developing decoy. This is done by injecting noise in VAEs that are tuned to ensure spatial coherence and ensure differentiability privacy. The federated learning is assisted by the transformers that give out the mandatory features and reduce the exposure of raw information. Further, transformer-based intrusion detection system is applied to analyse CAN messages to identify cyberattacks like denial-of-service and spoofing. All these innovations enable autonomous systems to withstand high-level threats within distributed and multi-agent systems without compromising the integrity of operations (Rathod & Tanwar, 2023; H. Du et al., 2023; B. Du et al., 2023).

4.7 Vehicle Safety and Fault Detection in UV Swarms via Generative AI

4.7.1 Ensuring Operational Integrity and Fault Diagnosis in UV Clusters Using Generative Intelligence

The security of UV swarms depends on the external movement control as well as internal diagnostic resilience to operate continuously. Unlike autonomy-related safety measures, fault management focuses on identifying vulnerabilities arising from algorithmic inconsistencies, hardware malfunctions, and sensor degradation. The goal is to enhance operational reliability by enabling UV systems to detect and mitigate faults before they compromise mission integrity or system performance.

Table 13.6 Generative AI Techniques for Vehicular Privacy and Security.

Model Type	*Reference*	*Application Summary*	*Advantages*	*Limitations*
GAN (ADGAN)	(Ha & Jeong, 2022)	ADGAN employs image-to-image translation to obscure background structures in vehicular camera feeds, preserving visibility of critical elements like traffic signs and pedestrians for autonomous navigation.	• Maintains object recognition fidelity • Multi-discriminator setup improves synthesis realism	• Indirect data may still reveal sensitive locations • Possible degradation in driving performance
GAN (TrajGAN)	(Fuertes et al., 2023)	TrajGANs generate synthetic mobility paths that mimic real trajectory distributions while concealing user-specific location and identity data.	• Preserves statistical patterns • Adaptable across varied datasets	• Difficulty in modelling dense path clusters • Vulnerable to overfitting and rare event omission
GAN (LSTM-TrajGAN)	(Kobeaga et al., 2018)	LSTM-TrajGAN synthesizes trajectory data to prevent re-identification via TUL algorithms, which exploit spatial-temporal correlations to link users to movement patterns.	• Maintains mobility semantics • Superior to traditional geomasking	• Requires robust validation to avoid overfitting • Trade-off between privacy and data utility
GAN (Object Replacement)	(Miao et al., 2025)	GAN-based framework replaces dynamic entities in street-view imagery with realistic backgrounds to anonymize visual data.	• Effective anonymization of moving subjects	• Risk of unintentionally removing static, context-relevant elements
VAE (Differential Privacy)	(Rathod & Tanwar, 2023)	VAE generates synthetic vehicle trajectories by injecting differential privacy noise, thereby masking individual location traces while retaining overall realism.	• Produces diverse and plausible data • Configurable privacy thresholds	• Noise addition may compromise analytical precision
Transformer (Federated Learning)	(H. Du et al., 2023)	Federated vehicular transformers integrate decentralized learning with multi-modal data fusion (e.g., trajectories, images, point clouds) for secure collaborative processing.	• Balances privacy with performance • Supports heterogeneous data types	• Increased system complexity and resource demands
Transformer (CAN Bus IDS)	(B. Du et al., 2023)	Transformer-based intrusion detection system examines CAN bus traffic using attention mechanisms to classify multiple attack types without needing labelled datasets.	• High detection accuracy across attack categories • Operates efficiently with unlabelled inputs	• Extended training duration • Susceptible to novel, unseen threats

Table 13.7 Advanced Generative AI Techniques for Fault Diagnosis in Intelligent Vehicles.

Generative AI Technique	*Reference*	*Application Summary*	*Advantages*	*Limitations*
VAE-CGAN Hybrid	(Song et al., 2018a)	A composite model where VAE initializes and denoises incomplete time-series sensor inputs, while CGAN's discriminator refines the output quality. This setup is tailored for fault-tolerant data recovery in sensor networks.	• Maintains sample fidelity across varying data loss rates • Enhances prediction precision	• Extended training duration required
Variational Autoencoder (VAE)	(Zou et al., 2023)	VAE compresses standard UAV telemetry into a latent representation, reconstructs it, and flags anomalies by measuring deviation from expected reconstruction norms.	• Capable of identifying previously unseen fault types • High anomaly detection accuracy	• Operates offline • Limited adaptability across diverse datasets
LSTM-based Models	(Dhakal et al., 2023)	Sequential sensor data is processed using LSTM to uncover temporal patterns linked to system faults in unmanned vehicles. This approach leverages memory of prior states to detect irregularities.	• Strong predictive performance • Captures time-dependent fault signatures	• Demands extensive training datasets • High computational overhead
Transformer-Based (BERT)		BERT architecture is adapted to extract multi-scale spatio-temporal features for diagnosing battery anomalies. It identifies five distinct fault categories using onboard sensor inputs.	• Robust fault prediction capability • Enables early intervention strategies	• Resource-intensive • Potential for misclassification of battery health states

A promising approach involves the integration of Long Short-Term Memory (LSTM) networks with autoencoders to monitor time-series performance data (Dhakal et al., 2023). This hybrid framework continuously learns from operational metrics, generating synthetic fault scenarios to enrich training datasets. It achieved 90% fault detection accuracy and 99% classification precision for drone misoperations in simulation environments. The temporal modelling capabilities of LSTM make it particularly effective in dynamic conditions, where fluctuating parameters influence system behaviour. Subsequent research (Dhakal et al., 2023) demonstrated a fourfold increase in fault classification speed using Field-Programmable Gate Array (FPGA)-based acceleration, with a 50% reduction in energy consumption—highlighting the potential of generative AI for real-time fault management in swarm deployments.

The VAEs in Table 13.7 provide another effective approach for anomaly detection. By training on normal operational data, VAEs learn to reconstruct expected input patterns. Deviations in reconstruction error indicate potential faults (Dhakal et al., 2023). This approach achieved an average detection accuracy of 95.6%, with the additional advantage of detecting previously unseen anomalies. The ability of VAEs to generalize beyond the training set makes them valuable in unpredictable environments. However, their performance depends on model complexity, data diversity, and threshold calibration.

Transformer-based architectures have also been applied to fault diagnosis, particularly in battery health monitoring. A spatio-temporal transformer model (Zhao, Feng et al., 2023) was developed to analyse sensor data across multiple scales, enabling early detection of battery degradation. This model supports predictive maintenance by forecasting failures within a 24-hour to one-week window, optimizing scheduling and reducing downtime. The UV systems require battery health and constant data flow to operate effectively. Hybrid generative models such as VAE-CGAN are also used in situations where sensors are failing or a sensor input is missing, and the time-series data is needed to maintain functionality. In case of critical faults, adaptive, where-to-crash strategies are used to execute the safe shutdowns based on real-time swarm analysis. Transformer-based frameworks increase decision-making by interpreting dynamic conditions. Such generative systems facilitate fault detection, recovery, and emergency planning, maintain resilient performance and safety under diverse conditions with no loss in continuity of operation and integrity in data.

5. Open Issues and Future Research Directions

Nonetheless, with much improvement to be noted, there are still unresolved challenges of scaling, coordination, and adaptability in UV swarms using generative intelligence. It is necessary to fill in these gaps by concentrating on the research on dynamic modelling, real-time decision systems, and resilient architectures.

5.1 Scalability in Large-Scale Swarm Deployments

The coordination of the unmanned swarms is complicated by scaling because of latency and signal interference in dense networks. Federation and distributed control of segmentation allow effective cooperation, and it is decentralized in making decisions among swarm leaders.

5.2 Adaptive Generative Intelligence for Dynamic Environments

The unpredictability of the environment of unmanned swarms increases the model flexibility as well as the learning efficiency. By incorporating meta-learning, transfer learning, and real-time reinforcement, it can be enhanced to become more adaptable with minimal retraining costs.

5.3 Towards AI-Native UV Networks

Semantic communication will also increase efficiency as it only sends mission-critical data in unmanned networks. The construction of robust, knowledge-rich UV systems requires encrypted adaptation of knowledge and real time coordination among limited, mobile agents.

5.4 3D Interference Management in High-Mobility Networks

Unmanned swarms operating in three-dimensional space must be able to withstand dynamic conditions of interference that can negatively impact communication and coordination. Adaptive generative models are optimized transmission models, where spatial-temporal patterns are learned, allowing transmission to be stable at minimum energy.

5.5 Security and Privacy in Adversarial Settings

Generative tools enhance security of swarms but are vulnerable to changing adversarial threat and resource constraints. Scalable defences in the form of dataset recovery, federated learning, and adaptive feedback systems are important in resilience.

6. Conclusion

This chapter presented a systematic and detailed study on the application of generative AI in UV swarm systems. It began with a historical overview of UV architectures and operational areas, providing the background for the relevance of generative AI in enhancing autonomous capabilities. The core generative models are discussed regarding their significance for swarm dynamics, including data synthesis, behavioural modelling, and adaptive control.

Later paragraphs offered a rigorous evaluation of generative AI–based solutions on the basis of essential operational aspects, which included the estimation of states, perception of the environment, autonomy, task distribution, inter-agent communication, safety, and maintenance of privacy. Each application was applied in the context of real-world constraints, showing how generative frameworks can be used to scale and make UV swarms resilient and intelligent.

In addition, the chapter came up with major research challenges to full-scale deployment, such as coordination in the small scale, adaptive learning in uncertain conditions, semantic communication in limited networks, interference control in three-dimensional systems, and cyber resilience in adversarial conditions. These gaps were addressed by proposing strategic directions to consider the following: decentralized architectures, federated learning, meta-adaptive frameworks, and lightweight security protocols.

Overall, this chapter provided a vision of the future of the generation of healthy, context-sensitive, and mission-deployable UV swarms through generative intelligence. The knowledge provided within this chapter will serve to stimulate future studies on scalable, secure, and intelligent autonomous systems.

References

Adeboye, O., Dargahi, T., Babaie, M. et al. (2022). DeepClean: A robust deep learning technique for autonomous vehicle camera data privacy. *IEEE Access*, 10, 124534–124544.

Arvinte, M. and Tamir, J.I. (2022). MIMO channel estimation using score-based generative models (No. arXiv:2204.07122). arXiv.

Bandela, S. and Cao, Y. (2023). Drone navigation in unreal engine using generative adversarial imitation learning. In *AIAA SCITECH 2023 Forum*. American Institute of Aeronautics and Astronautics.

Bentley, P., Lim, S.L., Arcaini, P. and Ishikawa, F. 2023. Using a Variational Autoencoder to Learn Valid Search Spaces of Safely Monitored Autonomous Robots for Last-Mile Delivery. In *Proceedings of the Genetic and Evolutionary Computation Conference* (GECCO '23). Association for Computing Machinery, New York, NY, USA, 1303–1311. https://doi.org/10.1145/3583131.3590459.

Chaalal, E., Reynaud, L. and Senouci, S.-M. (2021). Mobility prediction for aerial base stations for a coverage extension in 5G networks. *2021 International Wireless Communications and Mobile Computing (IWCMC)* (pp. 2163–2168).

de Curto, J., de Zarza, I. and Calafate, C.T. (2023). Semantic scene understanding with large language models on unmanned aerial vehicles. *Drones*, 7(2), 114. https://www.mdpi.com/2504-446X/7/2/114

Delecki, H., Kruse, L.A., Schlichting, M.R. and Kochenderfer, M.J. (2023). Deep normalizing flows for state estimation (No. arXiv:2306.15605). arXiv.

Dhakal, R., Bosma, C., Chaudhary, P. and Kandel, L.N. (2023). UAV Fault and Anomaly Detection Using Autoencoders. *2023 IEEE/AIAA 42nd Digital Avionics Systems Conference (DASC)* (pp. 1–8).

Du, B., Du, H., Liu, H. et al. (2023). YOLO-based semantic communication with generative AI-aided resource allocation for digital twins construction (No. arXiv:2306.14138). arXiv.

Du, H., Li, Z., Niyato, D. et al. (2023). Diffusion-based reinforcement learning for edge-enabled AI-generated content services (No. arXiv:2303.13052). arXiv. https://arxiv.org/abs/2303.13052

Du, H., Zhang, R., Liu, Y. et al. (2025). Enhancing deep reinforcement learning: A tutorial on generative diffusion models in network optimization. Available at https://arxiv.org/html/2308.05384v2#abstract (accessed on 16 December 2025).

Duan, C., Zhang, S., Yin, P. et al. (2023). SCMA-TPGAN: A new perspective on sparse codebook multiple access for UAV system. *Computer Communications*, 200(C), 161–170.

Duplevska, D., Medvedevs, V., Surmacs, D. and Aboltins, A. (2023). The synthetic data application in the UAV recognition systems development. *2023 IEEE 10th Jubilee Workshop on Advances in Information, Electronic and Electrical Engineering (AIEEE)* (pp. 1–6).

Fuertes, D., del-Blanco, C. R., Jaureguizar, F. et al. (2023). Solving routing problems for multiple cooperative unmanned aerial vehicles using transformer networks. *Engineering Applications of Artificial Intelligence*, 122, 106085.

Ha, S. and Jeong, H. (2022). Learning heterogeneous interaction strengths by trajectory prediction with graph neural network (No. arXiv:2208.13179). arXiv.

Islam, Z., Abdel-Aty, M., Cai, Q. and Yuan, J. (2021). Crash data augmentation using variational autoencoder. *Accident Analysis & Prevention*, 151, 105950.

Jha, N.K. and Lau, V.K.N. (2024). Temporally correlated compressed sensing using generative models for channel estimation in unmanned aerial vehicles. *IEEE Transactions on Wireless Communications*, 23(3), 2112–2124.

Kobeaga, G., Merino, M. and Lozano, J.A. (2018). An efficient evolutionary algorithm for the orienteering problem. *Computers & Operations Research*, 90, 42–59.

Krajewski, R., Moers, T., Meister, A. and Eckstein, L. (2019). BézierVAE: Improved trajectory modeling using variational autoencoders for the safety validation of highly automated vehicles. *2019 IEEE Intelligent Transportation Systems Conference (ITSC)* (pp. 3788–3795).

Krajewski, R., Moers, T., Nerger, D. and Eckstein, L. (2018). Data-driven maneuver modeling using generative adversarial networks and variational autoencoders for safety validation of highly automated vehicles. *2018 21st International Conference on Intelligent Transportation Systems (ITSC)* (pp. 2383–2390).

Li, X., Duan, H., Tian, Y. and Wang, F.-Y. (2022). Exploring image generation for UAV change detection. *IEEE/CAA Journal of Automatica Sinica*, 9(6), 1061–1072.

Liu, X., Chen, H. and Andris, C. (2025). trajGANs: Using generative adversarial networks for geo-privacy protection of trajectory data (Vision paper).

Miao, S., Xu, X., Zeng, T. et al. (2025). Exploration of microorganism and metabolites relation to the egg production of Shanma ducks based on 16S rRNA gene sequencing and metabolomics. *Poultry Science*, 104(12), 105880.

Nguyen, T.P., Nam, H. and Kim, D. (2023). Transformer-based attention network for in-vehicle intrusion detection. *IEEE Access*, 11, 55389–55403.

Rao, J., Gao, S., Kang, Y. and Huang, Q. (2020). LSTM-TrajGAN: A deep learning approach to trajectory privacy protection [application/pdf]. *LIPIcs*, Volume 177, *GIScience 2021*, 177, 12:1-12:17.

Rathod, T. and Tanwar, S. (2023). Autoencoder-based efficient resource allocation in device-to-device communication. *Physical Communication*, 60, 102133.

Shi, Y., Han, L., Han, L. et al. (2022). A latent encoder coupled generative adversarial network (LE-GAN) for efficient hyperspectral image super-resolution. *IEEE Transactions on Geoscience and Remote Sensing*, 60, 1–19.

Song, J., Ren, H., Sadigh, D. and Ermon, S. (2018b). Multi-agent generative adversarial imitation learning. *Proceedings of the 32nd International Conference on Neural Information Processing Systems* (pp. 7472–7483).

Tian, Y., Wang, J., Wang, Y. et al. (2022). Federated vehicular transformers and their federations: Privacy-preserving computing and cooperation for autonomous driving. *IEEE Transactions on Intelligent Vehicles*, 7(3), 456–465.

Uittenbogaard, R., Sebastian, C., Vijverberg, J. et al. (2019). Privacy protection in street-view panoramas using depth and multi-view imagery. *2019 IEEE/CVF Conference on Computer Vision and Pattern Recognition (CVPR)* (pp. 10573–10582).

Xie, Y., Shao, Z., Chen, F. and Lin, H. "Harmonic State Estimation Based on Network Equivalence and Closed Loop GAN," *2023 8th Asia Conference on Power and Electrical Engineering* (ACPEE), Tianjin, China, 2023, pp. 1688-1693, doi: 10.1109/ACPEE56931.2023.10135862.

Xing, D. and Tzes, A. (2023). Synthetic aerial dataset for UAV detection via text-to-image diffusion models. *2023 IEEE Conference on Artificial Intelligence (CAI)* (pp. 51–52).

Xu, D., Wei, C., Peng, P. et al. (2020). GE-GAN: A novel deep learning framework for road traffic state estimation. *Transportation Research Part C: Emerging Technologies*, 117, 102635.

Yu, X., Liao, W., Qu, C. et al. (2022). UAV cooperative search based on multi-agent generative adversarial imitation learning. *2022 International Conference on Machine Learning, Cloud Computing and Intelligent Mining (MLCCIM)* (pp. 441–446).

Zhang, M., Zhang, Y., Zhang, L. et al. (2018). DeepRoad: GAN-based metamorphic testing and input validation framework for autonomous driving systems. *Proceedings of the 33rd ACM/IEEE International Conference on Automated Software Engineering* (pp. 132–142).

Zhao, J., Feng, X., Wang, J. et al. (2023). Battery fault diagnosis and failure prognosis for electric vehicles using spatio-temporal transformer networks. *Applied Energy*, 352, 121949.

Zhao, J., Zhai, Q., Zhao, P. et al. (2023). Co-visual pattern-augmented generative transformer learning for automobile geo-localization. *Remote Sensing*, 15(9), 2221.

Zharkovsky, Y. and Menadeva, O. (2020). End-to-end change detection for high resolution drone images with gan architecture (No. arXiv:2006.00467). arXiv.

Zou, H., Zhao, Q., Bariah, L. et al. (2023). Wireless multi-agent generative AI: From connected intelligence to collective intelligence (No. arXiv:2307.02757). arXiv.

14 The Dual-Use Conundrum: Analysing How Generative AI Empowers Both Malicious Cyberattacks and Advanced Defensive Mechanisms in Modern Digital Security

Ritu Sindhu[1] and Jatin Singh Rajawat[2*]

The rapid evolution of generative artificial intelligence (AI) has created a profound dual-use dilemma in cybersecurity, simultaneously strengthening defensive capabilities while enabling increasingly sophisticated cyberattacks. This research examines how generative AI transforms both sides of the cybersecurity landscape through enhanced anomaly detection, synthetic data generation, and automated incident response on the defensive front, while empowering cybercriminals with automated phishing campaigns, polymorphic malware, and synthetic identities on the offensive side. The democratization of AI technologies has dramatically lowered entry barriers, accelerating the velocity, variety, and impact of cyber threats. Through critical analysis of large language models, adversarial networks, and autonomous agents, this study highlights emerging risks related to data privacy, model manipulation, and autonomous agent behaviour. We propose a vision-driven governance framework integrating AI safety protocols, ethical oversight, and adversarial testing approaches to mitigate threats while fostering innovation. This research provides actionable insights for cybersecurity professionals navigating an increasingly complex digital ecosystem where technological advancement presents both unprecedented opportunities and existential challenges.

1. Introduction

Imagine waking up to find your identity perfectly replicated digitally—your voice, your writing style, even your facial expressions—all synthesized by artificial intelligence (AI) to empty your bank account or manipulate your loved ones. This is not science fiction; it is the emerging reality powered by generative AI. As these technologies become increasingly sophisticated, we find ourselves at a critical juncture where the same innovations that promise to revolutionize healthcare,

[1] https://orcid.org/0009-0004-4052-1721
[2] https://orcid.org/0009-0004-4646-6970
* Corresponding author: jatinsr310304@gmail.com

DOI: 10.1201/9781003688174-14

education, and creativity simultaneously create unprecedented vulnerabilities in our digital infrastructure (Hyra & Premti, 2024).

The meteoric rise of generative AI represents one of the most transformative technological shifts in human history. What began as experimental systems capable of generating simple text and images has evolved into powerful platforms like GPT-4, DALL-E, and Midjourney that can produce human-quality content across virtually any domain. These systems have moved beyond novelty applications to become integral components of our digital ecosystem, fundamentally changing how we create, communicate, and interact with information (Arifin et al., 2024).

In cybersecurity, this transformation presents both extraordinary opportunities and alarming risks. On one hand, generative AI offers defenders powerful new tools to predict, prevent, and respond to cyber threats with unprecedented speed and accuracy. On the other hand, it provides malicious actors with equally powerful capabilities to launch attacks that are more sophisticated, scalable, and difficult to detect than anything we have seen before (Dunmore et al., 2023). This dual-use nature creates a fundamental paradox: every defensive innovation enabled by generative AI simultaneously creates new offensive possibilities.

Consider the case of Sarah, a cybersecurity analyst at a major financial institution. Last year, her team implemented an AI-powered anomaly detection system that reduced false positives by 60% and identified three previously unknown threats within its first month of deployment. Yet, in the same quarter, the institution faced a sophisticated phishing attack that used AI-generated voice cloning to impersonate a senior executive, successfully convincing an employee to transfer $250,000 to fraudulent accounts (Polra, 2023). This scenario encapsulates the dual-use conundrum—the same technology that protects us can also be weaponized against us.

As we stand at this technological crossroads, the choices we make today about how to develop, deploy, and govern generative AI will have profound implications for the future of digital security. The path forward requires balancing innovation with caution, embracing the transformative potential of these technologies while implementing robust safeguards against their misuse (Nag et al., 2024). This is not merely a technical challenge but also a societal one, demanding collaboration across disciplines, sectors, and borders to create a digital ecosystem that is both secure and equitable.

2. The Evolution of Generative AI in Cybersecurity

2.1 From Rule-based Security to AI-Augmented Defence: A Historical Perspective

The journey of cybersecurity reflects the broader evolution of technology itself—from simple mechanical systems to complex, adaptive networks. In the early days of computing, security was primarily physical: locked doors, guarded facilities, and restricted access to mainframe computers. As networks emerged, security evolved into rule-based systems designed to enforce access controls and monitor for known threats (Bui Thu et al., 2025).

The 1980s and the 1990s saw the rise of signature-based antivirus software and firewalls—systems that operated like digital bouncers, checking incoming traffic against lists of known malicious patterns. These systems were effective against the threats of their time but struggled with zero-day exploits and sophisticated attacks that could bypass static defences. The turn of the millennium brought intrusion detection systems (IDS) and intrusion prevention systems (IPS), which added behavioural analysis to the security toolkit, but still relied heavily on predefined rules and signatures (Navidan et al., 2021).

The real transformation began in the early 2010s with the advent of machine learning (ML) in cybersecurity. Systems could now learn from data rather than relying solely on pre-programmed rules, enabling more adaptive threat detection. However, these early ML systems were limited by their need for large labelled datasets and their inability to generate new insights beyond their training data (Arifin et al., 2024).

Generative AI represents the next quantum leap in this evolution. Unlike traditional ML systems that classify or predict based on existing patterns, generative models create entirely new content—text, images, code, and even malware variants—that did not exist before. This creative capability fundamentally changes the cybersecurity landscape, enabling both defenders and attackers to innovate at unprecedented speeds (Khan et al., 2025).

2.2 The Emergence of Generative Models: Architectures and Applications

Generative AI encompasses several distinct architectural families, each with unique capabilities and implications for cybersecurity.

Large language models (LLMs) like GPT-4, LLaMA, and Claude represent perhaps the most visible face of generative AI. These systems process and generate human-like text through complex neural networks trained on vast amounts of textual data. In cybersecurity, LLMs can analyse security logs, generate detection rules, simulate phishing attacks for testing, and even assist in reverse-engineering malware (Microsoft Corporation, 2023a). Their ability to understand context and generate coherent responses makes them invaluable for security operations centres drowning in alert data.

The story of LLMs in cybersecurity begins with early experiments in natural language processing for security log analysis. Researchers quickly realized that these models could not only parse complex technical language but also identify subtle patterns that human analysts might miss. Today, systems like Microsoft's Security Copilot leverage GPT-4 to help analysts make sense of overwhelming amounts of security data, turning what was once a needle-in-a-haystack problem into a manageable workflow (Freitas et al., 2024).

Generative Adversarial Networks (GANs) consist of two competing neural networks—a generator that creates synthetic data and a discriminator that evaluates its authenticity. Originally developed for image generation, GANs have found surprising applications in cybersecurity. They can generate synthetic network traffic for testing IDS, create adversarial examples to probe the robustness of security models, and even produce deepfakes for social engineering attacks (Dunmore et al., 2023).

The cybersecurity applications of GANs emerged from an unlikely source: digital art. As artists began using GANs to create realistic images, security researchers realized that the same techniques could generate realistic-but-fake network traffic patterns. This led to breakthroughs in testing security systems against sophisticated attacks that would otherwise be impossible to simulate safely (Randhawa et al., 2021).

Autonomous agents with memory, such as those built on frameworks like LangChain and AutoGPT, represent the cutting edge of generative AI. These systems combine language models with memory, planning capabilities, and tool use, enabling them to perform complex, multi-step tasks autonomously. In cybersecurity, they can conduct persistent threat hunting, coordinate incident response across multiple systems, and adapt their strategies based on new information (Reddy & Gujral, 2025).

2.3 The Dual-Use Turning Point: When AI Became Accessible

The year 2022 marked a watershed moment in generative AI's evolution with the public release of ChatGPT. Suddenly, powerful AI capabilities that were once the domain of specialized researchers became accessible to anyone with an internet connection. This democratization of AI technology accelerated the dual-use dilemma exponentially, as both defenders and attackers gained access to sophisticated tools (Polra, 2023).

Before this turning point, using AI for cybersecurity required significant technical expertise and computational resources. Now, a teenager with a laptop can generate convincing phishing emails or create polymorphic malware using publicly available tools. This levelling of the playing field has profound implications for cybersecurity, fundamentally changing the threat landscape (Khan et al., 2025).

This accessibility has created what some experts call the "script kiddie 2.0" phenomenon—individuals with limited technical skills who can nonetheless launch sophisticated attacks using AI tools. At the same time, it has empowered small businesses and under-resourced organizations to implement advanced security measures that were previously only available to large enterprises (Schmid et al., 2022).

The dual-use nature of generative AI (shown in Figure 14.1) is perhaps best illustrated by the story of WormGPT—an unrestricted version of ChatGPT developed specifically for malicious purposes. While OpenAI implemented safeguards to prevent ChatGPT from being used for harmful activities, WormGPT removed these restrictions, allowing users to generate malware code, create phishing emails, and develop attack strategies (Polra, 2023). The existence of WormGPT demonstrates how quickly defensive technologies can be repurposed for offence in the generative AI era.

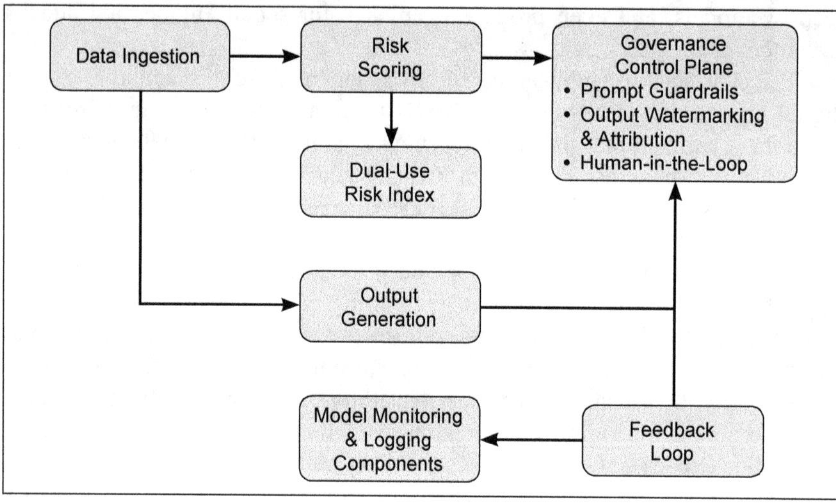

Fig. 14.1 Architecture of dual-use generative AI in cybersecurity, showing offensive, defensive, and governance layers.
Source: Korimilli et al. (2025)

As we navigate this new landscape, it is clear that generative AI represents not just another technological tool but a fundamental shift in the cybersecurity paradigm. The same systems that help us protect critical infrastructure can be turned against it, creating a complex chess match where every move creates new possibilities for both attack and defence. Understanding this dual-use nature is essential for developing effective strategies to harness the benefits of these technologies while mitigating their risks (Rogowsky, 2024).

3. Generative AI for Cyber Defence: Building the Digital Shield

3.1 Enhanced Anomaly Detection: Seeing the Invisible

Imagine trying to find a single fraudulent transaction among millions of legitimate ones—it is like searching for a specific drop of water in the ocean. Traditional security systems struggle with this challenge, relying on predefined rules that often miss novel or sophisticated attacks. Generative AI transforms this paradigm by learning what "normal" looks like in complex systems and identifying subtle deviations that might indicate malicious activity (Arifin et al., 2024).

The power of generative AI in anomaly detection lies in its ability to model the intricate patterns of legitimate behaviour in ways that humans and traditional systems cannot. For example, in a corporate network, normal activity varies dramatically by role, time of day, department, and even individual work habits. A rule-based system might flag unusual login times or large data transfers, but generative AI can understand the context—recognizing that a marketing executive accessing the customer database at 2 AM might be unusual, while a database administrator doing the same is perfectly normal (Dunmore et al., 2023).

Consider the case of a major healthcare provider that implemented a generative AI system to monitor network activity. The system learned the complex patterns of legitimate behaviour across thousands of employees, devices, and applications. One day, it flagged a seemingly minor anomaly: a nurse's workstation was accessing patient records at a rate 30% higher than usual, though still within normal limits for her role. Traditional systems would have missed this, but the AI recognized that the pattern did not match the nurse's typical behaviour. Investigation revealed that her credentials had been compromised and were being used to slowly exfiltrate patient data—a breach that might have gone undetected for months without AI's contextual understanding (Freitas et al., 2024).

3.2 *Synthetic Data for Training: Solving the Data Scarcity Problem*

One of the greatest challenges in cybersecurity AI has always been the scarcity of high-quality training data. Real-world attack data is often sensitive, incomplete, or simply unavailable—organizations cannot share details of breaches without revealing vulnerabilities, and novel attacks by definition lack historical data. Generative AI addresses this fundamental limitation by creating synthetic data that captures the essential characteristics of real threats without exposing sensitive information (Bui Thu et al., 2025).

The concept of synthetic data is not new, but generative AI takes it to unprecedented levels of sophistication and realism. Where earlier synthetic data generation techniques often produced artificial-looking examples that were easily distinguishable from real data, modern generative models can create datasets that are statistically indistinguishable from authentic ones. This breakthrough enables organizations to train robust security systems without relying solely on historical incident data (Randhawa et al., 2021).

Consider the challenge of training AI to detect ransomware attacks. Real ransomware samples are dangerous to handle and difficult to obtain legally, and each attack variant is unique. Generative AI can create thousands of realistic ransomware samples with different encryption methods, payload delivery mechanisms, and evasion techniques—all without posing any actual threat. These synthetic samples allow security systems to learn from a diverse range of attack scenarios that might otherwise take years to encounter naturally (Dunmore et al., 2023).

Synthetic data also addresses privacy concerns that often limit data sharing in cybersecurity. Organizations can generate realistic but artificial data that captures the statistical properties of their networks without revealing sensitive information about their actual infrastructure. This enables collaboration and benchmarking across organizations and sectors, accelerating the development of more effective security tools (Schmid et al., 2022).

The applications of synthetic data in cybersecurity continue to expand:

- *Malware Analysis*: Generative AI creates diverse malware variants for testing antivirus systems and training detection models, helping defenders stay ahead of evolving threats (Bui Thu et al., 2025).
- *Phishing Simulation*: Realistic phishing emails generated by AI help train employees and test email filtering systems without exposing them to actual malicious content (Polra, 2023).
- *Network Traffic Modelling*: Synthetic network data allows organizations to test IDS against sophisticated attack scenarios in safe, controlled environments (Navidan et al., 2021).
- *User Behaviour Analytics*: Artificial user activity patterns help train systems to detect insider threats and compromised accounts without monitoring real users (Arifin et al., 2024).
- As these applications demonstrate, synthetic data generation represents one of the most powerful defensive applications of generative AI, solving fundamental data challenges that have long limited the effectiveness of AI in cybersecurity. By creating realistic, diverse, and safe training data, generative AI enables the development of more robust, adaptable, and effective security systems (Khan et al., 2025).

3.3 Automated Threat Intelligence and Incident Response: From Data Deluge to Actionable Insights

Modern security operation centres face an overwhelming challenge: processing thousands of security alerts per day, each requiring analysis, prioritization, and response. Human analysts simply cannot keep up with this volume, leading to alert fatigue and missed critical threats. Generative AI transforms this landscape by automating the analysis of security data and enabling rapid, coordinated incident response (Freitas et al., 2024).

The power of generative AI in threat intelligence lies in its ability to understand context and generate human-readable insights from vast amounts of technical data. Where traditional systems might present analysts with raw log files or simple alert notifications, generative AI can provide comprehensive threat assessments that include attack patterns, affected systems, potential impacts, and recommended response actions—all in natural language that is immediately understandable (Microsoft Corporation, 2023).

Consider the experience of a mid-sized e-commerce company that implemented an AI-powered threat intelligence system. Previously, their security team of five analysts struggled to process over 2,000 daily alerts, with an average response time of 12 hours for critical incidents. After implementing generative AI, the system automatically correlated alerts across multiple sources, identified genuine threats, and generated detailed incident reports with prioritized recommendations. Critical response time dropped to under 30 minutes, and the team could focus their expertise on the most complex threats rather than routine alert triage (Freitas et al., 2024).

Generative AI enhances threat intelligence through several key capabilities:

- *Natural Language Summarization*: AI systems can ingest technical data from multiple sources—security logs, threat intelligence feeds, vulnerability databases—and generate concise, human-readable summaries that highlight the most important information. This transformation of technical data into actionable insights dramatically reduces the cognitive load on analysts (Microsoft Corporation, 2023).
- *Threat Correlation*: By analysing patterns across disparate data sources, generative AI can identify connections that human analysts might miss. For example, it might correlate a minor network anomaly with a new vulnerability report and suspicious domain registrations to identify a coordinated attack campaign in its early stages (Dunmore et al., 2023).
- *Predictive Analysis*: Generative models can extrapolate from current threat data to predict likely future attack vectors and targets. This predictive capability enables organizations to implement defensive measures before attacks occur, shifting from reactive to proactive security posture (Arifin et al., 2024).
- *Automated Reporting*: AI systems can generate comprehensive incident reports that include technical details, business impact assessments, and compliance implications—all formatted according to organizational requirements. This automation saves countless hours of manual documentation while ensuring consistency and completeness (Freitas et al., 2024).
- The impact extends beyond just efficiency. A global financial services firm reported that their AI-enhanced threat intelligence system identified a sophisticated supply chain attack that traditional systems had missed for months. By correlating subtle anomalies across multiple third-party connections, the AI detected patterns indicating that a software vendor's systems had been compromised, potentially exposing the financial institution's network. Early detection allowed them to implement additional controls before any actual breach occurred (Khan et al., 2025).

In incident response, generative AI enables coordinated, automated actions across complex environments. When a threat is detected, AI systems can:

- *Automate Containment*: Isolate affected systems, block malicious IP addresses, and disable compromised accounts—all within seconds of detection (Microsoft Corporation, 2023).

- *Coordinate Response*: Orchestrate actions across multiple security tools and teams, ensuring that containment, eradication, and recovery activities happen in the correct sequence (Freitas et al., 2024).
- *Generate Playbooks*: Create detailed response procedures tailored to specific threat types, incorporating organizational policies and regulatory requirements (Stroppa, 2023).
- *Communicate Stakeholders*: Automatically generate notifications for leadership, legal teams, and affected departments, providing clear information about the incident and response actions (Nag et al., 2024).
- The story of a major university's response to a ransomware attack illustrates this capability well. When the attack was detected, the AI system immediately isolated affected systems, blocked command-and-control communications, and generated a detailed response playbook. It simultaneously notified the IT security team, university leadership, and legal counsel with situation reports tailored to each audience's needs. The coordinated response enabled the university to contain the attack within 15 minutes, with minimal data loss and no ransom payment (Freitas et al., 2024).
- Microsoft's Security Copilot exemplifies this approach, combining GPT-4 with security-specific tools to assist analysts throughout the incident response lifecycle. Analysts report that the system helps them understand complex threats faster, identify connections between seemingly unrelated events, and implement effective response measures more efficiently. One security team leader noted that Security Copilot had reduced their average incident resolution time by 40% while improving the thoroughness of their investigations (Microsoft Corporation, 2023).

4. Generative AI for Cyber Offence: The Dark Side of Innovation

4.1 AI-driven Phishing and Social Engineering: The Art of Deception Perfected

Phishing attacks have long been the bane of cybersecurity professionals, relying on human psychology rather than technical exploits to breach defences. Traditionally, these attacks had telltale signs—grammatical errors, generic greetings, or suspicious links—that savvy users could recognize. Generative AI has eliminated these weaknesses, enabling attackers to create highly personalized, contextually relevant, and psychologically compelling phishing communications that are nearly indistinguishable from legitimate messages (Polra, 2023).

The transformation of phishing through AI represents one of the most immediate and dangerous applications of generative AI in cyber offence. Where previous phishing campaigns might have succeeded in tricking 1%–2% of targets, AI-enhanced attacks can achieve success rates of 50% or higher by tailoring messages to individual targets with unprecedented precision (Hyra & Premti, 2024).

Consider the experience of Maria, a mid-level executive at a technology company. She received an email that appeared to be from her CEO, referencing a recent conversation they had had about a potential acquisition. The email contained specific details about the discussion, used the CEO's exact writing style, and included a seemingly legitimate request for Maria to approve an urgent wire transfer. The email was so convincing that Maria processed the transfer without hesitation—only to discover later that she had been deceived by an AI-generated message that had analysed her recent communications and created a perfect forgery (Polra, 2023).

This scenario illustrates several ways in which generative AI enhances phishing attacks:

- *Personalization at Scale*: AI systems can analyse vast amounts of data about targets—their social media posts, work history, communication patterns, and even writing style—to create highly personalized messages. This level of individualization was previously impossible at scale, requiring attackers to manually research each target (Khan et al., 2025).
- *Contextual Relevance*: By understanding the context of a target's work and life, AI can create messages that reference recent events, ongoing projects, or personal details that make them seem authentic. For example, an AI might generate a phishing email that references a target's recent business trip, mentions a colleague they work with, and uses terminology specific to their industry (Polra, 2023).
- *Linguistic Perfection*: Unlike human attackers who might make grammatical errors or use awkward phrasing, AI systems can generate flawless prose in any language or style. They can mimic the writing patterns of specific individuals, making it virtually impossible to distinguish fake messages from real ones based on language alone (Microsoft Corporation, 2023).
- *Multichannel Coordination*: AI can coordinate phishing attacks across multiple channels—email, social media, messaging apps, and even voice calls—creating a consistent narrative that reinforces the deception. For instance, an AI might follow up a phishing email with a convincing phone call using voice cloning technology (Hyra & Premti, 2024).

The emergence of tools like WormGPT and FraudGPT has democratized these capabilities, making sophisticated phishing accessible to criminals with minimal technical skills. WormGPT, an unrestricted version of ChatGPT developed specifically for malicious purposes, allows users to generate convincing phishing emails, create malware code, and develop attack strategies with simple prompts. On dark web forums, criminals share techniques for using these tools to target specific industries or individuals (Polra, 2023).

Defending against AI-enhanced phishing requires new approaches. Traditional email filtering and user awareness training are no longer sufficient. Organizations must implement:

- *Advanced Authentication*: Multi-factor authentication that does not rely solely on knowledge-based factors (like passwords) can help prevent account compromise even when credentials are stolen (Microsoft Corporation, 2023).
- *Behavioural Analysis*: Systems that analyse communication patterns can detect anomalies that might indicate AI-generated messages, such as unusual timing, atypical language patterns, or inconsistencies with previous communications (Arifin et al., 2024).
- *Verification Protocols*: Establishing clear procedures for verifying sensitive requests, particularly those involving financial transactions or access to critical systems. For example, requiring in-person or video verification for large wire transfers (Stroppa, 2023).
- *AI-Powered Defence*: Using AI to detect AI-generated content by identifying subtle artifacts or patterns that might indicate synthetic communications (Dunmore et al., 2023).

As these defensive measures evolve, so too will offensive techniques. The result is an ongoing arms race between attackers using AI to create more convincing deceptions and defenders using AI to detect them. These dynamics underscore the fundamental dual-use nature of generative AI in cybersecurity—every defensive innovation creates new offensive possibilities, and vice versa (Khan et al., 2025).

4.2 Polymorphic Malware and Adversarial Attacks: The Shape-Shifting Threat

Malware has been a staple of cyberattacks since the early days of computing, but generative AI has transformed it from a static threat to a dynamic, adaptive adversary. Polymorphic malware—malicious software that changes its code to evade detection—has existed for years, but AI takes this concept to unprecedented levels, creating malware that can evolve in real time based on the defensive measures it encounters (Bui Thu et al., 2025).

The traditional cat-and-mouse game between malware authors and security vendors has been fundamentally altered. Where once security companies could develop signatures to detect specific malware variants, AI-generated malware can create countless unique versions of itself, each with different code structures, encryption methods, and behavioural patterns. This makes signature-based detection virtually useless and forces defenders to rely on more sophisticated—and resource-intensive—analysis methods (Dunmore et al., 2023).

The power of AI-generated malware lies in several key capabilities:

- *Automated Code Generation*: AI systems can create functional malware code from simple prompts, allowing attackers with limited programming skills to generate sophisticated threats. These systems can produce code in multiple programming languages, target different operating systems, and incorporate various evasion techniques (Polra, 2023).

- *Self-Modification*: Malware can use AI to analyse its environment and modify its behaviour accordingly. If it detects sandbox analysis or security monitoring tools, it can alter its execution path, change its communication methods, or even lie dormant until the environment appears safe (IBM Research, 2018).
- *Adaptive Evasion*: By learning from defensive measures, AI-enhanced malware can develop countermeasures in real time. For example, if a security system starts blocking certain network communications, the malware can switch to different protocols or encryption methods to maintain its connection to command-and-control servers (Dunmore et al., 2023).
- *Polymorphic Payloads*: The malicious payload itself can be transformed continuously, changing its encryption, obfuscation, and delivery methods to avoid pattern recognition. This creates a moving target that is nearly impossible to pin down with static signatures (Bui Thu et al., 2025).
- IBM's DeepLocker, while a proof-of-concept rather than actual malware in the wild, demonstrates the potential of AI-enhanced threats. DeepLocker was designed to conceal ransomware within a benign application, only activating when it recognized specific triggers—such as a particular face via webcam or a voice command. This targeted approach makes the malware extremely difficult to detect during static analysis, as its malicious behaviour remains dormant until the exact conditions are met (IBM Research, 2018).

The economics of AI-generated malware are particularly concerning. The cost of developing sophisticated malware has plummeted, while the potential impact has increased. A single AI system can generate thousands of unique malware variants, each with different evasion techniques, targeting multiple platforms, and organizations. This scalability makes AI-generated malware an attractive option for everyone from individual criminals to nation-state actors (Khan et al., 2025).

Consider the story of Alex, a university student with limited programming experience but a strong interest in cybersecurity. Using publicly available AI tools, Alex created a polymorphic malware variant that could evade most antivirus software. While Alex's intent was educational—demonstrating the vulnerability to university administrators—the ease with which this was accomplished illustrates the new reality. What once required teams of experienced programmers can now be achieved by individuals with minimal technical skills (Polra, 2023).

Defending against AI-generated malware requires a fundamental shift in security strategies:

- *Behavioural Analysis*: Instead of looking for specific code patterns, security systems must analyse the behaviour of software in real time, identifying malicious actions regardless of the code's appearance (Dunmore et al., 2023).
- *Sandbox Evolution*: Dynamic analysis environments must become more sophisticated, using AI to detect evasion techniques and force malware to reveal its true nature (Bui Thu et al., 2025).
- *Memory Integrity Monitoring*: Advanced techniques that monitor system memory for suspicious changes can detect malware that attempts to modify itself during execution (Arifin et al., 2024).

- *AI-Powered Defence*: Using AI to detect AI-generated threats by identifying patterns that might indicate automated or synthetic code generation (Microsoft Corporation, 2023).
- *Collaborative Intelligence*: Sharing information about emerging threats across organizations and industries can help defenders identify patterns that might not be apparent to individual entities (Schmid et al., 2022).
- As these defensive measures evolve, so too will offensive techniques. The result is an ongoing arms race where each side leverages AI to outmanoeuvre the other. This dynamic underscores the dual-use nature of generative AI in cybersecurity—the same technologies that enable more effective defence also empower more sophisticated offence, creating a complex and ever-changing threat landscape (Khan et al., 2025).

4.3 Synthetic Identities and Deepfake-enabled Fraud: The Illusion of Authenticity

Identity has always been central to security—both physical and digital. We rely on identity verification to protect our assets, our privacy, and our systems. Generative AI has fundamentally challenged the concept of digital identity by enabling the creation of synthetic identities that are virtually indistinguishable from real ones, and by allowing the impersonation of real individuals with unprecedented accuracy (Hyra & Premti, 2024).

The implications of this capability are profound. In a world where seeing is no longer believing and voices can be perfectly synthesized, traditional methods of identity verification become increasingly unreliable. This creates opportunities for fraud, manipulation, and deception at a scale previously unimaginable (Polra, 2023).

Consider the case of a financial services firm that fell victim to a deepfake-enabled fraud scheme. Attackers used AI to generate a video of the company's CEO appearing in a live video call, instructing the finance department to initiate an urgent wire transfer. The deepfake was so convincing—capturing the CEO's appearance, voice, mannerisms, and even the background of his office—that the employees processed the transfer without question. It was not until they followed up with the real CEO that they realized they had been deceived (Hyra & Premti, 2024).

This scenario illustrates several ways in which generative AI enables identity fraud:

- *Deepfake Video and Audio*: AI systems can create realistic video and audio of anyone, using only a few minutes of sample footage. These deepfakes can be generated in real time, enabling live video calls that appear authentic. The technology has advanced to the point where even experts struggle to distinguish sophisticated deepfakes from genuine recordings (Hyra & Premti, 2024).

- *Synthetic Profile Generation*: AI can create entirely fake digital personas with realistic photos, biographical information, social media histories, and even voice samples. These synthetic identities can be used to establish credibility, manipulate online discourse, or bypass identity verification systems (Polra, 2023).
- *Document Forgery*: Generative AI can create convincing fake documents—IDs, passports, certificates, and more—that include appropriate security features and pass visual inspection. When combined with synthetic identities, these forgeries enable attackers to establish false credentials that can withstand casual scrutiny (Khan et al., 2025).
- *Behavioural Mimicry*: Advanced AI systems can analyse and replicate the behavioural patterns of real individuals—their typing cadence, mouse movements, communication style, and decision-making patterns. This behavioural mimicry makes impersonation even more convincing, as it extends beyond appearance to encompass the subtle ways people interact with technology (Reddy & Gujral, 2025).

The geopolitical implications are equally concerning. Nation-states can use deepfakes and synthetic identities to influence elections, destabilize governments, and create confusion during crises. During the 2024 US election cycle, for example, researchers documented numerous instances of AI-generated content designed to mislead voters, including fake videos of candidates making inflammatory statements and synthetic social media accounts spreading disinformation (Hyra & Premti, 2024).

Defending against these threats requires a multifaceted approach:

- *Advanced Verification Technologies*: Developing new methods of identity verification that are resistant to spoofing, such as liveness detection that can distinguish real people from deepfakes, or behavioural biometrics that analyse unique patterns in how individuals interact with technology (Microsoft Corporation, 2023).
- *Digital Watermarking*: Embedding imperceptible markers in authentic media to help distinguish it from synthetic content. Several technology companies are developing standards for watermarking AI-generated content, though implementation remains challenging (Arifin et al., 2024).
- *Media Literacy Education*: Helping people develop critical skills for evaluating digital content and recognizing potential manipulation. This includes understanding the capabilities of generative AI and maintaining healthy scepticism about digital media (Nag et al., 2024).
- *Legal and Regulatory Frameworks*: Developing laws and regulations that address the creation and distribution of malicious synthetic media, while balancing concerns about free expression and innovation (Stroppa, 2023).
- *AI-Powered Detection*: Using AI systems to detect AI-generated content by identifying subtle artifacts or patterns that might indicate synthetic media. This creates an ongoing cat-and-mouse game between generation and detection technologies (Dunmore et al., 2023).

The challenge is particularly acute because the same technologies that enable malicious use have legitimate applications. Deepfake technology, for example, can be used for creative filmmaking, education, and accessibility applications. Synthetic identities can help protect privacy in online interactions. This dual-use nature makes it difficult to regulate these technologies without stifling beneficial innovation (Schmid et al., 2022).

As we navigate this complex landscape, it is clear that our concept of identity and trust in digital interactions must evolve. The old assumption that seeing (or hearing) is believing no longer holds true in an age of generative AI. Developing new paradigms for establishing authenticity and trust in digital communications will be one of the great challenges of the coming decades, with profound implications for security, privacy, and social cohesion (Rogowsky, 2024).

4.4 AI-Powered Offensive Automation: The Relentless Digital Adversary

Perhaps the most concerning aspect of AI-enabled cyberattacks is the potential for automation and autonomy. While human attackers need rest, make mistakes, and have limited attention spans, AI systems can operate continuously, adaptively, and without fatigue. This creates the possibility of persistent, autonomous attack systems that can probe defences, exploit vulnerabilities, and achieve objectives without human intervention (Reddy & Gujral, 2025).

The concept of autonomous cyber weapons has long been discussed in security circles, but generative AI makes this capability accessible to a much broader range of actors. Where once developing such systems required nation-state resources and expertise, now even small criminal groups can leverage AI to create sophisticated attack automation (Khan et al., 2025).

Consider the concept of an AI-driven "worm"—self-propagating malware that can identify vulnerabilities, exploit them, and spread to new systems without human guidance. Traditional worms like Code Red or Slammer caused significant damage, but they followed predefined patterns and could be contained once identified. An AI-enhanced worm could adapt its propagation strategy based on the defences it encounters, change its attack methods when detected, and even lie dormant to avoid analysis (Bui Thu et al., 2025).

The AI-powered offensive automation extends beyond just malware propagation. Attackers can deploy AI systems that:

- *Continuously Scan for Vulnerabilities*: AI can systematically probe networks, applications, and APIs (Application Programming Interfaces) are interfaces that allow different software systems or applications to communicate and exchange data with each other for weaknesses, testing thousands of potential exploits per second and prioritizing findings based on potential impact (Navidan et al., 2021).
- *Automate Exploit Development*: When vulnerabilities are discovered, AI can generate custom exploit code tailored to the specific environment, increasing the likelihood of successful compromise (Polra, 2023).

- *Coordinate Multi-Stage Attacks*: Complex attacks involving multiple systems, time delays, and conditional logic can be orchestrated by AI, creating sophisticated attack chains that are difficult to predict or defend against (Reddy & Gujral, 2025).
- *Adapt to Defensive Measures*: When security systems block an attack, AI can analyse the defensive response and develop countermeasures, creating an ongoing arms race between attacker and defender (Dunmore et al., 2023).
- *Maintain Persistence*: AI can create backdoors and maintain access to compromised systems over extended periods, even as defenders attempt to clean and secure their networks (Bui Thu et al., 2025).

The implications of this capability are particularly concerning for critical infrastructure. Imagine an AI system targeting an electrical grid, systematically probing for vulnerabilities and capable of disrupting operations without human intervention. Unlike human attackers who might be deterred by the potential consequences, an AI system would simply pursue its programmed objectives relentlessly (Stroppa, 2023).

Consider the story of a criminal group that developed an AI system to automate business email compromise attacks. The AI would:

1. Identify target companies through public data sources
2. Research key executives and their communication patterns
3. Generate personalized phishing emails using AI-generated content
4. Monitor responses and engage in follow-up communications
5. Guide victims through wire transfer processes using natural language interactions
6. Launder the proceeds through cryptocurrency networks

The system operated 24/7, targeting hundreds of companies simultaneously and achieving a success rate more than three times higher than human-operated campaigns. The criminal group's profits increased exponentially while their operational costs decreased (Polra, 2023).

Defending against autonomous attack systems presents unique challenges:

- *Speed and Scale*: AI attacks can operate at machine speed, exploiting vulnerabilities in seconds rather than the hours or days human attackers might take. Defences must be equally fast and scalable to keep pace (Microsoft Corporation, 2023).
- *Adaptability*: As AI systems learn from defensive measures, they can develop new attack techniques faster than traditional security teams can respond. This requires defences that are similarly adaptive and learning-oriented (Arifin et al., 2024).
- *Attribution*: Autonomous attacks can be designed to obscure their origins, making it difficult to identify who is responsible and where the attacks are coming from. This complicates deterrence and response efforts (Stroppa, 2023).

- *Persistence*: AI systems can maintain access to compromised networks indefinitely, even as defenders attempt to remove them. Eradicating autonomous threats may require fundamentally new approaches to network security (Bui Thu et al., 2025).
- *Resource Asymmetry*: Well-resourced actors can develop more sophisticated autonomous attack systems, creating an imbalance that smaller organizations or less developed nations may struggle to overcome (Schmid et al., 2022).

The emergence of autonomous cyber weapons raises profound ethical and strategic questions. How do we deter attacks when the attacker might be an AI system with no fear of consequences? What are the rules of engagement when machines are making decisions about cyber warfare? How do we maintain human control over increasingly autonomous systems (Stroppa, 2023)?

As we look to the future, it is clear that AI-powered offensive automation will continue to evolve, becoming more sophisticated, more accessible, and more autonomous. Defending against these threats will require equally advanced defensive capabilities, new approaches to security architecture, and international cooperation to establish norms and restrictions on the most dangerous applications (Khan et al., 2025).

4.5 The Expanding Threat Landscape: Democratization of Cyber Offence

Perhaps the most significant impact of generative AI on cyber offence is the democratization of sophisticated attack capabilities. Where once advanced cyberattacks required significant technical expertise, resources, and time, AI tools now enable individuals with minimal skills to launch complex, effective attacks. This levelling of the playing field has profound implications for the threat landscape, creating new risks for organizations and individuals alike (Polra, 2023).

The concept of "script kiddies"—inexperienced attackers who use pre-written scripts to launch attacks—has been around for years. But generative AI has created what some experts call "script kiddie 2.0"—individuals who can leverage AI to generate custom attack code, create convincing phishing campaigns, and develop sophisticated malware without understanding the underlying technical details (Khan et al., 2025).

Consider the case of Jake, a 16-year-old with an interest in hacking but limited programming knowledge. Using freely available AI tools, Jake was able to:

- Generate functional ransomware code by describing what he wanted in plain English
- Create convincing phishing emails targeting his school's administration
- Develop a basic keylogger to capture passwords
- Find and exploit vulnerabilities in the school's website

Within a few weeks, Jake had compromised several school systems, accessing sensitive student data and causing significant disruption. While Jake's intent was partly educational curiosity, the ease with which he accomplished these tasks illustrates the new reality (Polra, 2023).

5. Future Outlook: Navigating the Next Frontier of Dual-Use Generative AI

5.1 The Evolution of AI-Enabled Cyber Offence

As generative AI continues to evolve, the offensive capabilities it enables will become increasingly sophisticated, autonomous, and difficult to defend against. Several emerging trends suggest a future where cyber threats are more persistent, adaptive, and potentially more dangerous than anything we have seen before (Reddy & Gujral, 2025).

Autonomous attack agents represent perhaps the most concerning development. These AI systems can operate independently to identify vulnerabilities, develop exploits, and maintain persistence in target networks without human intervention. Unlike traditional malware that follows predefined patterns, autonomous agents can adapt their strategies based on defensive measures, learn from failed attacks, and even collaborate with other AI systems to achieve their objectives (Bui Thu et al., 2025).

A security research team demonstrated this potential by creating an autonomous agent tasked with compromising a target network. The agent independently identified a zero-day vulnerability, developed a custom exploit, established persistence, and began exfiltrating data—all without human guidance. What made this particularly concerning was the agent's ability to modify its behaviour when it detected security monitoring, changing its tactics to avoid detection (Reddy & Gujral, 2025).

Deepfake social engineering at scale will transform how attackers manipulate human targets. Current AI-generated phishing emails and voice cloning are just the beginning. Future systems will create fully interactive, personalized deception campaigns that can engage targets in extended conversations while maintaining perfect consistency across multiple channels. Imagine an AI system that can impersonate a trusted colleague through email, phone calls, and even video conferences, referencing shared experiences and current projects to build trust before attempting to manipulate the target (Hyra & Premti, 2024).

The implications for organizations are profound. Traditional security awareness training will be insufficient when employees face highly personalized, emotionally compelling deception campaigns that are virtually indistinguishable from legitimate interactions. A cybersecurity researcher studying these emerging threats warns: "We're approaching a point where seeing and hearing will no longer be believing. The foundation of trust in digital interactions is eroding, and we don't yet have good alternatives to replace it" (Polra, 2023).

A military cybersecurity expert describes the emerging landscape: "We're entering an era where AI systems will be making decisions about cyber attacks at machine speed, far faster than human operators can intervene. This creates a fundamental shift in the dynamics of cyber conflict, with implications for international stability that we're only beginning to understand" (Khan et al., 2025).

Weaponization of synthetic data represents another concerning trend. Generative AI can create vast quantities of realistic but fake data that can poison machine learning systems, manipulate decision-making processes, and create false realities. Attackers could use synthetic data to corrupt training datasets for autonomous vehicles, financial trading systems, or medical diagnostic tools, potentially causing catastrophic failures (Navidan et al., 2021).

5.2 The Future of AI-Powered Defence

Just as generative AI enables more sophisticated attacks, it also drives the development of next-generation defensive capabilities. The future of AI-powered defence will be characterized by greater autonomy, collaboration, and adaptability (Microsoft Corporation, 2023).

Autonomous cyber defence systems will shift cybersecurity from reactive to proactive by continuously monitoring environments, predicting potential threats, and implementing defensive measures without human intervention. These systems will use generative AI to simulate attack scenarios, identify vulnerabilities before they can be exploited, and even heal compromised systems automatically (Arifin et al., 2024).

A technology company is developing a self-healing security architecture that uses AI to detect anomalies, determine their root cause, and implement corrective actions in real time. Early tests show the system can contain and remediate certain types of attacks within seconds, far faster than human response teams could react. However, the challenge remains ensuring these autonomous systems do not cause unintended harm while taking defensive actions (Microsoft Corporation, 2023).

Collaborative AI ecosystems will enable organizations to share threat intelligence and defensive capabilities in real time, creating a collective immune system against cyber threats. Generative AI can synthesize and analyse data from multiple sources, identifying patterns that would be invisible to individual organizations and generating coordinated defensive responses (Schmid et al., 2022).

Explainable and trustworthy AI defences will be essential for maintaining human trust in autonomous security systems. Future AI systems will need to provide transparent reasoning for their conclusions, allowing human analysts to understand and validate their findings. This is particularly important for high-stakes security decisions where errors could have significant consequences (Goerdat & Schirrmacher, 2025).

Researchers are developing new approaches to explainable AI for cybersecurity, including techniques that allow AI systems to generate natural language explanations of their reasoning processes. These explanations help analysts understand why the system flagged certain activities as suspicious and provide context for evaluating the AI's recommendations (Arifin et al., 2024).

Integration with quantum-resistant security will become increasingly important as quantum computing capabilities advance. Generative AI will play a crucial role in developing and testing quantum-resistant cryptographic methods, simulating quantum-capable attacks to identify vulnerabilities before they can be exploited (Navidan et al., 2021).

A government agency is using generative AI to model potential quantum attacks on current encryption systems, allowing them to prioritize the transition to quantum-resistant algorithms. The AI system can simulate various quantum computing capabilities and identify which current cryptographic methods are most vulnerable, helping to guide the agency's quantum transition strategy (Khan et al., 2025).

5.3 Emerging Risks and Ethical Dilemmas

The future of generative AI in cybersecurity will bring not only technological advancements but also complex ethical and societal challenges that require careful consideration (Stroppa, 2023).

Escalating the cyber arms race is perhaps the most significant risk. As both attackers and defenders deploy increasingly sophisticated AI systems, the digital landscape could become a perpetual battlefield where automated systems continuously probe and counter each other's defences. This dynamic creates risks of accidental escalation, particularly when autonomous systems make decisions without human oversight (Rogowsky, 2024).

A case study from 2024 illustrates this risk: a small criminal group with limited technical expertise used freely available AI tools to conduct a sophisticated supply chain attack that compromised hundreds of organizations. The attack's complexity and scale would have required significant resources just a few years earlier, demonstrating how AI is levelling the playing field between sophisticated and unsophisticated actors (Khan et al., 2025).

5.4 Pathways to a Balanced Future

While the future is uncertain, several pathways can help navigate the challenges ahead and steer towards a more balanced and secure cybersecurity ecosystem (Rogowsky, 2024).

Embedding ethics in AI research is essential for ensuring that future technologies are developed with consideration for their potential impacts. This involves integrating ethical training into computer science curricula, establishing ethics review processes for research projects, and creating incentives for responsible innovation (Goerdat & Schirrmacher, 2025).

A leading university has redesigned its AI curriculum to include mandatory ethics courses for all computer science students. The programme covers not just abstract ethical principles but also practical case studies of AI misuse and strategies for responsible development. Early results show that graduates are better equipped to consider the broader implications of their work (Nag et al., 2024).

Promoting global governance requires building on existing international frameworks to create more effective mechanisms for addressing AI security challenges. This includes developing norms for responsible state behaviour in cyberspace, establishing international standards for AI safety, and creating platforms for ongoing dialogue among stakeholders (Stroppa, 2023).

The Global Commission on the Stability of Cyberspace has proposed a framework for responsible AI development that includes principles for transparency, accountability, and international cooperation. While not legally binding, these principles provide a foundation for more formal governance arrangements as the technology evolves (Schmid et al., 2022).

5.5 Modelling Emerging AI-enabled Cyber Scenarios

As generative AI continues to evolve, understanding its potential future impact requires new approaches to modelling and simulation. The probabilistic nature of AI-generated content makes traditional threat modelling insufficient, necessitating new frameworks that can account for the adaptive and unpredictable characteristics of AI systems (Reddy & Gujral, 2025).

The output of a generative model can be formalized as:

$$P(x) = {}^{T}\prod_{t=1} P(x_t | x_{1:t-1}) \quad \text{...(14.1)}$$

where:

- x represents the sequence generated by the AI (e.g., a phishing email, malware payload, or synthetic identity),
- T is the total length of the sequence, and
- $P(x_t | x_{1:t-1})$ is the probability of the t-th element in the sequence, given all previous elements.

This formulation (14.1) enables quantitative analysis of how AI generates realistic and adaptive attack content, allowing researchers to simulate potential threats and anticipate the evolution of cyber offensives. For example, security researchers can use this model to generate thousands of phishing email variants and test them against defensive systems, identifying patterns that make certain approaches more effective (Polra, 2023).

Conversely, the same probabilistic framework can be applied to defensive scenarios. AI-driven detection systems can use similar models to predict likely attack sequences or evaluate the probability that suspicious activity indicates a genuine threat. By modelling both offensive and defensive outputs probabilistically, organizations can prepare for emerging threats while strengthening adaptive defences (Arifin et al., 2024).

A financial institution applied this approach by creating a probabilistic model of AI-generated phishing attacks. The model incorporated various factors including target characteristics, message content, and delivery methods to calculate the likelihood of success for different attack variations. This information helped them prioritize defensive measures and train their security team on the most threatening scenarios (Khan et al., 2025).

These modelling approaches represent important tools for navigating the uncertain future of AI-enabled cybersecurity. By providing quantitative frameworks for understanding and predicting AI behaviour, they help organizations develop more effective strategies for both defence and governance (Reddy & Gujral, 2025).

6. Conclusion: Reconciling Innovation and Risk in the Dual-Use Era of Generative AI

Generative AI has irrevocably transformed the cybersecurity landscape, creating unprecedented opportunities for defence while simultaneously enabling new and more dangerous forms of attack. This dual-use nature represents not merely a technical challenge but also a fundamental paradox that touches upon ethics, governance, and the very nature of trust in digital systems (Khan et al., 2025).

6.1 Revisiting the Central Tension

Throughout this research, we have explored how generative AI enhances defensive capabilities through improved anomaly detection, synthetic data generation, automated threat intelligence, and advanced red-team simulations. These technologies promise a future where cybersecurity is more proactive, adaptive, and effective than ever before (Arifin et al., 2024).

Simultaneously, we have examined how the same technologies empower malicious actors through AI-driven phishing, polymorphic malware, synthetic identities, and autonomous attack systems. The democratization of these capabilities means sophisticated attacks are no longer the exclusive domain of nation-states or well-funded criminal groups but are accessible to individuals with minimal technical expertise (Polra, 2023).

This duality is not accidental but inherent to the nature of generative AI. The creative capabilities that make these systems so valuable for defence also make them powerful tools for offence. Every advancement in generative AI simultaneously equips both sides of the cybersecurity equation, creating a persistent tension that defies simple resolution (Dunmore et al., 2023).

6.2 Lessons from the Past, Signals for the Future

The history of cybersecurity has always been characterized by an arms race between attackers and defenders. What distinguishes the current moment is the speed, scale, and autonomy introduced by generative AI. Where previous technological shifts took years or decades to fully manifest, AI-driven changes are happening in months or even weeks (Microsoft Corporation, 2023).

This acceleration creates several critical challenges:

- *The Pace of Change*: Organizations struggle to adapt their security practices quickly enough to keep pace with evolving AI capabilities. A Chief Information Security Officer (CISO) at a major financial institution describes this challenge: "By the time we understand and implement defences against one AI-enabled threat, two new ones have emerged. We're constantly playing catch-up in a game where the rules keep changing" (Arifin et al., 2024).
- *The Scale of Impact*: AI systems can operate at a scale that dwarfs human capabilities, both for attack and defence. A single AI system can generate thousands of malware variants or analyse millions of security events per second, creating asymmetric advantages for whoever leverages AI most effectively (Dunmore et al., 2023).

References

Arifin, M.M., Ahmed, M.S., Ghosh, T.K. et al. (2024). A survey on the application of generative adversarial networks in cybersecurity: Prospective, direction and open research scopes. arXiv. Available at https://doi.org/10.48550/arXiv.2407.08839. Accessed on 9 April 2026.

Bui Thu, L., Thanh Nam, H., Duy Trung, P. and Le Minh, N. (2025). A survey on generative adversarial networks for malware analysis. *Journal of Computer Science and Cybernetics*, 41(2), 135–161.

Dunmore, A., Jang-Jaccard, J., Sabrina, F. and Kwak, J. (2023). A comprehensive survey of generative adversarial networks (GANs) in cybersecurity intrusion detection. *IEEE Access*, 11, 1–22.

Freitas, S., Kalajdjieski, J., Gharib, A. and McCann, R. (2024). AI-driven guided response for security operation centers with Microsoft Copilot for security. arXiv. Available at https://arxiv.org/abs/2407.09017. Accessed on 9 April 2026.

Goerdat, S. and Schirrmacher, N. (2025). Ethical tensions: The role of AI in ethical hacking. In *ECIS 2025 Proceedings*. Vrije Universiteit (Amsterdam) & The University of Sydney.

Hyra, A. and Premti, F. (2024). The double-edged sword of AI in cybersecurity: Boosting security while addressing privacy risks. *Smart Cities and Regional Development (SCRD) Preprints*, 1(1).

IBM Research. (2018). DeepLocker: Concealing targeted attacks with AI locksmithing for Black Hat USA 2018. Available at https://research.ibm.com/publications/deeplocker-concealing-targeted-attacks-with-ai-locksmithing. Accessed on 9 April 2026.

Khan, M.A., Ali, F., Tahira, K. et al. (2025). Securing the future, the dual role of artificial intelligence as a threat and a tool in modern cybersecurity. *Spectrum of Engineering Sciences*, 3(7), 205–218.

Korimilli, S.K., Rahman, M.H., Sunkara, G. et al. (2025). Dual-use of generative AI in cybersecurity: Balancing offensive threats and defensive capabilities in the post-LLM era. Available at SSRN: http://dx.doi.org/10.2139/ssrn.5437776 (accessed on 20 February 2026).

Microsoft Corporation. (2023a). Introducing Microsoft Security Copilot: Empowering defenders at the speed of AI [Blog post]. Microsoft Blog. Available at https://blogs.microsoft.com/blog/2023/03/28/introducing-microsoft-security-copilot-empowering-defenders-at-the-speed-of-ai. Accessed on 9 April 2026.

Microsoft Corporation. (2023b). What is Microsoft Security Copilot? Microsoft Learn. Available at https://learn.microsoft.com/en-us/copilot/security/microsoft-security-copilot. Accessed on 9 April 2026.

Nag, Y.M.N., Vishruth, M.H., Aiyappa, T.B. and Kher, U. (2024). Ethical concerns of using artificial intelligence in cybersecurity. *International Journal of Advanced Research in Computer and Communication Engineering*, 13(11).

Navidan, H., Moshiri, P.F., Nabati, M. et al. (2021). Generative adversarial networks (GANs) in networking: A comprehensive survey & evaluation. arXiv. Available at https://arxiv.org/abs/2105.04184. Accessed on 9 April 2026.

Polra, V.F. (2023). Decoding the threat landscape: ChatGPT, FraudGPT, and WormGPT in social engineering attacks. arXiv. Available at https://arxiv.org/abs/2310.05595. Accessed on 9 April 2026.

Randhawa, R.H., Aslam, N., Alauthman, M. and Rafiq, H. (2021). EVAGAN: Evasion generative adversarial network for low data regimes. arXiv. Available at https://arxiv.org/abs/2109.08026. Accessed on 9 April 2026.

Reddy, P. and Gujral, A.S. (2025). EchoLeak: The first real-world zero-click prompt injection exploit in a production LLM system. arXiv. Available at https://arxiv.org/abs/2509.10540. Accessed on 9 April 2026.

Rogowsky, E. (2024). Governing socio-technical risk in an era of dual-use technology. Doctoral dissertation, University of Virginia. Available at https://libraetd.lib.virginia.edu. Accessed on 9 April 2026.

Schmid, S., Riebe, T. and Reuter, C. (2022). Dual-use and trustworthy? A mixed methods analysis of AI diffusion between civilian and defence R&D. *Science and Engineering Ethics*, 28(2), 12.

Stroppa, M. (2023). Legal and ethical implications of autonomous cyber capabilities: A call for retaining human control in cyberspace. *Ethics and Information Technology*, 25, 7.

15 | Business Models and Commercialization of Defence AI

Priyanshu Mishra[1*], Shrutika Mishra[2*], Danish Hussain[3] and Mokhtar M. Hasan[4]

The rapid rise of generative artificial intelligence (AI) is reshaping industries across sectors, but perhaps nowhere is this transformation more complex—or more consequential—than in the defence domain. This chapter explores the emerging intersection between defence innovation and commercial enterprise by analysing how generative AI is being developed, monetized, and scaled by defence-oriented startups and public–private partnerships. The focus is placed on understanding how dual-use technologies, originally created for national security purposes, are now entering civilian markets, bringing with them a host of ethical, legal, and operational challenges. Drawing on a broad set of peer-reviewed academic sources, the chapter uses a qualitative thematic synthesis approach to map existing research, highlight methodological gaps, and explore how scholars have approached questions of intellectual property, licensing models, commercialization pathways, and regulatory oversight. A real-world case study from the EdTech sector is used as a reflective parallel, illustrating the organizational tensions and risks involved in adopting generative AI tools—insights that are highly transferable to the defence startup environment. The findings reveal that while legal scholars have made strides in identifying governance gaps, and business theorists have proposed models for monetizing generative systems, a clear integration of technical, ethical, and strategic frameworks remains underdeveloped. The chapter concludes by proposing future directions that include hybrid research designs, culturally inclusive ethical models, and interdisciplinary education pipelines to better prepare stakeholders for the long-term implications of generative AI commercialization in defence. Overall, this work advocates for a more nuanced and collaborative approach—one that balances innovation with accountability, and profit with public interest—recognizing that the tools we build today will likely outlast the policies currently designed to govern them.

[1] https://orcid.org/0009-0005-0401-1609
[2] https://orcid.org/0000-0003-3029-6503
[3] https://orcid.org/0000-0001-7617-3280
[4] https://orcid.org/0000-0002-4702-4320
* Corresponding author: priyanshu@bhu.ac.in[1]; shrutika.bhu@gmail.com[2]

DOI: 10.1201/9781003688174-15

1. Introduction

In the last decade, generative artificial intelligence (AI) has transitioned from an emerging research area to a foundational technology shaping both national defence and commercial enterprise. Its ability to autonomously create text, images, data simulations, and operational strategies has introduced new levels of efficiency, agility, and autonomy across industries. What sets generative AI apart is not just its functionality, but also its cross-sector impact—where the same models driving national security innovations are also powering product development, marketing, and service delivery in business sectors (Li et al., 2025).

In the military domain, generative AI is currently used for combat simulations, autonomous vehicle navigation, cyber-threat modelling, and decision-support systems, enabling real-time, data-driven actions in complex environments (Blowers et al., 2024). At the same time, commercial sectors are leveraging similar tools to streamline supply chains, personalize consumer experiences, and automate financial analysis. This growing overlap has given rise to a category of dual-use technologies, where systems originally developed for defence are re-engineered for civilian markets—a dynamic that has both commercial promise and regulatory complexity (Oniani et al., 2023).

These developments are not occurring in isolation. They are driven by a rapidly expanding ecosystem of defence technology startups, many of which are funded by private venture capital and operate at the intersection of government partnerships and market-driven innovation. Such companies are building business models around subscription platforms, data services, and modular AI toolkits that can be adapted across sectors (Alijoyo & Reddy, 2024).

However, monetizing and managing AI technologies at this scale presents serious challenges. Questions surrounding intellectual property rights, licensing structures, and training data ownership remain unresolved. Generative AI models often rely on massive datasets—some of which may include copyrighted, confidential, or sensitive content. This introduces significant legal ambiguity, particularly as companies attempt to sell or repurpose outputs beyond their original context (Samuelson, 2023).

At the same time, issues of data compliance and cybersecurity remain critical—especially when AI systems handle classified or biometric data. Organizations must balance innovation with adherence to evolving global standards such as (General Data Protection Regulation) (GDPR), national defence regulations, and AI safety guidelines (Ajiboye, 2023).

These commercialization efforts are further shaped by geopolitical dynamics. Export control laws like the US International Traffic in Arms Regulations (ITAR), China's AI restrictions, and the European Union's AI Act all influence how—and where—AI models can be sold or deployed. These regulations do not just apply to military-grade applications; they also affect tools with dual-use potential, thereby influencing business strategies globally.

To accelerate innovation while managing risk, governments are increasingly relying on public–private partnerships (PPPs). Agencies such as DARPA and

NATO's DIANA initiative are collaborating with private firms to co-develop generative AI systems tailored for security, intelligence, and logistics. These partnerships provide startups with funding, technical validation, and integration pathways while also serving as springboards for broader commercialization (Blowers et al., 2024).

Table 15.1 Historical Evolution of AI Adoption in Defence and Commercial Sectors (1950s–Present).

Year/Period	*AI Evolution in Defence*	*AI Adoption in Commerce*	*Examples*
1950s–1960s	Early AI research for Cold War applications	Limited to academic theory and lab demos	Military logic engines; Chess AI by IBM
1980s	Rule-based expert systems in defence logistics	Basic automation in factories and banks	DARPA projects; financial fraud detection
1990s	Simulation & training tools for battlefield planning	E-commerce platforms using simple algorithms	Military flight simulators; Amazon's early recommendation systems
2000s	AI in surveillance, drones, and image recognition	AI in supply chain, CRMs (Customer relationship management), and customer data analysis	Predator drones; Walmart's inventory AI
2010–2015	Machine learning for predictive threat detection	AI in marketing, fintech, and customer service	Cyber threat models; chatbots in banking
2016–2020	Deep learning in autonomous systems and cyber defence	Rise of AI startups and SaaS platforms	AI-driven navigation for UAVs; Salesforce Einstein
2021–2023	Generative AI for mission simulation, drone swarms, and defence cybersecurity	Generative AI for content creation, e-commerce, and healthtech	AI in swarm robotics; ChatGPT for business content; DALL·E in advertising
2024–Present	Business models emerging in defence AI; increased private sector involvement	Licensing, IP battles, and dual-use commercialization accelerate	OpenAI licensing deals; Defence tech startups like Shield AI & Anduril

Yet, no discussion of commercialization is complete without addressing the human capital challenge. A key barrier to deployment remains the shortage of skilled professionals who can translate theoretical AI models into secure, ethical, and market-ready products. Whether in military command centres or corporate innovation labs, the success of generative AI will increasingly depend on interdisciplinary teams that can balance technical proficiency with legal, ethical, and managerial competence.

This chapter aims to explore these complex intersections—between defence and commerce, ethics and business, innovation and regulation. By analysing real-world business models, policy frameworks, and risk factors, it provides a comprehensive look at how generative AI is transforming not only how we defend nations but also how we build markets. In doing so, it argues that the future of defence AI commercialization lies not only in code—but also in the strategic decisions made by managers, entrepreneurs, and policymakers.

2. Literature Review

The commercialization of generative AI in defence contexts has sparked a wide spectrum of scholarly debate, particularly around the business models, dual-use ethics, and legal frameworks underpinning this transition. At the heart of this discourse, Li and Li present a compelling argument that generative AI tools are no longer limited to R&D silos but are now actively influencing advertising strategies, enterprise planning, and autonomous systems across sectors (Li et al., 2025). They support the idea that commercial scaling of generative AI can be achieved through platform-based delivery models, but they do not deeply engage with the ethical or regulatory dilemmas involved in repurposing AI for non-defence markets.

Addressing this gap, Ajiboye (2023) emphasizes the importance of data compliance and secure system design in AI deployment, especially when transitioning from military to civilian environments. While Ajiboye agrees with Li and Li on the scalability of generative AI, he pushes the argument further by warning that without proper regulatory frameworks, commercialization may lead to data breaches and loss of public trust. His critique highlights a major blind spot in business-centric literature that often treats compliance as a secondary issue.

On the legal front, Samuelson 2023 raises pressing concerns about intellectual property rights, arguing that AI-generated content poses fundamental challenges to conventional copyright structures (Samuelson, 2023). He positions generative AI as a legal anomaly—neither fully owned by developers nor end users—and calls for international consensus on licensing standards. This is strongly supported by Irfan et al. (2024), who extend the debate by performing a comparative legal analysis across jurisdictions and noting the inconsistencies in how AI-generated works are classified under current intellectual property (IP) laws. They argue for a more function-specific copyright framework, which we personally believe could unlock fairer revenue models for defence-originated commercial AI.

Conversely, Jain and Verma (2025) challenge the optimistic stance taken by Li et al., 2025, stating that the absence of uniform global regulation may create strategic vulnerabilities, particularly in defence applications. They propose a multi-stakeholder governance model that includes defence agencies, private firms, and civil society. While their framework is ambitious, it aligns with Nasr and El-Deeb's (2025) argument that the future of AI development will rely heavily on ethical collaboration between humans and machines.

From a technical standpoint, Vadisetty and Polamarasetti (2024) provide empirical support for the military value of generative AI, demonstrating its effectiveness in cyber threat simulation and real-time network defence. Their findings validate the commercial potential of generative AI–powered security tools in both public and private sectors. We would argue that this creates a unique opportunity for startups to offer dual-use AI products with built-in compliance and adaptive threat modelling—a market niche largely underexplored in current research.

Interestingly, Hutson (2023) introduces a more philosophical critique, questioning what originality means in a world of AI-generated outputs. Though primarily focused on educational and creative sectors, his work has implications for defence AI as well—especially when generative tools are used for mission planning or strategic simulations. If originality and authorship become fluid, the accountability of decisions made using generative AI must be reassessed—a nuance not yet fully addressed by business scholars.

Taken together, these studies reveal a vibrant, evolving field where technical, ethical, and commercial perspectives intersect. There is strong consensus around the utility and promise of generative AI, but significant divergence in how its risks are prioritized and managed. From our point of view, a more integrated model of commercialization—one that accounts for innovation, governance, and transnational law—is urgently needed to balance growth with global security.

The academic discourse surrounding the commercialization of generative AI in defence and adjacent industries is growing rapidly, with scholars offering diverse yet intersecting viewpoints on business models, ethical deployment, IP, and legal frameworks. Ramamoorthy, (2025) argue that generative AI is no longer confined to the realm of research and development but is now a strategic tool for commercial scalability—particularly in marketing, enterprise planning, and product innovation. They propose that platform-based delivery models, including subscription AI and modular toolkits, are key to unlocking long-term value from defence-grade generative AI technologies (Ramamoorthy, 2025). However, their optimistic framing largely overlooks ethical and legal vulnerabilities in such commercialization. The summary of the key literature on the commercialisation of Gen AI is described in the table (Table 15.2).

Table 15.2 Summary of Key Literature on the Commercialization of Generative AI in Defence and Dual-Use Applications.

Author(s)	*Year*	*View Point/Intent*	*Methodology*	*Key Focus*
Ajiboye	2023	Cybersecurity in the era of generative AI	Conceptual Analysis	AI compliance frameworks in business
Samuelson	2023	IPR Challenges in Generative AI	Legal Review	Balancing innovation and IPR

Contd...

Table 15.2 *Contd...*

Author(s)	*Year*	*View Point/Intent*	*Methodology*	*Key Focus*
Irfan et al.	2024	IP Laws & Generative AI	Comparative Legal Analysis	Copyright reform for AI authorship
Hutson	2023	Plagiarism & GenAI	Statistical and Pedagogical Review	Redefining originality in education
Vadisetty & Polamarasetti	2024	GenAI in Cyber Threat Defence	Experimental Simulation	Cybersecurity enhancements via GANs
Wang et al.	2024	IP Infringement in Visual GenAI	Empirical Evaluation	Mitigation of copyright risks
Jain & Verma	2025	AI & IP Rights	Comparative Jurisdictional Analysis	Redefining ownership and legal boundaries
Nasr & El-Deeb	2025	Societal Impact of GenAI	Thematic Literature Review	Human-machine collaboration, ethical risks
Li et al.	2025a	Commercial Use of GenAI	Quantitative Modelling	R&D and Advertising strategy via AIGC (Artificial Intelligence Generated Content)

Addressing this limitation, Ajiboye (2023) provides a critical lens by emphasizing the urgent need for robust compliance architectures, especially in dual-use contexts. His work underscores how poorly governed transitions from military to commercial use may lead to privacy breaches, regulatory violations, and erosion of public trust (Ajiboye, 2023). While both Li and Ajiboye agree on the strategic potential of generative AI, the latter critiques the business-centric approach for underestimating the operational risks involved in unregulated deployments. We believe this tension points to a fundamental gap in the literature: the need for integrated frameworks that consider legal safeguards as core components of commercialization, rather than afterthoughts.

This gap becomes even more apparent when examining the legal challenges of IP in generative AI. Samuelson (2023) explores how traditional copyright law fails to accommodate AI-generated content, especially when authorship is ambiguous or when training datasets involve copyrighted material. His analysis, however, is extended by Irfan et al. (2024), who conduct a comparative legal study across jurisdictions, highlighting inconsistencies in how AI-generated work is recognized globally. They advocate for a function-specific model of IP attribution that could address both civilian and defence use cases. In contrast, Wang et al. (2024) focus empirically on visual generative AI tools and suggest technical solutions—such as watermarking and content tracking—to mitigate infringement risks. These legal debates collectively highlight how IP regimes must evolve in tandem with commercial generative AI deployment. In our view, the future of AI commercialization hinges on adaptive licensing models that reflect the diverse contexts in which AI outputs are used—from autonomous combat systems to consumer apps.

The ethical implications of generative AI in defence–commercial transitions are another area of debate. Oniani et al. (2023) stress the importance of embedding ethical principles like transparency, accountability, and human oversight in the development of generative models for security applications. However, Nasr and El-Deeb (2025) argue that ethical adoption cannot be siloed from commercialization—it must be operationalized through co-designed governance models that involve regulators, businesses, and civil society. Their extension of Oniani's work points to a more collaborative paradigm of generative AI development, one that our own view aligns with. Ethical AI is not just about moral principles—it is about business risk mitigation, especially when reputational damage and legal exposure are at stake.

Security concerns take centre stage in Jain and Verma's (2025) work, which critiques the over-commercialization of generative AI without adequate international controls. They caution that AI tools, especially those originally built for defence, could create new attack surfaces or be exploited in conflict zones if not properly regulated. Their call for multi-stakeholder governance models challenges more techno-optimist perspectives like those of Ramamoorthy, (2025). From our standpoint, their position underscores a vital truth: in the AI age, national security is not just about weapons—it is about data, code, and control.

Adding a technical dimension, Vadisetty and Polamarasetti (2024) empirically validate generative AI's utility in cyber threat simulation and response. Their findings offer practical proof of concept for both military use and commercial cybersecurity products (Vadisetty & Polamarasetti, 2024). In light of their work, I suggest that generative AI–based cybersecurity solutions—especially those using generative adversarial networks (GANs)—could become a pivotal dual-use market.

Finally, Blowers et al. (2024) shift the discussion from individual firms to ecosystems. They advocate for stronger PPPs, particularly between defence agencies and AI startups, to build secure, scalable platforms through shared funding and risk allocation (Blowers et al., 2024). Their perspective supports Nasr and El-Deeb's co-governance model and aligns with our belief that meaningful commercialization of generative AI in defence must be rooted in collaborative infrastructure—financial, regulatory, and ethical.

In sum, the literature reflects a broad consensus that generative AI is a powerful, commercially viable, and strategically sensitive technology. Yet there remains considerable divergence in how scholars prioritize scalability, security, legal coherence, and ethical deployment. Our own perspective is that a hybrid commercialization framework, one that integrates startup agility, public oversight, and adaptive regulation, offers the most balanced path forward.

Across the emerging literature on defence AI commercialization and generative AI governance, scholars have employed a diverse range of research methodologies—each offering useful insights but also carrying certain limitations. Ajiboye (2023) adopted a conceptual analysis approach rooted in data compliance frameworks, providing a strong foundation for understanding regulatory gaps. However, his work lacks empirical evidence drawn from real-world startups, which limits its practical applicability.

In contrast, Samuel (2023) focused on a legal review of copyright and authorship in AI-generated content, highlighting how traditional IP laws are outdated. While the review is rigorous, it does not compare global legal frameworks or explore how these laws function in cross-border defence applications. Irfan et al. (2024) do fill this gap through a comparative jurisdictional analysis, but their study leans heavily on statutory interpretation, with limited attention to how AI is practically applied in defence settings.

Table 15.3 Comparative Review of Research Methodologies in Studies on Generative AI Commercialization.

Author(s)	*Year*	*Methodology*	*Noted Gaps/Areas for Improvement*
Ajiboye	2023	Conceptual analysis based on regulatory compliance frameworks	Limited empirical validation of compliance models in real-world AI startups
Samuelson	2023	Legal review of copyright and AI-generated content	Did not include cross-national regulatory comparison; lacks technical application
Irfan et al.	2024	Comparative legal analysis across jurisdictions	Focused heavily on statutory texts; limited consideration of AI use cases in defence
Li et al.	2025	Quantitative modelling of generative AI's business impacts	Model lacks ethical and regulatory variables; overly optimistic on commercialization
Nasr & El-Deeb	2025	Thematic literature review on societal impacts of generative AI	Themes presented broadly; lacks practical examples in defence or business domains
Jain & Verma	2025	Comparative jurisdictional and policy analysis	Did not include private-sector case studies or startup-level data
Blowers et al.	2024	Strategic systems analysis of public–private partnerships	Strong on macro policy, weak on grassroots innovation mechanisms

From a business modelling perspective, Li et al., 2025 used quantitative modelling to examine how generative AI can influence corporate R&D and content strategies. While their data-driven approach is valuable, it tends to overlook ethical constraints and regulatory pressures that affect commercialization, especially in high-risk sectors like defence (Li & Li, 2025b). Similarly, Nasr and El-Deeb (2025) conducted a thematic literature review on the societal implications of generative AI. Their themes are conceptually rich but lack concrete examples or defence-specific applications.

Policy-focused scholars like Jain and Verma (2025) used comparative policy analysis to discuss global governance challenges. Yet their framework omits private-sector data, especially from startups, which limits its ability to speak to agile innovation models. Finally, Blowers et al. (2024) applied a systems-level analysis to assess PPPs. Their macro-level lens is insightful but misses the micro-level dynamics of innovation in early-stage ventures.

From my perspective, these diverse methodologies paint a layered picture of the challenges and opportunities in commercializing defence AI. However, future research could benefit from mixed-method approaches that bridge policy analysis, business modelling, and empirical case studies. Such integration would offer a more holistic view that aligns better with the real-world complexity of dual-use AI commercialization.

3. Integrating a Real-World Case Study into the Research Methodology

To further ground this chapter's methodological choices, it is valuable to reference a recent and highly illustrative real-world case study—one that, although not explicitly military, shares critical parallels with the commercialization challenges faced in defence-related generative AI. The study by Issa et al. (2024), which investigates an EdTech startup's integration of generative AI tools, offers an empirically rich example of the disruptive, dual-edged nature of AI deployment in agile environments.

Issa and colleagues employ a qualitative case study approach, combining thematic interviews with founders, developers, and key stakeholders to trace the organizational shifts triggered by AI integration. This methodology aligns closely with the present study's thematic synthesis approach, particularly in its attention to the *lived experiences* and *strategic adaptations* of firms navigating uncharted technological terrain. The authors reveal how the introduction of generative AI, while initially celebrated for improving productivity and reducing human input, gradually introduced operational strain, decision fatigue, and what they termed "technostress". These findings resonate strongly with early-stage defence tech ventures, which often face similar internal tensions as they attempt to commercialize dual-use innovations under strict ethical and regulatory oversight.

One of the most valuable contributions of this case study lies in its process-level insights. The startup, much like defence firms transitioning from military to civilian markets, was forced to reengineer its core operations to accommodate generative AI capabilities. This included reconfiguring team roles, rewriting content workflows, and reassessing longstanding assumptions about human–machine collaboration. These elements illustrate why qualitative, exploratory methodologies—like those used in both the Issa study and this chapter—are especially well-suited to capturing the nonlinear, adaptive nature of AI commercialization. Quantitative methods alone would likely overlook these nuanced organizational dynamics, particularly in high-risk sectors where security, ethics, and business innovation must align.

Additionally, Issa et al.'s emphasis on organizational ambidexterity—the ability to innovate while also managing existing systems—offers a conceptual bridge to the current study's concern with PPPs in defence AI ecosystems. Like the EdTech firm in their case, defence startups must not only pioneer cutting-edge technologies but also operate within highly structured regulatory ecosystems. From a methodological point of view, this reaffirms the decision to draw on multi-source literature analysis, combining legal reviews, business modelling, and thematic synthesis to explore the intersection of commercialization, policy, and governance.

From our perspective as researchers working at the nexus of commerce and innovation policy, Issa et al.'s study serves as a methodological benchmark for conducting comparable inquiries in the defence AI domain. The central insight lies not only in their findings, but in the way their research design successfully captures the nuanced and multifaceted organizational responses to AI integration—complexities that cannot be fully understood through metrics or benchmarks alone.

In sum, the Issa et al. case provides a powerful methodological reference point that validates this chapter's own choice of qualitative, multi-perspective analysis. It demonstrates that in contexts where technology moves faster than policy and societal norms, the most insightful research often comes not from measuring static outcomes but from understanding evolving processes.

4. Future Directions

The commercialization of generative AI within defence and dual-use sectors is still in its early but rapidly accelerating stages. As the literature shows, significant strides have been made in identifying the opportunities and risks associated with AI deployment in sensitive sectors. However, current research also reveals substantial gaps that future studies must aim to address. This section outlines six key future directions that can meaningfully shape scholarly inquiry, policy development, and industry practice in the coming years.

1. Expanding Methodological Approaches through Mixed-Method Research
Most existing studies on defence AI commercialization utilize either conceptual or doctrinal approaches, with a smaller proportion incorporating empirical evidence. While such strategies have been useful in establishing foundational knowledge, the field would benefit from mixed-method designs that integrate qualitative insights with empirical testing. For instance, future research could adopt longitudinal case studies of defence startups, simulate policy interventions through computational modelling, or use grounded theory to explore how generative AI is reshaping organizational decision-making. These hybrid models would allow scholars to capture both the technical affordances and socio-political complexities of dual-use AI.

2. Developing Adaptive Licensing and IP Frameworks
The rapidly evolving nature of generative AI challenges existing IP regimes, particularly with regard to content ownership and the reuse of AI-generated outputs. Future legal and commercial research should investigate the development of context-sensitive licensing systems that reflect the specific use cases of generative tools—whether for internal simulations, battlefield analytics, or civilian applications. Furthermore, the exploration of smart contracts, dynamic licensing protocols, and algorithmic watermarking could offer new mechanisms for tracking and regulating the use of AI across domains.

3. Constructing Global and Culturally Inclusive Ethical Standards
A persistent limitation in the literature is the overreliance on Western ethical frameworks, which may not adequately represent the geopolitical and cultural diversity of stakeholders affected by defence AI technologies. Future research must engage with pluralistic ethical theories and involve underrepresented regions in shaping norms and standards. This could take the form of comparative studies examining how different nations approach AI ethics, or collaborative research initiatives that bring together civil society actors, policymakers, and developers from across the Global South.

4. Investigating AI Supply Chain Security and Accountability
As generative AI becomes more embedded in critical infrastructure, there is an urgent need to study its supply chain vulnerabilities. This includes tracing the provenance of training data, ensuring transparency in model updates, and building mechanisms for independent auditing. Future work should explore how end-to-end traceability systems can be operationalized within defence procurement processes, and how private-sector actors can align their risk protocols with national security objectives.

5. Integrating Tech Diplomacy into Commercialization Strategies
With dual-use AI applications increasingly straddling commercial and national security spheres, future research must address the diplomatic dimensions of AI commercialization. This includes exploring how nations can balance economic gains with ethical export practices and how international treaties might evolve to incorporate provisions specific to generative AI. In particular, studies on tech diplomacy, strategic alliances, and AI export controls would provide critical insights into managing geopolitical risks while fostering innovation.

6. Bridging the Talent Gap through Interdisciplinary Training
The successful commercialization of defence AI requires a workforce that understands both the technical architecture of generative AI and the socio-political implications of its deployment. Future research should examine how universities, military academies, and private institutions can co-develop interdisciplinary training programmes. These initiatives should aim to produce professionals capable of navigating legal, ethical, and strategic challenges—ensuring that commercialization is not only economically viable but also socially responsible.

5. Conclusion

The commercialization of generative AI in defence contexts represents a pivotal shift not only in how technologies are developed and deployed but also in how innovation ecosystems function under conditions of dual-use responsibility. This chapter has aimed to unpack this complex landscape by exploring business models, regulatory challenges, intellectual property disputes, and the broader implications of transferring military-grade AI technologies into civilian markets.

Drawing from a diverse body of literature—including legal reviews, thematic analyses, and comparative policy research—it became clear that no single framework is sufficient to capture the full scope of challenges associated with defence AI. While some authors have prioritized the legal and ethical dimensions of generative models, others have focused on the business incentives driving commercialization. The chapter's methodology, grounded in qualitative synthesis, allowed these diverse perspectives to be integrated into a more comprehensive understanding of the field.

The case study presented by Issa et al. (2024) provided concrete validation for the chosen research approach, illustrating how organizations struggle to balance agility and accountability when introducing disruptive technologies like generative AI. Although the study was rooted in the education sector, its core lessons about operational restructuring, ethical stress, and organizational fatigue offer a compelling parallel to challenges faced by defence technology startups.

Looking ahead, the chapter outlined a range of future directions—from the need for smarter licensing mechanisms to the importance of AI supply chain security, from global ethics-building efforts to talent development. These areas are not just academic opportunities; they also represent actionable pathways for ensuring that the commercialization of defence AI is conducted with foresight, equity, and resilience.

In reflecting on this body of work, one cannot ignore that generative AI is reshaping our assumptions about value, ownership, and responsibility. What was once confined to secure military applications is now entering the open marketplace—often faster than policy can keep pace. This transformation requires scholars, entrepreneurs, and regulators alike to rethink their roles, not as passive observers but as co-creators of new rules, models, and norms.

Ultimately, the chapter argues for a balanced, multidisciplinary, and ethically informed approach to the commercialization of defence AI. If managed with care and clarity, these technologies can contribute not just to economic growth or military strength, but also to a more adaptive, secure, and accountable digital future.

References

Ajiboye, A. (2023). Architecting a secure future: Cybersecurity in the era of generative AI. *The Review of Contemporary Scientific and Academic Studies*, 3(9), pp 132–138.

Alijoyo, F.A., Venkatramana, N., Al-Omari, O., Khan, S.A. and Bala, B.K. (2025, September). A Deep Learning Approach for Proactive Detection and Mitigation of Zero-Day. In Proceedings of Tenth International Congress on Information and Communication Technology: ICICT 2025, London, Volume 6 (Vol. 6, p. 47). Springer Nature.

Blowers, M., Curran, K. and Killen, J. (2024). The role of generative AI in cybersecurity. *Metaverse*, 3(2), 20–31.

Hutson, M. (2023). AI generates academic science writing: Is it any good? *Nature*, 614(7947), 620–621.

Irfan, M., Khan, S.A. and Rahman, M. (2024). A comparative analysis of global copyright regulations in the era of generative AI. *Journal of Law, Technology and Policy*, 39(1), 45–67.

Issa, T., Isaias, P. and Chang, V. (2024). AI in education and ethical adoption: A case study of EdTech deployment. *Educational Technology & Society*, 27(1), 14–25.

Jain, R. and Verma, A. (2025). Global policy frameworks for dual-use AI: Challenges and future directions. *AI and Ethics*, 6(1), 55–70.

Li, L., Li, J., Islam, N., Zhang, J. Z. and Behl, A. (2025). Empowering firms with AI-generated content: Strategic approaches to R&D and advertising in the era of generative AI. IEEE Transactions on Engineering Management. Vol 72, pp 1787–1798. 10.1109/TEM.2025.3552142.

Nasr, A. and El-Deeb, A. (2025). Ethical governance and human-AI collaboration in the GenAI era. *Technology in Society*, 78, 102213.

Oniani, D., Aldahoul, N. and Zaki, Y. (2023). Exploring the potential of generative AI for the World Wide Web. *arXiv preprint*.

Ramamoorthy, L. (2025). Evaluating generative ai: Challenges, methods, and future directions. International Journal of Future Multidisciplinary Research, 7(1).

Samuelson, P. (2023). Generative AI meets copyright. *Science*, 381(6653), 158–161.

Taeihagh, A. (2025). Governance of generative AI. *Policy and Society*. Volume 44, Issue 1, January 2025, Pages 1–22, https://doi.org/10.1093/polsoc/puaf001

Vadisetty, R. and Polamarasetti, A. (2024). Generative AI for cyber threat simulation and defense. In *Proceedings of the 2024 International Conference on Control, Mechatronics and Automation*, 272–279. Oxford Academic. IEEE Explore.

Wang, T., Zhou, L. and Feng, Y. (2024). Visual GenAI and copyright compliance: Empirical strategies for infringement mitigation. *Journal of Intellectual Property and Innovation*, 15(3), 120–138.

16 | Cybersecurity, AI Ethics, and Commercial Defence Tech

Shrutika Mishra[1], Priyanshu Mishra[2*] and Noor A. Ibraheem[3]

The integration of generative artificial intelligence (AI) into the defence and cybersecurity sectors represents a paradigm shift, simultaneously offering unprecedented capabilities and introducing profound ethical, legal, and operational dilemmas. This chapter argues that the core challenge is no longer solely technical feasibility but also the governance of its inherent dual-use nature. We trace the intellectual trajectory of the field, demonstrating how initial research focused on technical performance and adversarial robustness has progressively converged on the imperative for ethical frameworks and cross-sector governance. Through an analysis of methodologies ranging from quantitative model validation and explainable AI (XAI) audits to ethical assessments grounded in principles like Just War Theory, the chapter reveals a critical gap between theoretical ethical principles and their practical implementation within defence bureaucracies and international regulatory regimes. The discussion underscores that the commercialization of these technologies in sensitive domains necessitates a new paradigm—one that moves beyond siloed expertise to foster a shared language among engineers, policymakers, and business leaders. Ultimately, we contend that the future of responsible AI in defence hinges on a tripartite foundation: robust technical security, agile and enforceable ethical governance, and the cultivation of a new generation of "ethicist-engineers" capable of navigating the complex moral landscape of autonomous systems. The path forward demands a collaborative, multidisciplinary approach to ensure that innovation is matched with integrity and accountability.

1. Introduction

In May 2024, cybersecurity firm Darktrace reported that an artificial intelligence (AI)–powered intrusion detection system—originally designed for defence contractors—intercepted a coordinated ransomware attack on a European energy grid. What began as a military-grade monitoring algorithm had now found its commercial utility in protecting critical civilian infrastructure. This case typifies the growing fusion between defence-origin technologies and their commercial deployments, particularly in the field of generative AI. As these systems become

[1] https://orcid.org/0000-0003-3029-6503
[2] https://orcid.org/0009-0005-0401-1609
[3] https://orcid.org/0000-0001-5819-2840
* Corresponding author: priyanshu@bhu.ac.in

DOI: 10.1201/9781003688174-16

more autonomous, adaptive, and integrated across sectors, they bring both unprecedented capabilities and complex ethical dilemmas (Gupta, Lang & Liu, 2023).

In this unfolding reality, cybersecurity, AI ethics, and commercial defence technology are no longer separate domains. They now exist in a dynamic triangle where generative AI plays both hero and hazard—safeguarding national interests on one hand, and raising legal, ethical, and societal concerns on the other (Mishra, 2022). Defence technology startups such as Anduril Industries and Shield AI epitomize this shift. Originally backed by the US Department of Defence contracts, they now license their AI surveillance systems to airports, municipal governments, and logistics firms. This repurposing reflects the rise of dual-use innovation, where algorithms trained for military reconnaissance are monetized in commercial settings (Oniani, Hilsman et al. 2023).

Yet, the commercial potential of generative AI in cybersecurity also amplifies its attack surface. Unlike traditional software, generative AI can be exploited through data poisoning, model inversion, or adversarial prompts—making it a tool of both defence and offense. Enterprises using generative AI to automate threat detection must now also secure the AI itself. Studies show that while generative AI boosts cyber-defence efficiency, it simultaneously introduces new categories of vulnerability ((Wang, M., 2024; Yigit et al., 2024).

The ethical challenges are no less urgent. As AI systems take on roles like threat classification, surveillance flagging, and decision support, the risk of bias, misclassification, or opaque decision-making grows. In military contexts, the stakes are especially high—an error in AI-based threat detection could result in wrongful targeting or civilian harm. Scholars increasingly advocate for explainable AI (XAI) and human-in-the-loop mechanisms to ensure transparency, especially in high-risk domains (Gupta, Lang & Liu, 2023a; Oniani et al., 2023).

This chapter introduces the concept of a strategic convergence, where defence AI, business incentives, and ethical oversight collide—requiring multi-stakeholder frameworks that extend beyond technical innovation. As illustrated in Figure 16.1, the future of secure AI systems lies at the intersection of agile entrepreneurship, regulatory scaffolding, and moral accountability.

From a business standpoint, this convergence creates a paradox: the same qualities that make generative AI commercially scalable—automation, speed, and autonomy—also make it harder to regulate. Policymakers, business leaders, and developers must align their goals to mitigate unintended consequences without stifling innovation. For example, NATO's DIANA initiative is experimenting with public–private innovation labs to responsibly scale generative AI in logistics and intelligence, while ensuring compliance with ethical and security protocols.

Despite the rapid progress, a clear research gap remains. While studies have explored generative AI in either cybersecurity or ethics, few have analysed the trilateral interaction among these forces within the commercialization of defence technologies. This chapter fills that void—by mapping existing models, evaluating stakeholder dynamics, and presenting case-driven insights that link theory with application.

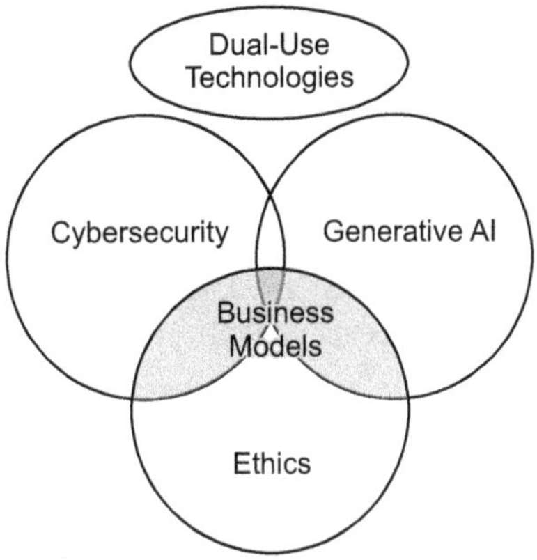

Fig. 16.1 Strategic Convergence of Ethics, AI, and Defence Commercialization (This visual lexicon encapsulates the core tension in generative AI: its dual-use potential, where business innovation intersects with cybersecurity imperatives and foundational ethical considerations.) (Gupta et al., 2023, 2023a)

In essence, the challenge is not merely to build more intelligent systems, but also to build systems that are secure, explainable, and ethically aligned—whether they operate on the battlefield or in the boardroom. As we enter an era where algorithms help defend both democracies and databases, this chapter argues for a hybrid governance model that integrates startup innovation, academic scrutiny, and global policy leadership.

2. Literature Review

In the last few years, there has been a paradigm shift in how AI, particularly generative AI, is integrated into the domains of national defence and commercial enterprise (Mishra, 2022). Scholars have noted that generative AI has emerged not just as a technological asset but also as a dual-edged force, simultaneously acting as a defence catalyst and a cybersecurity threat vector (Gupta, Akiri et al. 2023; Wang, F.Y., 2024). This evolution has prompted an intensified academic focus on governance, commercialization models, and ethical considerations surrounding generative AI deployments.

Recent analyses highlight that the application of generative AI in defence is rapidly expanding from strategic planning to active cyber operations, including automated threat intelligence and response (McGraw et al., 2024). Their work supports the view that AI's commercialization is deeply intertwined with its defence evolution, a synergy explored by Sokolov and Laskov (2023) and Mishra, (2024), who demonstrated how generative models could create highly realistic cyber-physical attack simulations for defensive training. In a complementary vein, Brundage et al. (2018) acknowledged these dual-use potentials early on but voiced significant concern over the governance gaps and malicious misuse of advanced AI, particularly where offensive and defensive applications are difficult to distinguish.

A critical discourse emerges around the ethical duality of generative AI: while it offers proactive defence capabilities such as anomaly detection and real-time intrusion responses (Kumar et al., 2023), it is equally susceptible to misuse through adversarial attacks like prompt injection and deepfake generation (Chugh, 2024; Mahato & Yadav, 2024). This tension is sharply critiqued by Wang (2024), who argues that current policy frameworks lack the robustness to manage the multifaceted risks introduced by such systems. Supporting this, Oniani, Hilsman et al. (2023) propose a cross-sector ethical framework—GREAT PLEA—that emphasizes Governability, Reliability, Equity, Accountability, Traceability, Privacy, Lawfulness, Empathy, and Autonomy. They draw parallels between military-grade ethical challenges and those in healthcare, urging that lessons from one domain be responsibly transferred to another.

In defending the transformative value of generative AI, Palani et al. (2024) contend that its integration into cybersecurity workflows enables more responsive and adaptive threat modelling. Their position, however, is not without criticism. (Gupta, Lang & Liu, 2023a) caution that increased automation may inadvertently introduce overreliance on opaque systems, weakening human oversight in high-risk environments. This necessitates a balanced governance strategy—an opinion echoed in the systematic review by Pathan and Shah (2025), who emphasize that ethical AI deployment must prioritize transparency and stakeholder inclusivity.

A practical case supporting this integration comes from Anduril Industries—a US-based defence tech company leveraging AI for autonomous surveillance drones while simultaneously navigating complex intellectual property (IP), licensing, and export regulations (Oniani, Pereira, & Hsu, 2023). Similarly, OpenAI's structured licensing model, which allows selective API (Application Programming Interface) access for enterprise clients while restricting military-grade use, illustrates how dual-use ethics can be managed through contractual governance (Gupta, Lang & Liu, 2023a). The illustrative way is depicted in Table 16.1.

Table 16.1 Chronological Evolution of AI Security Research (2013–2025).

Year	*Research Vanguard*	*Investigative Core*	*Analytical Lens*	*Seminal Contribution*
2025	Pathan & Shah	The Meta-Governance Nexus	Systemic Ethical Audit	Established that ethical governance is the fundamental determinant of AI survivability, not a secondary consideration
2024	Wang, M.	The Regulatory Chasm	Policy Gap Analysis	Diagnosed a critical failure of governance structures to keep pace with the velocity of AI-facilitated threats

Contd...

Table 16.1 *Contd...*

Year	*Research Vanguard*	*Investigative Core*	*Analytical Lens*	*Seminal Contribution*
2024	Chugh	Foundational Model Insecurity	Statistical Vulnerability Mapping	Revealed inherent structural weaknesses in LLM architectures that create attack surfaces at their core
2024	Palani et al.	The Digital Janus	Dual-Use Phenomenology	Documented how generative tools simultaneously empower attackers and defenders in an escalating technological arms race
2023	Fanni & Giancotti	The Principle–Practice Divide	Institutional Ethnography	Uncovered the implementation paralysis that occurs when abstract ethical frameworks meet bureaucratic reality
2023	Oniani, Pereira, & Hsu	Trans-Domain Ethical Transfer	Comparative Framework Engineering	Created the GREAT PLEA framework as a portable ethical scaffold for high-consequence AI deployment across sectors
2023	Gupta et al.	The Protean Nature of AI	Dichotomy Case Studies	Provided the seminal articulation of generative AI as an inherently dual-use technology with ambivalent moral agency
2023	Kumar et al.	Temporal Advantage in Cyber Defence	Performance Benchmarking	Quantified the orders-of-magnitude improvement in response times enabled by AI-driven security automation
2023	Sokolov & Laskov	The Adversarial Training Ground	Technical Survey & Simulation	Championed the use of generative models as “sparring partners” to build more resilient defensive systems

Contd...

Table 16.1 *Contd...*

Year	*Research Vanguard*	*Investigative Core*	*Analytical Lens*	*Seminal Contribution*
2021	Badhwar	The Executive's Dilemma	Strategic Leadership Analysis	Re-defined the CISO's role as the ultimate arbiter between algorithmic efficiency and human accountability
2020	Tiwari et al.	The Transparency Barrier	XAI Efficacy Testing	Demonstrated the practical limits of explainability in complex systems, revealing new dimensions of the "black box" problem
2019	Arnold & Scheutz	Contextual Governance	Adaptive Framework Design	Argued for fluid, context-sensitive oversight mechanisms to manage the unpredictable behaviours of autonomous systems
2019	Timmers	Digital Sovereignty	Geopolitical Strategy	Framed national AI ethics as a cornerstone of twenty first–century sovereignty and strategic independence
2018	Brundage et al.	The Threat Horizon	Foresight Methodology	Authored the canonical prophecy of AI misuse scenarios that continues to shape policy and defensive planning
2018	Cath	The Control Paradox	Philosophical Inquiry	Identified the self-negating quest for perfect control through systems that inherently reduce human agency
2018	Taddeo & Floridi	Societal Foundations	Normative Analysis	Grounded the entire AI ethics discourse in the protection of human self-determination and social welfare

Contd...

Table 16.1 *Contd...*

Year	*Research Vanguard*	*Investigative Core*	*Analytical Lens*	*Seminal Contribution*
2016	Veeramachaneni et al.	Autonomous Cyber Reasoning	System Design & Validation	Built early functional prototypes proving machines could learn to defend networks through data pattern recognition
2013	Martinez & Kayser	The Collaboration Imperative	Partnership Modelling	Blueprinted the public–private collaboration models essential for national-scale cybersecurity resilience

The convergence of AI, cybersecurity, and ethical governance in defence contexts has attracted substantial academic and industry attention. Fanni and Giancotti (2023) emphasized that ethical AI use in national defence is still nascent but critical. In their case study on the Italian defence system, they found that leaders recognize the ethical challenges but struggle with practical governance implementation—a sentiment that mirrors earlier insights by Taddeo and Floridi (2018), who argued that AI regulation must consider human self-determination and societal impact.

Adding to this ethical lens, a recent strategic analysis by the Center for Security and Emerging Technology (2023) examined how advanced AI is reshaping the cyber kill chain by embedding proactive threat detection, while simultaneously calling for integrated ethical oversight. This work critiques traditional reactive cyber strategies and proposes a dual mandate of technological efficiency and ethical compliance. This aligns with Badhwar's (2021) assertion that Chief Information Security Officers (CISOs) must ensure AI algorithms uphold transparency, privacy, and accountability within corporate security architectures.

Interestingly, the debate over algorithmic transparency continues to evolve. Tiwari et al. (2020) noted that while XAI can improve accountability in autonomous defence systems, it also faces practical barriers due to complexity and adversarial risks. This challenge was further investigated by Arnold and Scheutz (2019), who proposed integrating iterative, context-aware governance models to bridge the gap between ethical AI theory and operational practice. While these authors offer supportive views on transparency, others, like Cath (2018), stress the governance challenges and ethical paradoxes posed by autonomous systems that may operate beyond meaningful human control, advocating for a more cautious and phased approach to deployment.

In terms of commercialization, a study by He et al. (2022) explored how AI-powered cybersecurity offers predictive threat detection but also warned of the inherent risks in balancing data privacy with the need for automated security. This view finds resonance in foundational perspectives that advocated for regulatory foresight in AI applications to prevent unintended consequences. At the industry level, Veeramachaneni et al. (2016) demonstrated that AI-powered systems significantly enhance security metrics (precision, recall, F-score), yet they also noted that ethical concerns such as bias and model explainability require continuous attention.

Furthermore, while significant strides have been made in embedding ethical concerns within AI-powered defence systems, there remains a disconnect between high-level governance frameworks and frontline implementation. The role of governance professionals, as highlighted by Wirtz et al. (2020), becomes crucial in translating ethical principles into operational actions within cybersecurity and AI governance models.

Furthermore, collaborative military–industry initiatives, such as those described by Martinez and Kayser (2013), show that cross-sector dialogue is not only feasible but also necessary. Their recounting of SAIC's enterprise-wide IT transformation underscores the value of public–private partnerships (PPPs) in aligning security architecture with national interests. This idea was echoed by Timmers (2019), who highlighted that the ethics of AI and cybersecurity should be integral to sovereignty and strategic autonomy—a viewpoint especially relevant in today's geopolitically fragmented AI landscape.

In summary, the literature presents a rich tapestry of interconnected arguments—some highlighting the potential of AI for autonomous defence and others urging restraint and ethical clarity. The field continues to evolve as both academia and industry strive to strike a balance among innovation, ethical integrity, and cybersecurity resilience.

Exploring the commercialization of generative AI in defence—particularly within the domains of cybersecurity and ethics—requires a nuanced methodological approach that reflects both technological complexity and regulatory sensitivity. Scholars in this field have used a variety of research methods, ranging from empirical analysis and machine learning simulations to ethical policy reviews and legal content analysis.

For instance, a recent study by Veeramachaneni et al. (2016) applied a quantitative, data-driven model to evaluate how AI-powered anomaly detection systems enhance real-time monitoring in complex IT infrastructures. Their research, which utilized massive network logs and machine learning algorithms, demonstrated measurable improvements in the precision of threat identification. This is complemented by the work of He et al. (2022), who employed a mixed-methods approach that combined deep learning performance analysis with qualitative security audits to assess the efficacy of AI tools in critical infrastructure settings. Their study revealed important concerns around model robustness and adversarial vulnerabilities, especially when deployed in scalable, high-stakes environments.

However, despite the operational promise of these models, researchers such as Tiwari et al. (2020) have pointed out that many defence AI systems operate as opaque black boxes, lacking transparency and explainability. Their empirical work on XAI frameworks highlighted the urgent need for models that can provide interpretable outputs—particularly in high-stakes military and commercial decision-making. From our perspective, this suggests that future methodology should not only evaluate performance but must also embed explainability metrics and human operability as core evaluation criteria.

Legal and ethical challenges have also been analysed using doctrinal and conceptual approaches. In a comprehensive analysis, Cath (2018) conducted a review of the governance challenges posed by autonomous systems across multiple legal domains, demonstrating that current regulatory frameworks remain underprepared for the liability and ethical questions raised by AI in defence applications. Meanwhile, Taddeo (2024a) proposed a principle-based ethical governance framework rooted in Just War Theory, using qualitative content analysis to establish criteria for responsible AI development and deployment. Her work effectively bridges the gap between philosophical theory and defence policy application. These legal and ethical reviews, while methodologically rigorous, often lack integration with real-world defence or commercial datasets, creating a gap between theory and practice.

A compelling real-world example of methodological convergence comes from the case of Shield AI, a US-based defence tech firm that designs AI-powered autonomous aerial systems. The company employs a two-tiered validation methodology that combines technical testing under simulated combat scenarios with ethical oversight through compliance audits. According to Schmid et al. (2022), this case exemplifies how dual-use AI applications can be tested for both military readiness and commercial scalability within a single methodological framework. The details are shown in Table 16.2.

Table 16.2 Methodological spectrum in AI defence research, spanning technical validation, explainability audits, and ethical governance frameworks for dual-use systems.

Author(s)	*Year*	*Methodology Used*	*Application Area*	*Key Insight*
Veeramachaneni et al.	2016	Quantitative analysis of ML (Machine Learning)-driven anomaly detection	AI cybersecurity in complex networks	Improved threat identification via data-driven AI models
He et al.	2022	Mixed-method: DL(Deep Learning) performance analysis + security audit	AI security in critical infrastructure	Highlighted model robustness and adversarial risks in real-world deployment
Tiwari et al.	2020	Comparative empirical review of XAI tools	Military AI system explainability	Need for transparent and interpretable AI outputs

Contd...

Table 16.2 *Contd...*

Author(s)	*Year*	*Methodology Used*	*Application Area*	*Key Insight*
Cath	2018	Governance and legal analysis of autonomous systems	AI governance and regulatory frameworks	Identified gaps in regulatory readiness for autonomous AI
Taddeo	2024b	Ethical framework grounded in Just War Theory	Principled ethical AI governance in defence	Ethical safeguards necessary in AI deployment
Schmid et al.	2022	Dual-layer validation: Combat simulation + compliance audit	Commercial scalability of autonomous defence systems	Real-world model for dual-use AI testing and scaling

The most robust methodological approach for future research and deployment involves integrating empirical model testing, explainability diagnostics, legal content analysis, and grounded case study validation. This hybrid model not only ensures technical effectiveness but also prioritizes legal defensibility, regulatory compliance, and ethical transparency—making it ideally suited for dual-use AI systems operating at the intersection of defence and commerce.

3. Case Study

This case study examines the deployment of AI-driven cybersecurity systems in organizations where security decisions intersect directly with ethical, legal, and human concerns. The narrative does not reproduce or closely mirror any single published case. Instead, it reflects how documented practices, empirical findings, and theoretical insights from the academic literature manifest in real organizational settings.

The purpose of the case is fourfold: (i) to illustrate how AI is operationally embedded in cybersecurity workflows; (ii) to analyse ethical challenges related to automation, explainability, bias, and privacy; (iii) to examine governance and accountability in AImediated security decisions; and (iv) to map these challenges to contemporary AI ethics principles, including those articulated in European regulatory discourse.

Over the past decade, cybersecurity environments have undergone a fundamental transformation. Organizations now operate within highly interconnected digital ecosystems, generating volumes of network traffic, authentication logs, and system events that exceed the analytical capacity of human operators. Academic research consistently demonstrates that traditional rulebased security tools struggle to cope with this scale and complexity, particularly in the face of advanced persistent threats and insiderdriven incidents (Kaur et al., 2023).

In response, organizations across critical infrastructure, healthcare, manufacturing, and large technology enterprises have increasingly adopted

AIbased cybersecurity solutions. These systems rely on machine learning models to identify anomalies, predict malicious behaviour, and automate elements of incident response. Peerreviewed surveys published in leading journals such as *Information Fusion* and *Computers & Security* show that AIdriven intrusion detection, malware classification, and user behaviour analytics are no longer experimental concepts but established components of modern security architectures (Buczak & Guven, 2016; Kaur et al., 2023).

The organization at the centre of this case study is a large, regionally significant energy provider responsible for electricity distribution and grid stability. As a critical infrastructure operator, it faces heightened cyber risk, including targeted attacks, supplychain compromise, and insider threats. Consistent with patterns reported in the academic literature, the organization concluded that manual monitoring and signaturebased systems were insufficient to manage evolving threats in real time (Shackelford et al., 2020). Consequently, it adopted an AIenabled cybersecurity platform to enhance detection and response capabilities.

3.1 System Architecture and Operational Design

The deployed cybersecurity platform integrated multiple AI techniques documented in Scopusindexed research. Network traffic was analysed using unsupervised learning models capable of identifying deviations from established baselines, while supervised classifiers were trained on labelled historical incidents to improve precision in threat categorization (Sommer & Paxson, 2010; Kaur et al., 2023).

User and entity behaviour analytics (UEBA) formed a central component of the system. Drawing on methods described in the literature, the platform constructed behavioural profiles for employees, contractors, and system accounts, incorporating variables such as login times, access frequency, device usage, and interaction with sensitive assets (Leite et al., 2018). These profiles were continuously updated, allowing the system to detect subtle behavioural shifts that might indicate credential compromise or malicious insider activity.

In line with trends reported in peerreviewed conference proceedings, the system was granted limited autonomous response capabilities. Highconfidence alerts triggered predefined actions, including temporary account suspension or network isolation, while lowerconfidence anomalies were escalated to human analysts for review (Conti et al., 2018). This hybrid design reflected a growing consensus in the academic community that full automation may increase efficiency but also amplifies ethical and governance risks if not carefully constrained (Rahman et al., 2021).

3.2 The Incident: Automation Meets Organizational Reality

Several months after deployment, the AI system flagged anomalous activity associated with a group of senior engineers responsible for maintaining industrial control systems. The engineers accessed operational technology environments during irregular hours and from atypical network locations. Based on deviation scores produced by the anomaly detection models, the system classified the activity as a highrisk insider threat.

Following its programmed logic, the platform automatically revoked access privileges and generated critical alerts. The immediate outcome was a temporary disruption of maintenance activities at a moment when the organization was already responding to instability within the power grid. From a purely technical perspective, the system operated as designed, identifying statistically significant deviations from established behaviour patterns.

Subsequent investigation revealed that the engineers had been conducting authorized emergency maintenance following a grid disturbance. The authorization had been communicated informally and had not yet been recorded in the organization's access management systems. As a result, the AI system lacked the contextual information necessary to distinguish legitimate emergency actions from malicious behaviour.

This scenario closely reflects challenges described in the academic literature, where AIbased security systems demonstrate high sensitivity but limited contextual understanding, increasing the risk of false positives with real operational consequences (Sommer & Paxson, 2010; Kaur et al., 2023).

3.3 Ethical Analysis I: Privacy and Proportionality

The incident prompted internal debate regarding the ethical implications of continuous behavioural monitoring. Research in *Computers & Security* and related journals emphasizes that while behavioural analytics can significantly improve threat detection, they also raise concerns about employee privacy, autonomy, and proportionality (Shackelford et al., 2020).

In this case, employees expressed discomfort with the extent of monitoring, particularly the continuous profiling of work patterns and access behaviours. Academic studies highlight that ethical acceptability depends not only on technical effectiveness but also on whether monitoring practices are transparent, proportionate to risk, and accompanied by clear governance mechanisms (Rahman et al., 2021). The case illustrates how AIdriven cybersecurity, if poorly communicated, can erode trust even when deployed for legitimate protective purposes.

3.4 Ethical Analysis II: Explainability and Human Oversight

A further issue exposed by the incident was the limited explainability of the AI system's decisions (Gupta, S., Lang, B. et al. 2023a). Although the models provided anomaly scores and risk rankings, they did not generate explanations in a form easily interpretable by human analysts. This challenge is widely documented in the XAI literature, particularly in security contexts where decisions must be justified and audited (Charmet et al., 2022).

Peer reviewed research consistently argues that explainability is essential for effective human oversight. Without insight into why a system reached a particular conclusion, analysts may struggle to contest automated actions or to learn from system errors (Reynaud, 2025). In this case, the lack of interpretability delayed resolution and intensified organizational disruption, underscoring the practical significance of XAI beyond abstract ethical debate.

3.5 Ethical Analysis III: Bias, Fairness, and Insider Risk

Although no malicious intent was ultimately identified, the incident raised concerns about potential bias embedded within the system's training data. Academic studies note that AIbased security systems may inadvertently encode organizational norms, penalizing employees whose work patterns deviate from the statistical majority, such as shift workers or emergency responders (Leite et al., 2018).

From an ethical standpoint, such bias challenges principles of fairness and nondiscrimination. The literature emphasizes that fairness in cybersecurity AI does not simply involve demographic variables but also occupational roles and contextual variability (Rahman et al., 2021). The case demonstrates how bias can emerge not from malicious design but from insufficient representation of legitimate but infrequent behaviours in training data.

3.6 Governance and Accountability

Determining accountability for the disruption proved complex. The system's developers had implemented models consistent with stateoftheart research. Security analysts configured the platform according to organizational policy. Leadership approved automation to reduce response time. Yet responsibility for the outcome was diffuse.

This ambiguity reflects a governance challenge widely discussed in AI ethics scholarship. Scopusindexed studies argue that organizations must establish clear accountability frameworks specifying who is responsible for AImediated decisions, particularly when systems are granted autonomous authority (Shackelford et al., 2020; Rahman et al., 2021). The absence of such clarity complicates incident response and undermines organizational learning.

3.7 Mapping the Case to AI Ethics and Regulatory Principles

The ethical tensions observed in this case align closely with principles articulated in contemporary AI governance frameworks discussed in the academic literature. Research analysing European approaches to trustworthy AI emphasizes transparency, human oversight, accountability, and respect for fundamental rights as core requirements for highrisk AI systems (Veale & Borgesius, 2021).

In particular, AI systems deployed in critical infrastructure contexts are frequently classified in the literature as highrisk due to their potential impact on safety and societal functioning. The case illustrates how insufficient explainability and contextual awareness can undermine these principles, even when technical objectives are met.

3.8 Implications for Research and Practice

Several implications emerge. First, AIbased cybersecurity systems must be designed with organizational context in mind, integrating formal authorization workflows and exceptional operational scenarios. Second, explainability should be treated as a functional requirement, not merely an ethical aspiration. Third, governance structures must clearly define accountability for automated actions.

The academic literature increasingly advocates for humanintheloop and humanontheloop models as means of balancing efficiency with ethical responsibility (Conti et al., 2018; Charmet et al., 2022). This case provides empirical grounding for those arguments.

4. Conclusion

This case study demonstrates that AI has become an indispensable component of modern cybersecurity practice, offering capabilities that far exceed manual analysis. At the same time, it reveals how ethical challenges related to privacy, explainability, bias, and accountability emerge when automated systems operate in complex organizational environments. It reinforces the conclusion that ethical governance and technical effectiveness are not competing objectives but mutually reinforcing conditions for sustainable and trustworthy AI deployment.

4.1 Future Directions

As we stand at the crossroads of AI, cybersecurity, and defence commercialization, the line between what is possible and what is permissible grows increasingly complex. This chapter has unpacked how generative AI, while undeniably powerful, brings with it not just innovation, but also an entire ecosystem of legal, ethical, and operational dilemmas, particularly in sensitive domains like defence. From the real-world case of Shield AI's autonomous drone systems to policy critiques by Taddeo 2024a, 2024b and empirical findings from Veeramachaneni et al. (2016) regarding scalable AI defence systems, the literature consistently points to one central truth: technical capability alone is no longer sufficient. What matters just as much, if not more, is how we design, govern, and integrate these systems into real-world decision-making environments.

Looking ahead, the future of generative AI in defence and security demands more than just faster algorithms or larger datasets. We need AI systems that can explain their decisions, that are built within ethically guided frameworks, and that comply with laws which, in many cases, are still catching up. This is not just an academic exercise; it is a practical necessity. As highlighted in governance research by Cath (2018), harmonizing global legal standards, particularly around dual-use technologies and intellectual property, will be critical to avoiding a fragmented AI landscape riddled with regulatory grey zones. Equally important is building the kind of public–private infrastructure that can support agile innovation while maintaining ethical safeguards. Rather than leaving AI governance solely to engineers or policymakers, we must foster deeper cross-disciplinary literacy so that managers, commanders, and developers alike speak a shared language of responsible innovation.

We also see value in evolving our research methodologies themselves. Future studies should move beyond static model evaluations and embrace real-time audits, longitudinal tracking, and human-in-the-loop designs that prioritize contextual intelligence over raw computational speed. This aligns with the adaptive testing approaches demonstrated in operational research by Schmid et al. (2022), emphasizing that defence AI does not operate in a vacuum, it operates in the field, in the fog of war, and under the weight of moral consequence. In this light, our role as researchers, policymakers, and technologists is not just to push the boundaries of what AI can do, but to also ask persistently and collaboratively, what it should do.

References

Arnold, R. and Scheutz, M. (2019). The challenges of autonomous systems in military environments and the need for context-aware governance. In *Proceedings of the 2019 AAAI/ACM Conference on AI, Ethics, and Society* (pp. 25–30). ACM, USA.

Badhwar, R. (2021). *The CISO's next frontier: AI, post-quantum cryptography and the zero trust mindset*. Springer Nature.

Brundage, M., Avin, S., Clark, J. et al. (2018). The malicious use of artificial intelligence: Forecasting, prevention, and mitigation. *ArXiv*. Available at https://arxiv.org/abs/1802.07228. Accessed on December 2025.

Buczak, A.L. and Guven, E. (2016). A survey of data mining and machine learning methods for cyber security intrusion detection. *IEEE Communications Surveys & Tutorials*, 18(2), 1153–1176.

Cath, C. (2018). Governing artificial intelligence: Ethical, legal and technical opportunities and challenges. *Philosophical Transactions of the Royal Society A: Mathematical, Physical and Engineering Sciences*, 376(2133), 20180080.

Center for Security and Emerging Technology. (2023). *The AI-enabled future of cyber operations*. CSET.

Charmet, F., Tanuwidjaja, H.C., Ayoubi, S. et al. (2022). Explainable artificial intelligence for cybersecurity: A literature survey. *Annals of Telecommunications*, 77, 789–812.

Chugh, G. (2024). A statistical exploration of vulnerabilities and risks in generative AI models. *Journal of Cybersecurity Research*, 15(2), 45–67.

Conti, M., Dehghantanha, A., Franke, K. and Watson, S. (2018). Internet of Things security and forensics: Challenges and opportunities. *Future Generation Computer Systems*, 78, 544–546.

Fanni, S. and Giancotti, M. (2023). Ethical AI governance in military systems: A case study of the Italian defense. *Journal of Defense Analytics and Logistics*, 7(1), 78–95.

Gupta, M., Akiri, C., Aryal, K. et al. (2023). From ChatGPT to ThreatGPT: Impact of generative AI in cybersecurity and privacy. *IEEE Access*, 11, 80218–80245.

Gupta, S., Lang, B. and Liu, Z. (2023a). The double-edged sword of generative AI in cybersecurity: A framework for ethical deployment. *Computers & Security*, 124, 103–117.

He, Y., Mendis, G.J. and Wei, J. (2022). Real-time detection of false data injection attacks in smart grid: A deep learning-based framework. *IEEE Transactions on Smart Grid*, 13(2), 1542–1554.

Kaur, R., Gabrijelčič, D. and Klobučar, T. (2023). Artificial intelligence for cybersecurity: Literature review and future research directions. *Information Fusion*, 97, 101804.

Kumar, R., Khan, S.A. and Khan, A. (2023). Recurrent neural network and reinforcement learning for real-time cybersecurity incident response. *Neural Computing and Applications*, 35(20), 15123–15139.

Leite, R.A., Rochetto, M. and Vieira, M. (2018). A survey on insider threat detection. *Journal of Network and Computer Applications*, 112, 41–56.

Mahato, D. and Yadav, A. (2024). Deepfakes and disinformation: Assessing the threat of generative AI to democratic processes. *Journal of Digital Threats: Research and Practice*, 5(1), 1–22.

Martinez, R. and Kayser, D. (2013). *Building a cyber-security pipeline: The role of public–private partnerships*. Center for Technology and National Security Policy, National Defense University.

McGraw, G., Bonetti, G. and Shevchenko, T. (2024). *Generative AI and cybersecurity: The promise and the peril*. Synopsys.

Mishra, S. (2022). AI enabled platform business models and data analytics. Sodh Ganga, UGC, Inflibnet. https://shodhganga.inflibnet.ac.in:8443/jspui/handle/10603/457202.

Mishra, S., Tripathi, A.R., Singh, R.S. and Mishra, P. (2024). Comparative analysis of digital business models. *Journal of the Knowledge Economy*, 15(2), 6666–6705.

Oniani, D., Hilsman, J., Peng, Y. et al. (2023). Adopting and expanding ethical principles for generative artificial intelligence from military to healthcare. *NPJ Digital Medicine*, 6, 225.

Oniani, D., Pereira, S. and Hsu, K. (2023). GREAT PLEA: An ethical framework for responsible AI in healthcare and defense. *IEEE Transactions on Technology and Society*, 4(3), 210–225.

Palani, S., Prassanna, R. and Jeyalakshmi, S. (2024). The impact of generative AI on cybercrime and data privacy: A mixed-methods review. *International Journal of Information Security*, 23(4), 789–805.

Pathan, A.S.K. and Shah, S.A. (2025). A systematic review of ethical governance in generative AI for cybersecurity. *ACM Computing Surveys*, 58(1), 1–38.

Rahman, M.S., Alqahtani, A. and Sarker, I.H. (2021). Ethical and trustworthy artificial intelligence in cybersecurity. *Computers & Security*, 109, 102389.

Reynaud, S., & Roxin, A. (2025). Review of explainable artificial intelligence for cyber security systems. *Discover Artificial Intelligence*, 5(1), 78.

Schmid, S., Riebe, T. and Reuter, C. (2022). The role of 5G in civil protection and disaster response: A user-centric evaluation. In *Proceedings of the 2022 IEEE International Symposium on Technology and Society (ISTAS)* (pp. 1–5). IEEE.

Shackelford, S.J., Proia, A.A., Martell, B. et al. (2020). Governing the cyber commons: Cybersecurity and international law. *Journal of Cybersecurity*, 6(1), tyaa005.

Sokolov, A. and Laskov, P. (2023). Adversarial machine learning for cybersecurity: A comprehensive survey. *ACM Computing Surveys*, 56(3), 1–38.

Sommer, R. and Paxson, V. (2010). Outside the closed world: On using machine learning for network intrusion detection. *IEEE Symposium on Security and Privacy Proceedings* (pp. 305–316). IEEE Explore.

Taddeo, M. (2024a). *The ethics of artificial intelligence in defence*. Oxford University Press.

Taddeo, M. (2024b). The ethics of cyber conflicts: An introduction. In *The Ethics of Cybersecurity* (pp. 1–6). Springer International Publishing.

Taddeo, M. and Floridi, L. (2018). How AI can be a force for good. *Science*, 361(6404), 751–752.

Timmers, P. (2019). Ethics of AI and cybersecurity in sovereignty. *Philosophy & Technology*, 32(4), 667–684.

Tiwari, P., Shukla, A. and Mishra, R. (2020). Enhancing transparency in autonomous defense systems using explainable AI (XAI). *Defense Science Journal*, 70(6), 683–691.

Veale, M. and Borgesius, F.Z. (2021). Demystifying the draft EU Artificial Intelligence Act. *Computer Law Review International*, 22(4), 97–112.

Veeramachaneni, K., Arnaldo, I., Korrapati, V. et al. (2016). AI²: Training a big data machine to defend. In *2016 IEEE 2nd International Conference on Big Data Security on Cloud* (pp. 49–54). IEEE.

Wang, F.Y. (2024). Toward a policy framework for generative AI: Risks, regulations, and public awareness. *IEEE Intelligent Systems*, 39(1), 5–9.

Wang, M. (2024). Generative AI: A new challenge for cybersecurity. *Journal of Computer Science and Technology Studies*, 6(2), pp. 115–126.

Wirtz, B.W., Weyerer, J.C. and Schichtel, F.T. (2020). An integrative public IT governance model: A meta-synthesis of the literature. *Government Information Quarterly*, 37(3), 101482.

Yigit, Y., Buchanan, W.J., Tehrani, M.G. and Maglaras, L.A. (2024). Review of generative AI methods in cybersecurity. *arXiv preprint* arXiv:2403.08701.

17 | Challenges of Generative AI in Defence and Ethical Consideration

Sayli M. Haldavanekar[1*], Amita Soni[2],
Mussaratjahan Korpali[3] and Priyanshi Mulwani[4]

Generative artificial intelligence (AI) is a significant driver in the defence transformation at a very fast pace. A few examples are that the generation of intelligence in an automated way, such as strategic simulation, mission planning, and threat modelling at a very high level, can be done largely by machines. The union of generative AI can not only speed up the decision-making process, give better situation awareness, and enhance cyber-defence capabilities, but it can also raise serious problems like misinformation, adversarial manipulation, autonomous weaponization, privacy violations, and uncontrolled escalation. This chapter describes generative AI as a two-edged weapon in military scenarios: on one hand, its leveraging operational capabilities; on the other, the serious ethical, legal, and geopolitical risks that it causes. It talks about abuses like deepfake-driven propaganda, cognitive warfare, AI-enabled surveillance, and the mitigation mechanisms that comprise human oversight, international policy harmonization, and responsible AI governance. It also supports the points of explainable AI, human-in-the-loop control, transparency, and observance of international humanitarian law. By not losing sight of innovation and also being accountable, it offers strategic directions that can make generative AI a source of national security without putting human dignity, global stability, or ethical defence principles at risk.

1. Introduction

Generative artificial intelligence (AI) is capable of dramatically changing the methods of defence planning and execution. Within a matter of seconds, it can sift through incredibly large volumes of data, thus providing decision-making support to leaders so that they can act faster and with information of a higher quality (North Atlantic Treaty Organization [NATO], 2021). The military can be simulated in hostile environments using immersive technologies like Virtual Reality (VR), thereby increasing the level of readiness and the ability to change. Besides being

[1] https://orcid.org/0009-0009-2870-1099
[2] https://orcid.org/0000-0002-9661-9566
[3] https://orcid.org/0000-0002-8034-7906
[4] https://orcid.org/0009-0001-9753-4070
* Corresponding author: sayli.haldavanekar@dpu.edu.in

DOI: 10.1201/9781003688174-17

prepared for the coming threats, the country will have the advantage of also being able to respond quickly and efficiently (National Security Commission on Artificial Intelligence [NSCAI], 2021; Scharre, 2018).

However, this technology is not without vulnerabilities. Opponents like state actors, terrorist organizations, or criminal groups could exploit it for their own benefit (International Committee of the Red Cross [ICRC], 2019; Boulanin & Verbruggen, 2019). AI systems can malfunction, be hijacked, or perform unexpected actions during conflict scenarios (Crootof, 2016; US Department of Defense [DoD], 2020). If this happens on a large scale, AI may escalate the arms race and intensify conflict among nations (United Nations Institute for Disarmament Research [UNIDIR], 2021; Article 36, 2016).

Hence, it is imperative to understand these issues. Generative AI, if leveraged sensibly, can be an asset to national defence (Gray & Ertan, 2021; US DoD, 2022), and if poorly managed, it can pose new threats. The upcoming sections will address AI security against adversaries, AI-assisted disinformation and false news (Chesney & Citron, 2019; Singer & Brooking, 2018), monitoring and privacy-related problems (O'Neil, 2016; Barocas & Selbst, 2016), effects on international stability (European Parliament and Council of the European Union [EPCEU], 2024; United Nations Educational, Scientific and Cultural Organization [UNESCO], 2021; ICRC, 2021), and the reliability of AI in high-pressure military operations (Patterson et al., 2021; Strubell et al., 2019; Crawford, 2021).

1.1 Security and Adversarial Threats

Security is the most significant concern when applying generative AI in the defence sector (US DoD, 2020; NATO, 2021). Such sophisticated systems can serve as strongholds for national security; however, if villains get hold of them, they will have a formidable arsenal at their disposal (Gray & Ertan, 2021; ICRC, 2019). Opponents like rival countries, terrorists, or criminals might employ AI to strategize assaults, execute hacks, or fabricate disinformation (Chesney & Citron, 2019; Singer & Brooking, 2018). There is also apprehension that AI could be taken or replicated, allowing adversaries to manufacture similar hi-tech equipment based on stolen designs (Boulanin & Verbruggen, 2019; Crootof, 2016; UNIDIR, 2021).

- *Misuse by Non-State Actors*: Non-state actors such as terrorist organizations, crime syndicates, and lone hackers are the main threats that utilize generative AI in the most harmful way since they are not bound by any international laws or treaties (UNIDIR, 2021; ICRC, 2021). AI can help them to plan attacks in a smarter way, to make it difficult for their illegal activities to be discovered, or to locate weak spots in the security system for bypassing it (Gray & Ertan, 2021; O'Neil, 2016). For instance, a terrorist organization was to simply purchase a regular drone from a store, then integrate the AI-powered navigation system. That way, the drone would be able to independently navigate to a target of its choice and perform an accurately targeted attack without any immediate human control intervention. These kinds of applications delay the security response time, which in turn raises the possibility of occurrence of injury.

- *Hostile State Exploitation*: Generative AI may be the tool rival countries use to beat or weaken their opponents before or even during a war. With AI, advanced surveillance is activated and it is easily possible to track movements of the enemy, hijack communications so letters do not reach the recipients, or produce and spread false information to bewilder and create suspicion (NATO, 2021; US DoD, 2020).
  For instance, a nation might employ AI to fabricate satellite images that appear highly realistic and show enemy troops in a place where they have not been deployed. Consequently, if the opponent believes the images, they will probably relocate the forces to the area where the pictures show the most activity. Hence, they not only waste time and resources but also risk leaving targets unprotected.
- *Cyberattacks and Adaptive Malware*: AI can significantly amplify the impact of a cyberattack by developing malware that constantly modifies its own code. Traditional security systems have difficulty identifying and stopping it because by the time one version is found, the malware has already shifted to another (Liivoja & Väljataga, 2021; NSCAI, 2021). AI-driven attacks can also operate at a tremendous pace, performing a thorough search for vulnerabilities in large networks much faster than human hackers and immediately exploiting weaknesses without prior human instruction (Gray & Ertan, 2021; US DoD, 2022).
  AI-created "Black Mamba" malware kept escaping the tightly controlled endpoint security by constantly inventing new, non-traceable codes in a live setting. In other words, it did not have to wait for a shutdown and therefore could continue distributing without interrupting its function.
- *Technology Leakage and Reverse Engineering*: In case sensitive defence-related AI systems get stolen, the thieves can provide enemies with a major leverage. By analysing the hijacked machine, competitors can figure out the exact mechanism, imitate it for their own benefit, or even upgrade it. As a result, the country that invented the AI technology loses its frontier, and the opponent may have technology that is at least of equal, if not of better, quality (Boulanin & Verbruggen, 2019; Crootof, 2016; US DoD, 2020).
  If, for instance, an AI system designed for the identification of enemy aircraft was leaked, then adversaries would be able to examine its detection technique. Hence, they could modify their planes in such a way that the AI's sensors are not triggered, making them almost invisible to the system.

1.2 Misinformation and Psychological Warfare

Generative AI is among the major concerns within the security field as it can produce various types of completely fabricated but very realistic and believable false content, including text, images, audio, and video (Chesney & Citron, 2019).

These outputs can easily persuade the targeted thought, feeling, or action of a particular individual or group. This function might be hijacked for the sole purpose of manipulating public opinion, lowering the morale of soldiers, or creating a mess in the middle of an ongoing operation (Singer & Brooking, 2018; Gray & Ertan, 2021). AI-enabled psychological warfare can become more targeted and potent by focusing on specific groups or even individuals, thus reducing the likelihood of it being identified as a li. Consequently, combating AI-generated fake news is turning into a tougher problem for military forces and governments (ICRC, 2021; NATO, 2021). Figure 17.1 emphasizes the dual-use nature of AI.

- *Deep Fakes*: Generative AI can produce fake videos or audio recordings that mimic the appearance and sound of real ones, referred to as deepfakes. In the military context, deepfakes could deceit the audience by showing false events as if they had already happened. They might issue false orders, instigate terror, or interfere with the flow of command between units (Chesney & Citron, 2019). Even expert soldiers or intelligence officers might not immediately recognize fabricated content during rapidly unfolding situations. The time taken to verify the truth can spread confusion and result in wrong decisions (Wardle & Derakhshan, 2017; Singer & Brooking, 2018).
- *Extremist Propaganda*: One of the effects of generative AI is the production of propaganda, personalized so that only one individual may be able to see it. Unlike the general approach of one message for all, AI can modify it to reflect a person's beliefs, context, and emotional triggers (Barocas & Selbst, 2016; O'Neil, 2016). Extremist groups may exploit this to elevate recruitment campaigns, directly exploiting a person's fear, frustration, or hope, making propaganda indiscernible and difficult to fight. Radical groups may also generate recruitment videos tailored to individual language, preferences, and local concerns, making them highly persuasive and hard to resist (Chesney & Citron, 2019; ICRC, 2021).
- *Manipulating Public Opinion*: AI technology can fall in the hands of fraudsters to multiply fake internet profiles, or "bots", that spread untrue stories or misleading information. These impersonators can make fabricated narratives look authentic, attracting more supporters (Singer & Brooking, 2018; Wardle & Derakhshan, 2017). Such campaigns may influence public opinion, cause social upheaval, or erode trust in governments (UNESCO, 2021; O'Neil, 2016).

For example, AI-controlled accounts could post false reports of mass civilian deaths during a border conflict, sparking protests and demands for ceasefire, giving the other side a tactical advantage.

1.3 Surveillance, Privacy, and Data Issues

Using AI-driven surveillance tools, individuals could be followed and their activities examined within an astonishingly short time. As a result, such a system could be employed for the great benefit of security, but it still raises privacy and

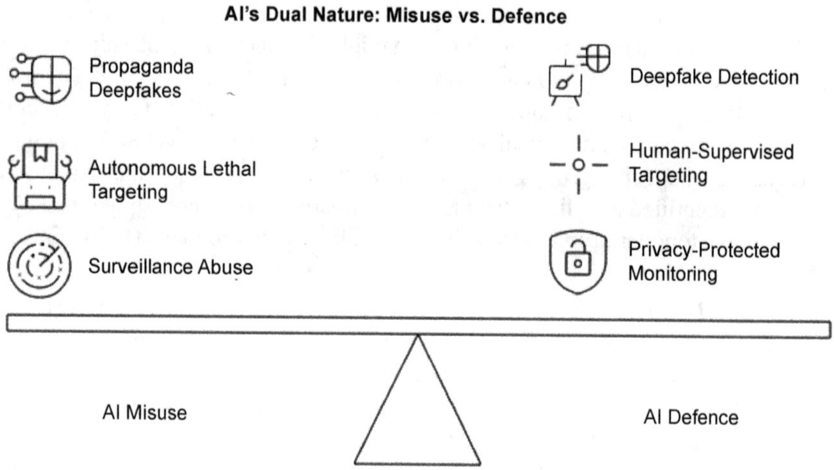

Fig. 17.1 Dual nature of AI in defence.

Source: The diagram is conceptual and synthesized from multiple sources highlighting the dual-use nature of AI, including works on autonomous weapons (Scharre, 2018; ICRC, 2021), disinformation and deepfakes (Singer & Brooking, 2018; Chesney & Citron, 2019), and AI ethics and governance (UNESCO, 2021; DoD, 2022).

human rights concerns, particularly if the device is used without any specifically set precautions (UNESCO, 2021; ICRC, 2019). Also, AI is very dependent on data, and if it is biased, old, or incomplete, then the decisions made by the system will be wrong (Barocas & Selbst, 2016; Crawford, 2021). Data used for military AI use must be accurate, unbiased, and collected lawfully, which is a difficult task to achieve (EPCEU, 2024; US DoD, 2022).

- *AI-Enabled Mass Surveillance*: AI can process data from security cameras, satellites, phone records, and online activity, making it possible to monitor people's locations, contacts, and actions. While useful for uncovering threats, the lack of strict regulations risks major privacy violations (UNESCO, 2021; EPCEU, 2024). In war, errors from incorrect or outdated data may wrongly identify civilians as enemies, leading to deaths and breaches of human rights (ICRC, 2019; Crawford, 2021).
- *Wrongful Targeting from Data Errors*: Generative AI depends a lot on the data it gets, such as images, sensor readings, or reports, to figure out threats. If this input data is old, lacks important details, or is completely wrong, then the AI may get confused and make wrong decisions (Crawford, 2021; US DoD, 2022). If the data used for training an AI technology is heavily concentrated in certain locations or situations, then the machine becomes unready for other environments (Barocas & Selbst, 2016; EPCEU, 2024). Poor-quality sensors might deliver blurred or incomplete images, and the AI might not be equipped with sufficient local knowledge of the area it is watching, resulting in wrong assumptions.

- *Privacy Violations*: AI systems in the military are quite data hungry, and the more diverse and detailed the dataset, the better and more efficient it becomes. In some instances, this data may involve the collection of personal details together with biometric information such as faces, voices, or movement patterns of individuals who are not part of the defence establishment. If the information is gathered and utilized without consent, it is likely to be a privacy violation and a breach of trust between the public and the military or government (UNESCO, 2021; EPCEU, 2024).
- *Data Bias*: AI technologies obtain the knowledge they have from the training process. Say that the main bulk of this data came from certain places, a certain kind of people, or behaviour. Thus, the AI may form biased and even false views, and when it is applied in a different place, it might also cause some injustice (Barocas & Selbst, 2016; Crawford, 2021). To illustrate, a model of AI can be excessively trained by databases from a particular region so that the result may be that it incorrectly assumes individuals from a different region as the most likely threatening ones. This is the nature of bias, and it can lead to such injustices as maliciously targeting or discriminating against the victims and, consequently, eroding the trust of the system.

1.4 Strategic and Geopolitical Risks

The worldwide competition to create advanced military AI that can reshape global security is very likely. Without strict control, states might compete to develop highly efficient AI weapons so as not to be left behind, a scenario that could lead to instability and heightened chances of conflicts (Scharre, 2018; Boulanin & Verbruggen, 2019). Besides, the difference in the availability of AI technology between the rich and the poor could deepen the gap between powerful and weak countries, resulting in the creation of new power imbalances (ICRC, 2019; US DoD, 2022). Such risks associated with geopolitics signify that the employment of generative AI in defence is no longer an issue of national security alone but rather also a matter of global security.

- *AI Arms Race and Global Risks*: With the understanding of AI strength in the military, there is a possibility of a race to an AI armoury all over the globe. If there are no global regulations or treaties, countries may hurry to build and use these systems to prevent them from lagging behind their competitors. Such rivalry could result in going through less comprehensive safety checks or overlooking the issue of morality just to be the first ones (Scharre, 2018; Boulanin & Verbruggen, 2019).

  Suppose a nation was the first to release AI-driven autonomous tanks, then other countries would accelerate their similar projects to not be left behind. They might put these weapons into action even before they have completely figured out the safety and the reliability of the weapons, which would make the danger of accidents or unintended consequences bigger.

- *Lowering the Threshold for Conflict*: One consequence of AI-powered autonomous systems in warfare is that they can make it easier for authorities to decide to initiate a conflict or launch an attack. With fewer troops directly exposed on the frontline, political leaders may perceive the risks as minimal, viewing military action as less costly or dangerous (Boulanin & Verbruggen, 2019; Crootof, 2016; Gray & Ertan, 2021; US DoD, 2022). Consequently, the likelihood of wars breaking out could increase since the use of force appears less hazardous (Article 36, 2016; ICRC, 2019; Scharre, 2018). However, such interventions can escalate political tensions, increasing the possibility that the conflict could intensify.
- *Capability Inequality among Nations*: It is a fact that different countries do not have the same resources to use for the development of sophisticated AI systems. Richer nations are in a position to create more advanced surveillance, weapons, and intelligence instruments, while less affluent countries may find it difficult to attain a similar level (Boulanin & Verbruggen, 2019; Gray & Ertan, 2021). Such a condition leads to differences in the technological capabilities of the armed forces, which may entail the occurrence of unfair advantages, possible abuses, and the domination of areas that are less equipped with behind-the-scenes power in international relations (Crootof, 2016; ICRC, 2019; Scharre, 2018). As a result, the adversaries that are less technologically advanced are substantially at a loss since they are not in a strong position to protect their rights effectively.

1.5 Operational and Reliability Concerns

It is found that even a very sophisticated AI cannot deal with battlefield scenarios that are chaotic and change rapidly (Boulanin & Verbruggen, 2019; Gray & Ertan, 2021; Scharre, 2018). Crootof (2016) along with the ICRC (2019) stated that a minor fault in the system, a failure of the hardware, or wrong understanding of the information can make the AI violate the law of the land in a big way, which constitutes the most serious mistakes. On the other hand, human interactions with AI also have some issues: too much reliance on AI may make soldiers follow a wrong set of instructions whereas doubting it might cause them to disregard correct warnings (Gray & Ertan, 2021; US DoD, 2022). It is a major precondition that AI should be able to function without failure and should be trusted as a security measure before they can be used conventionally in the defence industry.

- *Black Box Decision-Making*: Almost all AI systems are "black boxes", which means that they produce outputs or recommendations without revealing the reasoning behind them. Not even the developers fully understand why the machine makes certain decisions (Boulanin & Verbruggen, 2019; Crawford, 2021; Gray & Ertan, 2021; Crootof, 2016; ICRC, 2021). The absence of transparency is the reason why the use of these tools is limited in the military, where commanders need to trust and verify information before they can make their decisions that could cause the loss of human lives (US DoD, 2022; NATO, 2021). When an AI system designs a plan but is unable to provide an explanation of its logic, the people who make the decisions are in a tricky position: they may decide to follow the suggestion even though they are not sure whether it is supported by the evidence, or they may choose to ignore it and risk missing the opportunity.

- *System Failures in Combat*: In a real war scenario, AI systems could make mistakes if they come across situations that they are not completely equipped for (Boulanin & Verbruggen, 2019; Gray & Ertan, 2021; Scharre, 2018). For example, a system that relies on a malfunctioning sensor, that uses poor quality data, or is affected by violent weather will, in all cases, be led to a wrong interpretation and, therefore, to the execution of wrong operations by the system (Crootof, 2016; ICRC, 2019). In a situation like this, the system technology may be incorrectly performing the mandated task, with the consequence that disaster may be in the offing (US DoD, 2022; NATO, 2021). A machine learning–based air defence system that relies on radar that gives false information may wrongly identify a friendly plane as a hostile fighter. This confusion could lead to the occurrence of firing on friends, i.e., forces are attacked by the enemy and also unintentionally by their own side.
- *Human–Machine Coordination Issues*: One of the main features of AI that can lead to an improvement in military defence is the effective collaboration between human and machines that is a combination of human judgement with the speed and other capabilities of AI (Boulanin & Verbruggen, 2019; Gray & Ertan, 2021; Scharre, 2018). The problem is that soldiers sometimes overestimate or underestimate AI to such an extent that they either follow an AI-guided operation without any validation, or they completely neglect it (Crootof, 2016; ICRC, 2019). The above-mentioned mistakes can happen more often if there is no sufficient training or if clear operational instructions are missing, especially when the situations are changing rapidly and there is chaos in the battlefield. This, in turn, can be used to argue for the necessity of not only trust in AI but also proper training and clear rules for the use of AI in military operations. Table 17.1 summarizes the challenges of generative AI in defence.

Table 17.1 Key Challenges of Generative AI in Defence.

Challenge Area	*Description*	*Example*
Security & Adversarial Threats	AI systems are vulnerable to misuse by hostile states or non-state actors	Terrorists using AI-guided drones
Misinformation & Psychological Warfare	Deepfakes, propaganda, bot campaigns	Fake video of leader surrendering
Surveillance & Privacy	Mass data collection with errors or bias	Facial recognition misidentifies civilians

Contd...

Table 17.1 *Contd...*

Challenge Area	*Description*	*Example*
Strategic & Geopolitical Risks	AI arms race, capability gaps, lowering war threshold	Autonomous weapons race among nations
Operational & Reliability Concerns	Black box decisions, system failures, human–AI mistrust	Friendly fire due to AI misclassification

Source: Key challenges and risks associated with artificial intelligence, synthesized from prior literature on AI security, ethics, and governance (Singer & Brooking, 2018; Scharre, 2018; NATO, 2021; UNESCO, 2021; DoD, 2022).

2. Solutions for Challenges of Generative AI in Defence

To handle security and adversarial threats, defence agencies must develop AI systems that are inherently resistant to hacking and manipulation (US DoD, 2020; Boulanin & Verbruggen, 2019). One step towards this goal is teaching AI systems to identify counterfeit data or attacks (Brundage et al., 2018; Gray & Ertan, 2021); then, by implementing robust encryption, technologists can deter theft and, by maintaining operation "kill switches", allow fast deactivation of AI in case of malfunction (ICRC, 2021; NATO, 2021). Nations must collectively negotiate agreements restricting the use of AI for hostile purposes, like nuclear weapons regulations (Scharre, 2018; UNIDIR, 2021).

The issue of misinformation and psychological warfare may become manageable by creating technologies that can identify and verify deepfakes and fake news before they go viral (Chesney & Citron, 2019; Singer & Brooking, 2018). AI-powered fabricated content should be stamped with covert authentication labels or digital signatures to verify authenticity (UNESCO, 2021; NATO, 2021). A team of experts should be available around the clock to handle false propaganda, and awareness programmes should train soldiers and civilians to detect AI-based manipulation (Wardle & Derakhshan, 2017).

When it comes to surveillance, privacy, and data risks, AI implementation should be accompanied by strict regulations to ensure personal data is not exploited (EPCEU, 2024; Barocas & Selbst, 2016). Defence apparatuses should gather information only for short periods and limited purposes to avoid mass surveillance without consent (Crawford, 2021; US DoD, 2022). Privacy-friendly AI approaches like federated learning and synthetic data can enable training without revealing real individuals (O'Neil, 2016). Continuous inspections should ensure AI is not biased or making unjust assumptions towards certain communities (Crawford, 2021; Barocas & Selbst, 2016).

The best way to prevent AI weapons from targeting us secretly is for countries to collaborate and address strategic and geopolitical risks together (Scharre, 2018; Boulanin & Verbruggen, 2019). International agreements should define where AI can be used and where humans must have full control, especially in life-and-death situations (ICRC, 2021; NATO, 2021). Technology-sharing partnerships can reduce the AI power gap between rich and developing countries, lowering the chances of geopolitical imbalance and sudden conflict escalation (Gray & Ertan, 2021).

To rely on AI with confidence, the technology must undergo testing in extreme, unpredictable military scenarios before real missions (Scharre, 2018; Cummings, 2021). AI should always be supervised by a human; humans must be able to instantly override or stop AI decisions (US DoD, 2022; ICRC, 2019). Clear procedures should define when AI can act autonomously and when it needs human approval (NATO, 2021). If AI failure occurs, then there should be an impartial investigation to determine the cause and ensure that it does not happen again (Gray & Ertan, 2021; Jobin et al., 2019).

3. Ethical Considerations in Generative AI for Defence

Generative AI is a powerful tool for the defence sector, yet its use must always be accompanied by careful ethical considerations. In the armed forces, predictions made by AI systems can directly influence decisions regarding targeting, tactics, and intelligence gathering that may affect human lives (Boulanin & Verbruggen, 2019; Crawford, 2021; Gray & Ertan, 2021). AI should be deployed in a manner that is just, accountable, and respectful of human rights, while complying with international law and the rules of war (ICRC, 2021; UNESCO, 2021; US DoD, 2020). Ethical safeguards ensure that AI systems intended to protect a nation are not misused to harm civilians, spread disinformation, or cause destruction with long-lasting consequences (Chesney & Citron, 2019). They act as a guiding framework, helping military authorities understand not only what AI can do but also what it should do (UNIDIR, 2021; Crootof, 2016). Key ethical issues include bias in AI algorithms, fairness in decision-making, accountability for errors, respect for human dignity, ethical handling of information, minimizing environmental impact, and safe deployment. Figure 17.2 shows the ethical considerations in generative AI for defence.

3.1 Bias, Fairness, and Cultural Sensitivity

Generative AI is very dependent on the data it is given, and if the given data has biased aspects that are not apparent, then the AI will come up with biased decisions (Barocas & Selbst, 2016; Crawford, 2021; O'Neil, 2016). As a result, it could escalate to being negative in a considerable way, leading to some groups, for instance, being targeted unfairly and certain cultural elements being misunderstood and then perceived as threats (Chesney & Citron, 2019). In addition, biased AI-generated content will not only fail to be helpful but may also become a source of misunderstandings, or even offences, which could ultimately damage the relationship with local populations, make military operations difficult, or lead to an increase in the level of hostility in the region. The problem of making AI both fair and culturally aware is beyond a single technological issue and is a moral challenge as well (UNESCO, 2021; US DoD, 2020).

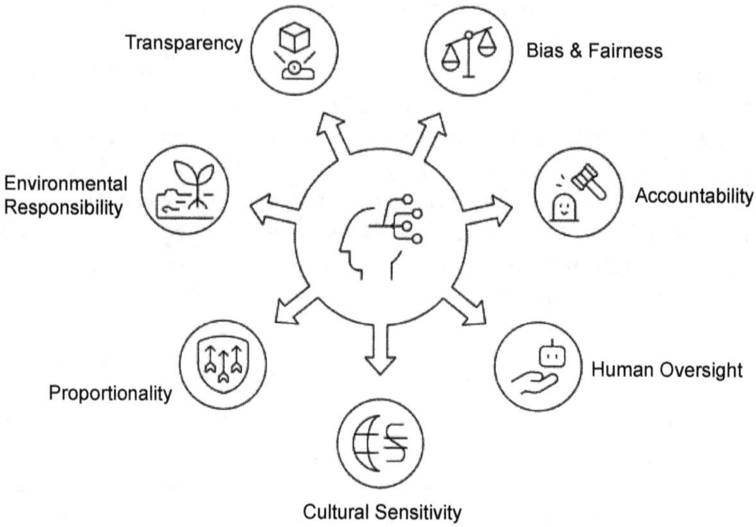

Fig. 17.2 Ethical considerations in generative AI for defence.
Source: Ethical principles of artificial intelligence, adapted from UNESCO (2021), DoD (2020), and EU AI Act (2024), highlighting key dimensions such as transparency, fairness, accountability, human oversight, and sustainability.

- *Bias in AI Outputs*: Generative AI essentially produces patterns based on the data it has been trained on, and if such training data is biased, e.g., certain regions, ethnic groups, or behaviours are overly represented, then the AI will carry those biases to its output (Barocas & Selbst, 2016; Crawford, 2021; O'Neil, 2016). Hence, it may wrongly identify people as suspicious or threatening without any cause. These biases are very dangerous as they have the potential to lead to the inaccurate targeting, discrimination, and harming of innocent communities (Gray & Ertan, 2021; Singer & Brooking, 2018).
  - In a case where a machine learning surveillance system is fed with data heavily representing crowded urban environments of one country, it might perceive normal activities in the countryside of another country as unusual or threatening. Consequently, this can create false alarms, lead to the misuse of resources, and, in certain cases, cause the taking of improper military actions.
- *Fairness in Decision-Making*: AI systems deployed in warfare need to be fair and should not discriminate against any individual on account of nationality, ethnicity, or background (Barocas & Selbst, 2016; Crawford, 2021; O'Neil, 2016). Rules must be enforced equally, and any distinctions in the way people are treated must come from impartial, fact-based logic rather than prejudice or bias (ICRC, 2021; UNESCO, 2021). The consequence of an AI machine intentionally attacking certain groups is that it could hurt the country's image,

result in loss of public trust, and go against international laws (Chesney & Citron, 2019; Gray & Ertan, 2021).

For example, at a border checkpoint, an AI-powered intelligent scanner which is forcibly selecting individuals of certain nationalities for additional searches without a legitimate reason may cause people to be dissatisfied and enraged. People might feel that they are being discriminated against or that they are being treated unfairly, thus making it harder for the relations between the governments to be good, and finally, security in the long run will be getting weaker.

- *Cultural Awareness in AI Content*: AI-generated content for military or psychological operations, such as leaflets, messages, or images, should not violate the culture, traditions, or social values of the local (Crawford, 2021; Gray & Ertan, 2021; UNESCO, 2021). Each community is unique in its customs, symbols, and ways of communication. When AI fails to consider such differences, the resulting communication may be perceived by the locals as offensive, derogatory, or even indifferent (Chesney & Citron, 2019; Singer & Brooking, 2018). This can jeopardize the relationship with the local people; thus, the military will have a hard time winning their trust or support (Boulanin & Verbruggen, 2019).

  Pysops (Psychological Operations: planned operations used by governments, militaries, or organizations to influence the emotions, beliefs, attitudes, and behavior of target groups). The materials could thus, instead of the intended influencing, raise antagonism, disobedience, or even rage against the military forces.

3.2 Legal Accountability and Responsibility

One of the biggest challenges in the environment of war is figuring out which party seriously bears the onus for the wrongs when AI makes a mistake after its incorporation in military decision-making (Crootof, 2016; Gray & Ertan, 2021; Scharre, 2018). Should it be the case of an AI error, for example, wrongly identifying an enemy or giving a false navigation, the issue of blaming developers who built the system, operators who use it, or commanders who authorize its deployment would be so vague (Boulanin & Verbruggen, 2019; ICRC, 2021). The problem with AI is further complicated by the fact that autonomous systems, as they can act faster than humans can intervene, are disrupting the traditional chain of command where decisions are reviewed step by step (Gray & Ertan, 2021; NATO, 2021). However, besides the challenges that hinder operations, there is a legal dimension, as the employment of AI technologies or data developed by the civilian sector without proper military authorization may raise lawsuits or result in international disputes (UNIDIR, 2021; Article 36, 2016). Thus, it is of great importance to lay down appropriate accountability measures to guarantee that AI is used in a safe and lawful manner.

- *Unclear Responsibility for AI Actions*: Whoever is to blame for an AI error during a military operation might not be clear right away (Crootof, 2016; Gray & Ertan, 2021; Scharre, 2018). The term "accountability gap" is used in this case to describe the inconsistency between the location of rights and that of responsibility (Boulanin & Verbruggen, 2019; UNIDIR, 2021). The engineers who wrote the AI might be held responsible if it was their product that malfunctioned, the soldiers who used it might also be considered accountable, or it might even be the commanders who gave their consent for the AI to be used (ICRC, 2021; NATO, 2021).
  For example, in case a missile operated by AI was to strike a non-combatant building unintentionally, one might say that the people responsible for developing the software are to blame, the soldiers might be blamed for carrying out the action, or the commander who approved the attack might be blamed by the one who got hit (Boulanin & Verbruggen, 2019; Scharre, 2018). To respond to these kinds of threats, it is necessary to have clear-cut rules and regulations that not only define the roles but also serve as a guarantee that mistakes will be dealt with in a just manner (US DoD, 2022; UNIDIR, 2021).
- *Chain of Command Disruption*: AI systems can handle an enormous amount of data and they can make a move within a few seconds, which is a capability far beyond that of humans (Boulanin & Verbruggen, 2019; Gray & Ertan, 2021; Scharre, 2018). However, this speed, although it is helpful, can also be dangerous because AI can perform actions before commanders or operators have a full understanding of the situation (Crootof, 2016; ICRC, 2019). In the military with its tightly organized chain of command, these autonomous actions which are outside control could, thus, be considered as going against the decision-making structures and at the same time eroding the issue of accountability, i.e. the capacity to be held accountable.
  Illustratively, a defence mechanism can, on its own, eliminate an unknown aircraft from which it is not receiving any data, but still, without the commander's green light, it can erroneously fire at a friendly or a civilian plane. This, in turn, calls for the establishment of the safeguards that ensure that there are clear demarcations of the AI limits so that unexpected rapid responses do not result in the infliction of harm on innocent people.
- *Intellectual Property Issues*: To function effectively, several military AI systems need data, software, or models that are owned by private companies, universities, or other organizations (Crawford, 2021; Gray & Ertan, 2021; Patterson et al., 2021). These assets have ownership rights associated with them and generally require permits or licences (Strubell et al., 2019; US DoD, 2022). If the military happens to use them without proper authorization—by ignoring permissions, licences, or usage rules—it may face legal action, financial penalties, or limited access.
- When it comes to the international stage, the situation becomes more serious. Unauthorized use of technologies that belong to another country may cause diplomatic disputes, trade restrictions, or political tensions (Boulanin &

Verbruggen, 2019; NATO, 2021). As an example, a defence AI program that takes high-resolution satellite images from a commercial company without consent may be sued for copyright infringement, and if the company is from a foreign country, there may be a cooling of relations between the two countries.

3.3 Human-centric Ethical Dilemmas

Generative AI might make a decision that is morally questionable but logically coherent (Boulanin & Verbruggen, 2019; Gray & Ertan, 2021; Scharre, 2018). For instance, in the military field, such a machine could unintentionally target non-combatants, suggest measures that inflict excessive harm, or prioritize efficiency without considering humanitarian aspects (Crootof, 2016; ICRC, 2019). People are also involved in this equation because soldiers and officers may experience moral distress if AI-assisted decisions lead to harm without justification (UNESCO, 2021; US DoD, 2020). Incorporating the productivity of AI together with human morality is arguably one of the most intricate ethical problems faced in the defence sector.

- *Target Misidentification*: Defence AI systems are designed to gather an enormous volume of data, such as images, sounds, or location changes, and then they decide or suggest actions. Yet, AI is not perfect and might in some instances incorrectly interpret or confuse its data (Crawford, 2021; US DoD, 2022). In a military environment, such errors could lead to the loss of human lives, for instance, if biased, old, or incomplete training data cause algorithms to mistakenly identify civilians, hospitals, or schools as military targets (Barocas & Selbst, 2016; ICRC, 2019). Should AI training data be predominantly focused on specific wars or areas, the machine might take the same patterns everywhere, even in places where there is no danger, just because it is not aware of them (Boulanin & Verbruggen, 2019; EPCEU, 2024).
  As an example, the AI looking for threats may find that a school is transmitting unusual radio signals and because similar signals in the training data were always associated with enemy bases, it falsely classifies the school as a hostile entity. The innocent people living in the area could then become victims of the violence.
- *Proportionality in Use of Force*: The principle of proportionality in international law states that military action should not cause greater harm than the expected advantage, particularly avoiding unnecessary suffering for non-combatants (ICRC, 2019). Defence AI systems, however, are designed mainly for efficiency, often selecting the "best" path based on speed or resource savings without accounting for ethics or humanitarian values (Crootof, 2016; Scharre, 2018). What AI defines as "effective" may be unacceptable from a human perspective, as it cannot fully grasp cultural or humanitarian implications (UNESCO, 2021; Crawford, 2021).
  For example, an AI technology tasked with stopping an enemy fighter might propose an airstrike on the entire district to eliminate the target quickly. While

efficient, this could destroy homes, kill civilians, and cause mass trauma which is disproportionate under international law and morally unacceptable.

- *Moral Injury to Operators*: When soldiers or commanders use AI as a tool during war, they generally assume that it will provide them with the right guidance. However, if the outcome of the decision is the killing of innocent people or the destruction of places that were considered safe, then it can cause them to experience emotional and psychological trauma (Scharre, 2018; US DoD, 2022). This type of trauma, which is called moral injury, refers to an injury of the conscience and the value system caused by the occurrence of a situation wherein a person feels that they have done something against their moral code, even though they may not be entirely responsible (Shay, 2014; Litz et al., 2009). Moral injury can make the members of the personnel community experience guilt, horror, and depression, particularly in situations where the horror was a consequence of the passing of a machine's recommendation and it was then trusted without question (Singer & Brooking, 2018; Crawford, 2021).

  For example, in a case where AI signals that a place is an enemy camp and there is a need to bomb it, but later the place is found to be a school, the commander who gave the go-ahead for the operation might be haunted by the feeling of guilt for a long time even though he did not intend to harm the civilians.

- *Over-Optimization without Ethics*: AI algorithms are structured to be very result-oriented, frequently choosing the quickest or most efficient method to achieve a goal. However, what may look "effective" by the numbers may not necessarily conform to rights or fairness when looked at from a human perspective (Crootof, 2016; Scharre, 2018). As AI has no empathy and merely processes data, it could come up with plans that make sense to a machine but cause human beings to suffer unnecessarily (Crawford, 2021; UNESCO, 2021).

  This is risky in a situation of war wherein the AI could be deciding on a few actions that not only defeat the enemy but also kill innocent people, demolish facilities, or cause prolonged suffering. While humans can weigh efficiency with compassion, AI is incapable of doing that without being overseen (EPCEU, 2024; ICRC, 2019). As an example, a machine learning algorithm may suggest that the cutting of food and medicine provision is a way to weaken the enemy, while it may be totally unaware that such a move would cause starvation of the innocent population, with children and the aged being among them.

3.4 Information Warfare and Disinformation Ethics

Generative AI helps to fabricate believable false information, such as fake papers and realistic deepfakes, more easily than ever before. On the one hand, these instruments could be employed for the purpose of achieving military objectives; on the other hand, their misapplication might result in the disintegration of trust, hurting of reputations, and the emergence of political problems that might last for a long time (Chesney & Citron, 2019; Singer & Brooking, 2018).

Simultaneously, the adversaries can perform a similar thing, i.e., they can utilize the same techniques for your side, thereby lowering your team's morale or causing disorientation (NATO, 2021). The issue of where to set the ethical boundary of the use of AI for deceptive purposes is fundamental to the task of retaining trust over time.

- *Offensive Use of AI-Generated Disinformation*: AI can create various types of fakes, including news articles that look authentic, as well as photos and videos that are almost impossible to distinguish from reality. Such tools may be employed to trick people, confuse adversaries, or convince the public to accept false information, as they hold the power to influence thoughts and behaviours on a large scale (Chesney & Citron, 2019). Yet, the use of AI in this way creates serious problems—lies can spread quickly, public trust can erode, and it becomes increasingly difficult for people to separate truth from deception (Singer & Brooking, 2018; Crawford, 2021). In the context of war, for example, AI could generate a fake video showing enemy leaders calling for surrender. If opposing troops believe this fabricated message and halt their operations, then the deception would directly benefit the creators of the fake content.
- *Defensive Risks from Enemy Disinformation*: AI has the potential to generate various types of fake content without giving away the fact that these are fabricated. AI can write fake news that sounds almost real and create photos and videos that deceive people's eyes. These fakes can be used to trick people, disorient adversaries, or make a lie look like simply a fact already accepted by the public. What makes them dangerous is the fact that they have the potential to change people's opinions and even their behaviour (Chesney & Citron, 2019).

  On the other hand, such use of AI technology is problematic on a large scale. Lies get viral at a lightning speed, the trust people have in each other is adversely affected, and people have more difficulties in distinguishing between truth and lies.
- *Establishing Ethical Boundaries*: Governments should introduce strict regulations defining when AI-generated disinformation may be used, especially in war, and how it should be implemented. Without such limits, false content could spiral out of control, causing distrust in truth-telling institutions, damaging diplomacy, and harming a state's reputation (Crootof, 2016; NATO, 2021). Clear rules would help ensure that AI use remains controlled and avoids unnecessary harm. These could even become part of military codes, alliances, or global treaties (ICRC, 2019; Scharre, 2018).

3.5 Environmental Responsibility

One of the factors that contribute significantly to the environmental impact of AI is the hefty amount of energy that goes into building and managing large AI models. The energy largely used in the process of AI projects is the "hidden cost" of the defence sector, particularly when the same models are being retrained or used for large-scale simulations (Strubell et al., 2019; Hao, 2019). Practising energy efficiency and investing in renewable-powered infrastructures are steps that a company can take in order to decrease the environmental footprint while still enjoying AI's advantages (Vinuesa et al., 2020). Sustainability in AI is not only for safeguarding the earth but also for keeping the transition of military technology accountable in all aspects (UNESCO, 2021; Crawford, 2021).

- *High Energy Consumption of AI Models*: Conventional or large-scale generative AI systems and their offshoots can produce lifelike text, images, or simulations from any domain and usually need very powerful computing hardware. The training, as a rule, is done on hefty machines which keep running for several days or weeks, consuming a lot of power, which in turn raises the expenses together with the carbon emissions—the major cause of global warming (Strubell et al., 2019; Patterson et al., 2021; Henderson et al., 2020).
  The carbon emissions related to heavy training of such models are not the only reason for concern. The energy consumption due to the deployment of such power-hungry models in situations requiring heavy and frequent use, for example, live predictions or battlefield simulations, is raising the long-term footprint. To give an example, it is stated that the electricity used during the training of one AI model with a focus on war scenarios equals that of thousands of homes in a year, and the regular military simulations might further push the demand and emissions (Hao, 2019; UNESCO, 2021).
- *Sustainable AI Practices*: Military organizations may reduce the environmental harm caused by AI through the implementation of energy-saving measures, such as exploring methods of using less electricity while still maintaining efficiency (Patterson et al., 2021; Schwartz et al., 2020). A significant way is to produce more efficient AI algorithms that require less computing power for the same task (Strubell et al., 2019; Henderson et al., 2020). Besides that, data centres can get their power from clean energy sources like solar, wind, or hydropower instead of fossil fuels (UNESCO, 2021; Vinuesa et al., 2020). Besides that, the military can cut down on the use of resources if they only deploy the models that are necessary for the task at hand and not run the redundant ones (Crawford, 2021).
  Likewise, they could decide on smaller and more efficient AI models that provide results similar to those provided by large, power-consuming models. This would conserve energy and lower the budget and carbon emissions; thus, no compromise would be made on the performance.

3.6 Best Practices for Ethical Deployment

The moral use of generative AI in the military, first and foremost, is to prevent damage to society and the environment (Cummings, 2021; Brundage et al., 2020). Moreover, it implies the implementation of systems that are open for inspection, unbiased, and have a clear link to those held responsible (Floridi & Cowls, 2019; Jobin et al., 2019). Such an approach includes humans in the decision-making process, efforts to make AI decisions understandable, rigorous testing of the systems before their use, and collaboration with other countries in setting common rules (Winfield et al., 2021; Scharre, 2018). It is possible that by adhering to the best practices, the armed forces will be able to employ the advantages of AI technology while the dangers to people's lives, public confidence, and international stability will be reduced to the minimum level (Cath, 2018). Figure 17.3 summarizes the entire ethical governance framework.

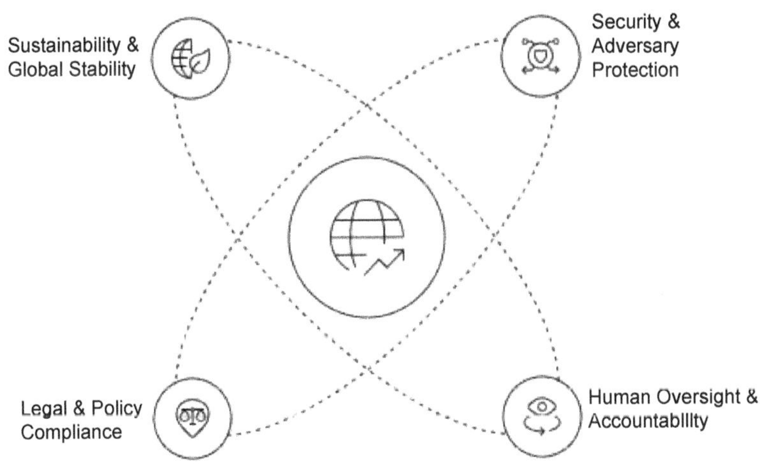

Fig. 17.3 Generative AI ethical governance framework.
Source: Generative AI ethical governance framework, synthesized from international AI ethics guidelines and policy frameworks including UNESCO (2021), EU AI Act (2024), DoD Responsible AI Strategy (2022), and NATO AI Strategy (2021).

- *Human Oversight in Critical Decisions*: By working fast and with accuracy, AI can be very useful in the army (Scharre, 2018; Horowitz, 2019). Still, if there are situations of life and death, it must be a human who takes the last responsibility, not AI (Cummings, 2021; Winfield et al., 2021). The role of AI is to give the data, the alerts, and the choices, but it should not decide on its own without the human saying yes (Roff, 2019).

  Artificial intelligence can misinterpret a situation or make a mistake (Jobin et al., 2019). The consequences of the mistake can be very severe if it happens

at a critical moment, especially since political, ethical, or human dimensions are beyond AI's understanding (Cath, 2018; Brundage et al., 2020). Human judgement is needed to solve these problems.
As an example, an AI radar system detecting the launch of a missile aimed at an enemy should inform the commander, who through other means can verify the fire and decide on the interception. AI here is used to make the detection faster, but the final decision is still with humans.

- *Transparency and Explainability*: It has been argued that AI systems should not be such that they operate in a "black box" manner, where nobody understands how decisions are made (Burrell, 2016; Doshi-Velez & Kim, 2017). Trust being a vital element in the military, it calls for the AI to give clear explanations of its reasoning (Cummings, 2021; Floridi & Cowls, 2019). This is done to assure human beings that they can verify whether the AI's advice is indeed based on sound data.
When examples of reasoning are provided, humans are able to confirm AI outputs, notice faults, and decide wisely (Miller, 2019; Mittelstadt et al., 2016). On the other hand, the absence of openness may lead people to follow AI commands without question, which might lead to devastating consequences (Rahwan, 2018).
For instance, if AI recommends a military strike, then it should also offer the evidence, like satellite pictures, radar data, or intercepted communications, so that commanders can verify the correctness before taking the action.
- *Robust Testing and Red-Teaming*: Real-life military missions incorporating AI are typically subjected to amazing stringent tests before they are allowed to proceed (Scharre, 2018; Brundage et al., 2020). This is essentially the AI introduced into scenarios that are close to the most challenging anticipated situations, and this includes unpredicted issues and complicated scenarios.
One significant method is "red-teaming", where a team of experts pretends to be the adversary and looks for weaknesses in the AI. The objective is to monitor the system response to the most rigorous test and then uncover any possible defects before it gets deployed in the field. Testers could simulate a cyberattack on an AI-powered targeting system to see if it can be tricked by fake signals. If they find that the AI can be tricked, then the engineers can solve the problem before the system is used on the mission, thus avoiding the occurrence of accidents that can be dangerous (Galliott, 2021).
- *International Cooperation and Treaties*: To get going effectively, countries should work together to establish definable international principles on the way AI can be deployed in military conflicts (Boulanin & Verbruggen, 2017; Scharre, 2018). If such agreements are absent, then the chances of nations misusing AI in dangerous ways are high, which may result in misunderstandings, accidental attacks, or escalation of conflict. Joint efforts ensure that countries operate according to the same standards, so no nation gains a secret or reckless advantage from unsafe AI use (Altmann & Sauer, 2017). These laws can be part of international treaties, just like existing agreements for nuclear or

chemical weapons (Docherty, 2012). Such regulations would guarantee that life and death decisions remain in human hands, reducing the likelihood of accidental or uncontrolled violence.

4. Path Forward for Responsible Generative AI in Defence

One of the most significant changes in how the defence sector works is the introduction of generative AI. For instance, such a mmachine can process large amounts of data, creating realistic simulations, and even helping the decision-making leaders by giving them more options in less time (Cummings, 2021; Horowitz, 2019). Unquestionably, it is an excellent method of security enhancement. But the same technology could be utilized for the purpose of starting wars that extend beyond escalation. Therefore, the main challenge is not just the focus on AI, but rather the assurance of its correct and decent usage. This means the setting up of strict regulations, having ethical safeguards, and encouraging interaction and common understanding among nations. In fact, generative AI as a tool of responsible innovation can contribute to saving lives, protecting human rights, and fostering sustained global peace (Roff, 2019; Human Rights Watch, 2020).

4.1 Strong Policies and Human Control

Rules are like guardrails on a highway that help the use of AI in defence to be ethically compliant. Guidelines of this sort must highlight the areas where AI is allowed to function, how it ought to operate, and the places where it is absolutely forbidden (Altmann & Sauer, 2017; UNIDIR, 2021). These rules should not simply be the outcome of deliberations among national defence authorities, but they also ought to be recognized worldwide so that all the countries have the same standards (Boulanin & Verbruggen, 2017).

AI, even when it is the most advanced, should not be allowed to decide the fate of human life. The authority of making such decisions should rest with the personnel who are well trained and capable of making judgements (Cummings, 2021). AI may give a helping hand, offer a choice, or make a prediction, but after that, the humans are the ones who must decide. The role of a human supervisor is still very important to be a safety measure against a dire error when AI wrongly evaluates a circumstance.

4.2 Ethical and Safe AI Design

Artificial intelligence must be constructed with the features of safety and justice as the primary attributes and not as some add-on characteristic (Winfield & Jirotka, 2018). The starting point for this is the data that the system will learn from. This data should be validated to make sure that it does not contain any prejudices that will lead the AI to unfairly treat or ignore those groups which have been less represented in the data (Mehrabi et al., 2021). Equally important is a sound security setup. The system should be granted well-fortified protection against the attacks of intruders who might try to take control over it or engage it in evil activities (Brundage et al., 2018). Just as people require regular health check-ups, AI also requires regular testing and audits. These exercises serve not only to identify the problems early but also to repair the problems that have been caused by the system and confirm that the system is functioning as expected (Jobin et al., 2019).

4.3 Collaboration and Transparency

Generative AI in defence is not only a matter of local concern, but it is also something that affects the safety of the entire world. That is the reason why no country should develop or use it entirely and secretly (Cummings, 2021). By sharing knowledge and agreeing upon common safety standards, not only can nations avoid mistrust, but also lower the risk of an AI arms race, where the countries compete to build the most powerful systems without considering the consequences (Brundage et al., 2018). Such agreements may even facilitate the imposition of restrictions regarding the use of AI, in particular those that may cause harm to the innocent (UNESCO, 2021). Transparency is a big factor as well. Some military secrets, of course, must be kept for security reasons. However, being open about safety regulations, methods of testing, and oversight systems can lead to the establishment of trust—both between the public and the authorities and among the various countries (Altmann & Sauer, 2017). Table 17.2 shows how challenges link to solutions.

Table 17.2 Challenges versus Ethical Mitigations.

Challenge	*Ethical Safeguard*
AI misuse by adversaries	Strong security, international treaties
Deepfakes & misinformation	Clear ethical boundaries, rapid verification protocols
Surveillance overreach	Data accuracy checks, privacy protections
Arms race & inequality	Global cooperation, responsible innovation
System unreliability	Human oversight, robust testing, red-teaming
Accountability gap	Defined legal responsibility & chain of command
Environmental impact	Energy-efficient models, renewable data centres

Source: Challenges of artificial intelligence and corresponding ethical mitigation strategies, synthesized from global AI governance frameworks including UNESCO (2021), NATO (2021), DoD (2022), and EU AI Act (2024).

5. Emerging Directions and Strategic Preparedness

Generative AI in defence is still new; however, it is advancing very quickly. New possibilities are emerging every year; for example, more precise threat detection, AI tools that can facilitate the planning of complex missions, and systems that can accept information at a much faster rate than humans (Horowitz, 2019; Payne, 2021). These innovations might have changed the way defence operations worked.

However, the benefits are accompanied with serious risks as well. For instance, AI might allow attackers to carry out quicker and more powerful cyberattacks. It might become easier to distribute false information, or AI might act in unexpected ways that cannot be easily controlled (Brundage et al., 2018; Cummings, 2021). This is the reason why strategic preparedness— being prepared for both dangers and opportunities—is very important.

Defence agencies need future-oriented policies, ongoing research and creativity, and the ability to adjust quickly with the change of technology to get this result. By preparing today, they can therefore be able to prevent threats from emerging, secure the country, and avoid dangerous surprises in the future (Boulanin & Verbruggen, 2017).

5.1 Anticipating Future Capabilities

Generative AI is getting better at a rapid pace, and tools considered cutting-edge today may become old-fashioned within months. Being strategically ready means forecasting where the technology will be by analysing research papers, monitoring industry progress, and observing changes in global defence (Horowitz, 2019; Scharre, 2018). Soon, AI might scan and process massive satellite or sensor data within seconds, giving defence forces early alerts of unusual activities. It may also produce intricate and real battle simulations, allowing commanders to test tactics without risking human lives (Payne, 2021). Additionally, AI can fully control logistics, manage supply movements, and predict equipment failures before they occur (Boulanin & Verbruggen, 2017).

5.2 Building Rapid Response Systems

Even the most perfectly constructed AI system can encounter issues such as software bugs, data errors, hacking attempts, or weird behaviour from its complex decision-making process. If these problems are not dealt with promptly, the consequences may be severe. That is why having a rapid response system is essential (Cummings, 2021). A good rapid response system keeps the AI under constant surveillance, so any odd behaviour is detected without delay. If the AI starts giving wrong instructions or acting unexpectedly, there must be clearly defined emergency steps for halting the operation or switching it off without causing harm (Boulanin & Verbruggen, 2017). Fast communication is equally essential. As soon as trouble arises, the military teams, AI engineers, and policy leaders must work together without delay, with predetermined channels, roles, and responsibilities ensuring no misunderstanding.

5.3 Continuous Training and International Readiness

Technology is only as strong as the people managing it. This refers to AI in the defence sector where it means very frequent and regular training so the personnel can use the systems with confidence and are able to handle the fast changes in technology. The training must be practical work with the most recent AI tools, lifelike exercises that simulate possible emergency situations, and learning not only for AI capabilities but also for the threats it could bring (Horowitz, 2019; Scharre, 2019). However, the readiness must not stop at the national borders. Most AI-related threats, such as hacking, the dissemination of false information, or the use of advanced surveillance, can lead to multiple countries being affected simultaneously. Hence, international cooperation is vital. Besides building alliances, joining global working groups is another way countries can share the most important intelligence, agree on common safety rules, and react more quickly and efficiently to global AI challenges (Boulanin et al., 2020; Cummings, 2021).

6. Conclusion

The modern defence landscape is being redefined by generative AI by enabling rapid decision-making, intelligent simulations, enhanced surveillance, and advanced threat detection. This transformative power comes with equally significant risks that include adversarial misuse, misinformation, privacy violations, operational failures, and geopolitical instability. The dual-use nature of these systems has made it essential to establish strong ethical frameworks, certain international regulations, and human-in-the-loop oversight to prevent any unintended harm. It is essential and critical to ensure transparency, accountability, and adherence to humanitarian principles as nations integrate AI into security operations. Ultimately, responsible governance and global cooperation are important to utilize generative AI's benefits while safeguarding human dignity, stability, and long-term peace.

References

Altmann, J. and Sauer, F. (2017). Autonomous weapon systems and strategic stability. Survival: Global Politics and Strategy, 59(5), 117–142. https://doi.org/10.1080/00396338.2017.1375263 . https://www.tandfonline.com/doi/full/10.1080/00396338.2017.1375263. Last accessed on 08 April, 2026.

Article 36. (2016). Key areas for debate on autonomous weapons systems. Available at https://article36.org. Last accessed on 08 April, 2026.

Barocas, S. and Selbst, A. D. (2016). Big data's disparate impact. *California Law Review*, 104(3), 671–732. https://papers.ssrn.com/sol3/papers.cfm?abstract_id=2477899&download=yes. Last accessed on 08 April, 2026.

Boulanin, V., Saalman, L., Topychkanov, P., Su, F. and Peldán Carlsson, M. (2020). Artificial intelligence, strategic stability and nuclear risk (Stockholm International Peace Research Institute Report). Stockholm International Peace Research Institute. https://www.sipri.org/sites/default/files/2020-06/artificial_intelligence_strategic_stability_and_nuclear_risk.pdf. Last accessed on 08 April, 2026.

Boulanin, V. and Verbruggen, M. (2019). *Mapping the development of autonomy in weapon systems*. Stockholm International Peace Research Institute.

Brundage, M., Avin, S., Clark, J., Toner, H., Eckersley, P., Garfinkel, B., Dafoe, A., Scharre, P., Zeitzoff, T., Filar, B., Anderson, H., Roff, H., Allen, G.C., Steinhardt, J., Flynn, C., Ó hÉigeartaigh, S., Beard, S.J., Belfield, H. and Amodei, D. (2018). The malicious use of artificial intelligence: Forecasting, prevention, and mitigation (arXiv:1802.07228). https://arxiv.org/pdf/1802.07228.pdf". Last accessed on 08 April, 2026.

Brundage, M., Avin, S., Wang, J., Belfield, H., Krueger, G., Hadfield, G., Khlaaf, H., Yang, J., Toner, H., Fong, R., Maharaj, T., Koh, P.W., Hooker, S., Leung, J., Trask, A., Bluemke, E., Lebensold, J., O'Keefe, C., Koren, M. and Anderljung, M. (2020). Toward trustworthy AI development: Mechanisms for supporting verifiable claims. arXiv. https://arxiv.org/pdf/2004.07213.pdf. Last accessed on 08 April, 2026.

Burrell, J. (2016). How the machine "thinks": Understanding opacity in machine learning algorithms. Big Data & Society, 3(1), 205395171562251. https://doi.org/10.1177/2053951715622512. https://journals.sagepub.com/doi/10.1177/2053951715622512. Last accessed on 08 April, 2026.

Cath, C. (2018). Governing artificial intelligence: Ethical, legal and technical opportunities and challenges. Philosophical Transactions of the Royal Society A: Mathematical, Physical and Engineering Sciences, 376(2133), 20180080. https://doi.org/10.1098/rsta.2018.0080. Last accessed on 08 April, 2026.

Chesney, R. and Citron, D. K. (2019). Deep fakes: A looming challenge for privacy, democracy, and national security. *California Law Review*, 107(6), 1753–1819. https://papers.ssrn.com/sol3/Delivery.cfm/SSRN_ID3505043_code119080.pdf?abstractid=3213954&mirid=1. Last accessed on 08 April, 2026.

Congressional Research Service. (2020). Artificial intelligence and national security (R45178). Available at https://crsreports.congress.gov. Last accessed on 08 April, 2026.

Crawford, K. (2021). *Atlas of AI: Power, politics, and the planetary costs of artificial intelligence*. Yale University Press.

Crootof, R. (2016). The killer robots are here: Legal and policy implications. *Cardozo Law Review*, 36(6), 1837–1915. https://www.cardozolawreview.com/wp-content/uploads/2018/08/CROOTOF.36.5.pdf. Last accessed on 08 April, 2026.

Cummings, M. L. (2021). Rethinking the maturity of artificial intelligence in safety-critical settings. AI Magazine, 42(1), 6–15. DOI:10.1002/j.2371-9621.2021.tb00005.x. https://ojs.aaai.org/aimagazine/index.php/aimagazine/article/view/7394. Last accessed on 08 April, 2026.

Docherty, B. (2012). Losing humanity: The case against killer robots. Human Rights Watch. https://www.hrw.org/report/2012/11/19/losing-humanity/case-against-killer-robots. Last accessed on 08 April, 2026.

Doshi-Velez, F. and Kim, B. (2017). Towards a rigorous science of interpretable machine learning (arXiv:1702.08608). arXiv. https://arxiv.org/pdf/1702.08608.pdf. Last accessed on 08 April, 2026.

European Parliament and Council of the European Union (EPCEU). (2024). Artificial Intelligence Act (Regulation (EU) 2024/1689). Official Journal of the European Union. Available at https://eur-lex.europa.eu/eli/reg/2024/1689/oj. 8. https://eur-lex.europa.eu/legal-content/EN/TXT/PDF/?uri=CELEX:32024R1689&from=EN. Last accessed on 08 April, 2026.

Floridi, L. and Cowls, J. (2019). A unified framework of five principles for AI in society. Harvard Data Science Review, 1(1). https://hdsr.mitpress.mit.edu/pub/l0jsh9d1. Last accessed on 08 April, 2026.

Galliott, J. (2021). Toward a positive statement of ethical principles for military AI. In J. Galliott, D. MacIntosh, & J. D. Ohlin (Eds.), Lethal autonomous weapons: Re-examining the law and ethics of robotic warfare (pp. 121–136). Oxford University Press. https://doi.org/10.1093/oso/9780197546048.003.0009. Last accessed on 08 April, 2026.

Gray, M. and Ertan, A. (2021). Artificial intelligence and autonomy in the military: An overview of NATO member states' strategies and deployment. NATO CCDCOE. Available at https://ccdcoe.org. 9. https://web.archive.org/web/20220921174418/https://ccdcoe.org/uploads/2021/12/Strategies_and_Deployment_A4.pdf. Last accessed on 08 April, 2026.

Hao, K. (2019). The future of AI research is in Africa. MIT Technology Review (blog). https://www.researchdatashare.org/sites/default/files/artifacts/media/pdf/www-technologyreview-com-2019-06-21-134820-ai-africa-machine-learning-ibm-google-.pdf". Last accessed on 08 April, 2026.

Henderson, P., Hu, J., Romoff, J., Brunskill, E., Jurafsky, D. and Pineau, J. (2020). Towards the systematic reporting of the energy and carbon footprints of machine learning. Journal of Machine

Learning Research, 21(248), 1–43. https://jmlr.org/papers/volume21/20-312/20-312.pdf. Last accessed on 08 April, 2026.

Horowitz, M.C. (2019). When speed kills: Autonomous weapon systems, deterrence, and stability. Journal of Strategic Studies, 42(6), 764–788. https://doi.org/10.1080/01402390.2019.1621174. https://papers.ssrn.com/sol3/papers.cfm?abstract_id=3348356&download=yes. Last accessed on 08 April, 2026.

Human Rights Watch. (2020). World report 2020. Human Rights Watch. https://www.hrw.org/world-report/2020. https://www.hrw.org/sites/default/files/world_report_download/hrw_world_report_2020_0.pdf. Last accessed on 08 April, 2026.

International Committee of the Red Cross (ICRC). (2019). Artificial intelligence and machine learning in armed conflict: A human-centered approach. Available at https://www.icrc.org. https://www.icrc.org/en/download/file/96992/ai_and_machine_learning_in_armed_conflict-icrc.pdf. Last accessed on 08 April, 2026.

International Committee of the Red Cross (ICRC). (2021). ICRC position on autonomous weapon systems and human control. Available at https://www.icrc.org. https://www.icrc.org/en/download/file/166327/icrc_position_on_autonomous_weapon_systems.pdf. Last accessed on 08 April, 2026.

Jobin, A., Ienca, M., and Vayena, E. (2019). The global landscape of AI ethics guidelines. Nature Machine Intelligence, 1(9), 389–399. https://doi.org/10.1038/s42256-019-0088-2. https://arxiv.org/pdf/1906.11668.pdf. Last accessed on 08 April, 2026.

Liivoja, R. and Väljataga, A. (eds). (2021). *Autonomous cyber capabilities under international law*. NATO CCDCOE Publications. https://ccdcoe.org/uploads/2021/05/Autonomous-Cyber-Capabilities-under-International-Law.pdf. Last accessed on 08 April, 2026.

Litz, B.T., Stein, N., Delaney, E., Lebowitz, L., Nash, W.P., Silva, C. and Maguen, S. (2009). Moral injury and moral repair in war veterans: A preliminary model and intervention strategy. Clinical Psychology Review, 29(8), 695–706. https://doi.org/10.1016/j.cpr.2009.07.003. https://www.penncerl.org/wp-content/uploads/2022/01/4603-moral-injury-and-moral-repair-in-war-vets-litz-et.pdf". Last accessed on 08 April, 2026.

Mehrabi, N., Morstatter, F., Saxena, N., Lerman, K. and Galstyan, A. (2021). A survey on bias and fairness in machine learning. ACM Computing Surveys, 54(6), Article 115, 1–35. https://doi.org/10.1145/3457607. https://arxiv.org/pdf/1908.09635.pdf. Last accessed on 08 April, 2026.

Miller, T. (2019). Explanation in artificial intelligence: Insights from the social sciences. Artificial Intelligence, 267, 1–38. https://doi.org/10.1016/j.artint.2018.07.007. https://www.sciencedirect.com/science/article/pii/S0004370218305988. Last accessed on 08 April, 2026.

Mittelstadt, B. D., Allo, P., Taddeo, M., Wachter, S., & Floridi, L. (2016). The ethics of algorithms: Mapping the debate. Big Data & Society, 3(2), 2053951716679679. https://doi.org/10.1177/2053951716679679. https://journals.sagepub.com/doi/full/10.1177/2053951716679679. Last accessed on 08 April, 2026.

National Security Commission on Artificial Intelligence (NSCAI). (2021). Final report. Available at https://www.nscai.gov. Last accessed on 08 April, 2026.

North Atlantic Treaty Organization (NATO). (2021). NATO's artificial intelligence strategy. Available at https://www.nato.int. https://operationnels.com/wp-content/uploads/2021/10/NATO-Summary-of-the-NATO-Artificial-Intelligence-Strategy-22-Oct.-2021.pdf. Last accessed on 08 April, 2026.

O'Neil, C. (2016). *Weapons of math destruction: How big data increases inequality and threatens democracy*. Crown. Last accessed on 08 April, 2026.

Patterson, D., Gonzalez, J., Le, Q. et al. (2021). Carbon emissions and large neural networks. arXiv. Available at https://arxiv.org/abs/2104.10350. https://www.kathimerini.gr/wp-content/uploads/2024/07/2104-10350_1.pdf. Last accessed on 08 April, 2026.

Rahwan, I. (2018). Society-in-the-loop: Programming the algorithmic social contract. Ethics and Information Technology, 20(1), 5–14. https://doi.org/10.1007/s10676-017-9430-8. https://link.springer.com/article/10.1007/s10676-017-9430-8. Last accessed on 08 April, 2026.

Scharre, P. (2018). *Army of none: Autonomous weapons and the future of war*. W. W. Norton.

Scharre, P. (2019). Killer apps: The real dangers of an AI arms race. Foreign Affairs, 98(3), 135–144. https://cset.georgetown.edu/wp-content/uploads/CSET-AI-Safety-Security-and-Stability-Among-the-Great-Powers.pdf. Last accessed on 08 April, 2026.

Shay, J. (2014). Moral injury. Psychoanalytic Psychology, 31(2), 182–191. https://doi.org/10.1037/a0036090. https://www.penncerl.org/wp-content/uploads/2022/01/4602-moralinjuryshayexcerptpdf.pdf". Last accessed on 08 April, 2026.

Singer, P.W. and Brooking, E. T. (2018). *LikeWar: The weaponization of social media*. Houghton Mifflin Harcourt. Last accessed on 08 April, 2026.

Strubell, E., Ganesh, A. and McCallum, A. (2019). Energy and policy considerations for deep learning in NLP. In *Proceedings of ACL 2019* (pp. 3645–3650). https://aclanthology.org/P19-1355.pdf. Last accessed on 08 April, 2026.

United Nations Educational, Scientific and Cultural Organization (UNESCO). (2021). Recommendation on the Ethics of Artificial Intelligence. Available at https://www.unesco.org. https://digitallibrary.un.org/record/4062376?v=pdf. Last accessed on 08 April, 2026.

United Nations Institute for Disarmament Research (UNIDIR). (2021). *The weaponization of increasingly autonomous technologies: Considerations for meaningful human control*. UNIDIR. Available at https://unidir.org. https://www.stopkillerrobots.org/wp-content/uploads/2014/11/considering-how-meaningful-human-control-might-move-the-discussion-forward-en-615.pdf. Last accessed on 08 April, 2026.

US Department of Defense (DoD). (2020). Ethical principles for artificial intelligence. Available at https://www.ai.mil. https://www.ai.mil/docs/Ethical_Principles_for_Artificial_Intelligence.pdf. Last accessed on 08 April, 2026.

US Department of Defense (DoD). (2022). Responsible Artificial Intelligence Strategy and Implementation Pathway. Available at https://www.ai.mil. https://www.ai.mil/Portals/137/Documents/Resources%20Page/DoD%20Responsible%20AI%20Strategy%20and%20Implementation%20Pathway.pdf. Last accessed on 08 April, 2026.

Verbruggen, M. and Boulanin, V. (2017). Mapping the development of autonomy in weapon systems. Stockholm International Peace Research Institute (SIPRI). https://www.sipri.org/sites/default/files/2017-11/siprireport_mapping_the_development_of_autonomy_in_weapon_systems_1117_0.pdf. Last accessed on 08 April, 2026.

Vinuesa, R., et al. (2020). The role of artificial intelligence in achieving the Sustainable Development Goals. Nature Communications, 11, Article 233. https://www.nature.com/articles/s41467-019-14108-y". Last accessed on 08 April, 2026.

Wardle, C. and Derakhshan, H. (2017). Information disorder: Toward an interdisciplinary framework for research and policy making (Council of Europe Report No. DGI(2017)09). Council of Europe. https://rm.coe.int/information-disorder-report-november-2017/1680764666. Last accessed on 08 April, 2026.

Winfield, A.F.T., Booth, S., Dennis, L.A., Egawa, T., Hastie, H., Jacobs, N., Muttram, R., Olszewska, J.I., Rajabiyazdi, F., Theodorou, A., Underwood, M.A., Wortham, R.H. and Watson, E. (2021). IEEE P7001: A proposed standard on transparency. Frontiers in Robotics and AI, 8, Article 665729. https://doi.org/10.3389/frobt.2021.665729. https://www.frontiersin.org/articles/10.3389/frobt.2021.665729/full. Last accessed on 08 April, 2026.

Winfield, A.F.T. and Jirotka, M. (2018). Ethical governance is essential to building trust in robotics and artificial intelligence systems. Philosophical Transactions of the Royal Society A: Mathematical, Physical and Engineering Sciences, 376(2133), 20180085. https://doi.org/10.1098/rsta.2018.0085. https://redi.anii.org.uy/jspui/bitstream/20.500.12381/443/1/20180085.full.pdf. Last accessed on 08 April, 2026.

18 Threats of Generative AI in Cognitive Warfare

Shillpi Mishrra[1*], Sauvik Bal[2] and Debasis Chaudhuri[3]

Cognitive warfare is a new kind of conflict that involves influencing what people think and feel. This does not refer to any kind of attack on either buildings or weapons; this is an assault on the mind. Thus, it is gaining further strength in light of emerging generative artificial intelligence (AI), which is able to create messages, videos, and images indistinguishable from reality. These can shape beliefs, decision-making, and trust. AI manipulates language, culture, and emotions to spread disguised misinformation. This manipulation undermines trust in government, the military, and institutions, and creates fear, anger, and internal conflict within a country. Assaults take the form of information overload, confusion, and mixed messaging as tactics to stop clear thinking and drive people to feel uncertain and make wrong choices. In particular, this could lead to grave situations for defence and military operations, where every little mistake may affect the performance of the mission. This chapter illustrates the way these threats affect air, sea, and space operations; provides examples of how AI can alter the mental states of decision-makers; and also suggests ways to protect minds, restore confidence, and integrate cognitive security into military planning.

1. Introduction

Generative artificial intelligence (AI) is changing the future of information warfare. Wars used to be fought with bombs and bullets. Today, a different kind of war is rapidly emerging: cognitive warfare. It is a form of warfare that does not harm the body but aims at influencing the human mind. The goal is to change what people believe, think, and feel in order to control decisions without their awareness. Modern AI systems are able to generate messages that seem real and valid, including fake videos, fake voices, fake news articles, and even completely fictitious online personas. Large language models and deepfakes learn how people speak, mimic cultural behaviours, and imitate emotional styles, which make information appear credible (Deppe & Schaal, 2024; Gambín et al., 2024). This is what makes cognitive attacks dangerous and hard to detect. Generative AI can also monitor online reactions. First, it analyses what people click on, what they read,

[1] https://orcid.org/0009-0007-5509-5595
[2] https://orcid.org/0000-0001-5569-1855
[3] https://orcid.org/0000-0002-6895-456X
* Corresponding author: shllpimishrra91@gmail.com

DOI: 10.1201/9781003688174-18

and how they make decisions. After that the messages are adjusted according to people's thinking and it tries to provoke the people. This real-time manipulation aims to push individuals towards incorrect beliefs or actions. Attackers have at their disposal several tactics (Lahmann et al., 2025; Fihri et al., 2019). One tactic is to flood social media with too much information to overwhelm users. Another tactic is to tell contradictory stories of the same event in order to make people lose track of truth and lies. When truth starts to blur, decision-making weakens. And this is quite dangerous in a defence and military environment (Shashank & Patil, 2025; Hoadley et al., 2018). A bad decision on a mission may lead to defeat, failure, or escalation. Imposter accounts and bot networks increase this problem by impersonating real users while amplifying fake messages and attacking accurate information. Such activities can sway public opinion, incite anger and fear, and erode trust in leaders and defence systems. If people's mental resilience declines, national security becomes more vulnerable. This chapter explains how generative AI creates cognitive threats in air, sea, and space defence. It gives examples where AI can mislead a pilot, a ship commander, or a satellite operator (Fenstermacher et al., 2023). Even a small confusion can spread across connected systems. The chapter finally discusses protection. Minds must be defended just like borders. We need awareness training, ethical rules, and strong safety checks for information. We must build cognitive strength in both civilians and military teams. Cognitive security is now a key part of national defence.

2. Early Works

Researchers have explored the ways in which AI can be used to cause harm. Brundage et al. were among the first to issue a warning regarding the dual-use nature of AI, with the key observation that the same technology helping people can also be used to manipulate them (Brundage et al., 2018). They described how AI can scale psychological attacks with unprecedented speed, producing a high volume of fake content in a very short time frame and creating new perils in information spaces. Chesney and Citron described the "liar's dividend", whereby deepfakes need not be perfect to cause their harm: the general awareness of fake videos can engender doubt about the veracity of real videos, too, undermining confidence in news, court evidence, and information in the public domain (Chesney & Citron, 2019). Wrongdoers may therefore escape blame by claiming true content was fake, increasing the harm: deepfakes spread lies and undermine trust in truthful information. Indeed, many international security groups are focusing on the threat today. NATO's Strategic Communications team took a deep dive into how disinformation spreads itself online (Brundage et al., 2018; Chesney & Citron, 2019; Hwang, 2020). They found that fake stories gained traction when they felt emotively resonant. AI will help craft messages that reflect the beliefs and emotions of different groups, which in effect makes lies much harder to detect while being easier to believe. Center for Security and Emerging Technology (CSET) warned that deepfakes can be very dangerous when part of a broader influence campaign. The issue is much more than the quality of the fake videos. In fact, the real power has to do with using deepfakes at times of elections, protests, and conflicts. With perfect timing, one fake message can influence a country's response to a crisis. The central idea of cognitive warfare, as underlined by NATO's Innovation Hub, is that a new frontier of war has turned the human mind into a battlefield. If an enemy can get an idea about a person's thinking, then it will be very easy for them to win a battle without firing a single shot. By creating continuous influence, confusion can be generated step by step. Research from the RAND Corporation connects automated propaganda, targeted advertising, and AI-generated messages with "truth decay" (Deppe & Schaal, 2024; Vasilescu, 2023). Truth decay can be characterized as when people cannot agree on basic facts about what is real, thus undermining society. Similar fears have been given voice by law enforcement groups like Europol, which pointed out that it is extremely hard to detect fake media (Sareen, 2022; Drmotová & Kutěj, 2024; Łabuz, 2024). The attackers are improving their tools all the time, and even experts may struggle to work out what is true, making it harder to hold the right party responsible for misinformation. Thus, criminals and foreign actors can keep hidden attacks running. The potential dangers become magnified in relation to global security. Byman et al. illustrated how deepfakes can cause a loss of confidence among state actors—a manipulated video of a leader making threats could provoke an actual military confrontation, and if the truth is unknowable, diplomatic relations become tenuous (Byman et al., 2023). Goldstein et al. examined the use of large language models (LLMs) and how they can be used in support of impact operations, detailing an entire process in which AI generates counterfeit news, establishes fraudulent social media accounts, and sends tailored messages to trick individuals (Goldstein et al., 2023). This makes propaganda campaigns cheaper and faster, meaning attackers can reach millions in multiple languages all at once. It was not long before these concerns were based on real evidence in the open. OpenAI reported on cases where state-linked groups used AI to spread political messages and build up numbers of fake online personas to manipulate others (Byman et al., 2023; Goldstein et al., 2023; Pauwels, 2024), and RAND later verified that similar (Zeng, 2025) techniques have been utilized by Chinese operations in attempts to interfere with the course of elections and public opinion.

3. Threat Landscape of Generative AI in Cognitive Warfare

3.1 Attack Vectors Enabled by Generative AI

Propaganda is being turned on its head by generative language models, which enhance content fluency, speed, and expense (Pauwels, 2024). The technology can create localized messages in multiple languages, reword stories for different constituencies, and generate huge volumes of influence material. It also optimizes emotional triggers and framing, as well as permitting simultaneous A/B testing. By automating posting and rapid translation, generative AI could potentially influence operations both across platforms and languages. Generative AI can spread any disinformation faster and cheaper. It can rewrite the same story in many versions and in many languages. It can automatically post on different platforms (Ienca, 2023). AI can also create fake identities and deepfakes. These can impersonate real leadership or figures of trust. They could destroy reputations, confuse commands, or trick people into harmful actions. It also results in something called the "liar's dividend", where actual evidence can be denied, saying that it is fake (Chesney & Citron, 2019; Hwang, 2020). Security agencies warn these tactics are on the rise in fraud, in election processes, and in national security threats. While detection models evolve and generation models incorporate countermeasures reducing detector effectiveness, defenders are confronted with an arms race problem (Argyle et al., 2025). Technical, operational, policy, and social controls are the primary targets of mitigation methods. A productive road map for these activities is set by National Institute of Standards and Technology (NIST) guidelines concerning forensic standards and transparency for synthetic content (Pauwels, 2024). Perhaps the most novel risk is not a single deceptive artifact but the creation of closed-loop influence systems that observe, model, adapt to, and exploit human responses in near-real time. Generative AI, combined with analytics and user-level telemetry, enables pipelines where content is generated, audience reactions are measured (engagement, spread patterns, sentiment), models are retrained or prompted to favour higher-engagement framings, and subsequent content is optimized accordingly (Goldstein et al., 2023; Luceri et al., 2024). This continuous observation → adaptation → targeting loop amplifies psychological operations because it allows adversaries to discover precisely which framings or persuasive hooks move target audiences and then scale those hooks rapidly. LLMs and influence operations implement this pipeline as a key through which AI could materially improve the persuasive strength of campaigns (Goldstein et al., 2023). Adaptive influence in real time uses three interconnected capabilities. The first is automated content creation like LLMs and multimodal models. The second is analytics and behaviour models like user profiling, micro-segmentation for maximum engagement. For an influence system, the third part is automated delivery through bots and Application Programming Interfaces (APIs) (Silva et al., 2012). This becomes a very powerful system if joined with AI content creation and analytics. Table 18.1 defines threat vectors and cognitive effects of generative AI in cognitive warfare.

Table 18.1 Threat Vectors and Cognitive Effects of Generative AI in Cognitive Warfare.

Dimension	*Specific Mechanism*	*Cognitive/Operational Impact*
Attack Vectors	LLM-generated text (propaganda, multilingual narratives), Deepfakes (audio/video impersonation), Synthetic personas (fake identities & profiles), Botnets & automation, Closed-loop adaptive influence	Scalable, cheap, adaptive disinformation "Liar's dividend"; Mass amplification and rapid dissemination; Real-time optimization of persuasive narratives

Contd...

Table 18.1 *Contd...*

Dimension	*Specific Mechanism*	*Cognitive/Operational Impact*
Cognitive Effects	Confirmation bias exploitation; Emotional triggers (fear, anger, outrage); Information overload; Strategic ambiguity & confusion by design	Reinforces existing beliefs, lowers resistance; Heightens persuasion, polarization; Decision fatigue, reduced analytic capacity; Paralyzes decisions, erodes situational awareness

Source: Goldstein et al., 2023; Chesney & Citron, 2019; Byman et al., 2023; Pauwels, 2024

3.2 Cognitive Effects and Vulnerabilities

Human minds can be influenced in a strong way by the use of generative AI. Nowadays, it has become a common weakness. It gets them to feel strong emotions. It uses the familiar cultural ideas. By this, the false information looks true. It is very hard to identify it in practical time. Attackers are taking advantage of the following:

- Overload the Information: The information is pushed everywhere at a very large scale. People are getting tired of finding the actual true information.
- Strategic ambiguity: Different stories are told about the same event. This halts people from arriving at a definite decision.
- Confusion by design: The spreading of fake rumours and mixed signals is deliberate. It dismantles awareness and sows doubts.

Combined, these effects lead to decision paralysis, trust erosion, polarization, and mental fatigue, degrading both civilian and military resilience. Because these attacks exploit deep cognitive biases rather than technical vulnerabilities, their impacts are often invisible until severe, making anticipatory defences critical.

3.3 Multi-Domain Threat Application

Generative AI completely changes how influence operations work. It makes them faster, cheaper, and much bigger in scale. By using generative AI, messages can be modified person to person. So, it is very easy for attackers to make the messages more personal. By synthesizing text, audio, images, and video at low cost and in many languages, generative models enable adversaries to operate across military, political, and civilian domains in parallel and with high specificity. Military or command-and-control, political (elections), and civilian (public trust and polarization) are the three domains. These domains demonstrate different attack surfaces. They also highlight the sequential harms that can result when generative capabilities are combined with networked dissemination and social amplification.

3.3.1 Military: Command-and-Control Disruption

Generative AI creates risks to command and control. It enables convincing forgeries of human communications. It also produces synthetic intelligence products that can be inserted into decision loops. Challengers can fabricate or manipulate voice messages, video orders, situation reports, intelligence summaries, and even believable images of battlefield events. When delivered to front-line units or headquarters through compromised or spoofed channels, such fakes can produce misdirection, paralysis, or misallocation of forces. Scholars and policy analysts have noted scenarios in which deepfake orders, or falsified ISR (intelligence, surveillance, reconnaissance) streams cause units to reposition, stand down, or respond to non-existent threats, outcomes that degrade combat effectiveness and raise the risk of fratricide or strategic surprise (Hwang, 2020; Sareen, 2022). Three technical and operational features make C2 disruption feasible and dangerous: (i) multimodal synthesis, audio/video/text that mimics commanders or trusted systems; (ii) hyper-personalization, messages tailored to cultural, linguistic, or unit-level cues that increase perceived authenticity; and (iii) automation + scale, the ability to generate many slightly different variants to evade simple pattern-matching detection (Huang et al., 2024; Lahmann et al., 2025). Coupled with platform vulnerabilities (e.g., poorly authenticated chat or social feeds used informally inside units) and human cognitive biases (authority heuristics, time pressure), these capabilities substantially raise the probability that synthetic messages will be acted upon before verification (Ienca, 2023; Deppe & Schaal, 2024). Analysts have documented both theoretical and observed cases where synthetic media was used to try to influence military audiences or public perceptions around military events; even when rapidly debunked, such content can produce short-term confusion that adversaries can exploit tactically and strategically (Fenstermacher et al., 2023; Vasilescu, 2023). Beyond immediate wrong orders, generative attacks can be designed to degrade morale (e.g., synthetic video of a unit's families in danger), to harvest or provoke reactions that reveal dispositions and locations, or to create false narratives that justify escalation. These effects compound when generative content is combined with cyber intrusions that alter official feeds, or with social amplification by bot networks and sympathetic proxies (Silva et al., 2012).

3.3.2 Political: Election interference and narrative shaping

Generative models dramatically lower the cost of producing persuasive political content: micro-targeted ads, multilingual messaging, synthetic audio/video of candidates or officials, and large volumes of tailored narratives adapted to different audience segments. Where earlier influence efforts required skilled copywriters, multilingual teams, or bespoke video production, modern LLMs and image/video models can produce persuasive text and believable media quickly and at scale. This changes two things: (i) adversaries or malign domestic actors can run many parallel, A/B-tested narratives; and (ii) the marginal cost of experimenting with extreme or tailored messaging is reduced, increasing the pace of narrative iteration.

3.3.3 *Tactics and Playbooks*

Typical AI-enabled election playbooks have four features. They are persona seeding, micro targeted persuasion, timed release of deepfakes and fabricated audio/ video content, and narrative laundering. Persona seeding is creating synthetic influencers or local "citizen journalists" who publish tailored content. Micro targeted persuasion uses LLMs to draft messages adapted to narrow demographic slices. Deepfakes and fabricated audio/video content are released at carefully chosen times before elections. This is done to influence public opinion during the most critical period leading up to voting. Narrative laundering is building a cover story across fringe and mainstream channels so that a manufactured claim attains apparent credibility. Intelligence provides an intricate picture. Synthetic content is everywhere, but little is absorbed by receptive audiences. The real danger is a "breakout" scenario, artificial content cuts loose from echo chambers and spreads far and wide. This is the greatest risk. In regions with limited media resources or lower media literacy, even simple fake content can strongly influence people. AI attack vectors on social media, including LLMs, deepfakes, personas, and botnets, are shown to spread in Figure 18.1. These attacks mislead and create an information overload on one's mind, obscuring the truth. The countermeasures to address this will be tools for fake content detection, tracking the origin of information, and policies, along with training for making people mentally resilient.

3.3.4 *Civil: Collapsing Public Trust*

Many researchers use the term "truth decay" to describe the outcome of generative AI. The concept here is that people progressively lose a shared reality about fundamental facts. Opinions begin to take on the appearance of fact and real evidence. AI-generated videos and messages capitalize on human biases, such as confirmation bias. Deepfakes are also going to lead to something called the "liar's dividend", which means actual evidence will be declared fake. Over time, confidence in the media, leaders, and institutions becomes fragile.

So, the flow is like: synthetic content → targeted amplification (bots, closed groups, influencers) → local belief formation → behavioural effects (voter abstention, violence, distrust of institutions).

This can produce persistent polarization, de-legitimization of media and expert institutions, and slower or fragmented collective responses to emergencies (public health crises, disasters, or security incidents). Law enforcement and judicial systems face practical difficulties as well: synthetic evidence complicates investigations and prosecutions, and detection/attribution lags create legal and operational gaps. Why does multi-domain interaction matter? The damages in each domain are not isolated: military C2 confusion can be amplified by political narratives that mischaracterize events; political disinformation can increase civilian polarization and reduce willingness to cooperate with public safety directives; and societal distrust can reduce the legitimacy of military or civic institutions that need public support in crises. In short, generative AI makes cross-domain cascades more probable and harder to arrest once begun.

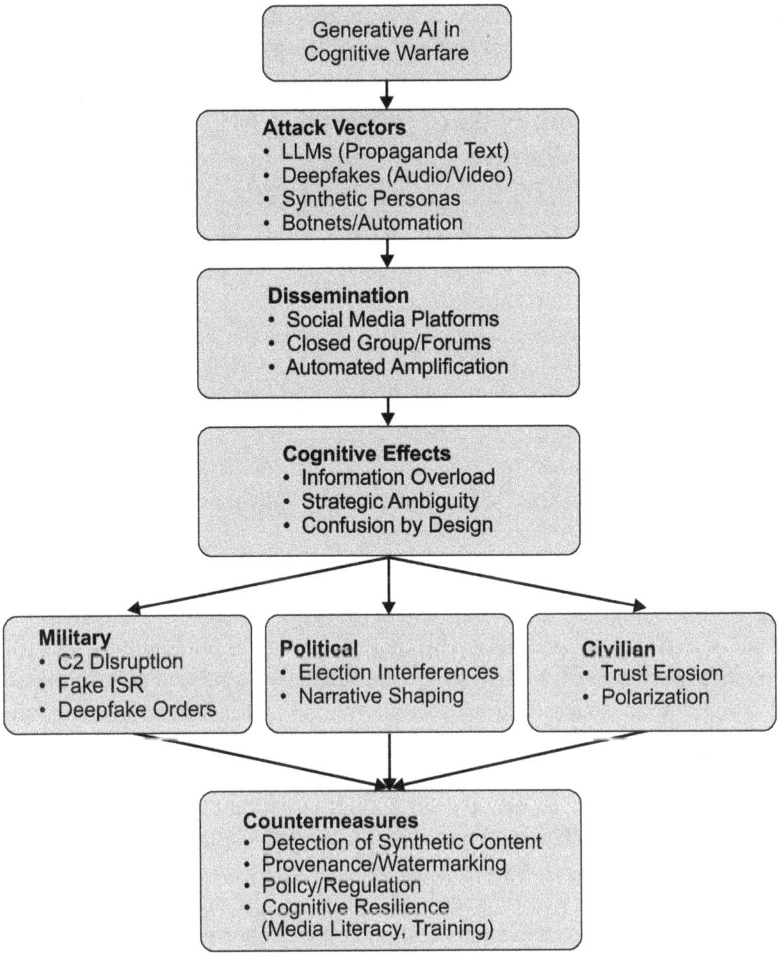

Fig. 18.1 Conceptual framework of generative AI in cognitive warfare.

3.4 Cross-Domain Cascade Effects

The threats of generative AI do not stay in one place. While they might begin in the military domain, they soon spread into the political and civilian spaces. For example, a deepfake military command could mislead soldiers or officers. Soon after, the same fake message might be used by various political groups to create fear or outrage. Civilians then start to feel confused and lose trust in their leaders. This is how a minor incident escalates into a huge problem for the entire nation. These scenarios reflect the one attack with multi-system impacts, bringing down the level of public trust, slowing down decision-making processes, and amplifying conflict within society. This makes for compound risks that are much difficult to contain. For that reason, defence strategies must not focus on one domain. They have to think of how the threat evolves among domains and strengthens. In sum, understanding connectivity is essential in preventing future crises from happening.

4. Technical Capabilities of Generative AI for Cognitive Warfare

Generative AI has evolved into a toolkit that attackers can mix and match to attack human cognition at scale. The following capabilities outline the key technical building blocks of what they do, how they produce cognitive impact, and why they are important for defensive planners. They all engage with social-platform affordances (amplification, recommendation, and monetization) and with human cognitive weaknesses (biases, heuristics, information overload) and have second-order effects that far outlast the naked model outputs (Łabuz, 2024; Ienca, 2023; Deppe & Schaal, 2024).

4.1 Language models (LLMs): Narrative Generation, Translation, Sentiment Shaping

Large pre-trained models that are transformer architecture–based and trained on large text corpora can generate human-level fluent context-sensitive text. A number of important features are what make them useful for cognitive operations. Auto regressive text generation using controllable prompts or metadata to govern tone is the first approach. The second, fine-tuning and instruction-tuning, allows the model to take on particular rhetorical goals. The third, few-shot or zero-shot prompting, enables rapid adaptation without the need for retraining. Such mechanisms enable an adversary to generate coherent articles, social media posts, comments, translations, summaries, and reply chains. The content can be tailored to the language of the audience and generated in volumes and speed that human teams cannot match (Byman et al., 2023). LLMs also lower the barrier to stylistic mimicry and source impersonation. A generator can produce material that mirrors a target outlet's register, such as headline conventions, quoting style, and idiomatic phrasing. This increases the perceived veracity and shareability of the content. LLMs have translation and localization capabilities. These capabilities allow multilingual influence campaigns. Such campaigns can rapidly A/B test narratives. They operate across jurisdictions and subpopulations (Goldstein et al., 2023). Importantly, instruction-tuning and reward-based fine-tuning (e.g., Reinforcement Learning from Human Feedback) permit models to be optimized for specific behavioural signals, such as engagement or persuasion metrics. This means that outputs can be explicitly shaped to maximize affective resonance or distrust. They are not limited to optimization for grammaticality or factuality alone. Operationally, LLMs' principal hazards for cognitive warfare are scale, adaptability, and plausibility. Scale refers to the cheap and fast generation of tailored narratives. Adaptability means that models can modify tone and framing in response to near-real-time feedback. Plausibility indicates that the generated text routinely passes cursory human scrutiny or platform moderation unless systems are specifically designed to detect synthetic language.

4.2 Deepfake Technology: Visual/Audio Manipulation for Trust Erosion

Modern image, video, and audio synthesis methods (generative adversarial networks, diffusion models, neural vocoders, and waveform models) produce increasingly photorealistic or voice-accurate artifacts. These methods create short video clips, audio snippets, or composite media that appear to show a targeted person saying or doing something they did not. Visual and audio cues carry strong evidentiary weight for lay audiences. As a result, deepfakes can produce immediate credibility shocks. They also create a lingering "liar's dividend" effect, whereby genuine evidence later becomes suspect because people think "it could be a deepfake". From a technical standpoint, developments in face re-enactment, lip-syncing, and cross-modal conditioning are considerably enhancing multimedia manipulation. Cross-modal conditioning is conditioning an audio model on a target speaker or matching a synthetic voice track to an altered video. Detection, however, remains an arms-race issue. Models that are trained to detect artifacts can be circumvented by better synthesis techniques, distribution washing (resampling, compression), and adversarial post-processing. Detection models tend to generalize badly to generators or unseen artifacts during training. There are two components to the combined effect. On the one hand, believable synthetic media elicits an immediate, visceral response. On the other hand, whether detection and provenance follow up to the quality of synthesis, there is long-term epistemic erosion.

4.3 Synthetic Botnets and Automation: Coordinated Influence at Scale

"Botnets" for information operations are not just scripts that retweet anymore. They are now automation networks that organize content creation. They also oversee personas, dictate timing, and echo content to various sites. Early research into social bots tracked how automated agents distort conversation and amplify marginal narratives. Generative AI shifts the math by providing each automated account smooth, context-aware output. It also makes credentialed or hijacked accounts look "human-like" in content and behaviour. Automation tools can connect AI models with systems. Automatically, different posts can be scheduled; locations can be hidden. Also, it can control many fake or stolen accounts. For improving the campaigns, it can also track the engagement. These campaigns may seed narratives, track traction, and automatically escalate or pivot successful lines. Platform affordances such as recommendation algorithms and trending indices amplify the impact. Planned content can quickly shift and shape social norms. Through encryption or use of ephemeral messaging, combining fake content with real accounts, establishing information cascades via private conversations, and rendering forensics and legal responses more challenging, automation has the ability to anonymize attribution.

4.4 Reinforcement Loops: Adaptive Persuasion and Feedback Systems

One important technical multiplier for cognitive operations is the ability to "close the loop", by observing human reactions to content, interpreting those signals, and using those signals to adjust future messages. This can be done with A/B testing, multi-armed bandit optimization, and reinforcement learning (policy optimization) where reward signals can be defined by engagement, conversion, sentiment shift, or downstream behaviour. While RLHF and other alignment approaches are often expressed in a defensive approach, an agenda for encouraging alignment of model behaviours to human values, these same mechanisms can be used for persuasive purposes. Reward models can be implemented with proxy signals of persuasion. Reward models can steer generation towards a stronger effect on the target population. At the social level, psychographic profiling research shows that tailored persuasive appeals can substantially increase behavioural response rates. These appeals are matched to personality traits inferred from digital traces. When such targeting is combined with automated generation and live feedback, a campaign can perform continuous refinement. Different variants are tested first. Then, it selects the best performers according to reward criteria. It continuously amplifies the messages that can work in the best way; then it gathers new reactions and repeats this in a cycle. With every iteration, these messages become not only more powerful, but also more focused on the target's particular weaknesses as well. This creates a persuasion system which can learn what changes people's minds. It learns in what situations what exactly works. And this makes defence very difficult because the attacks continuously improve themselves. Closed-loop adversarial systems operate significantly faster than human analysts can observe or counter. They can discover and exploit subtle persuasion vectors that evade coarse, rule-based moderation. Countering them therefore requires real-time signal-level monitoring. It also requires provenance tracking and platform frictions. Human resilience measures are essential. Additionally, research into adversarial-robust detectors that consider the generation–dissemination–feedback pipeline as a whole is needed (Kamoun et al. 2020).

4.5 Synthesis: Multimodal and Socio-technical Coupling

In reality, adversaries seldom apply a single capability alone. Multimodal synthesis including, for example, LLM-generated text, synthetic audio/video, and automated persona networks along with iterative and cross-modal feedback optimization is a socio-technical weapon. A socio-technical weapon draws from technical proficiency, platform exploits, and precision social engineering expertise. If defensive scenarios only treat models as stand-alone artifacts, then our defence planning would ultimately overlook the systemic risk. The systemic risk arises from orchestration and adaptation across modalities and perhaps platforms. A socio-technical risk can be enabled through modelled incentives or through measurement loops that convert online attention into cognitive effect. LLMs can strengthen existing cognitive biases and influence how narratives are formed. In this way, they link generative AI capabilities with their effects on human thinking (Table 18.2). The impact of deepfake information is to decrease the believability of evidence, while botnets, with AI, increase the psychological component with a sense of social consensus. Techniques of persuasion are continually updated with closed-loop adaptive influence systems, with multilingual generations exerting impact beyond cultural boundaries. Although multimodal fuse detection is increased, the goal of emotional targeting is to prioritize the affective over the factual in manipulation. The findings indicate that generative AI is a systemic threat that demands a corresponding defence against cognitive warfare.

4.6 Adaptive Adversary Dynamics

A defining feature of generative AI in cognitive warfare is its capacity for continuous adaptation. The implication is that static defences will prove insufficient. Effective resilience requires dynamic and layered systems that evolve in parallel with adversarial tactics, as well as international collaboration to share intelligence on emerging offensive methods.

5. Case Studies

This case study section examines two classes of evidence. One is documented, real-world influence operations where generative techniques or AI-assisted workflows were observed or credibly reported to have been used. Second is simulated attack scenarios that combine generative text, synthetic audio/video, and platform amplification. They demonstrate how cognitive effects can be produced end-to-end. The cases were selected for their relevance to modern cognitive warfare. They include electoral interference, wartime information campaigns, and crisis escalation. They were also chosen because they illustrate different parts of the pipeline described in the literature. That is LLM/deepfake → dissemination → human cognition. Taiwan's elections have been a target for foreign information operations, with adversaries using social media, messaging apps, and local information ecosystems to disseminate false narratives and influence voter attitudes. During the 2020s, this activity added complex messaging and AI capabilities to produce multilingual, locally relevant content. Taiwan's small, highly connected electorate, extensive reliance on private messaging platforms, and continuous, multi-vector campaigns make it a prime location for studying cognitive warfare.

Table 18.2 Generative AI Capabilities and Their Cognitive Impact in Cognitive Warfare.

Generative AI Capability	*Underlying Technical Mechanism*	*Primary Cognitive Impact*	*Operational/Security Risk*
Large Language Models (LLMs) (Goldstein et al., 2023)	Transformer-based autoregressive text generation; prompt tuning; fine-tuning	Narrative shaping, belief manipulation, confirmation bias reinforcement	Mass-scale propaganda, erosion of trust in official communication
Deepfake Audio & Video (Gambín et al., 2024)	GANs, diffusion models, neural vocoders, face re-enactment	Authority deception, emotional shock, credibility distortion	False command issuance, diplomatic escalation, mission disruption
Synthetic Personas (Byman et al., 2023)	Automated profile generation; behavioural mimicry; identity spoofing	Social trust exploitation, peer influence	Infiltration of online communities, narrative seeding
Botnets & Automated Amplification (Silva et al., 2012)	API-driven posting; scheduling; engagement optimization	Information overload, perception of consensus	Rapid viral spread of disinformation, agenda setting
Multilingual Content Generation (Pauwels, 2024)	Neural machine translation; localization via LLMs	Cultural resonance, cross-border persuasion	Influence across ethnic, linguistic, and national boundaries
Closed-Loop Adaptive Influence Systems (Luceri et al., 2024)	Feedback analytics; A/B testing; reinforcement learning	Progressive persuasion, decision fatigue	Real-time cognitive manipulation, strategic paralysis
Emotional Targeting Models (Ienca, 2023)	Sentiment analysis; affective computing	Fear, anger, polarization	Destabilization of social cohesion and morale
Multimodal Content Fusion (Huang et al., 2024)	Text–image–audio–video synthesis	Heightened realism and immersion	Reduced detection probability, delayed response

5.1 Operational fingerprint and impact

Operatives used swift production of brief stories. They used translation and localizing of themes. They seeded talking points via local surrogates. They used platform features that supported swift transmission. Analysts mentioned recurring utilization of burst messaging coordination that was coordinated to debates, leaks, or scandal news so that false frames would own early opinions. Once a belief is formed, it is often resistant to change due to cognitive biases such as confirmation bias (Ienca, 2023). Instead, campaigns typically tried to undermine confidence in institutions and raise indecision or bewilderment among swing voters. This is the kind of cognitive warfare that generative AI tools make faster and cheaper. As a result, such operations become easier to carry out on a large scale.

5.2 Lessons from the real world

In all these instances, the common thread was not that generative AI "won" the information campaign all on its own, but rather that it creates a lower barrier to entry and faster turnaround time for adversaries to more easily fabricate plausible, customized content and quickly iterate their narratives. On microtargeted platforms and within closed groups, enemies can rapidly explore, experiment, and modify themes, which often dissolve confidence and create an operating context where defenders are forced to rapidly verify, immunize populations, and strengthen institutions against repeated narrative shocks.

Simulated attack: LLM-generated propaganda + deepfake integration + social amplification

To make the threat concrete, consider an end-to-end simulated campaign (actor, aim, method, amplification, and expected cognitive effect). This scenario synthesizes empirical patterns documented in threat reports and the model-to-Information Operations (IO) pipeline described in the literature. Table 18.3 compares case studies across Taiwan, Russia–Ukraine, US, and African contexts, illustrating commonalities and differences in generative AI–enabled cognitive warfare.

Actor and objective: A state-aligned influence cell seeks to (i) erode public trust in a target country's military leadership, and (ii) slow political consensus around supporting an allied partner. The campaign is designed to create uncertainty and paralyze timely political decisions. *Preparation and reconnaissance*: The team harvests open-source data (public social posts, comment threads, local media), uses social listening to identify salient grievances and cultural fault lines, and builds audience segments (by age, region, political leaning). LLMs are used to synthesize talking points in the target language and to draft micro-posts, comments, and targeted messages suited to each audience segment. *Content production* (LLM + multimodal): For authenticity the cell generates three content types: (i) a series of short, localized narratives (text threads and comment replies) produced by

Table 18.3 Comparative Case Studies of Cognitive Warfare Campaigns.

Case/Region	*Methods Used*	*Cognitive Effects*	*Unique Features*	*Lessons Learned*
Taiwan Elections (2020–2024)	AI-generated multilingual posts, meme campaigns, LINE app disinformation, localized narratives (Pauwels, 2024; Luceri et al., 2024)	Confusion among undecided voters, erosion of institutional trust, delayed response to scandals	Small, networked electorate; reliance on private messaging channels	Highlight need for response fact-checking; resilience training in networks
Russia–Ukraine Conflict (2022–2025)	Deepfakes of leaders, botnets amplifying pro-Russian narratives, AI-assisted propaganda on Telegram (Byman et al., 2023; Gambín et al., 2024)	Undermining morale, distorting battlefield perceptions, fuelling international polarization	Integration of cyber intrusions with synthetic media; high use of Telegram	cyber + info war provenance systems call to verify ISR feeds
US Elections (2016, 2020)	Targeted ads, automated persona seeding, AI-generated memes, selective narrative amplification (Goldstein et al., 2023; Ienca, 2023)	Polarization, distrust in media, reinforcement of existing biases	Resource-rich environment but strong media literacy	Microtargeting and algorithmic amplification reshape discourse
African Disinformation Campaigns (2018–2023)	Fake news websites, WhatsApp chain messages, AI-based image/video fakes in low-resource environments (Vasilescu, 2023; Sareen, 2022)	Rapid rumour spread, violence incitement, public distrust of officials	Lower digital literacy and weak content moderation	AI disinformation outsized impact in resource contexts on grassroots mediacy
Simulated Attack (Chapter Example)	LLM propaganda + deepfake video + bot amplification (timed before parliamentary hearing) (Goldstein et al., 2023; Pauwels, 2024)	Suspicion of official sources, delayed political consensus, decision paralysis	Demonstrates full pipeline from generation to persuasion loop	AI makes attacks cheaper and easier to carry out. Therefore, defence measures must be flexible and able to respond quickly

LLMs and slightly edited for idiomaticity; (ii) synthetic audio clips that mimic an aide's voice to "leak" an out-of-context admission; and (iii) a short deepfake video showing a senior officer apparently contradicting public statements. Open-source video/image software and freely accessible face/voice cloning models are utilized in deepfake creation. LLMs subsequently produce fabricated "witness" quotes and supporting texts to authenticate the clip.

Seeding and amplification: Content is seeded onto fringe forums and low-moderation platforms where initial uptake is likely; simultaneously, a network of inauthentic accounts and previously established proxy pages repost material to mainstream platforms, leveraging paid ads and microtargeted boosts for key demographics. The campaign times the largest burst to precede a parliamentary hearing so that the fabricated content becomes part of the early news cycle and pressures mainstream outlets to react before full verification is possible.

5.3 Feedback, adaptation, and measurement

Using analytics and small-scale A/B tests, the cell measures which frames generate most engagement and updates subsequent LLM prompts to improve persuasion (e.g., shifting from accusatory frames to fear-based frames in certain communities). This rapid iterate-measure loop is a distinctive affordance of automated generation: it dramatically shortens the "test, learn, and scale" cycle compared with pre-AI workflows.

Expected cognitive effects: The joint effect can result in mass belief and acceptances of the manufactured material, but not necessarily; instead it brings about fragmentation of the epistemic environment, and that fragmentation includes an increase in suspicion of official sources, slower decision-making based on competing "facts", and diminished public willingness to support policies that require urgency. The degradation of the cognitive environment is itself a strategic goal of cognitive warfare. *Why are detection and attribution hard?* Three technical and operational difficulties make this type of campaign difficult to decipher. One challenge is that the generative content might be idiomatic or localized, which minimizes signals of obvious detection. Another factor is that encrypted channels like messaging apps and closed groups limit the ability of the platform to monitor communications. Finally, brief, irregular campaigns produce a "verification lag" in which audiences are exposed to the content before platforms or authorities can fully attribute its source or false claims. These factors have been consistently presented in recent threat assessments and empirical research.

5.4 Implications for defenders

The case studies indicate that the defenders have the following as their priority. First, they need telemetry and rapid validation for private or closed channels. Second, they need to institute provenance and content-watermarking protocols.

Third, they need to build strong public messaging that is capable of penetrating narrative probes. Finally, they must establish cross-industry threat intelligence sharing among industry, civil society, and government in order to detect short, adaptive bursts typical of AI-facilitated campaigns. Such answers are discussed in the literature of mitigation. But the case studies illustrate an urgent need. Adversaries are combining low-cost generative tools with thoroughly proven amplification tactics to create new, hard-to-track cognitive impacts.

6. Countermeasures and Defensive Strategies

Day by day, the cognitive warfare is getting stronger with generative AI. So, better defence strategies are highly needed to protect the mind.

6.1 Detection of Synthetic Content

Deepfake detection systems are highly essential for the identification of the fake AI-generated content. Those systems apply forensic analysis in order to confirm the authenticity of the content. These methods help protect the security of the content by detecting the misuse of deepfake technology and avoiding it.

6.2 Watermarking and Provenance Tools

Mechanisms for content provenance, including cryptographic watermarking and metadata verification, have played a crucial role in establishing the authenticity of media sources. Efforts such as the Coalition for Content Provenance and Authenticity (C2PA) have developed standards that allow platforms to track both the origin and manipulation chain of digital assets. Future research on blockchain-based provenance systems will also provide tamper-proof verification.

6.3 NATO and National Strategies for Cognitive Resilience

Military alliances and nation-states are increasingly viewing cognitive security as a strategic priority. NATO's Cognitive Warfare Concept makes clear the necessity of information domain situational awareness, cross-domain deterrence, and civil–military cooperation to meet influence operations. National defence strategies, including those of the United States, United Kingdom, and European Union (EU), all emphasize multilayered defence architectures to address cyber, information, and psychological security.

6.4 Human-in-the-Loop Verification

Though there have been technological improvements to automate, it is human judgement that makes the final call on judging uncertain or high-risk information. Human-in-the-loop (HITL) systems blend human supervision and AI-facilitated judgement of decisions. At times, this may help prevent automated data detection systems from producing false positives and being manipulated by adversaries.

6.5 Psychological Resilience Programmes

A fundamental element of the defensive strategy is building cognitive resilience in the military corps, policymakers, and the population. Programmes might be set up to promote media literacy, adversarial simulations, and stress inoculation to mitigate the effects of manipulation. Psychological information operations (PSYOPS) training could be adapted to include AI-enabled information threat scenarios to more fully prepare people to identify and withstand disinformation and manipulation tactics in a real-time indications-and-warning scenario.

6.6 Cognitive Sovereignty and Human Rights in the Age of Generative AI

Generative AI in cognitive warfare raises a host of ethical and human rights issues. It attacks the way people think, focus, and decide, taking away cognitive sovereignty from a person. These are, for the most part, clandestine attacks that people cannot recognize when regular influence turns into destructive manipulation. This opens a whole different understanding of what should be allowed in military and civilian contexts. According to many experts, cognitive sovereignty needs to become a legally protected right in the future. Protection against clandestine manipulations of one's mind is not only a security issue but also basic human freedom. Table 18.4 represents the importance of generative AI in cognitive warfare for countermeasures and strategic responses.

Table 18.4 Importance of Generative AI in Cognitive Warfare for Countermeasures and Strategic Responses

Category	*Examples*	*Purpose/Outcome*
Technical Defences (Chaitra et al., 2025; Łabuz, 2024)	Deepfake detection, watermarking, provenance systems (e.g., C2PA, blockchain-based tracing)	Authentication of media, limits deception
Operational Measures (Hoadley et al., 2018; Kamoun et al., 2020)	Human-in-the-loop verification, authentication protocols for critical communications	Prevents false positives and disorders
Policy & Governance (Deppe & Schaal, 2024; Jacobs, 2022)	NATO cognitive warfare doctrine, national defence strategies, regulation of synthetic media	Institutional and cross-domain resilience
Cognitive Resilience (Gustafsson et al., 2023; Lahmann et al., 2025)	Media literacy training, adversarial simulations, stress inoculation, PSYOPS adaptation	Reduces susceptibility to manipulation
Future Directions (Huang et al., 2024; Argyle et al., 2025)	AI-for-defence (counter-propaganda models, adaptive counter-messaging), ethical/legal frameworks	Anticipatory defence; balance security vs free speech

6.7 *Policy and Governance Gaps*

While generative AI is growing very fast, the rules to control it are still weak and scattered. Cognitive warfare is a serious threat now, according to groups like NATO and the EU. But strong laws that bar AI from manipulating people's thoughts remain to be agreed upon among countries. There are no global rules that clearly explain how to trace the originator of fake content. In addition, many places fail to apply the same standards for an identical proof of what is real. It is also not widely accepted as a right in the thinking of individuals to be able to protect their own thoughts. In order to solve these problems, the public sector, international organizations, and technology companies must work together. They have to frame clear rules for honesty, responsibility, and mental protection.

7. Future Research Directions

The rapid evolution of generative AI introduces a spectrum of challenges and opportunities in the cognitive domain. As adversarial capabilities progress, research must address the sophistication of emerging threats while simultaneously developing robust defensive and governance frameworks. Three critical future research trajectories are identified: emerging multimodal AI threats, counter-AI with AI-based defences, and the ethical and legal dimensions of cognitive warfare.

7.1 *Emerging Threats: Multimodal AI and Autonomous Propaganda*

Multimodal AI systems that combine voice, text, image, and video synthesis will be employed in the next phase of cognitive warfare for the generation of coherent cross-media narratives for influencing misinformation campaigns. Such technologies as Gemini and GPT-4V allow context-aware propaganda, which develops an engaging message that considers linguistic and cultural idiosyncrasies. Moreover, autonomous propaganda systems represent an escalatory threat. Leveraging reinforcement learning and real-time behavioural analytics, such systems could continuously optimize influence strategies based on the target audience's responses. Integration of different LLM-based content engines with social media APIs would empower the autonomous bots to conduct influencing operations without direct human supervision. Future research must investigate the detection frameworks for finding coordinated, multimodal disinformation campaigns and also propose system-level interventions that can disrupt automated cognitive attacks before they reach virality.

7.2 *Threat Countering with the Help of Generative AI*

Only stronger protection measures can counteract this bad information. This is done through technologies such as cryptographic watermarking, which help verify that digital content comes from a reliable source. AI counter-propaganda systems can correct messages immediately, changing in light of public responses. And besides this, AI counter-propaganda systems can quickly correct messages based on public responses.AI-based training systems also help people identify and avoid manipulation, which builds trust and resilience in society.. All in all, these are the means—content verification, counter-messaging, and cognitive training—that keep the public and military aware and prepared to improve national security.

7.3 *Ethical and Legal Implications of AI in Cognitive Warfare*

In case of conflict, the use of generative AI creates serious ethical and legal problems. It secretly manipulates how people can think and feel. There are no international laws that can protect the human mind, and new rules are urgently needed. Governments face the challenge of balancing security with freedom of speech. Too many limits may harm free expression, while too few may result in hazardous manipulations. Far more research is required to define clear guidelines and ways to check the AI systems. Policymakers, technology experts, and ethicists have to collaborate in protecting human thinking.

8. Conclusion

Cognitive warfare is a paradigm shift in war, transposing the battle space from physical to psychological. Generative AI has further accelerated this shift by making it possible to deliver scalable, adaptive, and very persuasive influence operations based on linguistic, cultural, and cognitive weaknesses. In contrast to conventional information warfare, campaigns driven by AI are defined by velocity, automation, and customization, making it possible for opponents to operate persistent psychological operations without drawing on much resource.

This chapter has viewed the threat landscape through an examination of foundational research, actual-world case studies, and simulated attack scenarios. Actual-world evidence in recent conflicts, such as the Taiwan elections and the Russia–Ukraine information environment, demonstrates how generative AI technologies such as deepfakes, synthetic personas, and automated propaganda pipelines are already being weaponized to influence narratives and erode trust. These trends emphasize the imperative of anticipatory defence because retrospective measures will not suffice in a field where manipulation takes place in real time. To protect against AI-based threats and propaganda, we need tools that can verify content, track its origin, and help people think critically and resist manipulation. To protect decision-making under information contest environments, defensive operations must include AI-powered verification and ethical and legal structures. There must be a whole-of-society effort addressing cognitive warfare under generative AI environments, connecting technological innovation, doctrinal adjustment, and global governance. Interdisciplinary integration involving AI, military science, psychology, law, and ethics know-how is essential in weaponized information environment resilience strategy formulation. Previous research on generative AI threats has largely been siloed into one dimension or another. This chapter demonstrates how attacks can cross military, political, and civilian lives simultaneously. It uses examples and simulations to explain the way in which these chain effects work and adds a suite of policy and ethical considerations from which to frame defence planning with a view to protecting human thinking and cognitive freedom as part of national security.

References

Argyle, L.P., Busby, E.C., Gubler, J.R. et al. (2025). Testing theories of political persuasion using AI. *Proceedings of the National Academy of Sciences*, 122(18), e2412815122.

Brundage, M., Avin, S., Clark, J., Toner, H., Eckersley, P., Garfinkel, B. and Amodei, D. (2018). The malicious use of artificial intelligence: Forecasting, prevention, and mitigation. arXiv preprint arXiv:1802.07228.

Byman, D.L., Gao, C., Meserole, C. and Subrahmanian, V.S. (2023). Deepfakes and international conflict. Available at https://www.brookings.edu/wp-content/uploads/2023/01/FP_20230105_deepfakes_international_conflict.pdf. Last accessed on 16 January 2026.

Chesney, B. and Citron, D. (2019). Deep fakes: A looming challenge for privacy, democracy, and national security. Calif. L. Rev., 107, 1753.

Deppe, C. and Schaal, G.S. (2024). Cognitive warfare: A conceptual analysis of the NATO ACT cognitive warfare exploratory concept. *Frontiers in Big Data*, 7, 1452129.

Drmotová, K. and Kutěj, L. (2024). Cognitive warfare as a new dimension of security. A fictional concept or a real silent threat? *Vojenské Rozhledy*, 33(1), 63–83.

Fenstermacher, L.H., Uzcha, D., Larson, K.G. et al. (2023). New perspectives on cognitive warfare. *Signal Processing, Sensor/Information Fusion, and Target Recognition XXXII*, 19.

Fihri, W.F., Ghazi, H.E., Majd, B.A.E. and Bouanani, F. E. (2019). A decision-making approach for detecting the primary user emulation attack in cognitive radio networks. *International Journal of Communication Systems*, 32(15).

Gambín, Á.F., Yazidi, A., Vasilakos, A. et al. (2024). Deepfakes: Current and future trends. *Artificial Intelligence Review*, 57(3), 64.

Goldstein, J.A., Sastry, G., Musser, M., DiResta, R., Gentzel, M. and Sedova, K. (2023). Generative language models and automated influence operations: Emerging threats and potential mitigations. arXiv preprint arXiv:2301.04246, 1.

Hoadley, D.S., US Air Force, Lucas, N.J. and Congressional Research Service. (2018). Artificial intelligence and national security (No. R45178). Congressional Research Service. Available at https://a51.nl/sites/default/files/pdf/R45178.pdf. Last accessed on 16 January 2026.

Huang, K., Wang, Y., Goertzel, B. et al. (2024). *Generative AI Security*. Springer Nature.

Hwang, T. (2020). Deepfakes—Primer and forecast. Questa Soft. Available at https://www.ceeol.com/search/book-detail?id=940530. Last accessed on 14 January 2026.

Ienca, M. (2023). On artificial intelligence and manipulation. *Topoi*, 42(3), 833–842.

Kamoun, F., Iqbal, F., Esseghir, M.A. and Baker, T. (2020). AI and machine learning: A mixed blessing for cybersecurity. *2020 International Symposium on Networks, Computers and Communications* (pp. 1–7).

Łabuz, M. (2024). Deep fakes and the Artificial Intelligence Act—An important signal or a missed opportunity? *Policy & Internet*, 16(4), 783–800.

Lahmann, H., Custers, B. and Scott, B. I. (2025). The fundamental rights risks of countering cognitive warfare with artificial intelligence. *Ethics and Information Technology*, 27(4), 49.

Luceri, L., Boniardi, E. and Ferrara, E. (2024). Leveraging large language models to detect influence campaigns on social media. *WWW '24: Companion Proceedings of the ACM Web Conference 2024* (pp. 1459–1467).

Pauwels, E. (2024). Preparing for next-generation information warfare with generative AI. Available at https://www.econstor.eu/handle/10419/311791. Last accessed on 10 January 2026.

Sareen, M. (2022). Threats and challenges by deepfake technology. In Gaur, L. (ed.) *DeepFakes* (pp. 99–113). Boca Raton: CRC Press.
Shashank, K. and Patil, H.Y. (2025). Deepfake technology: Emerging threats and countermeasures for military security using AI. In Kamboj, S., & Tiwana, P. S. (eds) *Innovations in Computing* (pp. 258–265). London: CRC Press.
Silva, S.S., Silva, R.M., Pinto, R.C. and Salles, R.M. (2012). Botnets: A survey. *Computer Networks*, 57(2), 378–403.
Vasilescu, C. (2023). "Truth" decay in the digital age. Potential implications for the field of security and defence. Questa Soft. Available at https://www.ceeol.com/search/article-detail?id=1243085. Last accessed on 16 January 01 2026.
Zeng, J. (2025). ChatGPT as a security threat: US–China security dilemma in the generative AI race. The British Journal of Politics and International Relations, 13691481251389415.

Index

About the Editors

Jeetendra Kumar has a PhD in Computer Science from GLA University Mathura, India. He has been an Assistant Professor in the Department of Computer Science and Application at Atal Bihari Vajpayee University, Bilaspur, India for the last 11 years. He has published research articles in reputed journals and conferences, including topics like sentiment analysis, fall detection using machine learning techniques, IoT applications, automatic question generation, etc. He has also contributed book chapters on topics related to neuroscience, smartphone applications, and fog computing in healthcare. He has recently published an edited volume. Dr. Kumar has completed a couple of significant research projects. He is also a member of prestigious academic societies such as IEEE, the Indian Science Congress, the International Association of Engineers (IAENG), the International Computer Science and Engineering Society (ICSES), and the International Association of Academicians (IAASSE).

Rashmi Gupta holds a PhD in Computer Applications from the NIT, Raipur, India. Currently, she is an Assistant Professor in the Department of Computer Science and Application at Atal Bihari Vajpayee University Bilaspur, Chhattisgarh, India. She has over 11 years of teaching experience, her research interests encompass Natural Language Processing, EEG signal processing, and Human activity recognition. She has published over 25 research papers, conference papers, and book chapters. He has been awarded grants by AICTE to organize the ATAL Faculty Development Program and by the Science and Engineering Research Board, DST, for conducting High-end Workshops and Internships. Demonstrating her commitment to mentorship, Dr. Gupta has guided over 30 PG and 20 UG students in their research-related major projects. She has published one edited volume. With over 10 years of teaching experience, her research interests encompass Natural Language Processing, EEG signal processing, and human activity recognition. She is also a member of prestigious academic societies such as IEEE, the Indian Science Congress, the International Association of Engineers (IAENG), the International Computer Science and Engineering Society (ICSES), and the International Association of Academicians (IAASSE).

P. K. Mishra is Professor at the Department of Computer Science, Institute of Science, Banaras Hindu University, Varanasi, India. He is a Fellow of the Institute of Mathematical Analysis (UK) and a Senior Member of IEEE (USA). His research interests include AI, Generative AI, Advanced Machine and Dep Learning Algorithms and Applications in Next generation of Computing, Internet of Things, High performance computing, Data Analytics etc. Prof Mishra has published 6 books with reputed publishers. He has published more than 150 publications in SCI/ Scopus and Q1/ Q2 listed journals. Prof Mishra has executed many extramural projects and visited many countries for academic and research purposes.

Gaurav Dhiman has a PhD in Computer Engineering from Thapar Institute of Engineering & Technology, Patiala, India and has also completed his Master's Degree of Computer Applications from the same institute. He is an Assistant Professor in the School of Sciences and Emerging Technologies, Jagat Guru Nanak Dev Punjab State Open University, Patiala, India. His research has been recognized at the highest level, as he has been named one of the world's top researchers by Stanford University, USA list of world's top 2% scientists prepared by Elsevier. He is the senior member of IEEE. He has also received accolades for his outstanding reviewer work from Knowledge-Based Systems (Elsevier). He has authored over 300 peer-reviewed research papers, all of which are indexed in SCI-SCIE, and 10 international books.

Valentina E. Balas is a Full Professor in the Department of Automatics and Applied Software at the Faculty of Engineering, "Aurel Vlaicu" University of Arad, Romania. She holds a PhD Cum Laude, in Applied Electronics and Telecommunications from Polytechnic University of Timisoara. Dr. Balas is author of more than 350 research papers in refereed journals and International Conferences. Her research interests are in Intelligent Systems, Fuzzy Control, Soft Computing, Smart Sensors, Information Fusion, Modeling and Simulation. She is the Editor-in Chief to International Journal of Advanced Intelligence Paradigms and to International Journal of Computational Systems Engineering, member in Editorial Board member of several national and international journals and is evaluator expert for important projects and PhD Thesis. Dr. Balas is the director of Intelligent Systems Research Centre in Aurel Vlaicu University of Arad and Director of the Department of International Relations, Programs and Projects in the same university. She served as General Chair of the International Workshop Soft Computing and Applications in nine editions organized in the interval 2005-2020 and held in Romania and Hungary. Dr. Balas participated in many international conferences as Organizer, Honorary Chair, Session Chair, member in Steering, Advisory or International Program Committees and Keynote Speaker. Recently she was working in a national project with EU funding support: BioCell-NanoART Novel Bio-inspired Cellular Nano-Architectures - For Digital Integrated Circuits, 3M Euro from National Authority for Scientific Research and Innovation. She is a member of European Society for Fuzzy Logic and Technology, member of Society for Industrial and Applied Mathematics and a Senior Member IEEE, member in Technical Committee – Fuzzy Systems (IEEE Computational Intelligence Society), chair of the Task Force 14 in Technical Committee – Emergent Technologies (IEEE CIS), member in Technical Committee – Soft Computing (IEEE SMCS). Dr. Balas was past Vice-president (responsible with Awards) of IFSA - International Fuzzy Systems Association Council (2013-2015), is a Joint Secretary of the Governing Council of Forum for Interdisciplinary Mathematics (FIM), - A Multidisciplinary

Academic Body, India and recipient of the "Tudor Tanasescu" Prize from the Romanian Academy for contributions in the field of soft computing methods (2019).

Kamila Zarychta-Romanowska is a lawyer with a degree in International, EU, and Comparative Law from Strasburg, France, and an LLM from the Faculty of Law, Wroclaw, Poland. She holds a PhD from the same university, where she focused on EU Criminal law, migration, border criminology and policing, human smuggling and trafficking, transnational organised crime, and EU humanitarian and security law. She is a former Senior Legal and Political Advisor with the European Parliament (LIBE, REGI, CRIM, SEDE, TERR,DROI); a recognised arbitrator and mediator for WIPO ADR as well as in Arbitration Court in Poland; an internationally renowned criminologist and expert/consultant on i.a.: Gender Matters/Global Security Strategies, WMD, and Emerging Security and Defence Technologies (NATO-MARSEC COE), Maritime Security, Gender/SDG Awareness (Polish Naval Academy, Kuwait and Qatar Coast Guard), EU Commission, and Polish Border Guard Agency CoE; visiting Fellow in Border Guard College in Koszalin, an international consultant on intelligence, counterintelligence, and cyber intelligence; and a Tech Legal Expert Member of Quantum Standards Group, EITCI, Brussels. She is a member of the Center of Study and Education for Security, University of Wroclaw, and a recognised author and international expert on European border intelligence, migration, EU criminal and police law, security and defence, digital intelligence, and digital/cyber criminology. She is passionate about WPS, the EU, and Global innovation at the ITC for disaster risk reduction, human security, and intelligence.

www.ingramcontent.com/pod-product-compliance
Lightning Source LLC
LaVergne TN
LVHW010607120926
847902LV00003B/34
* 9 7 8 1 0 4 1 1 2 3 4 9 1 *